THE TALE OF
KHUN CHANG KHUN PHAEN

COMPANION VOLUME

CHRIS BAKER formerly taught Asian history in Cambridge University and has lived in Thailand for over thirty years. PASUK PHONGPAICHIT is professor of economics at Chulalongkorn University, Bangkok. Together they have written *A History of Thailand*, *Thailand: Economy and Politics*, *Thaksin*, and published several translations.

MUANGSING JANCHAI, a native of Suphanburi, the cradle of the tale, was trained in Thai painting, and studied further in Tibet, India, Nepal, Burma, Laos, and China. He has executed several temple murals, including a series on the tale at Wat Palelai, Suphanburi.

The Tale of

Khun Chang Khun Phaen

COMPANION VOLUME

TRANSLATED AND EDITED BY

CHRIS BAKER AND PASUK PHONGPAICHIT

ILLUSTRATED BY

Muangsing Janchai

SILKWORM BOOKS

This publication is funded by The James H. W. Thompson Foundation.

The Tale of Khun Chang Khun Phaen
© 2010 by Chris Baker and Pasuk Phongpaichit
Illustrations © 2010 by Muangsing Janchai

Jacket: From *Khun Phaen and Kaeo Kiriya*, oil painting by Chakrabhand Posayakrit, 1989–90.

First edition published in 2010

Silkworm Books
6 Sukkasem Road, T. Suthep
Chiang Mai 50200 Thailand

ISBN: 978-974-9511-95-4 (Main volume)
ISBN: 978-974-9511-96-1 (Companion volume)
ISBN: 978-974-9511-98-5 (Two-volume set)

info@silkwormbooks.com
http://www.silkwormbooks.com

Typeset by Silk Type in Minon Pro 10.5 pt.
Design by Trasvin Jittidecharak

Printed in China
10 9 8 7 6 5 4 3 2 1

CONTENTS

INTRODUCTION

After some brief preliminaries, the first chapter of *Khun Chang Khun Phaen (KCKP)* announces: "This is the story of Khun Phaen, Khun Chang, and the fair Nang Wanthong." That story, ending with Wanthong's death, is presented in the first volume of this edition. But there is a lot more to the *KCKP* tradition, including alternative versions of various episodes in the story, and additional episodes which extend the story down through several generations. In this volume, we offer a sampling of these. We also include a translation of Prince Damrong's major study on the origin and development of the *KCKP* story, and listings of flora, fauna, costume, weaponry, and food mentioned in the poem.

In Thai literary tradition, a story is often not the property of a single author, but something more like a raga in Indian classical music—a theme which individual performers can elaborate into their own version. Owing to its huge popularity in late Ayutthaya and early Bangkok, *KCKP* is the best example of this process. We surmise that an Original Story with certain key incidents—romance in a cotton field, Phlai's departure on campaign, Chang's subterfuge, the jealous quarrel, Khun Phaen equipping himself for revenge, the abduction of Wanthong, trial and execution—was very widely known. Various performers improvised their own versions of these episodes, adding detail, dialogue, and incident to entertain audiences that wanted to hear a familiar story with some fresh touches. Performers also seem to have responded to this audience demand by adding new episodes which extended the story, often with ingenious links back to the well-known original.

Part 1 of this companion volume presents extensions to the story beyond the death of Wanthong. In his edition, Prince Damrong included seven further chapters before ruling that "subsequent chapters . . . are of no literary value in either story or poetic style and thus will not be revised and printed" (see below, p. 1370). These seven chapters focus on Khun Phaen's second son, Phlai Chumphon. Here we present translations of these seven chapters, based on the Prince Damrong (PD) edition with small additions from the Wat Ko (WK) and Khru Jaeng (KJ) versions.

Many other episodes were added, probably in the nineteenth century, though no details are known about timing or authors. The hook for the extension of the story is the marriage of Khun Phaen's son, Phra Wai, to two contrasting wives—his Phichit sweetheart, Simala, and the beautiful but brittle princess of Chiang Mai, Soifa. From this contrast, authors developed a story of two contending factions of Khun Phaen's lineage descended from these two wives. At the start of this sequel, the remaining key characters from the main story die in an epidemic. The main characters of the sequel are the grandsons and great-grandsons of Khun Phaen. Descendants of several other characters from the main story appear in supporting roles. These additional chapters have been printed in two collections which have only minor differences. Here we offer a summary of the plot, and translations of the chapter headings and sub-headings which give a synopsis.

Parts 2 and 3 offer alternative versions of certain episodes of the main story. Prince Damrong judged that Khun Phaen's abduction of Wanthong from Khun Chang's house in chapters 17–18 is the "high point" of the poem because it has "many moods—admiration, lovemaking, complaint, grief, humor, anger—combined in one passage" (see below, p. 1366). As a result, this episode was more widely memorized and performed than any other, resulting in many versions. Two old versions were printed in 1925, and are presented in translation here. Comparing these two variants and the version in the main volume gives insight into the development of the poem.

The jealous quarrel between Wanthong and Laothong in chapter 13 is another of the most famous episodes. The quarrel between Simala and Soifa in chapter 37 is in many ways a reprise of this original. Here we present both these quarrel scenes in alternative versions which seem to be earlier and earthier.

Khun Phaen's search for a sword, horse, and spirit son in chapter 16 is an axial point in the main story. Prince Damrong admitted having great difficulty choosing between alternative versions. Here we present alternative versions of all three episodes in Khun Phaen's search.

In his commentary on *KCKP*, Kukrit Pramoj reproduced a passage of parental advice which he claimed was authored by Khru Jaeng. Kukrit claimed that he had memorized the passage from a book which he had lost and which was already impossible to find twenty years ago. We have been unable to locate either the book or a manuscript version, but the passage is interesting enough to reproduce.

In his preface, Prince Damrong describes in detail how the performance of *KCKP* changed over the nineteenth century with the incorporation of music. The final passage in part 2, in which Khun Chang listens to a *mahori* performance, may have been developed to showcase musicianship.

In the mid-nineteenth century, the account of the military campaign against Chiang Mai in chapters 27–32 was substantially revised, with Khru Jaeng among the authors. The older version, found in the Smith and Wat Ko printed editions, is fascinating in its own right. Much of the campaign is told from the viewpoint of the ordinary soldiers. On the march, they live off the land. In battle, they kill and are killed. In victory, they loot property and seize women. It may be one of the most graphic evocations of pre-modern warfare in the region. Prince Damrong considered it "vulgar." In the revised version in his edition, the looting, raping, and much of the violence of combat were expunged. We have imported a few key passages from this earlier version into our translation in the first volume. In part 3 we offer the full account.

Prince Damrong wrote a preface distributed across the three volumes of his 1917–18 edition. This preface is the most important study on the development of *KCKP*. For the second edition in 1925, Prince Damrong wrote a revised preface which has much new material as well as some revised judgments. Although it results in some duplication, we offer full translations of both prefaces in part 4.

KCKP teems with life—human, plant, and animal. Part 5 has listings of all the flora and fauna mentioned in the poem. One convention of *KCKP* and other Thai poetry is detailed description of dressing before major events such as lovemaking, ceremonies, or battle. As a result, the poem mentions a large array of cloth, costume, and personal ornament. Part 5 also contains a listing of these articles, another listing of weapons and military terms, and a listing of prepared forms of food.

PART 1

THE STORY CONTINUED

In his 1917–18 printed edition, Prince Damrong included seven chapters beyond the death of Wanthong.

Six of these chapters were among the first collection of *KCKP* manuscripts assembled in the palace in the Fourth Reign. For the seventh and final chapter about a giant crocodile terrorizing the Chaophraya River, Prince Damrong chose Khru Jaeng's version, based on an episode in the palace manuscripts but extensively rewritten. These seven chapters recount a quarrel between Phra Wai's two wives, and the childhood and youth of Khun Phaen's second son, Phlai Chumphon. The plotting and detail are much less accomplished than in earlier chapters. Soifa lacks any sign of her royal origins. Phlai Chumphon, aged only seven or eight, undertakes extraordinary journeys. Khun Phaen leaves Ayutthaya promising to be back within weeks but fails to return for eight years. Simala's pregnancy seems to last that same length of time. Phlai Phet puts in an appearance even though he is not born until a later episode. Distances are wildly underestimated, and the geography is faulty.

Yet individual episodes in this segment of *KCKP* have been popular, particularly the quarrel between Soifa and Simala, Wanthong's reappearance as a netherworlder, and Elder Khwat's rampage as a giant crocodile.

37: SOIFA MAKES A LOVE CHARM

Now to tell of Phra Wai. He was incomparably happy and fulfilled—as bright and cheerful as the moon. His taste for love was undiminished, day or night.

But Soifa tended to be moody. If she got less attention, she would sob. If her husband came to sleep with her, she swallowed every spoonful, but if he missed a night, she became gloomy.

A young man with two wives tends to lose vigor, and the wives tend to compete over him, so rivalry arises between them, particularly if one wife makes matters worse by provocation.

Simala was generally wreathed in smiles because her husband loved her. Soifa got very worked up but hid it out of fear and respect for Thong Prasi who would not spare anyone, son or wife.

Soifa controlled her feelings like a tiger hiding its claws, but if provoked, she would flare up. If another person crossed her, she would explode like a raging fire. If the other stayed quiet, she would pounce.

pancake making

On the afternoon of the day when the trouble arose, Phra Wai and Phlai Chumphon were relaxing in the sitting hall, comforted by a cool wind.

Chumphon crawled up holding a chessboard. "Will you play chess with me? If I lose, I'll let you pull my eyelashes. You say what you'll do if you lose."

Phra Wai said, "If I lose, I'll have them make sweets for you—delicious little *khanom bueang* pancakes."[1] He promptly gave the orders.

Soifa and Simala said, "Yes, sir!"

They got busy lighting a fire and putting on skillets. They cracked eggs, added

---

1. ขนมเบื้อง, small pancakes, made with a batter of rice flour, wheat flour, bean flour, palm sugar, and duck egg yolk, filled with a sweet or savory filling, then folded. A specialty of the central area, hence Soifa's lack of skill in making them.

waffle stove

flour and good sweet sugar, and chopped some shrimps.

Simala spread the batter very thin, and scooped the pancakes onto a plate for serving. Soifa was frustrated by her lack of skill. She added too much flour and spread the batter too thick.

Phlai Chumphon said, "Soifa makes pancakes as thick as *paengji* waffles!"[2] Phra Wai retorted, "Thick ones are good." Thong Prasi said, "I never heard such a thing.

The Lao make pancakes different from the Thai. When flat, they're like boiled frogs. Folded over they look like bent frog legs." Phlai Chumphon shook with laughter.

Simala shot a sidelong glance. Even the servants could not stop themselves smiling. I-Mai[3] called out, "How shameful! I forgot. I thought we were making *khanom khrok*."[4]

Chumphon shouted, "You keep correcting yourself. Before long it'll turn into *ho mok*!" Soifa shook with anger. She knocked over the flour, banged down a skillet, and flounced into her apartment.

Thong Prasi shouted, "You pestilential Lao! What a racket, you mangy dirty bitch! Spilling flour all over the house, and throwing the skillet about, you evil Lao!"

Soifa heard her grandmother-in-law's scolding and felt angry almost to weeping. Simala put out the stoves and went inside. Chumphon went into his grandmother's apartment.

❦

At nightfall, a bright moon floated through the clouds, and a refreshing breeze made Phra Wai feel frisky. He was aroused by thoughts of Simala.

A fresh fragrance, wafting from the pots of *phutthachat* flowers, overwhelmed his heart with sensual feelings. He walked into Simala's room, sat down close to her, and hugged her gently to excite her passion. He extinguished the bright light of the lamp, and asked her to lie down.

Simala said, "I'm shy. Lots of people are still awake." Phra Wai soothed her. "Don't be sulky. My love is as hot as a raging fire."

---

2. แป้งจี่, a deep-fried pancake made with a batter of glutinous rice, coconut, salt, and sugar.

3. Soifa's servant, who here takes it on herself to try to protect her mistress.

4. ขนมครก, a sweet made with a batter of flour and coconut milk, poured into the cupped rounds of a special skillet.

Simala said, "Tcha! So hotheaded. The sun hasn't set yet. Little children are still awake all over the city. It's easy making pancakes with your mouth."[5]

Soifa caught the mention of pancakes, and thought that Simala was gossiping about her. Aching with anger from her lungs to her stomach, she flared up like gunpowder touched by fire,

calling out, "Miss Pancake Maker is good at raising issues to show off to her husband. Miss Pancake Maker is good at spreading things out wide, I fear. When it's over, she still stirs it up again.

My, my! I've never made it tasty so the result's all messy, not scrumptious at all. My pancake roll is as big as an arm so husband doesn't get thrilled and ask for more."

Simala said, "Oh Buddha! You're beating me up for nothing, my dear. The old itch remains as itchy as ever. Pandan bushes look beautiful but it's their nature to have thorns.

On a canal bank, the bush can become a stump, and boats going up and down have to scrape past. Oh dear! What did I say? Not fitting. My neck will be throttled in anger.

I don't want to get into a hornets' nest because hornets are known to be fierce as fire. Such clever talk attracts notice—like a stump that gets in the way of boats.

The flotsam and jetsam that eddies around in a pool gets into everything, like a dose of salts.[6] I'm sick of people talking so much that the spittle flows with betel."

Soifa said, "Yes, I'm a thorny pandan. Whoever paddles a boat carelessly will get scratched. Those who don't keep an eye out deserve to have their ears smashed to pieces.

True, I'm the salts found in every dose. I can cure a bloated belly,[7] or reduce a heavy fever. Without me, you'd be stopped up tight and close to death.

My method may not be as good as the Farangs' beeswax, but astringent

---

5. Meaning, it's easy to sweet-talk.

6. ดีเกลือ, *dikluea*, mirabilite, Glauber's Salt, hydrated sodium sulfate. This is salt that appears through salination of paddy fields, or the fine, white, intensely flavored crystals found at the lower levels of salt fields. It is used in many herbal medicines to treat constipation, sore throat, mouth ulcers, skin ulcers, and wounds.

7. ท้องยุ้งพุงมาน, *thong yung phung man*, ricebarn gut dropsical belly, a swelling caused by accumulation of fluid, once called edema or abdominal dropsy.

water is very good for anything infected. Mix it with a lump of nutgall[8] and a little cutch,[9] and it'll close the flesh up tight.

Even if there's a painful cyst inside, it'll suck up the oily itchy pus,[10] right down to the liver, and close it up as tight as the surface of the earth."

Phra Wai liked this answer and was bent over with laughter. "Eh, you get so worked up over sweets that it finishes up with nutgall!

The Farang doctor's prescription is disgusting. They grind it up to put on boils. If you had a wound infected with pus, would you try it, Soifa?"

Soifa cried out in reply, "I don't know why I should use any medicine. I don't have any wound, and I don't have to study prescriptions.

If you get the clap,[11] use Simala's medicine. That'll cure it. Her medicine's been good for a long time. As for me, I'm afraid of Thai prescriptions."

Grandmother Thong Prasi heard the racket and could not restrain herself. She opened a window, looked out, and called, "What's this about medicine formulas, Soifa?

Oh, you're Lao. So Lao! Why are you so sulky, so quick-tongued you seem to know about everything? I've never learned what medicine is for what.

People around here are hollow-eyed from having to listen to you—even louder than the claves of Jao To. How can the husband sit listening quietly without concern?

Oh Grandson, you're no lieutenant of the pages. You should be netting shrimps and hawking shrimp paste on the Maeklong River.[12] Aren't you ashamed in front of the neighbors? Still want two wives, you pus ball?"

Soifa's face fell. She said, "Grandmother is taking sides. One person scolds and the next person joins in. The wind blows but has nowhere to go.

Why does the water flow uphill instead of flowing down to the lowland, Grandmother?"[13] Thong Prasi said, "Hmph! Making insinuations. This Lao mouth is too much!

---

8. เบญกานี, *benkani*, a growth that appears on the leaves of an oak, *Quercus infectoria*, as a result of eggs laid by the gall wasp, *Cynips tinctoria*. Used to make ink and medicines.

9. สีเสียด, *si siat*, black cutch, a dark tannin-rich extract from the tree, *Acacia catechu*.

10. หนองไหน, *nong nai*, near homophone and maybe alternative spelling of หนองใน meaning gonorrhea but more likely a pun, since the correct spelling of gonorrhea appears four stanzas down.

11. หนองใน, *nong nai*, gonorrhea, literally "inner pus/infection."

12. River running down the western side of the lower Chaophraya delta, with an old fishing port at its mouth (see map 2).

13. The high ground is the major wife, Simala, and the low ground the minor one, Soifa. As

You're making such a racket, you rude Lao, it fills the whole house, you busted beam. I'm fed up with you, you seven hundred dogs. You're past loving—just a disgruntled, noisy, upland Lao."

Hearing her grandmother's scolding, Soifa bent her head and fell onto her pillow. Thong Prasi trumpeted, "Such a sulky little thing!" Tired by all the cursing, she fell asleep, snoring.

The sun's chariot loomed up and dawn brightened all the continents of the world. Cocks crowed and birds called.

Tailorbirds twittered, weaverbirds warbled, and crows cavorted, cawing and cackling. Simala opened her eyes and washed her face, then made preparations for her husband.

She placed a bowl ready for him to wash his face, along with powder and makeup articles, mirror, and comb. She brought a change of clothes carefully arranged on a salver. Then she hurried out to call the servants.

"The sun's risen already. Wake up, all of you. Why are you still asleep?" The servants got up, quickly washed their faces, went into the kitchen, lit fires, and prepared food.

I-Moei got up and called out, copying her mistress, "Hey! Don't sleep late, or you'll get slapped," Simala said, "You dumb girl! I've never seen a servant who apes her mistress."

Phra Wai awoke and left the bed. He took a bowl and washed his face to freshen up. He combed his hair, powdered himself, got dressed, then walked out in front of the apartment.

Food was ready, and he sat down to eat. Servant girls crouched and crawled all around. Simala gave instructions. Soifa looked bitter and said nothing.

At the time for the morning entry into the palace, Phra Wai ordered clothes brought, changed his lowercloth, left the house, and went to the palace.

Servants walked behind him, overflowing the road. Other people coming and going made way for Phra Wai out of respect for his status. He entered the Chakkaphat Audience Hall.

Soifa was presented by the king, she would normally be ภริยาอันพระราชทาน, *phiriya un phra-ratchathan*, a royally granted wife, a special category under the law, and would automatically become the major wife and have other superior rights. The fact that this is not the case, and that Phra Wai maltreats her later in this scene, may be because she was seized in warfare and thus her status is ambiguous. It might also be because this episode was adapted from a story that was not about a wife of royal lineage at all.

Now to tell of the king, avatar of Vishnu's lineage,[14] upholder of Ayutthaya, the crown of monarchs. When a golden light lit the jeweled spire and illuminated the whole earth,

he walked out to the golden audience hall like a god king in his heavenly palace, accompanied by celestial maidens. The curtain was drawn to reveal the king,

seated on a jeweled throne under a lofty and majestic white umbrella. Conch, horn, gong, and fiddle played in melodious harmony.

All the nobles prostrated with clasped hands and waited, crouching, to respond to the king's commands. The king roared like a lion, "What's in Chinaman Thong's petition?"

Phraya Khlang[15] responded to the king. "My liege. Chinaman Thong stated that in the past he asked for the hand of Amdaeng[16] Sang, got the mother's consent, and took her to his house.

Chinaman Thong went to her five times but she resisted him forcefully. When he eventually wrestled her down, she abused him in front of the neighbors shamefully and beyond reason.

Hence he lays charges in the petition to be judged right or wrong. If he does not speak the truth, he offers his life. May Your Majesty have mercy."

The king smiled and laughed. "This evil Jek can't talk with his wife. She just scolds him, and he lays charges. I want none of this.

Maybe in China he can lay charges. Kick him out of the court." Then the king made inquiries on every division, and was well pleased with government business.

On completion, he walked from the splendid jeweled audience hall up to the inner residence in a joyful mood.

The officials of various departments came out. Some went to sit in the official sala on government duty, and those who were free returned home.

Phra Wai was happy to have finished his work. He left the palace and went straight home.

---

14. จักรกฤษณ์วิษณุวงศ์, Jakkrit Wisanuwong, wheel of Krishna from the lineage of Vishnu. Jakkrit is an old Indic royal title, which appears in Thai literature as the title of the grandfather of Unnarut (KW, 534).

15. In PD, พระยารักษ์, phraya rak but in WK, พระยาคลัง, phraya khlang, head of the treasury ministry, in charge of trade and foreign relations, and hence also of foreign residents such as the Chinaman in this passage.

16. อำแดง, title for a commoner woman.

Now to tell of Soifa. When the sun was shining brightly, she awoke feeling anger, as if some six fires were burning in her breast

with flames raging. Like a fierce tiger stalking its prey,[17] she waited around, spying through a gap to watch Phra Wai leave the house.

Then she stamped down onto the terrace and shouted loudly to summon the servants. "Why are you hiding your heads in your rooms so I have to call you? Why isn't I-Mai here? Where's she skulking?[18]

Just cuddling from early evening until late morning, wallowing shamelessly in lust, floating your face and flaunting your figure like a dancing swan. You should be chopped to pieces like a fish!

What's the problem about getting up in this house? Last night, a tray and bowl were left out. They were knocked over and broken to pieces by some black cats chasing and biting one another.

They made a mess of the roof, dislodging the thatch, and caused the bolts to slip and shake. You sleep so well you didn't drive them away. Ai-Sijan let loose the horses and donkeys.

They chased around knocking into the pillars and almost shaking the house down. The water jars were rattling around but you were just billing and cooing.

Your eyes saw nothing and your ears heard nothing because the two of you were sitting, stroking, and sighing all the time. When in favor, you can stand and leap at the same time. Delirious with desire. Oily-eyed."

I-Mai knew the meaning behind her mistress's abuse, and played up to her by picking up the thread and wagging her own tongue. "I woke late because I was happily lost in dreams.

I dreamed that Lord Rahu, who looked as big as an arm, grabbed the moon and swallowed it.[19] I opened my eyes and didn't know what was happening. Something was burning as bright as a row of paperbark torches.

Then mistress called out, startling me. I was still sobbing out of pity for the

---

17. A tiger that has eaten a human is believed to be possessed by that person's spirit, with the result that the tiger appears to other people in human form, and wants to eat more human flesh (KW, 689).

18. In this quarrel, the metaphors and allusions are sometimes abstruse. It is worth reading another version of this passage ("Soifa and Simala quarrel," see below, pp. 1169–73), an earlier version in which the issues and the imagery are much more straightforward. Probably this version is the result of a nineteenth-century revision intended to make the quarrel less crude and more "sophisticated."

19. The traditional explanation of an eclipse is that the god Rahu is swallowing the sun or moon.

lovely moon. I didn't know whether Rahu would shit it out, spit it out, or keep it swallowed until the next night."

I-Moei listened to I-Mai, feeling so hurt and ashamed for her mistress that her breast burned as if flaming with fire. "All this spitefulness is sinful."

She called out, "Hey, I-Mai! Where's this Lord Rahu as big as an arm? The mistress scolds and now the servant joins in! I've never heard of people dreaming in the middle of the day."

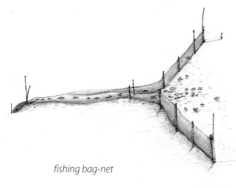

fishing bag-net

Simala called, "Hey, Moei! I didn't ask you so don't play up to your mistress by biting back with these loudmouthed insinuations. You're wiggling like the post of a fishing bag-net.[20]

However much abuse is being showered, why do you barge in? Is it your business to get in the middle? You're like a bramble blocking the road, you loose lady. I wasn't asking you so don't create an issue by getting involved."

Soifa felt hurt and needled as if stuck with a thorn. She rushed out of her room roaring. "Yes, I'm a thorn in a fence, you pet poppet.

Stop complaining for everyone to see. You wiggle like a dancer, a real expert. Nobody can say anything without you cursing back. The pillar in a preaching hall isn't as sturdy as your pillar.

I'm a toad that's fallen in a pond. Go on, stab me, I won't prevent you. It's your turn so enjoy it. Please powder your face to be fair, and rule the palace.

Truly it's you who is the post for a bag-net. Even though you dodge around, you seem to get knocked very often. You're so good at pleading and inviting pity. You babble like a bulbul and stay as moist as a mud snail."[21]

Simala sat listening quietly. "See. Karma catches up with one so easily. This cursing isn't right. You've got so used to it, you keep doing it.

---

20. โพงพาง, *phongphang*, a bag-net, fixed with stakes across the current of a river.

21. จุ๊บแจง, *jup jaeng*, salt water edible gastropod, *Cerithidea obtusa*, obtuse horn shell, horn snail, mud snail, blunt creeper. A 3–5 cm long spiral shell, especially found in mangroves, clinging to tree roots. They make a gurgling noise, reflected in the sound of their name.

What a pity. I didn't curse you even a little bit but you abuse me unjustly. It's true as you say, I've been wiggling since yesterday. An itch won't go away unless you cure it.

Ram in the pillar of an ordination hall or pillar of a wat! Why not choose to play as one likes? If husband comes, grab him quick, take him into the room and cure the itch for a couple of nights.

The issue arose because of the sweets yesterday evening, and flared up until late at night. The horse and the donkey created chaos, reducing everything to firewood. A little bit of water got turned into crashing waves.

Oh, whose heart wouldn't feel hurt? You're so good at picking and scolding. The more I stay quiet, the more you curse. Have you finished flinging abuse at me yet?

Why don't you be mistress of the house? Anyone in need will have to come crawling to you. I'm not the one who's a minor wife because a city fell,[22] so don't stamp everything to pieces, even slashing the shadows."

As maddened as if a kris had been stuck in her throat, Soifa blazed up like a smoldering log when kindling is added.

She clapped her hands, shook her head, and laughed uproariously. She hitched up her lowercloth, scratched her rear, and bounded forward in long strides. Trembling, she wagged her finger in Simala's face, raised her voice, and shouted.

"Hey, I'm the one that wiggles—all over. That's why he can't leave my room. Why don't I drag him out of your grasp? Please hold onto him for a while.

It's true, I'm a prisoner of war in this city. But let's not talk about a story that's spread far and wide, about an army turning up, and—baboom!—that evening there was a scandal in the house.[23]

When the army came home, it had a prisoner of war too. You're so good at covering up misdeeds. It wasn't worth teaching you about preserving virginity. When night fell, you made the move by yourself."

Simala also felt mad, as if hit a hundred blows with a stick. "You're good at flaunting yourself and merrily making mockery. You address me without respect.[24]

You have a loose mouth, good at sarcasm and slander. You deserve to have your face slapped. If my husband doesn't want to keep me, so what. However much he canes me, I don't care."

---

22. Meaning the fall of Chiang Mai, which resulted in Soifa being taken to Ayutthaya.
23. Referring to Phlai Ngam's escapades with Simala in Phichit in chapters 28 and 31.
24. Literally, "you use *ku, eng*," forms of I and you that are intimate rather than formal.

Soifa stamped forward, tightening the cloth over her breasts and tucking up her hair. Chumphon ran up, and tried to pull her away. Soifa pushed him so he spun round and fell down a gap in the floor.

Phlai Chumphon pulled up his leg, his face pale. Simala screamed in distress. Thong Prasi ran up shaking and shouting wildly. "Damn you!"

Coming close, she asked Simala, "Did the little fellow break his leg?" Phlai Chumphon wept, covered with blood. Soifa stood speechless.

Thong Prasi wagged a finger in her face and shouted, "Damn you! You big bully. You deliberately hurt my grandson, yet you're still flaunting your face and laughing enough to show the tendons in your neck.

You're like a nettle vine that goes around stinging people. You abuse people until they lose patience. You carry your head high like a chameleon,[25] you grinning ninny. You've been dancing around like someone possessed from yesterday till now.

chameleon

You're like a tusker in musth, wildly charging a wall down even though its own tusks are broken and trunk badly crushed. I'll slap you down, you scourge!"

The grandmother's scolding made Soifa's temper worse. Her mouth itched to let rip to the full. Instead she burst into tears and wailed.

"It's true. I'm an elephant in musth. You all club together to abuse me for fun. I'm alone with no kin so you beat me to your heart's content.

Your grandson ran up, grabbed my hand, pushed and pulled, but nobody said anything. When he fell down a hole, you blame me. Did I ask him to run up to me?"

Thong Prasi shouted, "You make such a racket, you forest Lao! I saw you push the child over with my own eyes, but you're talking as if I'm trying to shift the blame onto you.

Oh, you're so good, really, really good. You dance as if you had a band playing, as if you were a medium trembling under possession by a spirit. Did an ancestor spirit enter your orifice?"

---

25. กิ้งก่า, *kingka*, tree lizard, chameleon. They tend to stand with their neck stretched and head slightly cocked.

At that moment, Phra Wai reached the house and heard the loud sounds of quarreling and the voice of Soifa shouting. He strode up to the central hall.

Soifa was deep in argument with his grandmother. When she turned around, her mouth fell open in embarrassment. In fear that she would be found at fault, her whole body stiffened, and her fierceness evaporated.

Phra Wai stood glaring. The sight of Soifa depressed him. He tried to choke back his anger but it just flared up stronger, like fire or poison.

He asked his grandmother, "What's happening here? The racket is shaking the whole house. What were you arguing about just now? Who caused this uproar?"

Grandmother called out, "I'm totally fed up. Has the spirit possessing her gone yet? She dances around flaunting her face, putting on such an act. If you blow the flute and I beat the drum,

she'll dance and prance like old Bunjan[26] in a mask play. She doesn't fail to bash into everyone she meets, like a dugout boat blocking a canal.

In the beginning, she had an argument with Simala, and came running and shouting up to the door of her room. Chumphon stopped her, and she burst on him, so he fell down a gap in the floor and hurt his leg.

This happened because King Chaiyachet wanted some sweets, so round-eyed Suwitcha began shouting unstoppably.[27] She danced around the terrace, hitting and stabbing. I'm just a little finger that got chopped to pieces.

I don't know what they were arguing about before. Ask Simala, Grandson. Your women are tedious. Before long, you'll be the same."

Phra Wai asked straightaway, "What happened to reduce the house to such a noisy shambles, Simala? What was the quarrel about?

Why don't you think? You don't have even a little shame. If I don't complain. you'll get worse. Let's see who was in the wrong."

Simala replied, "The row started after you left the house. I was still sitting in my apartment. She came out of her room and began shouting wildly—

all kinds of complaints and abuse. It was too much, intolerable, nothing like it. Complaining about dogs and cats, all muddled up together. Saying some bowl and betel tray had been knocked over and broken.

Something about driving in the pillar for an ordination hall, a wat. Just

---

26. บุญจัน, probably a famous contemporary actor.

27. See p. 460, note 18 on Chaiyachet. Thong Prasi is using the names of characters from this drama for effect. There is no scene in the drama about sweets.

hammering on about nothing. Then the servant joined in with her mistress. Some sarcastic insinuation about an eclipse of the moon.

Then about going to war and taking someone prisoner in a bedroom. All very spiteful and abusive. Only when she saw you coming did she stop hurling it around. Her mouth is intolerable."

Soifa felt stabbed with thorns. "Tcha! This wife's good at telling all kinds of stories. True, your love for me is fading. She has the advantage so she can sound off happily.

I'm just a single lonely clove of rotten garlic. Nobody seems to have heard what she shouted at me, but they all pile in from every direction to bury me. When I argued, she tried to slap me.

I was telling I-Mai off in my apartment. It had nothing to do with Simala. I didn't do anything but got attacked on conjecture. Over a year ago, an astrologer predicted this misfortune."

Phra Wai said, "Mm! You're easily hurt and you make a lot of noise. Others were talking and you butted in. I know everything about your kind.

Even to my face, you dare to raise your voice. Behind my back, who'll argue with you? You're easily hurt yourself, yet you like picking on others. Nobody can match your wiliness.

Even when a child tries to stop you, he ends up injured. You snap at your elders without shame. You're a cruel, stupid loudmouth who shouts at people without respect for anyone.

Simala has helped you a lot but you still wag your finger in her face and mock her. Why should I keep you any longer?" He picked up a stick and went for her,

thwacking her so she was marked all over her back and shoulders. Soifa ran to escape in panic. "Please forgive your wife just this once."

Simala's anger turned to pity. She rushed forward and grabbed the stick. "Why are you hitting her? It'll leave marks." Soifa ran off to her inner room,

closed and bolted the door in fear, and lay down, writhing and sobbing, aching all over, weeping and wailing as if to die.

"How pitiful I am! When my father brought me to present to the king, I didn't think I'd be beaten and abused almost to death. This is terribly shaming.

My father and mother are too far away to turn to. Who can relieve my suffering? I entrusted myself to my husband, but it's like throwing myself into fire. He mashes me up like he'd mince fish.

Oh my golden bo, your beloved's shelter. Despite your protection, the sun is blazing. The branches are broken and the leaves withered. It remains only to kill me, my lord.

At first, I thought it would be eternal. I didn't know you were no better than a porter of kapok baskets. I think my life will crumble into dust. My merit is used up and I'll pass away.

I feel I'm floating in the middle of an ocean, too far to swim to the shore. I cling to a big post but it breaks. I have to hide away like a bedbug.

Oh my golden scales, why are you tilting to one side? Who can your wife rely on in a time of trouble? All my family is far away in another city.

How can I let them know, when they're at the ends of the earth and the yellow sky? Now my situation is hopeless. Who'll straighten things out?

There are only bad people who all act the same. If they saw me drowning, they'd beat me and push me further down so I flailed around until life departed. I think it's too much to expect to survive.

I'm like a jet gemstone fallen from its setting and shattered into dust. Everything looks black. How many years before the gem will be reset?"

She grieved with a troubled heart, her tears flooding down, her restless mind preventing any sleep. She grew ever more darkly angry until she began to think of taking revenge on Simala.

Late at night, she had an idea. "That teacher of mine is very able. For a long time, he hasn't come by. Is he still around or has he gone wandering off?

I must discover which is the wat where he's staying. If I can find Elder Khwat,[28] he'll be what I need. No problem."

She grieved until almost the start of the third watch, lying in deep thought with her left hand thrown across her forehead and her mind restless and anxious, until she finally fell fast asleep.

When the golden light of a brilliant sun brightened the sky, Soifa awoke feeling ever more incensed,

downcast, and vengeful because her beloved husband Phra Wai had believed Simala. "She incited him to almost kill me."

"I'm furious about what she told him, and how she sang her own praises to the full. If I stay quiet, this will be repeated until I'm destroyed, left to be blown

---

28. In chapter 32, the King of Chiang Mai left this man in Ayutthaya to help Soifa. In Thai, his title เถน, *then*, is rooted in a Pali word for a thief, which can be used for a monk in breach of the precepts. The title is used earlier in the poem for an old man who stays in a wat and feeds off the offerings (see p. 64, note 40). But it is also a homophone in Thai of the word เถร, meaning an elder, especially an elder monk. The usage here seems to play on these two meanings. He is an old man and he is addressed by Soifa and his own acolyte with words that mean a teacher or monk but he is clearly not an average monk.

away on the wind.

I'm like a fishing boat[29] with a pirate sail. When the wind blows, I keep skimming along through the stormy waves without sinking. Even when the sail looks limp and sad, let it be.

fishing boat

Though in a hopeless state, I can struggle through, but I have to know whether I'll live or die. I need an able person to serve as pilot and plot a course across the waters.

Elder Khwat is clever, superhuman. I should cling to him as my pilot. Simala wronged me first and made me angry. Now, rather than putting up with this, I'll take revenge."

With this thought, she called, "Hey, I-Mai! Come here quick. I'm so hurt it's not right. If you want to side with my accuser, that's up to you.

What are you thinking in your heart? Have I lost out or not, I-Mai? Are you going to side with Simala? Don't just listen quietly. Tell me the truth."

I-Mai listened with tears trickling down. "I've been your servant for a long time. Your mother, the queen, raised me in the palace since the time when my mother was still a servant.

When you had to leave Chiang Mai, I was by your side, facing the hardship too. I saw their bullying and lack of respect, and my own anger hasn't retreated for a minute.

If I could, I would've helped you yesterday, even if my back had been caned to death. How are you thinking of crushing Simala in revenge?"

"Don't worry, Mai, I already have an idea how to trample her to dust. This fellow, my teacher, is invulnerable, just like Old Lord Tiger Spirit.[30]

If you want to know who's good at spirits, it's him. If you want to summon up someone, he can do it. If you want someone to live, they'll live comfortably. If you want someone to die, they'll die in front of your eyes.

---

29. กุ๋ไล, *kulai*, an alternative spelling of กอและ, *kolae*, Malay *golek*, a brightly decorated Malay boat, once used in warfare, now for transport and fishing. A variant made in Pattani is known as ปตะกือระ, *patakuera*.

30. ปู่เจ้าสมิงพราย, *pu jao samingphrai*, an ascetic well-versed in the supernatural arts in the poem *Lilit Phra Lo* (see p. 344, note 31). The next couplet closely follows a famous passage describing this ascetic in *Lilit Phra Lo*: "He says, 'Die,' and it dies, instantly. He says, 'Live,' and it lives, immediately. If he calls anyone, they come." (Bickner, *Introduction*, 13).

He's expert at love charms. Hurry off to find him. Tell him the trouble that's arisen. If Elder Khwat still has some respect for me, let him not delay.

Out of consideration for King Chiang In, he must help me take revenge without fail. I'll reward him with five tamlueng of gold, and the same amount for you."

I-Mai said, "Oh! Don't say that. I won't take such payment. Truly this fellow is important. I'll take leave immediately."

She paid respect, got up, and left. She put Tani oil on her head and body, and dressed in a pretty uppercloth of parrot color,

a lowercloth of silk woven with a checkered pattern and a delicate pink lining. She picked out some excellent fruit to take along, ate her fill of breakfast, and left.

᪥

Now to tell of Elder Khwat, a royal teacher, who was formerly at Wat Wiang in Chiang Mai.[31] He was adept in various branches of knowledge, and known throughout the capital for his powers.

When the Thai army invested Chiang Mai, he was in the forest looking for fluid metal[32] of special power. Once he heard the news, he went to fight the enemy but was disappointed because the Thai had already taken the city,

and the King of Chiang Mai had offered full allegiance. Elder Khwat was upset enough to writhe to death. Then when the Lao were swept down to Ayutthaya, the King of Chiang Mai took him along as a companion.

Because of his belief in the old teacher's knowledge, the king retained him to overcome misfortunes using mantras and devices so the king would survive any dangers and return home.

When the King of Chiang Mai later returned home but Soifa had to stay in the south, the king was very concerned over his child and hence commanded the royal teacher to stay as her companion.

"In case any trouble should arise, you can overcome it. Don't let anyone know what you're up to. Find a way to behave like an itinerant monk[33] who has come down south."

Elder Khwat followed these orders. He went to stay in Wat Phraram[34] for

---

31. There is no wat of this name but it means the "city temple" and could refer to Wat Chiang Man, supposedly founded by Mengrai at the foundation of the city in 1296.

32. See p. 318, note 18.

33. พระธุดงค์, *phra thudong*, a monk who travels to expose himself to hardship as a way to control desire.

34. One of the major wat of Ayutthaya, almost central to the city (see map 8). According to

almost one rains retreat. He continued to behave like a Lao from Lanna, din-
ing and drinking liquor in the evenings.[35]

He would appear drunk in the ordination hall and create trouble until the
abbot, Phra Phimon,[36] could not tolerate it and said, "You fake elder, you drunk-
ard, I can't keep you." He was expelled from the chapter of Wat Phraram,

and so wandered around with Novice Jiw looking for a wat where they
could hide and escape their reputation. Eventually they arrived at Wat Phraya
Maen,[37]

and saw an abandoned kuti beside a graveyard. Few monks or novices were
around. For want of alternatives, they stayed there. The almsround did not
provide them with enough to feed themselves,

but Novice Jiw had a good idea. He went around telling people that his mas-
ter had knowledge and special powers that the spirits feared, and so had cured
sick people wherever he stayed.

Men and women, villagers and townsfolk, flocked to consult him. Some
asked for amulets, some for medicine, and some for bandeaus inscribed with
images of the Buddha.

Some had been affected by lore[38] and asked him to counter it by pouring
sacral water on their heads. In return they offered food, which solved the pair's
problems of hunger.

But some days after the forenoon meal, Elder Khwat still liked to dine and

---

the Luang Prasoet Chronicle, it was founded either at the death of the first king, Ramathibodi I,
in 1369, at the start of King Trailokanat's reign around 1448 (RCA, 11, 16).

35. In parts of northern Thailand and Laos, monks eat in the evenings and take liquor, though
usually covertly. Bizot argues that these and other practices are remnants of an old Southeast
Asian monastic tradition which, especially in areas remote from the main religious capitals, has
never been wholly replaced by "Sinhalese" practice (Bizot, *Le figuier*, especially 33).

36. In the listing of monastic titles from the Ayutthaya era, Phra Phimontham was the title
of the abbot of Wat Ramawat, and Phra Thepkawi that of Wat Phraram. In the Narai reign, a
Phra Phimontham, abbot of Wat Rakhang, acted as the king's astrologer (RCA, 280–81; KW,
542; KLW, 221).

37. Around 1.5 kms north up Sa Bua Canal from Wat Takrai (see map 8). According to the
chronicles, the future King Phetracha (r. 1688–1703) entered the monkhood here, and the abbot
predicted his future greatness, so after accession Phetracha restored and embellished the wat.
The early eighteenth-century Valentijn map shows the wat (as Wat na Maen, keyed as 65, see
Thawatchai, *Krung si ayutthaya*, 102). Its presence on this map suggests its importance, and the
thumbnail sketch, showing two stupas, an ordination hall compatible with the present remains,
and other buildings, suggests it was a substantial complex. The design of the ordination hall,
with no roof pillars, four tiers of lamp niches in the walls, and long oblong windows, suggests
it dates back no earlier than the Narai reign. (RCA, 321–22, 326, 332, 356–57; Busakorn, "Ban
Phlu Luang Dynasty," 44, 273; SWC, 9:4176; *Boranasathan*, 1:187–88)

38. ไสย, *sai*, a Pali word for supernaturalism, used today in the form *saiyasat* but rather rare
in *KCKP*.

drink liquor in the evening. He could not give it up. They had to keep dogs that guarded the stairs and barked to let them know someone had come.

If any evening Elder Khwat had got himself drunk, the novice would craftily help by saying his master was sick and had passed out. Only when the elder was well would the novice tell him to come out.

Because Novice Jiw knew this fault, he was not afraid that his master would scold him. Because he had fallen in love with knowledge, Jiw stayed with the elder as a favorite pupil, acting as his eyes and ears.

That day, Mai turned up in the morning and went in to ask whether the teacher was there. The dogs spotted her and ran up to surround her, barking fiercely.

Novice Jiw called out, "Get away, you ghost dogs. You there, have you come to see me or the teacher?" Timidly trying to evade the dogs, Mai called out, "Please help me!"

Novice Jiw shooed the dogs away, grabbed her wrist, and dragged her up the stairs away from them. Knowing Mai from before, he raised an eyebrow, narrowed his eyes, and grabbed the tail of her cloth. "Do you mind if I have this?"

Mai swatted his hand away and said, "Hey! So a fish that's been de-scaled[39] can still wriggle." Novice Jiw said, "An anabas[40] never gives up. Even when the scales are stripped away, the heart is still good."

Mai said, "Hey, Novice Jiw, why are you acting like a scissortail nibbling on shit."[41] She walked into the kuti and found Elder Khwat sitting cross-legged.

She sank down, put down the basket, wai-ed him, and said, "My mistress sent me to see you." She lifted the basket of fruit as an offering. The novice unloaded the fruit and returned the basket.

Elder Khwat greeted Mai. "It's such a long time, we're like strangers. Why did you leave me waiting here every day and night with no delight until I'm old and decrepit?

You came down from Chiang Mai. Are you well? You look cheerful. Two matching colors in the pattern of your uppercloth. Two lovely full cheeks.

If you were somewhere in Chiang Mai, your ears would be full of earrings. Now that you've come to the southern city, you're following the Thai. You've let the holes in your ears close up, like them.

---

39. ปลาขอด, *pla khot*, a "de-scaled fish," slang for someone who has shed worldliness by entering the monkhood (KW, 689).

40. ปลาหมอ, *pla mo*, "doctor fish," known for being very durable, not dying easily (SB, 558).

41. Referring to the proverb, ให้จระเข้กัดดีกว่าให้ปลาซิวตอด, *hai jorakhe kat di kwa hai pla sio tot*, better to be bitten by a crocodile than nibbled by a scissortail, better to be reprimanded by a superior than tutored by an inferior (Giles, "On Siamese Proverbs," 233).

Why did your mistress send you? Is she well too? Is there any problem, misfortune, or sickness? Do you have a husband yet?"

Mai wai-ed teacher Khwat and replied, "I don't think it's happy to be without relatives. Things are so hard, it's beyond me. Living alone, servant and mistress, is not pleasant.

As for having a husband and child, I'm too afraid. I don't go anywhere, not even the market. I can't count cowries like a Thai. I only come out when my mistress sends me.

She and her husband, Wai, have become badly estranged. Wai believes everything Simala tells him. Simala incited him to abuse and beat my mistress like a servant.

Master, please help. Bring his soul back without fail. Have him sleep with my mistress and cheer her up. She'll give you five tamlueng of gold."

Elder Khwat laughed. "Is that all she wants! I'll invite Wai's soul to return so he sleeps with your mistress and cuddles her, and this tension will disappear.

On this matter for which she sent you to me, I'll help her over the worry and sorrow. But my own problem is near fatal. If your mistress is kind, it'll ease matters.

Talking one on one and bluntly, if I can cure her sorrow, I'll ask her to let me keep you to be my partner and steam the rice for my forenoon meal in place of my pupil."

Mai said, "Hey, Master Khwat! I'm not willing to talk about having you as a husband. Your eyes are as white as rice water. Vultures come to ask for news every day, yet you're still flirting with me.

If you thought about yourself, you wouldn't want a girl. Do you wish to take off the robe and put on a shroud? Ninety years old and toothless. Even female flies don't settle on you."

Elder Khwat said, "I'm aged but I like to admire girls with their fragrant cheeks. I'm an old person, not an overripe fruit. Even if parrots flock around, I don't fall.

When can you say a human being is done for? Though I'm old, I can still keep my end up. You can't say I stink of fish yet. I've got the strength to do a job.

I just tend to get tired and short of breath.[42] When I'm collapsed, Mai could help revive me, by lying here to rub-a-dub-dub me through to daylight.

---

42. The remainder of this stanza is taken from WK, 32:1282; PD has: I have to put down the

Shift over here, Mai." He begged her to come close, and pass him a robe. "Let's talk straight. Why not have a peek at my lower robe? It's truly terrific!"

Novice Jiw poked his head round the door and said, "Master, don't talk about having a woman. It's not that I'm competing with you, I tell you. As a rule, I see you lying quietly in the wat.

What do you know about all of this? Better to leave off talking, and stick to dreaming. The day you went on almsround and tried to flirt with a woman, she just bowed her head and spat."

Elder Khwat cried, "Hey, Ai-Jiw! You're speaking nonsense, you ugly villain. Blathering on shamelessly. It's afternoon. Go and find the meal, you dumb novice."

Novice Jiw got up feeling annoyed. "I'll leave you to flirt on your own. Don't you fear the sin and karma?" Elder Khwat shouted, "I'll beat you, you idiot!

Mai, don't let this continue any longer. Ask Soifa to come here. Tomorrow is auspicious. Please come in secret to avoid trouble."

Mai made her farewell. "I'll come early tomorrow." She left the wat, walked back, and saw her mistress sitting looking out of a window.

Soifa nodded and smiled. I-Mai entered her room tiptoeing carefully. Beaming, she whispered the news. "I went to find the old teacher.

He thinks he can cure the problem for sure. Don't lose heart. He's willing to help. Tomorrow you're to go and speak with him. He'll make it a success."

Soifa was delighted. She lay thinking about achieving her wish. At dawn she got up promptly,
washed herself, and scrubbed her face smooth and bright. Seeing traces of the beating on her arm made her feel vengeful. She stroked her back and shoulders, feeling bruised and hurt.

"These wounds ache but not as much as my heart. Unless I have revenge on Simala, the hurt won't disappear even though the marks of the cane fade. As long as I live, I'll seek revenge. I'm not losing to her."

She changed clothes and went back into the bedroom, still feeling unsettled. She combed her hair, powdered her face, polished her teeth, and put on a two-layer sabai.

She passed a betel box to I-Mai, handed good things appropriate for presents to trusted slave girls, and went out.

---

spade and sit, talk, smoke tobacco, drink some water, have a bite to eat, and so on. When the strength returns, I can keep going until nightfall.

As Phra Wai had gone to audience, Soifa left without anybody noticing anything suspicious. She reached Wat Phraya Maen and happily went up to the kuti.

Sinking down, she prostrated to the teacher and presented her many offerings. The servants went to wait in the sala, leaving only Soifa and I-Mai in the kuti.

Soifa implored the teacher, "My suffering is more than I can suppress. My husband beat me and shamed me in front of Simala.

She provoked this discord by making up all kinds of accusations. Wai believed what she said, and now we're permanently estranged. If our eyes meet, he looks away coldly in anger.

Also, Grandmother Thong Prasi stirs up trouble and abuses me relentlessly. Please get me out of this difficulty, master. Make Phra Wai come back to sleep with me."

She took out her purse. "I'm counting out your fee in advance. If Wai comes back, don't worry. I'll carry everything over here for you."

Elder Khwat sat listening quietly to Soifa, and then replied, "Why suffer? If I fix this for you, Phra Wai will become good again within less than a day."

Saying no more than that, he lit incense and candles, and did the rite on the spot. He picked up a bronze bowl. At an auspicious time, he filled it with water, chanted a mantra,

held his breath, and then blew. The water seethed. Froth and foam bubbled up and overflowed. He passed the bowl to Soifa. "The time is auspicious. Make your wish immediately."

Soifa happily raised the bowl above her head. "May this lore succeed in bringing a grave evil to its end.

Please turn the heart of Phra Wai so he blindly comes to my room, so he no longer yearns for Simala but hates her, and so he becomes besotted with me under the influence of the mantra."

After the wish, she washed her hair, and began to brighten up. The gloom disappeared from her face, and she talked happily with the teacher.

The royal teacher examined the time and was pleased. He took beeswax recently used to cover the mouth of a corpse, and mixed it with ash from a cremation.[43]

---

43. According to old custom, during the ceremonies prior to cremation, the face of a corpse was sometimes covered with a layer of beeswax around half an inch thick, perhaps to disguise any ugliness. For rich people, the beeswax might be covered with gold leaf, or substituted by a

He traced letters with the powder, enchanted them, blew a formula, and then molded two figures, placed side by side. On one he inscribed a yantra with the name Simala,

and on the other, the name Phra Wai. He placed the two figures with backs together, facing away from each other, inserted thorns all over the bodies, then tied them tightly together, like binding a corpse.[44]

He drew another yantra, wrapped the figures in a fishtail palm leaf,[45] and sent Novice Jiw to bury them in the main graveyard. Then he molded figures of Soifa and Phra Wai, and placed them on amora leaves inscribed with yantra.

love charm

He sat chanting a formula and blew it. When his breath hit the two figures, they turned to face each other, hugging tightly. He fastened them together with sacred thread.

"Bury these figures under the place where you sleep. Within a day, he'll rush to you." He enchanted a mixture of powder, sandal oil, medicinal herbs, and spirit oil,[46]

and handed it to Soifa. "Go now. It's getting late. If this is effective, send Mai to bring a forenoon meal tomorrow."

Soifa responded, "No need to be impatient. I ask only that this will fulfill my hopes." She took leave of the elder and novice, left the precincts of the wat, and returned home.

At the house, she did everything the elder had ordered. That evening, she lay down on her bed feeling anxious and apprehensive.

Asleep in his room, Phra Wai had a turbulent dream that Soifa came and asked him to go and sleep beside her in her room.

He mumbled blearily in his sleep, woke up, and saw Simala at his side. His

---

sheet of gold. This mask would be taken off before cremation, and the beeswax used by spirit doctors as a powerful ingredient (Anuman, *Prapheni nueang nai kan tai*, 47–48; KW, 550). "Some methods [of making love charms] must draw on the power of the spirits. For candle meditation, the candle should be placed on a skull, and for making figures, beeswax from the face-mask of a corpse should be used" (PKW, 2:27). Some manuals prescribe the use of a skull for mixing the ingredients of such a love charm. In chapter 41, when the charm is discovered, a skull is mentioned, suggesting that a skull was used in some versions of this scene.

44. See p. 48, note 79.

45. เต่าร้ง, also เต่าร้าง, *taorang, Caryota mitis*, a palm with sap that causes itchiness to the skin and blindness if it enters the eyes. The *rang* syllable can mean "abandoned."

46. See p. 795, note 18.

heart flashed hot as if hit by fire. He turned away, feeling repulsion, and could not look at her.

The room flickered in the lamplight. Through his drowsiness he saw shadows, and strained forward to look. A breeze wafted pollen. His heart leapt and nerves tingled.

A bright moon shone. The sky sparkled with a profusion of bright stars. He went to embrace Simala but when he came close he knew she was the wrong person.

"Oh! Sweetheart, life's blossom, I'm surprised."[47] He felt uneasy. His skin crawled and his hair stood on end. "Am I being possessed by a bad spirit?" He went to Soifa's apartment, babbling deliriously,

hid close to the wall, and heard the quiet inside. Nothing stirred. Lamps burned brightly. He pushed the door but it stuck halfway. He tapped and waited to see what would happen.

Soifa did not make a sound. She realized the power of the lore was working exactly as the elder had ordered.

"If Wai comes, don't be afraid. Wait and see how the royal teacher's power has affected him. Will he explode in rage like before, or be submissive?" She said, "Who's sneaking around there? Are you spirit or person?

Aren't you afraid of my husband, Phra Wai? He's already thrashed me to pieces beyond what I can bear. Are you the spirit of my grandfather? I'll make offerings.

Have you come to see me because I was caned? Tomorrow I'll make offerings to feed you. I will, I promise. I'm not telling lies. Don't worry about coming into my room. I'll sleep."

"Oh Soifa, my eye's jewel, I'm not a spirit come to play tricks. Don't be afraid. Your soul is weak but don't fret.

You're frightened and confused because on the day you were beaten as punishment, your soul bounded away. I've come to embrace you and make your soul return to your fair body.

My beauty, please open the door. Don't keep the room closed and ignore me. Stop being hurt and sorrowful. Ease your mind and forget about the punishment."

---

47. This line is taken from WK, 32:1288; PD and SS both have: "I thought it was you. I didn't realize it was just the shadow of a plant." Possibly this discrepancy arose from copyists trying to interpret a damaged part of a manuscript.

"Is it you? I didn't realize. I didn't think you could come. Aren't you worried about Simala? Did you take leave of her or not?

If she wakes up and can't find you, she'll be hopping mad. She'll come after her man, shouting out loud. It's a pity but this meeting will come to nothing.

Please return to her room, and don't feel disappointed. I'm not a heavenly maiden but a bad person—bad in every possible way. Enough! What has happened has happened.

My back is swollen and my whole body smashed. I don't think I can be happy with you. The marks of the stick are all over me. I'm hurt inside and outside beyond what I can bear.

Yet you come to create even more karma. In a moment, your wife will arrive and make a scene. I'll be shamed in front of others yet again. This will create something else for Simala to rake over in the future."

"Oh light of my eye, don't think I'm like that. I love you as much as my own heart. I haven't stopped loving you for one minute.

You were in the wrong so you were beaten. Did I scold you for nothing? You raised your voice, trumpeted wildly, and wagged your finger with unblinking eyes. I was angry so I beat you.

The cause was your own rashness, your wild behavior, and lack of respect for my feelings. I've calmed down now and I'm feeling very merciful, but you still accuse me as if I'm breaking things off.

I may be wrong but please think of the time we were in love. Where will this aggression and anger get us? Please calm down and be less sorrowful. Don't break off the relationship. I'm true to you."

"Don't try to soften me up. I'm still angry. This has all affected me very deeply. While I was good, all I got was hatred. The lady put you up to being contemptuous of me.

You complained about everything and wanted to break it off. You picked at me without any consideration. I survived only because of Chumphon. If I hadn't been able to escape and hide in my room, I'd have breathed my last.

Even then, you grabbed your sword, and Simala went on shouting. You scolded and abused me for her to hear. The neighbors must be fed up with listening to all this.

That wasn't enough. You accused me of quarrelling. You raised your sword to cut off my head. You complained and complained to intimidate me because the lady provoked you to do so.

When you're kissing and cuddling her, I feel humiliated and heartbroken. Who could tolerate this? You've come here talking a pack of lies and wanting me to forget. I know I have nothing every morning and night.

Were you to file gold for me to eat, I wouldn't be happy. From now on, I don't want to see you—a man who can't keep his wife under control, and whose tongue is only good at trickery."

"Eh? Are these words worth listening to? You like rambling on about matters from the past. Once you've raised your voice, you don't ease off. You started it first so who are you to complain?

I told you off but did you restrain yourself? No, you kept stubbornly on with too much sarcasm and innuendo. The question is, who is trying to break this thing off?

I stopped you but you just made a bigger, angrier scene—insisting on arguing on and on. I come to see you but you complain and act sulkily. My love for you is too hot to bear.

I call out to you, eye's jewel, but you won't open up and receive me. You just keep on complaining until I'm crushed." While speaking, he chanted a formula that sprung the locks and bolts.

Soifa pushed the door open. "Look here, Wai, sir, what's all this—disturbing me in such an angry state? In a moment what will be will be."

"Tcha, my darling! Your eloquence never dries up. My hand is itching for some satisfaction." He made as if to grab a stick to beat her.

"Hit me if you dare. You're not listening. Why don't you punch me? Watch out that I don't scratch and draw your blood." She pushed him away, pretending not to let him get near her.

"Tcha! Why are you really so stubborn?"[48] He embraced her round the neck, pushed her down onto the bed, wrapped himself around her, kissing and stroking her precious parts. "I won't hit and hurt you again."

"Stop playing with me like this." "Why are you stopping me?" He clutched her close to his chest. "Your cheeks are more fragrant than a *phayom* flower."

He cradled her breasts, still tight and full. His hands felt, fondled, and kneaded. She pushed, pulled, and scratched. "Hey, don't squeeze me hard, it tickles."

"Oh, peak of love, sweetheart, why are you resisting, being shy and

---

48. From here until the end of the section, "grinding each other to bliss," is taken from WK, 33:1294, replaced in PD by: He took her by the neck, bent her over, lifted her in his arms onto the bed, and said beseechingly, "I won't hit and hurt you again. / Stop being angry. Why are you flailing around?" At the same time, he thrust in tune with an inner rhythm. He experienced joy before falling asleep with her.

hesitant?" Then they came together in the customary way, gradually grinding each other to bliss.

To north and south, a golden light lit up the sky. The sun's rays shone through a central window. Phra Wai and Soifa awoke immediately,
got up from the bed, and went together to rinse their mouths. Mai crawled in and set up a betel tray. She caught Soifa's eye and they exchanged a glance. Phra Wai prepared to go to the palace.

He changed clothes, grasped an umbrella, and descended from the house. His youthful retainers thronged along behind. All the way to the entrance of the golden audience hall, his heart was in turmoil with thoughts of Soifa.

Chaophraya and lesser nobles swarmed into the audience. The king, upholder of the three worlds, was feeling merry.

He roared like a lion, asking, "Phlai Ngam, why are you looking so murky? Your face is dark and badly freckled.[49] What are you unhappy about?

Perhaps your two wives are jealously bickering and insulting each other. People with two wives tend to be miserable. You can't find a single one that's happy.

Having three or four is better. According to the manual, that's bliss. I say you must watch out or there'll be trouble in the future."

Phra Wai bowed his head. Lost in befuddled thought, he said nothing. Under the influence of the mantra, he felt dull and so did not address the king.

---

49. A sign of being under the influence of a love charm.

Now to tell of the young Lao woman, Mai. When Phra Wai left the house, she flashed a broad smile and whispered a question to Soifa.

"Today you seem cheerful. He came last night as planned, didn't he? Was it as good as before? Myself, I lay worrying and couldn't sleep."

Soifa smiled and shyly averted her face. "His fierceness was gone, you know. I was hard on him for a long time but he didn't argue back at all. He just tried to placate and please me.

I saw with my own eyes that the monk had got rid of the problem. I'll break Simala for sure. I'll row with her in front of him, and provoke him to cane her to the point of death."

I-Mai laughed and said, "Perfect! Now the lady's arrogance will disappear. We have the wind in our sails and will get anything we desire."

After the king left the audience, Phra Wai thought of Soifa. Every minute his mind was on her and her alone.

Towards Simala, he felt anger and hatred. "Will she be jealous?" He arrived home, went up to the central hall, and found the two wives sitting there together.

Simala was lifting a salver of cloth. Soifa pretended to bump into her, stumble, and fall down. "Oh, how about that! Look, my dear Wai.

She blocked me with her arm. She spat on my head. She hissed at me with her mouth open, dribbling betel spittle. She pushed me with her foot for her husband to see."

Phra Wai had been looking the other way and had not seen, but heard this loud appeal. He glanced at Soifa fallen down beside Simala,

and felt as angry as if licked by fire. He stood quivering with rage. "Mm! This is vicious behavior—pushing her with your foot like a servant.

Did I redeem you for many chang[1] to be a bully? You don't fear me at all. You hit and spit at will, even worse than you'd treat a war slave."

---

1. He uses the verb meaning to redeem a slave, particularly a debt slave, presumably as an insult.

Simala said, "I didn't do it. Lightning strike! My karma is very troubled. She feigned this craftily. She pretended to fall over, then said I kicked her."

"Eh! You're arguing again are you, you trickster? You kick Soifa down and then you lie to shift the blame, you evil, big-mouthed, fibber!

I saw it with my own eyes but you won't admit it. You like twisting words, Miss Sweet-talker, but I caught you out, Miss Tricky-tongue. At first, I thought you were good.

On the day you had a quarrel with Soifa, you made many, many complaints. You egged me on and pretended to cry until I beat her. But that wasn't enough to satisfy you.

Today you're trying to frame her again. I should rip your flesh. If I don't, it'll become a habit." He took a stick and chased after her,

thwacking her all across her back. Simala went to hide behind Thong Prasi, who shouted out, "Don't come here! He's hitting you because you're a disrespectful loudmouth.

What's all this trumpeting about! You should be tied by your hands and thrashed to death. He warned you but you argued back at the top of your voice. And you kicked and bullied Soifa."

Thong Prasi pushed Simala forward, saying, "Hit her again, Wai." Chumphon said, "Please don't, Brother." He came up to shield Simala. Phra Wai attacked again violently,

hitting Simala repeatedly, and catching Chumphon with several strokes. Simala ran into her room crying. Thong Prasi danced around.

She picked up Chumphon and shouted loud enough to shake the house, "Why did you hit my grandson? It's your wives who are having a jealous row. Why don't you hit them, you idiot?

You're afraid of your wife, afraid of losing face, you dirty madman, full of rubbish. You close your ears and close your eyes. You're raving, dumb, useless—drunk on women."

She tenderly carried her grandson away to bathe him. "Your back and shoulders are a mess, as if they were scratched by a chicken. That bighead hit you instead of his wife." Mumbling on through her tears,

she carried Chumphon into her room, and glumly looked at the mess on his back and shoulders. She soothed him, wiped away his tears, and applied casumunar. Then she took him to sleep on the big bed.

At dusk, Phlai Chumphon was lying on the bed with his grandmother, lost in gloomy thoughts.

"Oh Wai, brother of mine, I didn't think it'd be like this. You went astray and sided with Soifa even though her accusations were all lies.

You didn't make inquires, and so believed the wrong person. I suspect you've been affected by some love charm. Your face is dark and dull with freckles.

As for dear Simala, you actually love her well, Brother Wai. Yet she got beaten with the cane all over her body. Even Grandmother was urging you to beat her.

If even your dear wife can get tattooed with the cane, why should my back escape? We're not siblings of the same womb.[2] How much do you really love me?

If I stay, I'll be like a pig for the slaughter. I should go to find my parents. I'll take Goldchild,[3] and the two of us can stumble our way through the forest to Kanburi."

With these thoughts, he stifled his sadness, and hugged, kissed, and stroked Thong Prasi. "Your flesh is as soft as cotton, Grandma. Today I'll sleep here, and gaze on the supreme merit of your face. Please tell me a story, Grandma." Thong Prasi laughed merrily. "Lie down, dear grandson. I'll tell you a story.

How about the tale of Chaiyachet? How does it go? I don't know. Maybe I've forgotten. I remember only the bit where he goes into a forest and his wife, left behind, gives birth to a baby that turns into a cat.

Oh, that's wrong, that's not it. I'm lost, dear Grandson. I haven't seen this story played for a long time. Was it a cat or a log? I don't know."[4]

Phlai Chumphon laughed and praised her, "Beautifully told, Grandma!" Thong Prasi hugged, kissed, and stroked him, then fell asleep snoring on the bed.

Little Phlai Chumphon lay listening carefully. When he saw his grandmother was fast asleep, he slowly slid away, stood up, and looked around by the bright light of a lantern.

He felt very sad about leaving, and tears glistened on both his cheeks. He took off the bangles, bracelets, and *sema* chain that his grandmother had dressed him in.[5]

He bent his two anklets open, and took out the hairpin that fastened his topknot. Examining these things, he felt even gloomier. "If I keep them on, it'll be risky."

He piled them up at his grandmother's feet, then bowed his face and cried. "Oh, karma forces me to leave. I was hurt beyond endurance.

---

2. Phra Wai was born to Wanthong, and Chumphon to Kaeo Kiriya.

3. Khun Phaen must have left Goldchild behind in Ayutthaya to look after the family.

4. It was a log. See p. 460, note 18 on the drama *Chaiyachet*. The author is perhaps gently lampooning the outer dramas that are so full of such improbable transmutations that it is difficult to remember which is in which story.

5. He removes these valuables so as not to attract the attention of robbers.

I had hoped to depend on Grandma's merit but Brother Wai hit me violently. I must leave and find my way through the forest to Kanburi to tell my father.

My beloved grandma, when you wake up and find me gone, you'll cry out loud and brim over with tears." He embraced her feet, sobbing.

When a cock crowed, he stifled his sobs. Fearing she would wake and prevent him from leaving, he got down from the bed and went into an inner room. He put on a colored shirt and red leggings,

fixed his topknot, tied a bandeau tightly round it, cinched a belt, strung on an amulet, and carried a small kris. Tiptoeing stealthily out to the terrace,

he went into Simala's apartment, found her fast asleep, and felt sorry for her. Waking her up to say goodbye would take too long, so he parted the curtain, sat next to her on the bed,

and prostrated at her feet, sobbing softly with a heavy heart. "Oh, I have karma and must go away. Stay well. I take my leave.

I feel sorry for you. Soon you'll be lonely. This misguided man will beat and abuse you without respect. You'll waste away with misery. I'll disappear from your sight from today.

I think you'll weep and wail about me because you're used to seeing my face. We both still carry the marks of his beating. Thinking about it chokes me with anger.

Even if I stayed, I couldn't help you. I'll hurry to tell Father to come down here." Forcing himself to stifle his sadness and swallow his tears, he went out to the brightly lit central hall.

He saw some sweets on a little salver. "Perhaps Simala prepared these for me. I'll eat them along the way through the forest." He put them in a waist pouch and left the house.

The spirit called Goldchild walked along beside as companion. The sky was bright with moonlight. After descending from the house, they strode quickly

to the road that crossed the plain. At dawn, the bright light of the sun caught a film of dew on the ground. They walked along at a robust pace.

Goldchild led him into the forest under the shade of fine tall *yung* and *yang* trees. Little Phlai began to feel better. They made for Kanburi.

Let us interrupt the story of Phlai Chumphon to tell of Thong Prasi. While she was fast asleep at night, a cock flapped its wings and crowed loudly.

She dreamed that a big tiger came roaring after her and pounced on her back, clawing and biting. She flailed around on the bed, crying out loud in her sleep, and then woke up.

On opening her eyes, she realized it was a dream, but still trembled uncontrollably with fear. She looked to left and right and was worried at not seeing little Phlai.

She got up and shouted out, "Phlai Chumphon, where have you got to, you naughty boy?" She looked around and saw the bracelets, hairpin, anklets, and *sema* chain

all in a pile at the end of her bed. She was shocked almost to death. "Perhaps he's run away to his parents without taking leave. My dear grandson, why is this?"

She searched around without finding him. "Perhaps he woke up and is lying hidden somewhere." She got up from the bed and summoned the servants frantically.

"Hey, I-Mi, I-Mao, old I-To, and Ai-Pho! My, you like to sleep late. I'll cane your backs into stripes, damn you, lying around with your bottoms in the air."

The servants heard and woke in alarm. They groped around for their clothes, and got up quickly. Drawing the bolts, they sleepily poked their faces out to look.

Thong Prasi wagged her finger at them, shouting, "Your mother's clan! Phlai Chumphon has run off somewhere and you're just standing around. Go and find my grandchild. Quickly!"

The servants rushed all over the house. Some shouted out Phlai's name. Some ran to make inquiries at the wat and returned to tell their mistress they had not found him.

Thong Prasi sobbed, beat her breast, and fainted down on her back from worry. Servants rushed up and frantically helped to revive her.

Soifa and Phra Wai were asleep in their room when they heard people shouting and shrieking. In panic that a fire was burning on the roof, they got up and grabbed their things, shouting out loud.

They tumbled out of the door and saw there was no fire but people running wildly around the terrace. They asked, "What's the matter?"

Thong Prasi wagged a finger at Phra Wai and shouted, "You sleep late, you evil villain. Because of your wives' jealousy, Phlai Chumphon got beaten, and so he's run away.

Still you dare to poke your face in and ask questions. Your mother's clan! You've got to find him and bring him back. If I don't have my grandson, many people will have their heads slapped, don't you worry."

Then she turned on her granddaughter-in-law, Soifa. "Karma has arisen because of this Lao, this northerner, ranting on until her voice is hoarse. A lovely face but the heart of a tiger. Unbelievable!"

Then she fell to lamenting. "Oh my dear Phlai Chumphon, if you were here now, I'd enjoy being with you. In the daytime, you'd ask me to make figures of cattle.

Morning and evening you'd run around playing, making a merry din. Today it's quiet, my beloved. Why should I go on living to be miserable?" She lay down and flailed around on the terrace.

Seeing his grandmother cry made Phra Wai concerned. He cast a horoscope following a teacher's manual. "A Tuesday with a remnant of Saturn entering the time of the moon.[6]

He'll go and return with no problem. He'll meet his parents and be joyful." He went inside, wai-ed his grandmother, and said, "I find no problem for Grandson Phlai.

I looked at the horoscope according to the manual. In the details it says he'll go to stay with his parents. He misses his mother and father for sure, so he probably went to Kanburi.

In fifteen days we'll get news. No need to make a big fuss. Nobody can do anything about it. He'll come back before long."

Thong Prasi sat quietly listening to Phra Wai. She saw the truth in what he said, and calmed down. "Well, you've looked at the horoscope by the manual. If things are as you say, I'll stop worrying.

---

6. This is a variant of the ทักษา, *thaksa* or *mahathaksa* method, a form of astrological divination based on age and day of birth (see p. 793, note 15). A life is dominated by eight planets—the seven day planets plus Rahu—set out in a three-by-three diagram. The day of birth dictates the starting point, with Rahu assigned half of Wednesday. Each planet rules for a certain period then is succeeded by the next in clockwise order, for a total of 108 years. Thus someone born on a Monday will be ruled by the moon for fifteen years, then Mars for eight years, and so on. However, the ruling planet rules alone for only a fraction of its span, and then other planets exert a secondary influence, again in clockwise order, beginning with the next planet in clockwise sequence. This secondary influence operates for the same fraction of the span as in

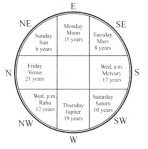

the division of years. So for someone born on a Monday, the moon rules solo for 15/108ths of the fifteen years, then Mars exerts secondary influence for 8/108ths of the fifteen years, and so on. The four planets at the cardinal points (moon, Mercury, Jupiter, and Venus) are generally favorable, while the others are not. Here Phlai Chumphon is in the cell dominated by the moon, and Saturn is exerting secondary influence, which happens after (15+8+17)/108ths of the moon's fifteen years have passed—about five and a half years. This position would not usually be considered favorable (Thep, *Horasat nai wannakhadi*, 521–29).

But if you're not sure and are fibbing to me, may your mother's clan all drop dead like a downpour. My grandson is not yet a grown man. Walking through the forest alone,

he'll be scared by the sounds of wild animals, and won't be able to avoid feeling lonely. Paddy fields are overgrown with grass and weeds, and swarming with all kinds of snakes."

She went grumbling back to her room. The sight of his things made her miss him even more. She found a little cord strung with cowries and prayed. "All the shrines and all the spirits,

please protect my grandson. I'll make offerings of duck, chicken, rice liquor, and two pig's heads. I'm not pretending." She made a garland of cowries and hung it on the head of the bed.

From morning to evening, she grieved for her little grandson, sadly hugging a pillow. At sundown, she wept with worry every passing day.

Now to tell of Phlai Chumphon walking through the forest. When they came to the region of Suphan town, Goldchild turned himself into a little boy,

and walked along with Phlai Chumphon, chatting as his companion. When the sun sank in the afternoon, Phlai became sad.

"I feel so sorry for dear Grandmother. She'll fuss and fret from missing me. By now the house will be in uproar, with everyone arguing angrily.

The neighbors will have come to inquire. I sympathize with you, Simala. Now that I've left, who'll be your friend? You used to tell me to fix my topknot all the time.

You'd bathe me, apply turmeric, and feed me. I love you greatly for this kindness. Though you're a sister-in-law, you didn't take sides but looked after me like a mother.

Karma, oh karma made me part from you. Now you'll sit weeping, and we won't see each other for days." He walked through the forest grieving.

Seeing his sadness, Goldchild encouraged him to enjoy the fine forest trees. "There's a cabal of crows cavorting on a *tumka* with a crowvine. Those cawing crows are gazing at a *kalong*.[7]

---

7. As usual in these passages, the sound is more important than the meaning. This line plays with a string of near homophones to imitate the cawing of crows. The next couplet plays similarly with the sound *khang*, langur, and the following one with *ling*, monkey, a bit like: monkish-looking monkeys were monkeying around in a monkey-puzzle tree.

That *khang* tree beside the hill is full of langurs, scratching their chins, covering their faces, and spreading their legs.

In the cucumber tree, monkeys are chasing other monkeys. And there's a monkey scampering up a *langling*."

There were stands of great tall *yung* and *yang* trees, with untidy looking lianas snaking through their branches, wound round one another in funny shapes. Some hung down like a forest swing that beckoned them to play.

Goldchild got Phlai Chumphon to sit and swing. A cool wind blew under the shade of the big trees. Phlai ate the sweets and felt refreshed. They hurried onwards before sunset.

Seeing wild cocks, they ran after them, throwing earth and grabbing at them playfully. When evening came, dew fell and a bright moon rose.

Scattered stars glittered around the moon and ornamented the whole sky. Goldchild led Phlai Chumphon along, telling him to admire the moon.

"See, the moon has a halo. It looks perfect. There's nothing like it. In the future, when you're grown up and seeking a wife, it would be really good to find one with a face like the moon."

Phlai Chumphon said, "I want to be an abbot. I'm not interested in getting a woman. If you have a beautiful wife, men try to grab her. I don't want all that bother."

Both of them laughed. The sadness and gloom lifted. To cut a long story short, they reached Kanburi in the dim before dawn.

Goldchild led him along a road, looking at the houses and people on both sides. Goldchild pointed out the residence of the governor of Kanburi, saying "That big house with the pot plants and the ornamental fish ponds,

that's the house of your mother, Kaeo Kiriya, and father, Khun Phaen. Mark it well. Go straight in to see them." With that, Goldchild disappeared. Phlai Chumphon walked along the road

and went straight up into the big house without stopping. Seeing his father and mother sitting in the cross hall, he ran forward to prostrate and said through his tears, "You abandoned me and let me be shamed."

Khun Phaen, great master, and Kaeo Kiriya were shocked. They hugged their son. Khun Phaen asked, "Why did you brave the forest to come?

Your grandmother asked to keep you in Ayutthaya. What troubled you so much that you dared walk through the forest? Don't cry. Tell your father. I want to hear."

Phlai Chumphon told the story from start to finish. "Grandmother looked after me affectionately and fairly. She loved me like her own eyes.

The problem arose because the tricky Lao wife created a lot of nonsense, confusion, and anger. Soifa and Simala quarreled. Wai took the side of the minor wife,

and beat Simala badly, making a mess of her back and shoulders. I pleaded for Simala so he turned on me. My back still has the marks of his beating—look here.

This made me so furious that I ran away to find you, Father and Mother. Wai and Grandma don't know what's going on so there's nobody to counter the mantra

that is causing all this big trouble. Goldchild knows what's behind it. If there's delay, I think Phra Wai will be lost. It all started because of the Lao, both mistress and servant."

Khun Phaen, great warrior, flared up in anger. "Tcha! Phra Wai is not a man, just a dumb, stupid field turtle.

I gave him all my knowledge but he's still outdone by a woman—to his shame. On top, he's beaten Simala. Her father, Phra Phichit, will be very hurt.

Before I left, I entrusted her to Wai. It's bad it turned out this way. Why did that accursed Soifa do this? Where was Goldchild? Why didn't he tell me?"

Goldchild heard Khun Phaen's question, and whispered in his ear. "Soifa ordered I-Mai to seek out a teacher who's an elder living in Wat Phraya Maen.

His name is Elder Khwat and his lore is very strong. He molded figures for burying. Terrible! This has created the trouble and discord. Khun Phaen, you should hurry down there."

Khun Phaen, great valiant, felt sorry for Simala, and shed tears. "How come Wai didn't act properly? He was careless to let Soifa make him besotted.

I must go in order to tell them how to solve this before matters get worse. I'll catch the villain and have the king cut off his head at the execution ground."

He thought deeply, shaking and sighing. The sun rose and shone brightly. Servants prepared curry and carried the meal in.

Khun Phaen invited his wives and son to eat. When they had finished and felt content, he went down to sit in the sala. Local officials came to discuss matters.

"The buffalo thieves are blaming other people." "They weren't telling the truth so we tied them up and caned them for interrogation." "People have been sent after those that escaped." Several matters were discussed in a just manner.

Kaeo Kiriya saw that little Phlai Chumphon was looking sad. His topknot and hairline had not been oiled. She kissed and comforted him,

bathed him, applied turmeric, gave him food, and took him into her room to tie his topknot. "I'm glad you've come. I'm happy now I can see you.

When Grandmother first asked to look after you, I was reluctant to let you go. But when your father agreed, my hand was forced and I was parted from you."

Phlai Chumphon saw he had an opening and said, "Lots of Father's relatives live in Ayutthaya,

but not even one of Mother's. Why? Do they live in some far place? Or is there not a single person left?"

"Oh, you're still very inquisitive! I've never told you the story of when I was poor and hard up. I'll tell you from the beginning.

Your grandfather is Phraya Sukhothai. He had to find fifty chang of fine money.[8] Because he was fifteen tamlueng short of paying the total, he was jailed at the guardhouse beside the treasury.

He sold me to Khun Chang. I had to face poverty and hardship for a year and a half, toiling on frame embroidery. Your father acquired me by paying the debt to redeem me.

I've many relatives but they're very far away in Sukhothai. I think about your grandfather and grandmother all the time."

Phlai Chumphon felt desolate after hearing this story. He thought, "What a pity she fell into great difficulty and had to be parted from her family. That's very sad.

This evening I'll run away to find my grandmother and grandfather, and get to know them." He put on an act of talking sweetly, sitting on her lap, and chattering to play up to her.

He pleaded, "My mouth's sour. Please chew a bit of betelnut for me. I'll recite some *sepha* for you beautifully!" They both laughed and played together.

When the sun descended behind the trees and the moon shone brightly in the center of the sky, he lay on the bed alongside his mother, pretending to shut his eyes and stay still without blinking.

At midnight when a cock crowed, everyone was fast asleep. It was still. He summoned Goldchild in a whisper, and tucked the little kris in his waist.

He prostrated at his mother's feet, weeping. "I'll leave you while you're sound

---

8. This story was first told in chapter 17.

asleep. I want to tell you but I fear you might prevent me so I have to run off without saying farewell.

Oh mistress of your beloved child, you'll miss me sadly, but I'm only going to see my grandparents." He suppressed his feelings, walking away from the bed,

and called to his companion, Goldchild, "Let's go." Opening the door, he stepped out to the verandah, and went down to the ground with Goldchild at his side. They slipped out through a fence,

and walked along a path across the plain in the dim light of early dawn. He chatted and fooled around with Goldchild, with no fear of the wild animals.

When the sun rose at dawn and birdsong echoed around the forest, Kaeo Kiriya felt lonely and apprehensive.

She slept hugging a soft, warm pillow to her breast, thinking it was her own child. When she woke, she looked around with an empty feeling in her breast, and was worried when she did not see the face of little Phlai.

His clothes and kris had disappeared. "Eh, something's wrong. Where's Phlai gone?" She got up, walked out, and asked the servants, but nobody knew anything.

She returned to the room, feeling distraught. She woke her husband and told him. "Last night Phlai Chumphon came to sleep on my bed but he's disappeared."

Khun Phaen felt fearful. "Eh, this is wrong. Where's he gone?" With doubt in his heart, he looked at the horoscope as usual. "Last night, time of the moon, day Tuesday.

The manual says this is a Conjunction of Eternity,[9] meaning happiness and enjoyment, not sorrow. He'll go to meet elders in the family. Before long we'll see his face again."

With this analysis, he said to his wife. "I've looked at the horoscope. Don't be sad. Goldchild has gone along, so nothing will threaten him.

There's an ancient saying that it's the destiny of this lineage to be soldiers. I think he'll grow up to enter royal service. Don't be burdened by worry about him.

I predict that before long he'll bring you a daughter-in-law." He laughed and teased her to allay the sadness over their son.

---

9. อำมฤคโชค, *amaruekkhachok*; according to the *Tamra wong* method (see p. 319, note 23), this is a time free from deadly influences, promising victory, prosperity, success. As this is a Tuesday, this would be the 9th day in either the waxing or waning phase of the lunar month (Thep, *Horasat nai wannakhadi*, 61–62).

Now to tell of Phlai Chumphon. Walking through the forest with Gold-child, he missed his home and mother greatly. His heart was heavy and tears bathed his face.

In the dense forest along the way, branches swung and swayed. He walked along feeling lonely but cheered himself by admiring the trees.

Chalut vine intertwined with branches of *ulok*. Raintree, pine, heartache tree, banyan, sappanwood, *sak*, *masang*, *khae foi*, tall *yung* and *yang* swayed to and fro.

Parakeets flew on high through the wilds, with flocks squawking and others crying in reply. Parrots fed their young on a *chongkho*, and flew off shrieking noisily.

The sight of a mother bird made him think of his grandmother. "I used to chatter to please you." Flocks of mynas perched in a row on a *kaelae*. "Just like Grandmother beside me, caressing."

He saw a greenpigeon perched alone looking lonely. "Uh oh, a bird like me. Pitiful. I have to walk alone and lonely. Everything that was happy has become sad."

Goldchild comforted him. "Don't be doleful or you'll waste away. Over there, the nutmeg are so plentiful, the branches are weighed down." He urged Phlai to pull down a branch, pick, and smell them.

To cut a long story short, the spirit led Phlai Chumphon along quickly, meeting no dangers or obstructions along the way. In the evenings, they halted and slept overnight.

In three days they arrived at Sukhothai.[10] In every house they heard the guttural northern accent.[11] Goldchild spotted the governor's residence with a timber roof. He told Phlai Chumphon,

"See the house with six or seven cages of parrots hanging and a strong-looking barrier across the gateway. That's the house of your grandparents. Go and see them without delay."

With that, Goldchild disappeared from view and became a shadow following behind. Phlai Chumphon went up to the terrace with Goldchild at his back, invisible to the people sitting there.

He saw his grandparents sitting in a cross hall, and walked gingerly in. His spirit companion advised him, "Crawl in and wai your grandparents."

---

10. The distance from Kanchanaburi to Sukhothai by road today is 555 kilometers. Three days is a huge underestimate.

11. เกื้อไก่, *kuea kai*, an imitation of the sound of the northern accent.

The governor of Sukhothai thought that a party from some court case was sneaking in to visit him. He put on his spectacles to see for sure, and looked at the face of Phlai Chumphon.

Seeing no gift, he feigned annoyance. Grasping a stick, he turned, and thwacked Phlai twice. "Tcha! Who's this naughty child with a topknot? Why did you come up to my house?"

His wife ran over and pulled the stick away. "Ask to make sure where he comes from. He doesn't look like the child of folks from around Sukhothai. What's his name and family? Please inquire."

The governor asked loudly and menacingly, "What's the name of your parents, child? Where's your home? Tell me. If you don't, I'll have you clapped in chains."

Phlai cowered in fear, "Forgive me, sir. I tell no lie. My mother's name is Kaeo Kiriya. She was sold by my grandparents to Khun Chang.

Khun Phaen paid to release her from bondage. I was born as your grandson and lived in a house at Wat Takrai. Mother gave me the name of Phlai Chumphon.

Father is now the governor of Kanburi.[12] I inquired and was told that my grandfather is a governor in the north so I came through the forest alone.

I didn't know where you lived. I saw a huge house so I came to look. Sir, if you're not my grandparents, don't be angry. I beg your pardon."

Phraya Sukhothai and Phenjan[13] hugged him and said, "Oh beloved, this is your grandparents' house, have no fear. What a pity, your grandfather is truly awful.

I beat you before asking properly. Your back looks badly marked." He embraced his grandson and carried him into the house.

He called the servants, male and female. "I-Ming, I-Mi, Ai-Muean, where have you got to, you lazy lot?" They all crowded in.

"Our grandson has come. We'll have a soul ceremony." He ordered the servants to make a *baisi*. The local officials of the place all turned up to hear the news.

When the sun sank at dusk, torch-lighting time, the old governor of Sukhothai, along with all his kinsfolk,

made a soul ceremony for Phlai Chumphon. Everyone cheered loudly. Granny Suk, Granny Sai, and Granny Chiang sat in a row calling the soul.

---

12. กินเมือง, *kin mueang*, literally he eats the town of Kanburi, meaning to be the governor and thus live off its revenues.

13. เพ็ญจันทร์, full moon.

"Soul, oh soul of Phlai Chumphon,
if you dwell upon a tall *yung* tree,
you'll feel alone and so lonely.
Soul, don't flee to the hills to stay
among spirits, reeds, and tangled thorn,
where swan, fawn, parrot, and peacock play.
Soul, come to stay in a house and be gay.
Come, pray, to enjoy silver and gold,
and a long stay of ten thousand year.
Be of good cheer with grandparents old,
Be a monk with robes, a bowl to hold,
and cane tipped with gold, when preaching sermons."

All the relatives brought cash and patterned cloth to give Phlai. "May you be cool and happy every night and day." "Your grandparents love you so much."

They kept asking questions about the past. "Phlai, can you read and write?" He replied, "My paternal grandmother taught me up to a point but I've neglected it so it's rough and ready."

Phenjan said to her husband, "Go and entrust him to the wat so he can learn to read and write again." Then she asked Phlai, "Dear child, can you live in a wat?"

Phlai said, "Yes, and I'll study hard. In truth, I've been thinking I'd like to be ordained to gain merit. I'll come to give you a sermon every day."

His grandparents said, "Please become an abbot to help your relatives go to heaven. Grandfather will have Ai-Phuk, son of Ai-Jan, go to stay in the wat with you."

Orders were given to find incense, candles, flattened young rice, flowers, betel, and pan as offerings. Phlai was bathed, powdered, and dressed in a patterned lowercloth and an uppercloth in purple silk with a hibiscus pattern.

Phenjan wore a lowercloth in checkered silk and an uppercloth of embroidered Tenasserim silk, befitting her standing. The governor wore a silk lowercloth presented by the king, and a wool uppercloth that suited him.

They took little Phlai to walk with them. Everybody held batwing umbrellas[14] for shade. Servants carried a pestle on a golden salver. They trooped out to Wat Kraphang Thong.[15]

---

14. ปีกค้างคาว, *pik khangkhao*, name for a style of umbrella, made of fabric with braces curved like a bat's wings, part of the insignia of noble rank.

15. A massive wat on the eastern edge of the old city of Sukhothai. Traphang/Kraphang is a Khmer word for a pond, and the wat's design—an island in a square pond—suggests Khmer

At the abbot's kuti, they questioned a novice, who said the abbot was in his room. The grandparents stepped inside, with their grandson carrying the golden salver. They prostrated to pay respect.

The abbot looked and thought it was one of his pupils so called out, "Is that Monk Khong? Why don't you come on in."

The governor heard the question and laughed. "Don't you know me, Lord Abbot?" The abbot was surprised. He put on his spectacles. "Oh Governor, I thought it was someone else.

At the back there's your lady wife too. Please come up close and have some betelnut. My legs are badly stiff so I don't go begging on almsround.

Both of you look bright, healthy, and full of energy!" The monk scrutinized the governor. "Looks like you could manage another couple of wives . . . '

The governor of Sukhothai sat laughing. "I could—there are plenty around. But my wife won't stop being jealous. It's intolerable." All three doubled over with laughter.

The governor turned his face and called Phlai to prostrate, wai, and present the incense and candles. "I've brought my grandson to place in your care. Please have him study the teachings thoroughly."

"If he's your grandson, as you say, whose lad is he and where from?" The governor of Sukhothai prostrated, wai-ed, and then informed him, "He's the son of Kaeo Kiriya.

When I had to raise money for fines, she went to stay at Suphan in great difficulty. Khun Phaen loved her, gave her the cash, and took her to live with him in a house at Wat Takrai.

That's how this Phlai Chumphon was born. Later Khun Phaen volunteered and went to attack Chiang Mai. Now the clever fellow has been favored by the king to be governor of Kanburi."

The abbot said, "Oh golden Kaeo Kiriya. Has she got a husband and child already? When you brought her to the kuti, I put a cap on her but she wouldn't have it and threw it off.

cap

---

influence. Unlike most of the old Sukhothai monasteries, the wat is still in use today, and probably was at the time of *KCKP*. This may explain why this wat was chosen for Phlai's education. By late Ayutthaya, Sukhothai had declined and dwindled. This surviving wat with the cachet of age must have been one of its most important religious places. Even today, the wat covers a large area. The island in the pond has an old Sukhothai-era stupa and a preaching hall that probably dates back to Ayutthaya. To the east of the pond, the wat extends over a large area including a massive sala, extensive kuti, a kindergarten school, and a major market.

When I last went to your house, I saw her still wearing a *jap-ping*. Truly, how time passes! Both boys and girls are growing up faster.

Here, Governor, you and I are getting dismayingly old." He stroked Phlai back and front. "The lad looks very lovable.

Make the effort to study both reading and writing to become a soldier like your father, young lad. I'll have you sleep in an inner room near me so I can keep an eye on you."

Phraya Sukhothai and Phenjan chatted until it was almost time for prayers. When the evening bell tolled, they entrusted Phlai to the abbot's care, took leave, and returned home.

$\sim$

Now to tell of Simala. She was incomparably miserable. Within a month of little Phlai leaving, she stayed in her apartment, feeling her breast was as hot as if lying in fire.

Because Phra Wai had gone to live with the minor wife, and because the grandmother kept abusing her with no respect, Simala was wasting away, gloomily weeping for Phlai Chumphon.

"You used to be my companion. You'd tell me everything that happened, good or bad. When you saw them beat me, you were upset. When you helped grind casumunar to put on my wounds, your eyes were wet with tears.

I love you to the bottom of my heart. You've crossed the forest to find your father and inform him about all the scolding. I'd have forbidden it, but you didn't wait.

You'll be in a pitiful state now, little Phlai. Sad and gloomy. You've never traveled through the forest before. When the dew falls, you'll be forlorn.

Who'll comb your hairline and coil your topknot? The fragrance you once had will fade away. You'll be lonely facing hardship and discomfort. By the time you reach your father's house, you'll look strangely thin.

Oh Father, Khun Phaen, when you know, you should rush down here. Yet I've been waiting several days and you haven't showed up. Perhaps you've forgotten Simala.

I'm living here alone and lonely, seeing no one. They've beaten my back until it's swollen. From the whole household all I get is hatred. Now, the only thing left for me is to die.

Mother and Father are in Phichit. Oh, the more I think, the more I feel desolate." Every day without fail, she sobbed softly, feeling weak and troubled.

"I must send someone to tell Mother and Father to come down here, learn the truth, and stand up for me. If Wai no longer loves me and breaks it off, I'll bow my face, go home, and become a nun."

She called an old servant from Phichit. "Ai-Thit! Where are you? Come in here." Ai-Thit answered, "Yes, mistress," and came immediately. "What is Mistress Simala calling me for?"

She said, "Come close here," and whispered to him through her weeping. "Please help me. Go up to inform my parents to save me however they can.

Inform them that I'm sick and my spirit's broken. Don't talk about the quarrel and beating. Please convince my father and mother to come down, but leave the big matter for me to tell them myself."

Ai-Thit felt sorry for her and wept too. "Mistress, they grabbed you to bully, hit, and abuse without respect. Me and the wife were upset.

I'll slip up there, don't worry. Once I've told the governor and his lady, they'll come for sure." He walked out without speaking to anybody. He picked up a big sidebag and put in food,

betelnut, pan, tobacco, pots, and a hookah. He tied a cloth with a *chalang* pattern round his belly, and grasped a Lawa lance. He put the big bag on his shoulder and hurried off.

Standing with legs apart, he hitched up his lowercloth Khmer-style, and looked for the route, which he could recall from his time as a buffalo thief. He went out to Three Bo Trees Plain and entered the forest. At night, he paid respect to his teachers for protection, and slept in a tree.

In the morning, he came down and found a stream, made a pile of firewood, lit a fire, and put on the pot. When the rice was done, he grilled salted mackerel. After eating, he left without delay.

In the heat of the sun, he rested and smoked a hookah. High on ganja, he walked along, laughing blurrily. A rustling sound made him hunch over in fear. A footfall on leaves sent him galloping ahead.

Three and a half days of walking brought him to Phichit.[16] Friends greeted him. "Ai-Thit, where are you going?" He pretended not to hear or see anyone but went straight up to the big house.

Phra Phichit was talking with Busaba in the sitting hall. Ai-Thit came in with his sidebag, looking a mess. He prostrated, and sat with his face bowed and eyes narrowed.

Phra Phichit's face paled when he saw Ai-Thit come up. He shouted, "You should get about eight hundred strokes of the cane. You look filthy. Fancy coming up here in such a mess.

---

16. The distance by road today is 258 kms. Again the journey time is vastly underestimated.

What's that in the bag? Oh, a hookah? Ai-Thit's been smoking ganja till his eyes glaze. You like getting wrecked at night. Why did you wander up here, you jailbird?

Why aren't you with your mistress? Did you come looking for some fun thieving buffaloes? Perhaps they caught you. Your face looks troubled. You deserve to be flung in jail."

Ai-Thit sat quietly listening to his master's scolding. He scratched his head, rubbed his eyes, and wept. "I've no intention of stealing anyone's cattle and buffalo. The mistress sent me to pay respects to you, sir.

She's sick. The lady has cramps and a cold shiver. Her stomach is bloated from time to time. She's not well. The spirit doctor was consulted and said she's under a charm.

Royal doctors and common doctors are all over the house, frantically treating her. She won't eat and I think she's reaching the end of her merit. Master should hurry down there."

Phra Phichit and Busaba wept and beat their breasts. She said "Thit, oh Thit, I'm disappointed. How did it come to this?"

She summoned servants frantically. "Hey, Ai-Ban, Ai-Bao, old Ai-Si! Go and get the canopy boat out. We're going down to Ayutthaya."

The whole house was in uproar. They shouted for others to help. Some grabbed paddles and poles and ran down to bring the canopy boat,

and moor it at the big jetty in front of the house. They put in a bamboo bed and tied up a backrest of woven bamboo and rattan. The northerners had never paddled a boat or raft. They haggled noisily among themselves over who would steer.

Women brought mats, tables, trays, crockery, silk, raw rice, cooked rice, and stoves to place in the stern.

Phra Phichit and Busaba were full of misgivings. They gave orders to the servants and phrai to take care of the house, cattle, and buffaloes. "All of you, men and women, help to look after things."

They went down from the main house. Ai-Thit walked behind carrying a fire set.[17] At the landing, they boarded the boat. Phra Phichit settled himself down comfortably.

Ai-Thit waved a hand to have them cast off. The northerner oarsmen said in their guttural accent, "Never done this before. How d'you paddle?" They blundered around, getting in one another's way.

---

17. ชุดไฟ, *chut fai*, presumably flint, oil, materials for torches.

Some took long strokes, and others were not skilled enough to follow. Those at the bow and those at the stern tried to steer this way and that. They were all over the place. The boat rocked and rolled.

Ai-Thit squatted on his heels and cried out, "These oarsmen are hopeless, sir." Phra Phichit wielded a cane and thwacked them. "You puppies, you're not pointing the boat downstream."

Seeing their master holding the cane, the men got up onto their haunches, and made big strokes. Ai-Thit raised his head. "Eh! What's that? Any moment we'll thump into that clump of bamboo!"

The bow broke. The seat collapsed. The canopy crumpled. Phra Phichit fell bang on his rear, and got up scowling and scolding loudly. Ai-Thit leapt up to steer.

They switched around and practiced in the middle of the river. It was late afternoon by the time the whole boat was ready. Then they paddled quickly downstream without stopping, and reached the capital smoothly.

Now to tell of Khun Phaen, great romancer, whose famed powers made the world tremble. He governed Kanburi securely and loved his two wives well.

Laothong and Kaeo Kiriya stayed close by his side, attending to his needs, and making love morning and night without fail. Yet he remained irritated and gloomy

because of the trouble created by Soifa. "She conspired with that elder to lead my son astray. If I sit here doing nothing, it's likely that Phra Wai will be destroyed and reborn as a crow."[1]

He summoned Laothong and commanded her to stay and look after the house. He got dressed, called Kaeo Kiriya, and mounted a fine tusker

with an ornate howdah and elegant canopy. Surrounded by a mass of servants, they left the house and plunged into the forest. Crossing hills, plains, and streams,

they reached Ayutthaya in three and a half days, at the time Phra Phichit and Busaba arrived also. Khun Phaen spotted them. "That's my patron!" He got down from the elephant, went to pay respect,

and asked straight out, "Sir, what business brought both you and Busaba down here? What is it you want?"

Phra Phichit and Busaba spoke. "Simala has fever. She's so sick she might pass away." "She sent Ai-Thit up to tell us, so we came."

Khun Phaen said, "It's not fever. Please come up to the house to hear the good and the bad news about Simala." He led the way.

Phra Phichit, Busaba, and their servants crowded into a big sitting hall. Annoyed at seeing his father arrive, Phra Wai went out to wai his elders.

When Simala, who was in a miserable state, heard that her parents had both come, she came out of her room

and prostrated at their feet. Sobbing sadly, she told them the whole truth.

---

1. Perhaps meaning he will go to one of the hells. Crows, including some "as large as an ox cart," appear in the description of various hells in the Three Worlds, and often appear in the depiction of these scenes in wat murals (RR, 73).

"It's beyond me. I can't stand it any more.

Look at the marks of the stick on my poor back. It's covered with them. They said little Phlai Chumphon and I were lovers. Phra Wai believed what people told him.

If they'd said a crystal appeared in my stomach, he'd have cut it open. With matters in this state, I'm likely to die." She sobbed pitifully.

Phra Phichit and Busaba felt so sorry for her that they could not restrain their tears. With eyes glistening, Phra Phichit said, "How did this come about, dear child?

Because I love Khun Phaen, I agreed to give you away in marriage. From the beginning I made him promise that because my daughter did not know much—

she's just a provincial without the proper speech and manners—she was not to be berated and beaten if she made any mistake.

Given that promise, why has she been flogged and abused like a war slave captured from a defeated army? It was a waste to have loved you so much, Phra Wai.

When I was looking after your parents, I took great care that their feelings were not hurt. I love my daughter like my own heart. Not even a midge was allowed to bother her.

Even when she was beaten, it was never heavy. When she'd grown up enough to have a husband, I entrusted her to you, but you've acted badly, and shamed her in front of others."

Phra Wai felt anger in every pore of his body. "Hurling all these accusations is very sudden. I don't know what to say.

According to the ancient and accepted saying, one shouldn't have two wives. For them to compete and quarrel is normal. It's not because I don't treat them equally.

I made Simala my major wife. All the servants know not to offend her. Even Soifa has to listen to her. Also I have Simala take the water oath each year.[2]

I've entrusted her with whatever money and possessions I have—the whole house. But when I saw something I didn't like, I complained, and she argued back loudly,

pretending to scold her servant but really getting at me. I couldn't ignore that so I beat her, but only enough to make her fear me and listen to me, not

---

2. See p. 123, note 28. Taking the oath with him amounted to a public display of her status as the major wife. On the status of Simala and Soifa, see p. 976, note 13.

to persecute her as she claims.

The Lord of Life has raised me to this position. Having a wife who is no good shames me. My noble colleagues will all gossip. It's not that I don't love her.

Did you and my mother, Busaba, never quarrel and come to blows? These are old practices. Not everyone can become a stream-runner.[3]

It's commonly said that we mortal humans still tend to get lost in delusion. It's beyond my wisdom to rid myself of anger.

Father, think of the tongue and the teeth. How many times do they get in each other's way? Not to beat her is beyond me. You want to grind me up alive, and scatter me to the winds."

Hearing his son's words, Phra Kanburi could not stay still. "Don't talk like this. You realize I came to find out what's happening.

I rushed here because I love you, and now I've been shown where the trouble lies. I can see your face is freckled as if painted with indigo. The warning against having two wives is age-old,

like in the tale of Lord Yotsawimon.[4] He had two queens, left and right, called Janthewi and Jantha, both from the same mother.

Even sisters from the same womb can act like this. Jantha conspired with an evil, lying old woman to use all kinds of devices and love charms so that the lord became obsessed.

Though Janthewi had done nothing wrong, Jantha sowed so much discord that her sister was driven away. You know this story in your heart so why are you paying it no attention, my son?

The good people of Ayutthaya are not finished.[5] Don't be arrogant. Listen

---

3. โสดา, *soda*, meaning *sodaban*, someone who has entered the stream or the first stage on the path to enlightenment. The term is used here with the same looseness as saying, not everyone can be a saint.

4. This is a reference to the outer drama *Sangthong*, The Golden Conch (see p. 258, note 56). King Yotsawimon is the father of the hero. He has two wives who are sisters. Janthewi is the major wife and favorite, which makes Jantha jealous. When Janthewi's son is born as a conch shell, Jantha bribes an astrologer to tell the king that this is an inauspicious sign that will bring disaster. The king has Janthewi and her conch-child abandoned in the forest. After the conch is broken, Sangthong returns to the city. Jantha then employs an old woman, Sumetha, to put a love charm on the king who orders the child to be drowned, but Sangthong is saved by a naga king and *yak* giant. He then undergoes many adventures before marrying Princess Rojana and being restored to his princely status.

5. คนดีอยุธยาหาสิ้นไม่, *khon di ayutthaya ha sin mai*, a proverbial saying, repeated with many variants, of obscure origin. The name "Ayutthaya" can be interpreted as meaning "undefeated." Probably the saying originates from the early Bangkok era and meant that though the capital had been destroyed in 1767, the people and spirit of Siam still survived. Some believe the saying originated among Burmese frustrated that the 1767 sack had not been final.

to me. I know for sure you've been put under a charm. If you don't believe me, you'll be ruined."

In their room, Soifa and I-Mai listened with scalps crawling and hair standing on end. Soifa opened a window, poked her head out, and said heatedly, "Who used lore? Bring that person here.

From my side, I already knew that Phra Wai had been affected by a love charm that made his face dark. Every morning and night I've been waiting anxiously for his father to come down and deal with it.

Now that you've arrived, I'm glad. You'll catch whoever did this mantra and we'll see what that person is like. Don't delay or it'll be nightfall."

mirror yantra

Phra Kanburi wagged his finger at her, and shouted, "Mm! Don't provoke me, you little phrai. Hey, I-Moei! Go and bring the mirror that Phra Wai uses, right now."

I-Moei went into an inner room and picked up a big Batavia[6] mirror, a genuine foreign one of good quality, fine clarity, and high price. She brought it out to Khun Phaen, who turned to take it. He took up a large slate, drew a yantra, collected the powder, and placed it on the mirror.

He put his hands together against his forehead and chanted a mantra. "I call on the power of lore. If someone has made a charm with unjust intentions, let it now be revealed."

In the mirror, images appeared of two figures, breast to breast, face to face, wrapped tightly together by an amora leaf. Khun Phaen laughed out loud and said, "How's that?"

Phra Phichit, Busaba, the servants, and the whole household all saw that the charm was for real. Khun Phaen handed the mirror to Phra Wai. "Look at this and tell me what it is."

Phra Wai averted his face and did not look. "I understand. Don't go on. I could do that the same as you. It's not that I'm stupid and can't see through it.

If I weren't able, how would you have been pardoned? Because the king asked me to attack Chiang Mai, you now live in comfort every night and day. Because you love Simala,

---

6. กะหลาป๋า, *kalapa*, Sunda Kelapa, river of coconut forest, an early name of Batavia, now Jakarta, the principal Dutch settlement in Southeast Asia. In early nineteenth-century Siam, Batavia was known as a source of European artifacts and its name was used, as here, as an epithet for European (SWC, 1:228).

you'll take her side, no matter how much she does wrong. I can't do as you wish. If someone is truly in the wrong, they must be blamed."

Khun Phaen wagged his finger and shouted, "Mm! You rake up the past to challenge me." He jumped up, grabbed a *samae*[7] stick, and rushed forward. Phra Wai ran off to Thong Prasi for help.

Thong Prasi leapt around angrily. "Tcha! Damn you, you loudmouthed madman! Why are you threatening my grandson, you villain? You boast that you're able, that you have knowledge.

You speak arrogantly and make this reflection in a mirror. I think you talk big to show off to dogs. I'm used to seeing what you can do. I don't want to believe it.

It's just a trick for people to see. The Terengganu[8] Khaek do this sort of thing. Throwing up a golden ball that divides into four. Fire eating."

Phra Phichit and Busaba were shocked. Phra Phichit pulled as hard as he could on the tail[9] of Khun Phaen's cloth to restrain him, and shouted until he was hoarse. Busaba grabbed the stick.

Khun Phaen stopped, not knowing what to do since he respected Phra Phichit like a parent. Busaba said to Phra Wai, "I'd like to take my daughter away for a year or so.

She's in unbearable discomfort because of the pregnancy. After the delivery, I'll send her back. If you go on using force and beating her, Simala is likely to die."

Phra Wai was as angry as if seared by fire. "Everybody is attacking me. Why delay, Simala?

Pack your money and possessions and have them carried down to the landing. Go and stay in Phichit with your father until you've delivered around five children,[10]

then come back to live with me as before. Your mother will teach you well. Go, my eye's jewel, my sweet-faced one. Carry things down to the canopy boat."

---

7. แสม, *samae*, name for several trees in the Avicennia family that have aerial roots similar to mangrove, and very straight branches suitable for sticks.

8. A Malay state on the lower east coast of the peninsula.

9. กระเบน, *kraben*, the end of a lowercloth when it is passed between the legs and tucked in the waist at the back.

10. There is a saying that a husband should not let his mother-in-law take his wife away as the mother-in-law will give the wife to someone else—hence the sarcastic reference to five children (SB, 573).

Busaba said, "Son-in-law, why are you being so spiteful and sarcastic with me? If you don't want her to go, then say so nicely.

We didn't come down here to get into an angry shouting match. I'm an old lady but I understand what's going on. You rake up the past to get at me. I know.

You're a big officer in the royal pages, and I'm just a poor mother-in-law, so you can stab me with all this sarcasm. Think about the past a bit. Everything except delivering you into this world . . .

Even if you pay no attention to my kindness, consider things from my side. I've already got a fine head of grey hair because of Simala. I feel hurt.

In the city where I live, nobody can bully me like this. You sent Ai-Thit up to tell us, pretending she had a fever, and so we came.[11]

If I'd known she was quarrelling with her husband, I wouldn't have bothered my big toe to show up here. From this day forward, I won't come again. It's our fate to be severed from each other.

If you're sick, don't tell me. For sure, I won't see your corpse. Even if you live in a brick house buzzing with servants, I'll bump along fine as a pauper.

It was a waste to have thought of depending on you. Marrying her to you was profitless. You've turned into an enemy who attacks me. Why worry about you at all?

If the blood in my own body is evil, I can scoop it out.[12] I wouldn't care. I'd think the Burmese took it away. I've no more thought for you until my dying day."

Phra Wai said, "Oh enough, Mother! Such a lot of noise, it's shocking. You think I don't respect you as a mother-in-law so you make up these comparisons.

For better or worse, husbands and wives quarrel, but they don't slash each other to death. When the anger passes, they're happy together again. Parents should help them to reconcile.

But that's not the case here. You want to drag her away from this house. You sound off like a trumpet, encouraging her to be aggressive. It's very irritating.

Why are you so quiet, Simala? Why don't you raise your own voice and argue back? Your mother here is asking questions. Things are not as she wishes so she's angry.

I'll be afraid of you from now on. If you offend me at all, I won't complain because it might annoy your mother enough to sever relations.

The wife fears the husband and treats him with respect, but her mother argues in her stead, on and on. The daughter stays quiet and never makes

---

11. Simala sent Ai-Thit. Perhaps Busaba did not realize this. More likely this is one of the many continuity errors in this section.

12. A stock saying meaning a parent can disown a bad child.

a fuss, but the mother comes to teach her how to be angry.

She picks on me about everything. Who's saintly enough to put up with this? I should respond in kind so you have a taste of your own medicine, but I restrain myself because you're my mother-in-law.

Father, why aren't you saying anything? Everyone else is lashing out so readily. She scolds her daughter but really she's casting aspersions on me, even dragging in the Burmese and the Mon!

When we asked for her hand, the parents agreed. How come they didn't choose better from the beginning? Now they're angry, picking at everything, strewing sarcasm around to their heart's content.

I'm now a Burmese! In the beginning you didn't realize that because I cut my hair to look like a Thai, so you made the mistake of giving me your daughter.

Now that you know I'm not a Thai, you want to drag her away in front of my eyes. Because I won't let her go, you're angry. Don't think it's because there's only a few of you.

Even if you brought some five thousand men to crush me to dust, I'd fight to the death. So let's find out who's able!"

Khun Phaen, great romancer, stared angrily. "Eh, Wai, how come you dare to issue threats before my very eyes, as if you were just mixing a salad?

You shit on my head as if it were a tree stump. You pick and scold without making any sense. I can't count you as a son, you blackguard. Your words are coarse and contemptible.

You think I'm not wealthy so you can answer back with no respect. You're abusive to your mother-in-law. Phra Phichit and Busaba are like parents to me.

You know the story from the past because I told you everything. When I stole your mother away from Khun Chang, if I hadn't been able to depend on them, who knows?

I'd probably have faced disaster and a bad death. And you, where would you have found a wife? But now you're all threats and contempt, you ungrateful slave.

You're only Phra Wai but you're this bad. If you rise higher in the future, you'll be worse. What will be will be. Let's see. I'm also Phra Kanburi.

Your father-in-law is Phra Phichit. Right or wrong, you should know your place. I'd like to elbow you just once, you arrogant fellow." Khun Phaen got up and rushed at Phra Wai.

Thong Prasi came between them, angrily brandishing a pestle for pounding betelnut. "You're making no sense, you thick-faced, excitable fellow. Son-in-law and mother-in-law are arguing.

What business is it of yours, you oaf? You join in and bark your head off. You arrogantly want to elbow him without shame. You shout challenges at my grandson.

I brought Wai up since he was a child. You have two eyes but you don't see, you lowlife. You buried your head inside a jail.

You got out because Wai went to ask the king. You marched up to attack Chiang Mai, and then were happy. You went to govern Kanburi without a care. Yet you come back and attack the person who helped you.

You may be gentlefolk but what level? Even now, they still call you 'Ai-Khun.'[13] You should be grateful for being governor of Kanburi, but you forget your debt to Phra Wai for asking the king.

If you don't get out of this house, I'll bash you to pieces." She tucked up the end of her lowercloth and bellowed, "Come on, if you dare. What are you waiting for?"

Phra Wai hid behind his grandmother and called out, "This is not right, Father. All this anger and insult will make the neighbors roar with laughter.

For better or worse, wife and husband quarreled. Mother-in-law joined in and threw her weight about, wanting her way alone, forcing others to follow her words.

Her daughter was hopeless but her mother said nothing about that, just scolded the son-in-law over and over about all sorts of things. Quite a pounding. Anyone not bruised by this wouldn't be human.

She even scolded her daughter to get at me, and raked up the past to pulverize me. It's intolerable. Even a lousy slave isn't treated like this.

If she had bought me out of slavery to become her son-in-law, I'd not argue and create a fuss. I'd endure it with a thick face all year round. Even if she shouted at my mother, I wouldn't feel hurt.

But she didn't buy me out at all. I'm not the son of anybody's slave. When she raises her voice to trumpet pitch, and scolds me like a servant, don't imagine I'll ignore it.

When warring with enemies, north and south, I've never once fled from the sound of gunfire, even one inch. I can match the power of others in hundreds of thousands. Only to the Lord of Life will I succumb."

Khun Phaen roared at his son, "You have no respect for your parents-in-law. You're too proud of your powers, not afraid of anyone in the realm,

---

13. Khun was a low noble rank but the prefix Ai was a conventional form of address for a commoner with no rank.

ready to fight to the death with no retreat! Even me you fear not one bit, because you think you don't have to depend on anyone. You show contempt for others even now.

If you become a big nobleman of some kind, you'll trample the heads of your elders into dust. The more Thong Prasi goes along with you, the worse you get. From today we're severed, until death.

If I die, don't come to cremate me. If you lose your life, I'm not coming anywhere near your body. All I want is to take your life.

When there's a war, we'll fight. Bring me the Skystorm sword I gave you. If you don't hand it over, I'll attack you right now!"

Phra Wai ran inside, crying, "Father isn't himself. He's in bad enough a temper to strike me without shame.

It feels like someone else is putting him up to abuse me and sever relations like this." He picked up the sword and raised it over his head in utter panic, terrified his father would slash him if he went out.

"Grandmother, please come in here." Thong Prasi took the sword and held it awkwardly. Eyes blazing, she shouted at Khun Phaen,

"I thought you were good, you suffering ghost. You gave this away but now change your mind and want it back. You're broken-toothed, grey-haired, and unreliable. Who can talk like you?

How many fueang is this sword worth—a city's ransom? Pah! Move your head away so we can see the sun. You couldn't slash a fish with this. Here, take it.

You disgrace! You're not real." She tossed Skystorm to him. "Fancy siding with your beaten daughter-in-law against your own son Wai, you jailbird."

Khun Phaen angrily picked up the sword, raised it reverently above his head, and moved away. Kaeo Kiriya followed him, then Simala and Busaba.

Phra Phichit went after Khun Phaen, flowing with tears of concern for Simala. They arrived at the boat mooring and held a discussion.

Phra Phichit said, "Busaba and I are very concerned about what will take place here. You're going to be far away and won't know what's happening to Simala.

When Phra Wai sees her face, he feels hatred. It wasn't like this before. He believes everything from Soifa, and she'll put him up to abusing and beating Simala some more.

We can't rely on the grandmother who goes along totally with this bullying. There's nobody Simala can depend on. Being so far away, I'll worry about her."

Khun Phaen prostrated at his feet and said, "Sir, don't look on the black side.

Listen to me. Nothing will happen to Simala. She's like my own heart.

After you return home, I won't neglect her. I should find a solution. I won't let her be lonely. I'll send two spirits to protect her.

Wai is befuddled by a love charm. The effect has also reached the grandmother so she takes his side. In fifteen days, I'll return here.

Leave this distressing matter to me. If I can't find a solution then you can complain. I'll catch the person making this mantra, and restore your honor."

Phra Phichit said, "I've always thought of you as an honest fellow with no crookedness. I've trusted you for many years.

Stay well, Simala. Listen to your father's words and don't cry. It's not that I don't love you. If I could, I'd remain with you."

Phra Phichit and Busaba consoled Simala, then boarded the boat, full of grief at the parting. Simala's eyes brimmed with tears. Phra Phichit and Busaba left.

After Phra Phichit had disappeared from sight, Khun Phaen, great romancer, drew Skystorm, brandished it in the air, and went back to the house.

Phra Wai's servants, men and women, ran off in alarm and hid themselves. Khun Phaen was extraordinarily angry. "Hey, Wai! Come here and fight with me.

I'm no longer your father. That's final. Though I'm old, I'm not afraid. Dead or alive, for better or worse, I'll slash you—and your stupid wife too. Watch out.

Where are you hiding up there?" He picked up lumps of brick and hurled them to clatter against the bedroom, several times over. Phra Wai stayed inside the apartment and kept perfectly quiet.

Thong Prasi poked her face out with eyes blazing. "Help! Thieves plundering in the middle of the day. Since I was little, I've never seen such a thing. Hey, servants! Go and tell the town officials to come."

Khun Phaen was so enraged by her, he picked up a brick and threw it against the wall. Thong Prasi shouted, "Ow! I'm done for!" She closed the door and ranted noisily.

Seeing the turmoil, Kaeo Kiriya could not stay still. She tried to calm and placate her husband. "It's nearly dusk. Don't stay around and create more trouble."

Khun Phaen listened to her and walked off. Simala followed him out of the house. When they reached a graveyard, she prostrated to Khun Phaen.

"My lord and master, you're leaving me. Whose merit will I depend on when you're far away and out of sight? Soifa will play all sorts of tricks.

Phra Wai is like a blazing fire, and she keeps stoking it with more kindling and oil. Before long, this fire will burn me to ash.

If I'm here alone, and his fury continues, how can I stay alive?" She hugged her chest, sobbed, and flailed around at his feet.

Greatly concerned, Khun Phaen consoled his beloved daughter-in-law. "I'll give you two female spirits to stay and protect you against dangers.

For certain, I'll come back with an army to capture Wai, take revenge for this harassment, and truly put Soifa to the question.

Whatever she did to you, I'll repay in full measure. I'll extract the revenge that she deserves. I'll rip her flesh and rub in salt. Now it's almost nightfall.

It's not good for you to be walking around alone in a graveyard where there are fierce and crafty spirits. My jewel, please listen to me. Go back."

Simala paid respect and took leave, wet with tears. She walked off alone, turning to look back forlornly. Khun Phaen sighed, and mounted his elephant.

He left, riding Phlai Kang with Kaeo Kiriya, and a great crowd of servants following behind, singing wild-chicken songs along the way.

In three and a half days, they reached Kanburi, halted the elephant, and went up into the house with all the servants. Kaeo Kiriya went into an inner room.

Phra Kanburi stayed in the residence. The anger and turmoil did not leave him. Vengeful feelings towards his son, Phra Wai, made him hot with frustration as if licked by fire.

He was almost mad with rage. Every day, morning and night, sitting or sleeping, he was steeped in gloom, thinking only of how to make an attack.

Now to tell of Phlai Chumphon who had made his way to Sukhothai where he was greatly loved by his grandparents. He had now been a novice for some time.

He studied Khmer and Thai well, and could translate texts skillfully. He was always in a happy mood. Morning and evening, he took a broom to sweep the wat grounds.

One day as he was sweeping the dirt, a Khmer who had tunneled his way from Hongsa carrying a golden palm-leaf book of knowledge with the aim of making inquiries on Mon teachings,[14]

surfaced in the middle of the wat grounds.[15] He posed questions to novice

---

14. ปริศนาของรามัญ, *prisana khong raman*. *Raman* is Mon; ปริศนาธรรม, *prisanatham*, means debates or inquiries on religious teachings. According to some historians, Buddhist teachings came to the Chaophraya Basin through the Mon country. In the mid-nineteenth century, the future King Mongkut launched a reform of Siamese Buddhism by using Mon texts and practices assumed to be "purer" than local equivalents.

15. This tale is adapted from one of the stories about the legendary King Ruang that were

Phlai Chumphon about the teachings, and Chumphon replied forthwith. The Khmer gave him the palm-leaf book in return.

Phlai Chumphon studied the knowledge in this book to become expert. He had the power to be invisible, to be invulnerable against all weapons, and to dive into the earth.

He was fifteen years old and full of vigor. Still with the strength of youth, he was known to have mastery without rival. Sukhothai quailed at his abilities.

Late one night, the novice woke up with his chest trembling and his mind agitated. He tossed and turned, unable to sleep a wink. He lay still thinking

about his grandmother and his parents, becoming more and more miserable. "After I faced being beaten by Wai, I fled up here in tears.

That's over eight years ago. I've now been parted from my parents for a long time. I don't know how they're aging. Grandmother must be quite doddery.

It's a long way to visit them but I'm missing them very much." He fretted in frustration and turmoil. When the sun caught the mountaintops

and flooded the world with brilliant light, birds burst into song, and the novice got up from his bed, washed his face,

went down from the kuti, and walked away. He tied up grass in the form of a standing giant with robust legs and arms. He shaped a mouth and fangs,

and trussed up bamboos as a stave to put in the giant's two hands. When he was finished, he went up the stairs, took some paper, and entered the kuti.

With a blackclay stick[16] he wrote a letter to his father asking for information. He folded it tightly, walked quickly out to the terrace,

and prepared all kinds of offerings. Descending from the kuti, he built a shrine, circled it with a sacred thread, chanted a mantra to activate the demon,

and scattered rice. The giant sprung up as high as a mountain, and leapt around displaying its powers. The novice shouted at the giant to sit down.

He tied the letter tightly on its neck, and gave orders, "Take this immediately to my father in Kanburi."

The giant prostrated to take leave and loped away, crossing hills and mountains, smashing *yung* and *yang* trees to powder, and trampling tigers and elephants under its feet.

It ran like a whirlwind, treading on mountain peaks which collapsed with a thunderous roar, shaking the earth, and making forests sway.

---

collected into the *Phongsawadan nuea* (see p. 649, note 74).

16. See p. 124, note 30. In this case, the clay is mixed with wood soot to make a black stick, like a stick of chalk, which is sharpened and used to write on light-colored paper.

It crossed streams, rivers, woods, and plains making for the lofty forest. In the evening when the sun weakened, the giant entered Kanburi.

Shocked out of their senses, the townsfolk fled away with their wives and children. Even Phra Kanburi was alarmed.

"What's that great crashing sound?" He rushed down from his residence, saw the giant, and knew it was created by lore.

He enchanted a thin white cloth, and threw it. The cloth turned into a big monkey that bounded over and attacked the giant. All the townsfolk watched the fight.

The monkey gamboled around, luring the giant on. The giant brandished a club and struck. The monkey crawled up the club, bit the giant, grabbed its neck, and squeezed.

The monkey pushed the giant away, raised the giant's club, and snapped it in two. The giant kicked. The monkey caught its foot, and the giant fell. The monkey hung on without letting go.

The giant's power weakened. The monkey magically tied it up with its tail. The giant changed back into grass. The monkey disappeared and became cloth again.

Khun Phaen looked at the sheet of paper. "Eh, this is strange." He unfolded it and looked at the elegant lettering. "From your son in Sukhothai.

I haven't seen you, Father and Mother, since we parted. I do not know if you are alive or dead, enjoying happiness or hardship. Is the king still well-disposed or angry?

Are you still happy in royal service? Have sickness or threats been mild? Are things between Simala and Phra Wai good or bad? I've had no news.

Since I left, is Grandmother alive and healthy or has she met with sickness and suffering? A long time has passed since I parted from her. Has her sorrow over her grandson diminished?

Kaeo Kiriya and Laothong, are they both well? I'm particularly concerned about my mother, Kaeo Kiriya.

As for me, I'm well and flourishing, with no discomfort and only joy every day. I was able to depend on the merit and kindness of my grandparents. I've devoutly entered the monkhood as a novice.

Let me share the merit with my parents, brothers, grandmothers, and other kin." When Khun Phaen finished reading, he folded the letter and went back up to the residence.

Musing on the contents, Khun Phaen went into a small room in the house and thought sadly about his beloved son, his eyes brimming with tears.

"Oh, I have a son but matters did not go as I'd hoped. I loved Wai like my own eyes but he turned out to show contempt for me.

He became extremely arrogant over his rank and status. I fear I cannot rely on him for my cremation. I think Chumphon is truly good, and I could entrust my body to him.

Though still small, he has a good heart. I think I can depend on him in the future." He promptly wrote a letter to tie on the neck of the giant.

He found rope and tied it tightly across its shoulders. Then he activated the giant, which sprung up, trampling many trees flat.

Borne on the wind, it bounded away in paces, each one *yojana* long, crossing rivers, forests, and cart tracks so fast it almost flew.

In a trice, the giant arrived in Sukhothai and entered the wat. The novice saw it coming from afar, and happily untied the grass spirit at once.

He saw the paper strapped across its shoulder and knew his father had replied to his letter. Very happy to have news from his father, he unfolded the letter and read it straightaway.

The lettering was very fine. "To the diligent novice, Chumphon. The fact you sent a mantra giant through the forest to carry an important letter to your father,

telling the news that you are well, has made your mother and father very happy. We are also glad that you have entered the monkhood, and offer respect to receive the merit you have shared.

You asked how things are here, good or bad. Your father is immersed in suffering because of the contemptible Wai who has forgotten his father's kindness, my eye's jewel.

You know about him being affected by a love charm. I wanted to release him from the charm and so went to Ayutthaya. Phra Phichit and Busaba came at the same time.

I warned him as a parent, and made a reflection in a mirror to show the cause, but Wai became even more enraged and stubborn. He raised his voice and argued loudly with no respect for anyone.

He dragged up the past to get at me. He said I was released from jail because he made a request. He abused me for all the people sitting around to hear. From that time onward, I've been very angry.

If that day your grandmother had not got in the way, I would probably have killed Wai. Grandmother has also been badly affected by the charm. Wai thus got the advantage and became vicious.

Since returning to Kanburi, I have not been happy. I suffer every morning and night without relief. If I do not take revenge successfully, I will probably die. As my son, you can help.

The fact that you made a giant figure to send to me shows that you have powers and knowledge. Please make soldier dummies, disguised as New Mon,[17] and send them down here.

Have them charge down and invest Doembang,[18] which is not far from Suphan. The news will spread to Ayutthaya. King Phanwasa will probably send Wai to do battle,

and will probably recruit me to go along to help him. You and I can cooperate to attack Wai in a pincer, and slash him to pieces. Then you escape back to the north.

Do not kill anyone else except Wai. If you care for your father, Phlai Chumphon, hurry to make the dummies and march them down."

When he had finished reading the letter, Chumphon felt very angry. Pity for his father made tears well up in his eyes. "Tcha! Wai is no good.

He even shows contempt for his father. He'd have the same feelings for me as for a midge. In the future I can't be concerned about him. We no longer count as brothers.

With my knowledge of lore, I'll repay the kindness of my father. It's a pity the plain is wide and the journey long. If I could fly, I'd go down there right now."

His breast felt bruised black with anger. At dusk, he went into his room but could not sleep soundly for thinking of his father's suffering.

---

17. Mon have lived in western Siam since the Dvaravati era. From the time the Burmese overthrew the Mon capital of Pegu in 1539, Mon periodically migrated to Siam to escape increasing Burmese domination, and were generally welcomed by the Thai kings as additional manpower. Many were settled in the west of Siam, and others along the Chaophraya River system. The older settlers were sometimes called "Old Mon" and the later arrivals "New Mon," a distinction clear from language as the later migrants spoke a version of Mon more influenced by Burmese. Later, this old-new distinction acquired different meanings. Under the Thonburi kingdom (1767–1782), King Taksin recruited the support of Mon groups around Thonburi and appointed their leader as Phraya Ram Jaturong. In 1775, there was a large migration of Mon led by Binnya Sein, a younger brother of the last ruler of Pegu. These new arrivals refused to accept Ram Jaturong's leadership. The old-new terminology was applied to this division. The New faction was recruited by the rebels who overthrew Taksin in 1782 and founded the Chakri dynasty. In 1814–15, another large group of Mon from Martaban under Saming Sotbao fled from the Burmese, and were sent by King Rama II to settle in Pathumthani, Nonthaburi, and Paklat. These were again sometimes called "New Mon." (Halliday, "Immigration"; KW, 690 from the Second Reign chronicle; Nidhi, *Kan mueang thai nai samai phrachao krung Thonburi*, 410–16, 470)

18. Now amphoe Doembang Nangbuat on the Suphan River in the north of Suphanburi province (see map 2).

At dawn, novice Phlai Chumphon still felt very unsettled. He put on his robe in open style, belted to his body, went into the house,

and informed his grandparents. "I can't be happy with my father and mother so far away. I miss them terribly. Allow me to take leave."

The governor and his wife agreed. "Take leave of the abbot and disrobe, as you wish. Please delay a little, and I'll arrange some servants to go with you."

Chumphon answered, "I was able to come here alone. I ask only for a good horse to ride, one that's fast with a good rhythm."

His grandfather said, "I think there's only Blueblack,[19] a spirit horse that's very swift. Anyone who wants to ride him has to currycomb him and feed him grass for a whole year or else he'll buck terribly.

He bit the son of I-Paen and almost took his arm off. The lad's still got yaws.[20] It's never gone away. As you have powers, you should be able to ride him. Let's see."

Chumphon took leave of his grandfather. He picked some grass and enchanted it with a formula, went into Blueblack's stable, and proffered the grass while chanting a mantra.

Stroking the horse's back, he said, "My beloved, will you be of service to me? I'm facing great hardship and I want to escape it today."

Iron-backed Blueblack listened, accepted the proffered grass, and whinnied loudly. Chumphon untied him and put on a saddle blanket, good saddle, harness,

stirrups, and flanchards—all very gently. He jumped onto the horse's back, dug in his heels, and whipped as a signal. The horse turned around and galloped away like a spear.

He was as swift, agile, strong, and fearless as hoped. With a little touch, he was also obedient. Chumphon rode him to the residence where his grandfather hollered loudly,

danced with glee, and clapped his hands. "You're a tiger cub or else you couldn't have done this!" Happily, he called his grandson upstairs and presented him with a sword.

"This sword is from the time of my grandfather. He attacked a group of Mon and Burmese, putting them to flight, so he named the sword Victor.[21] It's

---

19. กะเลียว, *kaliao*, horse-specific adjective for a bluish or greenish tinge.

20. A tropical skin infection, caused by bacteria entering through a lesion in the skin.

21. ชนะไพรี, *chana phairi*, defeat enemy. Possibly this refers to the Burmese attack in 1765–67. The Burmese northern army, led by Nemiao, spent the rainy season of 1765 in Chiang Mai and

a valuable heirloom passed down to me.

I'm old now and I'm concerned about you. I fear my merit will soon be up, and I have no son. Please take it, Phlai Chumphon."

Chumphon took the sword, and prostrated to take leave. He had a servant stable the horse. At sunset he arranged a *baisi* and offerings,

and had servants carry them to a graveyard. He cut bamboo as posts for a shrine, set out incense and victory candles on a salver, and strung sacred thread round the graveyard.

At an auspicious time, he performed the rite of opening the *khlon* gate,[22] chanted a very powerful formula, scattered rice, and summoned the spirits from every place.

Spirits from caves, ponds, streams, canals, forests, and woods all called out to one another in turmoil. In fear of his lore, they hurried over,

every one of them, to take the offerings. Chumphon finished making offerings and then chose only the fiercest spirits and sprites. "Tomorrow I'm going to Suphan.

All of you will come along to join my military column and take charge of the soldier dummies." The spirits all accepted, and Chumphon returned home happy.

At dawn, Phlai Chumphon went into the main house and prostrated to take leave of the governor of Sukhothai. Both grandparents gave their blessing.

He bathed his body, put on a lowercloth, splendid shirt, belt cinched tight, and powerful amulets.

He clasped his hands above his head, took up his grandfather's sword, and leapt onto his horse. At an auspicious time, he galloped away from Sukhothai,

---

then attacked the northern cities. According to the Thai chronicle, "The Phraya of Sukhothai and the Phraya of Sawankhalok took the families and troops of their municipalities and fled into the forests." Subsequently, there was a confrontation with the Burmese forces around Sukhothai which ended when the Burmese left to invest Ayutthaya. According to the Burmese chronicle, Sawankhalok was taken by force and Sukhothai surrendered to the Burmese. (RCA, 496–97, 500; Nidhi, *Kan mueang thai samai phrajao krung Thonburi*, 20–21)

22. โขลนทวาร, *khlon thawan*, a ceremonial gate used when a white elephant is taken from the forest and when soldiers leave for war or return from war. The gate is an open frame decorated with fresh leaves to mimic a forest. A monk sits at either side on a platform to sprinkle sacred water on the soldiers passing through. There is an example in stone, made in China, at the Phralokanat preaching hall in Wat Pho. At the rite of "opening the *khlon* gate," as prescribed in the *Tamra phichai songkhram*, the Manual on Victorious Warfare, offerings are made and prayers chanted for the success and safe return of the army. (CK, 103; SWC, 2:826)

surrounded by the swarm of spirits that were his only troops. His horse was strong, and he rode along as if blown by the wind.

Halfway along the journey, he halted and went to sit in the shade. He instilled a yantra in the horse's hooves, and sprinkled them with powerfully enchanted oil.

He cut grass, tied it into a thousand dummies, scattered enchanted rice, and the dummies came to life as people

with weapons in their hands, filling the forest with noise and movement. All prostrated to wai Phlai Chumphon. He mounted Blueblack,

and gave orders to his army of mantra dummies. "You will march as an army into battle. Cheer loudly like New Mon. There is one strict command:

Only round up people and hit them, don't kill." With that order, he galloped away.

They crossed streams, roads, rivers, forest, and plain, hollering war cries and stirring up clouds of dust. Villagers woke in alarm and scattered into the forest before the army could catch them,

carrying or dragging their children away to crawl into the undergrowth, clothes slipping from their trembling bodies, stumbling, tripping, and falling over one another. At every place, villagers were in turmoil.

The army soon reached Doembang, and set up a huge camp in the forest. They waited quietly and kept watch as they were close to Suphan.

The governor of Suphan heard the news and was very afraid. He recruited men to go up and secure the frontier with a fortified camp,

walls, spikes placed in the ground, and trenches suitable for a grand moated camp. Guardposts were placed all round the perimeter. Post horses were dispatched to relay information.

The governor quickly prepared a report, and sent Khun Phaeng to gallop through the forest to reach Ayutthaya at dawn, enter the inner official sala,

and deliver the report to Nai Chamnan[23] of the army. The duty officer took it, broke the cylinder open, and went to inform the minister of Mahatthai. The contents were copied.

The minister of Mahatthai pondered the matter and consulted urgently with his officials. Having reached an agreement, they went to attend on the king.

---

23. Chamnan Krabuan, a duty officer in Mahatthai, *sakdina* 200 (KTS, 1:225; KW, 476).

40: PHRA WAI IS ROUTED

Now to tell of the almighty king, eminence of the city and outer territories, who resided in a glittering crystal palace thronged with palace ladies and inner consorts,

all beautiful, fair, delicate, and radiant, reciting songs and playing fiddle music harmoniously, enhancing the royal pleasure. When the sun brightened the sky,

the king was bathed, arrayed in raiment and regalia, and proceeded to a window at the front. All the high nobles in attendance prostrated.

The minister of Mahatthai paid respect to the king. "My liege, Your Majesty, my life is under the royal foot.

A report has come from the governor of Suphan, brought by several local officials, saying that a bandit troop of almost one thousand has appeared,

and has created great confusion and nuisance by attacking people. Spies sent to investigate say they have established a camp in the forest at Doembang.

The governor has made preparations to defend the town but the bandits have not approached and invested it. The governor would go out to engage them but thinks that, as he has not yet informed the royal foot,

he could be held seriously at fault if officers and men were killed in an engagement. Anybody who saw the troop that has come would know it wrong to call it an army,

as it has only marched here but has not started a fight. Hence it should be called a gang of simple forest bandits. The sight of so many men is abnormal."

Hearing this, the king smiled. "This report is a lot of mumbling. Doembang is almost to Suphan.

If this army came from somewhere far away, why does it wait there? If it has the opportunity, it should approach, make a base camp, and take the town.

The governor of Suphan doesn't go out to fight but is hiding in the forest. This doesn't seem like a stray gang of forest bandits. They're bolder than that.

The governor of Suphan doesn't want to go out to fight because he's a coward. He sends this report to excuse himself for fear of me. I understand this silver-tongued fellow completely.

Send Phaen to take a look. He'll easily capture them in an instant. Have this Suphan governor serve in Phaen's army." The window was closed.

The minister came out of the palace and had sealed orders prepared, one to send to Suphan,
and another for Phan Phao[1] to take to Phra Kanburi. Phan Phao took the cylinder and went by boat, reaching Kanburi in three days.

Khun Phaen, great master, received the order with a Ratchasi seal. In the presence of his local officials, he unfolded and read the message.
When he knew the contents, a smile spread across his face. He told Phan Phao to go quickly. "Why this fuss over a few forest robbers?
They won't be able to put up much of a fight. If I go, I fear they'll run away. If they dare to stand their ground, we'll finish them off and should get rich.
We'll capture many war prisoners to use as servants, as well as elephants, horses, gold, and silver. We'll get a lot of pretty New Mon girls with chignons for the officers!"
He ordered the deputy governor, magistrate, registrar,[2] and others to quickly organize troops to march to battle on the following day.

The deputy governor, magistrate, and other officials busily arranged matters. Lists were drawn from the recruitment rolls, and the registrar promptly issued the call-up.
Those who fled or evaded were thrashed without discrimination. Oxen, horses, and elephants were assembled, along with all kinds of weaponry.

Hearing there would be fighting, Kaeo Kiriya prepared various supplies. Khun Phaen came into the inner room
and summoned Kaeo Kiriya and Laothong for a talk. "You both stay back here and don't be alarmed. This campaign will take some time.
Chumphon, our darling son, is now very knowledgeable. I had him come in disguise in the hope of luring Phra Wai out to be killed for revenge."

Kaeo Kiriya was distressed to hear this, and could not stay quiet. "You're angry at your own child enough to threaten him! Where do his flesh, blood, and innards come from?

---

1. Phan Phaonurat, see p. 21, note 7.
2. สัสดี, *satsadi*, officer responsible for keeping records of phrai, and for judging disputes over control of phrai (Akin, *Organization*, 7).

For better or worse, you could thrash him for his wrongdoing, but don't think of taking his life. Have sympathy for the lovely Wanthong. On the day she died, she entrusted

the now motherless child to depend on his father. Still you want to go this far! Tell Chumphon to take his troops back. Don't create more anger and confusion."

Khun Phaen clenched his teeth in exasperation. "I'm incensed that Thong Prasi stopped me out of compassion for my son. How many hundred days before I'm gone?

You think Phaen is old and will die soon. You're looking forward to depending on Phra Wai's kindness. From way back, you loved Wanthong greatly.

You always advised me to reconcile with her, which is why I agreed to bring her back to live with me. But now you've fallen in love with her son and wish to protect him. Though he's being arrogant, you refuse to hear it.

Don't try to stop me. I'm not listening. I'm through with Wai. If I fall dead on the earth, please turn to depend on him."

Kaeo Kiriya replied, "Oh sir! Don't make such abominable accusations. I try to stop you out of pity and concern. If you won't listen, that's up to you.

Why not slash and kill each other? Don't bother me with this talk. Whatever I say, you'll make accusations the whole year through. Don't keep on at me because I don't feel like replying.

I fear your mouth. I don't want to argue. Fly away, I don't want to talk to you. The supplies are all set out, ready—including food. Go off and have fun killing each other."

Khun Phaen, great master, snapped his face away, and went into the main apartment. He dressed, decked himself with amulets, and walked out. He mounted Color of Mist, and left at an auspicious time,

with crowds of local officials following behind, and the troops hollering loudly and banging gongs. They quick-marched away from Kanburi.

The governor of Suphan received his orders, and prepared troops, both officers and men. He waited for Khun Phaen, then joined forces with him.

They proceeded to Nangbuat[3] where they planted a flag and set up camp

---

3. Now merged with Doembang as one amphoe. Nangbuat was about 6 kms south of Doembang. The name means "the lady who became a nun." According to legend, a woman who was trying to avoid the amorous attention of a leper first cut off her own breasts, which are now the

with units arrayed by rank, trenches around the perimeter, and detachments posted as guards.

Chumphon, a warrior of great power and expertise, saw the camp being established and was not afraid. He posted a line of dummy troops as guards.

He had Phlai Phet[4] and Goldchild enter into the bellies of two dummies disguised as Suphan villagers, and sent them to the other camp

with orders to act like villagers who had been captured. "Tell them I sent you with a letter to their senior officer.

If they inquire, tell them we are New Mon from Hongsa, and ask them who is leading their troop." The spirits took leave and hurried away with the letter.

Reaching the front of Phra Kanburi's camp, they kept their distance, pretending to be scared. The troops were surprised to see them coming from afar, and swarmed out to meet them.

Phlai Phet and Goldchild sank down on their heels and cried out, "We're villagers from around here. That army captured us,

and sent us with this letter to the commander of your army. Two of us had to come since we're afraid. I wai you. Please take us to him."

Without realizing they were spirit dummies, the soldiers tied their arms tightly, and took them to report to Khun Phaen. He asked, "Who are they?"

The soldiers informed him. "We caught them. They say they came from the New Mon. When asked, they told us in Thai that they're bringing a letter."

Phan Phao and the governor of Suphan interrogated them with menace. "What village do you come from?" "How many troops have they got?"

Pretending to fear a beating, the spirit dummies raised their hands in wai. "We live in the forest village of Banyan Landing.[5] We didn't run away in time and were captured.

Their troops are about a thousand plus. We overheard them saying they came from Hongsa, far away.

---

hills called Khao Nom Nangbuat, hill of the nun's breasts, 4 kms northwest of Amphoe Doembang Nangbuat. When this did not deter him, she entered a monastery as a nun (SWC, 2:703; see map 2).

    4. This name is perhaps the most glaring of several continuity errors. Phlai Phet is the son of Phra Wai and Simala, born in chapter 42 below.

    5. ท่าต้นไทร, *tha ton sai*. Unidentified. Probably this is an internal literary reference to the place where Wanthong and Khun Phaen fled in chapter 18. That would be far south of the current position.

They had us bring this letter." They handed it over. Khun Phaen put on his spectacles, unfolded the letter, and read the contents.

"I, an army chief by name Saming[6] Matra the splendid, from the region of Hongsa, am not a royal servant,
   but chief of my own troops, and feared by people for my power and bravery. I am no base villain but uphold compassion towards my fellow man.
   I have heard news that all the people of Ayutthaya villainously fight and kill one another, doing evil and creating karma. They attacked Chiang Mai in the north.
   I think this is wrong and I am concerned. I cannot close my eyes to people mired in suffering so I brought my troops here with the intention to teach you a lesson. If you act sensibly, supplicate, and do not resist,
   I will not kill you. My only aim is to impart instruction. If you do not surrender and act sullen, I will have my troops attack and slash you.
   You have come here and set up camp. If you want to fight, do so. If you want to surrender, come out immediately. If you stay there, I'll slash you to the last man."

Khun Phaen made a show of angrily throwing the letter away. He clapped his hands, "Tcha! These Mon! He's from far away and never been here so he speaks haughtily at length,
   like a puppy who's never had a sniff of a tiger. Who'd listen to him! He boasts of his military powers like a winged termite flying into a fire unawares.
   Reply telling him to come out in the morning. If he lazes around, I'll go and chop his skull. If he has eight thousand, I'll slash every one of them. Don't let them be stupid enough to believe they'll survive."

The mantra dummies saluted, took the letter, and hurried away into the forest. Coming to where Chumphon was, they dropped to the ground.
   Phlai Phet and Goldchild handed over the letter, saying, "The talented Phaen is the head of their army."

Phlai Chumphon gave orders to all the mantra dummies. "This evening, I'll attack my father's camp. Don't kill anybody.
   Just capture Phra Kanburi and bring him to me." They made preparations. As the sun sank at dusk,

---

6. *Saming, samin, smein, somoin*, a Mon title meaning chief authority or governor, used frequently in the Ayutthaya chronicles.

the two armies were drawn up ready. The sound of their gongs and cheers echoed around. A bright moon lit the forest. Cicadas trilled plaintively.

At around four in the morning,[7] the wind changed direction and the sky became overcast. Seeing this was an auspicious and appropriate time, Chumphon had the dummies drawn up in a column.

He harnessed Blueblack and put a yantra on him. He leapt onto the horse, and they made their way forward. Close to the enemy, he had the troops keep silent

and creep through the forest without making sounds underfoot until they arrived in front of Khun Phaen's position. Then they let forth a yell and fell on the camp. The soldiers were shocked.

Asleep and unaware of the enemy, they jumped up in chaos. Nobody was able to grab a weapon. The dummies attacked them hand to hand,

hitting them with the hafts of their pikes, thwacking them lightly with the flat of their swords, and landing kicks and punches not hard enough to kill them. The troops cried out in pain, and fled stumbling away to hide.

The governor of Suphan trembled all over and fell flat on his back, calling out, "Oh Grandpa, Grandma, lord, master! Come and help me!"

His cloth slipped off. Naked and bent double, he crawled under a shelter where he hid, curled up. Phan Phao squatted on his heels, looking around as the dummies swarmed over the army.

He picked up a pike and stabbed a dummy, which roared, grabbed the pike, and kicked him. Crying "I'm done for!" Phan Phao fell over with his head buried on his chest. Khun Phaen called out, "Hold the line! No retreat!

I'll slash dead any coward who turns tail, without exception!" He rode his horse at the attackers. His troops recovered themselves,

sent up a cheer, grabbed their swords, fired back, and piled into the attack, slashing and stabbing. Hollers and gunshots rent the air.

But their weapons did not pierce the dummies, or missed them altogether. The dummies spun around and leapt forward again. The troops brought powder bombs, lit the fuses, and threw them, but the figures still swarmed towards them.

The dummies came in waves. Khun Phaen rode his horse into the thick of the fray, chopping and slashing, driving forward until he arrived in front of his son. They were happy to see each other.

The troops began to break. "This lot aren't human." "You can't fight them." They took to their heels. The governor of Suphan came up to Phan Phao.

---

7. *Sip thum*, see p. 159, note 23.

"My eyesight's no good," he said, nodding his head, "Please let me ride on you, sir." Phan Phao angrily threw him off. "This oldster will be the death of me."

All were afraid and bent on saving themselves. They plunged into the forest and disappeared. Khun Phaen and his son summoned the dummies and spirits,

who gathered in a great mass and sent up a cheer that resounded through the forest. They set off across the plain towards Ayutthaya, passing Suphan town.

The inhabitants of houses and shops close to the road were scared witless. Every single household scattered and stumbled away in fright.

Khun Phaen and Phlai Chumphon led the army of dummies and crowd of spirits to Talan,[8] and set up camp at the edge of the forest.

The inhabitants of Talan abandoned their houses and fled trembling into the woods. Khun Phaen and his son were pleased. "Here's where we'll meet Wai."

After the army had scattered, Phan Phao ran through the forest, trembling with fear, stumbling and tumbling through the undergrowth, frightened by any rustling sound.

With two of his men following behind, he pushed on through the trees without stopping, reaching Ayutthaya near dawn, exhausted and heaving for breath.

He went to his house and called out to his wife, "Open up for me." In alarm, his wife lit a torch and came out. Phan Phao shouted, "Don't use the light!"

She shone the torch on her husband. "Oh, you look truly frightful. There's not a scrap left of your lowercloth." Phan Phao called out, "Hey! I almost died!"

At dawn, he wound a cloth round his belly and went straight to the sala. He informed the officials who were shocked into confusion.

When the king came out, they went into audience. Phan Phao stumbled in like a madman. The king saw him enter and asked,

"Heigh! Why did Phan Phao come back? Did Phaen catch the bandits or not? Your face looks pale. What's up? Why didn't Phaen come?"

Phan Phao prostrated elegantly three times. "My liege, Your Majesty. I took the order

to Phra Kanburi and Phra Suphan. Both brought troops that joined together as one large army. We hastened to Nangbuat. Just when we made camp, a letter was received

---

8. About 20 kms northwest of Ayutthaya, near Phak Hai, a crossing point on one of the north-south waterways, now called Phak Hai Canal (see maps 2, 4).

from one Saming Matra, saying that he was from the Mon country, the region around the city of Hongsa, and that he'd come to subdue the Thai.

Phra Kanburi replied, challenging him to a fight. That day at dusk, torch-lighting time, our army slept with guards posted. In the quiet close to dawn, suddenly

they invaded our camp, swarming all over us before we knew it. They attacked, slashing at our people. The camp broke and scattered.

Phra Kanburi went out to defend, and rallied the troops to strike back at them. We slashed at one another in the forest but they had great martial powers,

all invulnerable to piercing. We lost many men. Only Phra Kanburi had the powers to ride into the attack, slashing at them.

But they swarmed all over him. He was captured and hasn't returned. It's not known whether they killed him or not. Allow me to inform the royal foot of Your Victorious Majesty. My life is under the royal foot."

The king was furious. He stamped his foot and bellowed like thunder. "This doesn't sound like a skilled army.

The camps were close together but they trustingly put down their heads and nodded off to sleep, letting the enemy creep up and slash them dead without time to defend! All the torches had gone out so there was no light to see them.

I've never seen anything like this. It seems they were lazy and had no intention of fighting. Before long, this lot will become my enemy, and have the idea of making trouble for me.

Phan Phao came back first. He ought to be thrashed with two canes. This is going to grow into a major matter. They'll be minded to advance on the capital.

The more I think, the more I'm infuriated that they were able to capture my Phaen. I've lost a valiant soldier. The likes of him cannot be found.

He was bested because he's now old. Were he the same as in the past, this could never have happened. Tcha! These toasted turds will bare their teeth in glee that we've lost position to them.

They'll probably come to invest the city because they think we don't have any able people. Summon Wai immediately! I'll send him to catch these Mon."

A palace guard took the order and rushed out of the palace. He found Phra Wai and reported that the king had ordered him to present himself.

Phra Wai heard the matter was urgent, and he was stirred by the news of a fight. He wrapped a cloth round his waist and went to the palace with his servants following behind.

He put on a sompak, crawled in, made obeisance, and waited with face bowed. The king turned his head and said suddenly,

"The more I think, the more I'm furious. It's wrong because of Phaen for a start. He was sent to command an army but was careless and got defeated.

He ceded the position and let them capture him. We lost officers, lost men, lost troops. These Mon have advanced to Talan. Who will go out to repel them?"

The king looked at Phra Wai and thought sadly of his father. Tears bathed his face. The loss of such a supreme warrior riled his anger. Furiously he ordered Phra Wai,

"This Saming Matra has killed your father, Khun Phaen. Raise an army and go to capture him. You will leave at dawn tomorrow."

Phra Wai pondered for a time and then told the king his thoughts. "I think there's something wrong. What martial powers do these Mon have?

If they'd defeated anyone else it would be understandable, but it seems too much that they should have defeated Phra Kanburi since he's skilled in lore.

Even if it were beyond his powers to defend himself, he should have become invisible and returned in secret. Now that he's dead, why should I live? I'll go to engage them."

With that, he made obeisance to take leave, and returned home. He completed the arrangements for an army using the troops who earlier had gone to Chiang Mai.

He ordered supplies, horses, and elephants, then went to inform Thong Prasi. "These black-hearted new Mon have killed my father, Phaen."

Thong Prasi beat her breast, and fell down in the central hall, rolling on the ground as if dead and not breathing. It was a long time before she could be revived, and could get up.

"Oh, Khun Phaen of mine! You've abandoned your mother. My heart is trembling. This is the end of me.

You've been fatherless since you were small. I raised you until adulthood. I was happy that you went to govern Kanburi. I had intended to entrust you with my corpse.

But now you've fled away from me again. If only I could cremate your body, I wouldn't complain, but because of these New Mon you've died far from my sight without a scrap of dignity.

Now that my son is dead and my grandson has disappeared from my sight, there's only me left and how long will I last? Day and night I see only Wai. I don't know if it's good or bad that he'll lead this army.

Oh, I'm terribly sorry for you, Wai. Your little brother has run off. There's nobody to turn to. If I could go with you, I would.

The Mon killed your father, and there's nobody to help you fight. You're still a small child who needs instruction. Your grandfather, Khun Krai, was a great teacher.

Before you lead an army out, assess the position. When you halt to sleep, be very watchful. Study the enemy. If it's possible to attack and kill them, then attack.

If the enemy forces are formidable, build fortifications for a strong defense. In battle, be wary of risks. If it's possible to surround an enemy, then do so.

If under heavy pressure, force an opening to break out. If your troops scatter and flee, slash at them with your sword to drive them back into the fight. Before retreating, find an opportunity, don't just take fright.

As your grandfather, Khun Krai, was an old teacher, put your hands together at your head to ask his blessing. Go well, and be victorious." Wai made obeisance and left.

He went into a room to give orders to his two wives. "Don't be afraid. Listen to what I have to say. Act properly as the senior, Simala. Soifa is not a tricky person.

She's just a Lao from the upland forests. Help to instruct her. If she makes small mistakes, don't reprimand her. Let me return home first. Don't forget this."

Soifa and Simala raised their hands in wai. "Go well. We'll get along and not be thorns in your side." "We're fearful only because you're going to battle."

"Even Khun Phaen lost to them. Be careful and don't be led astray." "Look out for their lore and invulnerability. Keep your feelings under control, and defeat them."

Phra Wai walked out, glancing back at his two wives. He picked up a sword he had formerly used in battle, went up to a shrine hall,

and chanted powerful formulas. He bathed an image of Lord Narai with fragrant water infused with herbs in a bronze bowl, chanted a formula to summon his spirits,

and blew a conch as worship to the great power. When finished, he dressed elegantly, anointed himself with the sacred water from bathing the image of Lord Narai, and walked away.

Simala was concerned and upset. "Who is the enemy my beloved husband is going to fight? Father Khun Phaen is angry enough to be his enemy. Phra Wai should realize this is a trick.

He's besotted with Soifa, and still under the influence of a charm. If he goes to fight in this state, his father will kill him. My Wai is unaware of this.

Oh lord of honesty and purity,[9] please deflect weapons from my husband." She trembled in fear that Wai would be killed by his father.

Phra Wai found an auspicious time to march. The hollering of the troops echoed around. Elephants and horses packed the way. Phra Wai thought randily of Soifa.

"Oh my love partner, far from my breast, you'll be worrying and weeping. I'm suspicious that Simala might do something to you, eye's jewel.

Even when I was there looking after you from morning to night, she still hurt you. Now that you'll be alone and lonely, the servants will pile in to beat you.

If I didn't fear His Majesty, I'd abandon this campaign and return to the capital." Then his angry thoughts returned even stronger. "These New Mon killed my father.

It's good I have a chance to engage them. I'll clench my teeth in fury and attack!" He rode his bay, driving the mass of troops along to halt at Wat Lat.[10]

The phrai steamed rice and grilled fish. When they had eaten, it was torch-lighting time. Dummies were trussed together, and Wai scattered enchanted rice.

The dummies turned over and wriggled but did not get up. Wai had to enchant rice many times before they stood up straight like people, and still they oddly had no weapons.

Phra Wai was alarmed. "Am I going to die because of these Mon?" He looked at the horoscope. "Today is Wednesday with an inner blockage.

This is a time when the moon is dominant but a remnant of Saturn intrudes, meaning there's a major enemy.[11] According to the manual, the confrontation will be between people close in flesh and blood."

He again chanted and scattered rice. The figures now all had weapons in hand. Under a bright moon, he led the troops off in uproar.

---

9. Probably this means the Buddha.

10. Now Wat Ratbuakhao, still pronounced colloquially as "Wat Lat", around 4 kms northwest of Ayutthaya up the Chaophraya River on the west bank, just past the entrance to the Mahaphram Canal, formerly close to the Pak Khu customs house, which was where Wat Khanon now stands, three hundred meters to the southeast (see p. 398, note 9; map 3).

11. See p. 1003, note 6. Wales says this position means: "Not good; fear enemies; propitiate to avert evil" (*Divination*, 42). The next sentence may also indicate that Saturn's secondary influence is about to be superseded by Jupiter, which indicates dissension between close kin.

Now to tell of Wanthong. After she was found guilty and the king ordered her execution, her fate caused her to become a netherworlder, a suffering ghost. Even after death she still missed her son.

On the day Phra Wai went to war, Wanthong had a fearful premonition that he would be killed by his father. She transformed herself into the body of a woman

around fifteen years old, with clear skin, a fair face as radiant as a full moon, and exactly the manners of a palace lady.

She wore a meshwork sabai embroidered with lovely flowers in glistening purple-dyed silk thread, and a Tani yok lowercloth in two bright colors with golden thread

in a cross-branch pattern with seven-sided diamond lanterns, and a cone border in ruby red overlaid on orange with flower sprays that looked real enough to pluck. She deliberately ornamented her body

to look delicately seductive, with a belt around her slender waist, a glittering golden breast chain studded with sparkling diamonds,

and a flower tucked behind her ear. She cradled blooms in her uppercloth, and threaded them on a necklace to fasten to her firm budding breasts. Plaintively she sang

a slow *phatcha* about a lamenting prince, dew dripping down, and birds crying as the sun set. She sang sad *sakkrawa* and *doksoi*[12] songs, sounding sweetly forlorn in the forest.

Under a brightly shining full moon, Phra Wai rode up to the place and heard the sweet sound of a woman singing. He halted the troops on the road

and dismounted. He walked softly, hiding among the trees, not rustling the leaves, and spied the figure of a woman as slender as if she had been cast in a mold.

Her skin was as radiant as if lustrated with liquid gold. The ten fingers on her beautiful hands looked soft. Her hairline was neatly and prettily trimmed. Her whole body was attractive.

Her sweet singing soared around the forest like the call of swans flying across the sky. Mesmerized by her, Phra Wai hid in the trees and admired her beauty with unblinking eyes.

---

12. *Phatcha* (พัดชา), *sakkrawa* (สักระวา), and *doksoi* (ดอกสร้อย) are all traditional song genres. *Phatcha* may have originally meant "repelling spirits," and the songs may have had such a purpose (*Roi pi Khun Wichitmatra*, 99).

The netherworlder craftily pretended not to see him. She strung flowers for a garland and sang joyfully to the forest.

She pretended to be picking flowers unawares, and casually walked backwards without turning to look. When she reached the tree where Phra Wai stood, she started and shrieked in fright.

Throwing away the flower garland, she shouted in alarm and hugged her own soft breast but did not run away. She hid in the foliage, pretending to be scared, in order to lure him on.

Phra Wai was absolutely entranced. He walked towards her, smiling broadly and talking softly to seduce her.

"Eye's jewel, don't be frightened and upset. Where is this shrieking and slipping off going to get you? I fear your skin will turn sallow from fury, and your soul will fly far away in fear.

Your soul has gone bounding off into the forest. Come here and I'll bring your soul back to your body. Don't be dismayed.

It's lonely on your own in a forest with no companions to talk to. Sleeping in the forest will be chilly with nobody to hug you and keep you good and warm.

Some good deed has caused me to meet you. Let me embrace you and stay close by your side for around a hundred years. My jewel, don't be alarmed."

He spoke soothingly while walking slowly towards her. He ogled her as he came up close. "Give me your hand. Don't turn your face away. May I have some of the flowers you're threading?"

The lady netherworlder was unmatched in craftiness. Seeing her son courting her, she burst out in a roar that shook the forest,

bellowing, "Hey! Phlai Ngam, my son. You come to force yourself on me without respect out of lust and infatuation. I'm not just anyone, I'm your mother,

Wanthong, who was punished with execution on the order of the enraged king. Though I died, my heart remained attached to my son, so I've come after you with a warning.

The army you're leading is likely to be defeated and put to flight. The enemy will attack you fiercely, and the battle will be heavy and momentous.

Hang back and be careful. Don't rush forward out of bravery and lose position." With that, she leapt up into the air making an uproar that shook the whole forest.

She disappeared and was transformed back into a suffering ghost as high as the heavens, standing with an awesome body and no head. Then she turned around and disappeared from sight in a flash.

Realizing the apparition was certainly his mother, Phra Wai was very frightened. He shivered and his head swelled from fear of her. Glistening tears streamed down his face.

"Oh Mother, mistress of your child, your corpse was consumed but you've not gone. I made much merit to send to you but this hasn't yet overcome the evil that you did.

You're now in the form of a netherworlder, a suffering ghost, but you can transform yourself back at night. You always had kindness to teach your son morning and evening since the time you were human.

You've been dead and gone for many years. Today in this forest is the first time you've appeared to me. You warn me not to go to battle as I'll lose my life at the hands of the Mon.

But my father, Khun Phaen, has already died so it's beyond me to avoid this. If I take the army back to the city, the king will have me executed.

Whether I may live or die, as a soldier I can't withdraw but must avenge my father. Don't be worried, Mother." He prostrated, sobbing and swallowing his tears.

He remounted and led the troops across the plain and into the forest. When the moon descended and disappeared, they marched into Bang Kathing.[13]

They cut wood and made a camp complete with trenches, watchtowers, fences, and spikes driven in for defense. A horseman was sent to investigate.

Hearing the sound of hollering echoing around the forest, Phlai Chumphon talked with his father how to fight and win against Phra Wai.

From investigation, they knew he had set up camp at Bang Kathing out of fear that they might attack and take the city. The powerful Khun Phaen arranged to make offerings.

He set up paper flags, put a ritual balustrade around, and strung sacred thread around the pillars of a shrine. He lit incense and bright candles, and placed their devices and charged swords on the shrine.

He scattered enchanted rice to gather together the deities of all the directions, giants of the netherworld, Garuda and Wasukri, swarms of spirits and skillful spectrals,

rishis, hermits, masterminds, and crowds of deities. He invited them to take the offerings, and then he sacralized the weapons.

Amulets jumped up and down. Swords jiggled, turned over, leapt up like

---

13. Now Bang Krathing, about 7 kms south of Talan down Phak Hai Canal towards Sena (see map 2).

young chicks, and wheeled around in the air. Khun Phaen lit a flame for coating his son.

When the flame went out, he sprinkled herbal water on Chumphon to make his body tougher, more resistant, and invulnerable to all kinds of weapons. He used the water to make the horses invulnerable too.

When they were done, he dressed Phlai Chumphon in disguise to look like a New Mon, and blew a mantra onto him. Then he prepared himself to join the battle.

When Venus rose in a white sky, both the powerfully equipped armies left their camps, hollering loudly through the forest.

Riding a horse at the head of his troops, Phra Wai chanted a sacred formula. Chumphon rode his horse to engage him. Khun Phaen hid to watch.

When the two armies met, they slashed and stabbed at one another noisily with both sides aiming for victory and fighting bravely without ceding ground.

The dummy troops from each side closed on one another, spinning around, slashing and stabbing back and forth amid loud hollering. They rushed at one another, leaping and hitting relentlessly, but were all invulnerable.

The thirty-five soldiers advanced into the attack, brandishing pike and sword with no thought of retreat, but the dummy troops engaged them, spinning, chopping, and slashing until the humans were forced to retreat in frustration at such a lethal attack. "I can't take it." "These Mon are too much." Phra Wai saw his men were withdrawing so he grabbed rice with his right hand and scattered it.

When the enchanted rice touched Chumphon's dummy troops, they changed back to grass and collapsed down. Chumphon drove his horse at the head of his men and blew a formula at Phra Wai's dummy troops, which also collapsed back into bunches of grass. The two commanders signaled to their soldiers to halt the fighting.

Phra Wai caught sight of a little Mon but could not recognize him because of the mantra. "Tiny! A slim waist but very soldierly. Only just of age, and not yet aware of my skill.

He's puffed up with arrogance, fears no one, and boldly thinks he can fight me. I'd like to hear what he has to say for himself so I can see just how much knowledge he has."

He called out, "Hey, little Mon! Your body is as tiny as a child's and doesn't match your big overblown ideas. What's your name? Tell me the truth.

What monk was your teacher and how many things did he teach you? If you truly want to fight me, you'll end up running off to hide.

What are the names of your father and mother? What city are you from? Tell me everything. Who urged you to be so bold, rash, and fearless as to come here, and why?

You slashed Khun Phaen dead. What did he do to annoy you? Did he attack *your* city and capture *your* parents?"

Phlai Chumphon cleverly spoke with a Hongsa accent. "Me? I'm Saming Matra. My father is a powerful soldier
called Saming Maengtayakala-on. In the Mon country, nobody can match him. His fame spreads to every city. My mother's name is Moei Maengtaya.

My teacher of lore was Phra Sumet Kaladong from Hongsa city. I came to try out the skill of the Thai. If any dare, I'll slash them dead.

I've no desire for the treasure of Ayutthaya. Khun Phaen brought troops to fight me so I caught him and slashed him down.

You, who the Thai king employs as a leading soldier, what's your name? What monk was your teacher? What's the name of your father
and your mother? Don't try to deceive. Tell me so I have no doubts. What power and daring make you bold enough to oppose my skill?"

"Hey, Mon Saming Matra! I dare to bring these troops to fight with you, and shortly you'll know my powers. You ask about my teacher.

For knowledge, I was not the pupil of any monk as my father came from a lineage of soldiers. His name is Khun Phaen Saensathan. He gave me my knowledge.

My mother's name is Nang Wanthong. My own name—I do not lie—was originally Phlai Ngam but by appointment I'm Phra Wai.

Don't let catching Khun Phaen make you bold and careless. He was old and his powers were failing. I don't fear you as much as a fingernail!"

Chumphon slapped his leg and said, "What you say isn't true. I know something that Khun Phaen told me himself.

I asked him about the past, and he told me before I killed him that he had one son, just of age, called Chumphon, son of Kaeo Kiriya.

This son has fled off somewhere unknown. Khun Phaen told me the story from the beginning that there's another *step*son who the king appointed as Phra Wai.

Though his mother's name is Wanthong, he's not the son of Khun Phaen but of the villainous Khun Chang. Your father lives in Suphan.

He has a mess of hair on his chest up to his chin but a spirit scraped the top of his skull bare. Perhaps you're ashamed to say this and so claim Khun Phaen as your father."

Phra Wai was as angry as a blazing fire. "My! You tricky Mon, picking at me with these lies." He flew into a blind rage. Forgetting to chant a mantra formula first,

he brandished his sword and surged quivering into the attack, spurring his horse to charge wildly at Phlai Chumphon. They engaged and exchanged cut and thrust.

Sword clashed against sword. Slash, chop, slash, chop. Horse reared up against horse. Dummy troops leapt spinning and soaring into the attack, charging their opponents.

Dummy attacked dummy, stabbing and parrying, pushing and pulling, clashing pike against pike, wrestling hand to hand in uproar.[14] The thirty-five soldiers had had enough.

They fought the dummy troops until staggering at the end of their strength. The dummy troops spun forward, grabbed their hair, and pounded them with their pike handles. The soldiers slipped away to hide in the undergrowth.

Chumphon and Phra Wai charged each other but missed, fell, and lost grip on their swords. They wrestled together, hand to hand, chest to chest, staggering around chaotically.

As enraged as if struck by lightning, Khun Phaen spurred his horse to race forward like a windmill, shouting out from a distance, "Hold him tightly, Chumphon! I'll slash him myself!"

Phra Wai looked up and saw his father. In fright, he released his brother's neck, and leapt onto his horse to escape, but lost his balance, and Chumphon stabbed at him.

The pike hit his chest but broke without piercing. Phra Wai rode his horse away. Khun Phaen furiously charged in from an angle. The dummy figures spun and stabbed at the troops.

The thirty-five soldiers lost their clothing and all blundered fearfully into the forest, stumbling among the thorns and being scratched all over their bodies.

Rustling sounds made them dash out again crying, "Forgive me, oh lord and master!" When the light dimmed at dusk, they cried, "We've survived, Pa!" and hurried onwards.

---

14. The dummies were decommissioned a few lines earlier but have somehow revived.

Phra Wai rode his horse straight across the plain—face drawn, hungry, aching, and out of breath—and went straight across the river at Wat Thamma.

People who saw him ran away in shock, crying, "Catastrophe!" "We're dead for sure!" "Phra Wai's army is routed!" The whole city was seized with fear.

Having no word or sign to know which direction the enemy would come, people raced around chaotically. Phra Wai arrived at a gate of the palace.

As King Phanwasa emerged before a crowd of officials, he heard a loud sensation outside, and listened without knowing the cause.

"What's that commotion? Has Wai returned in defeat? Heigh! Someone go to find out." At that moment, Phra Wai dismounted and entered.

He prostrated, shaking with fear, hungry, aching, and with face drawn. He waited in silence without saying anything.

King Phanwasa watched Phra Wai enter but make no address, and so roared like a lion. "What happened to make you return?"

Phra Wai was terrified at the king's authority. He raised his face and addressed the king.

"My liege, dust under the royal foot, lord protector, royal creator. May I offer my life as penalty for error. My life is under the royal foot.

I led the army against the Mon enemy. There was a great battle. When we attacked and killed them, their bodies changed. They were grass figures that were clearly created by some device.

Their army chief and I fought one on one, slashing and chopping at each other many times at close range. I did not realize it was my own brother, Phlai Chumphon, until I saw Khun Phaen race out.

He called for Chumphon to capture me. My father intended to slash me dead. I managed to get away alive but I can't escape royal authority.

This Phlai Chumphon is not my brother by the same womb but is the son of Kaeo Kiriya. Khun Phaen is his father."

After listening to Phra Wai's account, the almighty king pondered back and forth, and then gave his command.

"What Khun Phaen has done this time, I don't know what to say about it. He has sworn loyalty. I do not think he's in revolt against me.

His mother, Thong Prasi, is still here so I doubt he's acting disloyally. Why would he change into my enemy? I think there's something strange going on.

I'm the pillar of the land. Though someone may have powers, he can't compete with me. It's known throughout the city that the guardian deities protect the royal lineage.

How can those who are mere servants of the dust crave the world? If they had ideas of seizing Ayutthaya, they'd have come to the capital by now.

Perhaps this fellow Phaen has a wish for revenge. He's not in revolt but angry so he employs some trickery. What do you have to say?

If he had evil and improper intentions, he would have killed the troops, but in this case not a single person died. The father and son were trying to kill you alone."

Phra Wai made obeisance, thought quietly, and saw clearly. "The king suspects the truth about everything. I can't squirm my way out of this."

He made obeisance to the king. "My liege, the royal foot covers my head. At the very beginning, this matter arose when I beat Simala.

Chumphon tried to stop me and, because I did not notice him in my anger, there was a fracas in which he also was hit. He became angry and fled through the forest to Kanburi.

He spoke to his father, Khun Phaen, who came down here and made a big fuss about Soifa having put a love charm on me. I had doubts about that.

My father was angry that I didn't believe him. He waved Skystorm around aggressively. If I hadn't escaped in time on that day, I'd be dead. He must have been angry enough to play this trick."

The almighty king listened to Phra Wai's account. "I think you look dark like someone affected by a potion. In the past, your father was never crazy.

If the dispute was only about this, it shouldn't have resulted in a battle. It's not enough to cause fighting and killing. There's still more to this.

I'll have him sent for so we can discuss the matter, make a decision, and clear it up. Who can be deputed to get him? Think up some appropriate ploy."

Phra Wai took the royal order on his head, and prostrated immediately. "I don't think just anyone can go.

When Khun Phet and Khun Ram went after Khun Phaen, there was a great battle.[15] Somebody that Khun Phaen likes must be found to persuade him and his son to come in.

I can think only of Simala, his daughter-in-law. Whatever she does, right or wrong, Khun Phaen never complains. May Your Majesty have the grace to send her."

---

15. In chapter 20.

The king listened carefully and then commanded palace guards to summon Simala immediately. Nai Jong[16] ran off and brought Simala back.

She saluted and made obeisance to the king. Seeing Phra Wai angrily throwing her a cold, sharp look, she backed away to put some distance between them, and averted her face to avoid looking at him.

The king glanced to left and right and saw there was something up between Phra Wai and Simala. He called them to come forward, close together.

"Their behavior somehow doesn't look normal. Simala is usually well-mannered. How are things between her and Soifa?" With this thought, he smiled and said,

"You must go and fetch Phaen and Chumphon here. Inform them that I ordered this, and that I'll not punish them with death."

Simala wai-ed and bowed her head. "As Your Majesty has the grace to send me, may I request royal power to protect me from danger and ensure my father, Phaen, and his son moderate their anger.

I'm afraid. Even Phra Wai had to run away through the forest. I, as a woman, have no knowledge. I'll steel myself to volunteer because Your Majesty commands."

She prostrated to take leave. Phra Wai hastened out to the front. Simala walked along, ill at ease and trembling. At the house, Phra Wai went straight in and strode up the stairs. Thong Prasi watched, not knowing if the news was good or bad. "Why did you flee from the army, Wai?"

Phra Wai spoke to his grandmother through his tears. "Who do you think the enemy was?" Tears of anger flooded his eyes. "How could my father act like this?

He and his wild son, Phlai Chumphon, meant to kill me. I survived because I fled. Now the king has ordered Simala to go out and fetch Khun Phaen and Chumphon back here." He was so pent up and choked with fury that he could say no more.

After listening to her grandson, Thong Prasi shook convulsively, gnashed her gums, rolled her eyes, and trumpeted loudly.

"These were thought to be New Mon from somewhere! I didn't know you were killing each other. Having a son and grandson fighting each other with pike and javelin is terrible. They didn't care that you were alone,

---

16. นายจง, a title used by various positions in the royal pages (SB, 590).

but piled in to attack you like a pack of dogs. You'd be dead if you hadn't fled. Those two teamed up to attack you with no respect for me. If I could, I'd have gone with you,

and bashed their heads to bits like chopped fish. Their mother's clan should weep! Heigh! Simala, what do you have to say? Where have you disappeared to?

You're the darling of your father-in-law. You flaunt your flesh, flaunt your body so much—stirring things up by sticking out your bottom beyond belief. You're in favor now! Hurry off to fetch them.

I can see you're in league with them. Wai fled in time and managed to come back, otherwise he would've been slashed to death, and you'd be delighted.

Go fetch your lords, both of them. If their heads don't get chopped to pieces, I'm not Thong Prasi." Slobbering spittle, she raised a pestle to pound betelnut but her mind wandered and she forgot to put in the lime.

Soifa knew the issue had not gone away. She fretted fearfully as if fire were flaring in her breast.

"Oh, what karma have I made? Things shouldn't have come to this. A war against the Mon turned into a war against the Thai. And now this wretched woman!

If Simala is allowed to go and fetch Khun Phaen and Phlai Chumphon, there'll be a row. Those two know the good and the bad of this matter, and I think there'll be a big uproar."

She called Khanan Ai and told him what had happened. "Find about ten of my servants, get prepared, and go off unseen.

Ambush Simala on her way to the army. Catch her and kill her." She took out five chang and gave it to him. "Don't let Simala bring them back here."

Khanan Ai said, "Don't worry." He boarded a boat and hurried away from the landing. He took companions who had been partners for a long time. All were armed, and made no noise.

They went to the sharp corner,[1] turned to the right, and hastened past Wat Tha.[2] When dusk fell and the water was high, they hid on Mahaphram Island.[3]

Knowing that the Lao were hiding at the river fork, the spirits protecting Simala went and roared at them menacingly, wrestled them down, and tied them all together by their elbows.

Simala's boat paddled past at nightfall. The spirits called out for them not to come close. The oarsmen scudded past, singing chicken-flapping songs along the way.

---

1. The area around the junction of the Chaophraya River at the northwest corner of the city was called *Ban pom hua laem*, the village of the fort at the sharp corner (KLW, 180). As they turn right here, they must have come from around the main palace.

2. Wat Tha Ka Rong, which appeared in chapter 24.

3. About 3 kms northwest up what is now the Chaophraya River, the Mahaphram Canal forked westward (see pp. 850–51). The large triangular area enclosed by this canal, and the Bang Ban Canal was called Mahaphram Island (see maps 4, 10).

They cut through the Bang Phong Pheng route,[4] with the men merry and noisy. Close to dawn, they paddled past Bang Kathing, and at sunrise arrived at the Talan landing.

∽

Phra Kanburi and his son were happily inspecting the camp when they saw a canopy boat. They conferred. "The king probably sent someone."

They saw a woman sitting amidships. "That's strange. What woman would be so brave?" Then they saw Moei sitting neatly at the front of the canopy. "This is Simala for sure." They went down to the boat,

and on arrival asked, "Why did you come? You're pregnant[5] and must be uncomfortable. I pity precious you sitting in a boat. What's the reason you're here?"

Simala prostrated at Khun Phaen's feet, and told the story truthfully. "His Majesty asked me to fetch you back.

After he was routed, Phra Wai came back to tell the king that you and Phlai Chumphon had surrounded and attacked him with the intention of slashing him to death. The king inquired about the story from the beginning.

Phra Wai said there'd been a quarrel. The king didn't believe it, and so ordered me to bring both of you back. As for any crime, great or small, the king will be favorable."

Phra Kanburi heard her account and flew into a rage. "Tcha! This Wai's an evil fellow. He likes telling the king only what makes him look good.

He fought, fled, and then looked for a patron. Let's fight this out one on one and see what happens! He's arrogantly making accusations that this old man here is devious.

The king hasn't executed me yet. He'll probably ask me a few things first. What's true and false we'll see for sure. If the king doesn't keep me, I'm done for."

Khun Phaen ordered his son to release the mantra on the dummy troops, then took him to board the canopy boat.

Simala boarded also. The oarsmen paddled boisterously along and quickly

---

4. Bang Phong Pheng is on the Chaophraya River in the south of Ang Thong, near Pa Mok. From here Bang Luang Canal branches southwest towards Sena (see maps 2, 3).

5. Simala was pregnant when her parents visited Ayutthaya in chapter 39. That was eight years earlier. Her child, born below in chapter 32, figures as Phra Wai's firstborn in the rest of the story. The episode of Phlai Chumphon's sojourn in Sukhothai seems to have been inserted clumsily into the plot.

arrived at the capital. They went straight to the audience hall.

Near the time for royal audience, all the nobles were gathered there. Phra Wai was afraid of paying respect to his father. He hid behind a pillar and kept watch.

When he saw his father turn around, Phra Wai leapt up, startled like a little mouse. Phra Kanburi wagged a finger at him, saying, "You tried to trick me!" Phra Wai said, "I won't fight you. I beg forgiveness."

When the sun dropped, the king, paramount protector, emerged. Officials including Khun Phaen and Phlai Chumphon all quailed and quivered.

The king saw the father and sons had come to audience. He looked closely at them and reasoned with himself. "The two brothers are very alike in talent.

Phlai Chumphon, the younger, is smart and diligent. Both have an imposing appearance very much like their father."

He spoke with menace. "Look here, Phra Kanburi. Because you have great belief in your own lore, you boldly brought a mass of troops to attack and slash people.

What were you thinking? Did you intend to seize the capital? Have you forgotten the oath of allegiance? I'd been very carried away with you.

When it was said a Mon had captured you and taken you off to kill, I couldn't hold back my tears. When Wai rushed out to take revenge, you and your son attacked him.

I was going to dispatch troops after you but realized you'd probably hide away, so I sent for you to come to the capital. First, I'm going to ask you to explain yourself properly.

Tell me the truth about what happened. If you're tricky and deceitful, you'll die. Even though I raised you to govern Kanburi, do you still think of rebelling against me?"

Khun Phaen, great valiant, prostrated with his face bowed, trusting in the powers of his teachers, and focused his mind, directing it towards the king.

"My liege, Your Majesty, eminence of the city and all the territories. I offer my life under the royal foot. I'll speak the whole truth.

Every morning and evening, I place your kindness above my head. I do not lie. I have not rebelled against your royal grace. I have always been honest.

When I was imprisoned, I did not break my word. The ruse I've played at present is due to the intolerable grievance I have against Phra Wai.

In the past, he was enraged at Simala. He both abused her and beat her badly. He also hit his younger brother, Phlai Chumphon, who fled through the forest to Kanburi.

When Phra Phichit and I went to complain, Wai made an angry fuss. He issued insults and challenges that were improper. He no longer felt of me as his father.

I thought something was wrong so I examined him, and saw his face was dark and freckled. I thus knew that Wai had been affected by a charm. When I told him this, he replied that he didn't believe so.

He dredged up the past in an insulting way, saying that I'd been released from prison because he made the request. I was extremely angry and hurt. I wanted to slash him dead from that day onward,

but my mother came between us so I had to restrain myself. I collaborated with Chumphon to make a thousand dummy troops and advanced.

I expected that Wai would come out to do battle. When we met as hoped, I attacked to kill. Once Wai was dead, I intended to submit to royal authority. If in the future an enemy appeared in any direction,

I would volunteer, and offer to the king the services of my son, Chumphon, who is knowledgeable, brave, and valiant. As for Wai, I want to fix him finally."

Hearing the reason, the almighty king pondered carefully and said, "Heigh! Kanburi, I've always trusted you.

In this military operation you didn't capture people or kill them. I've no doubt you're telling the truth. Wai is bold and haughty,

rash and pushy with his elders, very arrogant. He jests with people, even his father. Yet how much merit has he made?

He shouldn't rake up the past and have no respect for his elders. He seems to be getting stupider by the day. He doesn't look at his own face in the mirror.

At present, he's only been affected a little but in time he'll be crazy. Heigh! Khun Phaen, don't be vengeful against Phra Wai.

Because he was subjected to a love charm, he's not the same person he once was. He believes that with his powerful knowledge, he couldn't have been affected by any mantra.

If you asked him now, he'd probably dispute it. You have to expose it for all to see. Find whoever made the mantra, and reveal where the figures are placed.

If this crooked fellow can be caught, the matter will be out in the open and all doubts removed. I'll give the wrongdoers their just deserts—not a fine but their last will and testament!"

Phlai Chumphon replied to the king with no fear. "My liege, Your Majesty, allow me to capture him.

May I ask that Your Majesty provide a reliable witness? I'll get the person who cast the mantra, along with the figures, and bring them here without delay."

The king laughed. "This fellow is just perfect to be a soldier! Who can go with you as witness? He must be quick, clever, courageous,
and neutral between the two brothers. I think the only person of suitable character is Phramuen Si. Go off quickly and catch this fellow who's good with knowledge."

Phramuen Si and Phlai Chumphon bowed their heads, raised their clasped hands to accept the royal order, and left to return home.
The two of them arranged to pretend that they were Khaek who had come to the Thai country from Java. Each dressed as a Khaek, wearing smart britches,
yok lowercloth just down to the knee, a good-looking Javanese-style kris tucked in a very beautiful sash round the waist, shirt with epaulets[6]
and tight sleeves down to the elbow, and a cloth wrapped round the head. They looked exactly like Khaek from Java or Malaya.[7] Servants and phrai crowded along behind them,
all dressed up as Khaek and treated with mantra so people would not recognize them. Pretending to be seamen[8] come to the city, they carried toddy[9] and ganja along with them
as well as pipes, opium, and strong liquor in a square clear bottle filled to the brim. They spoke no Thai. When they walked through the market,
the young vendor girls looked at them and found them very unusual. "They're good-looking and stylish." "Their eyes look very similar to a Thai."
"Where do you live? I've never once seen you before." "Do you come from a sailing ship or what?" Some asked them, "What are you selling?" "Hatsi,[10] what do you have for us?"
"Eh? This is very strange. Khaek usually sell spices but how come you're car-

---

6. อินทรธนู, inthanu, Indra's bow, epaulets.

7. In Thai, the term แขก, khaek covers people ranging from Arabia and Persia through India to the Malay world. Although this sentence identifies their disguise as Malay, the following passage shows them as a pastiche of the whole region covered by the term khaek. Words used such as hatsi, mohurram, baniya derive from India and Arabia.

8. กะลาสี, kalasi, an Iranian word borrowed into Malay.

9. น้ำตาลเมา, namtan mao, toddy, wine made from sap of the sugar palm.

10. หัศรี. Khun Wichitmatra suggested that "Hatsi is similar to an Arabic word Hassari that was adapted in India into a form of address, like mister or sir" (KW, 599). We cannot find any confirmation for this. Hassari is an Arabic family name. In Tibetan, Hatsi is an exclamation, like "My goodness."

rying bottles of liquor?" "Perhaps you have some novelties from a junk?" The market people could not stop talking and joking about them.

They arrived at Wat Phraya Maen. Goldchild ran on in front and told Chumphon, "That's the kuti of the monk that cast the mantra.

He has a novice pupil who came with him from the Lao country. People know their reputation everywhere. Both are skilled in knowledge. Think how to weaken it."

Phlai Chumphon listened to the spirit, then turned to whisper to Phramuen Si. "The key person lives in this kuti. If we're not careful, we'll fail."

He chanted a formula to chase away the spirits of the old monk. The skillful spirits kept by the elder and novice leapt out of the kuti and frantically fled away.

The Khaek-in-disguise walked up. The dogs saw them and ran over barking. "*Hatsi,*" the Khaek called out, "Where are you, Novice? Please see to the dogs."

Novice Jiw stuck out his face and saw the Khaek. He threw a brick at the dogs, scattering them away, and opened a door to welcome the Khaek into the kuti. "Today, I'll get to eat dates!"

The two Khaek went in, sat down, and wai-ed the elder. They raised their gifts and said, "*Moharram.*"[11] Elder Khwat said, "I don't know this word. If you're bringing me a ram,[12] I don't want it."

The Khaek said, "Today is new year. I am bringing these gifts for monk. These are unusual articles from my country, come by junk. I have heard people say you're able.

If anyone sick or unwell comes for your treatment, they are not dying." Elder Khwat said, "There's no need to go on. What do you have for me?"

The Khaek picked up a hookah, filled the chillum[13] with ganja, and lit it. They smoked a chillum each, and smiled blearily. The elder asked, "What's making the sound in there?"

The Khaek said, "The inside is having water." Elder Khwat said, "What does it do? Let me try a taste. Is it all finished?" He took a light and tottered over.

The Khaek put in some ganja and passed it across. The elder stretched his

---

11. The first month in the Islamic calendar—hence "new year" in the next line—well-known to the Thai as a time of festivity, as seen by mention in the boat songs authored by King Rama II, but nonsense as a greeting.

12. In the Thai, the pun is on รำ, *ram*, meaning chaff.

13. In India, a clay pipe, or the clay bowl for burning on a hookah. The Thai จ้าหลิ่ม, *jalim*, is derived from this.

neck, raised his face upwards, and shivered. "I can't take it, don't want it. Hurts my throat terribly. Keep it."

Laughing heartily, the Khaek took back the hookah and passed him an opium pipe. Elder Khwat examined it closely and cried, "What's this you're giving me?"

They lit it, and he sucked with a plopping sound, smacked his lips, and said, "It's bitter." He got up unsteadily, slobbering. "What's that jar over there?"

The Khaek said, "This is good. It'll cure the harshness you are having just now, good sir. It is a sweet and sour sugary medicine." He picked up a bowl and ladled some out.

Elder Khwat glugged it down, and pushed the bowl back over. After five or six bowls, he was totally drunk but still not finished. "What's in that bottle. Let me see."

The Khaek poured liquor for him, and he gulped a whole cup. Wind blew out of his ears. His head spun, his mouth slobbered, and his mind was gone. He looked up at the roof and thought it was a whale.

He picked up the hookah, took another pull, and fiddled distractedly with the cover. He grasped a pestle and frantically pounded betelnut. He leapt up, stamped on novice Jiw, and said "Let's fight."

The novice said, "You're drunk enough to die badly."

The elder sat down, eyes bulging, and said, "I'm a drama master carrying a sword. Thotsakan kidnaps the lady Uthumphon."[14]

The two Khaek laughed merrily. Elder Khwat raised his leg in the pose of drawing a bow.[15] "I remember Hanuman when he was fighting. Was it a mask play or drama, I don't know.

Everyone carried a stick, stood legs astride in groups, and cried out 'I-lat-tat-tha!' and 'Pong-mang pong-khrum!'[16] I can see it. Today I'm having fun.

noble in robe and conical hat

---

14. Lady Uthumphon does not figure in the *Ramakian* but in the Sangsinchai story (see p. 102, note 25) she figures among several ladies enjoyed by the hero on his travels (*Bot lakhon nok*, 487).

15. A familiar pose in dance and drama. The actor stands on one leg with the other leg cocked behind, one arm extended forward as if holding a bow, and the other beside the ear as if drawing a bowstring.

16. Cries used in Mongkhrum, a ritualistic drum performance probably originating from India, played as part of royal ceremonial in the Ayutthaya period, and revived in early Bangkok. Players wearing *lomphok* conical hats and long *khrui* robes act as deities attending a festival at Mount Kailash. The leader calls out names such as "Lotus bud blooming," "Dragon lashing tail," "Wind blowing," and the team performs the appropriate drum sequence and dance. The name

I thank you, Khaek with your strange tongue. You know how to find good things for me. Since I came to the Thai country, I've not had such a good time as today.

Are you sick or something, little fellow? Is that why you came to see me? I can fix external and internal matters. Tell me what's up. Don't be shy."

The Khaek said, "I am coming to see you because I am very troubled beyond toleration. I abandoned my parents to take Thai wife. I gave her so much money, I lost the junk.

We lived together for less than year. She is attacking and beating me. Parents-in-law are abusing me. Wife is taking their side.

They call me coconut-head Khaek, man without religion who come by ship. I cannot enter house without beating. Every day, such trouble and strife.

So we are coming to see you, sir. Please help solve problem. Make her submissive like before. If can, I am giving piles of money;

making kuti with nine rooms, timber roof, and firm terrace; sending meals both morning and midday; and offering us two as your servants."

Elder Khwat laughed and said, "You want only that! It's no more than picking my teeth. You've taken the trouble to come begging for my help. Don't fret. I'll fix it within no time.

I'll make them furious at each other for eight years. If I don't put things right, you can complain. Phra Wai, Soifa, and Simala—I fixed that in less than an eye-blink.

I made Wai thrash Simala. Thong Prasi was affected too. Soifa was delighted. She's happy with Wai all the time."

Novice Jiw was shocked to hear him. He called out to warn the old monk. "It's almost time to eat the forenoon meal." He talked on other matters to change the subject.

Elder Khwat bellowed, "You dog! Butting in on your elders. Why tell me about the forenoon meal? Go to your kuti!"

Chumphon could see everything, including a skull.[17] He nodded to his phrai to storm the kuti.

They grasped sticks, hammers, and lumps of brick, and bounded up to catch

---

Mongkhrum and the calls cited here in the text come from the sound of the drums. (KW, 691; SB, 602; SWC, 11:5297; Flood and Flood, *Dynastic Chronicles*, 1:237)

17. From here onwards, it is implied that a skull was used in constructing the love charm, though no skull was mentioned in chapter 37.

the elder, shouting, "That's him! Get him before he goes!" Some stood guard at the door while others swarmed in.

Elder Khwat saw what was coming and shut the door. "Damn! These crazy Bayinu[18] are slitting a chicken's throat. They appeared all of a sudden but with the door closed what can they do?"

He scooped water into a bowl, enchanted it, and threw it over the novice's head so it splashed down his body. "Jiw, don't be afraid of these enemies. Grab round my waist and we'll be invisible."

The phrai came into the kuti but could not see the elder and novice. Chumphon shouted, "Don't be alarmed. Close the door tight again."

He lit a fire under the house and roasted chilies so the smoke billowed upwards. Unable to stand it, the elder came outside. "There he is! Get him!"

Elder Khwat bellowed like thunder, making the walls shake. The phrai trembled in fright, jumped down from the kuti, and rushed away.

When they had gone, Elder Khwat had the advantage and bellowed again. He stood swaying his waist in a circle, scattering rice all round the kuti.

"Hey, you Khaek peering through the wall, you popeyed coconut heads, what can you do, especially against *me*? All you're good for is killing one chicken a day to eat.

You oldie and you crazy kid! Do you still have some toddy left? Give me another bowl. You're arrogant enough to challenge the power of Thotsakan! You villains, I'll chop your heads off."

Chumphon bellowed, "You lowlife! Give me just an eye-blink, you disaster." He scattered rice, summoned his crowd of spirits to gather around,

chanted a stunning formula, and blew it with a roar. Elder Khwat froze. In surprise he said, "Tcha! This slave is trying to outdo me. Come on up! What's keeping you?"

Hopelessly drunk, he sat down and threw up. Mouth agape, he could not chant a formula. The men swarmed all around, seizing his shoulders, gripping his neck, thumping, and elbowing.

Under this assault, Elder Khwat shouted until his eyes almost popped out. "You bring me liquor to drink, then beat me up!" They tied the elder and novice together with hemp rope.

Bound around the neck and elbows, the elder shook so much he could not breathe. Chumphon asked him, "Where did you hide the enchanted figures?

Tell me how you did this to Phra Wai. Lead us over to dig them up." Elder

---

18. บ้ายี่หนุ่, *bayinu*; Khun Wichitmatra glosses this as "the name of a group of Khaek" (KW, 691). Possibly Balinese.

Khwat's eyes were as red as the light of a fire. He shouted, "Why should I? I won't."

Chumphon angrily drew his sword and slashed him between the eyes, drawing blood, which dripped down. In pain, the monk led them

to the graveyard of Wat Phraya Maen. They dug down about an arm's length and found the figures of Simala and Phra Wai with thorns stuck all over them.

The retainers said angrily, "You villain!" and hit Elder Khwat's skull with bricks that crumbled and smothered his body in red dust. "Why's your head so tough, you lackey?"

They took him to Phra Wai's house. "Tell us where the figures of Soifa and Phra Wai are." The spirits softly told their master to dig directly under where the couple slept.

They found the figures of Phra Wai and Soifa, faced towards each other and entwined in embrace. Khun Phaen, Thong Prasi, and Phra Wai all saw with their own eyes.

Watching them pick up the figures, I-Moei was so happy, she laughed merrily, nodded at Simala, and said, "Mistress, they've got them, the figures with the designs."

Soifa's breast trembled in alarm. The sight of the yantra figures turned her face pale. She ran off into the house with eyes narrowed. "This evil lowlife elder will get me killed!"

I-Mai consoled her. "Don't be afraid, mistress. Don't surrender to them easily. There are still lots of ways to evade, deny, and swear oaths to wriggle out of this."

As the mantra waned, Thong Prasi gradually recovered. Once all trace had gone and the blackness had disappeared from her eyes, she jumped up and shook convulsively.

"Tcha! Come out here, Soifa! We can't keep this evil Lao. Making little figures that had Wai blundering around besotted

to the point his father and Chumphon would not even look at his corpse,[19] and Chumphon ran away from the house, and Simala was shamed! I'd like to split your skull."

Phra Wai restrained her. "Don't, Grandmother. What's the point of making a fuss and driving her into a corner? In time, the case will be tried. If she's truly in the wrong, she'll be executed."

Phra Kanburi laughed, "Oh young Phra Wai! How come you were duped

---

19. Meaning they would not have even the sympathy to attend his cremation.

like this? It's shocking. Now that you know her bag of tricks, do you still want to protect Soifa?"

Phramuen Si listened and thought, "This won't do. It'll blow up before my eyes." As it was near the time for audience, he promptly took leave. His servants tied the hands of the novice and elder.

At dusk Phramuen Si took them to the guardhouse of the main guard, and informed them of the case. "We had king's orders to arrest them
for what Soifa made them do to Phra Wai. All the figures have been found. It's too late to inform the king now so I've come to place them in the safekeeping of the guard."

A duty officer of the royal guard ordered the warders to load the elder and novice with chains and cangue up to their necks—
the full five irons, locked tight. He informed them not to trust the old fellow. The guard listened. "Without delay, sir." They sparked fire and busily lit lamps.

Novice Jiw grimaced with the discomfort of not moving his body under the restraint of the five irons. "I complained and tried to stop you but you wouldn't listen.
As they expected, you tossed down enough of the toddy and ganja to fill you up to the ears. You were so drunk you slurred your speech and were careless. When I complained, you shouted at me.
You boasted and stupidly told them you're a master of love charms. But they won't cane you alone. I don't like listening to the sound of the cane. I'll have to spend money and I might die."
Elder Khwat clicked his tongue. "You can't take a bit of suffering, you disaster. I got drunk and muddleheaded on their toddy. If I'd been able, they'd never have taken me."

In the dead of night, when it was perfectly quiet and the torches shed a dim light, Elder Khwat thought of his teacher, stilled and focused his mind,
and chanted a Great Subduer formula. Everybody fell asleep like logs. He examined the movement of Rahu,[20] then used a Loosener to open the

---

20. This form of divination is similar to the Iron Spear (see p. 100, note 21). Over the course of a day, the demon-god Rahu resides for three-hour periods at each of the eight sub-points of the compass. One should avoid facing in that direction when performing an auspicious act, or setting off in that direction for travel. Beginning at 6 to 9 a.m., the directions occupied by Rahu are: east, southwest, north, southeast, west, northeast, south, northeast. The sequence is a series of knight's moves on a three by three diagram (Thep, *Horasat nai wannakhadi*, 91–92).

bolts and unlock the chains.

Everything slipped off, including the cangue. He repeated the mantra for chains and locks, and everything fell off Novice Jiw.

Using powerful knowledge, he enchanted a scrap of leftover pan leaf and lime, turning it into figures of a novice and elder lying in their place. The pair made themselves invisible and crept out of the gate.

Fearing they might be caught if they traveled by land as humans, the elder changed into a crocodile and swam through the water with the novice as a young crocodile on his back.

When dawn streaked the sky, the guards awoke and picked up bowls to wash their faces. They saw the elder and novice were both still lying down. "Hey, ha! Why don't you get up?"

"Everyone is awake but you're still covered with blankets." "How long are you going to sleep, damn you?" They grabbed canes and beat them. "They can stand a lot." "Don't move a bit."

The guards kicked them in the side. "Eh? How can they lie still with heads covered?" The guards bent down, pulled off the cloth, and got a shock. They cried out for others to come and see.

All arrived, including the head and deputy wardens, and saw the elder and novice lying flat on their backs, dead. In shock, they went to inform the official sala.

✧

Now to tell of the king, ruler of the world. When streaks of dawn lit every direction, he bathed and went out front

where all the ministers and officials attending audience prostrated at the head of the courtyard, to the royal pleasure.

Phramuen Si made obeisance and addressed the king in his turn. "My liege, lord of the earth. Yesterday, Chumphon and I

caught Elder Khwat and Novice Jiw, and found the enchanted figures. Elder Khwat said Soifa hired him to do this to Phra Wai, so he was arrested.

The figures, festooned with many yantra, were dug up in two places. It was past the time to inform Your Majesty so after consultation the culprits were sent to the palace guard."

The king was pleased with this news. "Eh, that was satisfactorily quick. Heigh! Guard, bring them here immediately."

The superintendent of the palace guard felt helpless. He made obeisance and bowed his head. "My liege, Your Majesty, the royal authority above my head.

Phramuen Si and Phlai Chumphon brought the elder and novice, along with the inscribed figures. Guards were ordered to put them under tight restraint.

Last night, both the elder and novice happened to pass away. News was sent to the official sala. May I inform the foot of Your Victorious Majesty."

King Phanwasa slapped his thigh and said, "This elder and novice are able. They were afraid of being thrashed,

so they died before it could be done. They fled on ahead to be spirits. That leaves only that scourge, Soifa. Now we'll get to the bottom of this."

He commanded Phramuen Si, "Bring Soifa here. I'll question her on this matter. If it's true, I'll have her executed today."[21]

Phramuen Si made obeisance, backed out, and gave orders to a guard to go at once to inform Soifa

that the king had sent for her. "If she resists, drag her here. Choose suitable people to bring her quickly, as the king commands."

The palace guard rushed to the house, went up, and called Soifa. When she emerged, he reported

that both the elder and novice had held their breath and died. "There's now an uproar. The king has ordered you to appear forthwith. Please come quickly right now."

Soifa felt as anxious as if a fire were raging in her breast. She quickly changed clothes. "Come here, I-Mai. Go with me."

The palace guard led the way from the house. They hurried along without stopping. People who saw her face went along to watch. On reaching Phramuen Si, she sank down, trembling.

Phramuen Si led Soifa into audience, bowed his head, and addressed the king, "Following the royal order to fetch Soifa, she has now come to salute the royal foot."

The almighty king looked at her, feeling hatred, and roared like a lion. "What's this, Soifa, you scourge?

---

21. The latter section of the Miscellaneous Laws, probably dated to 1784, is devoted to punishments for the malicious use of supernaturalism. Clause 69 runs: "Should anyone intend to make another person besotted by concocting a love philter with any materials to be eaten, inserted in any way, or as figures which are buried using any device of knowledge (วิทยาคุณ, *withayakhun*), that person, being found guilty, shall receive sixty lashes, be paraded on a cross by land or boat for three days, and then executed. If the potion was made for a lover or husband, and the person found guilty, the punishment shall be the same, and the body delivered to the husband, if so wished" (KTS, 3:180). The "cross," ขาหย่าง, *kha yang* was a diagonal X-shaped frame.

I give you patronage commensurate with your lineage, age, and birth but you lust for lovemaking terribly and make this evil love charm.

You sneak off to contact this elder and novice at a wat, and bury little figures inscribed with all kinds of yantra. But they've been found and brought to me.

Under your house, they dug up figures molded from beeswax, hugging together tightly, placed in an amora leaf and tied by cord to make him fall in love with you and you alone.

As for the figures of Simala and Wai, they were pierced with thorns from head to foot, and buried with the dead in a graveyard. Horrible! It made your husband so blithering stupid

that he beat Simala and also Phlai Chumphon, who fled from home and was estranged from his family and kin because of your wrongdoing.

It created great conflict with people running around all over the place, plunging the whole realm into confusion, and Wai almost losing his life.

Phaen and his son, Phlai Chumphon, attacked Wai, slashing to kill. Wai's army was routed and straggled home. I learned the reason only yesterday,

and brought the father and son in for questioning. They related the matter in detail. I sent them to arrest the people behind this, and to bring the spirit skull.

The elder and novice who did this were taken to find the figures. Several were retrieved. But you? How many years have you been doing this kind of thing, Soifa? Tell me nothing but the truth."

Soifa turned the matter over in her mind without fear. "As the elder and novice have lost their lives, there's nobody left." With this thought, she prostrated with clasped hands.

"My liege, lord protector, the righteous, excellent, and prosperous, I am but dust beneath the royal foot. Allow me to tell you the whole truth.

The facts were not like that. This is a conspiracy of lies. In the past, Chumphon and Simala secretly became lovers.

I know the reason why Chumphon ran away. He went to tell Phra Kanburi these trumped up charges that a love charm had been put on Phra Wai to make him beat Simala violently.

Without thinking, Phra Kanburi made up his mind to believe his beloved son. He turned up here shouting that he was going to catch the culprits, so they'd better look out.

I challenged him to go ahead. For better or worse, why should I cover things up? He made a reflection in a mirror and said he could see figures of me and Phra Wai.

Grandmother looked and couldn't see them. So Phra Kanburi danced around, gnashing his teeth at the old lady, stamped his foot, and went off home. He arranged with Phlai Chumphon to bring an army

to fight in alliance with himself. They pretended they were Mon troops, and agreed between themselves not to kill opposing soldiers but just beat and disperse them,

so that when Your Majesty sent Phra Wai out to give battle, they would combine to attack and scatter Wai's troops to the winds. They wanted to slash Phra Wai to death but he fled into hiding and so survived.

All this trickery was planned. They disguised themselves as Mon rather well. Then they fearlessly came to extricate themselves from their wrongdoing by catching this elder and novice from somewhere.

Phramuen Si, who was put in charge of this, is the father's bosom friend, hence both tell the same story. Perhaps they found a skull in a graveyard, inscribed it with yantra, and brought it to Your Majesty.

When the elder and novice were to be questioned to find the truth, they suddenly dropped down dead. These people think I'm just a forest Lao so they can tell you all this. May I request Your Majesty's assistance in this case."

King Phanwasa said, "Soifa is not being straightforward. From start to finish of her account, she's covering things up with blather, like using thorny bushes to plug every opening.[22]

She's the true daughter of a Lao lord. Any insinuation and over-claim she can get away with. So quick to put the blame on the plaintiff to captivate both the guards and the judges.

As a person of status, she's good at making use of people, and good at making up arguments that seem true. Since there isn't a single witness to the event, she's trying to wriggle her way out.

To make her admit the truth will be very difficult. We can't go on questioning only one side. It's no use catching a snake by its tail, because the head can still talk.

She must be confronted with the testimony of witnesses. Only then will the result be definite. Simala must be summoned to make a statement in order to see which side is telling the truth.

Heigh! Guard, summon Simala." A guard fetched Simala who came to bow and prostrate in audience.

---

22. See p. 594, note 18.

The king, upholder of the world, leaned forward and spoke loudly and clearly, asking Simala, "Soifa has made accusations against you,

that you were lovers with Phlai Chumphon. Soifa knew your secret so you became angry, and that was the cause of this whole uproar, to the point of wanting to kill Phra Wai.

I'm not bothered about the other issues but being lovers is a major matter. Are her words accurate? Are they true or not? Tell."

Simala prostrated and said, "It is not true, Your Majesty. When Chumphon went off to find his father, he was just a seven-year-old boy.

Who could teach a child such a thing? Making such an accusation is shameful. Is this the sort of thing the Lao do, teaching kids to be evil, as she said?

She's inventing wrongdoing to smear others and to cover up her own bad deeds. Were it true, keeping me would shame the royal foot, and I should be executed.

But if I stay quiet, who'll see through this? Even our husband is under suspicion. Let there be an end to this slur on me. My life is under the royal foot."

The almighty king, eminence and pillar of the world, spoke immediately after Simala.

"Look here, chaophraya and senior officials, I've listened to this affair and I'm surprised at its oddity. Words are being used to cover things up in a very involved way. What is the old law

in cases where there are no witnesses so that judges cannot get to the bottom of the matter? How can the case be examined so that we see the whole truth?"

The chaophraya in audience conferred together and then addressed the king. "My liege, Your Majesty, my life is under the royal foot.

When Khun Chang was so bold as to try to kill Phra Wai, the event took place in a forest without anybody else's knowledge.

After both sides gave statements, discussions were held on how some proof could be found. He and Phlai Ngam were submitted to ordeal by water. On this occasion, may it be according to the royal mercy."

After hearing all this information, the king asked Simala, "Heigh! What do you have to say?

The truth must be revealed through a test of honesty, otherwise there will be an objection that no proof can be found. I think the only way to get to the truth is ordeal by water or fire."

Simala bowed and prostrated with hope in her heart. "Oh, lord upholder of the palace, I am prepared to undergo ordeal by fire.

If I lose to Soifa, please execute me. If I'm bad, why should I live? Let the truth emerge through ordeal by fire."

The king laughed loud and merrily. "Did you hear that, Soifa? Simala accepts the ordeal by fire.

If you're telling the truth, you should contest. If you're lying, say so and I'll be lenient. Don't bow your face and say nothing. Tell me whether you'll contest or not."

Soifa's heart trembled and her hair stood on end. Fearing royal authority too much to admit guilt, she steeled herself, raised her face, and addressed the king.

"On the contention that I contacted the elder and novice to make a love charm to get my husband besotted, I'll undergo ordeal by fire to show my honesty."

As both of them accepted, the king, eminence and pillar of the world, gave his approval.

He ordered a pit[23] dug in front of the throne hall. The palace guards took the order as an urgent matter, conscripted officials, and hastily made all the arrangements.

When everything was settled, the king went inside and nobles left in order of rank. Guards ushered the parties to the case along to a swordstore, and placed them under confinement.

Guards were stationed on watch to prevent anyone coming and creating complications. Both Simala and Soifa were made to wear white upper and lower cloths. The provisions in confinement were arranged in the ancient way.

Galangal, lemongrass, rice, chili, ginger, chicken, duck, betelnut, coconut, rice pots, curry pots, and stoves were all provided.

Guards quickly dug a fire pit, while others fetched firewood, dirtying their faces and clothes. Some made themselves busy inspecting the work.

Some hitched up their lowercloths Khmer-style, and tottered away under loads of soil, mouths agape and eyes bulging with the effort, stumbling over and picking themselves up. When the pit was dug, everything was ready.

---

23. The Law on Trial by Ordeal stated: "In the case of ordeal by fire, have a pit dug six cubits long, one cubit wide and one cubit deep, and place charcoal one span deep" (KTS, 2:109; KW, 612).

42: SOIFA AND SIMALA UNDERGO ORDEAL BY FIRE

Now to tell of the king, turner of the wheel,[1] ruler over the wealth of heavenly Ayutthaya, resident of a crystal palace where inner ladies bowed with clasped hands.

He gave thought to Phra Wai's wives. On the previous day, he had commanded them to undergo ordeal by fire. "I must watch over this matter closely." He walked out to the window.[2]

All the chaophraya and officials of various ranks including Phra Kanburi, Chumphon, and Phra Wai were gathered for audience, prostrate at the front of the palace courtyard.

Thong Prasi shook with anger over the case. "Tcha! This accursed Lao has done such evil!" She scurried down the stairs and rushed along

the road in a daze. Great crowds of people talked about the matter noisily. "Let's go and watch the ordeal by fire."

Chinese, Khaek, and Farang who heard about it all went along. The palace parade ground overflowed with people. Thong Prasi entered and made obeisance.

The king acknowledged her presence, thinking, "Now she has sunken cheeks, broken teeth, and graying hair. As a young woman, she had square shoulders and a round rear. The poor state she's now in is pitiful.

Still, he was an old royal retainer. Thinking about it is dispiriting. I feel sad that Khun Krai had to die by royal punishment back then."

Then the king said suddenly, "Phaen, Chumphon, and Phra Wai, don't let people have doubt in their hearts. Take an oath before my eyes that you'll not take sides."

---

1. จักรพรรดิ, *jakraphat*, a term meaning the turner of the wheel, used prominently in the Three Worlds cosmology as the title of the supreme, ideal Buddhist sovereign (RR, 135–72). The wheel is the wheel of the law but also an abstract symbol of perfection reflecting the supreme merit of those few who "are born to be great rulers and kings who have splendor and majesty, who have a great and infinite number of attendants, and whose conquests extends over the entire universe" (RR, 135–36). The title was claimed by Buddhist rulers in Southeast Asia who aspired to rule over other rulers, and hence the term has come to be equivalent to "emperor."

2. See p. 509, note 49.

Khun Phaen, Phra Wai, and Phlai Chumphon all swore an oath for the king. "If I take any side, may I fall and be burned in the Lokanta hell.

I will set my mind to be straight and just to both Soifa and Simala, not leaning either way or having evil intent." At the end, they made obeisance.

A Brahman examined both ladies' feet to make sure there was no wound or dirt.[3] Both were seated beside the fire pit. An old teacher chanted a mantra to thwart any lore.

Both ladies were given popped rice and flowers.[4] Brahmans on each side offered *baisi* and food to the deities, and chanted prayers to the gods.[5]

"Om! Lord Buddha,[6] Brahma the great protector, mighty Krishna, Lord of Water, Lord of Fire of noble power,

Lord Ganesh, Lord Kantakuman,[7] Lord Indra,[8] Lord of the Winds, Lords of the Earth who oversee the four directions, please come to serve as witness.

Also the guardian spirits of the royal umbrella who nurture the religion, the powerful guardian spirits of the city and the city pillar of mighty Ayutthaya,

come to receive offerings of food. Do not side with either plaintiff or defendant. Let whoever has spoken untruthfully be burned by the fire and thus exposed by sacred power to the eyes of the people."

The two then had to make a prayer. Simala raised a salver of flowers, and prayed, "If Chumphon and I were lovers, may the fire burn me until blistered to destruction.

If I was faithful to my husband, may the fire not touch me, may the gods protect me as if I were walking on cooling water.

Let the gods uphold honesty. If I was evil, let me die by the fire." She had no fear in her heart, and her face was as radiant as a lotus in bloom.

---

3. "Have the feet washed, and have the wardens and judges inspect the soles and toes of the plaintiff and defendant for any injuries, new or old . . . and draw a picture of the toes and soles." The arrangements for detaining the parties and ensuring they were dressed and fed in the same way applied to both types of ordeal, fire and water (Law on Ordeal, clause 3, KTS, 2:109–110).

4. ข้าวตอกดอกไม้, *khao tok dok mai*. Nowadays this phrase means any offering, not necessarily including popped rice.

5. The law specified long invocations to be spoken before the ordeal. That for the water ordeal occupies almost four pages of the Three Seals Law, and that for the fire ordeal almost three. These invocations name every possible Indic god, shrine spirit, spirit of the place, malevolent spirit, and natural spirit to ensure a fair result. The short version here gives only a flavor (KTS, 2:116–22).

6. พระสยมภูวญาณ, *phra sayomphuwayan*, "the one who radiates light from himself," a common epithet of the Buddha.

7. พระขันทกุมาร, *phra khantakuman*, Kartikeya, Skanda, a six-headed son of Siva.

8. มัฆวาน, *makkhawan*, from Sanskrit Maghava, Maghavantu.

Soifa's face was dark. She raised her salver and mumbled her prayer so quickly it made no sense. "Oh, spirits and possessed people,[9] come to help me."

The Brahmans laughed, "Oh, that's droll! What a wish, my lady!" Thong Prasi shouted, "You blackface! Such a nonsensical prayer shows you up."

Soifa made another prayer. "If I concocted lore with the Lao elder by washing my hair and burying figures to make Phra Wai besotted with me,

and also if Phlai Chumphon and Simala are not lovers as I claim, let the fire burn and blister both my feet." She trembled white-eyed, and her heart felt icy.

pit for ordeal by fire

Khun Phaen, Phra Wai, Thong Prasi, and Phlai Chumphon sat at the edge of the great pit. The four pillars, city officials, inner and outer guards all crowded around.

Spectators were crammed together, jostling one another, arguing irritably, getting into noisy fights, falling on top of one another, pushing and shoving with trembling bodies.

Those with no view on the outside tried to barge in. Dust billowed up, cloaking the onlookers' heads. Children cried and hung onto their mothers. Some rode on shoulders, holding onto the hair and straining to see.

A Jek selling sweets stumbled and fell. A gang of riffraff yanked his pigtail. "*Aiya!* Don't tug that." He crouched down and huddled over to protect himself.

---

9. ปรางควาน, *prang khwan*, an animal or person possessed by a spirit of someone who died a bad death (KW, 692).

A Mon girl selling rice crackers trod on his leg. "*Aiya!*" the Jek cried, and jumped up. The Mon girl scolded, "Fuck your mother,[10] you villain! I want to see the fire ordeal but you're getting in my way."

Palace guards were positioned round the edge of the grounds to put a stop to any quarrels. Masses of people sat down to wait. Suddenly silence fell.

King Phanwasa sent down an order to summon Soifa and Simala to undergo ordeal by fire to reveal the truth.

Consorts and inner ladies poked their faces out of windows or peered through the strips of blinds to watch Soifa and Simala undergo the ordeal.

peering through blinds

On the king's order, Soifa and Simala approached either end of the pit, and made obeisance.

The charcoal was fanned bright red. Soifa was very frightened. Simala looked pretty and smiled brightly. After making obeisance, she walked into the fire pit,

pacing like a royal golden swan. Though she stepped on the fire, she felt no heat. Without fear, she walked back and forth three times.

The gods protected her because of her honesty. A wind blew, touching her like celestial water. Everybody cheered her loudly.

Soifa stood awkwardly at the head of the pit. The flames blazed up in front of her, making her frightened that the fire would burn and blister her. She steeled herself and clumsily stepped forward.

After two or three steps on the fire, her body shook and her feet were scorched. She jumped out of the pit. "Oh, it's so hot it'll kill me!"

I-Mai went and dragged her away. "Your feet are as red as little mice, I fear." The crowd was in uproar. Phra Wai came over, gnashing his teeth and quivering with anger.

He kicked Soifa in the side. Nobles shouted out to stop him, "Don't! Don't!" Phra Wai said, "Why keep her? Take her and cut off her head at the execution ground."

---

10. ต๊อกย่าย, *tok yai,* in Mon.

Khun Phaen felt mortified for Simala. "Soifa shouldn't have put you through this torment. She was intent on doing you harm. I knew already from some time ago,

but because nobody else understood, there was doubt. You've been hurt terribly. Now that all is revealed before the king and everybody else, this will put an end to the gossip."

Thong Prasi shook with fury at Soifa. She rolled her eyes, gnashed her gums, grabbed a *samae* stick, and rushed forward shouting, "I'll bash your head to my satisfaction!

Tcha! You maker of love potions and elephant medicine! Why are you lying there legs akimbo, whimpering? Are you hot? Use some *phimsen* to treat the burn.[11] You deserve this, you clever concocter of love charms.

You contacted that evil elder and novice to fix your husband, yet that wasn't enough. You also accused Chumphon of having Simala. Why are you pointing at your leg and whimpering?"

Chumphon ran up and grabbed the end of Thong Prasi's cloth. "Don't do this, Grandmother, I beg you." Thong Prasi angrily pushed his hand away. "I'm going to bash her head." She hitched up her lowercloth, Khmer-style.

"What will be will be. I'm not listening." Guards surrounded her back and front, and grasped her arms like children jostling in a tug-of-war.[12] Onlookers laughed uproariously. Thong Prasi sank down, still ranting with oily eyes.

Chumphon prostrated at Simala's feet with one hand wiping away tears. In a rage, he went over to Soifa and shouted, "You're full of holes! Your tricks shamed others.

Simala loves me like her own child. You spitefully told lies so easily, you forest Lao. You have no shame, lying on your back whimpering for the crowds to see."

He put an arm-lock on I-Mai's neck, and elbowed her. "I know how you were her accomplice and protector." He grabbed Soifa's hand and dragged her away. "I'll slash you at the execution ground."

Phramuen Si pulled Chumphon away by the hand. "Listen to me. Don't be harsh." The crowds stood around staring, all abusing Soifa.

King Phanwasa raged at Soifa like a blazing fire. "Now I see as if I can look into your heart, you evil trickster.

---

11. *Phimsen* (see p. 88, note 10) would make the burns hurt more.

12. ชักส้าว, *sak sao*, a tug-of-war game played by two players gripping each other's arms (SWC, 5:2003).

You used a love philter on your husband to make him fall so madly in love with you that his powers and knowledge were weakened. Even with him besotted and befuddled, you still weren't satisfied.

You provoked a quarrel between father and son that blew up into an affair big enough for them to kill each other, and for the father to challenge me.

Then you turned on Chumphon and Simala with false accusations to have them both executed. You think of everyone as an enemy. Truly you seem to be in revolt.

Ha! Heigh! Phraya Yommarat, take her away and slash her dead. Open her chest with an axe for public shame. Make an example of her to caution others."

Phraya Yommarat summoned the executioners immediately. They grasped Soifa's wrists, gnashing their teeth. She implored, "Please have mercy!

If I'm to die, let me take leave of my husband and grandmother. I must ask forgiveness of Simala so I don't carry the karma to my death."

Gripping her arms on both sides, the executioners took her to prostrate to her husband, to her grandmother, and to everybody there. Then weeping she went up to Simala,

raised Simala's foot onto her head, and flailed around without raising her face. "My lady and mistress, I'm bad. Please accept my apology and don't hold anything against me.

Let the karma end here. Make merit so I may be born in a new life. Though I carry my sin and bad karma, your forgiveness will ease the burden.

Karma gave me such a bad heart that I stupidly contacted the novice and elder, and let myself be ruled by jealousy and desire for revenge. I couldn't see my own wrongdoing.

That wasn't enough. I accused you of being lovers with Chumphon in the past. I laid false accusations to turn the king against you. I told insolent lies because I got carried away.

I am of low birth and a danger to the city. Everybody sees that now. I'm dishonored and shamed. I know that matters have come to this because I'm evil.

The guardian deities saw that I caused trouble and so sent me to my death. The king should execute me. He may have mercy only for the child in my womb.

Though just seven months and blameless, the child will die inside me without ever seeing either sun or moon, without us knowing whether boy or girl.

Oh mistress, please don't harbor revenge against me. Help request a pardon. Keep me as your servant until death. Think that you are helping the little baby in my womb."

On hearing this, Thong Prasi's tears fell. "Who made you like this, you beggar? Only when heaven's anger hits you in the back,[13] do you have remorse. I can't hold back my tears.

However much I taught you, it didn't get into your head. Instead you bullied me with your big mouth. I've never met anyone as arrogant, but now you hug her feet and ask for mercy.

Have a care for me, dear Simala. She was bad to you and your husband but if you spurn her, the baby will die. For better or worse, have mercy on the little child in her womb."

At this, Simala's heart softened and her tears streamed down. Now that Soifa admitted her guilt, Simala felt pity. "I'll ask the king to give her a reprieve, and then let merit decide.

If it's not yet her fate to die, sending merit should help her. I don't aim for anything in return. I'll use my merit to help save a life.

Don't imagine I'm vengeful. Don't fear but devote yourself to prayer." Simala promptly made her plea. "Oh gods! I have made some merit.

I wish to free myself from the cycle of rebirth[14] and take the path towards nirvana in the future by helping a living creature to evade death." With this prayer, she walked

over in front of the throne, prostrated, raised her clasped hands, and said, "My life is under the royal foot. Whatever pleases or displeases.[15]

At present Soifa, who is under penalty of execution by Your Majesty's order, is around seven months pregnant and will take Phra Wai's child to its death.

My heart feels pity for a child who must follow its mother to death. Please grant pardon to Soifa so that the child may survive."

The king was shocked. He had not known a child would die. Righteousness made his anger abate.

Soifa's fate was not to die. Simala's good deed came to her rescue, and the merit of the child in her womb protected her and enabled her to escape the threat.

The king said, "Thank you, Simala. You're not vengeful but honest and fair in the extreme. Though this villainous woman has an evil heart,

you ask for her pardon and so I'll grant her life. Yet to keep her here would be a public danger. Before long she'll create trouble. I'm loath to see you undergo ordeal by fire again."

---

13. ฟ้าเคืองสันหลัง, *fa khoeng san lang*, meaning, when something catches up with you (KW, 693).
14. สงสาร, *songsan*, Pali *samsara*, the cycle of birth, life, and death.
15. See p. 497, note 12.

He gave orders to Phraya Yommarat, "Simala has pleaded for Soifa's life, but Soifa is a menace and cannot be kept. Expel her from the city."

Phraya Yommarat made obeisance, backed out, and gave orders. "The king has pardoned Soifa's life. Expel her from the city within three days."

King Phanwasa wished to console Simala. He commanded the treasury to arrange money and various articles,

two chang of silver, two sets of cloth, a gemstone ring for the little finger, a washbowl, and an enamel betel box with a votive-deity pattern as royal gifts to Simala.

He also gave golden armlets and bracelets as gifts for the baby in the womb. "Simala, you have acquitted yourself well on this occasion and won favor. I reward your good deeds.

Phaen and Chumphon came back because you went to talk with Phaen, otherwise the old man would have done wrong in a fit of anger, and then fled away."

The king issued commands. "Phaen and Chumphon, don't waver around. Drop the quarrel with Wai. Let bygones be bygones, I beg you."[16]

Phra Kanburi, Phra Wai, and Phlai Chumphon all took the king's order on their heads. The king left, and others trooped out of the palace.

I-Moei said to Soifa, "Never forget the goodness of my mistress." Simala angrily reprimanded her, "Shush, you evil Mon! Keep quiet!"

The local people all showered Simala with praise. "Mistress Simala is so good." "She wasn't vengeful but asked the king for Soifa's life." "The likes of her are hard to find."

Someone said, "If it were me, I'd have had Soifa's head cut off and stuck up over there." With face drawn and feet hurting, Soifa walked gingerly home.

Hanging onto I-Mai's back, she went into her room. The burns were hot, swollen, messy, and painful. "I'll soon leave this house. All the possessions must be left here."

At dawn, Soifa went in to see her husband. In tears, she prostrated to ask forgiveness. "I did evil to myself.

Please absolve me of blame. I'm leaving and going far away to drift on the ocean. I'll miss the warmth of depending on your merit. My lord protected me since I came down here.

My parents also depended on you when in trouble. You helped a great deal by speaking to the king, otherwise the whole city of Chiang Mai would have been reduced to dust.

---

16. This call for reconciliation does not appear in the Wat Ko edition.

The king favored me to be your partner. Whether I did right or wrong, you kindly never complained, but karma from the past intervened and made me think wrongly.

Since leaving my city, I've been with you and depended on you. Now I return home and you'll be far from my sight. Morning and night, I'll think of you in desolation. Traveling alone through the forest will be hard.

I came down with many people. I return alone. Along the way through the forest, there'll be elephants, terrible tigers, fierce rhinos, buffaloes, and cattle.

I must pick my way through streams, gorges, and ravines, with thorny under-growth all around. When I came down, my father gave me an elephant to ride. On return, I must travel by foot.

There'll be nobody to carry goods. I must stagger along with my big belly, battered by sun and wind. I'm distressed that the child in my womb

must be dragged through this hardship. Both rice and water will be unknown. Whether the child lives or dies, whether it's boy or girl, the father will not know.

In the evenings, I must sit hiding in the bushes with nobody to fetch fire-wood. I must lie on the earth with a log as a pillow, praying out of fear of the forest animals.

I'll hear only the bleating of deer, the cries of birds, and the whooping of gibbons echoing around the great forest. Not only will I think of the dangers around me but I'll be sad from missing my husband."

She lifted his foot onto her head. The pain of parting overwhelmed her and she wept as if her heart would shatter to dust until her eyes were clouded and bloodshot.

"Oh pity, pity! Because of karma I must suffer. How could I leave you? Were it possible, I'd stay with my husband even though I'd face hardship and penury.

Look at me while I'm still here, my lord and master. You'll not see me again. I'll disappear from your sight until death."

Phra Wai sighed heavily out of pity and sadness for his wife. His tears flowed and he hastily wiped them away in shame.

Steeling himself, he consoled Soifa. "Please shed this sadness. Every man and woman faces both happiness and hardship. An inauspicious time must result in troubles.

Look after the baby in your womb. If in the future you're still alive, we should meet again. Don't flay yourself before the fever comes.[17] If you take care of yourself, we should meet again."

---

17. A proverb meaning, don't look on the bad side, don't be pessimistic ahead of time.

Hearing Phra Wai, Soifa's grief subsided. "All your words of instruction, I'll remember steadfastly until my dying day.

But my heart will miss you because of love. The further we are apart, the greater my dread, the deeper my desolation." With tears flowing, she fanned out her hair and bent down to wipe his feet.

"Oh lord and master! After today's parting, I'll not see your face. Stay well. Be in good health. May you live a thousand years."

She took her leave and went weeping to prostrate and wai Thong Prasi. "Mistress grandmother has been kind to me. For better or worse, you didn't abandon me to die.

You made Simala plead for me so that I was not destroyed. I wish to stay here to repay your kindness until death but that's against the king's order of expulsion.

Stay well, mistress of meritorious heart. I'll not return again to the southern city. Leaving you now is like dying. Far apart, we won't see each other again, dead or alive."

Thong Prasi trembled and wept as she listened to Soifa. "I pity you. You acted rashly without thinking.

The more I reprimanded you, the more you played with love charms, and did 108 senseless things.[18] Only when you faced death did you think. It was beyond my powers to help you.

I stayed with my husband into old age[19] without ever giving a thought to love charms. If he didn't love me, I didn't care. If I were you, I wouldn't have bothered with them."

Soifa wai-ed, bowed, and prostrated. "You hoped I'd be something of substance, Grandmother, but I was so bad I almost died. I can't blame my karma on others."

She raised Thong Prasi's foot onto her head, and shook with weeping. "I beg your forgiveness." She prostrated to take leave,

and went to pay respect to Khun Phaen. "Please absolve me from blame. I did such wrong I almost died. Though I angered you, don't burden me with the karma.

---

18. Literally: "108, mouth neck not connected." The number 108 appears often in astrology and lore, sometimes as a magic number, and in other cases to convey the meaning of "many."

19. In chapter 2, Thong Prasi's husband was executed when their son was a small child and she must have been in her early twenties, at the most.

I'm a stupid, simple, fumbling fool. In anger, I listened to the elder, and let myself be ruled by jealousy and revenge. I created karma that crushed me.

Phlai Chumphon too, stay well. Today I take leave. Be happy and bright. Achieve your wishes. I'm bad, and must take my leave according to karma."

After hearing this, Khun Phaen and Phlai Chumphon replied. "I helped you but you wouldn't listen. You created such karma and shame for yourself

that the whole city came to know about it. Everybody gossiped and criticized. It wasn't right to create a scandal for the whole realm. You heedlessly did vile things.

But why should we bear a grudge? Don't worry about past matters—like a living being who has erred and fallen into hell. We forgive you. Don't worry."

Soifa listened to both of them. "That is my due, my lords." She prostrated trembling before Khun Phaen, then took leave of Chumphon.

Entering Simala's room, Soifa embraced her feet in tears. "Karma forces me to go far away. I wai you. Stay well.

You had the goodness to beg the king on my behalf. Otherwise I'd have died. I'll keep your goodness on this occasion in my mind until death.

Today I'll leave, and it's unlikely I'll return. I won't miss my possessions. Please offer them to the monks and send the merit to me.

If I reach Chiang Mai alive, my family will support me. I'll think only of your goodness. I've depended on your merit and haven't been able to repay you.

If in the future I'm still alive, I should come back down here for sure, and I'll bow my face in repayment. Don't harbor revenge. I take my leave."

Simala replied, "If I were filled with thoughts of revenge, why would I have pleaded with the king?

There's no need to repay me. I don't wish it. I feel sorry for the baby in your womb. I've no anger and want only the merit.

I'll offer the possessions on your behalf. I'll dye the white cloth yellow, and present the cups, bowls, and other things for the monks' use."

Soifa raised her hands in blessing, and prostrated. "Your goodness is overflowing. You don't burden my karma with what I've done.

If I can share my merit, I'll give half to you. Forgive me. I take my leave. Don't let my bad deeds from the past become my karma.

All the trouble and anger I created, right down to the business with the elder, let it be dismissed from my karma from today." She offered a salver of popped rice and flowers.

Simala accepted the plea, and herself asked for pardon, passing the salver immediately back to Soifa who accepted the apology and said, "Please believe me. Don't have any doubts."

Having begged forgiveness of Simala, Soifa walked grieving back to her apartment and lay down on the bed.

"I've been in this apartment of mine for several years, and furnished it with many good things including powder sets and beautiful screens for the bed.

I think of my husband and think of myself facing hardship. Having to leave here, I'll be frightened and lonely. I'll remember living happily with Phra Wai." The more she thought, the more she writhed as if to die.

Steeling herself, she swallowed her sorrow. "I can't stay here longer or I'll be in the wrong. Because I was condemned to death, I must make up my mind to leave."

She packed money and valuables in a big back-basket, choosing the lower and upper cloths that she liked the most.

When done, she went out and ordered the servants, "Bring a boat down to wait at the landing." Khanan Ai took the order, and brought a three-fathom boat with an awning down to the mooring.

I-Mai carried chili, salt, rice, stove, kitchen utensils, and supplies to load in the boat. Soifa boarded.

Phra Wai opened his window on the side of the landing. He saw Soifa looking sad, and Khanan Ai and I-Mai accompanying her. The prow of the boat swung out and they paddled away.

He still thought of the past with love. "I feel sorry for you with your belly. You'll face much hardship having to walk a long distance through the forest."

He heard the sound of her pitiful weeping echoing clearly across the water. "Oh, our karma made in prior lives has forced this separation.

Were it not for fear of the king's authority, you wouldn't leave here easily, my jewel. Even though you did wrong, I'll still miss you. Oh, the ending of this love should not be!"

He craned to let his eyes follow her until the boat was hidden by a promontory. His tears splashed down. "From now on, there won't be a day that I don't miss you."

He closed the window, walked into the room, and lay down, still thinking of her sorrowfully. He felt choked as if someone had trussed him up. She stayed in his mind until he drifted into sleep.

Now to tell of Soifa, Khanan Ai, and I-Mai. They paddled quickly along the river past Ban Pom to Hua Saphan.[20]

In two days and two nights, they reached Ang Thong, then continued past many villages to reach Bang Kaeo,[21] and stopped in the evening at Bang Maeo.[22]

At nightfall, boatmen coming from north and south moored alongside one another in rows. They steamed rice and boiled curry by the flicker of lights. After cooking and eating, they chatted together

about a crocodile around twenty fathoms long that liked to show off its might by floating in the middle of the river. When it rose to the surface, it stirred up waves. Another crocodile was about nine fathoms long.

If any boat went alone at dusk and ran into them, the crocodiles would attack before their eyes, biting and breaking rudders and paddles. But the crocodiles had not been seen to eat people.

Soifa's boat was moored at the riverbank. The story made her hair stand on end. She cried out loud, "Oh, poor me! How to escape being bitten to death by a crocodile?

Our boat is very small. A big wave would sink it. Oh, this time I'm going to die." She flailed around, out of her senses.

Elder Khwat and the novice, who had fled by boldly making themselves invisible and going through the water as crocodiles, were staying at the entrance to Ban Nang Maeo.

At nightfall, they made roaring sounds, came to the surface, and played around in sprightly fashion, with eyes flaring like fire flashing. Boats could not go out,

but huddled together at the moorings around a bend. Seeing a cluster of craft, the crocodiles approached to look, wanting to hear news of Soifa. Hearing some weeping, they went up close

and recognized her voice. Diving down, they came up on the bank and transformed themselves back from crocodiles. Elder Khwat walked along with Novice Jiw following behind.

---

20. Ban Pom, fort village, a little northwest up the Chaophraya River; now Hua Taphan (see map 3).

21. Ang Thong provincial capital is now at the site of Bang Kaeo. There may have been another Ang Thong village slightly south of this site in the past (KW, 624; see map 3).

22. Just 2–3 kms north of Ang Thong. Below it is called Ban Nang Maeo.

He called out, "Hey, Mai! Bring the boat to fetch us. I'm the elder with the novice. We're both here. We escaped and still survive."

Mai looked up to the bank and recognized them in the moonlight. She got up, pulled up the stake, paddled over, and steered the stern in to receive them.

The elder and novice stepped down under the awning and saw Soifa sitting weeping. The elder told the story from start to end. "I survived because of my knowledge.

We became invisible to escape from prison, and went into the water as crocodiles to wait for you. We listened for news whether Soifa would live or die.

We recognized the sound of your weeping and came up to find you. Why did you come here? What punishment did the king give you? Where are the three of you going?"

In reply to Elder Khwat's question, Soifa related the story honestly. "At first, the king had me questioned to find out the truth—

whether I along with the novice and elder had made my husband besotted. I gave a statement that denied the matter evasively. I said the truth was that Chumphon and Simala

were lovers, I knew for sure, and that's why they provoked the parents to make accusations. There were no witnesses on either side so King Phanwasa ordered an ordeal by fire.

Because I'd done wrong, I lost and the king ordered my execution. But I didn't die on account of the child in my womb. The king had me expelled from the city.

I decided to go up to Chiang Mai. I'm pleased to have met you. It's a great blessing. You can be my companions and help save my life. In sickness or injury, we can see one another's faces."

She ordered Khanan Ai to steer the boat away from there.[23] The novice and elder went together with them in the boat, helping to paddle and punt upstream.

---

23. At this point in the Wat Ko edition (WK, 37:1456) and TNA mss 67: In mid stream the elder shouted out to echo around, / "I by the name of Elder Khwat can turn myself into a great crocodile. Currently we are going up to the city of Chiang Mai. / Should anyone found a settlement here, let it be called the Village of the Crying Crocodile, and be recorded thus in texts." With that, they hurried along.

The village of Jorakhe Rong is about 8 kms above Ang Thong. Probably this passage was omitted by Prince Damrong's editorial team because of the alternative explanation of this name in the following chapter (CS, 93–94).

Elder Khwat became apprehensive when he saw guard boats making inspections up and down the river, and people at customs posts watching by the light of fire-rafts[24] along the way. "If I get caught again, it won't be good."

He snapped off a branch of secretspirit,[25] chanted a mantra of the Rishi Transforming Matter,[26] and stuck the branch on the prow to disguise themselves from men at the guardposts.

They passed the river mouth at Bang Phutsa,[27] and continued on past many villages. Happily, nobody accosted them. They stopped at nightfall and set off again immediately at dawn.

In one month they reached Rahaeng, beached the boat at a landing, and continued by land through the forest. Soifa was in a pitiful state.

She had never walked through a deep forest. She had to step carefully because of her belly and was greatly troubled by the sun and wind. She felt lonely and afraid.

Sounds of deer and wild animals echoed around. Herds of elephants crashed through the bushes. Gibbons, monkeys, and langurs bounded around, leaping down onto the ground and gesticulating.

Serow leapt along the hills, fell, and licked away their wounds.[28] Wild dogs trailed tigers, intent on eating their leftover prey.

When the sun cooled, they arrived at a narrow pass.[29] Sunset lit the sky red like cinnabar. They piled up leaves to lie on. The elder made a prayer before they slept.

The moon shone brightly in the center of the sky, surrounded by masses of stars. Dew fell in a soft spray,

touching the flowers in the forest. Petals bloomed in dazzling bunches. Breezes wafted fragrances to ease their fatigue. Yet her heart still dwelled despondently on what she had left behind.

She missed Phra Wai greatly. "Oh pity, pity! We loved each other intimately.

---

24. Rafts with torches were anchored midstream to allow guards to inspect the night traffic (SB, 628–29).

25. หิงหายผี, *hinghai phi, Crotalaria laburniflora,* a bush with yellow or purple flowers, often seen along riverbanks, used in lore because the name sounds like "the spirit that disappears" (KW, 625).

26. ฤษีปลอมแปลงสาร, *ruesi plom plaeng san,* a mantra to obscure other people's senses (KW, 693).

27. Now Singburi. The river mouth is the entrance to the Lopburi River.

28. See p. 411, note 34.

29. This could be a place name, Chong Khaep, of which there are several but none obviously on their route. The nearest is in Amphoe Phop Phra, Tak, which would mean they went west from Tak and up through the mountains, which is unlikely. More likely this means a defile or pass crossing the ridge south of Lampang.

He took care of me and made me happy. It's not right we have to be parted.

Feeling slighted made me act very badly. I was obsessed with revenge and intent on causing trouble. Because of my wrongdoing, I almost lost my life."

In her melancholy, tears welled up and flooded her eyes.

She wept through to dawn without sleeping. The elder got up to wash his face, took an almsbowl, and went off with Novice Jiw to beg. They got some sticky rice and pumpkin curry from forest villages.

After traveling a long time, their supplies of rice were finished, so they had to beg from villagers. They walked ahead with determination, and reached the city after two and a half months.[30]

⤙

Now to tell of Simala, who was heavily pregnant and about to give birth. All the relatives gathered around. Thong Prasi prayed to the spirits. Hearing Simala moan, she trembled and called out loudly for this and that servant to come.

"She's about to deliver. Quick, quick! Where have you put the firewood and the banana leaves we bought? Servants, light the fire and put on a pot to boil water.

Fetch the turmeric, tamarind, and raw oil, and get pounding. Where has Wai got to? He mustn't be late enchanting water for loosening."[31]

Phra Wai enchanted water for his wife to drink, and poured the rest on her head. By the power of these formulas, the child in the womb was delivered.

It was a delightful son with pleasing features, plump and very lovable. The greatgrandmother, Thong Prasi, quickly took him to bathe and rubbed him with turmeric.

She called servants to bring good cloth to make a canopy. Settling him in a basket with a little mattress under him, she lullabied him to sleep.

She made arrangements for Simala to lie by the fire, daubed her with ground turmeric, made her drink hot medicine, gave milk to the infant, and admired him.

Three months later, the son's head was shaved, and all the relatives came to perform a ceremony for his soul. Khun Phaen brought *sema* wristlets and bangles to give his grandson.

---

30. At this point in the Wat Ko edition, Soifa is welcomed by her parents and relatives. She explains truthfully why she was expelled from Ayutthaya and is reprimanded by her father the king for her folly. A soul ceremony is held, led by a female spirit-medium who gets drunk and dances herself into a trance. Her mother loads Mai, Khwat, and Jiw with gifts (WK, 37:1458–64).

31. See p. 572, note 84.

Phra Wai said to Phra Kanburi, "What's a good name to give him in line with family practice, Father?" Thong Prasi said, "The name of a jewel is smart."

Khun Phaen gave him the name Phlai Phet,[32] using a trace of his grandfather's name. All the relatives approved. They lived in happiness and comfort.

჻

Now to tell of Soifa. When heavily pregnant, she was in pain and distress. With all her relatives gathered around, she easily delivered a lovely son.

He looked the image of Phra Wai. His grandfather, the king, loved him greatly and supplied a wet nurse and nursemaid to look after the baby every night.

He arranged to perform a soul ceremony with all kinds of food offerings, a *baisi*, musicians playing, and Brahmans, monks, and ascetics giving blessings.

The king commanded an old master of astrology to cast the child's horoscope and find an auspicious time. "I'll give him a name according to his Thai lineage. Tell me which day is auspicious."

On that good and auspicious day, the royal clan gathered together. The King of Chiang Mai named his grandson Phlai Yong Phong Noppharat.[33]

He furnished him with servants, diamonds, gems, and the ornaments of a king, including silver, gold, and several playthings. They lived in happiness and well-being every day.

---

32. พลายเพชร, bull elephant diamond.

33. พลายยงพงศ์นพรัฐ, great bull elephant of the lineage of the new city. *Noppharat* derives from นพบุรี, *nopburi*, Pali *navapura*, old versions of Chiang Mai, which means "new city."

43: CROCODILE KHWAT

Now to tell of Elder Khwat, adept at knowledge and famed for his powers throughout the realm of Chiang Mai. Since he escorted Soifa back to the capital, he had been feted like a brave lion,

because the Lao king praised and rewarded his goodness. "He has more merit than all the monks together!" He was appointed patriarch of the Lao chapter,[1] and stayed at Wat Phrathat Ratcharam.[2]

He was given the regalia of a patriarch including a bowl-sling, palm-leaf fan, and sidebag beautifully embroidered with gold wire. He traveled in a boat with curtains or in a palanquin sheltered by a ceremonial umbrella.

The King of Chiang Mai gave him Lao as wat slaves,[3] with great numbers in service on rotating months. His disciples numbered around a hundred, with Novice Jiw as his eyes and ears.

He lived in a kuti of four units like a palace, with each building crowded and busy. Tiers of half-moon tables were arrayed with articles of worship all made from Batavia crystal with gilt rims.

bed with lion legs

Large mirrors were fixed to the pillars in all directions. The windows were framed with mirrorwork. The room was richly furnished including a Chinese bed with the legs of a golden lion.

---

1. สังฆราชามลาว๎วงศ์, *sankaracha malawong. Sangkharat* is the title of the head of a monastic community. *Mala(o)*, is a variant form of Lao.

2. There is no such wat but the meaning—the great or royal wat with a relic—would make it equivalent to Wat Chedi Luang, one of the major wat of Chiang Mai.

3. เลขวัด, *lek wat*, people donated to a wat to take care of the upkeep, carry out rituals, cultivate wat lands, and other activities. The practice traces back to Angkor and to similar donations in India. It is found in Sukhothai-era inscriptions, and in fragmentary records from the Ayutthaya period. At the opening of Wat Pho in 1801, King Rama I donated 124 slaves at a cost of 95 chang and 11 tamlueng. A system of rotation, as cited here, was known at the Chomthong temple in Lanna in the late nineteenth century. (Flood and Flood, *Dynastic Chronicles,* 235; Sarassawadee, *History of Lan Na,* 227)

One day after the patriarch had eaten the forenoon meal, he went out to a verandah where his disciples prostrated all around. He reclined on a bed with a golden backrest

and a triangular cushion for support. He picked up a Batavia mirror to look at his reflection. His face was healthy, fair, and fine, the skin perfectly radiant.

He noticed the mark of the wound on his forehead where Chumphon had cut him with a saber. His anger rose immediately. "You're able, are you? Let's contest and see. I'll go down to Ayutthaya to catch and kill you." He leapt up from the bed, tossed away the pillows, and stumbled into the kuti.

He put on his robes in open style, and shouted to his disciples. Novice Phrom held an umbrella and fan, while Novice Si put a sidebag over his shoulder and followed the teacher.

Wat slaves came and waited by a palanquin with a colored roof. Elder Khwat walked grumpily over and clambered in. They carried him through villages to the palace,

elephant-ear gate

and stopped before an elephant-ear gate.[4] He descended from the litter, walked quickly into the palace, and gave orders to be taken for audience with Princess Soifa.

Soifa was living happily in a sandalwood pavilion, attentively raising her beloved son Phlai Yong.

When a servant girl reported that the teacher had come to the main palace, she led her son by the hand straight over there, and invited the patriarch to be seated.

She offered him betelnut and lime, and paid respect. "Your Lordship has taken the trouble to come here. I am blessed! What business brings you? Or can I be of some service?"

Elder Khwat sighed, gave a blessing, and said, "I have a big problem. These days, I'm fine on the outside, but inside I feel battered and bruised, all night and day.

---

4. Term for a gate in which the tops of the door panels protrude above the gateposts, often as twin half-moons. Many palace or city gates were in this style (CK, 305–6).

When I bite on anything, it's difficult to swallow. I start awake at night with my chest burning. If it goes on like this with no relief, I think I'll be at death's door.

I came with the intention of taking leave to rid myself of this irritation. Don't stop me and put my life in danger. Your Highness, have compassion for this teacher."

Soifa felt sorry for Elder Khwat. "I have devoted myself to you for a long time. Please explain the situation.

There was only one time when I stopped you—when you wanted to go down to the southern city to take revenge on Khun Phaen and Phra Wai. I stopped you because of concern for Phlai Yong.

I feared the child would become fatherless so I appealed to you against your wishes. If your intention is not for Phra Wai to die, then go ahead with your idea of going down there."

The patriarch was pleased to hear this. He shifted closer and whispered, "Morning and night, I've been thinking
ceaselessly about taking revenge on Chumphon. He treated me with great contempt in a shameful way. Since birth, I've never let anyone look down on me. Allowing him to get away with this is too much.

If I don't rid myself of this grievance by taking revenge, I must die of the pain. I intend to transform my body into a crocodile and go down to Ayutthaya.

I'll throw the whole city into confusion so that King Phanwasa is concerned. What able person will then come to face me? Probably the only volunteer will be Phlai Chumphon.

I'll lure him down into the water and deal with him properly by simply biting him to death. Once that is achieved, the worry will disappear and I can live happily in this northern city.

As for Phlai Yong's father, I've no thought of killing him. I came with the intention of taking leave. Please give your blessing for success in my aim."

Soifa was happy and laughed heartily because of her hatred for Chumphon from the past. "Your words scratch an itchy spot.

If you kill this fellow Chumphon, I'll thank you for sending me to heaven. I'll give you anything you want except the sun, moon, and stars, which are beyond me.

But be careful. Your body is old and Chumphon is very clever. When he disguised himself to fight Phra Wai, he alone chased everybody off into the forest.

He's a master of devices, there's no joking about it. He disguised himself and had you surrounded. Because you were at your peak, you survived. Had you not been able, you'd have died and not returned."

Elder Khwat replied, "Don't worry. I won't let him hurt and shame me. Though my body is this old, my knowledge is still excellent.

On that occasion I drank liquor and lost my senses, so he was able to approach and grab me. Had it been other people in thousands, they'd have died. Though I slipped up, I didn't lose.

If he and I can meet face to face, have no fear. Let him come riding on the neck of his father and brother. I'll reduce them to dust. If I'm not able, don't receive me back again.

Tomorrow I'll leave because it's an auspicious day of the ninth with Saturn at the fifth.[5] I'll hasten straight down to Ayutthaya and won't take long to accomplish the task."

Soifa raised her clasped hands and gave a blessing in elegant words. "May your powers be strong and forceful so that nobody can withstand your might.

May you overcome enemies so the villains are defeated and die as desired. May your every wish be fulfilled so that you succeed and return quickly."

Elder Khwat took his leave. "Stay well with young Phlai Yong." He got up and blundered off through the gate and into his palanquin.

The wat slaves carried the palanquin along quickly, trailed by disciples holding his umbrella and bag. In a short while, they arrived at the kuti. He went up the half-moon terraces into an inner room.

After changing his triple robe into old clothes, he called Novice Jiw over. "You stay here and look after the disciples on my behalf. I'm going to Ayutthaya to take revenge on Chumphon. I'll do away with him and return within fifteen nights.

You remain here while I finish this matter. Wait and count the days. If you see I'm taking longer than I said, follow after me without delay."

The clever Novice Jiw was alarmed, wondering, "How come the teacher suddenly wants to rush off and court danger?"

With this thought, he spoke. "Going off heroically like this isn't a good idea. This unruly Chumphon is smart. We saw that with our own eyes.

---

5. Possibly this means the ninth day of the month with Saturn in the fifth house (*rasi*), Sing (Leo).

Any power or device of lore that you have, he has better. Good people have not disappeared from Ayutthaya.[6] Don't be careless or you'll lose.

You're old now, in your late eighties, very comfortable with rank and status. You've come this far but don't know how to enjoy it. How many more years will you live?

Spend the rest of your life sitting, sleeping, and eating. You shouldn't be thinking of revenge. Why go and create hardship for yourself? Die in Chiang Mai and be cremated on a *meru*."

Elder Khwat sat listening with his face drawn. "Tcha, Jiw! You're a coward and you're insulting me by taking Phlai Chumphon's side. Am I not skillful, novice?

Even if he has powers as strong as iron, he's only a little child, no bigger than a testicle. His breath hasn't lost the smell of his mother's milk. Just how deep is his knowledge?

We got captured by him because of your mistakes, so now your head shrinks in fear like a boiled shrimp. If I hadn't been drunk out of my mind so the formulas got muddled,

if I'd been as able as I am now, I'd have slashed their necks off in droves. You stay here in the kuti for around half a month. If I take too long, hurry after me."

Novice Jiw's scalp crawled in apprehension but he was too afraid of Elder Khwat to stop him. He wai-ed to give his blessing as wished. "May you succeed in your intent. Go.

May you win victory over Phlai Chumphon. May your devices achieve your hopes. May the fame of your great powers spread. I'll stay to look after the kuti as your eyes and ears."

The patriarch was pleased to hear the novice comply, and laughed heartily. On this occasion, Elder Khwat was fated to die so he believed he had an advantage and would not lose.

He collected his martial devices—a *takrut* cord and golden prayer beads, both old things, a headband thread to ward off evil, a silk bandeau, and an important mercury amulet.

He stuffed them in a sidebag slung on his shoulder, changed his *sabong*, and put on a sabai in open style with a belt. He went to a shrine and made a prayer to take leave.

---

6. See p. 1019, note 5.

Grasping a walking stick, he stepped off. A *jingjok* dropped down dead in front of his eyes. A barn owl brushed over his head.[7] The monk stopped still with thoughts racing.

"Oh, what's this? These look like bad omens." He sat down to concentrate his mind, closed his eyes, and chanted a formula to counter the omens. Standing up, he changed direction to go north.

As he stepped down the half-moon terraces to a lower level, a cobra slithered up, hissing, swaying its head, spreading its hood, and blocking the way. The elder knew this was a bad portent.

He hugged his chest and looked up for a sign in the clouds.[8] Strangely he saw a body with no head or arms. He knew for sure this meant he would not return.

"If I pull out now, Soifa will call me a coward. A man must die sword in hand." He gritted his teeth, steeled his heart, and set off straight to a graveyard.

He sat cross-legged, focused his mind steadily, and activated a yantra with spirit oil. His body disappeared and was transformed into a vulture

with a bald head, hooked beak, and red ears.[9] He thrust his feet against the soil, and flew upwards, tail waving and wattle swaying. On a strong wind, he soared towards Ayutthaya.

He hovered down above Ang Thong where the Bang Maeo Canal cut a line through the forest.[10] The vulture turned back into a monk, sat, and prayed 108 times.

He enchanted his walking stick, attached it to his body as a tail, put his almsbowl over his head, leapt into the river, and turned into an enormous crocodile

with a body nine fathoms long and white fangs curving upwards from his jaws. He thrashed around, roaring with a sound like thunder, and disported on the surface of the water.

Dear listeners, have no doubt about this. The area had already been settled with houses. After Elder Khwat transformed himself into a fierce creature here, the village was known from then onwards as Ban Jorakhe Rong, the village of the crying crocodile.[11]

---

7. See p. 636, note 51.
8. On cloud omens, see p. 621, note 15.
9. Probably a red-headed vulture, *Sarcogypus calvus*, which has a rather bare, red head.
10. The canal joins the river from the northeast around 2 kms north of Ang Thong. Khwat and Jiw stayed here in the previous chapter.
11. About 8 kms above Ang Thong, south of Amphoe Chaiyo (map 3, and p. 1086, note 23).

This place, named after the story of the teacher, still exists today as a densely settled village in the district of Ang Thong.

Crocodile Khwat was as large and as long as Lord Chalawan.[12] He thrashed against the bank with his tail, making a loud noise and stirring up waves.

The old crocodiles who were lords of that locality hid themselves underground, or fled away into marshes, or clambered up onto dry land and concealed themselves in the undergrowth for fear of death.

He came down quickly past Ban Talat Kruat.[13] He thrashed at buffaloes and elephants blocking his path, and snapped them dead in piles, then chased on further downstream.

In a short while, he arrived in front of Ang Thong, waving his tail and groaning loudly. When villagers came down to the jetty to wash fish, he grabbed them in his jaws, and dived underwater.

He thrust half his body above the surface, waved his tail, and raised the corpses as an offering to Lord Isuan.[14] Then he rushed to the governor's residence with the bodies in his jaws, thrashed them to bits, and scattered them around.

District officials and villagers rushed around screaming in fright. They watched the crocodile with bodies still in his jaws go down the steps and thrash about in the middle of the river.

The crowds on the banks swirled in chaos. "Where are the spirit experts? Go and fetch them." Spirit experts who had no teachers and knew nothing in depth[15] thought they could stab the beast easily as usual.

Old teachers understood better and tried to stop them. "Forget it, you young fellows!" "This crocodile is big. Don't go." "If he brings his jaws down on your boat, you'll fall in the water and drown."

"There's an ancient saying: A crocodile three fathoms long has powers of

---

12. A massive crocodile in the Phichit-based folktale, *Kraithong*, which was converted into an outer drama by King Rama II. Chalawan seizes Taphaothong, daughter of a rich Phichit merchant, and takes her to his underwater Emerald Cave. Kraithong dives down, defeats Chalawan, and enjoys Chalawan's wife, Wimala. The merchant rewards Kraithong by granting him both Taphaothong and her sister in marriage. But Kraithong misses Wimala, and fetches her from the depths. Kraithong might be able to defeat a mighty crocodile but he cannot manage the demands and jealousies of three wives (*Bot lakhon nok*, 299–340).

13. Immediately to the north of Ang Thong (see map 3).

14. In legend, Siva went to travel in the water so his consort Uma brought him a crocodile as a vehicle. Square markings on a crocodile's head are the remnant of Siva's throne. Because the crocodile is Siva's mount, Khwat has to offer a body to Siva before eating it. In fact, Khwat does not eat people—he stuffs them under tree roots—but makes this gesture to terrorize onlookers (KW, 635).

15. งูงูปลาปลา, *ngu ngu pla pla*, "snake snake fish fish," meaning not knowing anything deeply.

lore. This one is a lot more than three fathoms. I don't think mantras will be enough."

Some saw this was true and ran back, trembling with fear. One stubbornly believed in his own skill. "Even if it's Chalawan, so what!"

He hitched up his cloth and sat in the bows of a boat holding a harpoon. In the stern, men paddled furiously without stopping. The crocodile glided around watching. When the beast came close, the man thrust the harpoon but it bounced off.

He tried again at full force but the crocodile seized the harpoon in his jaws and broke it in two. The man drew a spear and stabbed but it glanced off. The crocodile turned back with red jaws agape,

and snapped once with great power. The spirit expert's boat, almost three fathoms long, was crushed to powder in his mouth, along with five strong oarsmen.

The crocodile was so big that the boat, six people, and five paddles did not even fill his cheeks. He dived down, wedged them underwater, and swam away.

On the banks people ran around in confusion. Seeing the crocodile swallow the spirit expert, all took to their heels. The news spread to every place in Ang Thong.

Khmer, Mon, Lao, and hill people all heard the news and were terrified. Nobody went down to bathe in the waterways. The crocodile drifted downriver.

When he arrived at remote places with no houses in sight, the crocodile floated along slowly like a log. When he saw houses or people on the banks, he showed off his power by attacking.

Close to dawn he found a remote spot, landed, assumed the form of the elder, and went to beg for alms at houses. After eating, he quickly plunged back into the water and became a crocodile.

The villages where he had received alms were excluded from his killing. He floated along in no hurry, wishing the news to spread far and wide.

At Ban Hae he uttered a loud bellow. The attacks were the talk of the town. He came to the start of Ban Satue,[16] and dived down to hide underwater.

Villagers who were returning home after work in the paddy fields went down to clean their dirty feet at a landing in large numbers. The crocodile thrust up out of the water, clambered up on the mud, and pounced.

Flailing his tail, he chased and snapped people, displaying his power to the utmost. With three people in his jaws, he plunged back under the water.

---

16. Ban Hae, Fishnet Village, 2 kms below Ang Thong (see map 3). Ban Satue, named after a tree similar to a *pradu*, unidentified.

He showed off his powers to thrash and snap but did not eat the bodies, stuffing them instead in the roots of banyan trees. Then he chased off along the river.

He glided ahead to Pho Sa[17] and came upon an old monk on almsround. He thrashed his tail, grabbed the monk in his jaws, and tossed him onto the mud. Men and women on the bank ran around shouting.

All the boats and rafts fled up canals away from the river in turmoil, bunching together in mortal fear. The fierce crocodile came down to Ban Rakam,[18]

arriving as the sun dropped in the afternoon. People were herding many buffaloes down to a landing. The crocodile glided along hidden underwater, then thrust up suddenly in the midst of them.

A buffalo turned to butt with its horns. The crocodile snapped its neck off, and thrashed with his tail. With the body in his teeth, he swam away, raised his jaws, and tossed the buffalo onto the land where it fell in the mud.

People on land stumbled and slipped down in the mud. The crocodile came ashore, scrambled along, and attacked. Those on the banks ran off like crazy. The crocodile came to the end of a bend and plunged into the water.

He showed off his power by thrashing his tail around in mid river, and churning up waves by diving and surfacing. People on land rushed around wildly, falling over themselves in fright.

The crocodile arrived at Bang Thewa at the end of Mok Forest[19] where there was an expanse of deep water. He waved his tail and went to hide in undergrowth on a bank just beyond the wat.

Villagers had come to a festival for honoring the Buddha image. The river was packed with boats and rafts, racing one another up and down in front of the wat amid sounds of merrymaking. People sang chicken-flapping songs and boat songs.

Young girls showed themselves off in uppercloths of bright purple silk and shirts over the top. In the stern of boats, they set up footed trays in pairs, and laid out mats, skins, and pillows to lean on.

Fun-loving young lads came from every village in boats with roofs stretch-

---

17. Bo Tree Pond, 1 km below Ban Hae (see map 3).

18. Named after a tree, a further 3–4 kms south (see map 3).

19. Bang Thewa, village of the god, unidentified, but Pa (forest) Mok is now an amphoe with no forest in sight. *Mok* is a shrub, *Wrightia religiosa*, water jasmine, that figures in the life of the Buddha. The wat figuring here would be Wat Pa Mok Worawihan, a large wat on the west bank that had a famous annual festival with boat races. In the late 1720s, a large reclining Buddha in the wat was moved away from the river as the bank was threatened by erosion. (KW, 636; RCA, 409–13; see map 3)

ing the whole length, and soft mats and pillows laid out for reclining. They paddled round and round, flirting with the girls.

Drinkers arrived in boats full of liquor bottles with a Chinese table for snacks placed amidships. All of them had a new haircut, wore a *phakhaoma*, and hung marigolds from their ears.

Novices and monks came on board a *khon* boat, playing boat songs and making a loud noise. Young female market vendors had powdered their faces, trimmed their hairlines, and put on silk shirts.

They sold fried bananas, oranges, and *khanom jin*, or set up elaborate trays with elephants' feet for dressing.[20] The wat was jam-packed with people. Boats were moored together as rafts.

The local roughs swaggered around acting tough with tooled knives and axes in their belts. When they went into the crowded wat, the young women took fright at these playboys and went off by boat.

Crocodile Khwat saw the whole area was crammed with boats. He left the scrub on the bank, glided along underwater, then shot up with a bang among the people,

feet scrambling, jaws snapping, and tail thrashing. Some people collapsed, bodies smashed and necks broken. Others rushed around screaming in turmoil, jumping down into boats, and sinking them in the chaos.

The crocodile grabbed a *khanom jin* vendor and dragged her along by the feet. She shouted, "You old buffalo!" leapt up onto the bank, and ran off yelling. She squelched through mud and her lowercloth slipped off but she clung on to the end.

The crocodile barged in among musicians in the middle of playing. A woman fell on her back, dropping her lowercloth, losing her senses for fear of death, yelling, and scrambling wildly like a field turtle.

A male musician leapt up, dropping his cloth in the confusion. Now naked, he stumbled awkwardly away, jumped, and crashed into the field turtle.

The woman fell. He went head over heels on top of her. They pushed and pulled at each other, swaying and hitting. She wriggled. He thrust full force. Suddenly ashamed of their bodies, they sprung apart.

The crocodile seized a vendor in his jaws and showed his power by plunging loudly into the river. Only her head was in the jaws with her body waving around outside the teeth. Everybody on land shuddered.

The crocodile swam rapidly against the current with the woman in his mouth, and raised her up as an offering to Lord Isuan. All that could be seen was a white

---

20. แต่งแง่, *taeng ngae*. Perhaps for makeup, like a beauty parlor.

bottom and feet waving in the air. Not a single person knew what to do.

The crocodile floated down to Bang Phong Pheng, saw a flock of ducks, and thrashed them to death. He kept diving and surfacing along to Ban Kum,[21] where he hid in undergrowth.

Village girls came down to bathe. The crocodile approached them underwater, than sprang up suddenly. They screamed, grabbed at their slipping cloths, and hid in bushes. Covering themselves with their hands like *jap-ping*, they ran up onto a jetty.

The crocodile did not hurt them but plunged further along. Anxious people went out to pass on the news to every village. The crocodile floated down past Bang Ban to Ban Phi Mot[22] and took a buffalo.

Ai-Maduea raised a pole and stabbed. The crocodile thrashed his head off, and tossed it away. I-Moei jumped and squirmed, letting the paddle slip from her hand. She cried out loudly, "Oh mother!"[23] and scrambled away.

He went through Hua Taphan and Kopjao to Ban Tuek,[24] and chased a woman who ran off losing her lowercloth. She went down into the mire, swimming wildly and getting sucked down until her whole body was smothered in mud.

She feared the crocodile so much, she lost her strength, her legs turned to jelly, and she lay on her back. Fearing she would die, her husband scrabbled with his hands to push her bottom onto higher ground.

From Ang Thong down, terror gripped both sides of the river. News spread, making the villagers tremble. Boats and rafts would not go out in fear.

Spirit experts who came to look shook their heads when they saw how huge the crocodile was. "From the time of my grandparents, nothing like this has been seen."

People talked about it loud and long. The crocodile floated down towards the capital, thrashing and biting people into dust. The city people spread the news in uproar.

---

21. Bang Phong Pheng is at the junction of the Chaophraya River and the Bang Luang Canal, 5 kms below Pa Mok. Ban Kum is 2 kms south along the Chaophraya River below the junction with the Bang Luang Canal; named after a species of tree in the Crateva genus (see map 3).

22. Bang Ban, now an amphoe, down the Bang Ban Canal, about 3 kms south of where it branches from the Chaophraya River; Ban Pi Mot, village of the spirit experts, 1 km south of Bang Ban (see map 3).

23. อุยย่าย, *ui yai*, in Mon.

24. Hua Taphan and Kopjao are close together, further down the Bang Ban Canal, about 7 kms past Bang Ban. At Kopjao, Khwat branches eastward along the Mahaphram Canal. The village is now called Ban Tuek Mahaphram (see map 3 and accompanying note).

He came in front of Ban Pom and lay hiding in wait to snatch people and stuff them under the roots of banyan trees. He chased boats to Phu Khao Thong.

People could see this crocodile was fierce. In every house, the men and women ran off in fright. He came to the rafts of the Jek moored at the Ka Rong jetty,[25] and grabbed the wife of oil merchant Jek Jong in his jaws.

Her husband shouted, "*Aiya!*" and ran to help. The crocodile gripped her tightly round the waist. The cloth tied round her belly slipped off. Her husband turned to look, and bent over crying.

The crocodile saw the Jek crying and thought this was so funny he could not stop himself roaring with laughter. When he opened his jaws, the Jek immediately pulled and his wife escaped alive.

The crocodile went down from the raft and sped away. He saw a female vendor carrying goods and crying out her wares. When she started her pitch, he sprang up on the stern of her boat, scrambling with his feet, snapping with his jaws, and flailing his tail.

The Vietnamese woman was paddling the boat along standing up. The crocodile grabbed her paddle, smashed it to smithereens, and swung his tail to thwack the middle of the boat. She fell right on the paddle post,

impaling herself, wriggling and squirming as the blood flowed. Her husband was so shocked his eyes almost popped out. He could only cry out, "The paddle pierced her!"[26] and swirl round in the boat.

People on boats and rafts were in uproar. "This terrible crocodile is worse than a tiger!" Nobody could buy or sell. Boats from the north, big and small, took refuge up canals.

The crocodile saw people were afraid. He surfaced and floated along past houses, swinging his tail boisterously in midstream, until he came to the Floating Pavilion.

Officials trembled. Jek, Lao, Khaek, and Thai were in uproar. The banks were packed. Guards rushed into the palace.

One went straight to the official sala and informed the senior nobles, "There's a very fierce crocodile attacking boats in front of the boathouse.[27]

He's very long, about ten fathoms. The news is that he came from the north. He's been eating animals and snapping lots of people along the way. He looks much bigger than crocodiles in general."

---

25. The wat here, just northwest of the city up the Chaophraya River, appeared in chapter 24.

26. แจวกำจุ๋น, *jaeo kam jun*. Possibly *jaeo kam* comes from the Vietnamese *cheo cam*, meaning the paddle pierces (her); alternatively the phrase might come from *sau can xuong*, "A crocodile is biting the boat."

27. The palace boathouse was on the opposite bank of the river, just to the west of the palace (see map 8).

Knowing that this extremely fierce people-eating crocodile had come to the city, the minister[28] had to inform the king.

He put on a sompak, tied a prostration cloth round his waist, went to the audience hall, prostrated, and addressed the king.

"My liege, Your Majesty, eminence of the city, patron. There is currently a crocodile that has come from the north and is extremely violent.

His head alone is over five cubits long. He has shown his power by eating many people. He floats along the current to show off his body. He is now swimming against the stream in front of the boathouse."

The king thought, "A crocodile much bigger than normal has come from the north and is going around eating animals and snapping people to dust.

To ignore this would make the populace angry and sow confusion throughout the city." He ordered the minister, "Send for the major crocodile experts,

including both royal and common ones, to help capture and kill this crocodile. I'll give a reward to whoever catches it. Don't let it get away. Go now."

The noble prostrated, crawled back out, and immediately gave orders to city officials to fetch the major crocodile experts.

Officials rushed off to find them. Many came immediately, thinking of the crocodiles they were used to killing, and hoping for the reward.

They hung amulets round their waists, put on britches with belts cinched tightly on top, tied auspicious threads round their heads, and boarded boats brandishing harpoons.

In all there were twenty boats which went upstream and downstream in rows. The experts sat on raised seats with hands in wai holding their harpoons, praying and scattering water.

Unafraid of their lore, Crocodile Khwat did not dive down but floated with body motionless, watching to see what the experts would do.

They were too afraid to come close. Seeing his length, they shook their heads in awe. He looked fearful, baring his fangs and rolling his eyes. Some leaned out and hurled their harpoons from far away.

This one threw, and that one threw, but the harpoons bounced off his skin without piercing. Other boats came and threw in turn. The crocodile lay still until the harpoons were finished.

---

28. Not specified but it must be Chaophraya Yommarat, minister of the capital.

One expert, seeing the crocodile was not moving, approached closer and stabbed with a spear. Strangely, the spear did not penetrate even a little, and broke off, as powerless as if thrown at a teak log.

The crocodile showed off his power by jumping and thrashing around, then turned suddenly and slashed powerfully, breaking and sinking every one of the boats.

He spun round wildly like a whirlwind. All the spirit experts fell in the water and flailed around. The crocodile turned and thrashed with his tail, leaving every one of them crushed dead or drowned.

Watching the experts die to a man, the crowds on the banks were so terrified their hair stood on end. It was unthinkable that a crocodile did not respond to the experts' mantras.

Officials who had come to watch twitched and trembled on the pier. Some ran in to an audience with the Lord of Life, prostrated, and relayed the news to the king.

Knowing this crocodile was so fierce that many spirit experts had lost their lives, the king understood this was a very unusual affair.

"A crocodile this big boldly coming down here and finishing off all the city's spirit experts has never happened before."

He beckoned to Phra Wai, "Heigh! What about this fierce crocodile? You're an able person with knowledge. How do you think it can be killed?"

The brave and clever Phra Wai pondered. "This crocodile has unusual powers. It's not an ordinary crocodile.

I shouldn't lose this opportunity for Chumphon to win royal favor." With this sole thought, he addressed the king.

"My liege, lord of the earth. There is no real crocodile such as this. It has exceptional strength, and is much larger than usual.

It must be a mantra crocodile created by some villain. That's how it has killed all the experts. Please send my younger brother, Phlai Chumphon, to examine this beast."

The king immediately commanded, "Eh, Phlai Chumphon, come here. It has been many years since you were placed in royal service but you've not yet been assigned any task.

You come from a military lineage. On the occasion you captured the elder, you proved adept. When presenting you, your father said you're able. I can see you look suitable.

This crocodile has attacked, injured, and pulverized many people beyond estimation. Go and find out without delay what kind of crocodile this is."

Chumphon received the order, crawled back out, and rushed out of the palace. He arrived at the Floating Pavilion and stared down at the huge crocodile,
floating on the surface of the river, looking intimidating. Phlai Chumphon made an examination and saw it was different from ordinary crocodiles.

"It's like telling a chicken from a snake by looking at the feet. This is a mantra crocodile and hence vicious. Nobody realized it was an artifice that had come to challenge Ayutthaya."

With this insight, he rushed to tell King Phanwasa. "My liege, Your Majesty. This is not a crocodile in the river,
but a mantra beast. Some skillful person has adopted this form to come and test the capital's military. That's why it didn't shrink from the crocodile experts. I think this is an able person, for certain.

If Your Majesty will grant your servant his grace and permit me according to the royal wish, I beg to volunteer to the royal footsoles to capture it."

The king laughed loudly in high spirits. "That's it! This Chumphon, a man of knowledge, must volunteer to earn my favor. I thank you.

If you can catch this important crocodile, I'll reward you splendidly. Go immediately with your elder brother and your father, who is staying in the city,
to prepare devices for fighting. Wait on me at dawn at the Floating Pavilion. You'll fight him famously. Tomorrow I'll go to watch."

The two brothers prostrated to take leave. With their crowd of servants following behind, they went out of a gate and along to Phra Kanburi's house.

They informed their father about the royal order. "A fierce and powerful crocodile has been attacking people, and is now in front of the boathouse.

The experts who went to deal with it were thrashed and drowned, not one remaining. It has snapped many other people to death. Chumphon examined it and knows it's a person transformed.

There was an opportunity for Chumphon to volunteer to capture this fierce crocodile. The king instructed us to tell you to help prepare Chumphon for the fight."

Khun Phaen, great romancer, sat and thought carefully, then took his sons along to Phra Wai's house.

On arrival, he had his devices fetched, and commanded Simala to prepare everything for offerings. Powder, oil, and krajae were daubed on Chumphon's forehead.

In Phra Wai's shrine room, incense, candles, and flowers were arranged. An adept's knife, sheath, spear, and harpoon were laid out side by side.

Chumphon was sent to bathe. Khun Phaen chanted an *athan* formula, and daubed Chumphon with herbal medicine and oil to make him invulnerable against dangers from animal fangs.

In the golden light of dawn, Chumphon went into the quiet of the shrine room. He sat still, uttered incantations, held his breath, then blew to sacralize the weapons.

By the power of knowledge, the weapons shook. Chumphon was pleased to see this power. He got dressed and went down in front of the house.

Khun Phaen, Phra Wai, and Phlai Chumphon hurried along with their servants crowding behind. They reached the Floating Pavilion, and awaited the king on the riverbank.

꿏

Now to tell of the almighty king, whose powers were feared by enemies from all regions, who resided in a palace as great as Wetchayan, equal to the Bantukam throne of Indra,[29]

with heavenly maidens and consorts attending to his wishes by entertaining him with song and lyre[30] music so that the eminence of the earth was joyful.

At dawn, when he had completed the royal ablutions and ladies on duty had clad him in apparel, he thought about the matter of the crocodile, and said, "Today I'll go down to the Floating Pavilion

to watch Chumphon fight and capture the crocodile. This group of ladies will accompany me. Don't make too much noise." He proceeded to the Floating Pavilion with columns of guards in procession on both sides.

On arrival, he ascended a dais, took the royal seat, and laughed. The nobles prostrated. All the groups of lords and nobles,

palace governesses, every one of the inner ladies, royal relatives,

lyre

---

29. Wetchayan is Indra's palace, and Bantukam his throne (see p. 172, note 19, and p. 173, note 21).

30. พิณ, *phin*, a string instrument, akin to a lyre, with two or three strings, formerly made from animal skin, and a sound box often made from jackfruit wood.

servants of the dust under the royal foot from both the inner and front divisions had all come.

The king said, "Ha! Heigh! Phra Wai, where's Chumphon gone?" Phra Wai summoned Chumphon, who crawled up and prostrated beside his brother.

The king asked, "How is it, Chumphon? Can you capture this mantra crocodile?" "My liege, Your Majesty, if I cannot, I offer my life."

"That's it! That's what I like to hear. You just do as we expect. If you kill this crocodile,[31] I'll appoint you as an officer of the pages,

and present you with five chang in cash, along with wives and women as appropriate—whoever you like, just tell me. Catch the crocodile and you'll be rewarded."

Phlai Chumphon saluted to receive the order, backed out, and went off. He had a raft brought down to a landing, where he prostrated elegantly three times.

"I salute the Lord Buddha, and beg protection for his servant against danger. May the merit of the goddess of the earth, the goddess of the waters, my father, and my mother safeguard me."

He walked down to the raft. The watchers were both excited and terrified. Older people shouted their blessings. Young women were unable to drag their eyes away.

Phlai Chumphon, of exceptional powers and dignity, had a raft released to go out midstream. Spirits surrounded his body completely.

He chanted a Holy Regal Siva[32] formula, intoned the story of the crocodile race from the beginning until they were cursed to live in the land of men,[33]

---

31. From here until the end of the next stanza, "you'll be rewarded," is taken from WK, 38:1492–93; PD has: you will become rich on the reward.

32. พระสยมภูวนาถ, *phra sayamphuwanat*. Sayambhu is one of the names of Siva, and *phuwanat* is a word of Sanskrit derivation meaning lord of the land, king.

33. Uma, consort of Siva, populated the world with animals, including the crocodile. After the crocodile was chosen to be the mount of Siva, it got very puffed up about having a throne on its head (see p. 1096 note 14), and went around eating humans and other animals. Rishis and disciples living along the Godavari River (in eastern India) could not bathe or fetch water so the rishis complained to Siva, who in turn passed the buck to Uma. She made an iron harpoon cursed with magic, and plunged it into the crocodile's tail, rendering it paralyzed. The disciples of the rishi then trussed up the beast and tormented it. Unable to hunt for food, it lay with mouth open in order to catch anything passing by. The rishi took pity on the beast and explained that Uma made them do it because the water-dwelling crocodile had been eating land-dwelling animals. The crocodile complained that it was not fair to persecute him since land-dwelling humans were eating water-dwelling animals too. Realizing the beast would never relent, Uma enchanted a turmeric root and threw it into the crocodile's mouth where the root became a dis-

and pronounced a mantra for overcoming crocodiles.

"*Om*, crocodile![34] Don't stay still. I'm the Lord of Darkness come to kill you. The Lord Isuan sent me to take back your life.

Om, crocodile, courageous one! Come up quickly. Why are you lying low, oh crocodile?" He enchanted rice to counter evils, and scattered it around.

"Any spirits who have taken up position to give protection, get away from this place right now." He enchanted water and scattered it around. Elder Khwat's spirits fled away.

Crocodile Khwat could not remain lying low. Looking up and seeing Chumphon on the raft, he was happy things had turned out as expected.

"Chumphon has come as hoped! I'll take his life." He surfaced and floated along. The king watched in excitement.

People on rafts could not be prevented from crowding down to the front. Sentinelles from the palace chased them back. "You thick faces, don't you listen?

If you want to watch, just sit quiet and obey orders, or your beautiful appearance will be ruined by stripes on your back! The more you're told off, the less you listen. You palace ladies go over the top about men."[35]

The valiant Chumphon saw the crocodile surface as hoped. "Above the water, it can do damage. This villain knows I've come."

He enchanted three strands of sacred thread, tied them round his hand, and waited with the adept's knife at his side and a harpoon held ready to attack.

The monk-crocodile of good knowledge got into position and charged. Great waves crashed against Chumphon's raft, which looked as if it would capsize and sink.

The crowd gasped as the raft nearly broke apart. Watchers' eyes were glued to the excitement. Sentinelles shouted out, "You simpletons! You're too playful, shameless."

Crowds of people were watching and cheering. Khmer, Mon, Burmese, Vietnamese, Karen, Jek, and Farang had never seen such a sight. A Thai said, "Come and look if you dare!"

---

cus and cut out the crocodile's tongue so it was not able to taste anything. Hence the crocodile fears turmeric and harpoons, honors Siva, is always hungry, and lies with mouth open waiting for any food. (KW, 642–43; SB, 658)

34. นักกะพุด, *nakkaphut*; combination of a Pali-Sanskrit word for crocodile with a Thai word for "come to the surface"; a term used for crocodiles in literature and legend (SB, 658–59; KW, 642).

35. This last sentence is taken from WK, 38:1494; PD has: You palace ladies have no shame.

Shy Tavoy ladies turned their faces and said in dialect, "We don't dare look or listen to the crocodile."[36] A Mon said, "I'm leaving, sir,"[37] and left his pan and lime behind. A Lao said, "I don't know. I can't look. I'm really scared."[38]

On the riverbank, many people of many languages watched, sitting and standing. Jek and Khaek argued together in sing-song, "*Nung ning no na*," sounding so cute.

A Khaek said, "I am greatly fearful."[39] The Jek argued back, "I disagree, you pudding face."[40] He[41] pushed the Khaek over in front of the onlookers. A Khmer said, "Too much. Calm down."

Phlai Chumphon, with the powers of a lion, watched the crocodile approach, got himself into a good position, and stabbed so blood spurted.

The crocodile wheeled its tail round and crushed the raft with a great crack. Chumphon fell off. People screamed. The king was greatly alarmed.

He cried, "Wai, what's happening? This crocodile has knocked Chumphon down!" Nobles were badly shocked. Wai prostrated three times and said to the king,

"Chumphon hasn't lost to the crocodile. He should come up in a moment." None of the nobles was so confident. The palace crowd watched tensely in turmoil.

Young ladies who were in love with Chumphon were in a pitiful state of agitation. Some hid their faces and wept at the thought of him. "When will Phlai come up?"

Using a formula, Phlai Chumphon was able to dive down and stay under-water, where he drew the adept's knife. The crocodile came to confront him,

thrashing his tail. Chumphon defended with the knife. The crocodile turned and retreated, luring Chumphon on, then returned to the attack. Chumphon

---

36. แมงขะแวงเฉมะราฉามาหลู, *maeng khawaeng che ma ra cha ma lu*, literally "(we) dare not look at and do not want to listen to the crocodile," in the form of Burmese spoken in Tavoy (Thawai), which retains pronunciations from ancient Burmese that have changed in the "national" form of the language.

37. อาละกุล, *alakun*, in Mon, a farewell and an honorific.

38. ฮู้บ่หันข้อยยั่นจริง, *hu bo han khoi yan jing*, in Lao.

39. เมาะโมหะโยเปาะ, *mo moha yo po*, translation highly speculative, assuming *moha* comes from *maha*, and *yo po* is a mangling of *bhaya*.

40. อั๊วละไหม่อ้ายมู่ทู่, *ualamai*, "I disagree" or "I don't want it" in Teochew; *ai mu thu*, short-ened from the Thai อ้ายหน้าตามู่ทู่, someone with a round or bland face.

41. From here to the end of the stanza is taken from WK, 38:1485; PD has: At that moment, the crocodile surfaced, startling everyone. They packed together, jostling at the water's edge.

got a grip on his throat. The crocodile surfaced. Chumphon swung up to ride on his neck.

The king slapped his thigh and roared. "Get him! Such bravery. That's my boy. Take him for real! Don't wait!" All the nobles cheered Phlai Chumphon.

Khun Phaen and Phra Wai sat with eyes glued. The palace crowd ran up to watch in tumult. People's cheering echoed across the water. Gentlefolk mingled with riffraff without complaint.

Royal retainers in the audience shouted out loud, "Chumphon can ride the crocodile!" "Unbelievably fearsome!" "Both big and long." "Looks about nine fathoms."

Sentinelles told them to quiet down. "For pity's sake, you make a bit of noise and they tell you off." "They want you to watch something with your eyes only." "Let's go and cheer somewhere else. Come on."

Elder Khwat in his crocodile form twisted and turned angrily but could not shake Chumphon off his back. Chumphon kept his seat and stabbed strongly,

chopping repeatedly until the water was stained red with blood. The crocodile could not stand it and was at wits' end. Elder Khwat used lore,

chanting a formula 108 times, transforming himself into a fish. Chumphon disappeared and became a bird that dived down and searched for the fish in the waters.

The crowd stood watching in excitement. The Floating Pavilion was on the point of collapse. Concubines, palace ladies, and eunuchs[42] were creating uproar at the water's edge.

The king asked Phra Wai several times, "How did they both disappear? Is Chumphon winning or losing?"

Phra Wai's eyes were fixed on his brother. Knowing his brother's skills, he had no doubts. He said to the king, "The enemy transformed himself to get away. Chumphon transformed to give chase."

Just as he spoke, he saw the elder transform again into a great tusker that came ashore, making people scatter away in fright. Chumphon transformed into a tiger,

followed the elephant up onto the bank, and attacked, leaping up and get-

---

42. ขันที, *khanthi*. Eunuchs are little mentioned in accounts of the Thai court, perhaps surprisingly given the long contact with China. This mention, in the same sentence as concubines and palace ladies, strongly suggests they had a role in the inner palace. La Loubère wrote, "Tis reported that he [King Narai] has eight or ten Eunuchs only, as well white as black" (*New Historical Relation*, 101). The Ministry of the Palace included a department of eunuchs headed by Okphra Simanorat, *sakdina* 1,000 (KTS, 1:242).

ting a tight grip on the trunk. The elephant shook wildly and managed to break free. As the elephant turned, the tiger pounced at his throat.

Some spectators were so frightened they fled. Others stood their ground, watching with no fear. The tiger sunk its teeth in the elephant's neck and clung on. The elephant curled up his trunk and trumpeted loudly.

The nobles all cheered. The king was still assailed by doubts. "Which is our side, Wai—the tiger or the elephant?" "Sire, it's the tiger."

The tiger's bite brought the elephant to a standstill. Then the elephant disappeared and became a monkey in front of their eyes. Chumphon also transformed, becoming a cobra, and closed to attack.

The spectators understood they had transformed, and jostled forward to get a view. "Who's changed into a monkey and is causing havoc?" "Even though he's good, he won't escape Chumphon as a snake."

The monkey attacked. The cobra snapped its jaws, coiled round the monkey's body, and pulled him down to the ground. The monkey disappeared and became the monk-teacher. Chumphon changed from snake to human.

With his two hands he got a firm grip on Elder Khwat. "It's this villain! I thought he came from somewhere." Chumphon took Elder Khwat over in front of the king's seat, made obeisance, and awaited the royal command.

The almighty king, eminence of the great capital of Ayutthaya, saw the monk was held at the front of the palace courtyard. He clapped his hands loudly and said,

"Eh, you deserve favor, Chumphon. You're very brave and tough. On this occasion you've won royal favor utterly. I'll give you all you deserve."

Then he looked over angrily. "Tcha! You great rickety old wreck! What kind of holy man are you? Going around eating people is inhuman.

You came with the intention of challenging the capital with such arrogance and overconfidence. There must be some treacherous criminal gang that put you up to coming here transformed.

Ha! Heigh! Phramuen Si, take this elder off and interrogate him thoroughly. Don't fear sin. Clap him in yoke, fetters, and cangue, and find out why he came,

who sent him, what village and district he comes from, what's his name, and why he transformed himself."

The king turned and addressed Phra Kanburi. "I was not wrong to have taken this son of yours, Phlai Chumphon, into my service.

His knowledge was equal to this trickster who came transformed. He bravely volunteered to fight. We all watched his powers and they were worth seeing. He's fit to partner Wai on royal duty."

The king left his seat and went up into the palace. Inner ladies and royal officials entered the palace or went to their homes feeling joyful.

The common people went off home in crowds, talking noisily. They showered Chumphon with praise as an able person. "What exceptional powers of lore!"

"This old elder who came transformed is a rare and daring teacher. He destroyed spirit experts, punt poles, and paddles in thousands, but Chumphon knew how to tie him up and knock him down like a fairground monkey!"

One said "I enjoyed it so much I forgot to run away. Really fun, better than a mask play." Another said, "When I saw the snake I almost jumped. It swayed up less than a fathom away."

Khaek, Farang, Chinese, and Cham walked along, praising in their different languages. "Never seen anything like it anywhere!" Only one Jek said, "In China, this has happened before.

At the time Kiang Ju Yae overcame the enemy's strategies, fearsome bands of spirits fought one another.[43] But that was a long time ago, over a thousand years. To have seen this occasion was a treat for the eyes."

A woman complained, "I'm so fed up with fighting. I get the shivers and can't watch with my eyes open. I just made wishes for Phlai Chumphon.

He looks as frail as a whittled stick. I feared that accursed oldie would crush him." Another said, "I was so worried I was praying for him to escape danger."

While adults talked, young women kept quiet. They walked along with heads bowed but faces wreathed in smiles. They were too shy to open their mouths but thought of nothing but Phlai Chumphon all the way back home.

Phramuen Si, of peerless valor and skill, left the Floating Pavilion and called out to Phlai Chumphon,

"Beware of this old trickster. Watch over him. Don't let anyone interfere."

---

43. This story appeared in a Chinese work, *Hong sin*, ห้องสิน, which was translated into Thai in early Bangkok, and compiled with other Chinese works by Chaophraya Phrakhlang (Hon). The original is *Fengshen yanji*, "The Investiture of the Gods," a historical novel about the transition from the Shang to the Zhou dynasties, an event now dated as around 1046 BCE. The novel was written in the Ming dynasty, probably in the sixteenth century. "Kiang Ju Yae" is Jiang Ziya, a hermit who predicted and incited the Zhou overthrow of the last Shang ruler, and was rewarded by being made prime minister. Fox spirits, pheasant spirits, chicken spirits, and various deities descended to earth to take part in the fighting. After the war, both victors and vanquished ascended to the heavens and became part of the pantheon of deities, with Jiang Ziya as an overlord of the spirits. (KW, 646; SB, 663; Chew, *Tales*; http://en.wikipedia.org/wiki/Fengshen_Yanyi)

He commanded the palace guard to disperse the crowd, then went to a seat behind the boathouse

and had the monk brought for questioning. "Tell the truth and don't make things up. Why did you kill so many people? Who entrusted you to come here?"

The monk sat sad-faced, and gave a statement full of lies. "Nobody sent me. I wanted to see Ayutthaya so I came by myself."

Phramuen Si said, "This fellow is not telling the truth. He's stalling, trying to fool us with a lot of nonsense. Seeing the city and merrily killing people! You're a big liar. Why don't you say things straight.

Somebody must have sent him. Guards! Bring the pillory post[44] in here." The front guards ran up and busily set up the post at the boathouse,

along with chains and cangue, the whole set. The guards trembled and twitched as they tied Elder Khwat to the wooden frame, looping several times both inside and out.

The adroit Phramuen Si promptly began the interrogation. "Tell the truth. Don't keep quiet. Where are you from and who sent you here?"

In pain, the elder told the whole truth. "I live in Chiang Mai, sir. I used to be a servant of little Princess Soifa. My name is Elder Khwat. Let me tell you.

When I came down and stayed in Wat Phraya Maen, Chumphon, son of Khun Phaen, captured me and wanted to slash me dead, so I fled back to Chiang Mai, my hometown.

Nobody sent me. I had a grievance against Phlai Chumphon for capturing me so I transformed myself into a crocodile and came to Ayutthaya again.

I anticipated that if anyone volunteered to come out and fight me, it would be Chumphon. If I lured him with every trick and device, I could grab him and drown him underwater.

As for the king, I had no thought of revolt. That is the full truth. As for my punishment, have mercy."

Phramuen Si laughed. "This old fogey has lots of excuses. You resented Chumphon so much that you crushed and ate people for any old reason?

Don't you know that in the provisions of the law code, the penalty for murder is execution? You have bold ideas of treachery and revolt and you're wasting our time with these tricky excuses."

---

44. หลักคา, *lak kha*, a wooden frame with holes to clamp the wrists and ankles, similar to the stocks.

He had a clerk take down the elder's words. Close to midday, he went to the front of the audience hall. When the king arrived, he prostrated and told him what the monk had said.

Informed of the matter, the king pondered carefully. "This fellow was said to have died many years ago but now he turns up again.

Ha! Heigh! Phraya Anuchit,[45] at that time, you covered up things and lied to my face that the novice and elder had died, but now he comes back. What do you have to say?"

The superintendent of the guard did not raise his face. He feared royal authority so much that his sweat flowed. "I was stupid and simple. Because the palace warders said they were dead,

I took it on trust without checking, and carelessly had them thrown in a graveyard. If the king disapproves, may I be punished by death." At the end of his words, he prostrated.

The king said promptly, "Henceforth, let it be established as regular practice, that if an accused person dies,

a report is sent to the pages and guard, along with Kalahom and Mahat-thai, to make an inspection without fail, and only then is the body taken to a graveyard."

He ordered the ministers and judges of the royal court to confer about the punishment for the old trickster according to the provisions of the law code.

The councils of the court and royal court,[46] after consultation with each minister, ruled that Elder Khwat was guilty of a gross crime and should be executed.

The king listened to this advice and promptly commanded, "This fellow is devious and untrustworthy. Chumphon is entrusted to carry out the execution."

---

45. Phra Anuchitaracha, *jangwang* in the right department of the guard under Kalahom, *sakdina* 3,000 (KTS, 1:383; KW, 647). In the Wat Ko version, Phraya Yommarat is responsible for the error, not Phra Anuchit (WK, 38:1501).

46. ลูกขุนศาลาแลศาลหลวง, *luk khun sala lae san luang*. These were two councils of senior nobles. They are mentioned three times in the Three Seals Law in laws dated 1743, 1758, and 1783, and the membership is different in each case (KTS, 4:229, 261, 324). According to Vickery, the first was "a council of the officers in charge of the most important government departments," while the second was "a council . . . of judicial officials from various ministries," and may have been a kind of appeals court, as mentioned by Schouten and Van Vliet ("Constitution," 172–73).

The king went inside. The minister of the capital rushed off to relay the king's order that the elder was entrusted to Phlai Chumphon.

Phra Wai had wanted revenge on the monk from the beginning. "This elder has powerful lore." He advised Chumphon not to trust him.

Khun Phaen handed Skystorm to his son. Both Phaen and Wai gave Chumphon strict instructions. "You must carry out the execution, and then take care of the head.

When it's stuck up, there must be guards all the time. His men will want to take this fellow's head. Don't be careless and leave the place unattended. Station guards by bonfires."

Chumphon received the king's order and promptly took leave, leading the elder under escort with officers and men of the Ministry of the Capital as a rearguard.

Crowds of people gathered to watch. Guards inspected and kept order, not allowing anyone to approach closely.

They halted at the execution ground.[47] People milled noisily around. A post was set up. The elder was tied to it, seated and bent over. Chumphon flourished the sword and severed his neck.

Among the people who had come to watch the execution, no one felt pity. They said, "Got what he deserved." "What kind of monk eats people?"

Relatives of those he had killed crowded around shouting abuse. Everyone returned home. Chumphon ordered guards to keep watch.

"Stick up the head, and keep close watch. Able people may come to take it, so keep guard without fail." After giving orders, he returned home.

Now to tell of the mighty king, feared in every place in all ten directions, who resided in a bedchamber of the palace, surrounded by consorts like scattered stars,

some fanning to please him, others on duty to massage and loosen the royal tendons, and others to play music and sing beautifully for his comfort and pleasure.

In the golden light of dawn, when birds sang like the sound of a conch, and masses of consorts prostrated with clasped hands, the king left the golden bed

to be bathed and arrayed in splendid, glittering, nine-jeweled raiment before proceeding out front to sit on the throne at the window to deal with city affairs,

---

47. In the Wat Ko version, they carry out the execution at their house (WK, 38:1503).

looking as elegant as Lord Brahma riding on a swan.[48] All the nobles prostrated along with senior officials and royal kin. The king thought of Chumphon.

"By overcoming the crocodile, he has won royal favor. It is appropriate to confer rank on him as reward, and to take him into royal service. He's as clever as Wai."

With these thoughts, he roared like a lion, "Chumphon has won royal approval. I thank him. He volunteered without thought for his own life.

On this occasion he has earned royal favor on a large scale. If he had not got the crocodile, things would be difficult. He is appointed as Luang Nai Rit[49] to serve me closely.

City officials and palace soldiers will find a place to build a house for him to live. Wai, help look for somewhere. He's too young to know about houses."[50]

The king commanded treasury officials to arrange silk sompak, wool sabai, and five chang in cash on a salver. After the presentation, the king went back inside.

Luang Nai Rit smiled brightly in happiness over the royal grant. Phra Wai led the way out, and servants carried all the goods.

They went home to tell their father. Everyone was overjoyed. The whole family celebrated, and all lived happily from that time onwards.

---

48. ท้าวครรไลหงส์, *thao kanlai hong*, lord of the golden swan, meaning Brahma whose mount is a swan.

49. Nai Rit, *nai wen* in the right division of the royal pages, the same unit as his brother Phra Wai, *sakdina* 800 (KTS, 1:224; KW, 648).

50. In the Wat Ko version, the king orders the militiamen to build the house adjacent to that of Phra Wai (WK, 38:1505).

LATER CHAPTERS, SUMMARY AND SYNOPSIS

Probably in the nineteenth century, authors developed new episodes, extending the story beyond what Prince Damrong selected for his edition. Two collections of later chapters have been printed:

> *Sepha rueang khun chang khun phaen ton to jak chabap ho samut haeng chat* [*KCKP* continuation beyond the National Library edition], printed by Bunnak Phayukkadet at Sinlapa Bannakan, n.p., n.d. (SB).

> *Sepha rueang khun chang khun phaen phak plai krom sinlapakon truat sop chamra mai* [The latter part of *KCKP* edited by the Fine Arts Department], printed for the cremation of Khunying Chuea Chonlathanwinitchai, Wat Prayurawon-sawat, 10 January 1966 (FAD).

The SB edition has approximately 9,000 lines divided into twelve chapters. The FAD edition has approximately 11,000 lines divided into thirty-three chapters. The FAD edition includes the final chapter, chapter 43, of the Prince Damrong edition (Elder Khwat) and numbers its subsequent chapters in the same sequence.

The story is the same in the two editions. The FAD edition has more elaborate and longer treatment in the early chapters, and an extra few pages on the end, but is otherwise the same as the SB edition. The preface of the FAD edition states that the only corrections made to the manuscript versions were in spelling and versification.

THE STORY: THE CONFLICT OF PHRA WAI'S DESCENDANTS

The story revolves around the attempts by the Chiang Mai line, Soifa and her son Phlai Yong, with the help of Novice Jiw, to take revenge on the Simala side of the lineage.

Khun Phaen, Phra Wai, Phlai Chumphon, Laothong, Kaeo Kiriya, and King Phanwasa all die in an epidemic.

In Chiang Mai, Phlai Yong, son of Phra Wai by Soifa, studies with Novice

Jiw, goes to fight in China and returns with a wife, Wesio. Soifa persuades Phlai Yong to go to Ayutthaya to kill Simala for revenge. They raid Simala's house and believe they have killed her, but in fact she survives.

Phlai Phet and Phlai Bua, sons of Simala, find out about the attack. By chance they make contact with Luang Tang Jai, son of Laothong, who joins their cause. They attack Chiang Mai, take the city, and kill both Soifa and Phlai Yong.

Phlai Phet governs Chiang Mai. Phlai Yong's people go to Ayutthaya and tell the king that an army from Pagan has captured Chiang Mai. Ayutthaya dispatches an army, but Phlai Phet sends a missive that exposes the subterfuge. The Ayutthaya king appoints Phlai Phet to govern Chiang Mai as a tributary.

Phlai Yong is reborn as a Burmese prince. He allies with Jiw and takes Chiang Mai, then makes Jiw the governor as a tributary of Pegu, and returns home.

Phlai Suriyan is born, son of Phlai Phet. After a long series of adventures, he retakes Chiang Mai with the help of his father and his uncle, Phlai Bua. Jiw manages to kill Simala, and repeats his mentor's trick of turning into a fearsome crocodile, but Phlai Suriyan defeats him.

Phlai Phet has two wives. One of them, Soi Kaeo, daughter of the Uppahat of Lamphun, becomes jealous and uses a love charm on Phlai Phet. She is found out and expelled from the city. The Lamphun forces attack Chiang Mai, but are defeated.

SB EDITION: CHAPTER AND SECTION HEADINGS

1. Phlai Bua goes to China

    Novice Jiw searches for his teacher
    Novice Jiw steals Elder Khwat's head
    Elder Khwat's head disappears
    Soifa learns that Elder Khwat has died
    Phra Wai goes to Nang Waen Fa
    Phra Wai gets Nang Waen Fa
    Governor of Phimai presents Nang Soi Raya
    The presentation of Nang Soi Raya to Phlai Chumphon
    Phra Wai and Phlai Chumphon play polo before the throne
    Luang Phaen dies
    Phra Wai and Phlai Chumphon die
    Phlai Yong studies knowledge with Novice Jiw
    Nang Soifa puts herself in the service of Phlai Yong
    Nguan Bun Jeng brings an army to fight with Tang Jiw
    Governor Tang Jiw calls for help from the Thai army

Phlai Yong volunteers to go to China
Phlai Yong reaches China
Phlai Yong puts people to sleep and enters
Phlai Yong fights with Nguan Bun Jeng
Phlai Yong captures Nguan Bun Jeng
Governor Tang Jiw bestows Nang Wesio
Return to Siam
Phlai Yong presents tribute and Nang Wesio
Nang Wesio is presented to Phlai Yong who is appointed Governor of
    Chiang Mai
Phlai Yong goes to Wesio's room
Phlai Yong sends people to attack Simala's house

2. Phlai Phet and Phlai Bua

Nang Simala dreams she floats to the front of Wat Lelai
Phlai Phet and Phlai Bua have an omen
Sami Phet and Novice Bua visit their mother
Ai Thit tells a story
Phlai Phet and Phlai Bua plan revenge
Phlai Phet goes to fetch the sword, Skystorm
Phlai Phet and Phlai Bua travel to Chiang Mai
Luang Tang Jai takes his daughter to wash her hair
Novice Bua meets Nang Waen Kaeo
Phlai Bua gets Nang Phrai Tani
Entering the house of Luang Tang Jai
Phlai Bua abducts Nang Waen Kaeo
Phlai Bua acquires a horse and the sword Phrong Kaeo
Phlai Bua gets Nang Waen Kaeo
Luang Tang Jai follows Phlai Bua
Phlai Phet warns against war
Various people recognize their cousins
Phlai Phet gives battle
The army marches to Chiang Mai

3. Phlai Phet attacks Chiang Mai

Phlai Phet creates an army of spirits
Attack on the outpost of Chiang Mai
The spirit army attacks Chiang Mai
Luang Tang Jai fights with Saen Kham In
Saen Kham In is captured

Phlai Yong fights with Phlai Phet
Phlai Yong is captured
Phlai Yong vows eternal vengeance
The deaths of Soifa and Phlai Yong

4. *Phlai Phet governs Chiang Mai*
Phlai Phet governs Chiang Mai
Phlai Yong's people go to attend on the King of Ayutthaya
The Ayutthaya army marches to Chiang Mai
Phraya Yommarat attacks an outpost
Phlai Phet sends the king a missive
Phlai Phet is appointed governor of Chiang Mai

5. *Nilamalai attacks Chiang Mai*
Phlai Yong is reborn as Nilamalai
Elder Jiw visits his teacher
Nilamalai gets people to attack Chiang Mai
Elder Jiw volunteers
The spirit army attacks and takes an outpost
Elder Jiw fights with Phlai Phet
The spirit army attacks Chiang Mai
The burning of Chiang Mai
The fall of Chiang Mai
Nilamalai enters Chiang Mai
Elder Jiw is appointed Governor of Chiang Mai

6. *The birth of Phlai Suriyan*
Phlai Bua loses his way
Wesio and Simala meet Phlai Maninat
The birth of Phlai Suriyan
Phlai Suriyan destroys the dummies and finds a golden rod
Phlai Suriyan abducts Nang Bua Thong
Phlai Suriyan gets Nang Bua Thong
Phlai Suriyan and Nang Bua Thong lose their way
Phlai Suriyan asks to travel by the boat of Anlamang
Anlamang tricks Phlai Suriyan into an abyss
The ghosts of Khun Krai and Khun Phaen come to help
Phlai Suriyan follows to fight Anlamang
Anlamang flees

7. Phlai Suriyan fights with teacher Kewat

Anlamang flees to find Teacher Kewat
Teacher Kewat sends a magic crow to make a killing
Kewat and his pupils follow after Phlai Suriyan
Kewat fights with Phlai Suriyan
Phlai Suriyan is captured
The ghost of Phra Wai comes to the aid of Phlai Suriyan
Phlai Suriyan travels to find Phlai Bua

8. Phlai Bua fights with Chiang Mai

Phlai Suriyan meets Phlai Bua
Phlai Bua creates a spirit army
The spirit army attacks an outpost of Chiang Mai
The Chiang Mai outpost falls
Elder Jiw raises an army
Saen Rahu fights with Phlai Suriyan
Phlai Bua fights with Elder Jiw
Phlai Bua and Phlai Suriyan put the army to sleep and capture Elder Jiw
Phlai Bua governs Chiang Mai
Wesio and Simala enter the city
Phlai Phet and Luang Tang Jai return to Chiang Mai
The King of Ayutthaya orders the execution of Elder Jiw
Elder Jiw puts people to sleep, escapes from jail, kills Wesio and Simala
Elder Jiw as a crocodile rampages in Ban Thap Chang
The officials of Ban Thap Chang spread the news
Phlai Suriyan defeats the crocodile
Elder Jiw flees into the forest
Phlai Suriyan gets Nang Takhian Thong
Phlai Bua follows after Phlai Suriyan
Phlai Suriyan and Nang Takhian Thong are taken to the city

9. Phlai Phet is affected by a love charm

Phlai Phet gets Nang Soi Kaeo
Muen Wichai presents Nang Montha
Soi Kaeo is jealous at Nang Montha
Nang Montha makes a love charm
Phlai Phet expels Nang Soi Kaeo from the city
Novice Malai Krong takes Soi Kaeo away

PART 2

ALTERNATIVE VERSIONS

THE ABDUCTION OF WANTHONG

Two fragments, first published in 1925 from the Wachirayan Library collection, have come to be known as *Samnuan kao*, the old versions. They are earlier forms of chapters 17–18 in the PD edition. There are internal signs that the second was developed from the first, and that the final version in PD, a product of King Rama II's literary salon, was developed from the second. Comparing the three shows how the text developed at the hand of different authors.

The first fragment seems to be the earliest. Khun Wichitmatra thought it was composed by Chaophraya Phrakhlang (Hon), one of the great poets of the Bangkok First Reign, on grounds that there are similarities with lines in Hon's other works (KW, 166–69). Hon died in 1805. This first fragment covers only Khun Phaen's approach to the house, his entry, and description of the first tapestry. The account is mostly narrative storytelling, with limited dialogue. It may be close to a form transcribed from performers.

The second fragment continues the story further—up to Phaen and Wanthong's departure from the house and arrival in the forest. The part which is equivalent to the first fragment is over three times the length. A few scenes have been added but most of the extra length comes from greater detail—more inner thoughts, more dialogue, more description of the setting, more elaborate accounts of dress and ritual, more poetic metaphors.

The final version in chapters 17–18 of the PD edition is a little shorter than this second fragment because some sub-scenes have been cut. The language is more elevated, and the poetry more accomplished. In addition, the characterization of Phaen and Wanthong has changed. He is more violent, and she is more submissive.

Significantly, through these three versions the story does not change, but the telling changes dramatically.

This translation is based on Chotichuang et al., *Khun Chang Khun Phaen chabap yon tamnan*, 103–46. The text can also be found in *Khun Chang Khun Phaen chabap khwam kao*, and Atsiri et al., *Khun Chang Khun Phaen chabap nok thamniap*.

OLD VERSION I

A flock of egrets settled on a big *yang* tree. A *khla*[1] perched on a *khla* tree in the forest, and a woodpecker pecked in the undergrowth.

Pollen fell from the flowers of a *rang*. Masses of leaves blocked the light of the sun. Flowers bloomed on a *tabaek*, branches rustling in the breeze. Twigs of walkinglady[2] trembled in the wind.

"What a pity. Were you with me, I would not suffer, sleeping without love. I would bring you with me to enjoy the forest and hill, and to gather bunches of blooms—

pradu, lamduan, tasselfern. The fresh, fragrant scent wafting on the wind is like the scent of you. My breast is filled with sadness and longing.

There's waitinglady, smilinglady, *kalong, phayom*, and *phayong* with petals falling. There's milkwood, pupil tree, and gem jasmine in bloom, with masses of flowers scattered on the ground.

Seeing amora flowers suggests your love for me still lingers. Or have you tired of me totally now that you've gone to live with wild Khun Chang as a fair-weather friend? Have I gone from your thoughts and cares?

Oh, how to tell you the reason that I left the city to come through the forest, longing for you all the time." *[Manuscript damaged.]*

He used a Loosener on the locks of the gate, looked all around the house, and went to the cross hall. A crowd of slaves lay scattered around outside, sleeping and snoring oddly,

lowercloths and uppercloths tangled together, breasts exposed, and swathes of hair covering their faces. They looked pitiful. Arriving at a room, he caught sight of a woman

sleeping on a tiny bed. She had a slim waist, attractive slight frame, fair skin and breasts, hairline sharp and shapely,

face beautiful like a foreigner, and cheeks with the soft color of young *karaket*.[3] "Her face is very like my beloved Wanthong. Very strange. Who could she be?

Is she a relative of Khun Chang or kin on Wanthong's side? It's probably wrong to think her a wife of Khun Chang. She has the sheen of someone not

---

1. คล้า, unidentified.

2. นางกราย, *nang krai*, a plant that appears also in other Thai literary works, e.g., *Ramakian*, but is difficult to identify.

3. การะเกด, *Pandanus tectorius*. The petals and bracts of the young flowers have a curved shape and pale yellow color which are the basis of the simile with cheeks. A smaller pandanus with similar flowers, used for ground cover in gardens, is also called *karaket* or *karaket nu*.

yet touched by a man.

I must wake her to inquire and know everything." He ordered his spirits to release her, pronounced a mantra, and drew close to caress and enjoy her.

Kaeo Kiriya, sleeping . . . [Manuscript damaged.]

". . . I secretly admired you with feelings of love, and stole kisses and caresses—captivating.

You were sleeping soundly under a mantra, eye's jewel, and not conscious at all. I did wrong and I beg forgiveness. Please speak just a couple of words to me.

What is your connection to Khun Chang? Am I speaking with a wife who has had a water pouring,[4] or a lover under his patronage? Please tell me the truth without concealment."

Kaeo Kiriya listened to the question, thinking quietly to herself. "This is Khun Phaen for certain. He's come to seize Wanthong.

His lore is great. He boldly goes around every room. His business is with Wanthong so why did he sneak into the wrong room?

If I don't comply with his wish, he'll get angry and make a big fuss." This thought made her fearful so she said, "I'm not Wanthong.

It's a pity and it's laughable that you thought so. You got the wrong room and the wrong person, and so you flatter me by saying I'm like Wanthong. Don't sing my praises beyond reality.

Don't compare this bead to a gem. I know that I have little rank. I'm not gentlefolk, merely a slave of Wanthong.

I'm the daughter of the Sukhothai lord.[5] My father was pursued for twelve of fine money, and faced a penalty of imprisonment, so he mortgaged me here for a loan of fifteen tamlueng in cash. It's now half a year that I've not been ransomed. My name is Kaeo Kiriya and I've fallen on hard times. Now that you know, please leave without beating or killing."

"What a pity! Seeing your face, I feel sorry for you. Falling into difficulty for such a long time is bad, and all for only fifteen tamlueng. I can ransom you.

Some fate from a past life brought me to meet you in this room. Let me entrust my love to you here. I'll protect you against taint, my eye's jewel."

---

4. Pouring water is part of a formal marriage ceremony.

5. Meaning the governor of Sukhothai. The place is here spelled Sokothai, โศกโขไทย, turning the first syllable into a word for sorrow, perhaps as a play on words,

With these words he moved closer. "Don't be alarmed. Be merciful to me." He stroked her back to impart his love, filling her with turmoil and uncertainty.

Kaeo Kiriya glared at him, and pushed him away. "Don't assume you'll be my lover. You say you love me greatly but it's unreasonable. Using tricks to seduce is wrong.

You're a freeman. Should you consort with a slave who's not clean, not equal in rank? If you want to take revenge, that's up to you. Do it in the manner of gentleman against gentleman.

What do you want with me? You came here with business to settle. Why do you want to get involved with me?"

Khun Phaen said, "What a pity. I love Wanthong. That's the main thing. For better or worse, you know that fully. The accursed Khun Chang made me come for revenge.

Because of past merit I met Kaeo Kiriya, and I love you greatly, eye's jewel. I'm happier than if I were in heaven. Utmost love, I cannot delay a single day."

He embraced her, caressed her breast, lifted her onto his lap, and kissed her. "You're like heavenly cooling medicine for the heat that inflames my heart."

Kaeo Kiriya pushed and pulled. "Hey, what's this? Stop all that. I don't believe you. You choose pretty words, pleasant to the ear. Once you've had me you'll rush away.

While you float off and disappear, Kaeo Kiriya will be left waiting here, looking with unblinking eyes but seeing nothing. Friends will whisper and gossip together,

saying, it's her karma now and what's more, she's been fouled. She got what she deserved for softheartedly believing fine words. I'll bring shame to my father, and my master will scold me hurtfully."

Khun Phaen said, "You're good with words—so sweet, heavenly, incomparable, that they make my heart skip and become captivated by love. Any man who heard them would fall for you."

He took out fifteen in cash and proffered it to her. "Please settle this one matter. I'm not deceiving you. Don't worry about that." He removed the devices of lore from his body,

and hung them on the wall, then took her in his arms, and encircled her with mounting love. Though she pinched, scratched, and pushed, he would not let go, but pressed his body close to her.

A gentle breeze blew, wafting the scent of flowers through the window, fluttering the end of her sabai. A bright shining moon slipped in and out of the clouds, tinting them with gold, leaving the brilliant stars to replace the moonlight. Constellations peeked through the clouds. A breeze blew coolly as a sign.

He inhaled the scent of her cheeks mixed with the scent of flowers, hugging, kissing, and stroking intimately. The taste of love raced throughout their bodies. Both were in bliss.

Khun Phaen stood up and looked at the cross hall which Khun Chang had newly built. All around a sitting hall, screens were placed with Japanese-style clear glass in the center.[6]

In the glass was a picture of a Farang in profile. A cage of parrots hung by a window. "The eyes of the Farang look like the eyes of a woman glancing sideways in displeasure—so lifelike.

Someone was clever to draw that!" He walked around the picture, looking and touching. Opening a window to the soft breeze, he saw a crowd of sleeping women.

He used a Loosener to open the bolts and entered an apartment. Flickering lanterns lit the way. The sight of an embroidered curtain startled him.

"This curtain is Wanthong's handiwork. I recognize it." She had embroidered the Himawalai range, with the great mountain of Kailash like pure silver.

A flock of *kinnari* floated high in the sky, admiring the great mountains. Trees were hung with sprays and strings of flowers. Buds bloomed in bunches, with petals falling.

Gibbons gamboled among the trees. Monkeys swung from branches, looking for their young. Wind wafted, and langurs scattered leaves, so lifelike.

She had depicted maidenfruit trees with maidens of fair face that the masterminds came to admire every morning and evening.[7] Their skin and breasts were as attractive as if real.

Flocks of beautiful golden peacocks spread their

dragon-unicorn

---

6. Chotchuang Nadon found a collection of Japanese-style paintings on glass in the preaching hall of Wat Pratusan in Suphanburi (Atsiri et al., *KCKP* , 70).

7. นารีผล, *nariphon*, a mythical tree in the Himaphan Forest with young women as fruit. "Beyond this is a forest of trees that have women as their fruit; the fruits of these trees are very beautiful—they are like maidens who have just reached sixteen years of age. When men see them, they fall in love with them, and when they drop, the birds flock around to eat them like bears eating honey" (RR, 291–92).

wings and danced. Dragon-unicorns[8] played in the water with *norasing*. The whole scene looked beautiful and real. The more he stared, the more he was enthralled. "If I spend too long admiring this, I'll be late." Missing Wanthong badly, he quickly walked through, cutting the string of her curtain to fall in a heap.

He came to a second curtain. "This is Wanthong's handiwork too. Oh my love, you know how to depict Lord Garuda. It's so attractive."

Greatly in love with Kaki, Lord Garuda was spreading his arms to embrace her as they passed over the trees to the summit of Chimphli and entered his palace.[9]

She had depicted the Sithandon Ocean, with throngs of mermaids, snakes, and dragons floating on the surface in pairs, crocodiles, fish with human faces,

troops of nagas, sharks leaping one after another, water elephants rearing up in clouds of spray, and *orahan* flapping the water with their wings.

[The manuscript ends at this point.]

OLD VERSION II

Khun Phaen, great romancer, unmatched in mastery, was mournful and miserable at being apart from Laothong.

At times for sleeping, he would lie restlessly, sighing randily for her. "Oh, what must I do to have her sleep close by my side!" His breast was filled with loneliness and longing.

He slept alone and lonely in the room, his eyes flooded with tears from thinking of her. "Oh my love, you must be heavy-hearted. When will you ever be happy!

Now my jewel will be sorrowing, lying still on your pillow. Were you here, I could enjoy you happily. What a pity I've neglected you.

What a pity that Khun Chang was so mean-spirited and black with rage." Khun Phaen became so unsettled, upset, and maddened that he burst out to the terrace,

and gazed at the moon to lift his spirits, letting the breeze soothe his longing for his perfect love. A crescent moon lit the world. Stars sparkled, speckling the sky.

---

8. กิเลน, *kilen*, an animal from Chinese legend with a deer's body, a dragon's head, and a single horn.

9. On the Kaki story, see p. 350, note 49.

Looking at the moon, he missed the rabbit. "In the waning of the moon, the stars emerge, like Khun Chang envious of my lady love. And falling stars fall away like us, torn apart."

Thinking of the dispute made him angry, frustrated, vengeful. "You fixed me, and thought I'd let it pass, but I'm coming after you to do away with you to my satisfaction.

Wanthong was as dear to me as my own eyes. But when you wanted her, I consented. I had Laothong but due to your interference she was kept in the palace.

Right. That's how it is, Khun Chang." Thinking of the wrongs in the past made him realize that he should not hate Wanthong in anger and confusion. His love returned.

"Oh my Wanthong, you shouldn't have fallen into the mud, become so angry and jealous that we got into a fight and broke it off.

I tried to stop you but you were carried away by your own abuse and eloquence." Thinking of the day of their parting filled him with regret that the quarrel had left him high and dry.

"It was sweet that you knew how to minister to me. When our love was still young and fresh, you were so loving and intimate. You took the trouble to sit and massage me so nicely and regularly.

After we wed, everything was fine. You were perfection in a woman. Your heart loved me so truly. You wavered only because your mother had a change of heart.

Also, that old bushy-headed fellow with the hairy chest thought he could trample on me because I was poor. He dared to do that, and now that's his karma. But as I'm fearful of the king, guardian of the city,

I'll only take Wanthong away, and make a scandal talked about everywhere. If he follows me, once we're far from the city, I'll come back from the forest and slash him!"

Thoughts of revenge made his longing for Laothong recede. He pondered until sunrise, and then promptly summoned his retainers, slaves, and freemen to assemble.

He ordered them to enter the service of Muen Si Saowarat and Muen Wai Woranat.[10] "As for me, I say farewell. Please look after my mother."

After giving these orders, he went to his mother's apartment, raised his two hands above his head, prostrated at her feet, and informed her.

"That bald Khun Chang and I must fight to the death. I've come now to take my leave. Everything is already prepared.

---

10. Two of the four heads of the royal pages.

Mother, please take the servants away from this house. If you stay here there'll be trouble because of me. I can tolerate it no longer and must fight back, even to death. Please give me your blessing for success."

Thong Prasi opposed him. "Oh my topmost love, don't be careless. After Wanthong went off with Khun Chang,
why do you want anything to do with her? She's two-minded already. We can't keep her. Never chase after a two-minded person or a Khaek. Being two-minded is bad.
Just like a fine yak that will fight to the death to avoid losing its hair, a truly beautiful woman will not let other men enjoy her love.[11] This simile captures the essence of woman.
You come from a lineage of lions but she's from a lineage of the gutter. Run away from her. The Lord of the World has favored and supported you this far. You have a reputation among the people of the capital."

Khun Phaen, great romancer, pondered over his mother's advice, then corrected her, saying, "In truth, Wanthong is not two-minded. All her wrongdoing was due to her mother.
That crone, Siprajan, encouraged Khun Chang to close in. That's why he grew bold enough to seize her. Wanthong kicked him off the bed,
but that hag rushed in to beat and scold her daughter for maltreating her husband so much his head split. Wanthong found a knife but her old mother blocked it.
I know of this because of Saithong's letter, which told the whole story without omission. Even so I was not convinced. But now I'll have revenge on that crooked fellow.
He parted me from Laothong. I'll repay him in the same coin. I've been banned from the king's audience because this trickster thought up a story.
I feel greatly hurt, Mother. I beg you not to oppose me. I don't shrink from battle. If Khun Chang comes after me, I'm not afraid.
I have a superb mercury and diamond charm so I need not fear that anyone will do violence to me. If a thousand of his type come, I won't take fright but see each of them off with a single blow.
This Khun Chang is a shameful mole, Mother. He won't dare follow me. He'll just lie hugging a pillow, weeping, wailing, and beating his chest until death."

---

11. The exceptionally fine hair of yak is used for royal regalia. This saying reflects a belief that the yak will do anything to prevent loss of such beautiful hair; if the hair gets caught on a branch, the yak will not try to pull itself free for fear of losing some strands.

Knowing her son would leave, Thong Prasi felt desolate. She wept, splutter-
ing betel juice, but gave him a blessing through her tears,

barely able to speak from sobbing. "Do as you wish." She braced herself,
wiped away tears, and cursed, "May Khun Chang lose to your mastery.

I give you my blessing with a full heart, truly. Be successful in whatever
you plan. Overcome all your enemies. May a mother's blessing work for her
beloved son."

Khun Phaen received the blessing, bowed down, lifted his mother's foot
onto his head, and circled her to the right in respect. Then he went to a shrine
of the four-armed lord,[12]

lit candles as offering, placed flowers, spread a fine piece of lion's pelt, and
called upon the gods.

Wearing white lower and upper cloths, he stilled his mind, and pronounced
the full 108 verses with knowledge. The image was activated.

He blew a conch in worship of the lineage of Lord Narai, and bathed the
image with rosewater from a bronze bowl. He mixed powder from a yantra with
some of the bathing water, and made an auspicious mark on his forehead.

After washing his face, he prostrated, prayed, and asked for mighty pow-
ers. Then he ordered his servants to harness a horse. At an auspicious time,
he quickly got dressed

in a lowercloth with a glittering clashing-circles pattern, a belt designed
to match, an inner shirt coated with herbs and inscribed with yantra, and an
outer uppercloth in golden *attalat*.

He tied a foreign sash around his waist, and inserted a kris like a Javanese,
one of fearful power. He put on a filigree breast chain embroidered in gold,
gilded beads, and a *tumpi* cap instilled by a teacher.

He made offerings of food in the usual way, and carefully arranged a sacred
thread, incense, candles, umbrella, flag, and a roof of woolen cloth.

He put on several beautifully shining rings to look magnificent and powerful,
tied round his head a bandeau instilled with his usual charm, a Phakhawam,
and a sacred thread.

He bent down to grasp Skystorm and stood pronouncing mantra, waiting
for an auspicious moment. When it came, he walked off, mounted his horse,
and blew a formula to summon his spirits.

It was neither a day of the Obstructive Sun or of Yama's Portion,[13] but a slant-

---

12. Meaning Vishnu (Narai).
13. See p. 584, note 9, where almost exactly the same line appears.

ing conjunction of circles when the sun inclined down,[14] and the Iron Spear and the Great Spirit had passed beyond the evil time.[15] He ordered his spirits to shield him front and rear,

and used a knife to slice herbs and rub on his lips. He left the house and went straight into the forest, stilled his mind, and pronounced a prayer. Cutting through the forest to Nong Taphan stream,

he reached the Crocodile Pond at dusk. He let his horse graze and drink water. Before long he reached Ban Phlap, close to Khun Chang's house, and went straight there.

He cut wood and made a shrine with a roof, struck a flint to light incense and candles, and placed various offerings that he had brought with him.

He made a circle of sacred thread and a *khlon* gate,[16] hung yantra in all eight directions, brought cloth already instilled, and pronounced mantras.

Gods were aroused and gathered around, darkening the sky with rain. He invited the gods from every site. "Lords Itsaret[17] and Narai,

Indra, gods of the moon,[18] sun, and wind,[19] Wetsukam, Warunachai, Ramasun, Orachun, allow me to bow and wai you in invitation.

And all sixteen heavenly chambers of the sky, the trees and sacred mountains, streams, lakes, canals, peaks, ravines, spirits of the wild, guardian spirits of the city,

grandfather spirits of the hills and forests of red reeds, Jettakup[20] of famous mastery, the Lord of Darkness, and guardian spirits of the city pillar, please come to receive these offerings."

Then he composed himself for prayer. "Please be divine witness that Khun Chang has not acted justly. Though we were friends, he has done me wrong.

---

14. This and the previous clause refer to the "circles" method of divination, and indicate the day is on one of the slanting loops in the diagrams for this method of divination. These days are generally favorable (Wales, *Divination*, 128–29; see p. 319, note 23).

15. See p. 100, note 21.

16. See p. 1033, note 22.

17. A colloquial version of Isuan, Siva.

18. ศศิธร, *sasithon*, "the keeper of the rabbit," the moon.

19. พระพ(ร)าย, *phra ph(r)ai*. This list is clearly the guardians of the eight directions including Indra, sun, moon, waters (Warunachai), and wind (see p. 41, note 63). But the other three seem to have been imported from the *Ramakian*. Ramasun comes from the Mekhala myth (see p. 823, note 33), which appears in chapter 10 in the Rama I edition. Wetsukam is Visvakarman, Indra's craftsman, who is prominent throughout the story. Orachun is a deity who is the first to do battle with the villain, Thotsakan, after Thotsakan plunders his orchard (ch. 6 of the Rama I edition).

20. For all these guardians of the city, see p. 654, note 4, and p. 655, notes 10, 11, and 12.

He took away my wife to enjoy, but on that matter I controlled my anger. I had a new wife by my side but he villainously had her separated from me.

He concocted a story that made the king angrily bar me from audience. On top of that, he had my wife taken to be an embroiderer in the palace.

Today I've come to repay him, to take revenge on Khun Chang. If I do not speak the truth, please kill me—don't spare my life.

But if Khun Chang has truly done wrong, let me succeed in my intention. Gods and spirits, do not side with either of us. Whichever one was in the wrong, let it be revealed."

The gods, guardians, fierce spirits, sprites, spectrals, and demons that had come to take the offerings
conferred together and agreed that Khun Chang was evil and black-hearted for wronging and injuring a friend, and taking his wife to love.

"He's rich but never gives one little bit of money to reward us." "He's only good at drinking himself drunk and rowdy." "Never a tiny thing has reached us,
though we've given him no small amount of protection." "This time we'll let matters take their course, as befitting such a stingy blackguard." "He'll reach for her in vain, and not know why!"

Khun Phaen, great conjuror, as masterful as the bright shining sun, activated powers through lore, creating a commotion all around.

He looked at the clouds for an omen,[21] saw a body with a radiant complexion, white like the moon, and was pleased by the sign.

He took Skystorm between his palms in salute, and mounted his horse. Goldchild led the way. They soon reached a dyke at the boundary of the house. Khun Phaen stilled his mind and intoned a mantra
to put the guards on the gate to sleep. They curled up, mumbling and grumbling. Phan In Phatthaya burbled while sucking on a hookah and holding a flint.

Five lady spirits of Khun Chang on watch slid out to check on the threat and saw a man coming on a horse.

They said to one another, "That's Khun Phaen for sure." They happily weaved and danced over, concentrating their minds to disguise themselves with strange and fearful faces.

Tall and black, they stood blocking the horse. One went up into a jambolan

---

21. See p. 621, note 15.

tree and dangled her head down. Another threw her head in the air and ran along the top of a wall, crying, "Catch him, the man with lore!"

Another shot her head up taller than the treetops, and spread out her hair, making enough racket to collapse the earth, opening her mouth and emitting a wind like the era-destroying fire.

Khun Phaen, great valiant, of such fine skills, watched the lady spirits menacing him, blocking his way, and racing around wildly.

He unwrapped a packet of fragrant rice dyed with herbs, pronounced a powerful mantra, and threw the rice at Khun Chang's spirits, hitting them like deathly lightning.

None of Khun Chang's five lady spirits could stand it. They fell over, hid themselves, and scrambled up trees to hide, breaking the branches.

Realizing he was a young man with a fine, lovable face and powerful weapons of lore, they transformed their bodies into ladies of the palace, sneaked up on him, and coughed.

Staying hidden, they asked sweetly, "Where are you going at this time of night? Excuse me, sir, what's your name? Why did you come to make such a commotion here?

You seem unafraid of the guards on patrol. I feel very nervous on your behalf. Don't complain that I'm interfering. It's because of love that I want to warn you off."

Khun Phaen knew this was an illusion. "This is no small trick." Smiling he asked, "But if a palace lady like you is not afraid, why should a man such as I be?

Let me ask you—and please don't doubt me—which department do you five ladies come from? If the king would grant permission, I wouldn't miss a golden salver at all."[22]

"It's no small matter to lure a woman with such a ploy. So skillful, so smart. Anyone taken in by it would float on the wind, tricked into lovemaking.

Am I suitable to be a royal servant? Don't so overdo the smart talk that I get puffed up with myself. I wouldn't like being a palace lady. I fear my back would be thrashed, and I prefer having fun outside a palace.

Though I have to be a servant of Khun Chang, it's like being on my own. If I

---

22. Meaning he would go to present a golden salver to the king, a requirement when asking for the hand of a palace lady.

consent to your wish, I fear there'll be trouble—like making karma for myself, and I don't need it.

I'd like to know what is your desire. That's why I stopped you at the gate of the house. If Khun Chang sees you, it won't be good. Please go away quickly."

"I thank you for talking with me. As you don't know what I intend to do, I'll tell you from the beginning. Khun Chang and I were once friends.

Now he's taken my wife Wanthong away to enjoy, dishonestly breaking an oath, and today I intend to repay him.

So please allow me to enter. Don't cause obstruction and don't rise up against me. What do you fear from that villain? I'm being held up by you five ladies.

Your loyalty to your master is creating difficulties for me. I think he's using you improperly. To make ladies such as you stay awake and walk around guarding the way is not fitting.

I'm at a loss because you're on his side. If you come over to me, I'll look after you. I'll let you sit powdering your faces, making yourselves pretty, and chatting away merrily.

I'll make sure there's powder and oil to make you beautiful, and I'll provide hair quills, ivory tips, tweezers, a looking glass for doing your hairlines, and krajae and sandal oil to please you."

The lady spirits listened to him. "So sharp and incisive!" They sat wai-ing him, and glancing from the corner of an eye. "Your words are beyond belief.

I and the other four are with Khun Chang. We fear it would be wrong to run off with you. We thank you for your kind offer to take us away for intimacy,

but Khun Chang has supported us, and we shouldn't turn against him. It would be ungrateful on our part to flout Khun Chang who feeds us.

On the right or wrong of what Khun Chang has done, we don't know what to say. We won't make karma for ourselves by lodging accusations against our patron."

Khun Phaen saw things would be slow so he took out rice and threw it mercilessly. "You'll get hurt. Please move far off and stop blocking the way."

The proficient Khun Phaen used a Loosener to draw the bolts, open the gates, and kick open the doors at all three barriers. He ordered his spirits to enter.

"Go around everywhere, make sure people are sleeping, count how many there are, and then come back."

Goldchild and the spirits took the order and promptly raced one another inside. In an instant they reached Sonphraya's large house by the central gate.

Sonphraya was lying with his head reversed towards the tail of the bed, using his wife's bottom as a pillow, fast asleep, snoring. He and Khun Chang were a real pair.

Goldchild and the spirits crept around. They found guards by the doors, and gave their heads a shake. There were other groups of guards at each of the three barriers. They counted the people, ran back,

wai-ed Khun Phaen, and reported. "There are many servants and guards on watch. At each of the three barriers, there are fifteen sitting by lamps.

There's a solid wall around the compound, and many people at readiness surrounding the main house. Some are enjoying a game of chess. There are patrols to make sure they don't sleep."

Khun Phaen, great conjuror, was clearheaded. He whispered orders. "Go back in, draw the bolts, and put everyone to sleep,

all of Khun Chang's people without a single exception, everywhere and everybody, both upstairs and down. Don't let even dogs open their eyes."

Goldchild and the lady spirits paid respect, ran off as if blown by the wind, and carried out the orders.

All the servants, men and women, dozed off, some bent over double, others on all fours. One dreamed that robbers were getting in, grabbed a stick to stop them, and hit his wife by mistake.

Asleep facedown with her bottom in the air, she fumbled in her skirt, and murmured, "I've found a monitor lizard's hole." A child with a pigtail from a Jek's shop walked round the house in his sleep, crying out for his father.

Another started to dream he was setting a fish trap,[23] wading through foul water and getting dirty. In every house people dozed, befuddled with strange dreams because of the spirits.

Khun Phaen, great valiant, had angrily ordered Goldchild and the spirits to put everyone to sleep.

Khun Chang's house was now dead quiet. People slept in rows, not raising their heads. Khun Phaen mounted his horse and approached to inspect Khun Chang's compound.

On the outer rim was Sonphraya's house, a spacious and good-looking accommodation. Everyone was lying, snoring and dreaming. The thought came to his mind,

---

23. กร่ำ, *kram*, a circle of stakes enclosing smaller sticks which form a habitat that attracts fish.

"At dawn tomorrow, Khun Chang will lie hugging his pillows, moaning and groaning with tears flowing. He's had his pleasure with Wanthong. Today we'll meet face to face."

He rode around to see everything. Nobody challenged him. All were in their dreams. He came to the large house of Khun Chang, and turned to look towards the bedroom.

He put a yantra on Color of Mist to hide him from human eyes, blew a mantra, stroked the horse's back, and instructed him to hide in a corner, stay awake, stay hidden, and stay alert.

He ordered his spirits to sit on Khun Chang and little Wanthong until he woke them up, and then get off their bodies. "Don't let them or their servants raise their heads."

He lit a Subduer candle and affixed it to a post. The guardian spirits of the house could not stay. Khun Phaen dominated them, and drove them away by flinging herbed rice

across the roof three times. People who had woken up fell back to sleeping, snoring, and mumbling. He enchanted limes and threw them

across the roof three times. Khun Chang slumbered, snoring helplessly and hugging Wanthong in her sleep. The lady spirits all remained vigilant.

They helped to roll up a mortar for Khun Phaen to place his foot, and climb up a flower frame to the window. He stopped to admire Khun Chang's shrubbery. Glazed flowerpots were arranged on three levels.

There was orange, lightleaf, damascene, and gem jasmine with lingering scents; fragrant pupil flower; myrobalan pruned to have eleven levels of foliage; tamarind festooned with fine seedpods;

pine, lion's tail, ebony, pecking plum, and paperwood with ripe and ripening fruits; tasselfern with beautiful clusters of blossom; *prayong* with blooms among sprouting leaves;

lamduan smothered with delicate flowers; sprays of waitinglady, *saraphi*, and *phayom* with alluring fragrance; scented rose interspersed with *jampa*;

and Chinese ivorybell with masses of flowers spreading a cool fragrance. He stopped to enjoy the plants, but saw it would take time, and turned to admire the ornamental ponds with goldfish,

gliding through the water, dipping down and breaking the surface in the moonlight. Looking smoothly rounded like drums, the goldfish dived and rose heavily.

Some were all knobbly and bobbly, and swam languidly in pairs, looking funny. Many others bristled with spiny fins. From there he walked straight to the central hall,

used a Loosener to open the doors, and looked in every room, before coming to a cross apartment. Swarms of slaves were sleeping outside the central hall, some lying in strange poses,

lowercloths and uppercoths tangled together, breasts exposed and hair falling over their shoulders, looking pitiful. Walking further, he noted an unusual room.

Khun Phaen veered away to look. He saw little curtains hanging at the main door, and folding screens to block the way. Lotus-petal lanterns flickered.

He boldly pulled back the curtains and examined the fine decoration of the room: a bowl placed on a salver with a dipper floating on the water;

a pair of nak chests with a spittoon beside; a horse-stool with tweezers, hair quills, and other articles; a large clear mirror and looking glass; a little salver with a gold-capped powder set;

dipper

a pile of handkerchiefs; and a chest for cloth, placed to one side so as not to clutter the restricted space. Side pillows were lined up on a bed. He opened the mosquito net, saw a woman, and sat down to admire her.

"You're sleeping on a bed that's tiny like your slight frame. Face attractive. Eyebrows beautiful. Complexion and breasts fair. Hairline plucked sharp and shapely.

Features similar to a foreign face. Cheeks as fair as *karaket*.[24] Mouth breaking into a smile or speech. Neck like a *kinnari* gliding to land.

Fingers, hands, and arms as neatly drawn as a fine portrait. Slender waist as if sketched to please the eye. Bosom sweetly spread open.

A patterned lowercloth, and a little uppercloth in cream. She looks like an angel floating through the heavens. Though fast asleep, she seems composed. Very strange. Who could she be?

Is she a relative of Khun Chang, or kin on Wanthong's side? It's probably wrong to think her a wife of Khun Chang. She has the sheen of someone not yet touched by a man.

I must wake her to inquire and know everything." He ordered his spirits to release her, pronounced a mantra, and drew close to caress her.

Kaeo Kiriya awoke from deep sleep to find a man secretly admiring her. She wanted to cry out but was held by the mantra.

She got down from the bed, watching him from the corner of her eye. "Eh?

24. See p. 1125, note 3.

Where did this man come from? His body is slender but his mind is bold. I must ask to know."

She hid behind a curtain and said, "Who are you to dare this? You don't look like a villain. What made you think of coming in here?"

Her words made Khun Phaen's heart skip a beat. He replied in a roundabout way. "I'm not some rough villain. I came after Wanthong.

Khun Chang took her away to love, and I don't know where her room is. By my merit, I've met you. I thought you were Wanthong, my beloved wife.

You're just like her, down to the eyes and brows, and the refined manner in sleep. By mistake I sat down to admire your face and was so excited I kissed and caressed you.

You were fast asleep because of a mantra and were not conscious at all, eye's jewel. Don't take offense. Please forgive me, and explain in a couple of words

what relation you have to Khun Chang. Don't hide matters from me. And let me ask a couple of words about Wanthong. Please tell me the truth without concealment."

Kaeo Kiriya started in fear, then stilled her mind to think. "This is Khun Phaen for certain. He's come to seize Mistress Wanthong.

His lore is great. He dared to come into this room." She felt her hair bristle and her head swell. "I think we'll lose Wanthong for sure.

If I don't comply with his wish, he'll turn angry and make a big fuss. Think quickly in fear of the consequences. He came here because he's hurt over Wanthong."

With this thought, she replied, "It's laughable. You come to the wrong person and the wrong room too. It's not funny to say that I'm like Wanthong. Don't sing my praises beyond reality,

don't compare this bead to a gem when you know it's just colored glass. I'm not gentlefolk. I'm merely a slave of mistress Wanthong.

My father is Phraya Sukhothai. He got into difficulties over repaying money and faced a penalty of imprisonment, so he mortgaged me here

for cash of fifteen tamlueng. That was a year ago and he's still sent none. My name is Kaeo Kiriya and I've fallen on hard times. Now that I've told you, please leave nicely.

As a freeman you shouldn't consort with a slave. If you're not careful, you'll harm your reputation. Go and take your revenge today in the way that gentlefolk do among themselves."

"Your words are so lovable I want to caress and kiss your face to console you. You're modest and composed in every respect. Your way with words is appealing,

befitting the daughter of Sukhothai. I pity you for having no partner. Any man who made love with you would remember you with longing forever after.

Your difficulty is not so great. Out of love, I'll ransom you. Don't tell me that the difficulty is only fifteen tamlueng. Were it five chang, I'd ransom you."

He took out money to give her, and turned to kiss and caress her. "Please show me Wanthong's room. I won't forget your kindness until my dying day."

Hearing these words, Kaeo Kiriya sank down on the bed and turned her face aside. She pushed his hands away out of shame. "Why are you rough with me?

For ransoming me out of difficulty, you'll gain merit. Now that you've done me right, you want to do me wrong. I'm not a worthy partner. Don't bother me. My father commanded me to preserve myself.

However great the difficulties I might face, I should not consort with a lover or take a husband. I should not seek just bodily pleasure. If I take a lover or steal someone's husband, he won't support me.

Please inform my father and mother first and get their blessing. I took my father's instructions and I won't give in to you, so please don't talk any further.

What do you see in Kaeo Kiriya? She's a just an unfortunate, destitute person. Since you already have a love partner, you shouldn't force yourself on me.

Once you've had me, you'll cast me away, not caring which direction the wind blows me. On my part, I'll be hurt. It'll be like hoisting a sail and floating away lost on the breeze.

Once you've had a taste, you'll toss me away. A lotus wilts away from the stream. Bees take the pollen, and the bloom is battered and bruised.

My breast will be consumed with sorrow, as mournful as a gem that's lost its hue. I shouldn't get myself hurt but this will. I shouldn't invite shame but this will.

Friends will hurt me with their criticisms and insinuations. My lord and benefactor will pick at me critically. I'll join the ranks of the shamed forever.

If my mother and father know, they'll be furious, and cane me like they'd thrash a slave. You'll have the joy of entering a perfect heaven.

While Kaeo Kiriya waits expectantly, you'll float away and disappear. People who know will whisper among themselves, nodding as they censure me, even to my face, saying, she's his already, she fouled the cloth. How could I turn my face to argue back when that's the deserts for a softheaded fool? I'll have to hide behind a thick skin forever."

Khun Phaen replied, "How sweet, my utmost love. Your father gave you such instructions because he follows the ancient customs.

I won't deceive you into breaking your promise. I'll follow what you say, because I love you and feel sorry for you. I came to take revenge on Khun Chang,

and have already put the whole household to sleep. Please have some mercy for me, dear Kaeo Kiriya. I've lain close to your breast already. It's too late to try ending this between us.

Please let me entrust my love within you. Afterwards, I'll repay your kindness by going to wai your parents. Don't doubt me, Kaeo Kiriya.

If I deceive you into breaking your word, may my knowledge fail in every respect. I'll do as you ordered. Please accept my love."

He took off his devices and hung them on the wall, then lifted Kaeo Kiriya onto his lap, caressed and kissed her face, and would not listen however much she pushed him away.

A soft wind wafted the clean fresh fragrance of flowers, and fluttered the end of her sabai. A bright shining moon

slipped behind the clouds, tinting them with gold, leaving the brilliant stars to replace the moonlight. Constellations peeked through clouds. The breeze blew cooler as a sign.

In her breast, Kaeo Kiriya felt anxious and fearful of her master, Khun Chang. She clung close to Khun Phaen, feeling miserable.

"You force yourself on me like this, and now you'll abduct Wanthong away from the main apartment. You leave happily but I'll have only hardship.

Khun Chang will be furious and will curse his servants endlessly. He'll take his anger out on me without reason." She peered up at him with love and hurt.

Khun Phaen replied, "Oh eye's jewel, haven't your doubts disappeared yet? I won't deceive you. I'll come back later to collect you.

But now I'm going to repay that villain. I'm not intending to make love with Wanthong. I'll take my revenge on her too. Wait a bit and you'll understand.

Were the gods to fly down to forbid me, I wouldn't give you up. Don't rush to have doubt and suspicion." With these words, he embraced, kissed, and caressed her again.

"Hey! You're just using my cheeks like a war slave. You're so happy but I'm bruised black as a boil. Please have some mercy. Don't go too far. You're not letting poor me open my mouth."

Khun Phaen said, "Oh my eye's jewel, you protest too much. I love you greatly. Don't resist and make me angry. No matter how you object, I won't listen."

With these words, he hugged her tightly to him, with arms encircling her like a naga, breast to her breast, hand caressing her feverishly.

Passion stirred turmoil in their hearts as the pair clung together in ecstasy, wrapped around each other, experiencing the joy of their first lovemaking.

A breeze gently wafted pollen as if inviting them to love. Bees circled among flowers, caressing the blooms,

releasing their aroma to mingle with the scent of her cheeks, cloaking the pair in the fragrance of petals and pollen. He embraced her closely, feeling a warmth that urged them to lose themselves in love.

The first taste had left Kaeo Kiriya enraptured. She clung tightly to him, each wrapped around the other, both blooming with love.

But it was approaching dawn, and any further lovemaking would cause delay. Ruefully she had to suppress her love. She hugged, kissed, caressed, and then spoke,

opposing what he had come intending to achieve. "Give up your plan. Be cautious. Just thinking about it makes my whole body fearful.

If you get caught, you'll die, and I'll wish to die along with you. I'll be too sad to continue living." She clung to her husband in grief.

From his little finger Khun Phaen took a ring with a small cluster of diamonds, and passed it to her. "You can depend on a price of ten tamlueng. Keep it as a memento until I return."

He put back on the gear he had removed earlier, and got out another fifteen tamlueng to give her. "Keep this to support yourself until I return." He kissed her and moved off.

Kaeo Kiriya was grief-stricken. She sat pensively looking after him with tears streaming, feeling as if someone had plucked out her heart. She ran to pull her husband back out of love.

"Why are you abandoning me? Use your sword to cut off my head so I can be rid of this love." She sobbed and beat her breast wildly.

Khun Phaen, great romancer, quietly watched her while comforting her. "I'm not going away and abandoning you. Don't be sad, and please stay your hand."

"If you don't love me and abandon me, I'm ruined. You won't listen to me and keep pushing and pulling. Let lightning strike! I'll cry to my heart's content."

"But the karma's made, Kaeo Kiriya. It's a pity you're making an issue of it. I'm not deceiving you. I told you the truth from the start."

Kaeo Kiriya heard these words like sword blows on her head. She did not know what to reply as he had indeed explained his business from the beginning.

She bowed down and prostrated at his feet, feeling lonely and miserable. "To stop him would be wrong given the hardship he faces."

Khun Phaen led her back to the room and comforted her. "Don't cry. Don't worry that I'll abandon my beloved. Before long, I'll return."

With that, he left the room, turning back to look at her sitting with face bowed. He felt sorry for her without parallel but then his vengeful anger revived, hardening his heart.

He drew Skystorm and went out to the central hall that Khun Chang had newly built. In a sitting area were placed folding screens with Japanese-style clear glass in the center.

In the glass was a picture of a Farang in profile. A cage of parrots hung by a window. "The eyes of the Farang look like the eyes of a woman glancing sideways in displeasure—so lifelike.

Someone was clever to draw that!" He walked around the picture, looking and touching. Opening a window to a soft breeze, he saw a crowd of sleeping women.

He used a Loosener to open the bolts and entered the main apartment. Flickering lanterns lit the way. Curtains hung to both left and right. The design on one startled him.

"This curtain is Wanthong's handiwork. I recognize it." She had embroidered a picture of Mount Meru of great and imposing height,

with images of Ramasun, the Asuri, pursuing Mekhala,[25] the sun god coming to illuminate the earth and sea,

riding in a brilliant and magnificent chariot drawn by lions, and the goddess of the moon rising to light the world,

riding in a celestial chariot drawn by the Phalahok horse, with a floating pavilion[26] emitting light. Next, she had depicted Lord Indra moving through the universe, riding joyfully on the Erawan elephant

---

25. See p. 823, note 33.

26. บุษบก, *butsabok*, a decorative pavilion for a Buddha image or a king during a ceremony, often depicted in illustrations such as wat murals.

with his four queens as beautiful as perfection. There were the ranges of Winatok, Atsakan, Isinthon, Yukhunthon,[27] and magnificent Mount Kailash; Uma[28] with Lord Mahison; the grand Anodat Lake;[29] the four-armed lord riding the Ananta naga,[30]

with his queens, Lady Laksanawadi and Lakshmi, on left and right;[31] the *khonthan*, and divine *kinnon*, and beyond them the palace of Garuda;

along with masterminds, a large beautiful tree bearing maidenfruit in the form of humans,[32] the Sithandon Ocean,

groups of fish and naga playing in the water, and many water-elephants diving and jumping. After admiring the curtain, he felt a yearning. He cut the string so the curtain fell,

floating pavilion

and quickly walked straight ahead, thinking of her, sadly finding that his love had not died, intent on murderous revenge.

He came to a curtain at the second level. "This is also superbly embroidered . . ."

[The manuscript is defective at this point. The story resumes where Khun Phaen turns away from the last curtain.]

While looking, he thought of Wanthong, and his anger rose. "You should not have tired of my love." Fearing it was getting late, he made for the head of the bed,

and saw Khun Chang hugging Wanthong in her sleep. He drew his sword. "I'll cut him into about ten pieces!" His trembling spirit, Goldchild, stopped him. "Don't. Don't slash in anger."

khonthan *musicians*

27. Four of the seven mountain ranges around Mount Meru.

28. The wife of Siva, here called มหิศร, *mahison*, the great one, a contraction of Mahesuan.

29. See p. 343, note 30.

30. พระสิกร, *phra sikon*, Vishnu (Narai), on อนันตนาคา, *anantanakha*, Ananta, meaning eternity, the serpent on which Vishnu sleeps (*Hindu Myths*, esp. 221).

31. ลักษณวดี, *laksanawadi,* is probably originally a Thai-ification of Lakshmi, the goddess of fortune, wife of Vishnu. It became the name of a separate wife of Vishnu in the Thai tradition.

32. See p. 1128, note 7.

The spirit's restraint made his mood still blacker. "I'll slash him into shreds!" He kicked at Goldchild, who ran away. "Why spare this venomous snake?"

Goldchild replied, "Why kill him and put yourself in the wrong? He's a courtier of the Lord of Life. His Majesty will say you do not respect him."

Khun Phaen said, "I'll repay the force he used against me, and if I'm in the wrong, then I'm in the wrong. He thinks he can fix me without fear. This is none of your business. I want revenge."

He kicked Khun Chang in the chest so he fell off the bed with a loud thump. "Tcha! You treated me with contempt. You stole my wife away to sleep by your side."

Khun Phaen looked at Wanthong and heaved a great sigh. "You shouldn't allow him to sleep beside you. I should hit you and pinch your leg to avenge my anger.

But you have so little flesh, Wanthong. You've been squashed flat by him for sure. Your fair flesh should not be treated so. My fury against him is very fierce."

He looked from her bright cheeks to her bosom. "Your breasts are not a bit firm any more. When I left you on your own, I was pleased that you had no secret affair with anybody.

You waited until the army returned, refusing to go into a bridal house, so I thought you could be counted as a good person. But then you turned from good to terrible. I'd like to take out your heart to examine it.

When I was with you, I treated you very gently, fearing that a heavy touch would dismay you. But now you let this fellow wrestle you roughly. Why don't you protect yourself?

As for that crone, your mother, Siprajan, she didn't fear my sword. She thought she could treat me with contempt. I'd like to slit her open and chop up her heart for vultures to eat."

He lightly tapped the skull of Khun Chang with his sword. "You whining beggar, hiding your head in the earth. Then there's the old hag with a big mouth, Thepthong, who treated me with more contempt than she would a little child.

Now where have the mother-in-law and elder cousins got to? Why haven't they come for a look? The mother is only good at sitting idly around. I'll knock Khun Chang's head like a fish head with my sword,

and wound him to serve the mother right. Tcha! Then there's Phan Sonphraya. If I didn't fear King Phanwasa I wouldn't spare him either.

Tcha! You hide your head away like a log. Your belly bulges and gleams. I'd hit your head with my sword again and again, but you're fast asleep, you toad."

He shaved three lines across Khun Chang's skull, and used oil and soot to draw an adjutant stork with five fish in its beak. He rubbed the head with fresh fish so cats would lick it.

He scraped off Khun Chang's chest hair and smeared him messily with lines of vermilion. "I've had fun with you. That's what you deserve, you wife stealer, you ox stuck in a mud hole.

If Goldchild hadn't stopped me, your head would no longer be attached to this beautiful body." He ordered his spirits to release Wanthong and let her wake up. "Get up, look at your husband, and have a good laugh."

The beautiful Wanthong was asleep and dreaming when she woke up with a start and reached out to hug what she thought was Khun Chang.

As the effect of the mantra had not yet worn off, she was still dreaming blearily. She hugged Khun Phaen without thinking, her mind spinning,

and said, "My lord, I had a dream. Please interpret it for me. You lit an ember and in an instant it set light to the mosquito net at the head of the bed.

Flames flared up to the roof, then dropped down, burning up the mattress and pillows. My skin was singed and blistered. The fire spread to the laths and rafters, which collapsed down

onto us, burning our whole bodies. Nobody came to help put it out. The flames flared and flickered around. I thought I was dying.

In the dream, I was whimpering in such shock that I woke up. Please interpret this. I've never had such a dream."

Khun Phaen, great romancer, felt hatred towards Wanthong while he interpreted the dream. He stroked her breast and said, "Don't cry. The dream is good, not a worry.

The fire burning the mosquito net and flaring up to the rafters, mattress, and pillows means that you'll have a new house, and someone will give us a mattress and pillows.

That it fell on you and burned your head means you must go far away from the old bed, mattress, and pillows. That you were burned means a former friend will come to admire you.

You'll have to leave an evil man, and your old husband will come to live as your partner. Don't be concerned about hardship or happiness." He hugged, caressed, and kissed to please her.

Wanthong lay listening, growing ever more suspicious that this was not the voice of Khun Chang. She fumbled all over his chest. "Eh? Who's this? It's not Khun Chang.

He's plump with bushy hair all over his chest and chin. Who's this with a very different, slender figure, and a scent of krajae-sandal all over him, not the usual smell from drinking liquor?

His wrist is barely half a span, and he's no great fat lump. How did he come beside me on the bed tonight?" She turned over in alarm.

In an instant she recognized the face, and trembled even more in fright. Inflamed with fear, she looked for Khun Chang and saw him lying asleep under the bed,

his head shaven in stripes. She screamed at the top of her voice, and rushed down beside the bed to embrace him. Though she called at the top of her voice, he did not wake up.

Khun Phaen, great romancer, said angrily to Wanthong, "Don't try to shake him awake. Why don't you raise your face and greet me,

or do you think I'm a vagabond and so don't turn your head to talk? Because you now have piles of money, you don't miss the friend in difficulty who was parted from you.

You forget completely how we talked under a low *krathum* tree. You don't want to remember it correctly. You forget sleeping with a tree trunk as a pillow,

forget sipping water from a caladium leaf, forget sleeping in a room made from leaves, the hardship of lying on a bed of bamboo fronds, splitting a betelnut into two halves for each of us.

It's a pity I've come to find you when you're rich and don't even want to look at me. On top of that, you keep shaking Khun Chang to wake up and slash me with his diamond sword.

What an idea, Wanthong! It's a pity you cut me off so completely. You love the king, take the bishops, and then the pieces are all gone. You cut off a banana flower without leaving a strand of stalk.[33]

When it's time to fly off, you don't turn to look back, you don't think of me at all. You have no pity for my left arm that almost fell off because I let you sleep on it."

Khun Phaen's words made Wanthong weep uncontrollably. She pretended to address Khun Chang. "Why are you still sleeping?" She pushed, pulled, pinched, and said,

"How did you get down here, Khun Chang? You claim you don't love me and won't support me so why do you come back and sleep here? You're just pretending to be out cold.

First, you have thoughts of revenge, and then all your thoughts of revenge

---

33. See p. 83, note 7.

disappeared and jealousy arose! It's laughable. It's shameful that you're a man all over but you don't fear that people will laugh at you.

The time you lost your temper, you spoke very fiercely: 'Wanthong, don't think that I love you. I won't beg you ever again.' And now, who invited you to come here?

Tcha! This fellow is just like a man all right—not concerned about the promises he made. We women are better. Don't imagine that we would break our word."

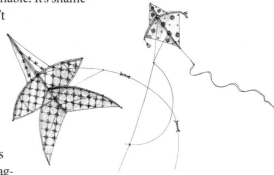

jula *and* pakpao *kites*

Khun Phaen, great valiant, skilled in all the arts of war, sat quietly pondering these angry words. He thought back to the past and said,

"Let everything between us come out clearly. Where did I break a promise, as you claim? It's normal for people to have a row. At the moment, who is copper?[34]

I thought I'd found a swan that, by nature, lives only in the mountains. I did not realize that a crow had led the swan astray, and when I followed in chase I couldn't trace the tracks.

As soon as I found out, my chest was choked with anger and my tears trickled down. When Khun Chang addressed the king and got the advantage, you became even more distant.

I understood that my partner had fallen out of love. When I met you, you turned your face away. Is this a woman's heart—tarnished, black, inconstant?

I was like a *jula* kite[35] that swoops down and gets cornered. When we clashed for an instant, I didn't jerk the string in time. You, a little *pakpao* kite, soared away and floated on the wind.

I kept thinking of the past. I set my face to wait and pine. Finally I was brazen enough to be blown back to your room, but you scowl at me in anger.

I look you in the eye but you never return a full gaze. It's a pity you can do

---

34. Perhaps a reference to the proverb, เหมือนทองแดงแฝงฝ้าเป็นราคี, *muean thongdaeng faeng fa pen rakhi*, like the copper (in a debased coin) which the air turns black (by oxidation) (Gerini, "On Siamese Proverbs," 213).

35. This passage refers to the popular pastime of kite fighting. จุฬา, *jula*, is a large five-pointed kite considered male. It is often pitted against ปักเป้า, *pakpao*, a smaller lozenge-shaped kite with a long tail of starched cloth, considered female. The *jula* competes using size and weight, as well as splints inserted in the string. The *pakpao* tries to foul the *jula* with its tail or with a loop attached to its string.

this without shame. If I say any more it will be irritating—like the saying, grasp a bull by the horns to make it obey.

Because you have a patron, you stay put, admiring your husband's wealth until you waste away. To you I look black and evil, not like this Khun Chang who pleases you.

You've got a good husband with wealth and reputation, no wonder you stay close. Through ups and downs, you just float along, never at a loss for hope or love.

Only now can I see the way you lean—just as your mother had hoped! Your whole face is blooming so radiantly not even a full moon can compete.

I still remember your promise in the cotton field—you'd fight to the death for our love, you'd stay by my side forever. That person was not two-minded.

Even if another man were to float down from the sky, you wouldn't seek love with anyone but me. So why do you now let this fellow pile on top of you and not get away from him?

If he sees me kissing you, I'll die for nothing with my neck lopped off. I didn't think it would come to this. I made a mistake to fall in love."

"So I'm bad, black, evil, fallen into mud. But that's because someone broke off our love, drew a sword, and threatened to slash me to death.

I was hurt and that's why I lean to this side. Why should I be ashamed that I did something wrong? Neither of us pined for the other, yet you're getting at me.

Who counts as good is up to you to judge. If someone is trampling, shaming, or bullying you, so what? As for me, I live my way.

I'm truthful about my heart. I disagree with what you said. Every day, I'm two-minded Wanthong. But I still remember, and pine with grief.

But on your side, you had somebody else—Laothong—and didn't spare me one thought. All of this is the fruit of karma. Why rake up our past?

In the cotton field I gave you a promise. But you also said you wouldn't abandon me, and so I secretly gave you money. Don't you remember where you got the bride price?

If I hadn't been taken in by your tricky tongue in the cotton field, you wouldn't have got Wanthong to embrace. I gave you my own money for the bride price. After you got the embrace, you bit me."

"Oh for sure, my lady, I can't argue with you. You pleaded with me to ask for your hand. You gave me money for the capital.

But on the day that you and I quarreled, you angrily went off with your lord. How much have you managed to recoup? Or does it not yet cover the amount you gave me?

I know that you love me, that until today your love has not died, and that you love me enough to sleepwalk, dream, and relate those dreams in Khun Chang's arms.

I've come to beg you to make up, but you still turn away, hide your face, show me your back. You love me, don't you, but you're pretending to hate me. You won't even sit and talk with me.

Because your heart loves that barbarian Khun Chang, when you see me, you avert your face and flee. Don't keep painting yourself in a good light. The curtain serves as a sign.

Because you've become loyal to Khun Chang, you have the leisure time to sit embroidering all the time, with no thought for matters of any importance. If that's not so, whose handiwork are those three curtains?"

"Why are you going on and on at me? In the past I didn't do embroidery. Later I took it up because I was unhappy. Am I wasting anybody's silk?

I'm simple and I embroider in a simple manner. I don't boast about it because I'm not skilled like Miss Chiang Mai. I just follow my mood.

Your wife is a skilled embroiderer. Why doesn't she stretch a cloth to embroider? You two could think of the content as you go along. Sew a bit and then look at it together.

Sit sewing and sleep sewing for three years. Are my complaints getting on your nerves? When you first came back, I didn't have time to see. I thought you'd rush in and slash.

From the time you returned from the Chiang Thong campaign until today I still dream. If you'd come in daytime, all would be fine. Why wouldn't I welcome you well?"

"Tcha, Wanthong! You weave words like you plait hair. I didn't come in daytime because I didn't have servants to carry me in a litter.

Would your lord and master greet me? He'd turn me away! Plus there are gatekeepers at every barrier who wouldn't allow me to enter.

Great love drove me to come and find you. I must beg your pardon over my anger. I wasn't hot-tempered because of hatred. Eye's jewel, don't have doubts.

It was our karma that we quarreled on that day, though we shouldn't have. There was no need to abandon our love. I still lie holding my forehead in grief and amazement.[36]

---

36. In this classic pose of grief, the person lies on the back with both hands, overlapping and palm upwards, resting on the forehead.

At home I couldn't think of anything but my resentment and revenge. I was sad because I couldn't stop thinking of you. When I arrived here, I heaved a sigh of regret.

I brazenly hoped that you would ease up, and we could recover our affection. Don't abandon our love to ruins. Please rethink a little, Wanthong."

"Don't say this, my heartmate. I thought you were unhappy. I preserved myself while waiting for you at home—right until your return from the Chiang Thong campaign.

I was happy to have evaded Khun Chang. I tried to stifle my sadness when I went down to meet you. Was it right for my lord and master to be so unkind as to let his Lao wife abuse me in so many ways?

On top of that, you drew your sword to end my life. If Saithong hadn't arrived in time, you'd have killed me in anger without a thought.

Even so, I still kept my word. I didn't cast you out of my heart. Only because Khun Chang used a mantra to put me to sleep was I violated by him.

Now I'm despoiled, bad. To go back to loving you would be wrong. Please forgive me, my lord, and don't be angry. The merit we have made is used up.

Please break off this love completely. There are lots of gorgeously beautiful women. I'll wai you and prostrate at your feet every day like a sister of the same womb."

"Oh pity, pity, Wanthong. Your heart is not like it was before. I'm full of love and unable to lose my yearning. Should you break it off without a care?

Khun Chang looks terrible. How could you love him so much and not think of the friend in hardship parted from you? Enough! I'll kill Khun Chang to put an end to all your care for him, my heartstring. I'll cut him in two to stop the yearning in your heart." He grasped his sword and stood swinging it to slash Khun Chang dead.

Wanthong screamed in fear, and threw her body across Khun Chang. Trembling she called out, "Forgive me. Why slash him dead and make karma for yourself?

This kind of person will not fight you but will end up dead, curled over with his head lopped off. I have another suggestion for you. Please chop me dead for angering you.

Kill me. I won't complain. Let me meet you again in the next life. In this one, I've given up hope of reuniting our love.

Even if you stick a broken bowl back together with glue, you can still make out traces of the join. People seeing my face will call me evil for not choosing, and being the wife of two men.

If you love Wanthong as a little sister, all will be sweetness and light. If you want three or so beautiful wives, I'll find them to meet your wish."

Khun Phaen's anger subsided and he replied, "You fell in love with me and we married. To treat each other as brother and sister is impossible.

Were we to have children together, two or three would be about right. But if you no longer love me, then that's it. Why are you talking of finding other women for me?

Were there ten thousand other women of outstanding beauty, I wouldn't exchange Wanthong alone for all of them. That's the truth. I wouldn't.

Is the old saying wrong, Wanthong? Even when love dies, a trace remains. Stay here, my love, I take my leave.

Because of little merit, I won't enjoy your love again. I say farewell to go into the forest, like Inao traveling after Busaba,[37] so nobody will see my face from now on."

While speaking, he intoned a mantra to captivate her heart and soul in an instant. He stroked her back, blew a Beguiler,

and got up as if he were really leaving. Wanthong ran after him, crying, "I'll go with you. Just wait while I get dressed and collect some valuables. I'll be your friend to death in the forest."

Khun Phaen stopped and stood waiting. Wanthong rushed into the main room, found a candle, lit it, picked up a key, and opened a chest.

In turmoil she picked out rings, opening and closing the chest several times, feeling regret about those she could not take, but knowing the whole lot was too much.

She picked out waist chains, breast chains, and diamond earrings, and pried out the gems to reduce the weight. Other gold and silver items were very heavy so she took only her favorites.

Then she quickly opened the central chest, looked at the cloth of many types, but took none. "These won't help avoid poverty in a forest." She took only some gold-brocaded silk

which she had woven herself, showing a naga with a coiled tail, and motifs of Inao asking for Busaba's hand, Chunnarat[38] riding a golden deer and embracing a young *kinnari*,

and in the middle of the piece an image of Lord Garuda coupling with Kaki

---

37. See p. 588, note 12.

38. ชุนรัตน์, hero of a Third Reign drama, now lost, but alluded to in other works (*Bot lakhon rueang unnarut roi rueang*, 2; Niyada, *Phinit wannakam*, 34).

in a room of the holy palace, then stealing her away to enjoy in his Chomphli abode.[39]

Another piece had an image of Unnarut joyfully embracing Usa, along with attractive motifs of beautiful animals.[40] Next she chose uppercloths from an inner chest.

There were many silk pieces in pink, ruby red, purple, green, and white but she did not touch them. She chose only enough tat and kimkhab pieces as coverlets for sleeping along the way.

She lingered so long in the room choosing the cloth that the effects of the mantra began to wear off. She thought of Khun Chang again. Putting down everything, she stretched out and grieved.

"Oh pity, pity, Khun Chang! You'll miss our lovemaking. When you call me, you always say 'mistress,' never make me unhappy by being impolite.

You provide me with everything. Whatever I want, you don't oppose. You truly love me, Khun Chang. Oh my lord and master, I'm at my wits' end.

What help can I get from spirits or from people? Oh beloved, what should I do?" She flailed around, beating her chest and crying in distraction.

Then she recovered her senses and promised the spirits to make offerings of duck and chicken. "Oh spirits, help me quickly by waking my husband up.

I'll give you gold-mouthed duck[41] and a chicken phanaeng including the feathers. If I don't give the rewards I promise, end my life."

The spirits of Goldchild all smiled happily, licking their lips at the words "duck" and "chicken." They wanted the chicken phanaeng and so accepted the promise.

"Once he wakes up, we'll eat our fill, drink ourselves drunk on strong liquor, and then put him back to sleep as before." They relaxed the mantra so Khun Chang would revive.

Khun Chang awoke, still confused and lost in dreams. He felt his head with a hand, and his body shook. "Oh Wanthong, come and hug me!"

He embraced the side pillow, mistaking it for her. "Is this Wanthong's cheek? I'm feeling feverish and confused. Why do you lie apart from me?

I want to make love with you but I feel as if there's a heavy slab of rock on

---

39. On the Kaki story, see p. 350, note 49.

40. See p. 724, note 31.

41. เป็ดปากทอง, *pet pak thong*, a duck with a gold chain hanging from its beak, used in offerings to the spirits, especially on occasions when a man has come to ask for a woman's hand (the chain is part of the bride price).

top of me." He lay hugging the pillow and whispering, "Khun Phaen will come to take you away.

Should he dare to come as far as this room, I'll stab him so his innards spew out." He mumbled and burbled, not opening his eyes, yawning blearily.

Khun Phaen, great romancer, angrily contemplated chopping Khun Chang into a thousand pieces. "Mm! Come on, you spirits, my fast friends. You don't fear punishment even a little.

If you let him wake up, look out or your heads will be off. Because you want chicken, you play around recklessly without thinking of your lives."

He tied the spirits and thrashed them with a cane. "You villains, you think only about eating chicken. I don't leave you to go hungry yet you still work against me without fear."

The spirits screamed and squealed, "Sorry. Please forgive us, lord and master!" "We just woke him for fun." "We'll sit on his head and put him back down."

"We're scared and we'll remember not to do it again." "Even if it's the best chicken, we won't take the bribe." "If in the future we do it again without fear, don't spare our lives."

Khun Phaen listened to the spirits' apologies and his anger calmed. He untied the four of them. "Tcha! I'm annoyed at you, Wanthong, for bribing the spirits to wake your husband up

so he can stab me so my innards spew out, and I have to plead with you to help stuff them back. Did he entice you? Why else did you rush here? Hug him to you heart's content.

I thought you'd gone to collect your valuables. I didn't know you were making offerings to spirits. Very cunning, Wanthong. The sun is almost up. Don't take too much time."

He pronounced a God-Arouser mantra, and made as if to walk away from the house. "I'm not going to force you against your will. If you love this home, don't come."

Again under the influence of a mantra, Wanthong grieved with tears falling. "I'm sorry. Soon I'll be ready to leave. Don't be angry, my lord. I'm coming."

She chose some *attalat* for the hard times ahead. "I should take a lot with me so even if we lack food, things are not too bad."

She lit a candle and went around opening up chests and boxes. Then she grew concerned and sorrowful about leaving her mother.

"Oh Mother, mistress of your child, I'll go away and not see your face. You carried me in your belly, yet I'll not see your funeral."

Khun Phaen heard her grieving and felt so sorry for her he could not ignore it. He enchanted water and rubbed it on her to cheer her up.

"Don't be too sad, Wanthong. Come cuddle close with me. That will be better. Don't delay too long. Dawn is almost up, and we must hurry away."

Wanthong sobbed with tears flowing down. She knew in her heart she must leave and go far away. She made offerings to say farewell.

"Oh lord spirits of the house, please remain here and keep watch. Karma from the past has caught up with me. I entrust my gems, rings, silver, and gold to you.

Guardian spirits, please keep watch. Lord spirits of the house, please pay heed. I say farewell because karma has caught up with me. When will I ever come back?

Please inform Khun Chang, in these words, without mistake: Don't follow me; it won't do any good; he'll kill you for nothing."

She made her farewell to the room and changed her clothes but pitifully got things back to front. She put on an uppercloth in the color of wilting lotus. She placed her valuables in a little basket given by her mother,

wrapped up the cloth and put that in too. Tears fell in streams. Sobbing, she said farewell to Khun Chang, grieving and beating her chest in distress.

Khun Phaen said, "You're very miserable. With such love and concern, how can you leave?" He took her hand and led her out of Khun Chang's great house.

Wanthong was almost too miserable to walk. She turned to look back towards Khun Chang, feeling overcome with sorrow.

She pleaded with Khun Phaen to stop. "We haven't taken any betel and pan. And we've forgotten tobacco. Please wait. I'll be back in a moment."

She rushed in, cut some betelnut and rolled pan leaves. She wrote a letter and attached it to the wall. She shook Khun Chang to open his eyes, then pushed and pinched him hard, but he did not awake.

"Khun Phaen is taking me away. Don't just sit still. Stand up and fight over me, can't you? The spirits gave me no help, and you lie still with your eyes closed, snoring.

Pity me! I fear I won't survive. I'll die in the forest. Because he's so angry and vengeful, once out of sight of people, he'll do away with me.

Oh, lord and master of your wife, you'll eat tears without relief." She lay down almost at the point of giving up her life.

Khun Phaen waited, knowing the time was late. "Where is she dithering now?" He returned in anger to look for her, and saw her crying out of love for Khun Chang.

"Is this how you fetch betel and pan?" He banged her with his hand, kicked the spirit Goldchild sitting on Khun Chang, and drew Skystorm in anger.

Not thinking of her own life, Wanthong threw herself on Khun Chang, and peered angrily up at Khun Phaen. "What will be, let it be, according to karma.

Whether I go or don't go, I'll probably die. I don't love this body. Please cut me down. Wherever you're taking me will be terrible. You'll hurt me for fun and pride."

Khun Phaen gripped her arm and dragged her away. Wanthong challenged him, "Slash me dead here in the room." Realizing her mood, Khun Phaen blew a mantra to soften her heart.

Wanthong was overcome with love. "Where are you dragging and pulling me? Stop it, you'll break my arm off. You have no heart. You just pretend to be kind.

The basket has spilled everything—hair quills, mirror, and comb. The betel box is knocked over." Khun Phaen said, "Never mind. Leave them. I'll provide."

From a hiding place in the shadow of a pillar close by, Kaeo Kiriya was watching with tears streaming. She feared Khun Phaen would abandon her and not return.

"Now that he has Wanthong, why should he come back? He'll never fetch me as promised." She thought of speaking out but feared Wanthong would think that she and Khun Phaen had planned this.

Yet she kept edging to go out, with heart thumping and tears streaming. Wanthong saw the shadow and immediately shuddered in fear that it was a spirit.

She saw the shadow flicker and then disappear, coming and going in flashes. She feared that the spirit would later inform Khun Chang, and in fear of the spirit, she hugged Khun Phaen.

Khun Phaen, great romancer, with power throughout the three worlds, was worried that Kaeo Kiriya was feeling hurt, and so pretended to address a spirit.

"Stay here. I'll return to fetch you. I'll not go back on my word. I gave the ring for you to admire in my stead. Stay here, spirit, don't be worried.

If it were not yet near the light of dawn, I'd linger to keep you company in the main room." With that, he led Wanthong away, feeling cheerful, and took her out through the main gate. She was crying pitifully. "Oh, I was happy here. I sat embroidering curtains for display.

You stay here, Kaeo Kiriya. Don't be sorrowful like me. All the guardian spirits and lords of this house, I salute you and bid you farewell."

Khun Phaen, great romancer, skilled in lore, saw she was miserable. He turned to her and teased her while blowing

a God-Arouser mantra to persuade her to go anywhere. Once Wanthong was affected by the mantra, the sorrow subsided in her heart.

They walked towards the horse, Color of Mist, who ran out and waited to receive them. Khun Phaen stroked the horse's back and said, "Wanthong is afraid of you.

She fears that you may be displeased and might throw her off in the forest. I beg you to allow her to ride." The horse licked Wanthong, causing her alarm.

She said, "I'm a woman. How can I mount and ride on your back. I'll walk along behind so as not to bother you."

Color of Mist licked her hand, as if to say: You don't want to bother me; I licked your hand with compassion; you've apologized, and may ride, no problem.

Wanthong prostrated at the horse's hooves, saying. "Don't feel bad, I beg you. If I don't lose my life, I'll be able to repay your kindness."

Khun Phaen lifted her onto the horse's back, and mounted in the front. He stilled his mind, intoned a prayer, and urged the horse ahead. The spirits followed behind.

Wanthong turned back to look at the house, almost ready to die with sadness. "Oh, from now on we'll be far apart. Today I part from so many things. Who can make you understand which way he took me?"

[The manuscript is defective here. The departure from Suphan is missing. The story resumes at the river crossing in Ban Phlap.]

. . . rocked it but was surprised it was stuck.

He gripped the gunwales of the boat and dragged it. "This boat is stuck in the mud and won't move." He went round to the stern and pushed. "Motherfuck![42] How did it get so stuck?"

He shoved with his shoulder until the bow moved and the boat slipped away, splashing himself in mud up to his shoulder blades. Happy to have freed the boat, he hurried across, panting with a shaking chin.

---

42. ตอกไย, *tok yai*, in Mon.

Coming close, he saw a beautiful lady and became apprehensive about approaching further. "Who's he got there? He talked lies to fool me.

He's abducted a lady from the palace, for sure, and tricked me into rowing for them. He's got the looks of a loverboy as far as I can see, though I didn't have time to wipe the sleep from my eyes."

Khun Phaen shouted, "I'm fed up with you, you scoundrel. Why not put on a tucktail cloth, master ferryman? You've got your valuables dangling on display. Please put on a lowercloth while you row."

Matho was shocked. He covered his belly with his hands, crying, "Who took my lowercloth? I'll tell them to lock him up in the city jail!"

Khun Phaen, great romancer, was worried that word would spread. "This accursed Mon will create trouble." He jumped down from the horse, rushed over,

blew a mantra into the boatman's face, and spoke amiably. "Please send us across safely. We'll pay a fee for your efforts."

He took from his little finger a ring with a scintillating pearl, and proffered it. "It's almost light. Please send us across quickly as we wish."

Matho laughed and took the ring. His head jerked back and his mouth fell open at the sight of the fine glittering jewel. "I'll sell this to redeem a slave I can hug in bed.

I'm in love with I-Khlai at the end of the village, and I-Phon with the dangling breasts, the wife of Phan Son. You're like a patron who has brought me a mattress to lie on. Quick, please get in the boat."

Khun Phaen boarded the boat, took up a paddle, and sat in the stern, paddling so hard his body shook. Color of Mist swam along beside the boat with his rope tied to Wanthong's wrist.

She was under the influence of a mantra that made her obliviously happy. At the landing, Khun Phaen carried her up from the water and put her on the back of the horse.

He pointed the horse in a northeasterly[43] direction through the forest to Ban Mai Phai Lawa.[44] Still angry, he carved messages on trees

all along the way. "Let Khun Chang chase after me so we can fight it out to see which one of us is able."

He teased Wanthong, "If Khun Chang loves you and dreams about you, I think he'll raise an army to chase after us with more than three million men.

---

43. More likely this should be northwesterly, towards the hills.
44. The village of the Lawa Bamboo. Unidentified.

I'll tell him, Wanthong, that you wept pitiably to come with me; that you gathered up your rings, silver, gold, and valuables, escaped from the house, and hurried after me;

that you said Khun Chang was vile with his sparse head in four stripes like a wild cat; that you clung on and would not let me leave without you, grabbing my cloth and refusing to let go;

that you wept, beat your breast into bruises, groped the flesh of both your breasts, walked along the way wiping away tears, pulled the tail of the horse, and ran begging me to take you."

Wanthong replied, "Thunder! You like shooting your mouth off and making up stories. Your lying is scandalous.

You don't fear the spirits of the forest, or feel shame in front of fishes and crabs. You put on a straight face, not scared the spirits will laugh at you.

Is this man speaking such sharp words the soldier that destroyed a Lao army? Anyone would think it laughable, though it sounds sweet to the ear."

Listening to Wanthong, Khun Phaen turned his face away as if not paying attention. He urged the horse ahead and they wended their way along the route, pointing out birds and trees in the forest.

"Over there is a big adjutant stork preening itself. Look, there on the cinnamon tree. What a fine head! Wanthong, my love, don't be upset.

He's as beautiful in appearance as Khun Chang. I thought your husband had come to collect you. Oh what a pity. Who has such love? He's come to fetch you back."

Wanthong cried, "What's this? It's not funny. Don't play around. If you knew I was bad, why did you bring me? You can talk like this because I'm in the palm of your hand.

You see only that great adjutant stork. But further on, don't you see that mound where there's a *soithong*[45] bird perched on a *satue* tree? Is that Laothong following us?

Somewhere I heard she went into the palace. You've lost her, and that's why you've come after me. Oh, are you getting annoyed? I'm jumping down from the horse. I'm not going."

Khun Phaen was affected by what she said. He smiled broadly. "We're even. Don't scold any more. Let's enjoy the trees in the forest."

A bevy of peacocks was strutting around. A flock of swifts cried through the

---

45. Unidentified.

forest. The call of a coel encouraged the sun. Wild cocks crowed to announce the sunrise.

Cicadas and crickets chattered and churred prettily without a break. Little by little the white moon slid down to set, and the sun rose into the clouds, brightening the forest.

Young cattle and deer emerged from their hiding places. Troops of monkeys gamboled, and rabbits danced among the trees. Gibbons dangled head down from branches and swung away.

Seeing red cloth, they leaned out to look, whooping to call their mates, joining up with the monkeys that scampered merrily in the treetops.

She[46] pinched, scratched, and glared at him, then turned her face away. "Tcha! You're enjoying yourself, my good fellow."

Khun Phaen said, "Look. You've never seen it before. I prompt you to look for fun but instead you're angry at me." Wanthong said, "I'm fed up with this. You're too good." Khun Phaen said, "We ran away together."

He turned to kiss and caress her. Wanthong fended him off and averted her face. They flirted and teased through the forest, both enjoying themselves and both becoming aroused.

∽

Now let's move to the next scene. Khun Chang was fast asleep in his house. At dawn he was startled awake by the call of a crow. He sprung up and groped around for Wanthong on the bed.

He hugged a pillow, caressed and squeezed it thinking he was cradling her in sleep. He kissed the pillow and begged her to scratch him in the old spot.

"I dreamed that I stepped on a loose plank. I was frightened that you were running away." He ran his hand across his head. "What's happened to my hair? Why is it so thin? Who took it?

Here I should have a lot of hair. Who came and plucked it away?" He peeked open his eyes and felt around in alarm. "Eh! This isn't the bed.

Why are things strange like this. Eh? This is a pillow." He beat his breast as if burned to ashes. "Oh Wanthong, these are both pillows!

Where's my wife gone? I don't see you, Wanthong. Where are you?" He ran, tripped over a tray, and scrambled back up, losing his lowercloth without knowing it.

"Where did you go without telling me? Oh Wanthong, you dare run away from your husband. How can I survive on my own? I'll box my head and die right now.

---

46. This first line of this stanza is missing from the original text.

What man on earth loves his wife as I do, with a love that's never-ending? Who on earth loves as I love Wanthong?

When I love you to the utmost, should you have run away just like that? With unending love, I never failed to caress you.

Only just now, I was kissing you. I got up and searched for you but you'd disappeared. You changed clothes and left your sabai for me, but you yourself have disappeared from sight.

The scent of your skin, of your breast, still lingers on the sabai. But where have you gone? Have you run away somewhere to test me?"

He went around searching everywhere. He saw the letter on the wall and his tears flowed. He kissed his beloved's handwriting and read the letter through tears.

The letter said, "Khun Phaen is very angry at you. He put people to sleep, broke into the house, and dragged me away against my will.

He abused me heavily but I countered that I would fight to the death not to go with him. He complained because I was still missing you, and drew his sword to kill you.

I pushed him, threw myself in the way, and agreed to go with him, and that's why you did not die. I kept hitting you to wake up till I had no more strength.

I took gold and rings so I can look at them as mementos. Don't delay. Think quickly. Inform the king and then come after me."

After reading the letter, Khun Chang recovered himself, raised the letter above his head, and cried, "It's my fault, mistress of my heart. I'm not angry at you.

As a result of karma, I was so oblivious that he could even shave my head. Our spirits—what happened to you? You didn't say anything but stood aside and let him do this.

It's a waste to love you and feed you with offerings of liquor, rice, turtle, fish, chicken *phanaeng*, curry, raw salad, and spicy fish salad every morning and evening. It's a waste for me to give you food.

Where have you gone, you lowlife? If I catch you, I'll cut all your heads off. Rogues attack this house regularly but when an enemy comes, you disappear."

He rushed around to summon his servants, thwacking their backs. One sprung up still asleep and stood without clothes. Another fell over on the terrace. Another mumbled in sleep, "You villain!

You dog, you hit me for nothing. Did I take your liquor bottle away?" Khun Chang grew even more enraged. "You sleep like puppies,

and allow Khun Phaen to get in. Why didn't you chop him up a bit? There are about a hundred of you but you didn't watch for an enemy breaking in.

That lowlife, that villain, that dog-heart has stolen away my Wanthong."

Weeping, he called for Sonphraya. "Round up the servants right now."

Still bleary with sleep, Phan Sonphraya grumbled, "Your wife has disappeared from the mosquito net and you come around beating and shouting. Why didn't you keep her under lock and key?

You hugged her through to dawn with eyes closed. Now she's disappeared and you come bawling at me." Sonphraya got up and went to call the servants and inform everybody.

The servants rushed off to find swords, pikes, and other weapons. They busily harnessed elephants and horses, and arranged over five hundred men including phrai, ivory taxpayers,[47]

Lao, Lue, and Tavoy people that they bought eaglewood from. All came with weapons ready. Sonphraya told his master immediately,

"I've arranged many men. Go to bathe and get dressed quickly. If we follow after him now, we should be in time. He can't have flown away."

Khun Chang saw everything was ready to set off for the forest immediately. With tears pouring down, he rushed off to bathe and dress, and came back in a flurry. The troops were treated to liquor and got noisily drunk.

At an auspicious time, they left the house hollering, with the sound of gunfire echoing around. In a turmoil of anxiety, Khun Chang urged them to hurry.

Halfway through the forest, the troops at the front saw a notice carved on a tree by the path, and bent their heads to look at it.

The message said, "You dumb turtle, you sluggard dolt who sleeps like a pig, you showed off that you could bully me without respect, with more contempt than for a little child.

You flirted around so arrogantly. Now you'll see a little of my handiwork. I'll make your tears drop until your eyes fly out.

Hurry after me along this path. Don't go astray and get lost. Mistress Wanthong of yours came to admire the forest. Come right this way. I'm waiting to receive you.

Are you coming or not, Khun Chang, you pickled toad? I'll chop you till I'm bored, you interfering lowlife. I'll beat you like a coupling cat. Don't fall asleep. Hurry after Wanthong."

---

47. ส่วยหน่องา, *suai no nga*, tax on tusks. *Suai* was a tax in kind, used especially for the collection of resources from forests and other remote areas—special timbers, metals, lac, benzoin, ivory, etc. Certain people specialized in collecting these goods, and were exempt from the labor services imposed on phrai. This passage hints that Khun Chang's wealth comes from trade in forest goods.

After reading the message, they conferred together. "It would be a bad mistake to let them come this way and allow the master to read this rude message. He'll get angry at us."

They asked the scouting party, "Hey! Is Khun Phaen around here or not?" They saw shadows among the waving trees, and nobody wanted to approach for fear of his power.

The troops of the vanguard ran off, some throwing away their cloths and running naked. A drunk whined, "I've got no strength." Another mistakenly cried, "He's coming! Over there!"

Khun Chang stuck his goad in the elephant until the goad broke. He bounced along on its rear, crashing up and down. Sonphraya's rear mahout, eyes wide in fright, fell off the elephant into the forest with a thump.

Sonphraya said to Khun Chang, "They're overexcited. Don't be misled by them. Wait until we see him for certain, then send the army through the forest."

At midday, they arrived at a lake and went out to a plain, kicking up dust. They came upon some cowherd boys playing in a field and asked them for information.

"When you were grazing cows at the end of the paddy field, did you see anyone, a man and woman riding a horse through the forest? If so, tell us."

The Lawa boys wai-ed and told them, "We saw a man and woman today. They were riding a horse and flirting as they went."

"The lady was riding at the back, and the man at the front. She had her elbows round him. He turned back to kiss her, and was all over her."

"She rested her face close to him. He kept turning back to sneak a smacker. Then they went off into the bushes hidden by the leaves, by that persimmon tree where I'm pointing."

At the boy's words, Khun Chang broke out in sweat and felt he was losing his mind. "Tcha! If we meet, I won't spare him. Today, what will be will be.

I'll slash him down with my sharp sword to serve this shameless fellow right for his lewdness. I'll chop him with this sword." He hit his brother bang in the chest.

Phan Sonphraya almost fell off. "What's this, master, almost stoving my chest in? Don't get too worked up. Let's rest the troops a little first and gather our strength."

Khun Chang halted the elephant. They sat down in the shade of trees beside a lake, placed guards, and gave the men liquor to get stumbling drunk.

❧

Khun Phaen, great valiant, took Wanthong into the forest. He had the idea to stop in the evening under the cool shelter of the dense foliage of a banyan tree.

He helped Wanthong down from the horse, and took her to sit under the shade of the banyan. He broke off leaves to lay as a cushion for their backs. Wanthong sat down and waved a fan.

He snuggled close to her and kissed her cheek. Feeling shy, Wanthong fended him off. But the mantra still induced her to love, and she attended to him happily as before.

A soft breeze wafted all the alluring scents of the forest. Flowers opened in bloom, releasing their scent to spread through the trees.

Coel and wild cock sang out. Peacocks and golden swans joined in a chorus. Cicadas trilled through the trees, and crickets crooned plaintively like the lilt of a lyre.

The music of the forest tugged at the heart. A flock of peacocks sang while circling in the air. The crystal clear call of a coel struck the heart like the gong of a *phinphat* ensemble.

The sounds harmonized like an overture. Wanthong listened, almost falling asleep. Khun Phaen was stirred with desire. He urged Wanthong to make an apology.

"We've come to stay at this holy banyan. I fear there'll be guardian spirits who may think us rude. Please make an apology."

Wanthong said, "Hey! What's this? It's shameful in the open air, without any cover. It's like you're disgracing me. This isn't a house. Are you without shame?

If it were dark, I might not mind. I'd easily consent to make love. I've nowhere to go to escape your clutches but this is very shameful. Don't do it."

"We traveled together, just the two of us. Who's going to come and watch?" With that, he cuddled up close to her. "Don't try to put it off so long."

He hugged her close to his breast, and covered her. Dark storm clouds gathered, blanketing the sky. Light flashed from Mekhala's alluring gem. Ramasun slowly drew back his arm,

approached, and hurled his axe to clatter on the rock.[48] Thunder boomed and rain fell in a swirling spray.

[The manuscript ends at this point.]

---

48. See p. 823, note 33.

WANTHONG AND LAOTHONG QUARREL

This is an earlier version of the famous scene in chapter 13, prior to the rewriting by the Second Reign salon. The extract starts after Laothong has emerged from the boat and been subjected to Wanthong's first, withering attack. The translation is based on TNA ms 132 (CS, 171–73).

Hearing this, Laothong was as angry as if engulfed by fire, maddened to distraction. "You pick at me on everything.

I restrained my husband because I feared something wrong would happen, not because of jealousy between us. I did not yet know how serious this matter is, but I feared letting my husband risk punishment.

I'm just a forest Lao who has come empty-handed, with no elephants, horses, buffaloes, or cattle. I did not think of any gifts for you. I have only my hands to wai you. There.

If later my relatives come down, they can bring lots of gifts for you like eaglewood, rhino horn, ivory, nettle vine, and antlers. Let me offer myself

to be used as a slave according to the wishes of my husband. Without knowing it, I wrongly stopped him. Now I'm afraid. Please, Husband, ask her to forgive me and end the matter.

Truly I spoke with honest intentions. Don't mistake my words for barbs. I wai you three times, fair lady. Please calm your anger."

Wanthong spat and said to Phlai Kaeo, "Having heard that, what do you have to say? Her words are so fine and so piercing they deserve a response of about five coconut shells.

I do not think I had such little merit, but this war prisoner dares to malign me. I sit quiet as a doll minding my own business but she goes mad and forgets herself.

She has lots of horn, ivory, elephants, and horses. Maybe she mixed some with the rice fed to you so a curse has seeped all through your body, absorbed even into the strands of your hair and your black bones.

Your face is freckled as if daubed with soot, and you're burbling like a little child all day and night. Before long you'll be crawling on the ground and she'll harness you up to use as a buffalo."

"Eh! Enough, Wanthong. You're over the top. You show no respect for your husband. You're stubborn, wrongheaded, thoughtless. Even if you don't fear me, at least show me a little respect.

For better or worse, I'm your husband, but you don't seem to want me to be. Don't overdo it or I'll get angry. Don't lose the fish by beating the water in front of the trap.[1]

If you love yourself and fear death, then simmer down. Don't make a racket because you'll lose face. If you don't listen to me and continue this abuse, you'll be shamed in front of the townsfolk. Wait and see."

Wanthong was enraged as if on fire. "Take my life, if you want. You dared bring her home to insult me. Now we're wise to Mr. Silver Tongue.

You've got only this war prisoner, and you're already making up stories to batter me. If you get someone better than this, I think I'll be under the foot-soles of this lowly Lao.

You approve of her making sarcastic remarks about me. If you came to my aid, this slave child would not trample all over me. She hits me in the head but you egg her on, and stab me at the same time. I don't care about the merit and karma, I'm going to get her.

Saithong, quick! Come and help. Thump this forest Lao so she has the face of a ghost and her sarcastic mouth can't eat anything sour. I'll take her teeth to play odds 'n' evens,[2] the witch."

Wanthong tightened her breast cloth and struck a pose. "Get out of the way, Husband, I'm going to slap her." Khun Phaen stopped her and scolded, "Stupid." Laothong ran off to the stern of the boat.

Khun Phaen blocked Wanthong following her. She pushed and pulled, seething with rage as if she could eat flesh and blood like a tiger. They struggled chaotically in the boat. Running out of tolerance, Khun Phaen clenched his fist and punched.

Wanthong scratched and pushed without giving up. Many blows were exchanged amidst grunting. He knocked Wanthong down flat, and continued to beat her on the back and shoulders to drive her away.

Wanthong was badly bruised but unrelenting. "Who cares! Today is my

---

1. See p. 272, note 26.

2. เล่นคู่คี่, *len khu khi*, play odds and evens, a game in which two players bet whether there is an odd or even number of items in a pile of beans or similar items.

dying day. The vows you gave so religiously have been tossed away. You're shameless, clever Phlai Kaeo.

I can still remember your promises. Now that you have a lover, you break your word so easily. Now you're drunk on power but not manly. As a woman I don't want anything to do with you."

In fury, Khun Phaen drew his sword, raised it, and stamped his foot hard enough to break the boat apart. "Why should I let you live, you fine talker, when you use threats to make me fear you?"

Wanthong was greatly shocked to see her husband with his face drawn taut and sword raised. She got down from the boat and ran up to her room, crying loudly and piteously.

"Oh Phlai, my heartstring, it shouldn't have come to threats of killing. I loved you and preserved myself until your return. I intended to care for you until my dying day.

This incident arose because that demoness stirred up such great anger. Both of us lost our tempers and created confusion. Oh, what a pity, I spoke wrongly by thinking only of myself.

Why didn't I swallow the slight? Instead, I let my itchy mouth heap insults on my husband. I fear I've lost the shelter I was pining for. Now anyone can come and trample me into the ground without fear.

I can't depend on my mother because she's on Khun Chang's side. In the end I've lost everything. By my calculation, it's not worth staying on this earth. Everything good is gone. Sorrow alone remains.

Just this old, and two husbands! So much badness, so much evil, in every strand of hair! I'll suffer only shame and endless grief. When I'm dead and buried, my name will still be talked about.

The pain won't lessen, and the shame will never disappear, like a tattoo on the back of a hand. Why should I love this body?

Death is finer." She dragged over a rope, climbed up, raised her hands, and prostrated three times. "In this life, I've lost you, Phlai.

In fear of shame, I'll die and wait for you. May we meet again in the next life. Don't let Khun Chang have a clue." She made a prayer, walked quickly across,

and climbed onto a roof beam. With two hands, she tied the rope tightly round her neck, and jumped, letting her body swing out, making the roof sway. Coming in at that very moment, Saithong was shocked.

SOIFA AND SIMALA QUARREL

An earlier version of the scene in chapter 37. The translation is based on TNA ms 79 (CS, 186–89).

Soifa awoke and roused I-Mai. "Why do you sleep so well, damn you? My breast feels as hot as a blazing fire, but you're still curled up like a bandicoot!"

I-Mai said, "Last night I didn't sleep. Hold off, I'm still comfy. Wait a while, I've still got sleep in my eyes." I-Mai got up, washed her face, and came to her mistress.

Soifa said, "Oh I-Mai, I'm so shocked about last night. I'm feeling hurt on account of this man, my husband. Whether I live or die is up to my merit.

You go over there and pass some sarcastic remarks. Today, whatever will be will be." I-Mai replied, "Yes, mistress. I'll go out and give them an earful."

I-Mai went out to sit on the terrace, leaning on one arm with her feet tucked beside her and her face raised. "Oh my! Last night in the starlight, if you could have been there, it was wondrous!

An evil toad took a ride on a chameleon, and a cat was climbing up and down a dog. What a scene! The house was shaking and quaking like a cradle rocked nonstop.

My head slipped off the pillow and bounced on my ear. For what reason, I don't know, every night they're at it without a break. I've never seen or heard anything like it, never had such a laugh."

On behalf of her mistress, I-Moei countered so fiercely that she foamed and spluttered at the mouth, lashing out with no restraint, bent over with her neck thrust out, singing a *thayae*,[1] berating the Lao.

"Fuck your mother![2] Why was there such a racket last night? I'm furious that this Lao bitch got into the room, and they were banging one another wildly.

The male wouldn't lick her so the female got mad, jumped all over him,

---

1. See p. 479, note 32.
2. ตอมินายนายเอย, *to mi nai nai oei*, in Mon.

sending him tumbling on his back, racing around, barking and scratching, scrambling and scrapping, knocking over many spittoons.

And that's not all. They chased after me, and before I knew it, my cunt got hit and split open.[3] I'll take a pestle and bash your cunt until you split open and die."

I-Mai lost her temper and lashed out. "This Mon cur is pissing—oh what a mess! I was happily singing a song. Why are you picking at me so sarcastically?"

Angered by I-Moei's mouth, I-Mai ran over and kicked her down flat. Soifa ran up in a rage and helped I-Mai beat I-Moei.

Simala came between them. "Why are you fighting, Sister? Hey! I've never heard such a noisy earful. As a mistress, you shouldn't get involved.

Let them go at each other, who cares? But why are you so worked up that you rage like a roaring fire and start shouting wildly? It's not becoming.

You're scolding and bullying a servant. You have no compunction about hitting my maid. Why so, Soifa? I-Mai started it before I-Moei.

Otherwise the row would not have arisen. Lashing out at me doesn't put you in the right, my dear. If my people are in the wrong, I don't side with them, and I never make up accusations.

Just because Phra Wai came to me last night, why does this lowlife attack me? She eats only red rice and cold curry[4] yet she always wants to behave like gentlefolk,

pretending to sing and make music, and showing jealousy over our husband too. Every day, I'm kind and forbearing but I'm being assaulted with abuse and sarcasm."

Soifa clapped her hands and laughed. "Is that so? You're using fine words to bully me. I think I should really be afraid of you!

Is this the behavior of a major wife? From this abuse, I now know you're *the* lady! Speaking is so easy, it's truly shameful. When you drink water, you see the leeches too.

When I was first presented by the king, did he order me to be the minor wife? You use fine words to bully me. Issuing threats to scare me is not funny.

As our husband favors you, I'm a little worried that you'll make many accusations against me to play up to him. When the man between us is so besotted, I'm at a grave disadvantage."

---

3. ฉิกูบิแบะ, *chi ku bi bae*, "cunt . . . open" in Mon, also "cunt" in next sentence.

4. Meaning she is only a servant.

"Tcha! Your words cover matters up so completely, Soifa. You're just a Lao war prisoner, captured from a defeated army and brought to the Thai country.

As for me, when the army halted at Phichit, Phra Wai came to be with me. Everybody talks about this. Where were you hiding your head so you didn't know?

Because Khun Phaen went to speak with my father to ask for my hand, we came to live together as a couple. Phra Wai was my husband before you turned up.

He had to be separated from me for a year because he went to capture this two-faced scourge, who he dragged down here by the hair, yet you're still acting angry and arrogant."

"Truly I beg your pardon. *[manuscript damaged]* It's said you made love together at the time of the war but secretly concealed it by splashing around three or four bowls of water for fear the word would spread.

Because you were already wounded, the matter had to be covered up and made to disappear. Your parents gave their consent readily and allowed things to happen without wait or obstruction.

They were afraid of what might subsequently come about—that a child would be born without a father. With that knowledge they didn't stand in the way, and let the bare ground serve as a bridal house, against the custom.

In my country I've never seen a single person who has married twice like you.[5] It's against ancestral tradition. Your fortune must be truly good!"

"You can speak well, Miss Lao, about anything at all. Who asked you to recount this story? Truly I'm in the wrong, not Phra Wai.

I'm not black-faced like someone who strips and bathes to fulfill desire indiscriminately. You were bored with the Lao country so you followed the Thai to try a new taste.

But you remain restless, frustrated, mad with fury and lust. When the husband lost interest and became distant, you couldn't stand it and got so heated with anger that people could see the smoke."

"True, I have lust, but that's because I'm frustrated, unlike you who are going at it all day and all night. If he doesn't go to sleep, you don't stop.

---

5. Probably this means that Muen Wai and Simala were married in Phichit and again in Ayutthaya. Prince Damrong edited this out of his edition (see p. 1369).

From nightfall onwards, you banter about Phra Rot,[6] knowing how to set the pace and the rhythm, moving and shaking through several rounds together. I'm afraid already. I don't wish to compete."

"Hey, you shameless hussy! Did I tie this man up by the waist? Your grudge is making you rage like a roaring fire and stubbornly spill out accusations.

He hates your mouth and doesn't want to lay a finger on you. Your anger is making you mad. It's pathetic. You feel no shame, but pick at me with insinuations and gossip,

slander and sarcasm. You're shameless, thick-faced, abusive, and jealous. Come on then.[7] I'm not backing down." Simala stepped towards Soifa.

Now to tell of Phlai Chumphon, who was playing up in the house. He saw his two sisters-in-law quarreling and intervened to block Simala.

"Whatever's up, hold off for a moment. It's better to wait and talk to brother Wai. Why quarrel? It's not fitting or necessary, and shameful in front of the servants."

Soifa called out, "My, my, Chumphon! What makes you interfere, you squirt? This is none of your business. Go away."

Old Thong Prasi, who was sitting behind a curtain, heard her grandson being scolded and had to respond. She leapt up as angry as a fire and called out, "Chumphon,

why do you let this hollow-eared Lao browbeat you? Is my grandson her servant? Come on then, don't let her get away with it. Make a scene in daylight for people to watch.

Chase her away. She's a waste on the land. I didn't ask to hear this racket. They're taking turns to strip naked for dogs to see. Anybody who hurts my grandson gets a kick with my foot."

Soifa called out, "Here, here! Why are you taking sides? You're older than the earth but still not dead. You don't think about impermanence[8] but still act fierce."

---

6. Hero of an old Thai courtly poem; a metaphor for lovemaking.

7. เอาเหวยเอาวะ, *ao woei ao wa*, a chant accompanying a long drum performance.

8. อนิจัง, *anijang*, Pali *aniccang*, a key term in Buddhist philosophy for the transience of this-worldly existence.

That made Thong Prasi even madder. "Your mother's clan, you disaster! It's you who wants to live forever so you can gad around quarreling to you heart's content."

"Yes indeed, Grandmother, all you have is a big, hollow mouth, good for scolding. You're already old, so I'm at a loss. But whatever comes out of your mouth goes straight back in your own face!"

At that moment, Phra Wai had left the audience and was hurrying back with his servants. He heard the sound of Soifa quarreling and stopped to listen unobserved.

Then he entered the scene. Soifa showed no fear. Phra Wai was as angry as a raging fire. "Stop it, Grandmother. I'll deal with this myself.

So this is how you are, Soifa. You're just a war prisoner throwing your weight around, showing off and arguing with no respect for your husband's grandmother, making such a noise.

You don't know what I'm capable of. Who are you and where are you from? What is the cause behind this? Tell me quickly, Soifa."

THE BIRTH OF GOLDCHILD, SON OF BUAKHLI

This version of Khun Phaen's quest for a spirit son does not appear in the first printed versions (WK and SS). Probably it was written down by Khru Jaeng during the Fourth Reign. Prince Damrong recorded that it was popular among performers, and included it in his printed edition.

This translation is based on PD chapter 16, starting immediately following the first section ending "sleeping along passes through the mountains."

Now to tell of Nai Det Blackbones who had established a big gang in a lair[1] at Ban Tham.[2] He was a leader of notorious skills, and had been given the title Muen Han, the valiant.

He looked fearsome—almost four cubits tall, with bulging eyes, a moustache curved up at both ends, eyes rimmed red as if painted with vermilion, firm flesh, thick skin,

curly hair, and a hairy chest. He was as tough and fearless as they come. His whole body was lumpy with charmed devices inserted under the skin.

He was invulnerable to guns and other weapons, and if he trod on spikes in

---

1. ช่อง, *song*, a settlement beyond the reach of government, usually in the forest. Such settlements may always have been common but certainly became numerous in the period after the fall of Ayutthaya in 1767. As the lines below suggest, such settlements attracted people with various reasons to escape these and other laws. Records from the early nineteenth century show the court dealing with such settlements in order to acquire forest goods for trade, and having to ignore that these settlements existed beyond the manpower laws of the time. Nai Det may have been given his title in an attempt at incorporation. Provincial governors were instructed to lure the residents of *song* to move to the towns (Damrong and Narit, *San somdet*, 2:315–16, 334).

2. "Cave village," on the southern bank of the Maeklong River, in Tambon Khao Yai, Amphoe Tha Mueang, about 7 kms southeast of modern Kanchanaburi (see map 2). Ban Tham is clearly marked on the early-nineteenth-century maps found in the royal palace (Santanee and Stott, *Royal Siamese Maps*, 95, 102). Local people believe that Muen Han was a real life figure and that they are his descendants. Wat Ban Tham sits at the foot of a craggy spur of hills that straggle away from the Tenasserim range. The wat now contains a series of murals based on this chapter, and a shrine to Buakhli, whose image is painted on the foot of a stalagmite. Local people believe the stalagmite developed because of the power of Buakhli's soul. Twice a month on holy days there are ceremonies at which devotees make offerings to the image, and others communicate with Buakhli through a spirit medium. (SWC, 4:1647–48)

the ground, they shattered. He had twenty good soldiers who were all invulnerable and could stand up to anybody.

His village was large, and teemed with cattle, buffaloes, elephants, horses, and servants. Houses were crowded together, and furnished as well as any princely palace.[3]

There were throngs of young Lao and Thai girl servants, all just of age and good-looking. The sitting halls were spread with soft mats, pillows, and carpets, and strewn with items of gold, silver, nak, and nielloware.

With his wife, Nang Sijan, he had a daughter called Nang Buakhli[4] who was fresh to maidenhood, about seventeen years old, and as beautiful as a palace lady.

Local nobles and officials had sent people to make their pledges and ask for her hand, but her father had refused them all. She looked after the servants on his behalf, and oversaw workers in the fields every day.

If any stranger came to the village, soldiers would lock him up, then after dusk take him into the forest, chop him down, bury him in the earth, and have done with it.

People who had stolen elephants or fled from their masters could gain entry into the forbidden camp, but their masters dared not follow, even if they were sure their men were there. They had to find an intermediary to go there and ransom them.

At dawn, the radiant Buakhli called servants to go to the fields. Both men and women went in a crowd to tend the vegetables and fruit trees.

They took hoes to dig water channels. In the heat of the day, they relaxed comfortably in a shelter built in the middle of the fields. Afterwards she put them back to work.

Khun Phaen, great master, had been walking through the forest for a long time, taking every path and visiting every village. Arriving at Muen Han's fields,

digging channels

---

3. The word used is กรม *krom*, department. In late Ayutthaya, royal relatives were allotted retainers as *krom*, and given titles prefixed by *krom*.

4. บัวคลี่, a lotus just on the point of blooming.

he found a *yang* tree cut down across the way, and posts driven into the ground to make a fence around the holding. Surprised to see the place teeming with workers, he concealed himself and crept up.

He saw Buakhli in the shelter. She was just of age, with an eye-catching slight figure, beautiful fair complexion, and attractive bearing.

His heart skipped a beat in sheer delight. Some merit drew him strongly to her. He set his heart to fall in love, and wanted her as his partner.

On looking at her closely, he saw that she fitted the requirements of the manual in every way. If they were to have a first child together, he would certainly get the son he wanted.

"Whose daughter is she? How can I find out? She has many servants. I'll have to make inquiries from them."

He pushed through the thorny undergrowth and went into the field. The Lao[5] and Thai men and women sitting around in groups caught sight of a stranger and ran up to take a look at him.

Some waved their hands and called out to him to go away. "Why do you come this way, you groaning ghost?[6] Our master's daughter is in the shelter by the bombax tree. Before you know it, your head'll be blown off your body."

"We're telling you to go somewhere else, so why are you standing there blinking, you abomination?" "Our boss is a fearsome man, as fierce as a tiger. You're going to die for nothing."

Khun Phaen, great master, stooped his body and feigned fear. "I didn't know who she was.

If men are forbidden to approach, she must be the daughter of the lord of some country. I'm a hill person from the forests. I beg forgiveness for walking straight in."

The Thai and Lao servants could tell that his accent and manners were not those of a forest dweller. They shouted back, "If our master came and saw this, it wouldn't do."

"Where did you blunder in here from? Mistress Buakhli here is the daughter of Muen Han, and he's not a man who trembles in fear of the district officials. He's put many passersby to death already."

"I'm telling you kindly to do you a favor. If our master comes and sees you,

---

5. The western side of the Chaophraya Plain was severely depopulated in the wars with Burma in the late eighteenth century. Bangkok resettled the area with war prisoners, especially from the Lao regions.

6. อ้ายผีผิว, *ai phi phiu*; ผิว = ผิวปาก, *phiu pak*, to make wordless sounds with the mouth, such as groaning. The phrase is especially used for fearful sounds heard in the forest and thought to be made by spirits.

it won't turn out well. Get away from here right now. I'm being kind to you because you act like a gentleman."

Khun Phaen, great romancer, had found out that her name was Buakhli, and that she was the daughter of Muen Han, who lived in this village and was an able person, famous for his skills.

"I could ask these servants to act as go-between. She probably wouldn't escape my clutches and I'd gain what I want. But I fear I wouldn't really get her because her father would be mad and tear us apart.

If it came to a fight, it would be a big fuss and destroy any chance of winning her and achieving what I have in mind. I must get close to the father,

act humble, and let him make use of me. After a while, he'll come to like me a lot and probably give her to me as wife. If I keep on the right side of him, I think I can gain what I want."

With this in mind, he said goodbye, walked back into the forest, and cut across to Muen Han's house. He arrived at a sala in the lane outside the gate, and went to talk to villagers going in there.

At[7] the time the sun was falling, the lovely Buakhli called to her servants and cut across the field to a path.

She saw someone sitting in the sala. Glancing at him shyly out of the corner of her eye, she walked into the house, ascended the stairs, and entered her apartment.

Khun Phaen watched Buakhli rush up to her rooms as if warning him against loving her too much.

He waited there for a long time without anyone from the house coming to question him. Then someone inside caught sight of him

and asked threateningly, "What are you up to?" Khun Phaen replied, "My master worked me too hard so I ran away.

I want to stay here and seek the lord's protection from now on." A villager said, "If you're telling the truth, wait here in the sala and don't wander around.

If you blunder into the house compound, the soldiers will catch you and slit your liver. We'll go talk to people inside to inform our boss, Muen Han."

They went into the compound and told the soldiers that someone who had

---

7. From here until "caught sight of him" is taken from TNA ms 117 (Sujit, *KCKP*, 224), and TNA ms 177, absent from PD.

fled from his overseer wanted to seek the protection of the boss.

The soldiers rushed inside to bow and say, "A man who has fled his master is waiting outside. We told the guards not to let him through the gate."

The head of the lair ordered the soldiers, "Bring him to my smart house." The soldiers grasped their spears, ran off, and returned dragging Khun Phaen by his arms.

He went up to the terrace and prostrated deeply.[8] Muen Han sat quietly examining his face. "He's studied the texts, and has the appearance of a clever man,

not some vagabond of lowly lineage. His skin is unusually fine and clean. Maybe he lost his cattle, buffaloes, and everything else gambling on the bean game,[9] and so blundered up here."

He asked menacingly, "Whose slave or servant were you? What name do you go by? Where are you from? Why did you stumble into our village?"

prostrating deeply

Khun Phaen made up a story. "My name is Kaeo from the six units.[10] I was on royal service at the frontier but it was tough and I was tired so I ran away.

I've no father, no mother, no wife. I'm destitute and penniless so I've been wandering around the forest, but I was afraid they'd chase after me so I came here.

I want to live in your lair and shelter under your protection from now on. If your lordship is kind and merciful, I'll be your servant until death."

Hearing[11] the sound of voices, the lovely Buakhli came out of the main apartment, and saw somebody on the terrace. She hid in a little room and

---

8. หมอบลงศอก, *mop long sok*, prostrating with arms from elbow to fingertips flat on the ground (KW, 671).

9. เล่นถั่ว, *len thua*, a gambling game. The host or banker pours out a pile of beans, or tamarind seeds, or similar small items, and the players place bets on 0, 1, 2, 3 at four corners of a square cloth. Using a small stick, the host removes the beans in sets of four until fewer than four remain, and the winner is decided by this remainder. More complex combination bets are also possible (SWC, 5:2420; Bastian, *Journey in Siam*, 262–63).

10. See p. 173, note 25.

11. This whole section down to "you and I will be dead" is taken from TNA mss 117 (Sujit, *KCKP*, 225–26) and TNA mss 177, absent from PD.

peered out.

Her heart leapt in excitement. She sat down and examined him for some time. She wanted to know where this fellow was from and why he had come,

so she called in Granny Khai and asked, "Where is this man from? To walk here through the forest on his own is brave and fearless."

Granny Khai bowed her head and said with a smile, "He's able. He knows about the boss and is not afraid. Mistress, I'll tell you.

At midday I was sitting behind the hut when this man blundered into the field. The servants ran to swarm around him. Some of them tried to chase him away by cursing quite heavily.

This able fellow got away and sneaked through to the house—brave and unafraid of the master's wrath. In his heart he wants to be friendly, no doubt. I'm not making it up but don't let many people know."

Buakhli's heart was churning. "You have no need to worry. Should this get to the ears of anyone, you and I will be dead."

Khun Phaen blew a Beguiler mantra that befuddled Muen Han and dispelled his doubts. The power of the mantra made him love Khun Phaen like his own son.

"Fine! You and I will live together. If you're loyal, I'll get you well-established here. If you have any crooked ideas, you'll be ground down into the dust of our district."

He arranged a house for Khun Phaen to stay, and gave him Granny Khai to take care of his food. Khun Phaen cunningly acted very timid—bowing, prostrating, and crawling about on his elbows and knees every day.

Muen Han liked him and took him into his personal service. Khun Phaen mingled with his daughter, wife, servants, and maids. He kept his feelings under control, and gave no clue of his intentions.

Buakhli took to calling Kaeo her elder brother, and brought him betelnut, pan, and tobacco. Muen Han's wife liked him too, and not once had the slightest inkling of what Khun Phaen was hiding.

Muen Han, who was skilled in the ways of the forest, had an idea to go and hunt wild gaur. He summoned Khun Phaen. "Will you come with me?"

Khun Phaen agreed, "Yes sir, I'll go along." Muen Han handed him a side-bag and a tooled pike to take into the forest. He himself put on a waistcoat and black trousers,

tied a powder horn and a box of fuses[12]
round his waist, slung a *sutan*[13] gun with
a tooled barrel on his shoulder, took some
rifled three-baht bullets,[14] and went straight
into the forest.

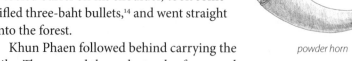

powder horn

Khun Phaen followed behind carrying the
pike. They passed through stands of *rang* and
bamboo. Seeing a red gaur hidden among the trees, they crept up and hid
crouched at the foot of a *lamphaen*.

Muen Han poured powder into the priming pan and closed the frizzen.[15]
He raised the gun to his shoulder, poked it through a rattan bush, and took a
steady aim, but did not notice the gaur raising its head to eat.

He pulled the trigger, the flint flashed, and the report echoed around, but he
missed the gaur. The animal tossed its horns and immediately came towards
them. Muen Han turned but fell down flat in the middle of a clearing.

The gaur charged. Khun Phaen leapt in and got a strong grip on its jaw and
horns. The gaur slammed into him and tossed its horns, but he was strong
enough to hold on.

He dodged the horns, lunged between the beast's legs, and grabbed its tail.
The two spun around wildly like a windmill. The gaur went to gore him but he
jumped out of the way in time. As the gaur raised its head, he darted in, got a
grip on its neck, and twisted.

The gaur sprang but Khun Phaen wrenched hard to choke it. The gaur's eyes
rolled up and it collapsed to its knees. Muen Han plunged a pike into the side
of the gaur's neck. The beast fell to the ground, mooing.

Rage gave the gaur strength to leap back up, spurting blood, but then it
shuddered and collapsed, thrashing about and splattering blood all over the
ground until it expired.

---

12. เต้าชนวน, *tao chanuan*, a box to hold lengths of cord used to touch off powder. "A num-
ber of accessories were required. These included a powder flask, bullet pouches, priming horn,
match-cord (flint or cap as the case may be) and steel. All these were attached to the leather belt
embroidered with gold" (Pant, *Catalogue of Arms*, 98–99, on flintlock guns).

13. สุตัน, possibly this word came from pistol, pronounced in Thai as *pitsatan*, then shortened
to *sutan*, and used as a general term for a gun (KW, 139; SB, 89).

14. Three baht may be the weight, which would make it elephant shot. พันลำ, *phanlam* is the
term for a longitudinal pattern that seems to mean rifling (KW, 139, 671).

15. To fire a flintlock, powder was poured into the priming pan, หูลับ, *hu lap*, secret ear, which
was then covered with a metal flap known as a frizzen, หน้าเพลิง, *na phloeng*, fire face. When the
trigger was pulled, the flint struck the frizzen, throwing sparks into the pan (Hogg, *Encylopedia
of Weaponry*, 58).

Muen Han pulled out the pike and said, "If you hadn't been here to help, and hadn't leapt in and grabbed it so handily, I'd have died in this forest."

He was so angry he did not take the gaur meat. "Leave it where it was speared, and let's go home." He shouldered the gun and set off brusquely through the undergrowth, still shaking with shock.

After a short time, they arrived at the house and went straight up the stairway. Muen Han threw the gun down with a crash and said to his wife, "I met bad fortune in the forest and nearly died.

We were stalking a gaur but I shot and missed. It charged and would have gored my arse if Kaeo hadn't come and tackled it. Between the two of us, we killed it.

If it'd been anyone else but Kaeo, I think I'd have had it. We owe him a lot. Look, Wife, don't feel demeaned.

We must repay him. We'll give him our daughter, Buakhli. They look just right for each other as husband and wife. Don't be disappointed. Tell me how you feel about that."

Sijan already loved Phlai Kaeo like her own eyes so she was happy that her husband suggested something that accorded with her own wishes.

She replied, "It's up to you to give her away, I don't have any objection. If you think this is good, I'll fall in with your wish. He's not a bad fellow."

Having agreed, the couple summoned Kaeo for a talk. "Are you going to be with me a long time, or do you have any thought of going home?

I'm thinking of making you a son-in-law, giving our daughter Buakhli to you. Or maybe that's not to your liking? Don't be polite. Speak the truth."

Phlai Kaeo replied eagerly, "I'm just a poor vagabond in trouble, and you're thinking of setting me up as your son-in-law!

If it pleases you, sir, I'll stay here and not run off anywhere until my dying day. I'm an orphan, on my own. I want to entrust my life to you and I have no thought of leaving."

Muen Han and Sijan were happier than they could imagine. They called the servants to get a house ready by sweeping, laying mats,

setting out bowls, pots, spittoons, trays, tables, covered trays, salvers, and pintos[16] neatly all around the apartment, and finding a good mattress,

---

16. ปิ่นโต, *pinto*; a food container, nowadays especially a multi-compartmented container used especially for travel or delivery. The word was possibly adapted from the Japanese food box, *bento*.

mosquito net, curtains, and pillows,

along with ornaments for the room including washbowl, spittoon, dressing table, mirror, and comb. "There's no wat here for prayer chanting. We make offerings to the spirits[17] in the ancient way."

Sijan prepared a large amount of food including pork, crab, fish, and liquor. Soon, all was ready.

On the following day, a Thursday, a shrine was decorated, offerings made to the spirits, a soul-scooping ceremony held,[18] blessings bestowed, and much advice given about looking after each other until death.

When the ceremonies were over, Kaeo went into the main house and was presented with cash, goods, and servants. Elders went to make a bed.[19]

Phlai Kaeo prostrated with his hands together in wai, and the parents stood giving guidance. When everything was finished, the parents left just as the light of the sun disappeared.

Late in the night under a bright, resplendent moon, Sijan went to soothe her daughter and give her advice.

"My darling, you're going to live with your husband. Look after yourself, and do as I instruct you. The time is right so don't be worried. I'll escort you over there to him."

Buakhli was still agitated at the idea of having a husband. Her mother's words frightened her. "Oh beloved mother of your child, have mercy.

Are you going to give me to this man just like that? I've never had a partner. Please allow me some more time. Put off going over there for a bit."

Sijan comforted her by saying, "Lovemaking with a husband is nothing to fear. Go along, darling, and don't worry.

When it comes to lovemaking, there are no teachers. You'll know it all without need for lessons. In a trice you'll be happy and your worries will all disappear. It was the same for your father and me.

---

17. ผีสาง, *phi sang*; *phi* means corpse, spirit, or ghost; *sang* means the smell of putrefaction from a corpse; together the two words means a spirit that has passed through death into another world.

18. See p. 224, note 3.

19. Part of the ceremonial. Those chosen for this task would be elders of the bride's and groom's families who were well-off and had children that were easy to raise and still alive (Anuman, *Prapheni kiao kap chiwit taeng ngan*, 148–49).

When my mother escorted me over, I was trembling with fright as soon as he came close. But your father was good at pillow talk and put me at ease.[20] He kept on saying that nothing would happen.

He wouldn't lie down. He wouldn't go to sleep. He just kept on at me gently, and soon I gave in to him. I was caught between fear and love, and so tense that sweat was pouring down my face and back.

I 'closed the door' and wouldn't let him enter, but he insisted and pushed. I clenched my teeth, and held my breath, and in half a tick he'd slipped in through the door. Then I knew the power of it. That was it!

Afterwards we did it again and I had no problem. I was only worried he'd get up and leap about. I wasn't afraid of doing it in any position. It's like a gambler playing the bean game. You get very excited.

The first time you play, you get bruised and have to cry off halfway through, because you're new to it and your heart's pounding. After three days, you get more daring and dive in. Even speared real hard, you can take it to the hilt without complaint.

You don't have to study from teachers. It's as easy as threading a needle. When you're still learning to sew, you have to concentrate. Once you've had a taste, that's it!

So go along, darling, and don't worry. Your husband will teach you sensitively, and you'll know each other in a trice. The cock's crowing already, Mother's jewel."

She hustled her daughter to bathe, comb her hair, powder herself, and get dressed. Once she was ready, Sijan walked ahead of her into the room.

Phlai Kaeo was lying quietly, waiting randily and glumly for Buakhli. He had not slept for more than half the night. "Why, oh why, hasn't she come yet?"

Hearing the creak of a door hinge, he turned over and raised his face to see her escorted in by her mother. He got down from the bed.

Entering the room, Sijan peered around and coughed to clear her throat and signal their arrival. Buakhli glanced around by the light of a lamp. Sijan went forward,

reached the bed, and sat down. Phlai sat with his hands together, and bent forward to prostrate. Buakhli hid behind a curtain in confusion. Never having been with a man, she was very shy.

---

20. From here until "take it to the hilt without complaint" is taken from TNA mss 12 (Sujit, *KCKP*, 198), TNA mss 117 (Sujit, *KCKP*, 229–30), and TNA mss 177; PD has: He kept on saying nice things to please me. After listening for just a short time, I was in love. I relaxed and gave in to him. Lovemaking has been like this forever, and that's why so many children are born.

Her mother spoke to Phlai. "Look after each other until death. May you be free from any illness. May you grow richer with every passing day.

My daughter is still a very little child. Be patient and take the trouble to teach her. May you both be happy forever. The cock is making a racket. I'm leaving."

Phlai Kaeo paid respect and received her blessing. When Sijan got up to go, Buakhli clung onto her mother and would not let her leave. Sijan soothed her to be let go.

Once free, she left the room, and walked away. Buakhli, trembling with trepidation, was too slow to follow her mother, and Phlai Kaeo blocked her way.

Unable to escape, the lovely Buakhli hid behind a curtain and stared at the wall. Phlai Kaeo spoke soothingly. "Why are you sitting silently and hiding your face?

Here, let me tell you the truth. When I saw you out in the fields, I fell deeply in love, and that's why I dared to come and serve your father.

Because of some merit, he gave you to live with me as man and wife. Please relax and talk with me. Don't be scared." But just his touch made her tremble.

Buakhli's thoughts raced and her heart fluttered. She began to shake with fright, and said nothing. The touch of a man made her act like a baby chick.

She turned her face away, her lips moving silently, ready to flee. Phlai Kaeo could see she was worked up and so said imploringly, "Please. There's no need to be shy and upset."

He clasped her at the same time as blowing a Beguiler breath onto her eyes. "I love you as much as my own life. Why are you pulling a face and pushing me away?"

He took her in his arms, lifted her onto the bed, cajoling and caressing her insistently. "Please turn your face this way. Is it a waste to love you as much as my own heart?"

Buakhli responded to his pleading with a sidelong glance. She tossed her head, and spoke with her face averted, "Why are you so insistent?

I know that Father gave me to you. I can't escape your clutches, can I? But please leave me alone for two or three nights. I've no experience of lovemaking at all."

Phlai Kaeo replied, "Why put it off? Lovemaking is nothing to be worried about, my darling. Even though you've never done it, you'll know all about it in no time."

He blew a God-Arouser mantra that stirred excitement in her heart. He kissed her cheek, nuzzled her breasts, and encircled her. "Don't struggle, you'll only bruise yourself."

Touched by the love mantra, Buakhli relaxed and her fear slipped away. Passion attacked her heart, making her feel shy. She turned her face away, glanced around the room, and kept silent.

Phlai Kaeo hugged her to him but she pushed against him, scratched, and tried to get free. Phlai Kaeo held her until she fell still. Then the two of them writhed around together, inflamed by near fatal passion.[21]

A storm broke wondrously. A typhoon wind[22] stirred up crashing waves. The deep ocean seemed on the point of destruction under a hellish gale. Waves of mighty power slammed

against a Chinese junk, almost sending it to the bottom. A sloop cut across to shelter close to the shore. A Hainanese,[23] heeling over with gunwales listing, cut across to a peninsula, and skirted along the shoreline.

Entering an estuary, it sailed straight towards a channel, hit an obstruction, and could go no further. Because the channel was tight and the water low, the junk was stuck dangling on the back of a turtle.

junk

A strong burst of wind slammed into the boat and lifted it clear. Half the boat entered the channel but then stuck fast again. The captain, afraid the ship would break up, tried to shift it free,

but the boat was too big for the small channel, and remained jammed halfway. When the sails were frantically hoisted and the cleats made fast, a stern wind drove the whole boat in on the flood.

Rain fell. The wind dropped. The ship coasted smoothly through the water away from the port. Both came together, refreshed and elated. They tasted joy cheek to cheek every day.

21. The next six stanzas, down to "cheek to cheek every day," are taken from TNA ms 12 (Sujit, *KCKP*, 200–201), absent from PD.

22. สลาตัน, *salatan*, a Malay word for "south," used in Thai for a southwesterly wind at the end of the rainy season, and more generally for any strong storm wind.

23. There seem to be a lot of boats around where only one would have been expected. The "Chinese junk" and the "Hainanese" could be the same, but "sloop" can hardly be, as this word *kampan* was used as a general term for European-style ships.

Phlai Kaeo and Buakhli lived together in total harmony. He put himself in Muen Han's service for some time, until Buakhli was several months pregnant.

Khun Phaen,[24] whose mastery was well-known and matchless, had been at Muen Han's house for many months, indeed over half a year.

His mind was consumed by thoughts of the past, and he still felt incensed as if licked by fire. "How can I overcome this? Being here accords with my idea

of getting a Goldchild to fulfill my intentions. I feel sorry for my darling Buakhli. What a pity. I think it's unfortunate,

as she ministers to her husband's needs very well, and her love and loyalty for me is undiminished. In the evening she comforts me with massage. Oh my heartstring, I'm heavy-hearted.

But for someone of a valiant military lineage, thinking round in circles like this is not good. I still have to make my way through the forest. I have not got a single one of the other things yet.

I must act like a fool who doesn't know how to do anything in order to annoy my father-in-law and draw him into a quarrel. I've been putting up this cover for several months."

Everyone else in the village—all the many soldiers, slaves, and servants—helped to make a living, but Phlai Kaeo sat around the house, acting like a clueless fellow who had never done anything.

Sijan and Muen Han took note of their son-in-law's attitude. "He doesn't do any work at all. The good-for-nothing has taken no interest for many months.

I mistakenly thought he was good but he's a disaster, not up to the others. He just buries himself in the house, dozing about. Does he want me to warn him with an elbow or what?"

After talking together, the couple summoned Phlai Kaeo. "Tell me, how are you going to feed yourself for the rest of your life?

Can't you see the example set by our men? If they spot something worth having, they go over there, steal it, run away, and bring it back—cash, cloth, silk, cattle, buffaloes, elephants, and horses. They seize everything, ransom it,[25]

---

24. The next six stanzas, down to "cover for several months," are taken from TNA ms 117 (Sujit, *KCKP*, 232), and TNA ms 177, absent from PD.

25. Robbers stole goods (especially cattle or buffaloes), then went to the owner and offered to "get them back."

and share out the proceeds. Then we all have food to eat and nothing to worry about, day after day.

You've been living in this house a long time but you haven't brought in one fueang. Aren't you ashamed in front of the servants? I've had my eye on you for a while."

Phlai Kaeo replied boldly to Muen Han. "I have in mind to devote myself to you until death, and I expect you to feed and protect me.

If I do anything good or bad, please tell me. If I don't listen to your words, if I'm pigheaded or devious or cheeky or lazy, then it's up to you to deal with me how you see fit.

But I won't steal elephants, seize people, rob houses, or go in for any other banditry. Yet if there's any danger, I'll bear the brunt so you're not affected."

Muen Han, forest expert, heard Phlai Kaeo out. "Tcha! You think you can get away with it like that? Just how much knowledge do you have?

The soldiers in my village can fight one man against ten. They're all invulnerable and can stand up to anything—slice them, stab them, or whatever and they won't budge.

For all your boasting, you're just a frail weakling. Your manners are like a woman. I don't think you could fight anybody. Just a puff of wind would bowl you over."

Khun Phaen, great valiant, listened to Muen Han's scorn, and his boasting about his own fierce, invulnerable soldiers, able to withstand any onslaught.

He smiled boldly and replied. "Just being invulnerable beyond compare is not enough in my opinion.

People can be so strong and tough that a blade will not penetrate but that doesn't count as able. If they're surrounded by people stabbing and slicing, then probably something will give way and they won't escape death.

To have true knowledge means being invulnerable to any type of weapon—so if completely surrounded by people firing guns, not even the tips of the hair are hurt one little bit."

After he had heard Phlai Kaeo, Muen Han's eyes turned fiery. "This fellow is really, really boastful! In a moment we'll put him to the test!"

He leapt down the stairs into the middle of the compound and loudly summoned soldiers and servants. "Load the guns you carry, every one of you. Come and shoot this fine fellow to test his lore!"

In response to their master, some twenty men ran up with their guns, loaded cartridges,[26] raised the guns, and cocked the triggers.

Muen Han called Phlai Kaeo, "Come on now! Why don't you come down from the house. Stop fooling around and hurry over here. If your knowledge is good, you've nothing to fear.

If you're really invulnerable to any weapon as you say, then you won't get hit by a single bullet when the guns shoot. But if you're not as able as you claim, you'll die riddled like a honeycomb."

Phlai Kaeo sat calmly. "Are you really going to shoot, Father? Please hold off for a little until there's an auspicious time, then test me out.

As[27] I'm going to my death, let me say farewell to Buakhli in the room. It was a waste for you to support me and have me married. As soon as I've said goodbye to her, I'll come down for you to test me."

Muen Han pointed angrily at Phlai Kaeo's face and growled, "How this arrogant fellow boasts! If you don't come down to face the shooting, I'll beat you to pulp and chase you out of the house."

Phlai Kaeo had dared to bait his father-in-law until he was red in the face but now could see that he had been given many warnings. He slid down the stairs, feigning reluctance.

"Maybe I spoke out loud without thinking and said the wrong thing, but if I don't comply, he'll beat me and drive me out." He quickly walked over. "Don't get angry. I'll let you shoot."

He composed himself, pronounced a formula, and meditated to still his mind and focus it unwaveringly in one direction. Then he raised his face to signal them to fire.

Muen Han called out, "Right, soldiers!" They raised the guns and took aim—twenty guns pointing straight at Phlai Kaeo. When they pulled the triggers, the guns flashed and roared.

Each man fired, reloaded, and fired again. Smoke enveloped the scene. The sound echoed off the rocks and shook the whole village.

Men and women ran up to look but could not see Phlai under a pall of smoke. Some thought he must be dead because the sound of gunfire was relentless.

The men reloaded and fired until their powder was exhausted. Phlai was

---

26. ปัดตัน, *patsatan*, powder and bullet wrapped in paper (PAL2, 635). Flintlock guns were inaccurate because the bullet fitted loosely in the barrel. One solution was to have a smaller shot wrapped in cloth or paper (Wilkinson, *Flintlock Guns*, 8). Damrong associates this charge with percussion cap guns such as the Enfield that came to Siam in the Fourth Reign (see p. 1366).

27. This stanza is taken from TNA ms 117 (Sujit, *KCKP*, 234) and TNA ms 177, absent from PD.

still sitting there, erect and fearless. Every one of the bandits shook his head in fear.

The villagers said, "This fellow is really able." "They've been loading and firing like a downpour." "All the powder and shot are used up, and he's not hit." "Not the tip of one hair hurt." "He's *able!*"

Muen Han was badly shaken to see Phlai Kaeo unscathed. He thought to himself, "This Kaeo is formidable! I used to think he just stumbled in here

to hide and conceal his identity. He acted humble like a mad fellow. I'm able with knowledge but it's humiliating that this fellow is better.

I don't think two fierce Lords of the Lions can live in one cave." The more he thought about it, the more he felt choked with anger. He walked quickly up the stairs to the house.

Phlai Kaeo was still focused unwaveringly. When the guns fell quiet, he opened his eyes and issued a challenge.

"Why are you standing still and not reloading? Aren't any of you going to shoot some more? Don't worry about my life. Please all take aim again."

The soldiers prostrated to Phlai Kaeo in fear. "The powder and shot are finished, sir." "Please forgive us for trying to shoot you." "Have mercy and don't punish us in anger."

Phlai Kaeo replied, "The idea wasn't yours. My father-in-law ordered you. You had to shoot so why should I get angry with you lot?"

With that, he went up to change clothes. His face was as black as torch soot, and his whole body was dirtied with gunpowder, but he was cool and unbothered.

The soldiers had fired over five hundred shots without piercing him or touching the tip of a hair. All the soldiers shook their heads in fear. "He's superb." "Superhuman." "Just the best."

Phlai walked into the house, picked up a change of clothes, and scrubbed himself with water to wash away the powder. Buakhli came to help him and please him.

She wrung out his clothes, led him into the room, and sat close beside him. Muen Han was so angry he could not take food, liquor, or tobacco.

Whether sitting up or lying down, he was in total turmoil. He called Sijan to talk. "Kaeo's knowledge is expert, more effective than mine.

He's a brave tusker and I'm a great tall war elephant. Can two such live in the same forest? Over time I'll be completely crushed.

The elephants, horses, people, wife, child, and whole village will all end up in his hands. He's overbearing enough already. I think he has to die."

Sijan's breast trembled with shock. "He's a venomous snake with evil powers, not at all how we thought. He'll cause trouble for us.

But if we make a wrong move, it'll be like beating a snake but only breaking its back.[28] He'll be as vengeful as a soldier. If you make a move, make sure he dies. Please think it out carefully."

Muen Han said, "We won't kill him with weapons. However much we stab and slash him, he has extraordinary lore. We must act friendly—and then poison him."

He ordered a female slave to go and call Buakhli over, and asked her gently, "Please, beloved daughter, I want to inquire about your true feelings.

Who do you really love more? Your father and mother who raised you from birth? Or the husband you met when you were already grown? I want to know your inner thoughts."

Buakhli spoke her feelings without any doubt. "The truth, with no pretending, is that I love my husband but not as much as I love my father.

How much does a husband love? He can just go down three steps and be gone.[29] But parents are never separated from their child into ripe old age, no matter how bad the child might be."

At these words, Muen Han and Sijan hugged and comforted her. He said, "It's no waste to love you like our own lives. If that's sincere, I'm thankful.

Recently we made a mistake in getting you married and established in a house. We have to begin again. Kaeo is a penniless pauper, and we won't have you living with him.

We'll set you up with a new husband and hand you all the property. We'll make sure it's a gentleman of good lineage with heaps of money to keep you happy.

You're still beautiful in every way. Why not get a new husband? We'll kill this Kaeo with poison. Tell me how you feel about this."

Buakhli listened to her father's question. She still loved Phlai like her own eyes. There had been no falling out between them so far.

But now that her father had mentioned heaps of money, her mind became fixed on possessions, and selfishness shaped her thinking. She was fated to die while pregnant, and so changed her mind.

"My parents have money by the bucketful. I don't need to worry about childbirth because I still look young and fresh. Crowds of people will come to ask for my hand every day."

---

28. A saying that the snake will live to take revenge (Gerini, "On Siamese Proverbs," 221).
29. See p. 775, note 31.

Because she was fated to die, she wearied of her husband, and believed everything her father said. With these thoughts she replied to him, "Up to you, Father. I don't object."

Once his daughter had agreed, Muen Han immediately concocted the poison, combining many ingredients according to a great manual from an old teacher.

"Take bile of peacock, bile of rat, bile of cobra; grind into a powder with rat poison;[30] add a squeeze of lime and bile of snake." He wrapped the concoction in a pan leaf and gave it to his daughter then and there.

"Prepare a meal of rice and curry. Add this poison to everything, and make sure to disguise it well to hide the aroma. Give it to him today. Don't delay."

Buakhli took the packet of potion, covered it with a cloth, and took leave of her father. She crept into her room and hid the potion in a secret place, then returned to the kitchen.

She made softshell turtle curry, lizard salad, *ho mok*, roast bird, and new rice in a lotus-petal bowl. She sprinkled the potion on all the dishes,

not letting anyone know. When everything was ready, she carried the food over and set it down along with a spittoon and water jug.

One of Phlai Kaeo's spirits had seen Buakhli adding the mixture, and immediately whispered to Phlai. "You just lost your wife. She's crooked.

She sprinkled powder over the rice and curry she prepared for you. It's poison for certain. Make sure you don't eat it."

Phlai Kaeo was perplexed. Since they had been together, there had been no problem, yet she treacherously intended to kill him.

Wanting to make absolutely sure, he picked a little from each dish—pork curry, fish curry, noodles, fishcake—molded them into one lump,

and threw it up onto a roof. A crow swooped down, swallowed it, flapped shakily, and died in an instant.

Any doubt disappeared. He believed the spirit. "It's true. She dares to kill me, the little demon. We've been living together for almost a year with nothing wrong. This must be Muen Han's idea.

If the spirit hadn't told me, I'd be dead. I must repay her as she deserves. I can no longer support her as my wife. I have to kill her."

He composed himself and concealed any hint of his intention. He slyly said to Buakhli, "I'm not well. I'm aching all over and I've got a bad case of the shakes.

---

30. สารหนู, *san nu*, usually meaning arsenic. As several commentators have noted, with this in the mix, it's not clear why all the other ingredients were needed.

Only two or three mouthfuls of the food went down, and now I feel nauseous and can't eat any more. Take the food away and put it over there. I'll sleep it off until the queasiness goes.

I can't sit up because my head's spinning." Buakhli noticed nothing unusual. She put covers on the dishes and carried the food away, then returned and sat massaging his back.

She had no suspicion about Phlai Kaeo. After sunset, Phlai kept up the pretence by fondling and caressing her. "Please give the little child in your belly to me."

Not knowing his intention, Buakhli replied innocently, "Why do you ask this of me? Surely the child in my womb is your child?"

Phlai Kaeo saw that she did not understand. He stroked her soothingly and spoke with cunning. "True, it's our child together. But I want the authority over the child,[31] so I'm asking you.

The newborn first child will belong to me, the father. I'm asking my darling not to oppose that. If you still love me with your whole heart, please give your permission with no objection."

Buakhli laughed. "Why are you pleading with me like this? It's our child together so it will be your child, whatever I say."

Phlai Kaeo replied, "What a pity, you oppose my wishes. This is all I ask and you won't consent. It's a waste of effort loving you. You don't think.

I just want you to say you agree that I have the authority.[32] I want to cherish the child as my partner for life, but if you don't care for me already, then let it go."

Buakhli was fated to lose the life she had been given, so she carelessly replied with too much sarcasm. "I agree with what you want.

You won't give up picking at me so slit me open and take it out." Khun Phaen said, "Good. You give me the power." Her permission accorded with what he had in mind.

He embraced, fondled, and aroused her. Buakhli was not at all dismayed. He hugged her tightly, kissed, and caressed her so that she trusted him completely.

---

31. สิทธิ, *sit*, which in modern usage means a right, but earlier meant power or authority. Pallegoix defined it as "Perfect, endowed with perfect strength" (PAL, 741).

32. กรรมสิทธิ์, *kammasit*, which in modern usage means ownership or right of ownership. Pallegoix defined it as "Under power; subject to; jurisdiction," and *pen kammasit kae* as "To be under the power of another" (PAL, 213).

Late at night when everyone was sleeping quietly, he blew a Subduer formula to immobilize people, and got up to get things ready.

He hastily put his devices, three candles, a flint box, sacred thread, and yantra cloths in a sidebag.

He grasped a tooled knife with a coral handle, and went straight to Buakhli. He parted the curtains and turned up the mosquito net. The lamp shed a dim light.

He stood up on the bed beside her and examined her sleeping form with a great sigh. "I didn't know such a body could have no heart. That she could kill her husband is unthinkable."

He raised the knife to strike but felt a pang in his heart, changed his mind, and relaxed his arm. Then he thought again about her giving him the poison. "Don't hesitate! Take her life."

He plunged the knife into her chest, piercing right through. She writhed and died. Red blood spurted out and spread all around like the killing of a buffalo.

He cut her belly wide open, and severed the umbilical cord. Examining the baby, he was happy to find it was the male he wanted.

He lifted the infant out of her belly. "Come, my Goldchild.[33] Go with your father." He picked up his big sidebag and hung it round his neck. He wrapped the son in a cloth, and slung him on his shoulder.

old wat

---

33. กุมารทอง, *kuman thong*, see p. 316, note 2. There are several methods for creating a *kuman thong*. According to one manual, the person must act alone; use an adept's knife to open the belly; invite the child to go; take him to an ordination hall, preaching hall, or somewhere within *sema* boundary stones so that the mother's spirit cannot enter and interfere with the rite; make a ritual area with posts of amora wood in the four directions, a ceiling of white cloth, and seven circles of sacred thread; place a Mongkut Phraphutthajao yantra on the roof, Trinisinghe and Itthipiso yantra in the four directions; make a frame with *chaiyaphruek* wood; use *marit*, *kankrao*, *kanphai*, and *rak* wood for kindling; grill the body evenly, and complete the rite before dawn; put lac and gold leaf on the body; and finish by pronouncing the *anissa* formula (SWC, 1:405–6).

Opening the door, he walked quickly away from the village through the forest to Wat Tai. He closed the door of the preaching hall, shot the bolt inside, and inserted battens to secure it tight.

He put down the sidebag and took out his flint box to strike a flame and light candles. He stuck pieces of victoriflora[34] wood in the ground to make a frame on which to lay the Goldchild.

He put a yantra cloth with a Narayana design of mighty power over his head, another with a Racha design on his lower body, another with Narai Ripping the Chest[35] on his middle, and one with Nang Thorani on the ground.

He drove amora wood into the earth as pillars of the four directions, attached more yantra cloths as flags, and circled them with sacred thread. As a canopy he put a cloth with the design of Indra's breast chain. Everything was prepared according to the manual.

To light a fire on the ground below, he made a bundle of goodwood, armorbark, and shieldvine.[36] He meditated to focus his mind, and sat grilling the Goldchild,

heating the whole body, turning it over front and back so the fat dripped and sizzled. Just as the dawn brightened and a golden sun rose, it was dry and crisp as he wanted.

๛

Buakhli's servant, Granny Lao, who was living in the area on the ground below the big house, saw a patch of blood soaking through. Shocked, she ran upstairs to look

and found the curtains opened, mosquito net raised, and Buakhli lying dead, her face already pallid, amid a spreading pool of blood. She ran out screaming,

banged on doors, and shouted loudly, "Mistress Buakhli's dead, master! Her

---

34. ชัยพฤกษ์, *chaiyaphruek*, *Cassia fistula*, golden showers. The text adds *phraya-ya*, prince of medicines. All the woods used in this ceremony have names in Thai that convey the qualities to be instilled in the spirit (KW, 146; SB, 102). *Chaiya* means victory, and *phruek* comes from the Sanskrit word for plants, used, for example, in the Thai word for botany.

35. นารายณ์ฉีกอก, *narai chik ok*. A *yak* demon Hiranyakasipu, หิรัณยกศิปุ, "golden garments," persecuted his son Prahlada, ประหลาท, Pralat, for worshipping Vishnu, so Vishnu assumed his incarnation as the man-lion, Norasing, and ripped open Hiranyakasipu's breast with a claw (*Hindu Myths*, 170; see image in Niyada, *Tamra phap thewarup*, 208).

36. มะริด, *marit*, *Diospyros discolor/philippensis*, in the ebony family, here rendered as goodwood on Suphon's suggestion that *marit* is used here because the name sounds like *samret*, success (SB, 102). กันเกรา, *kankrao*, *Fagraea fragrans*, tembesu, Burma yellowheart, here rendered as armorbark because the Thai word echoes *kankro*, กันเกราะ, armor. กันภัย, *kanphai*, *Afgetkia mahidolae*, a vine with bunches of purple and white flowers, found in Kanchanaburi, here rendered as shieldvine to convey the meaning of *kanphai*, "ward off danger."

whole body's slashed to pieces. And Phlai is nowhere to be seen."

Muen Han and Sijan jumped up with a start. They scrambled across in shock, and saw their dead daughter.

Rushing[37] over, they embraced her. "How can we lose you?" They hugged and rocked her, struck silent by the pain of Buakhli's death.

Servants shrieked and screamed wildly at the thought of their dead mistress. Muen Han sat speechless from sorrow, feeling his heart was choked.

"He cut her open! There's pools of blood! Damn! Kaeo thinks he can outdo me." He went out of the house and called the servants, who all rushed over.

"Kaeo has killed Buakhli and run off. Go after him, all of you. Search the whole village." They ran off wildly in all directions, both inside and outside the compound,

carrying every kind of weapon—pikes, cleavers,[38] lances, spears, guns, knives, tridents, swords, kris, and poisoned arrows. They followed traces of blood

left here and there on the grass straight through the forest to Wat Tai. Finding the door of the preaching hall bolted from the inside, they walked round to look through a chink.

By the flickering light, they saw Phlai Kaeo sitting in the preaching hall. They called out to one another to surround the place closely, and battered the door with a ram.

Khun Phaen recited mantra unperturbed. The spirit rose up and chattered. Khun Phaen leapt up on the spirit's neck. "Goldchild, help get me out of this spot."

Goldchild sprung up nimbly and took his father out through a chink. Because of the mighty power of Khun Phaen's lore,[39] Muen Han's people did not see them pass over their heads.

Khun Phaen arrived outside the ordination hall with Goldchild. "I'll show myself to Muen Han so he knows my mastery and expertise, then go to Kanburi."

---

37. The next two stanzas are taken from TNA ms 117 (Sujit, *KCKP*, 241) and TNA ms 177, absent from PD.

38. ตาว, *tao*, a large knife, probably the same as *dao*: "Most of the aboriginal tribes of Northeastern India use this weapon. It has a straight, heavy, square-ended, chisel-edged blade, narrowest at the hilt. This serves both the domestic as well as martial purposes" (Pant, *Catalogue of Arms*, 17).

39. ไสยเวทวิชาการ, *saiya wet wichakan*. This is one of the very few appearances in the poem of the word *sai/saiya*, that in the form *saiyasat*, is the usual modern term for supernaturalism.

Relaxing the mantra so people could see them, he stood looking as formidable as a lion with his right hand holding the powerful kris, and his left leading the Goldchild spirit.

The sight of them created an uproar. People shouted at one another loudly, and charged forward brandishing poisoned arrows, swords, staves, and clubs.

Khun Phaen yelled a Power of Garuda mantra. Weapons slipped from the assailants' hands. They fell down and could not get back up. Muen Han strode up holding a lance and drove his people to attack.

Khun Phaen called out, "You men have done me no wrong. I'll kill Muen Han alone. Don't insist on protecting your master or you'll die with your heads cut off and scattered across the earth."

The soldiers had witnessed his invulnerability and knew they could not fight him face to face. But they feared their boss too, so they put on an angry act by dancing wildly up and down.

In a rage, Muen Han waggled his finger at Khun Phaen, saying, "Hey, you scum! You don't show me any gratitude. What a waste of effort to have supported you.

I fed you every morning and night, and even gave you my beloved daughter, yet you commit this treachery. This time I won't spare your life."

Seething with anger, Khun Phaen took out his kris and danced forward whirling it. "You shout out these accusations but I don't hear you talking about your own crime.

You treacherously conspired with your daughter to poison me out of envy. If we'd been straight with each other, you'd still be my father-in-law, but you had crooked thoughts, so I killed your daughter.

Don't cling on to the idea that you have powers. Don't believe that you'll survive. Heads will roll, and faces turn white, both master and men." He came closer, flourishing his kris.

Muen Han stepped forward, raised his lance and struck. Because Phlai was invulnerable, it did not touch even the tip of his body hair. Phlai drew out his adept's knife and stabbed but it only creased the skin.

Muen Han slashed. Phaen parried, stabbed back with his kris, and twirled away, evading him nimbly. They fought a long time with neither giving ground.

As Muen Han's lance was longer than the kris, Khun Phaen had to dart in close then dodge away. When Muen Han lunged with the lance, Khun Phaen stabbed with the kris, but the blows missed every time.

Then Muen Han slashed, Phaen parried, and delivered a mighty blow with the kris. Muen Han staggered. Khun Phaen struck again and again until Muen Han fell flat on the ground, and Phaen put his foot on Muen Han's neck. "Now, Father-in-law!"

Some cowardly soldiers who feared death scattered into the forests, throwing away their weapons. The more daring ones rushed up to help their master, and were all destroyed.

Muen Han squirmed desperately. Other people did not dare come close. Khun Phaen raised his kris to strike and said, "Do you see my mastery or not, you blackguard?

Not one of your thrusts and lunges penetrated me. Stop believing *you* are invulnerable. I'll stick this kris in your mouth and cut out your tongue. Hey, if you're able, then wriggle your way free."

Muen Han squirmed as hard as he could, rolling his head until his back and shoulders were skinned. He did not want to die so cried out, "I submit. Spare my life.

It's the truth. I got angry because we couldn't shoot you. I had the idea of killing you with poison. That was wrong. Please forgive me."

Khun Phaen, great romancer, seeing Muen Han in fear for his life, spoke with menace. "Your wrongdoing deserves to be punished with death,

but on second thoughts, you fed and supported me in your house, giving me rice, curry, chili, and salt. For that kindness, I won't execute you.

Also your good wife, Sijan, gave me cash and clothing. If I didn't think of these things, your life would be dust. This time it's not your fate to die.

Stay here. I'm going home." He called Goldchild and all his spirits, sprites, and spectrals, which swarmed around his body. He nimbly leapt onto Goldchild's neck and instantly disappeared.

They went like a wisp of smoke, unseen by anyone, through the forest, over canals, lakes, and streams, to Kanburi.

Through the spirits' power, the distance of over a thousand[40] was covered swiftly in one instant. He went up to his house as happy as if he had acquired a precious gem.

Having seen the extent of Phlai Kaeo's mastery, including his martial skills, Muen Han was still trembling.

"I'm a person of some mastery but I don't have a fraction of his. I can't face

---

40. No unit is given. The distance from Ban Tham to Cockfight Hill as the spirit flies is about 27 kms. Probably the unit meant was a *sen* although a thousand of these would be 40 kms.

up to him. The servants who are still left will gossip.

Though I'm not dead, I'm finished. Wherever this news reaches, I'll be shamed. All my effort to build a name for myself has gone to waste. It'll be known for a long time to come that I lost my dignity and my reputation.

The more I think about it, the more I feel choked." He called out to the servants to return home. He had a coffin made for Buakhli in great haste, and sent his soldiers to bury it behind the wat.

Muen Han never lost the feeling of frustration in his chest, and never stopped seething with resentment. He still excelled in many branches of knowledge but was overwhelmed by gloom.

Khun Phaen, great romancer, now had powers that were unequalled. As he had hoped, he now had a skillful son, Goldchild.

For this episode in chapter 16, Prince Damrong elected to use a newer version composed by Khru Jaeng in the mid-nineteenth century. This translation is based on an older version found in the Wat Ko edition (WK, 13:489–95).

Now to tell of Khun Phaen, great romancer, of such resplendent powers. Having been separated from Laothong for several days, he was feeling mournful.

Sleeping alone, he pined for her in solitude and sorrow. Although there were crowds of young Thai and Lao servant girls, he was unwilling to taste their charms.

Instead he harbored resentment in his breast. "This Khun Chang has created such trouble for me. He stole my Wanthong, even though I thought he was a friend.

On top of that, he had Laothong separated from me by laying false accusations with the king. People in every direction fear my strong powers of mastery.

Unless I take revenge, he won't stop. He'll petition the king time after time. I'll slash him dead and chop him into little pieces to my own satisfaction.

At present I don't have the weapons or the tools." After thinking, he promptly sent for fifteen of his servants

to carry rice, fish, and other provisions. "I'm going into the forest to make myself a weapon. Ai-Phon, take some of my money along."

When he had said farewell to his mother, he left the house and cut across the plain, surrounded by his crowd of servants.

For many nights and many days he traveled through the wilds, shedding tears over missing his wife. Reaching a mine with a large deposit of fluid metal, he cut wood, attached cloth to make a canopy,

and set candles, incense, and offerings on the shrine for the deities to witness. "I beg you to allow me to take some metal away."

chalom *baskets*

Having made offerings of liquor, he sent his servants

down to collect as many small lumps of ore as they could carry. It was put in *chalom*[1] baskets that the servants carried along behind.

They came upon an elephant in musth at the edge of a path, blocking their way. He was oozing oil, breaking off branches, wheeling around, and thrashing about, filling the forest with noise.

Khun Phaen took a piece of fluid metal and threw it, hitting the elephant's flank and piercing through, leaving a huge hole. The animal trumpeted and fled, bumped its head into a tree, and tumbled to the ground.

Khun Phaen retrieved the metal he had thrown at the elephant and walked into the forest. In the evening they steamed rice to eat. Coming to a place called the Village of Rak Hill,[2]

they built a furnace, erected a shrine, and made offerings. They kindled a fire with bones from a corpse mixed with teak wood, and used liquor, lacquer, and bellows to melt iron in a crucible.

Khun Phaen dressed in white, covering his shoulders with a sabai of new white fabric. When they had put in all the iron, he cast a powerful mantra,

forbade the servants from walking around, and loudly summoned rishis. It was a Saturday with an auspicious time, open in all directions. The fire glowed brightly.

When the iron turned molten in the crucible, it was poured into a long narrow mold. Blown with the bellows, the metal glowed as red as fire. Big tongs were used to grip it.

The ingot was weighed at two chang and five tamlueng.[3] A salver was set up with a *baisi*, and offerings were made, then the smiths were asked to beat the metal forthwith.

There were seven persons—Ta-Phet, Rathaya, Ta-Nan, Ta-Jantachot, Ta-Phon, Ta-Kha, Ta-Phet—all dressed in white and arrayed with amulets.

The fluid metal was melted and added to the mix. Someone was deputed to light candles and activate the shrine. Once that was done, the charcoal was scraped away.

Metal of Chinese, Cham, Indian, and Farang origin was used to make a platform. At an auspicious time of victory according to the manual, Khun Phaen felt a trembling,[4] as should be.

---

1. ฉะลอม, ชะลอม, a container made of loose basketwork, often used for fruit or vegetables (Wibun, *Phojananukrom hatthakam*, 138–39).

2. บ้านเขารัก, Ban Khao Rak. There are many hills with similar names. The most likely is 16 kms southwest of U Thong in Amphoe Huai Krachao (see map 2).

3. 2x80 + 5x4 = 180 baht of 15.2 grams, about 1.22 kilograms.

4. เขม่น, *khamen*, an involuntary trembling of muscle or bone, especially of the eyelids, believed to be an omen.

The weight and proportions were exactly right. The matter was accomplished quickly, as desired. The place where the sword was beaten was given the fitting name of the Village of the Bell Spear.[5]

Because of the power of the fluid metal, while it was being forged into a sword, the metal made an almighty sound like that of a conch. The sword was beaten to be sharp and strong, polished to gleam like an emerald beetle,

anointed with spirit oil, and annealed for sharpness and strength. A handle was fashioned from pacifier wood. When it was done, he raised the sword to his head, and carried it away.

He journeyed through the Kanburi region, through hills and forests. Walking along a path, they came across a tall narrow rock.

Khun Phaen sat down and sharpened the sword with the intent it should defeat and kill his enemies. He declared, "Let this place be called the Village of the Whetstone.[6]

May it be well known in the future." He raised the keen, strong sword above his head with a swish and reduced the rock to fragments. He took the sword and led his men off.

He arrived in excitement before Wat Kajom,[7] rushed up to the sala, and entered the front of the ordination hall.

In the bright, glaring sunshine of midday, he chanted mantra without a break, and immersed the sword in spirit oil combined with all 108 medicines,

including frog herb, diamond-on-anvil, *sangkorani,* and rhino's hoof herb. After steeping, the sword was dried in the sun. A fly flew into the blade and died with its head severed.

The power of the metal and sharpness of the sword stirred the heavens. Khun Phaen stood up, gripping the sword, and brandished it to flash and dazzle. He walked away, holding the sword,

and entered a graveyard to instill in the weapon the power to defeat enemies. He made offerings with candle and incense, and paid respect to his father and teachers.

For protective *athan* power, the hair of a spirit, a Phakhawam, yellow sapphire, pearl, boar's fang, and powder already instilled with knowledge as a yantra were loaded into the sword to have the power to defeat and overcome ene-

---

5. บ้านทวนระฆัง, Ban Thuan Rakhang. Possibly this is now Phanom Thuan, an amphoe in Kanchanaburi, as this is around 15 kms south of Rak Hill where the ore was smelted, above, and on the way to Ban Hin Lap, which appears below (see map 2).

6. บ้านหินลับ, Ban Hin Lap, 30 kms northwest of Kanchanburi in the south of Amphoe Bo Phloi (see map 2).

7. Most likely this is Wat Sa Krajom, 4 kms north of U Thong.

mies. He offered a *baisi*, and anointed the sword with fragrant powder, scented oil, and krajae-sandal. Once done,

he prepared a ceremony for soothing the soul, and placed the sword on a shrine, while intoning mantra for invulnerability and expertise in battle.

He raised both spectrals and demons, creating uproar among the spirits in the graveyard. "Grant me power in battle, invulnerability, and invisibility.

I call on the sky, earth, and ocean, everything, to make this sword excellent, effective, splendid, auspicious, indestructible, and invincible."

As a result of lore, thunder and lightning struck seven times. Khun Phaen was untouched because of his mastery.

The sword rose up and vibrated with the power of its fluid metal and instilled spirit. He promptly gave it the name, Skystorm, raised it to his head, and hurried away.

For Khun Phaen's search for a horse in chapter 16, Prince Damrong elected to use an older version rather than Khru Jaeng's recomposition. This is Khru Jaeng's version. The translation is based on Sujit Wongthet's publication (Sujit, *KCKP*, 215–18, 246–50). Sujit published two documents from the National Archives: a typescript labeled number 12 in cupboard 116; and a *samut thai*, number 112. This passage is the same in both sources, except for minor copying errors.

Now to tell of Granny Krawae, a widow who lived on the bay at the mouth of the Tenasserim River. Since her husband had died many years earlier, she had sold horses and was rich with cash and servants.

She had a huge corral with a ditch and fence around to pen the horses. In the morning the corral was opened to let them out, and in the evening they were all rounded up again, all through the year.

Now to tell of a filly who went looking for food around the Tenasserim Bay, grazing where the grass sprouted at the bank of the river. That was the home of a water horse[1]

which was enormous, strong, and sturdy. When it saw the filly approach, the water horse leapt up to straddle its back. A Farang who saw the sight, loaded a gun and stood taking aim.

Normally when a water horse mates, it bites the filly to death afterwards. But on this occasion, the Farang let fire before it had time to bite, and the water horse leapt into the river.

The filly survived unscathed, and stayed at its owner's house until its belly was large. On a Saturday, a conjunction of great success,[2] a foal was born without fatality.

His coloring resembled the father—dusky grey like clouds in the sky. He was a very fine animal according to the manual, of the lineage of valiant steeds, tall with a broad chest, a rear like a *maprang*, a rounded midriff, and a beau-

---

1. See p. 325, note 45.
2. See p. 319, note 23.

tifully sleek tail. He pranced and danced around spiritedly. No other horse was strong enough to stand up to him.

When the corral was opened in the morning for the horses to go out and crop the grass, the string of horses waded across the river to the opposite bank, but this Color of Mist had the power to vault straight across without wading.

He jumped, pranced, and danced around in play, then sauntered slowly, then wheeled around, kicking up the dust, pawing the ground, and galloping headlong across the plain.

He was the bully boss of the herd. He chased the fillies in heat, and bit other colts, none of which could fight back but scattered and ran away. Every day the owner would pursue him to deliver a beating.

At that time, the quick-witted Khun Phaen was traveling around for a long time, searching every locality, but none of the horses he saw were to his liking.

When he arrived in the forest fringe by Widow Krawae's village, he saw the whole place was packed with horses of every color—coal black, green black, dun, chestnut, smoky grey, and light grey.

Khun Phaen liked what he saw, and approached to make an inspection. He noticed that the tall grey colt of an unusual color was chasing and biting the others, which scattered away in flight.

His coat was a dusky color. His flanks, tail, ears, and eyes were correct according to the manual, with no exception. He had a broad chest, stout rear, four firm fetlocks, and a suitably sleek, flowing body.

Finding him perfectly to his liking, Khun Phaen went into the compound and saw the old lady sitting up in a house. He sank down, wai-ed her, and asked about the horses. "Are they for sale?"

Granny Krawae said, "Yes, I'll sell. Which one do you like?" Khun Phaen replied straightaway, "I like the misty-colored one, Granny.

Whether he's cheap or dear, I won't complain. Tell me the price you usually sell for. I like him so much I won't be upset. Whatever Granny wishes."

"Oh, you like this Color of Mist, do you? No need to buy him. I'll let you have him for nothing. He's unruly. He bites and bothers the other horses. The lads have to chase him all day through to evening. Very tedious.

He's too frisky for anything, too good. Do you think you can ride him, my son? If you want him I won't stand in your way. Take him. I'll be glad to be rid of him.

He's strong but does not yet know the rope. He bucks and twists so much he's unridable. How will you take him home? He'll attack, kick and bite you to death."

Khun Phaen, great master, was immeasurably happy to hear this. "Though you say he's bold, strong, and wild, if you'll let me have him, I'll take him.

But as he's not used to a rope, I'm not sure how to catch him. I want to know how difficult it will be. Please catch him for me, Granny."

Granny Krawae said, "The horse hands can't get close to him. When they approach, he bounds away. He can jump seven fathoms, this horse. People have seen that and admired him for a long time.

At first he was going to be taken as a royal horse. The whole village crowded around to catch him. However many surrounded him made no difference. When they brought a rope and bridle near, he jumped over them and escaped.

If you want to take a good look at him, I'll call him for you to catch." She scooped up a handful of bran. When the horse came close, she held out her hand

and called out to him, "Come on, Mist." The horse leapt and pranced, came close, and licked the bran from her hand. She took a firm grip on his mane.

Khun Phaen pulled some grass from a sheaf, held his breath, intoned a mantra, fed the grass to the horse, and blew. Color of Mist was hit by the mantra and stunned. With his palm, Khun Phaen stroked his whole body.

Under the power of the mantra, the horse was induced not to flee. Color of Mist fell greatly in love with Khun Phaen. He stopped prancing around and began to calm down.

Khun Phaen quickly put on a harness while intoning additional love mantras to strengthen the horse's attachment. He strung on the straps and carefully tightened them well and properly.

Grasping the reins tight in his hand, he leapt onto the horse's back. Color of Mist wheeled around wildly, kicking up dust,

and reared up with his front legs to throw his rider off. When he rocked back down, Khun Phaen slipped into a riding position on the horse's back. When the horse turned to bite, Phaen punched him in the mouth. The horse bucked fore and aft without stopping,

rearing up wildly then curling his head down onto his chest. Khun Phaen shook the reins strongly and cracked the whip repeatedly. The horse took off in a fast gallop with long strides,

hooves pounding like a storm raging, streaking ahead like a howling gale. Khun Phaen slackened the rein, and cracked the whip. The horse galloped hard for a time, and then slowed.

Khun Phaen saw he was tiring and eased off, making him dance with his haunches lowered, neck arched, chest thrust forward, and face raised, looking splendid. He had stopped bucking and become calm and orderly,

no longer stubborn. Khun Phaen held him on a tight rein, making him step gently, beating a rhythm with his hooves, marking time on the spot. Next Khun Phaen shook the reins lightly and taught him the spear dance,

high-stepping for polo, long and short pacing, all the disciplines of a thoroughbred. Then he rode straight to Granny Krawae's house.

She saw and laughed loudly. "When he took off with you, my heart sank. I thought he'd buck you off to fall down dead. You're truly, genuinely good.

You had the strength and expertise to keep your seat. Color of Mist has learned to fear your powers for sure. He's calmed his prancing and lost his rowdiness. He's no longer difficult but is quiet and docile.

Seeing him hang his head shows he fears you a lot. I give him into your ownership. Now that I've seen your knowledge and expertise of military matters, I won't take a sale price."

Khun Phaen led Color of Mist away to swab him down. After stroking him, tethering him, and feeding him grass, he went straight up to Granny Krawae's house and poured out fifteen in silver.[3]

"I thank you for giving him to me for nothing. This fifteen in silver I give in return for your kindness. This is all the money I brought. Even five chang would be less than his worth."

Granny Krawae watched him pour out the pile of money. She smiled broadly and patted him, back and front. "You're expert with knowledge and lore. No human in the lower world is equal."

She gave him a blessing. "May you have long life, high rank, everything. May you defeat every region and country without harm from any weapon."

She called servants to bring food, both savory and sweet. Khun Phaen paid respect and ate. Once the meal was finished, he took his leave,

harnessed and decorated the horse with Burmese flanchards and tooled stirrups, said farewell, leapt onto his back, and galloped hard for some time to reach Kanchanaburi.

---

3. Probably the unit is tamlueng.

Kukrit offered an alternative version of Siprajan's advice to Phim before entering the bridal hall in chapter 7. He claimed this extract came from the published version of Khru Jaeng's contributions to *KCKP*, but he had lost the book and was reproducing it from memory (KP, 92–95). We have been unable to locate a copy of the book.

Sujit suspects that this passage was more likely to be part of Sijan's instructions to Buakhli in chapter 16, as written by Khru Jaeng, but the passage does not appear in the reprint of two manuscripts of the Khru Jaeng version in Sujit's book (*KCKP*, 126). Both passages are similar to Khru Jaeng's version of Busaba's advice to Simala at her marriage to Phra Wai (see chapter 33), but are also more elaborate and more direct. Did Kukrit "improve" them? As both poet and prankster, he was quite capable of it.

Late at night when all were sleeping quietly throughout the house, the mother consoled her beloved little daughter. "You're going to sleep with your husband.

My beauty, make an effort to listen to my instructions and remember them. If a woman ministers to her husband well, he'll not tire of her.

Humbly minister to him. When he's hard, don't go against his wishes. When you know how much he wants to love, move and shake to satisfy each other.

Siprajan then instructed Phim on the importance of cooking.

First, boiled pig's trotters. Make sure the meat is truly tender. Add peanuts fried golden brown. Moist tamarind is not enough. Add vinegar to round off the taste.

Second, chicken's eggs. Roast at some distance from the fire until they are thick and cloudy as baelfruit sap when cracked open. Stir with a stick until white as jelly. Pour in some Japanese soy sauce and chopped onion.

Third, eels. Grill on the fire until they have drops of sweat. Coil into a pot with peanut and cleaned white rice. Add pounded lemongrass and simmer on high heat until the soup is white, the rice swells, and the peanut is soft enough to be stirred into the eel. Pick a kaffir lime leaf, strip out the stalk, and add. Scoop into a thin Farang bowl.

Stir with a stick until the rice and eel are thoroughly mixed. Break the heads off and discard all the bones. Grill chili, shrimp paste, and garlic until brown, then pound together like medicine for a good taste.

Add just enough fish sauce to moisten the chili. When the garlic is cooked, add and pound further. Garnish with an onion boiled and chopped slantwise, coriander leaves, and fresh green lime for a truly good taste.

Try to remember these and cook for him to savor. All three are for increasing strength. Cook them for him often and he'll become more active. This is true and certain.

If you make them for him to eat every day, even a flabby one will be as stiff as a pole. When evening comes, he'll climb aboard without sleeping, and paddle along at a steady lick until the temple bell tolls.

KHUN CHANG'S *MAHORI*

The scene is part of a much longer and more elaborate account of Khun Chang's wedding in chapter 12. It takes place at Siprajan's house, immediately after the dowry procession has arrived and has negotiated entry past someone guarding the door. This translation is based on TNA mss 131 (CS, 167).

The guests came up to a spacious cross hall which was packed so tightly with people and goods that there was no room, and some people overflowed down the stairs. A *mahori* started without delay.

They played a piece about Garuda abducting Kaki to his Chimphli Palace to enjoy her.[1] Phrommathat searched for her, bathed in tears of lament. When Lord Garuda came to play *ska* dice,[2]

the *khonthan* transformed himself into a mite, traveled to the palace hidden in Garuda's feathers, and induced the beauteous Kaki to make love with him.

---

1. On Kaki, see p. 350, note 49. Kaki is married to King Phrommathat, Brahmadatta, king of Benares. Lord Garuda hears of Phrommathat's famed skill at *ska* dice, and issues a challenge. Every week, Lord Garuda comes in human guise to play against Phrommathat. Lord Garuda sees Kaki and falls in love. He waits until nightfall, uses his powers to create thunder and darkness, then goes to her room and persuades her to leave with him for his Chimphli Palace. Phrommathat is distraught, but the *khonthan*, a musician-retainer who is also smitten with Kaki, suspects that Garuda is responsible and advises his master to remain calm. After the next dice game, the *khonthan* transforms himself into a mite, stows away in Garuda's plumage, and is carried away to Chimphli. At night while Garuda is with Kaki, the *khonthan* hides. By day when Garuda is away, he makes love to her. The *khonthan* then returns to Phrommathat's palace by the same method, and, at the next dice game, boasts of his success with Kaki. Garuda is so enraged at Kaki that he decides to restore her to Phrommathat. Phrommathat is also so angry at Kaki that he floats her away on a raft. She has a short dalliance with a junk captain, and is then taken up by a forest bandit. The bandit's gang members so lust after her that they kill their leader and then fall to fighting among themselves. Kaki flees into the forest and is discovered by King Thotsawong on a hunting expedition. She tells him that she is the virginal daughter of a forest rishi, and is taken back to his palace. Meanwhile Phrommathat has died of grief at missing Kaki, and is succeeded by the *khonthan* who goes to war with Thotsawong, kills him, and reclaims Kaki. They live happily ever after.

2. สกา, *ska,* a game akin to backgammon where the players throw dice and move counters on a board.

On return he reported the matter to Lord Phrommathat, who was so enraged that he made arrangements for musicians and singers to recount the story from the abduction of Kaki from the city palace.

When Garuda came to play dice on the appointed day, the proficient musicians and singers played the piece for him to hear, inflaming Garuda with rage.

Lord Garuda was so in love with Kaki, and had no suspicions, carelessly assuming that nobody could come to Chimphli Palace as it was so remote.

The deities and masterminds could not cross the wide expanse of the Sithandon Ocean.³ The powerful and almighty gods had their own heavenly ladies to enjoy.

Seven days later, he went to play dice again, flying through the air like a windmill, gliding down to the city, and changing himself into human form.

He played dice with Lord Phrommathat while the *khonthan* arranged a well-trained ensemble. The *khonthan* prostrated and bowed to pay respect to the lords, and sang with the music,

saying, "Oh alas! I am parted from the caress which was once as fragrant as a *phayom* flower or a heavenly *montha*. Oh, since we made love together at Chimphli Palace, I have been apart from darling Kaki for seven days.

I miss the fragrance I once enjoyed so much that I lament with lust and longing. But today my heart feels refreshed again as I'm sure my nose senses Kaki.⁴

Someone has been intimate with her, and her scent has followed his body to this place. This someone is near at hand in this audience hall. Oh, I fear my heart is broken and my love lost."

A pipe intoned a mournful lament. A fiddle keened softly. A lute plick-plucked alongside. Cymbals slapped the rhythm with a sharp sound.

A lyre took up the tune following the cymbals. A *rammana* drum⁵ tripped out a sprightly tread, and a *thon* drum boomed. Listeners were absorbed with enjoyment.

---

3. สีทันดร, *sithandon*, Sidantara. In the Three Worlds: "Around the royal Sumeru mountain there is an expanse of water that separates it off; this water, which is called the Sidantara ocean, surrounds it, is 84,000 *yojana* wide, and is 84,000 *yojana* deep; and its circumference is 756,000 *yojana*." There are also vast oceans also named Sidantara surrounding each of the mountain ranges ringing Mount Meru (RR, 276).

4. Kaki's fragrance lingers on her love partners for seven days.

5. ร้ามะนา, *rammana*, a broad and shallow one-sided drum rather like a large tambourine, held vertical with one hand and tapped with the other to accompany many kinds of folk performance.

Siprajan watched, listened, and knew what she had to do. She took money out of the end of her cloth and offered it to the musicians. "Please play a bit more. It's delightful. I want to hear how the story ends."

Nang Soi Son, the singer, continued the story. The disguised Garuda turned this way and that in rage that the *khonthan* had sneaked into his palace and made love to Kaki.

Furiously he asked, "About this lovemaking with Kaki, is Garuda's palace near or far? Do you know, or are you guessing and making all this up to seem real?"

The *khonthan* laughed joyfully and said, "Everything I related is true." While the *khonthan* taunted Garuda with his claims, the ensemble played rousing *choet*,[6] and cymbals clashed to heighten the drama.

fiddle, lute, and rammana *drum*

A tongue teased a pipe and fingers fluttered flippantly on a flute, then switched to a deep tone that cut to the gut. Sticks stuttered on *ranat* strings, tripping along behind the tune of a fiddle,

which sobbed and sawed and sorrowed over the sound of the lead *ranat*, weeping and yawning, wailing and sighing.

A lute scurried and scuttled along, against the clash, clang, tinkle, and bang of the cymbals.

A *rammana* drum beat out a tattoo of bips, booms, and bungs. The music rang out loud and clear. They played through three rounds and were still not finished.

6. See p. 487, note 59.

PART 3

THE WAT KO VERSION OF THE CHIANG MAI CAMPAIGN

The account of the Chiang Mai campaign in the PD version was rewritten some time in the mid-nineteenth century. Khru Jaeng contributed, along with other unknown authors.

The recomposition begins in chapter 26 at the point where the King of Chiang Mai sends Kwan Mahabat to spy on Lanchang. However, in the early part of the recomposition, the changes are in detail rather than in plot. The language is more elevated. Several speeches, particularly the laments over Soi-thong's departure from Vientiane, are longer and more poetic. The geography is more accurate.

When the story moves beyond the diplomatic maneuvers, and the main characters of *KCKP* reappear, the recomposition is much more far-reaching, significantly changing the plot, characterization, and angle of vision. The change comes at the point where Phlai Ngam volunteers in chapter 27. This translation begins at that point.

This extract is translated from the Wat Ko text, beginning with the last stanza of volume 22, page 871, and ending at volume 28, page 1101, 3 lines up. There are no chapter divisions in the originals. Here the text has been divided into chapters to match the PD edition.

Phlai Ngam and Phramuen Si looked at the horoscope and found it was the time when the ogre captured Sida completely.[1] "If we address the king today, it will be easy.

I have been waiting to repay the debt of gratitude to my father. I will request to volunteer as I have intended. Now that Mercury is in a good position, the time of bad fortune is ended. Please help me by addressing the king artfully."

Phramuen Si laughed and said. "I've thought it out already. My dear son, listen with both ears. When I get the floor, pay attention so you know what I say to the king."

Now to tell of the almighty king, paramount in wealth and power, who resided in a palace of glittering crystal and lapis lazuli, enjoying perfect and continuous contentment,

because the gods were ever present to protect the king, upholder of the teachings. But he did not yet know about the royal missive which would greatly disturb his disposition.

When the sun moved to the time of three o'clock, the gong sounded for him to go to the audience hall. The chaophraya put on sompak and went together to attend on the monarch.

As the sun approached afternoon, the almighty king, ruler of the fortunate realm, went to bathe

in fragrant rosewater and be anointed with floral scents. Lady attendants crawled in, bringing his splendid attire.

Once dressed, he took up a short sword with brilliant diamond, filigree, and red gems. Loyal inner lady attendants prostrated to present a betel tray.

Once he had partaken, he walked elegantly, looking as splendid as the Lord

---

1. Another use of the Three-Tiered Umbrella method of divination (see p. 208, note 4). This is probably the number 7 in the southwest section dominated by Thotsakan. According to Wales, "A grand portent. First will be happy, but later rue the day" (*Divination*, 39).

of the Swans, surrounded by a circle of inner ladies, up to the Banyong Rattanat Hall.[2]

The curtain was drawn back. The audience was so crowded with Brahmans, officials, astrologers, lords, and judges prostrating on their knees that the hall looked about to burst.

Horn and conch sounded. Nobles prostrated in rows and groups. Palace guards drove away people who were waiting around the doors to see what would happen as a result of the report.

Chaophraya Jakri had the floor. He made obeisance, rose, and addressed the king. "My liege, my life is under the royal foot.

Chiang Mai has sent a royal missive, delivered to the outpost guards at Tha Kwian to forward on. The messengers returned through the forest. Sawankhalok had the missive sent here.

The matter concerns Phra Thainam, who has been captured by Chiang Mai but not killed. Phan Mano brought the report." Before the missive could be read, the king flew into a rage,

stamped his foot, and roared loudly. Throughout the audience hall, not a word was uttered. Some sat with scalps crawling in fear. "Heigh! Read the report at once."

"My liege, the missive states as follows. The great king, ruler over the territory of Chiang Mai, who cleaves to truth, honesty, and the teachings, a monarch of great splendor,

with power over all regions of the realm, before whom enemies quail and submit, whom a royal household text inscribed long ago on a golden sheet

described as a warrior king, the unparalleled eminence of the world, like the Lord of Darkness who destroys all enemies so he may be without any irritation,

dispatched an envoy with a missive to request the hand of the gracious Princess Soithong, daughter of Lanchang, according to ancient royal custom,

in the expectation she would be consecrated in marriage as a wife of the first rank, though, since she is still young and unfit to possess with joy, she would not be entertained close to the royal side.

The Thai city was heard to be honest, yet it has become woefully vain and carried away by power. Phra Thainam was sent to lead troops across the forest to infringe on our territory,

with no respect for us as ruler. This was insolent and imprudent. In addi-

---

2. See p. 540, note 22.

tion, he took away the Princess Soithong, our love.

Hence an army was conscripted and sent in defense. It was able to defeat the enemy and seize the princess. Phra Thainam and his phrai fled. We chased and captured them but have not put them to death.

If we did not inform you, you might have totally false suspicions. This gracious princess has been received in a sandalwood residence.

If you wish for this princess, leave home and bring an army. I invite the King of Ayutthaya to fearlessly bring troops for a duel on elephant back.

Whoever wins will get Princess Soithong to marry and enjoy with no hindrance. Phra Thainam and his troops are in prison as punishment for the offense committed.

If you do not come, all five hundred will be killed. We await your response. Stake your glory to be known forever. Do not delay but reply to this missive immediately.

This war will be decided according to past examples. The princess will not yet be joined in love. At the conclusion of the war, if the southern city succeeds, it shall have the princess to adorn the city,

and the power and glory. News will spread in all directions that it won the elephant duel and gained the princess as prize." At the end of the missive, the minister prostrated.

After listening, the king was choked with fury. He spoke out immediately, "This Chiang Mai is proud and arrogant."

Feeling as if an era-destroying fire were burning him to death, the king brandished his royal sword, and stamped his foot so angrily the sound echoed through the palace.

All those in attendance shrank backwards in panic and confusion. Betel dropped from waistbands. Sompak slipped and fell in disorder.

Nobles wanted to disappear into the earth. Some crawled backwards in despair. The king's voice thundered all through the inner palace where palace ladies huddled together in alarm.

"Mm! This Chiang Mai is evil. He captures my troops and arrogantly boasts he will fight me. He thinks a lot of himself.

Hundreds of countries, great and small, have respect for the soldiery of Ayutthaya. He's like a single, young deer come to die battling a lion.

I'm the ruler of a city which no country dares oppose. He's like a little firefly trying to compete with the flames of hell or the light of the sun itself!

I'm like Mount Meru. Can a little ant hill lean up against a mountain? His whole dynasty will be wiped out. He boasts he will fight an elephant duel with me.

He is thick-faced and shameless enough to make up stories that he asked for the hand of the princess. But when Lanchang presented the princess, it was to me.

I know who she was given to. If he had the power the missive claims, Lanchang would have fearfully sought Chiang Mai's friendship. Why then did Lanchang not do so but talked to me? He demeans this city.

He not only seized the princess on the way, but pulverized Thainam and our troops. This forest robber is a crow with nothing but a mouth, coming to seize a poor fledgling.

If he were bold enough to attack across the frontier, even at the loss of hundreds and thousands of men, he could be called a bold and mighty king. But he's a stupid, mindless commoner

who thinks he knows best, puffed up with arrogance, using his mouth as a gong to shout at the spirits. Why allow him to remain a burden on the earth? Heigh! Minister, raise an army immediately.

I will go to obliterate Chiang Mai. If I can't take the city, I won't return. Raise hundreds and thousands of troops from the dependent cities, great and small. Squeeze them to the last man.

Storm and besiege Chiang Mai. Slash them to dust wherever they are. Pulverize them so none remain. Raze their walls and fortifications."

For the four pillars, listening to the king's outburst was like being pierced by arrows. Chilled and trembling with fear, they nudged one another to have Chaophraya Jakri reply.

"My liege, ruler of the glorious city, perfection of royal authority, your humble servant begs to address the dust beneath the royal foot.

If Your Majesty is thinking of war, we see there is good cause and offer no opposition. But I crave Your Majesty's pardon that it will detract from the royal advance to enlightenment in the long run.

It is not fitting for Your Majesty to go to war against nothing more than caterpillars, mosquitoes, flies, and midges. Are there no military officers for such purpose?

The royal dignity may suffer. The people will gossip. The populace of all cities will criticize. It is not fitting to bring the sky down to the earth.

At the time of Lord Ram, the mighty Hanuman volunteered and succeeded as the greatest soldier of the land, making the demons fear his eminence.

What if, on this occasion, Your Majesty were to go to Chiang Mai and lose all the capital's troops? I beg Your Victorious Majesty to preserve his honor by emulating the time of Lord Ram."

The king, paramount ruler of the world, pondered on what he had heard, then ordered the courtiers, "As you oppose that I should go, who then do you see as suitable. Heigh! What then do you think? Speak out!"

Phlai Ngam nudged Phramuen Si and said, "This is the time to talk to the king on my behalf." Phramuen Si prostrated three times and raised his face to speak.

"My adopted son, by name Phlai Ngam, boldly believes he can undertake this war. He is the son of Khun Phaen Saensathan and grandson of Khun Krai. He has studied lore.

He hails from military stock with a reputation passed down the line. He wishes to volunteer, believing he will succeed. He is capable, daring, and has good knowledge."

The almighty king turned his face with a joyful smile, reflecting the happiness in his mind.

He said, "Ha! Heigh! Phlai Ngam, you think you can undertake this war, reduce Chiang Mai to defeat and destruction, and bring back Soithong and the two hundred phrai?

Should you succeed, I'll reward you handsomely, and employ you as a military commander in Ayutthaya so that your capability is made known."

Phlai Ngam made obeisance and said, "Great lord above my head, may I offer my life beneath the dust. In order that nothing should irritate the royal foot,

I shall overcome and crush this enemy that is a thorn in the side, and gain a fearsome reputation as a bold soldier. If I fail to defeat and take Chiang Mai, let my whole clan be executed.

Allow me to make one request for a life to be granted at Your Majesty's disposition. Khun Phaen, my father, is still undergoing punishment. Your Majesty in anger had him confined to the inner jail.

He has been festering there for fifteen years and almost lost his life in prison. Please grant him a pardon so he may acquit himself in the attack on Chiang Mai."

The king smiled. "This Phlai Ngam has good thinking. He looks bold, sharp, and not afraid of an enemy.

His features are taken straight from his father. By nature, fruit falls close to the tree.[3] This Khun Phaen almost died. I cannot think how I forgot him.

---

3. A well-known proverb meaning that characteristics are passed down from parents to offspring.

I blocked him out of my mind. Only when Phlai Ngam made his request did I think of him. When he asked for Laothong, I was angry and imprisoned him all this time.

Look here, all you nobles. It's not right for you to remain so quiet. Khun Phaen has suffered for fifteen years because not a single person liked him enough.

As he had no wealth, his case lay hidden, isn't that so? If he were rich rather than poor, all you fellows would be asking on his behalf every single day.

I pay you allowances for nothing. You stay quiet and let this soldier of mine die because you're jealous that your own knowledge doesn't equal his. You begrudge how he sliced you up when you went with Khun Chang,

and you all ran off in fright, heads nodding like flowers. You knew about his skills but you didn't seek him out. Phramuen Si, go off immediately and have Khun Phaen released."

The king ordered Phraya Yommarat, "Along with his father, release some tough robbers, up to forty of them."

The minister of the capital took the order and crawled away. Phlai Ngam crawled after him. Phramuen Si prostrated to take leave.

All three went out past the screens, and hastily removed their sompak. With their servants accompanying them, Phraya Yommarat got into a palanquin, Phramuen Si rode a horse, and Phlai Ngam followed.

Their servants jammed the road, almost bumping into the rears of the palanquin bearers. They carried a betel tray, the bundled document, and a flaming torch. Market vendors asked one another what was going on.

Ai-Rot said, "They're releasing prisoners. The king has pardoned them to fight Chiang Mai." Crowds of people came to sit at the roadside. Phramuen Si went into the jail,

unfurled the document, and gave orders to the keeper of the central rolls. Thirty-five men were checked off, all fearsome. "These prisoners are to be released,

along with the great soldier, Khun Phaen Saensathan, to join an army on the king's orders." The inspector of the rolls came to oversee, and the warden went in to remove their irons.

The chains and cangues on Khun Phaen and the thirty-five were unlocked and fell off with a clang. Pliers were used to pry open the manacles on each of them.

All were brought to prostrate before Phraya Yommarat. The inspection was rowdy and disorderly. Each name was read from the register, and the person was required to speak.

"My name is Ai-Phuk from Luk-kae. My wife's name is I-Tae, sir. I was convicted for robbery, forcing the victims to dance wildly, and making I-Ma dance single-handed."

"Next!" "Ai-Mi from Ban Yilon, wife's name I-Phon. I robbed Ta-Khiao, and stabbed I-Klae, making only a single wound. She grimaced and fell down flat, slobbering."

"Next!" "Ai-Pan from Ban Chi-hon, wife I-Son. I robbed Bang Kot, tied Ta-Jai and Granny Rot by the neck, and singed off all their hair."

"Next!" "Ai-Jan Samphantueng, wife I-Thueng, from Ban Mueang Mai, in the gang that robbed Khun Siwichai and shoved a stick up his anus so he died."

"Next!" "My name's Ai-Mueang Kaen, wife's name I-Saen, from Ban Nong Wai. I robbed Khun Si Jaeng and stabbed him to death, taking property and many water buffaloes."

"Next!" "I'm Ai-Jian Yok from Ban Talokbat, wife's name I-Kongrat, sir. I fell in with some Thai and robbed a gambling den, then murdered Ta-Pan from Ban Tan-en."

"Next!" "Ai-Thong from Chong Khwak, husband of I-Mak and a Lao wife called I-Thao Sen. I burgled an almsbowl and shoulder cloth from a novice, beads from an elder, and lowercloth from a nun."

"Next!" "Ai-Khaek Cham, husband of the Brahman, Sa. I burgled a partridge from Ta-Thi, taking all his money and goods—good stuff and no small amount, including jewels."

"Next!" "Ai-Ya, husband of I-Ngi, convicted for robbing Abbot Chi at Ban Klet, burgling Granny Khongphet, and selling fake goods with Ta-Sai at Ban Tuek Daeng."

"Next!" "My name's Ai-Mi Pok, wife's name I-Thong Ngok, from Ban Chumsaeng. I robbed Chi Dak Khanon, barricaded a road taking all I could carry, and killed Khun Thipsaeng, owner of the goods."

"Ai-Phet Suea Luang from Chainat town, wife's name I-Pat from Ban Khayai. I've robbed and killed about a hundred people, and stolen countless buffaloes to kill and eat."

"Ai-Rot with a mottled hand, formerly resident at Bang Chalong, wife's name I-Khong, a northerner. I've stolen just about everything including mortars and pestles, and robbed boats."

"Next!" "Ai-Thong from Nong Suang, wife's name I-Duang, I robbed Ta-Jop." "Next!" "Ai-Dam from Ban Thamnop,[4] wife's name I-Kop, I burgle at dusk."

---

4. Dam Village, a common name, probably the one in Amphoe Tha Tako, Nakhon Sawan.

"Ai-Mak Saklek. I robbed Jek Kue and his slit-eyed wife named I-Sao."
"Next!" "Ai-Bung from Khung Tapao. I stabbed I-Mao's husband and seized her as my wife."

"Ai-Kham, husband of I-Khong, from Kongdon. I killed a Mon and stole cloth."
"Next!" "Ai-Chang from Bang Hia. I couldn't find a wife so I robbed boats."

"Ai-Kling, husband of I-Klak from Dak Khanon. I stole elephants, robbed people, and plundered boats from the north." "Ai-Phao, husband of I-Phan from Ban Saphan Kluea. I poisoned Luang Choduek and cleaned out his house."

"Ai-Bua, husband of I-Prang, from Bang Namchon. I burgled Muen Thon, picking him clean." "Ai-Maeo, husband of I-Ma, from Tha Kwian. I went to Ban Thit Taphian to rob and steal.

Under questioning, I put the blame on someone else. Then I took things from Nang Thong Kramip." "Next!" "Ai-Nan, husband of I-Janthip, from Namdip. I robbed Abbot Phao,

but did not stab him as accused. The custodian's examination found it was an old wound." "Ai-Jan Niao, husband of I-Khiao, from Ban Kaphrao. I was convicted of robbing an old Chinaman and burning his shop.

I fired a gun, hollered, and hit the foot of a Chinese ironmonger." "Next!" "Ai-Noklek, from Thalunglek, husband of I-Di.

I barricaded roads to rob cattle around Khorat, and stabbed Ai-Chua, husband of I-Pat, who fell down in the dirt." "Ai-Mak Nuat, husband of I-Khuat, from Bang Phli. I was convicted of daylight robbery in Doembang."

"Ai-Koet Kradukdam, husband of I-Khamdang, convicted of burgling the Department of Elephants with mahout Mun, and robbing a forest Lawa. I'm invulnerable with copper testicles and a twisted scrotum."

The thirty-five pardoned convicts were all daring and strong. They stood, legs akimbo, lowercloths hitched up, with red eyes and ears, looking fierce and fearless.

For their karma, they had been imprisoned a long time. When Phlai Ngam asked the king for the release of his father, all of these were pardoned too.

Khun Phaen, with his powers as a warrior, boldly pronounced a mantra and blew a Beguiler breath to captivate all the officials.

Phraya Yommarat was affected by the mantra and felt loving. He hastily handed out silkwool cloths, carpets, mats, and shirts of foreign *attalat*.

Phramuen Si happily distributed brilliant, sparkling diamond rings and Malacca silkwool from overseas out of compassion for his friend.

Other people gave them sweets and sharp oranges. A widow, making eyes and laughing heartily, passed over enough baskets of bananas to feed all of them.

"May you defeat and destroy the demon enemy. May you glorify the city by having the weapons and strength to kill the foes just as bold Hanuman defeated Lanka."

Khun Phaen received the blessings, "May we have victory as you say, so our valor is reputed through the ages, as if the Great Elect[5] himself had given us a potent blessing."

∽

Kaeo Kiriya, who had remained beside her husband when they slept in the shelter at the slip gate, was now ten months pregnant.

When her husband was pardoned and able to leave the jail, their house was strewn with pots and pitchers and piles of raggedy cloth and torn mats. These were her old friends in hardship, but now she would be parted from them.

She prayed for her husband to avoid further harm now that his punishment was over. She came to find him, made a low bow and wai to Phraya Yommarat, and said to her husband, "Make some merit by distributing to the thirty-five phrai this big bundle of Surat cloth that I was given." The phrai quickly grabbed the cloth, and ate up all the donated bananas and sweets, making their cheeks bulge.

Kaeo Kiriya packed some money and valuables in a big wicker back-basket. The thirty-five phrai happily came and changed into upper and lower cloths of the Surat material,

back-basket

and threw away their shabby and raggedy old ones. "It shamed my wife. Unbearable. Close the front and nothing at the back. A flies' nest." Some took off sacking and threw it away.

"We'll be servants of Khun Phaen until we're dead and gone." With big piles of goods to carry, they sat waiting for Khun Phaen, then said farewell to Phraya Yommarat and left.

---

5. มหาสมมิตร์, *mahasommit*, distorted from *mahasommuti*, the Great Elect, the putative first king in the political theory outlined in the Akanya Sutra. The world was originally populated by undifferentiated beings, but after a pure food became available, they overindulged, became gross, lost their virtue, were differentiated into male and female, beautiful and ugly, were forced to plant crops, and fell into dishonesty, theft, and violence towards one another. At this point they called on the most handsome and virtuous among them to become king in order to control their conflicts and misdeeds. (Nidhi, *Pen and Sail,* 323–24; Rhys Davids, *Dialogues of the Buddha,* 3:82–89)

Phramuen Si mounted his horse and returned home. Crowds of people watched. Phlai Ngam walked along behind his father with the thirty-five to Khan Landing.[6]

࿐

King Phanwasa summoned Laothong. "Phlai Ngam asked for his father to be released and I had Khun Phaen freed from jail.

You've suffered for fifteen years. I can see you're not happy here so I shall free you to end your suffering. No more embroidery. Leave quickly and go to him."

Laothong was happy at the king's pardon. She prostrated to the royal foot, made her farewell, and crawled back out.

She went to take leave of all the seniors and female guards she had lived and eaten with, along with her circle of close friends. "I must say farewell to everybody."

She gracefully walked into a room to take leave of the head governess. She powdered her face in a mirror, applied oil, and put on a refreshing perfume to arouse anyone close to her.

She wore a fragrant Tani Sappadun[7] cloth in head-turning green, and a quilted uppercloth with a flowing *kanok* motif, and swans and dancing *kinnon* in a quatrefoil pattern.

She packed her betel box and articles of nak and gold, trays, nielloware bowls in the inner-palace style, rings and glittering ornaments, went out of the door, and cut through to leave by Din Gate.[8]

I-Thueng hurried along behind her mistress carrying the chest, with five others walking behind in a crowd, lugging the rest of her things. They came through Din Gate towards Khan Landing,

and saw Khun Phaen gazing around. "Over there! Who's that? He looks familiar but thinner, and his hair is long enough to sit on."

From a distance they peered across but neither mistress nor servants could recognize him. He resembled the sort of madman who throws dirt around. I-In called out, "Poor fellow,

my mistress is looking for her husband, but this fellow sitting and staring around turns out to be the husband of the lady with the heavily pregnant belly." I-Suk got up to look, "What?"

---

6. See p. 708, note 1.

7. From Machlipatnam, a port in eastern India which exported cloth to Siam (see p. 739, note 15).

8. See p. 418, note 41.

Khun Phaen could scarcely recognize Laothong but worked it out. He called out immediately, "Don't you know me? Why don't you come over?"

Hearing his words, Laothong could remember the voice. Going closer to him, she recognized his face, and clasped his feet, trembling. "I just heard the king gave you a pardon,

so I came to find you. You look so unfamiliar I didn't recognize you, so I was standing there. When you greeted me, I knew. You look so wasted and different.

Oh my dear lord and husband, by merit you've been released from suffering in jail, as if you'd died and now are born again to reunite us. I've cried all the time without missing a day.

At mealtimes, I couldn't eat a mouthful without being forced to swallow tears of sorrow. At night, I'd sleep thinking of love. I almost held my breath until I died.

I embroidered silk endlessly, beyond thinking when I would see you. In the past when it was hot, you brought me cool comfort, but I hadn't seen your face for fifteen years."

The crowd of people walking past stopped to look at them and tut-tutted to one another. "Oh good lady, you have a very lovely face. In every respect you look like a palace lady.

But falling in love with someone who's lost his mind is not befitting. Aren't you ashamed, I beg of you? Don't good people like us please you? Hanging around to consort with a madman is despicable."

Someone else said, "Hey! You crazy fart. Don't be so arrogant. When a tiger falls on hard times, nobody pays him attention. That's the mighty Phaen who has just been released.

Behind is Phlai Ngam, who has volunteered to go on military service. And that's Phaen's wife Laothong, who was punished but has been released to rejoin her love."

Laothong asked her husband, "My lord, who's sitting back there?" Khun Phaen said at once, "Her name is Kaeo Kiriya.

I got her as a wife when I fled away with Wanthong. While I was in jail, she looked after me. That's my son who asked the king for my pardon. His name is Phlai Ngam. His mother is Wanthong."

Khun Phaen led them into the palace. His son, wives, and servants all went along, and a crowd of people followed. At the gate, they walked straight in.

Ta-Ai the gatekeeper, who was weaving a wicker basket, raised his face and shouted in alarm, "Oh no! A lunatic is entering the palace. Push off."

Phlai Ngam cried, "Ha, gatekeeper, you don't recognize Khun Phaen, my father? He's not mad. The king has released him and requested his presence." The gatekeeper shrank down and wai-ed in surprise.

Khun Phaen ordered his wives and servants, "Sit in this sala for a moment while I hurry to the audience." He went off and soon reached the inner official sala,

which was packed with nobles going to audience. They raised their hands in wai to greet Khun Phaen. A chaophraya said, "Don't feel resentful for being forgotten until the king scolded us.

While you were hidden away, nobody came to speak with us, so none of us petitioned on your behalf." Khun Phaen said, "I harbor no resentment, but please present me in audience."

The chaophraya and other officials laughed, and gave him money and cloth as consolation. "I'll present you straight away. Put on a sompak. It's almost time."

When the time approached four o'clock, the almighty king, peak and pillar of the world, resident of a glittering crystal palace,

went to be bathed and arrayed in raiment. As he walked out to ascend the dazzling crystal throne, inner ladies prostrated with clasped hands.

Crowds of courtiers entered the audience and made obeisance. A *mahori* ensemble and Mon *piphat* played. Horn and conch resounded.

Chaophraya Jakri, a senior minister, was the first to address the king. "Khun Phaen has been granted a royal pardon.

With a heart of utmost loyalty, he volunteers to serve Your Majesty until death. He begs to attend on the king, upholder of the teachings, with Your Majesty's gracious permission."

King Phanwasa smiled and clapped his hands loudly. "Heigh! Now I think we have the means to go after that villain! Bring him in."

Chaophraya Jakri bowed to receive the royal order. A palace guard ran to fetch Khun Phaen and Phlai Ngam, who came to the front of the audience hall and prostrated.

From the magnificent throne, the king, ruler of the earth, turned to look at the bowed figures of the father and son, and roared like a lion.

"Heigh! Khun Phaen Saensathan, I forgot you and let you suffer heavily until your hair grew so long you can sit on it. But you did not die. When your son came to tell me, then I knew.

I scolded all my servants, as your son heard with his own ears. Now that you've requested to volunteer, how many people will you take?"

Khun Phaen Saensathan bowed and prostrated. "No troops will be needed, only the convicts pardoned and granted for us to take to Chiang Mai."[9]

The king shook with laughter. "If you return with victory over Chiang Mai, have no fear about my taking care of you.

But going on campaign with only thirty-five phrai seems very risky. I don't think you'll succeed. Maybe I need a chance to admire your command of mantra and knowledge in full measure."

Khun Phaen replied, "Pray allow me to display my men and knowledge. Pray allow me to bathe my body for comfort and return with the phrai."

The king said, "That would be to my liking." He ordered Phramuen Si to arrange a full display without delay.

Phramuen Si took the order, and prostrated to take leave. Khun Phaen and his son also went out to the sala. His wives and servants followed along.

They arrived at the house by Wat Takrai and paid respects to Thong Prasi, who turned to look and beat her chest with eyes streaming. "Oh, you've been reborn so we may meet again.

I thank you, Kaeo Kiriya, for taking care of your beloved husband. Now then, you and Laothong must be sisters. Don't be hateful towards each other from now on.

I feel for Phlai Ngam, who made the effort to ask for his father's pardon. It fits the ancient saying: To be a man, do not look down on any other man."

She stroked the back of Khun Phaen. "I'm shocked and concerned beyond toleration about your strange appearance. I'm happy you had the merit not to die,

but your hair is as messy as a madman, and flows down over your shoulders long enough for you to sit on it. Take a bath for your comfort." She ordered the servants to make preparations.

Khun Phaen and Phlai Ngam took their leave, mounted elephants, and rode away, taking salver, candles, and incense for offerings. Servants followed in a crowd.

Kaeo Kiriya and Laothong stayed with the grandmother while Khun Phaen and Phlai Ngam went in one day to Suphan to pay their respects to the abbot of Wat Palelai.

---

9. Khun Phaen addresses the king without any of the usual formalities.

They took offerings of incense, candles, betel, and pan. The abbot scrutinized them and asked, "Where are you from?" "My name is Phlai Kaeo. My son petitioned the king to have me released from punishment.

My wife's name is Wanthong. After I abducted her, she became pregnant in the forest." The abbot laughed, "Oh, that's right. I thought it was somebody else, some madman.

After I'd taught you everything, it was unnecessary for you to face such hardship. You can unlock manacles and any kind of restraint, be invulnerable, disappear, be invulnerable or invisible, and hold your breath.

Yet you still got yourself locked up in chains and cangue. What was up? Didn't you have faith in your knowledge? Or was it fun lying in jail? Why didn't you escape to find me?

If they'd come after you, I'd have put on a yantra cloth and fought back. Why did you sit doing nothing, not following what I taught you? You've got knowledge up to your neck yet you're still afraid of people."

Khun Phaen prostrated on the ground to the teacher. "I was not lacking in power, but I'd sworn to Phraya Yommarat and would not go back on the word I'd given.

He trusted me, and as a result I was not placed under restraint. It was unbefitting for me to disobey and put him in the wrong. I would rather die keeping my oath. You're disappointed because you're unaware of this.

I'm going to attack and take Chiang Mai. My hair is as messy as a lunatic. May I ask the master to cut it for me, and wash it so I'm comfortable?

After hearing Khun Phaen, the abbot changed his robe, picked up scissors and comb, parted the hair, and gathered it up with the comb.

However hard he tried, the hair resisted until Khun Phaen enchanted some water and wet it, after which the cutting was quickly done. Then the abbot had a fire made to bathe Khun Phaen's body.

Khun Phaen clasped his hands in prayer while the flames whooshed up to cover his head. When the fire went out, his body was not burned but looked as beautiful as a freshly blooming lotus.

The abbot anointed him with water. The father, son, and their phrai were happy. "Be victorious over Chiang Mai without fail!" They received this blessing, prostrated, and left.

Khun Phaen and Phlai Ngam went to Thong Prasi and entrusted beloved Laothong into her care. Thong Prasi blessed them in every possible way she could think of.

They prostrated, took the blessings on their heads, made their farewells, and went into the palace with the servants in train.

Phramuen Si ordered attendants to decorate the audience hall. The palace staff went into the treasury for materials to adorn the front and inside of the palace.

All the nobles put on sompak and gathered busily for the audience. Khun Phaen and Phlai Ngam erected and activated an eye-level shrine,

and made offerings on the inner grounds of the palace. They set up *baisi* on right and left, a balustrade with umbrellas and flags, and placed offerings including liquor,

powder, oil, popped rice, candles, and incense sent by his wives. The mighty warrior Khun Phaen wore a belt made with skin from the forehead of a corpse.

In his mouth, he put a mercury charm. He wore lowercloth and uppercloth in dazzling pure white, a splendid snake's fang, an enamel ring, and a sacred thread round his head for invulnerability.

Phlai Ngam finished dressing and walked grandly along. Weapons and devices of lore were placed on the shrine, and a white cloth spread as a canopy.

The thirty-five phrai, all dressed up well, sat around the shrine with their legs tucked under themselves and their hands in wai. Without delay, the candles were lit and Khun Phaen pronounced mantra.

He made a great ceremony of offering liquor to the crowds of spirits, then circled his hands above his head to convoke the deities. The heavens trembled up to the Brahma levels.[10] Storm clouds darkened the sky.

A mass of spirits, deities, and guardians of greater or lesser powers all came together to receive the offerings. The weapons shook and rattled.

Khun Phaen enchanted sacred water, whirled a flickering victory candle to extinguish the flame, and wafted the smoke to give power for victory. The phrai received the blessing. The rite was complete.

In the palace, King Phanwasa mused that he would like to see the display of knowledge. Bathed and decked in apparel and regalia,

---

10. In the Three Worlds cosmology, above the realm of men are six realms inhabited by spirits and deities, and then sixteen realms of the "World with only a Remnant of Material Factors," otherwise known as Brahma realms. Above them again are four realms of the "World without Material Factors" (RR, ch. 7, and especially the chart on 358).

he promenaded in splendor with the elegance of the Lord of the Swans, surrounded by the beauteous ladies of the palace.

The infants of the royal family were carried by wet nurses. Young men came with insignia and royal umbrellas. At the royal pavilion, those in attendance prostrated in ranks.

Attendants drew back the curtain, and beautiful music played. The four pillars, officials of the palace, palace guards, and royal pages all made obeisance.

The king, lord of the earth, seated magnificently on an elevated dais, roared like a lion.

"Now, Khun Phaen Saensathan and the thirty-five soldiers, demonstrate the knowledge you have learned. Show how good you are."

The father, son, and thirty-five phrai promptly bowed their faces and prostrated. Khun Phaen said, "Please have trainee conscripts[11]
bring in fifteen large guns, put in a great amount of powder, and stand to fire from around three fathoms. We'll come out to display one at a time."

Nai Bun of innate knowledge came out and sat focusing his mind. He recited a mantra three times, then had them fire the guns.

The conscript trainees stood and pulled the triggers. Sparks fell into the powder and exploded, darkening their faces, but the shots were blocked and did not emerge. All fifteen guns failed.

They opened the chambers and refilled with powder. Nai Mi stood smiling happily without concern. The guns were fired three times but made no sound. "Useless!" "He's really able!"

Nai Thuam came out carrying a flag, and called for them to stop standing around and fire. The conscript trainees loaded the guns and stood taking aim. Nai Thuam stilled and focused his mind.

The guns were fired with smoke billowing until the shot was exhausted. By controlling his mind, Nai Thuam was not hit. The shot flew off in other directions. His mental control was superhuman.

Nai Thuam had been tested and had survived. Now Nai Mo, who had trained to withstand anything, made obeisance three times, crawled over
into the arena, and prostrated again three times, pressing his head on the

---

11. เกณฑ์หัด, *ken hat*, or more fully *ken hat yang farang*, conscripts trained in the Farang fashion, a military unit headed by Phra Phiphit Decha, *sakdina* 800 (KTS, 1:299).

earth. The conscript trainees loaded tripod guns. Nai Mo called, "Ha, hey, shoot!"

The soldiers fired fifteen rounds from the tripod guns. All fifteen hit Nai Mo but it was like hitting a slab of stone.

The watchers urged one another to look, saying "His lore is very good." "His effort in study was no waste." They clicked tongues in appreciation, saying "What skill!"

After showing their abilities, the three came in front of the throne and made obeisance. The king showed his appreciation.

"These three famous fellows are fit to be soldiers. You have volunteered for royal service. I will reward you."

The three prostrated to receive the royal order, crawled forward, and made obeisance in a row abreast. The king said,

"These others soldiers have knowledge, similar to what you three have displayed. Although it will take some time for all thirty-five to display,

I will watch them all so I know what powers the father and son can command. Bring money and cloth for them. Having seen the display, I'll present gifts."

Phramuen Si received the order and spoke to the soldiers to make obeisance and crawl into the arena.

Nai Bua, who was adept with a sword, prostrated, rose up, and called on his friends to slash him with their swords, but the blades bent or crumpled.

Nai Thi with a dark skin and strong frame had them untie the waistband of his lowercloth and stab without restraint. After nine or ten concerted blows, every one had missed his body.

Nai Thang, who had great strength and tough skin, told them to attack his skull with an axe until all his hair was gone. They hacked at his head again and again, but he got up and ran his fingers through his hair.

Nai Mon lay down with his stomach exposed and had each person saw at it a couple of times but not a hair was cut.

Nai Jai had a chisel brought and hammered to pierce his stomach but the blows did not penetrate at all and the chisel crumpled.

Nai Thin had them slice his calf muscles with razors but the blades failed to pierce. Each person's ability was proven for all to see.

All thirty-five were invulnerable. All had their knowledge tested, and all were better than they revealed. They intentionally kept their true powers of invulnerability hidden and secret, but made a show for the audience to see.

All the rich men, monks, Brahmans, Khaek, Cham, Chinese, Vietnamese, Farang, Khmer, Mon, Thai, and Lao who witnessed the display were overawed.

"The knowledge of each of them is unthinkable." "They're fit to be servants of the king." "They'll fight the enemy without fear." "They've earned merit through study."

"The father and son are yet to be tested. They'll be even more accomplished." Their reputation was known far and wide. The palace courtyard was jammed with around fifteen thousand people, packed tight, jostling to get close, unable to move, and smothered in choking dust.

The king asked, "Where's Phlai Ngam gone, Phramuen Si? Have him put to the test right now along with all this group of soldiers."

Little Phlai received the king's order, raised his fingers in wai, and crawled forward. He took off his belt, and enchanted it with a yantra.

The belt disappeared and was transformed into a fierce-looking naga with eyes as red as the era-destroying fire. It opened its mouth, flicked its tongue,

reared up, baring its fangs, and slithered sinuously towards the onlookers. With hair standing on end at the sight of a naga weaving towards them, all the watchers fled,

shrieking and screaming, scared out of their wits. Even nobles were frightened. Many inner ladies were petrified

that the snake would slither into the royal pavilion, and were in total confusion. The king was concerned at the sight of people scared to death,

and thus ordered Khun Phaen, "Don't just stand there, get rid of this snake!" Khun Phaen received the order, took hold of a bandeau,

wound it round his head, uttered a mantra, and threw the bandeau in front of him where it turned into a huge Lord Garuda, which flapped after the snake, snapping its beak.

The father and son sat with smiles on their faces watching the snake and Garuda fighting. Using his knowledge, Khun Phaen uttered an instruction to Garuda, which seized the snake in its beak,

and flew down in front of Khun Phaen. The crowd of nobles in attendance all fled away in alarm, leaping, stumbling, and falling over one another.

The naga disappeared and became a belt again. Garuda, gripping the naga, vanished and reappeared as a bandeau. The king turned to look at Phlai Ngam.

Everyone present who had seen the apparition was greatly impressed and overawed. Some praised Khun Phaen and some Phlai Ngam, arguing together over who was better.

Khun Phaen, great valiant, of unequalled expertise in knowledge, walked into the courtyard, made obeisance three times,

and spoke his wish to the king. "Salutation to the lord above my head! Allow me to concentrate my mind and powers in order to pay gratitude to my mother and father,

to the seven rishis,[12] to the teachers who instructed me, to my son and wife for their blessings, to the regular guardians of the directions,

to His Majesty the King, the pinnacle and axis of the world, and to the deities who lent me insight." Then he uttered an eternity formula,

pulled up couch grass from the edge of the path, plaited it into the shape of an elephant the size of a pillow, inserted sticks as tusks, poured spirit oil on the tusks,

covered the figure with a black cloth, and uttered an activating mantra. The figure became a tall, imposing elephant in musth with ears spread, tail raised, and tusks with tips curving upwards and inwards in front of the trunk.

Its freckled cheeks were puffed out and its flanks swollen, making it look enormous. With musth oil drenching its face and trunk, it stood drowsily moving its eyes, looking fearsome.

The beast was six cubits and eleven inches tall.[13] It raised its face, swished its head from side to side, curled its trunk, flicked its tail, and rocked its body to and fro. Everyone without exception was terrified.

Whichever way the fierce musth elephant turned its head, the people fled in alarm. Its eyes ranged over the crowd.

Some people stood huddled together in fright. Some shrank away in utter panic. Others stood shaking with despair, waiting to flee if the elephant approached.

To overcome his father's elephant, the brave and bold Phlai Ngam acted on the knowledge he had gained from study.

He grasped a goad and danced back and forth to induce the elephant to attack. The mantra beast watched the goad dance, trumpeted, and charged at Phlai Ngam.

Phlai was chased several rounds until he was panting heavily. Then he grasped the goad, stepped onto the tip of a tusk, leapt up, and straddled the elephant's neck.

---

12. The seven rishis or Saptarshi are mentioned, but not named, in the Vedas as the carriers of the wisdom written down in these texts. Later Puranic literature attributes names to them, in various lists. Modern scholarship interprets them as a metaphor for the ancient tradition of learning.

13. Around 3.30 meters.

He struck with the goad to subdue the beast. The elephant drew in its neck in fright. People laughed. The elephant looked up, swung its tusks from side to side, raised its curled trunk, let its rear droop, and excreted.

Opening its mouth and trumpeting loudly, it dropped its haunches, broke a fart, spread its legs, and pissed. The onlookers roared loudly, and danced around to cheer Phlai Ngam.

After Phlai Ngam had struck the elephant for some time, Khun Phaen, who was watching from the grounds, ordered the elephant, "Shake Phlai Ngam off your back and trample him according to my instruction,

but do not injure or kill him. Let the guardian spirits protect him." The beast did just enough for it to look real and fool the onlookers.

Wetsuwan yantra

Having seen everything, the king announced, "Truly good! This father and son have great knowledge.

To display further will take too long. We must have the ceremony." Money and cloth was brought for the king to present to the father, son, and thirty-five men.

"They could take even a hundred and one cities. There's no way this Chiang Mai fellow will escape their handiwork." The king said, "Khun Phaen, you are the real thing. Phlai Ngam cannot yet surpass your skill.

Even so, he's without comparison, too—matchless. I've just seen your knowledge. Though out of anger I had you jailed for a long time,

you're still upright and faithful, still understand the meaning of the water of allegiance. You and I should be servant and master until death. I'll present to you first to make amends for your hardship.

If on this occasion you can take Chiang Mai, I'll have you well established. And I won't make your son ashamed either. Have no fear of facing poverty in the future."

He presented fifteen chang of money, cloth, a Farang helmet, and other items. Phlai Ngam received seven chang and ten tamlueng, and half the amount of cloth.

Each of the thirty-five men got one chang and a set of cloth. Khun Phaen was also rewarded with carpets, cushions, and an eleven-fathom boat.[14]

---

14. The text merely says an "eleven boat," but usually such numbers specify the length in *wa*.

Khun Phaen, Phlai Ngam, and the phrai prostrated and joyfully took the royal gifts.

Khun Phaen, great master, addressed the king, "My liege, lord of the realm, as Your Majesty has granted me pardon, I shall be a servant of the land.

May the royal power cover my head until my life's end, with no thought whether I should live or die. As for Chiang Mai, I should not speak as if it were already in the palm of my hand.

When I besieged Chiang Thong and slashed people dead in piles of hundreds of thousands, they ran off like nodding flowers, offering no resistance. Now they challenge for another war.

In a short time you'll see me slash them and truss them up like frogs." The king laughed and said, "Do it! Thrash them!" Khun Phaen made obeisance to take leave,

and went to the boat. The phrai grasped the paddles, sang boat songs at the tops of their voices, and churned up the water so the boat flew along like a bird.

Villagers and townsfolk came to watch. "Both the father and son look handsome." "The men are a sturdy-looking lot—muscular bodies,

curly hair, bulging stomachs, pointed noses, moustaches waxed to curl up at the ends, and flashing red eyes." "Like the soldiers of Lord Wetsuwan."[15] "They have hearts of Macassars[16] and won't shrink from anyone."

"Looking like that, they won't run away from a spear." Some opened their mouths and uttered hair-raising cries. "Every one of them was born a fine specimen." "Criminals, robbers, and murderers of householders."

They reached home and went to see Thong Prasi who opened her mouth and roared with laughter. She stroked the back of her beloved son, now pardoned by the king.

The money and goods were shared out. Phlai Ngam gave his portion to his grandmother. Khun Phaen paid respect to her. "I'm taking leave to go on campaign.

Let me entrust Kaeo Kiriya and Laothong to your care." Thong Prasi nodded in agreement and gave her blessing. "May Chiang Mai be destroyed and may you be untouched by weapons.

At 11 *wa* or 22 meters, this boat would be half the length of the premier royal barge, Supannahong.

15. A giant, lord of the giants, and guardian of the northern direction (see p. 42, note 64).

16. มักกระสัน, *makkrasan*, from Macassar, a people from the Indonesian archipelago. A settlement of Macassars in Ayutthaya instigated a famous massacre in 1688, and hence a byword for fierceness.

May you have each and every good fortune, and win victory for the honor of your descendants." Khun Phaen prostrated, and Phlai Ngam crawled forward to receive a blessing.

At dawn, they took leave of Thong Prasi and went first to the house of Phramuen Si, followed by their crowd of servants. Phramuen Si got up from his bed and invited his friends in.

Phlai Ngam followed his father to pay their respects. Phramuen Si laughed and called for his wife to bring betel for his friends. She rushed out with a salver,

sat down on a carpet, and proffered the nielloware article. Phlai Ngam prostrated and said, "May you be well and joyful. I come to take leave." She turned her face and gave a blessing.

Phlai Ngam bowed his head and made a wai to receive the blessing. "On royal service, one cannot delay." Phramuen Si took them off to choose horses from the inner stable.

They selected two fine steeds, Big Red and Great Fog, also Humpback, a keen animal. Whitey and Blondie were saddled up, along with Black Crow and Dapple.

Fancy Fetlocks, Palomino, and Pinto were all led out. They chose the good ones quickly, busily put on all the trappings,

and led them out through the palace gate. Crowds of people sat to watch. Khun Phaen galloped off merrily. Phlai Ngam and the phrai rode in pursuit,

all carrying their particular weapons at the ready. Young women crowded around to look. "Oh sir, this young and going to war already!"

"So slight I can't take my eyes away." "Such a pretty body, I'd not go to sleep at all." "I'd love to go to war with you but the action would make my clothes filthy!"

Widows fluttered their eyes at Khun Phaen. He still looked brisk, galloping along with his legs in the stirrups powerfully urging the horse ahead. "I'd like to jump up in his saddle for a ride."

The thirty-five volunteers tried to control unruly horses. One pranced sideways, frightening a Mon woman who fell down with a bump.

"Tcha, you slave horse, you trumpet flower! "Damnit, lord fuck me,[17] a pot of shrimp paste has broken." A fish vendor was knocked aside and her cloth fell open. "Don't bash me, you evil horse."

They arrived at Wat Chai Chumphon, tethered the horses, and went up to a big sala where they drank liquor, hollering rowdily without fear of anyone.

---

17. ดอก ขมิ อ่าง, *dok khami ang*, in Mon.

Don't have doubts about them staying at this place. Because its name alludes to victory, it is an auspicious place according to the Manual on Victorious Warfare.

Phramuen Si along with his major wife and all his minor wives came along to send off his friends. Loaded down with goods,

they busily boarded a boat. Phramuen Si reclined on a backrest, and oarsmen paddled with full strokes. Crowds of people watched.

Thong Prasi shouted at her servants to hurry with the fermented fish, *thian* sweets, chili, and ginger, along with white rice in great hampers.

They loaded the eleven-fathom boat. The paddlers sat waiting for their mistress to arrive. Thong Prasi came from the house

with Laothong, Kaeo Kiriya, and a crowd of servants following. They boarded the boat and set off. Thong Prasi told the oarsmen to row hard. As she stood unsteadily,

the oarsmen pulled so hard the boat leapt forward, throwing her onto the backrest with a thump. "You're thrashing about. I can't follow your rhythm." She sat swaying and calling out the pace,

but the paddlers still raced off noisily. They came across the boat of Phramuen Si, who laughed heartily. He greeted them, and they chatted on the way to Wat Chai Chumphon.

Khun Phaen and Phlai Ngam invited Phramuen Si and Thong Prasi to sit up in a sala while the servants staggered along behind carrying the goods.

Phramuen Si's wife summoned Phlai Ngam and gave him a good sidebag filled with tobacco, dry betel, fresh betel, and a punnet[18] with a flint set.

Phlai Ngam took the sidebag and made a wai. Thong Prasi had her servants harness ten elephants and load them with the articles that Phramuen Si,

Kaeo Kiriya, and Laothong had brought. The servants climbed up with the goods, opened the howdah, and loaded everything including chili, salt, and sundries.

When it was done, they went to sit in the north sala. Thong Prasi pounded betel with a pestle. "Hey Ai-Duea, you'll leave the house and go to accompany my son.

Ta-Muean, Ta-Men, old fellows, Ta-Man, Ta-Thai, and Ta-Phuk, go along to look after the elephants for them and keep watch that things are not stolen."

---

18. สมุก, *samuk*, a small lidded basketwork container (Wibun, *Phojananukrom hatthakam*, 300).

Khun Phaen called out, "Hey, Phlai Ngam, stand up to check the shadow.[19] I think it's almost the auspicious time. Hurry to take leave of Mother and friends."

Phlai Ngam prostrated to take leave. Khun Phaen examined the time by the shadow. They hollered, beat gongs, and fired guns, making a great racket.

Khun Phaen, Phlai Ngam, and their thirty-five comrades swarmed up onto their mounts. Just at the auspicious moment, Kaeo Kiriya gave birth to a son.

Thong Prasi came to see her grandchild. Khun Phaen turned to look. His mother held the grandson, and loudly called for fire.

Phramuen Si's wife ran to them, and servants scurried over with a stove. When Kaeo Kiriya had recovered comfortably, they lifted her into a boat and left.

There is no reason for doubt here. Kaeo Kiriya's pregnancy was advanced in the jail. She gave birth right at the auspicious time and so the son was named Phlai Chumphon.

When Khun Phaen knew that Kaeo Kiriya had given birth to a son without difficulty, he had the men holler, beat gongs to start the march, and fly red flags flapping above.

Gunfire echoed around. Birds flew off in fright, some plunging to earth and then flying up again. Bandicoots hid in holes.

Rabbits and squirrels looked up and bounded off. Monkeys and langurs jumped and swung away. Elephants, horses, and men set off, carrying pikes with flags streaming overhead.

Arriving at a junction on the river, the soldiers came upon a liquor boat and called out loudly, "Hey! We must get some." They poled and paddled over at speed, and collided with a Mon boat on the way.

The Mon shouted, "You sons of slaves, you tangerine flowers!" Ai-Phut and Ai-Ngok elbowed him. I-Tasoi cried loudly, "Hey, robbers!" They rushed towards the Jek, hollering,

punnet

---

19. *Chanchai*, see p. 10, note 51. This may refer to another form of divination. Make a stick using the joint on the middle figure of the right hand as the measure. The length in joints should be 3 on a Sunday and 12, 14, 17, 12, 11, 10 on the other days in sequence. Use the stick to draw a circle on the ground then plant the stick in its center. If the shadow falls within the circle, the day is auspicious (Wales, *Divination*, 127).

grabbed pitchers of liquor, and put them in their own boat. Northerners in the army went off to catch girls. Others took a whole field of cabbages from a Jek, Chinaman Lek, who ran up to ask, "What are you up to?"

The Thai grabbed hold of his pigtail. "Knock you dead.[20] Oh shit, please help me!" Elephants, horses, and people swarmed across the river and out to the plain.

Guards at the customs post rang a gong, called in their troops, and raised lances and swords to attack, but the robbers bounded away with flaming eyes, and all the guards could do was beat their gong and watch.

They marched out to the Maharat Plain and arrived at the landing where Skystorm was buried. They halted and had people dig. The sword was as bright and shiny as if it had never been buried.

Khun Phaen drew it from the sheath with a smile on his face. There was not a trace of rust. He spoke to his son, "I buried it when Phra Phichit sent us down."

Phlai Ngam asked his father, "But it's been buried for a very long time, up to fifteen years. It's odd it should have no rust. How can that be?"

Khun Phaen told his son, "Hundreds and thousands of swords cannot compete with this. Many metals were collected to make it good. At each stage, years ago, an auspicious moment was found.

It was anointed with 108 herbal waters and spirit oil. The haft was filled with a diamond, jet, yantra, and mantra. Once made, it was activated in seven graveyards. A damned spirit was inserted for protection,

and it was entrusted to the care of the gods and Krung Phali. How could it ever get rusty? The metal is good and has martial power. The fluid metal gives it the greenish sheen of a carpenter bee."

Having said that, he made a prayer, "Whoever should establish a village here, let it be called Sword Village[21] and be the boundary of the district of Lopburi.

Khun Phaen, great master, wished to instill the sword with the power of victory. He had an eye-level shrine erected with a good white cloth as a canopy,

set out various offerings, placed Skystorm on the shrine, lit victory candles, and pronounced mantra.

Spirits and deities swarmed around. Khun Phaen raised his arms above his

---

20. พะชี้ ไส้ บวย, *phachi sai buai*, in Chinese, see p. 43, note 69.

21. บ้านดาบ, Ban Dap, now Ban Dap Kong Thanu, is just north of the present-day boundary between Ayutthaya and Lopburi provinces (see map 2).

head in salutation. A wondrous, howling wind blew up a storm to shake the whole earth.

The troops shouted and hollered. "Will you go to war with our boss, damn you?" Skystorm slid out of its sheath and shook. The fierce-fanged spirit instilled in the sword

bellowed like thunder. The sword rattled and flashed on the shrine. Khun Phaen presented the offerings and extinguished the candles.

Skystorm slid into its sheath with a smack. Khun Phaen grasped it and raised it above his head. Now that everything was done, Khun Phaen mounted on his fine elephant, Phlai Kang,

and the army marched off, hollering and beating gongs, with gun smoke cloaking them like fog. Flags streamed in rows along the way. Elephants, horses, and troops swarmed forward.

Villagers shivered in fear. Some prostrated. Some peeked through gaps in their walls. In every district on the way, the troops were fed and looked after by villagers and local officials.

They passed through Chawai to Chalon[22] and stopped to sleep for a short while. At dawn, hollering and firing guns, they arrived at Mueang In.[23]

The villagers and local officials fed and looked after them. They entered the forest with the crackle of gunfire echoing around, and sent servants to collect anything, including gourds and melons.

They arrived at Ban Ngio,[24] walking along a path in file, and chewing sugarcane to quench their thirst. They took whatever they found to keep up their strength. The jailbird, Ai-Ta Daeng, went off for some mischief.

They halted at Chainat to visit the market. Seeing young women, they raised their eyebrows, winked, and followed the women's bottoms. The girls cried out, "Ha! Don't be lewd." One soldier mischievously grabbed some popped rice and chewed it.

The owner called out, "Where's the money?" The soldier mumbled from the corner of his mouth, "Oh, I just want a little taste." They went around in a noisy crowd to collect food. If they met anyone walking alone, they robbed them in broad daylight.

---

22. Chawai, ชะไว, to the east of the river, 3 kms north of Chaiyo in Ang Thong province. ชลอน, Wat Chalon, now called Wat Phrom Thephawat, 8 kms south of Singburi on the west bank of the river (see map 2).

23. Now Inburi (map 2).

24. บ้านงิ้ว, 12 kms north of Inburi on the east bank (map 2).

Villagers and local officials fed and looked after the army. They marched onward past Chi Dak Khanon, Nakhon Sawan, and Koeichai to Wat Yang.[25]

They reached Wat Jan[26] as evening approached. Khun Phaen put his foot in a stirrup and jumped down. The phrai unloaded supplies from the horses and elephants. A crowd of nobles and villagers arrived

to feed and look after the army. Once that was done, they returned home. Khun Phaen spoke to Phlai Ngam, "Tomorrow we'll go to see Phra Phichit.

His goodness when I brought your mother out of the forest was beyond belief. You don't know because you were still in the womb, but he and his wife took pity on us and fed us.

He loved me as much as their natural child. His words helped to make our severe punishment disappear. Color of Mist, the horse I rode into battle, was left here in the care of Ai-In.

A closed and roofed stable was built where he is fed plenty of hay and water. We'll go to visit Phra Phichit tomorrow so you can see, my son."

Phlai Ngam was happy to hear this. "We should certainly go, Father, so that they may know me and understand why we have come." They went in to sleep.

---

25. Dak Khanon lies 10 kms northwest of Chainat along the Chaophraya River. Koeichai, เกยไชย, is on the southern edge of Amphoe Chumsaeng on the Nan River close to where it meets the Yom in the northeast of Nakhon Sawan province. เกย, *koei*, is a royal mounting platform for elephants, boats, or other conveyances. Probably this was a common transition point between land and water on trips to the north. Wat Yang Jaroentham, about 8 kms north of Boraphet on the west bank of the Yom River (see map 4).

26. See p. 865.

At the third watch, Phlai Ngam dreamed that a leech as thick as a leg fastened onto him. In shock and confusion, he sprang up and hit his head on a horse saddle.

In surprise Khun Phaen called out, "Men, come and help! Phlai is going to a bad death!" Phlai Ngam related the dream to his father with staring eyes. Khun Phaen gave him a blessing, saying, "You'll have a wife."

While Simala slept, she dreamed that a snake coiled round her body, making her eyes stream. She sprung awake with bleary eyes. Her legs gave way and she fell smack on I-Moei.

I-Moei responded, "Oh, my cunt is showing![1] Did you think you were going to a bad death and so rushed here?" Simala recounted her dream, and I-Moei said, "Don't worry. You're in luck. You'll have a husband."

Simala shouted, "What in heavens?" I-Moei said, "If it's not a husband, you'll get something. But mark my words, given with good intentions, he'll come by the golden light of dawn."[2]

సౌ

Khun Phaen marched the army into Phichit, firing guns, ringing gongs, and hollering loudly.

All the woman vendors—young, old and widows—liked what they saw. They smacked their lips. "Just perfect! Figures good enough to eat."

The widows fancied Khun Phaen. "I think we would be just right for each other." The young girls thought Phlai Ngam was a dish. Their hearts were in turmoil.

When the men looked over, a young woman wriggled her shoulders to make her uppercloth slip down, and left it there with breasts bare, then jiggled her eyebrows as she turned her body away.

---

1. อุยมิซิ โล้ง โต้ง, *ui mi chi long tong*, in Mon.
2. Choomsai notes that a snake can be an omen for a good partner but that a leech is generally interpreted negatively and at best means a partner that will give problems (CS, 83–84).

Phra Phichit came out to sit in the central sala with his nobles and local officials to discuss the case of I-Moei Mua, who Ai-Jek Ngua tried to rape in broad daylight.

Phra Phichit looked over where horses, elephants, and men were arriving at the central sala, and saw Khun Phaen coming to see him.

"I think my beloved son, who went down so long ago, has arrived!" Khun Phaen prostrated with his heart thumping. "The king just pardoned me and sent me here."

Phra Phichit laughed, "What good fortune!" He grabbed Khun Phaen's hand and took him up to the house. Phlai Ngam trailed behind his father. They prostrated together to Phra Phichit and Nang Busaba.

Busaba streamed with tears. "I was desperately worried about you." They all talked together, relating the whole story.

Phra Phichit and Busaba stroked Phlai Ngam on the back, saying, "Your little son was fearless to address the king, asking for his father to accompany him to war.

He's a brave fellow from a lineage of powerful lions. A spark catching a little bit of fluff grows and grows into a spreading fire. Don't ruin your family's good name, my fine fellow."

As she said this, a thought jumped into her head—that she'd like Phlai Ngam as a son-in-law. She called to her daughter, "Simala! Come and wai these two gentlemen."

Hearing the call for her to come and wai the visitors, Simala was overcome by fear and shyness.

She walked over and opened a chest for a change of clothes. She put on a Tani lowercloth with a beautiful cone-pattern border[3] and a motif of fish embroidered in golden silk.

She wore a diamond ring on her left hand, and a radiant red ring on the right. Picking up a mirror, she looked at herself from this way and that, then powdered her face to look fair,

combed her hair, and trimmed her hairline straight with no bits sticking up and down like a gardener. She put on a soft ruby uppercloth with a gold pattern which matched well with her lowercloth,

and found a nielloware goblet[4] for pan leaves. In the manner of a charm-

---

3. กรวย, *kruai*, shorthand for the *kruaichoeng* pattern of elongated cones, popular as a border.

4. จอก, *jok*, a small bowl, usually with a base if used as part of a betel set (Wibun, *Phojanan-ukrom hatthakam*, 122).

ing young lady, she walked out of the room with head bowed, glancing from a corner of her eye.

She made obeisance, put the betel on a salver, lowered her face, and slid backwards to sit beside her mother, letting her eyes glance at the men.

The governor, Phra Phichit, could see she was drawn to Phlai Ngam but, though she might feel real love, as a woman she was bound to be shy. So he spoke out.

"Now then, Simala, that's terrible. You can't even wai Khun Phaen. How can you be shy of someone you should consider as an elder brother?[5] Wai him, dear daughter."

Khun Phaen, seeing how charming she was, turned to accept Simala's wai. Her looks and manners were beyond expectation,
    her whole body like a gleaming bar of gold with not a single flaw. He was greatly taken by her. While admiring her, he also examined his son,
    who was clearly love-struck, his youthful face lit up. The girl was radiant, and the boy brilliant.

"They deserve to be partners. Would such a match be found again? Why would Phlai not go for her?" He nudged his son with a smile.

As soon as Phlai Ngam looked over, his heart was captured by love. Once he saw Simala's face, he did not want to take his eyes off her.

But if he stared, he feared the Phichit governor would comment. He drew backwards behind his father in order to look at Simala to his heart's content.

She sat beside her mother. Her face was radiant, and her chignon[6] suited her well. Her breasts were full, her rear uplifted, her waist curvy,
    and her arms faultless. The fingers on both hands were elegantly rounded as if neatly molded from wax. She wore a ruby uppercloth edged in gold,
    and a Tani lowercloth in bee-wing green. He focused his eyes on the gap where her uppercloth opened and saw her two firm breasts.

"So this is this noble's child! She carries herself like a royal lady. If I could hug her to my breast, I'd hold on as long and tight as I could."

Simala's heart was trembling and she was overcome with shyness. Seated beside her mother, she saw lovable Phlai Ngam looking intently at her.

---

5. Phra Phichit had adopted Khun Phaen as his "son" (see ch. 21).

6. The text has ไรจุก, *rai juk*, topknot, but Simala would not have a topknot at this age, and the word is probably being used with poetic license because it fits the rhyme.

She turned away and shifted behind her mother. After a while, she looked at him again. "So this is the knowledgeable Phlai Ngam, sitting with his father, and looking as if made from the same mold.

He has a bright face and cheeks like nutmeg. His lips look as if painted with rouge. His black teeth gleam prettily. When he smiles, you can see a glimpse.

Hair as cute as a lotus pod. A rounded neck in proportion like a molding. Eyebrows curved like a bow. The black pupils of his eyes gleaming like jet.

A strong chest and curvy waist. Everything looks perfect. If he came to lie with me for one night, I'd gobble him up." They looked at each other without any shyness,

both with the same hope and intent. Then she came to herself, felt shocked and shy in front of him, rose and went up into the residence.

The governor, Phra Phichit, looked carefully at his daughter. He could see that both children were affected and happily aroused to mutual love.

He promptly sent his servants to invite the monks. "Deliver the invitation today that I'll have a feeding for around seven monks tomorrow."

Tell all the nobles to come for giving food to the monks. Also tell the servants and phrai in the family circle to come and help make merit."

The servants each went off to tell the local officials that all the friends of the governor should come on the following day to make merit.

Some left for the wat and went up to ask the abbot, who sent a novice to invite the monks. Within no time, seven monks were arranged for.

Phra Phichit then ordered his servants to prepare everything to feed and look after the army. Servants bustled off.

Phra Phichit's household lit fires, pounded chili, mixed spices, steamed rice, and made curries. Lizard, spider, and turtle were taken to the army commander.

The local officials and villagers fed the soldiers until they were full and happy. Khun Phaen and his son ate with Phra Phichit.

While taking a mouthful of rice, Phlai Ngam glanced around. Simala was waiting with her eye at a chink in the wall. As a result of some good deeds done in the past, their eyes met through the gap.

When the meal was over and removed, betel and pan were provided for their enjoyment. Khun Phaen asked, "Sir, is that horse still in sturdy condition?"

Phra Phichit said, "Color of Mist is still well and has no problems." Khun Phaen promptly took his leave. Phlai Ngam made obeisance and followed him.

They opened the door of the stables and went in. Color of Mist stamped and whinnied. Both horse and human shed tears. Khun Phaen spoke.

"I feel sorry that Color of Mist, my friend in hardship, who had the goodness to carry me and Wanthong through the forest, has been parted from me. It was a heavy punishment but I had to bear it.

I suffered in the inner jail until my son asked for my release and I could come to see you. I've just got over this trouble. Phlai Ngam here is the son of Wanthong.

The king has sent us to fight Chiang Mai, so we were both able to take our leave and come here together. I ask you with good intentions to help me gain victory on this occasion."

The horse was happy, loving, and trusting. He understood Khun Phaen's words and did not shrink from going to war.

Khun Phaen could see the horse had no fear. He turned to speak to Phlai Ngam, "My horse is raring to fight.

He's bolder than any other and fears nobody. If you visited all the cities of the north and south, you'd not find another that knows how to fight and maneuver tirelessly like him.

The crackle of gunfire doesn't scare him. This horse is strong. He's worth a hundred chang." He called for a saddle and harness

encased in red felt, tassels to hang left and right, a gold-embroidered brow-piece in the shape of a bo leaf with glittering stars to left and right,

water peonies on either side with a crabclaw pattern[7] made of yellow serge[8] and covered in brilliant red felt, as ornaments for battle.

Khun Phaen leapt up onto the horse's back, pulled the reins to make him circle, drew his saber, and galloped back and forth, performing a war dance.

The horse responded nimbly to both left and right. Then Khun Phaen reined him in to pace backwards, and finally gave him the whip to gallop.

The horse was still very fast, and arrived at the residence in no time. Khun Phaen tethered the horse, went in,

and walked up into the house. Everybody had gathered to admire the horse. In the late afternoon, the monks arrived.[9]

---

7. The water peony is a floral decoration fixed on the harness below the ear. Crabclaw pattern, ลายก้ามปู, *lai kam pu,* is a repeating motif giving the appearance of a serrated edge, found especially in the framing of Khmer statuary.

8. ประสะตุ, ปัสะตุ, *p(r)asatu,* serge, a type of twilled fabric. This passage is unclear, and also slightly different in the SS and WK versions, suggesting this place was damaged in a manuscript from which both were copied.

9. Above, the invitation is clearly for the following day.

They were invited up to sit in the hall as fitting, and people came to pay their respects. Food and medicine had been prepared for presenting to the monks. After the request for the precepts,[10] prayers were chanted.

Everyone was dressed up. Both men and women sat together. Phra Phichit and Busaba presided at the prayer chanting.

Phlai Ngam arranged a groom's party of five people from among the soldiers—Nai Thuam, Nai Mi, Nai Si, Nai Pan, and bald Nai Bua.

The elders in the household arranged a bride's party with five persons—Sang-Lao, Si, Son, Som, and Sa. Only the relatives of the house were invited, not outsiders, so everyone knew one another and all were relaxed and jolly together. Little children came along too. The water-sprinkling ceremony was very boisterous.

Nang Si flirtatiously squeezed up close to Nai Bua, giving him a shock. With his clothes and body totally soaked, he went up close to Nang Som and eyed her up.

As bald Nai Bua was a rogue, Nang Som, an old lady with droopy breasts, retreated behind Nang Sang. Everybody laughed out loud.

When the water sprinkling was over, the monks returned merrily to the wat. Food was carried in. People ate and chatted happily.

The governor, Phra Phichit, said. "I'll give that sitting hall for you to be together as a bridal house. I'll provide money and servants."

Khun Phaen raised his hands in wai and replied promptly, "Whatever you wish to give, Pa." They all wai-ed and left.

Khun Phaen took pitchers with water for the horse. Feeling very happy, they reached the sala where they stayed.

The thirty-five soldiers came to welcome them, asking to be told all about it, teasing and joking in the last light of the evening sun.

Smiling merrily, Khun Phaen called his son to come for instruction. "Beloved son, you'll be going to sleep up there. Go and see the parents before going into the room.

As for Simala, nobody like her can be found. She's suitable to take charge of a household, and she'll not shame you in front of friends.

She's wealthy from olden times, better than any villager. Protect and enjoy her, my son, and continue the line for a thousand years."

---

10. See p. 64, note 39.

Phlai Ngam raised his hands to receive the blessing, and listened to his father's instruction closely. "Let it be according to merit and fortune. As for me, I'm utterly happy."

With that, he saluted and left the sala where they stayed. Five soldiers followed him to the front of the great residence,

and saw him off there. Phlai Ngam entered, went to prostrate to his parents-in-law, and happily entered the sitting hall.

The monks had all returned to the wat. The villagers had gone wherever the mood took them. The local officials had taken leave of Phra Phichit. The sun sank behind a fringe of trees.

Busaba happily went to instruct Simala. "Now that you'll be with your husband, please remember what I now tell you and follow it for your own good.

Even if he's angry with you, don't be angry back, but be compromising so he appreciates your good nature. If he becomes doubtful, he'll leave you alone and abandoned.

It's said good people must have some shame. Don't take as your model those who are evil and shameless. Follow the saying that a good nature is the most important thing.

To give long instructions will take too much time. Your father is waiting to hear how you two get along. He'll say I talk too much without any meaning like a drunk coming home late, babbling nonsense."

After the instruction, she left and closed the door. Phlai Ngam knew what to do and wasted no time. He could now embrace Simala as he wished. He lifted her up and lay her down on the bed.

Simala pushed at him. "Hey, Phlai! Let all the servants go to sleep first." Phlai Ngam replied, "Don't worry, we won't bother them."

With that, he pulled her close and caressed her lovingly. Storm clouds gathered, the atmosphere thickened, and thunder rumbled. Ramasun[11] swirled through the clouds.

Mekhala's gem flashed and flared. Peals of thunder echoed through the skies. He admired her eyes, head, and cheeks. Both tasted ecstasy.

At cockcrow in the golden light of the sun, Phlai Ngam kissed Simala and said, "Stay well. Please don't feel hurt.

This morning I'll leave you and go with the army. Don't have suspicions that I want to run far away from you."

Her husband's words made Simala feel someone had slashed her head off,

---

11. On this myth, see p. 823, note 33.

but she knew how matters were and that she should not try to stop him.

It would be bad for both of them. Army service was a serious matter. Karma made it necessary, and a wife could not lament and complain.

At dawn, Phra Phichit arranged a force of two hundred and fifty men including servants, phrai, robbers, and serious bandits, all of them invulnerable,

with Muen At Narai, an expert and thorough brigand, as the unit head. They harnessed up twenty elephants and loaded them with panniers and packs.

When ordered to go with Phlai Ngam, these men proudly boasted that they were going to war, and got busy packing their devices of lore.

The quartermaster and deputy governors of both left and right, along with many minor officials, packed a great number of supplies and had their retainers lift them onto elephants.

Liquor, snacks, and sweets were brought to feed the thirty-five soldiers. They sat all around in the sala, happily eating and chatting.

Khun Phaen ordered everyone to get dressed quickly as it was an auspicious time for them to move off.

The thirty-five soldiers all decked their bodies with armor and devices[12]

that had served them well in the past, including auspicious bandeaus tied around their heads, black trousers, red shirts on their bodies,

tooled swords with engraved handles encased in red sheaths, quivers strapped smartly crosswise on their bodies, and flintlock guns for all to carry. They looked fierce and strong,

standing together, holding their guns, with powder horns dangling from their belts, ready to go, and complaining impatiently that it was time to leave.

Khun Phaen and his son said farewell to Phra Phichit, who had come along to see them off. Crowds of people sat in the central sala to give their blessing.

Khun Phaen, bold in warfare, looked as magnificent as the Lord of the Lions. He was dressed in colored silk britches with upturned cuffs,

lowercloth with a pattern of swans, shirt for traveling, soft *song praphat* hat,[13] belt embroidered with a pattern of dragons, golden beaded necklace presented by the king,

---

12. In both WK and SS, this stanza has lost the first hemistich.

13. ทรงประพาศ, a close-fitting military headgear made of soft material like felt with a pattern of *lamduan* petals, and a flap covering the back of the neck.

and a helmet with a fringe. To make his body powerful and bold, he put on a bright *phirot* ring. To seize and sack the city,

he carried Skystorm in a sheath covered with black velvet and decorated with yellow gems, and stuck a fine shining silver kris in his belt. He walked out to wait for his son.

Phlai Ngam, bold slayer of enemies, dressed magnificently in leggings of light moon-yellow, patterned britches,

yok lowercloth with a design of fighting Garudas on a red background and a brilliant cone-border in gold, a belt with sparkling diamonds on a flower-patterned pleated *attalat* cloth around his waist,

a helmet with a brim from the Farang city of Reo,[14] a foreign[15] saber in a scintillating golden sheath, and amulets strapped around his waist. He mounted an elephant.

Khun Phaen rode an elephant amid the troops. Phlai Ngam also rode an elephant with his red shirt and red helmet catching the sunlight. Red flags flapped and fluttered overhead.

Villagers and townsfolk flocked to watch them. Some cradled little children or lifted them above their heads to see. The clouds formed an omen of Lord Narai riding a flying Garuda, moving along ahead of the troops.[16]

At an auspicious time, the soldiers beat gongs and hollered loudly and raucously. The sound of gunfire crackled, and a pall of smoke hung overhead. With flags flying, the army marched off.

The volunteers rode horses, kicking up clouds of dust. The porters walked with loads bouncing along. Dried giant snakehead fish dangled down.

Boxes of chili and boxes of ginger clattered and creaked. A jumble of sacks and bags bounced and buffeted. Panniers swayed and swung to the rhythm, dancing up and down as they passed from district to district.

Braids of little dried leaf fish dangled down from the carriers, waving around like bunches of flowers. Snakehead fish lay flat. Pots fell off and bounced along the ground.

---

14. ฝรั่ง เมือง เร่ว, *farang mueang reo*, probably meaning Riau, now an island in the Malacca strait, just southeast of Singapore, but may in fact indicate Singapore. In the early nineteenth-century Thai maps, Singapore island is labeled as เร่ว, *reo* (Santanee and Stott, *Royal Siamese Maps*, 190–91).

15. เทศ, *thet*, which may mean foreign in general or the "western lands" of India, Persia, and Arabia.

16. On cloud omens, see p. 621, note 15.

A unit head used his whip to prevent people slacking. "What's up. You're not the boss so keep moving!" The troops ran off, knocking into one another, heads trembling, staggering and stumbling ahead.

Mahouts rode elephants with saddles and elephants with howdahs, swaying from side to side. Clusters of shields, bows, crossbows, spears, and blades jutted skyward.

Flags flew finely. Some men hoisted flashing swords aloft, hallooing and hollering to fill the forest. They soon left the city behind, reached Wat Chang,[17] went along the Phing,[18]

passed Tha Rong,[19] and entered Phitsanulok. They pilfered gourds, marrows, anything, making the owners jump up and down in frustration. "It's like a pack of monkeys turning everything inside out."

Phra Phichai, the officials of city, palace, treasury, and land, and the governor quickly organized to have them fed. Once finished, they left along a buffalo track

to Ban Trai[20] and Pa Faek. Along the way, people collected up their petty belongings and families, and fled into the forest to hide in fear of the army.

Triggering their guns as they went, they passed Tha Kasem and arrived at Wat Pa,[21] where they waited for the elephants, staying at the tail of the city, shooting their guns, cloaked in smoke.

The Chaophraya of Sawankhalok, local officials, village officers, and villagers came out to feed the army and then returned to the city. At dawn, a crowd of servants again brought food.

As soon as they had eaten, the soldiers set off, halting at Ban Tha Kwian where old Khun Krai fed them.

Though Simala had just had a new husband by her side, she was shy and fearful about going to see him off in front of the ordinary townsfolk.

"Oh, oh Phlai Ngam of mine, you've left for the ends of the earth and the yellow sky. When will you return to this city? I'll be gloomy and miserable."

---

17. Wat Rong Chang, between old Phichit and the site of the modern town (see map 9).

18. The canal linking the Nan and Yom rivers (see p. 538, note 13). Here they seem to have gone northwest from old Phichit towards the Yom River, then cut back east along the course of the Phing Canal to the Nan River, and then north towards Phitsanulok.

19. On the west bank, 7 kms southwest of the center of Phitsanulok (map 4).

20. Perhaps Krai(lat), now Kong Krailat.

21. วัด ป่า ข่อย, Wat Pa Khoi, on the south side of Sawankhalok.

Phlai Ngam felt hot and stifled as if burned by fire. In the evening when he lay down to sleep, he mumbled deliriously, hugging and manhandling Khun Phaen,

who cried, "Hey, damn you! You're climbing over me like a besotted Chinaman." He punched Phlai Ngam in the head. Phlai fell flat face-down and pretended to lie still like a sleeping crocodile.

At daylight, they had the officers of the outpost supply various articles for offerings, and construct a shrine with balustrade, umbrellas, and flags.

shrine

All the soldiers were mobilized to make five thousand grass dummies. In the ruddy light of the dawn sun, Khun Phaen carried out the ceremony.

Offerings were brought, and the grass dummies were placed on the shrine. Candles and flowers were set on a salver, and a circle made with sacred thread. Rice was hurled around to drive away spirits.

When Khun Phaen and his son had got dressed, they walked out looking as grand as the bold Lord Matjurat[22] going to end the lives of the Lao.

Victory candles were lit to activate the shrine. All around, spirits trembled and called out to one another, even the Lord of Red Ox Cave.[23]

Khun Phaen pronounced a mantra to convoke the deities. Dark storm clouds gathered, obscuring the moon. Villagers lit bonfires, fired guns, and shouted for help,

thinking the moon was in eclipse,[24] not knowing the darkness was caused by mantra. Swarms of spirits from every graveyard came rushing over,

calling out to grandfathers and grandmothers to come along as well. They prostrated rowdily around Khun Phaen, who said, "Hey! Will you go to war with us?"

The crowds of spirits were waiting open-mouthed to enjoy the offerings and white liquor. They replied happily, "We'll go, sir!" and devoured the offerings, soon becoming drunk and disorderly.

Only Khun Phaen could see the mass of spirits, not the soldiers and people

---

22. A name for *yom*, Yama, the god of death.

23. เจ้า เข้า ถ้ำ วัว แดง, *jao khao tham wua daeng*. Presumably this was a local spirit of the place, well-known at the time. There are several caves of this name, including in Ubon, Uttaradit, and Chaiyaphum.

24. According to belief, during an eclipse, the moon is being swallowed by the god Rahu who has to be dissuaded by making a racket.

packed around. He enchanted rice and hurled it. In a flash of flame, the mantra dummies turned into people,

complete with various weapons in hand. The dummies prostrated before Khun Phaen, who stood, legs apart, holding Skystorm, and pronounced a mantra ordering the spirits

to serve as a vanguard army. "You attack and drive away the spirits of the forest. If you meet any Lao spirits, do away with them. Help to protect us against all the Lords of the Plains."

At the end, the candles were extinguished. The spirits prostrated, and got busy organizing their army. Four of the spirits and four of the sprites were appointed as the eight commanders of the vanguard.

Ai-Mu, who had been gored to death, was in charge of the scouts to go ahead of the army. Old Phon, who had died in a collision with a buffalo, was in charge of the lookouts,

commanding a hundred spirits to provide intelligence. Nai Ban, who had been struck down by thunder, headed the signals brigade, and Ai-Ma, who had been killed by lightning, headed the victory brigade. These two officers were to command four hundred spirits.

The vigorous, fierce, daring, and fearless Ai-Daeng, who had been gored to death by an elephant, had charge of the vanguard of one thousand and six hundred spirits. Ai-Noi, who died falling from a sugar palm, took the left flank,

while the right flank fell to the rough, wild, and audacious Ai-Duea, who had been eaten by a tiger. Each had a thousand men. The army commander was Deputy Pan, who had died from fever.

Chinaman Hap, who had succumbed to cholera, was to carry the standard. Spirits of tigers, rats, snakes, deer, hinds, and many other kinds of fierce wild animals were also recruited.

They moved out immediately. The troops under the army commander numbered almost eleven thousand in several brigades. Many spirits who had died bad deaths joined up

to carry the supplies, arguing fiercely with one another. Spirits of Farang, Dutchmen, Kula, Vietnamese, and several spear-carrying Burmese came riding spirit horses.

Spirits of dead Lawa commanded the spirit elephants. Spirits of Karen squabbled over porterage. Spirits of Thai carried baggage bouncing along on shoulder poles. Spirits of Khmer, Chinese, and Khaek helped with transport.

Kuai[25] spirits rode on spirit oxen. Mon and Meng spirits served as porters.

---

25. Kuai, Kuay, Kui, a Mon-Khmer ethnic group that lived earlier in what is now southern Laos and northern Cambodia. They are traditionally associated with elephants.

Spirits of slaves and jailbirds hid themselves away, but Thai spirits chased them down

to carry baskets on their heads. The officers drew up the spirit army in the forest in a great mass, shouting and hollering, with horses neighing and elephants trumpeting. They waited for Khun Phaen to unfurl the standard.

Khun Phaen and his son organized the army according to the Manual on Victorious Warfare to be imposing, skilled, bold, invulnerable, and effective in battle.

Nai Sa from Ban Tha Sao[26] took charge of the scouts; Nai Ma from Ban Tha Khayi, the lookouts; Nai Kaen from Lopburi, the signals brigade; Nai Mi from Muang Bon,[27] the victory brigade;

Nai Rat from Kawatti,[28] the left flank; Nai Ni from Ban Chihon, the right flank; Nai Sa and Nai Yon, the vanguard; Nai Phon from Ban Pho Kluang,[29] the rearguard;

Nai Prang from Bang I-ra[30] as quartermaster; and Nai Da from the capital, as commissary. The large army was organized into units. Nai Duang from Bang Suea was deputed to carry the standard.

Volunteers riding post horses would go ahead to clear any obstacle. The dummy troops were placed at the front of the army. Gongs were beaten to announce an inspection.

At an auspicious time, a big gong sounded, and three cheers were raised for victory. Smoke from gunfire cloaked the column. Red flags were unfurled to flutter aloft.

The elephants and spirit troops led off, hollering raucously through the forest. Shouting war cries, they attacked Lao spirits,

stabbing and shooting so their enemies fell and rolled in the dust like jackfruit. Some foes got up and fought back, others ran away among the trees. The spirits of the forest fled and hid far away.

---

26. Village of the landing with posts, a common name, the two most likely candidates are 5 kms northwest of Ratchaburi and 3 kms northwest of Chainat.

27. A place in Amphoe Phayuhakiri, Nakhon Sawan, where remains have been found dating back to the Dvaravati era.

28. ก(ร)ะหวัด ตี, *k(r)awat ti,* not obviously a place name unless it means Gauhati in Assam, which seems unlikely. It could translate as "fierce in attack."

29. Village of the hollow bo tree; unidentified.

30. Now Bang Nangra, นางร้า, egret village, just north of Bang Pahan in Ayutthaya province (see map 3).

Spirits of the streams, rivers, mountains, and lakes gave protection to the troops. To describe would take too long so let's hurry on to admiring the birds and trees.

When they reached the defile,[31] an area of hills, Phlai Ngam was missing Simala sadly. "That smilinglady reminds me of Simala's cheeks when our eyes met and she smiled.

This lady's fingernail reminds me of my lady lamenting. That *lamduan* recalls how I had to lumber away with the army. The parrot calling from a gem jasmine mimics our joyless parting.

That barbet rocks back and forth like my darling when she grieves. Now it's darting up to catch a cricket and calling out so clearly. Doves cooing in couples, echoing around the forest, are like you weeping when I first departed.

The water in the stream splashes and spurts like your tears on our parting. There are *saraphi, jampi, khanang, yang,* jasmine, laurel, banyan,

in-jan, pring, maprang, changnao, jambolan, hundredtongue, armorwood, and rattan. Several *kot*[32] are perched on a *ket* tree. A row of lory on a *khontha,*

a flock of swans landing on a *krathan-han* tree,[33] crake on a forest *lamduan,* lorikeets in the trees, pheasant on *mafai.*"

Streams splashed down through levels of rock, and crashed through ravines. They halted at Thoen. The governor came out to welcome the army.

Grilled paddy frog, lizard, rat, mole, and warmed-up deer meat, along with liver soup, were brought to feed the army. Afterwards, the officers talked with the governor.

"So, you went to fight Chiang Thong. After you left, I was waiting for news. It's a good chance to see you again. Your body still looks robust, and your flesh youthful.

Why has Chiang Mai turned aggressive, invaded and captured all the Thai? This time they'll get slashed to pieces and left as prey for vultures, crows, and dogs."

---

31. ช่อง แคบ, *chong khaep.* As elsewhere in *KCKP*, this name is used to refer to the pass where the route from Sawankhalok across Thung Saliam crosses the ridge just east of Thoen.

32. See p. 526, note 13.

33. Both SS and WK have กระทัง หัน, *krathang han,* which is difficult to identify with a tree. It might be กะทันหัน, *kathanhan,* instantaneously, or กระทายเหิน, *krathai-hoen,* a tree also known as *mahahong, Hedychium coronarium.*

Khun Phaen replied to Phraya Thoen. "It was beyond our king's imagination. It would be hard for the king to come so far from the city. The two territories are not adjacent.

My face has already aged, and my beloved son has already grown up." The governor of Thoen greeted Phlai Ngam to make his acquaintance. Phlai Ngam wai-ed his elder in return, and called him grandfather.

When they were finished, the army marched off, firing guns grandly, filling the forest with shouting and gongs. They marched to camp at Chomthong.

Saen Kham Maen, the father of Nang Laothong, Khun Phaen's wife who had to become an embroiderer in the palace, looked up and was happy to see his son-in-law. He had things sent for,

and rushed out with Nang Si Ngoen Yuang, the mother, to provide food for the troops. Afterwards, the army marched onward towards Lampang.[34]

The father and son conferred together and agreed they should avoid villages, but should kill any Lao they happened to meet. At Lampang they stopped and made camp.

Some fell asleep while others chattered together. At cockcrow, they set up cooking pots, made a meal, and ate their fill, then set off again in the early morning.

In the light of dawn, the spirit army attacked a Chiang Mai outpost, surprising Lao spirits, which ran into the forest and hid.

The guardian deities of the boundary post were also taken unawares and raced away after the others. Then at dawn, hollering, firing guns, and loosing arrows, the mantra dummies overpowered the Lao,

who tried to run away, shouting loudly, losing their lowercloths, and exposing their white bellies. The soldiers cried, "Ha, you Lao. We've seen the red and white of your legs. Now taste my gun!"

Lao men and women broke and ran into the forest, pushing through the undergrowth. Thai chased after them, blasting away with their guns.

Some could not run fast but only limped along. "Slash and stab, mate, until there are none left." "If you find a young Lao girl, keep her. She can stroke your moustache and give us a nice massage."

They slashed and stabbed them down, captured Lao as war prisoners, and got wives to take along with them. About those captured by the soldiers,

the Mon laughed in unison, saying, "Take the cunts.[35] These girls say they're

---

34. Here called นคร, *nakhon*, short for the full old name, Nakhon Lampang.
35. เอาชี อี ตอก ขมิ, *ao chi i tok khami*, in Mon.

afraid of our spears." To describe everything would take too long. The army reached a lake and pitched camp

where there was water, young grass shoots, and dense forest gave shade, making a good hiding place. They established a main base.

✧

Now to tell of the Lao who had fled. When it fell quiet, they emerged to look around. Seeing the army had gone, they raced around to find their wives and children.

Some were still alive and saw their husbands coming to look for them. Others lay dead with their guts spilling out. In places, the bodies of husband and wife lay together, chopped up like fish.

Those still alive ran off, whole households together. Possessions were strewn everywhere. Floors and walls were shattered and scattered. The sight was pitiful.

Some lay dead in their own devastated houses amid the broken remains of pitchers and water jars. The floor in the center of some houses was full of corpses.

Petty possessions had been taken—boxes of chili and salt, vegetables, clothes, everything. Those who came to look wept for their loved ones, and hastily buried the corpses.

In shock, they went through the forest to the city and reported to the King of Chiang Mai that an army had attacked and destroyed the outpost village, but they had not seen how large the army was.

The King of Chiang Mai listened to their report. "If they attacked that village, they will set up camp there. Things are going according to my expectation. Conscript people from the ends of the territory.

Spy on their army from a distance. Establish a camp without disturbing them." Saen Kamhan and Khwan Phon-maen took the order and hurried off.

A camp was hastily established. As they did not know where the enemy was, bonfires were lit after sundown and patrols sent out to keep watch.

The King of Chiang Mai became greatly concerned over the Thai prisoners. He promptly issued an order, "Have all the Thai placed under full restraint.

Send out torch patrols on duty. Assemble local headmen and good soldiers, and issue them with big guns and other weapons. From evening onward, post guards."

The senior officials took the royal order and crept off. Officials of all ranks took up positions on the walls, beating the alarm, waving torches, and calling out across the city.

Heron-leg guns were placed at apertures. Inspection patrols were posted everywhere, carrying pikes and torches to give light. Turmoil reigned in the city for fear of the army.

City officials put full restraints on the Thai and kept them under lock and key. Torch brigades patrolled around with torches blazing. Nobody could sleep for the gongs and shouting.

Ta-Lo and Phra Thainam talked in whispers. "Damnit! Some Thai army is attacking. That's why there's all this commotion and sounding the alarm.

I pray that Khun Phaen has been released and ordered up here by the king. If he arrives tonight, I'll be comforted and have no fear. But if it's anyone else, we'll die tomorrow.

Other than Khun Phaen, there's no one who could come all the way here." Ta-Lo said, "Don't get happy yet, sir, in case Khun Phaen is still in jail.

With anyone else, it won't succeed. Your head and mine will be lopped off. At dawn tomorrow they'll slaughter the whole jail." Phra Thainam lamented. "Oh damn!"

He wept in self-pity with his head doubled over on his knees, praying and babbling. All five hundred trembled and wept, crying, "Tomorrow we'll die for sure," until they fell asleep.

29: KHUN PHAEN RESCUES PHRA THAINAM

Phra Thainam had a dream with an unmistakable omen. He dreamed that the king ordered an old ascetic to bring

golden receptacles along with royal victuals,[1] both sweet and sour, including delicious meats, pancakes, and sweet potatoes, all furnished by the king.

In the dream, the old ascetic proffered the victuals to Phra Thainam, who received them and ate them from the golden receptacles.

After eating, Phra Thainam wept from sorrow and distress. He collapsed over the golden receptacles, which filled with his tears.

The old ascetic brought celestial liquor with powerful qualities and poured it on Phra Thainam's head, dispelling his sadness. Nobody heard or interpreted the dream.

✧

Now to tell of Khun Phaen, great valiant, the greatest soldier on earth without equal, who had set up camp close to the city. When the sun sank into the forest,

and a splendid haloed moon illuminated even the ants on the earth, Khun Phaen came out in front of his lodging to meet with his son and the army commanders.

Officers of the spirit army massed around. Mantra dummies sat in front. Khun Phaen discussed matters with his troops.[2]

"Today Chiang Mai will have got the news. I don't think we can delay until morning. Whatever we do, they'll slash the Thai dead. I must go in there with my son

to release the Thai, bring them out, make our fame known, and ensure it was no waste for the king to send us here. Has anyone anything to say?"

---

1. สุพรรณภาชน์, *suphannaphat*, golden receptacles; and สุพโภชน์ *suphaphot*, royal victuals; and มังษา, *mangsa*, the *ratchasap* for meat.

2. With this passage, Khun Phaen is presented in the manner of a king. His name is followed by an invocation; his lodging uses a word, พระโรง, *phrarong*, which would normally mean a palace or royal hall; when he speaks, the verb is one normally used for an elephant trumpeting, rather as the king always "roars like a lion."

The mass of soldiers replied, "Agreed," and raised their hands in wai. "If the Thai are not released in time, they'll be killed and the king will condemn us for failing."

"We'll stay here to look after the camp, arrange lookout patrols, and prevent the enemy from causing trouble." "Please do as you wish, sir."

Khun Phaen grasped Skystorm and Phlai Ngam stood holding a Japanese sword with spirits swarming around them. Khun Phaen left the camp with Phlai Ngam following,

and the spirit army accompanying them. Khun Phaen and his son slung sidebags across their shoulders. Phlai Ngam put a small gong in his waist pouch for signaling to the army.

Khun Phaen gave orders to the officers of the spirit army, "Organize parties to gather intelligence. Do not let any danger befall the army. Only spirits are to come with us."

When he pronounced a mantra of Narai Transforming His Body,[3] both he and Phlai Ngam were turned into Lao, down to the hairstyle. They climbed onto the shoulders of a spirit and in an eye-blink reached a city gate.

The place was bustling with the sounds of Lao on guard. Khun Phaen said to his son, "Eh, what do you think?

Are things as I said, or not? When you go to war in the future, you should remember today as a manual. Concentrate on your expertise in military matters."

They walked ahead looking around and saw Ai-Bu, the gatekeeper, asleep. In disguise, they went in and beat a gong loudly.

In alarm, Ai-Bu dropped a torch, which went out, and raised his hand in wai. Khun Phaen said, "Why were you sitting asleep? I didn't trust you so I came to make an inspection."[4]

The sprites leading and the spirits behind lit torches for light, beat gongs, and called out loudly in Lao. "So why didn't you keep the fires going?"[5]

Hearing him speak in Lao, Ai-Bu thought Khun Phaen was a Lao soldier on inspection, and so replied, "I wasn't asleep, sir."[6] Khun Phaen lashed at him. He turned away and relit the torch.

---

3. See p. 812, note 15.

4. อีสัง นั่ง หลับ ใย บ่อ ไว้ใจ สู ให้ กู มา, *i sang nang lap yai bo wai jai su hai ku ma*, whole speech in Lao.

5. อีสัง จ้า ฟืนไฟ บ่อ ใส่เค, *i sang ja fuen fai bo sai khe*, whole speech in Lao.

6. ข่อย บ่อ เมิน นาย เจ้า นั่ง เซา เค่, *khoi bo moen nai jao nang sao khe*, whole speech in Lao.

They went to the back end of the city and found city officials setting bon-fires circling the main jail. As they crouched down to watch, they could hear the sound of the Thai in the jail,

snoring, groaning, weeping, sneezing, and coughing. Khun Phaen said, "They'll soon be out of trouble." Beating a gong, they approached the patrol.

The Lao thought Khun Phaen and his son were also Lao because they spoke the language without fault. Khun Phaen pronounced a mantra that could make even an elephant in the forest become friendly,

and would overwhelm the minds of mere squinty-eyed Lao in an instant. He approached and blew this friendship mantra to subdue their minds.

Khun Phaen said, "Ha, officials of the city. You don't know what's happening, so I'll tell you. We've been assigned to watch the Thai. The guards are not to be trusted, so I was sent for.

In the morning, the Thai will invade the city right up to the jail, killing people and trying to take the town. They've crossed the border already."

All the Lao accepted this story and thought they could hand over and go to sleep. "Don't worry about those Thai in the jail. They're all clapped in cangues."

Even before they had finished talking, the Lao were yawning, rubbing their faces, and closing their eyes. It was almost to the third watch. "As you've taken over, let us sleep a bit."

Khun Phaen called out, "Don't worry." The Lao fell asleep like blocks of wood. Phlai Ngam was also affected and yawned wearily, showing he could not yet match his father's expertise.

Khun Phaen blew a mantra three times, focused his mind, and scattered rice. He sent off spirits to drive away the city's guardians and then return to subdue the townsfolk.

All the Lao guardian spirits including the Lord of Darkness feared Khun Phaen so much they leapt away from their shrines. The Thai spirits attacked, creating uproar across the city. Both the spirit of the city's ancestors and the spirit lord[7] took off in alarm,

and ran howling into the woods. Thai spirits gave chase, creating turmoil through the forest. In the city, all without exception slept soundly.

---

7. See p. 654, note 4.

The Thai spirits came back and toured around, subduing everyone by sitting or riding on top of them so that they closed their eyes, snored, and would not awaken.

Khun Phaen, great and bold warrior, pronounced a mantra, grasped a fistful of rice, and hurled it like a destructive bolt of lightning.

He lit a Phraphirot[8] city-conqueror candle, and the gates of the jail crashed to the ground. Khun Phaen and his son entered. Phra Thainam cried, "Hey, my master has come!

Eh, how's that, Ta-Lo? You argued there was no chance he would come. Your words deceived me, so I was crying like I was going to die.

If he hadn't come tonight, in the morning they'd have slashed the whole jail to death." The Thai were happy to escape fatality. The whole jail was in uproar over this escape.

People put their hands together and raised them in wai. "You came to bring your children back to life, Pa." Khun Phaen cried, "Ha, men! I don't put faith in battle.

Instead I came straight in here. We couldn't wait until tomorrow. My thinking was right. Don't waste time. It's almost dawn."

He blew a Great Loosener mantra. Locks opened, chains fell with a clang, cangues crashed to the ground. All the restraints fell off every person as if someone had unlocked them.

Phlai Ngam produced whiteclay powder that he had brought along in a packet ready to use, put it in a tube, and blew it onto people to make them revive from sleep.

They stood up and stretched their stiff bodies, bending their backs forward and gripping their legs. Seeing Khun Phaen and Phlai Ngam, Ta-Rak rushed over to prostrate at their feet.

Phra Thainam stood up and danced for joy. He took his sword, slashed the head off a fire inspector, and chopped off his two feet. "This guy climbed up to inspect my cangue and cursed me so much. That's his lot."

Ta-Lo drew himself up, took three steps, and slashed a warden across the chest. Others went off to stab those who had angered them. Every corner was washed ruddy with blood.

Kueng Kamkong and his two hundred men[9] were also released from their

---

8. *Phraphirot* is normally the name for a ring or belt plaited from material instilled with yantra, but probably here it means cloth marked with a mantra that has been rolled (as in a *phirot* ring) and then used as the wick of a candle.

9. These are the Vientiane Lao who had escorted Princess Soithong.

suffering in jail. They went to loot pikes, swords, and guns from the armory,

and then swarmed into the stables to take away royal horses along with glittering saddles and harness. Every one of them found a mount and galloped away.

They came to a barrier[10] at a gate. Some Lao who were lying there leapt up and flew into the attack. Khun Phaen turned around and slashed with Skystorm.

The Lao could not escape in time. Two were lopped off at the neck. Khun Phaen took a palm leaf and wrote a summary of what had happened.

"Soldiers from Krung Si Ayutthaya volunteered fearlessly for this mission. By name they are Khun Phaen and Phlai Ngam. They volunteered to come with only thirty-seven men.

We disguised our bodies, put a Subduer on people, entered the city, and released all our men. The King of Chiang Mai should beware. If you conscript troops to follow us,

we will await you for about one day at the lake in the forest. If from fear you do not come after us, prepare to defend your city.

We shall return within five days, and slash you to dust. If the king loves life and cares for himself, he should return Soithong and the goods.

In that case, Chiang Mai will not fall, but will float up again from the depths it now faces. The king too will enjoy a long life. If you choose to resist, that's up to you."

The message was fastened on the end of the barrier. They hastened to a city gate and halted the whole force.

Khun Phaen enchanted rice and hurled it. The great gate across the main road opened wide. Khun Phaen looked through and saw the way was clear. "My mantra has flattened the couch grass!"

Pursing their lips and nodding their heads, the phrai cried out, "Oh, that's really able!" Phra Thainam laughed open-mouthed. "Pa's knowledge is beyond my belief."

Khun Phaen spoke with Phra Thainam. "We should make a racket to frighten them, undo the Subduer mantra, raise a cheer for victory, and then leave for our camp."

Phra Thainam replied, "I agree. Let's make their eyes bulge with terror!" They loaded their guns, hollered, and unleashed volleys of gunfire.

---

10. จ่าหล่อ or จังหล่อ, *ja lo* or *jang lo*, an old word for a barrier made by driving in two rows of stakes with rails to make people pass through an S-bend passageway.

Khun Phaen ordered the spirit commanders to lead the spirits out, and they went in a raucous crowd. Khun Phaen activated a Great Collection formula and the Lao woke up.

The Thai unleashed another hail of gunfire, while hollering loudly at the same time. Both men and spirits fired away all around. Khun Phaen marched out and led the way.

Spirits walked at the front making noise like thunder, and beating gongs as a signal to their colleagues ahead. The phrai at the camp heard the gongs and cried out, "The chief is coming!" They opened the gates for the troops to enter.

The Lao on duty in the city had been terrified by the racket of gunfire, men hollering, and horses neighing. In shock they called out to one another.

In the confusion, some stabbed other Lao, mistaking them for Thai. Unlucky ones dragged their innards along, or limped away on injured legs. Some fled. Some fell to fighting with one another. Some shouted and screamed all through the city.

The King of Chiang Mai fell trembling out of bed, swung his sword but hit a water bowl with a crash. Palace ladies ran around screeching in fright, knocking things over like baby elephants.

The King of Chiang Mai pulled himself together, "What's wrong, you low-life?" In the city, there was panic. People said fires were spreading.

Trembling with fear, a wife went to find her husband, but collided with a water jar and fell crashing onto the bamboo floor. The husband sprung over to help her.

A widow fell down from a bridge, her droopy breasts flapping. Before she could wipe off the dirt, her cloth slipped off completely, and she crawled off on all fours as quickly as she could.

Jail guards awoke and found corpses lying everywhere. They ran off in alarm to look for the Thai and discovered they had gone, leaving only Lao corpses behind.

Stable staff raced off without even wrapping their cloths properly, showing their white navels. When they found all the horses had disappeared, the Lao shouted, "What is going on?"

The lighting brigade, waving torches and firing guns, went to investigate and found that pikes and guns had disappeared. "Hey! How did they do that?"

The stable staff and lighting brigade ran around in wide-eyed confusion, bickering and backbiting with one another heatedly. They went into the palace
and spoke to royal overseers, "Our backs will feel the rattan this time." "It

was strange we slept through it all." "The prisoners in manacles have escaped
and taken weapons and other articles, leaving nothing behind." "On top of
that, they've taken horses, choosing all the good ones."

"Please help. If you're not kind, we'll die." "There was something strange
about us falling so fast asleep. To execute us would be unfair."

Senior officials of all departments quickly put on their sompak and gathered
at the front to investigate events and take evidence.

The King of Chiang Mai came to the outer sala in front of the audience hall.
Courtiers crawled in together, and prostrated flat.

The King of Chiang Mai in his splendor went up to the throne, and asked,
"Ha, soldiers! With this commotion all around us,

I was woken up and thought an army had entered. I listened for a moment
and it went quiet. Why have you come to speak here?"

A chaophraya prostrated and read a report. "The commotion that awoke
Your Majesty came from a group of Thai who were able enough to enter the
city, remove manacles and cangues, take the Thai prisoners away,

kill the prison warders and inspectors, put people all around to sleep, seize
weapons from the armory, and empty the stables of all the royal horses."

The King of Chiang Mai was so enraged that his mind seemed seared by
fire. He stamped his foot in anger and roared.

"Whether they were able or not, how could you lowlife carelessly let the Thai
escape! If an army came into the city, there must be tracks where they left.

Inner torch brigade, stable staff, city officials—what are you on royal ser-
vice for? Raise an army at once to follow and capture the Thai. If they escape
I'll slash you instead."

The chaophraya took the order and staggered off. The officials of the city
and inner torch brigade fearfully informed others that they had to chase after
the Thai and bring them back.

At the official sala, arrangements were made to conscript three thousand
people from three departments. But the chaophraya thought that would be too
few. He feared the Thai army would return to the attack.

While conscription was in progress, he went to speak to the king, who
replied, "I agree. Conscript a big army to engage the enemy in force.

Anyone who tries to evade the call-up is to be slashed dead, and their chil-
dren, wife, and house are to be seized." Notices were issued to conscript people
by royal order.

Saen Rahu, skilled in mantra, was appointed army commander, with the attacking Phetkla in command of the vanguard, Saen Kanji for the rearguard,

Nai Phlia Phet Phraya on the left flank, and Kamkong on the right. The good royal retainer, Saen Jop Mueang Man, was appointed quartermaster and commissary.

The outpost staff—Khanan Thong Thongfa and Khanan Ai—would serve as scouts and lookouts. Saen Pop Phaen Chang and Ngang Ko Khwai were appointed to head the signals brigade.

Nai Kaen Saen Traiphop, fast and thorough at patrolling, took the victory brigade. Thirty-one thousand phrai were to be conscripted and junior officers chosen from among the good soldiers.

Phlia Ruat of the palace guard was ordered to report to the chaophraya. He arrived, prostrated with a wai, and stood up. The chaophraya said, "All these notices have been issued on royal orders. Don't make trouble.

Go and conscript people. You must be very thorough—even make them lie down and strip off their mustaches to check. These are royal orders applying to everybody." The chaophraya and courtiers were included,

along with junior officials of the left and right, royal retainers, royal pages, and heads of departments. Everybody was informed of the royal order and busily set to the task of conscription.

The total was achieved, along with many horses and elephants, and masses of pikes, swords, shields, bucklers, bows, and guns.

Many war elephants were requisitioned along with horses, crossbows, bucklers, and shields. Once ready, they waited for an auspicious time.

At an auspicious time, the army of thirty thousand marched off, banging gongs, firing guns, and hollering, with victory flags hoisted amid the troops.

There were elephants with howdahs and elephants with saddles, lumbering along with mahouts aloft, swaying up and down. Elephants with fine tusks were placed in the middle of the column. The cavalry shouted and cheered as they rode along.

The foot soldiers looked like a trail of ants covering the plain. Supplies for the troops were carried on horses, mules, and oxen. Some people sneaked up on the backs of pack animals.

A cow with tired rear legs stumbled into another which took fright, galumphed off, and started a stampede, but it was brought under control.

Scouts and lookouts went ahead of the troops, skillfully spying out the lie of the land. The signals brigade used teams of post horses to deliver messages in stages.

As they approached the lake, they could see a pall of smoke and storks and vultures swooping down to feed on the corpses of dead buffaloes. Scouts were sent ahead to spy.

Hearing the sound of crows cawing, they went closer and saw the large Thai camp. Some Thai shot at them, so they ran off to inform their army commander.

He gave orders to halt at the edge of the forest and make a row of twelve camps close together with a chain of guns, sharp spikes and snares dug into the ground, trenches all around for defense, and emplacements for guns.

At the Thai camp,[11] the phrai who had shot the Lao came to make a report that they had heard the sound of people chopping wood, and had shot at Lao spies who had run away through the forest.

Khun Phaen laughed, "What sneaks! They won't get off a shot before we slash them. Nai Jan Samphantueng, you're a fast fellow. Go over there and spy on the Lao position.

Ai-Mo has come racing in to report that the forest is full of the sound of chopping wood. Go out there and somehow bring back information to help our attack."

Nai Jan Samphantueng made a wai and rushed away. He got dressed, took a sword in hand, mounted a horse,

dug in his heels, and galloped up close to the Lao camp. Some Lao in a dugout fired at him. He halted with shots pinging around him. The Lao climbed out of the dugout, shouting "What's this? Get him for sure!"

"Tcha, you bastard, a dog got at your mother." Nai Jan turned back to look, cursed the mothers of the Lao, dug in his heels, and galloped off.

Nai Jan returned, wai-ed Khun Phaen, and said, "They've already established a row of twelve camps. Some people in a dugout shot at me, and we exchanged curses.

I estimate from their position that they'll attack us in force with many horses, elephants, and around thirty thousand troops."

Khun Phaen, expert in warfare, said, "Even if they had ten times that, they needn't be hopeful. I'll get bored slashing them all." He turned to his son. "Have the officers and men get dressed and prepared."

Phlai Ngam saluted to take leave and went to give orders to the officers and men to get ready. He also sent orders to Phra Thainam.

---

11. This opening phrase has been inserted for clarity.

Phlai Ngam kitted himself out impressively with dazzling Farang equipment. He wore tubular britches in *mori*,[12] with a belt tied around the waist,

a golden *mot* shirt decorated with a grid of quartz, a bandeau tied round the forehead, buttons in the shape of *daorueang*, gooseberry fruit, and *mafueang* flowers in nielloware and lapis lazuli studded with diamonds,

a hat in bright red velvet with a back flap decorated with scintillating silver wire[13] in a pattern of *kanok* and birds in flight. Fully kitted out, he looked dazzling.

On his left side, he had twin sabers in sheaths, and on the right, Skystorm[14] instilled with a spirit. A kris with a gold sheath, nielloware handle,

and blade of crow's-egg green of Tani origin[15] was fastened to his body with a belt. With his weaponry, he looked slight but splendidly imposing. He leapt onto his dun horse

that was bold and fierce in battle, ready to lay back its ears, raise its tail, neigh loudly, kick, and bite ferociously.

The horse picked up its hooves and trotted rhythmically, as if it would leap and fly at the enemy with the agility to attack and withdraw at will. Phra Phichit had trained him to his own liking.

The clever and daring Khun Phaen quickly got dressed in a shirt inscribed with yantra, diamond and *phirot* rings on his fingers,

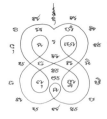

an inner shirt in dark purple,[16] and a helmet instilled with a *Namo ta bot* formula,[17] and with the fang of a Hanuman spirit[18] placed in its peak. In his mouth he had a mercury charm with power like the wind.

Namo ta bot *yantra*

---

12. โมรี, a type of cloth from India.

13. เลื่อม, *lueam*, metallic wire used in cloth design.

14. At the end of the next section, Khun Phaen also has Skystorm.

15. ชาติ์ ตานี, *chat tani*, possibly meaning from Pattani, a center of Malay Muslim culture.

16. สี มังโก, *si mangko*, possibly this comes from mangosteen, a fruit with a dark purple rind. The fruit came to Siam from the Moluccas, probably with its Malay name, which Thai speakers initially shortened, and only later adapted to *mangkut*.

17. มะโน (properly นะ โม, as in SS) ตา บอด, *namo ta bot*, a mantra and yantra for invulnerability, especially against gunfire, very popular on amulets, also used to protect rice crops against thieves. In full: นะตันโต นะโมตันติ ตันติตันโต นะโมตันตัน, natanto namotanti tantitanto namotantan. The name seems to be a mix of Pali (*namo*, praise) and Thai (*ta bot*, blind). Origin and meaning obscure.

18. หนุมาร เขี้ยว พราย, *hanuman khiao phrai*; possibly *hanuman* here is just a poetic flourish meaning a monkey; perhaps the charm is supposed to make the wearer as fierce and loyal as Hanuman.

He wore a spirit-skull belt made from the forehead of a corpse instilled with a Phakhawam, nielloware beads hanging round his neck instilled with the spirit of a monk by mantra, and an outer uppercloth in a pattern of golden flowers.

Both officers and men were all decked out. The superlative[19] mastery and might of Khun Phaen provided protection against everything. "I will contest with these Lao on this occasion.

Even if there's a rainstorm of guns and spears, I'll be safe because of mantra and will not give ground. Even if by bad fortune I'm struck, it will be like striking iron or diamond—nothing to fear.

If they grab me, I'll be slippery as an eel, and escape to fight back." Phra Thainam opened his mouth and chuckled. "You're like a mother and father come to save us."

Khun Phaen ordered everyone to harness horses for all officers and men and get prepared for battle. He spoke with Phra Thainam.

"Phlai Ngam and the thirty-five phrai will be placed as the vanguard, along with the retinue of two hundred and twenty men that were selected by Phra Phichit to join us.

Muen At Narai, expert at plunder and pillage, will be their unit head. As for the five hundred phrai, you and Phlai Ngam

will stay behind and enter the fray to provide fearless support. I would like to witness the knowledge of Phlai Ngam. If the battle is heavy, I'll join in myself."

Phra Thainam replied, "I agree, sir." Ta-Lo laughed gaily, leapt up, and danced around. "Father has come to be our mainstay. You and I will not go to our deaths."

He made a merry racket. Khun Phaen stood grandly holding Skystorm, and stilled his mind for a long while to find an auspicious time. When he found the time, he looked up

at the clouds moving above, and saw the shape of a Lao with no head.[20] Two egrets flew across the sky. He had the men beat gongs,

shoot guns, and holler loudly on and on. Phlai Ngam rode forward with the gold color of his shirt and helmet conspicuous from all around.

Phra Thainam led the troops off. The volunteers rode Thai horses out to battle, the ground echoing with the clatter of hooves.

Muen At Narai and his men rode Lao horses. Heavily armed, everyone went out to wait for Khun Phaen.

---

19. โกฏิ, *kot*, a very rare word, with the same meaning and root as crore, 10 million, here probably used as a super-superlative.

20. On cloud omens, see p. 621, note 15.

Khun Phaen, expert in battle, leapt up onto Color of Mist. The horse, in a harness glittering with gold, thrust out his chest, and neighed loudly.

In the camp, there were crowds of people, one thousand two hundred spirits, and a massive number of mantra dummies, all hollering and firing guns.

The sound of horses, troops, and spirits was deafening. All followed Khun Phaen. Mounted on horses, the chiefs of the spirits drove the mass of dummies and spirits along.

Khun Phaen pronounced a mantra to give the spirits such shielding that even if they were attacked by those possessing mantra power, they would be protected.

Only Khun Phaen saw the mass of spirits. The troops could not. The dummies hoisted flags and led the way, cheering for victory just like humans.

Saen Rahu, the Chiang Mai army commander, heard gunfire, and saw a pall of smoke over the forest. "Ah! They're coming." He immediately gave orders. "Vanguard! Lead out and engage them.

I'll bring the army in the rear, and wait at a distance to see what happens on the battlefield and estimate their strength. If they put up a fight, I'll come into the attack."

Phlia Phetkla of the vanguard busily organized horses and mules, while his skilled and expert troops harnessed elephants and horses.

They enchanted liquor, and blew mantras onto herbs, following the advice of teachers. Around their bellies they hung strings of amulets, including dangling eel heads in copper.

Some had bandeaus wound around their heads. Some were so decked out that they clinked and clanked. Some were drunk on liquor. Others had enchanted limes to make themselves invisible, or sang songs to build up their courage.

When ready, the army marched off, rending the air with gunfire. The cavalry advanced, mounted on neighing horses, carrying pikes decorated with beautiful peacock tails.

Elephant troops moved forward, trumpeting. Foot soldiers surged ahead in a mass. All were expert troops with the power of youth, numbering ten thousand.

In the vanguard, Phlai Ngam, with the power of his knowledge and the evident legacy of his lineage, cut a fine figure as the pride of the army.

Both attacking and defensive troops trotted along, looking as fearsome as

Macassars,[21] raring to engage the enemy and slash them down in piles.

Ta-Lo boasted in excitement, "Though I'm old and broken-toothed, don't you recognize a tiger?" Phra Thainam listened, mouth agape. "How come such a fierce tiger had to fester in jail?"

Ta-Lo cried, "Hey, what d'you mean? Even though old, I can get this horse to leap, prance, and buck. Who made us suffer in jail? They're going to taste some happiness today!"

The army came out of the forest, saw the Lao flag, and advanced, shaking the ground. The Lao saw the Thai flag and advanced noisily,

until the two armies could see each other clearly. Both forces halted and faced off against each other. Phetkla called out, "Hey, Thai brothers!

Some time ago we invited you to a contest on elephants but you did not reply to the message in the ancient way. Instead you sneaked in to steal horses and spirit away the Thai. Are you a royal army or a bunch of forest bandits?"

Phlai Ngam called in reply, "Those who seized a princess and imprisoned the Thai are the forest bandits. His Majesty would have come himself but he considered that to be excessive force,

so he sent me, Phlai Ngam, as his great fangs of war. The king doesn't bother with catching forest bandits. What's your name, you who will die soon?"

The Lao replied immediately, "I'm a great soldier named Phetkla. Some time ago, the Thai came up here to abduct the Princess Soithong.

This lady is someone of importance. Our lord had asked for her hand, and her parents had consented. So we raised an army to seize her back and capture the intruders. Why are you accusing others, you bandit?

You're just a tiny little kid who wants to ride a tiger and compete with his elders. We'll fight without retreat. As you're out of line, we'll deal with you."

Phlai Ngam asked, "Who did Soithong's parents present her to? Why don't you talk about that? Instead you say the Thai came up to abduct her.

Does a mere leaf fish dare lock mouths with a crow?[22] This princess is the daughter of a high-ranking lord. The palace wall is well guarded. How could they get in and abduct her? Please tell me, you prick!

Everyone knows Lanchang presented the princess to Ayutthaya. You're talk-

---

21. มักกระสัน, *makkrasan*, from Macassar, a people from the Indonesian archipelago. A settlement of Macassars in Ayutthaya instigated a famous massacre in 1688.

22. The verb บิด, bit, twist, is used to describe when fighting fish lock mouths and twist around.

ing a pack of lies. You're white-haired already and you don't make sense. Are you boasting because you have invulnerable spirits?

If you want to see my power, let's fight one on one until death so as not to cause suffering for the troops. I'll demolish you like chopped fish."

Phlai Ngam spurred his horse to leap ahead, calling out, "Let the troops watch to see what happens. Hey, you villain! A short sword against a long spear."

Phetkla was enraged. "How dare this Thai youth challenge me!"[23] He charged on his horse, raised both hands high, and hurled his spear but missed the Thai and collapsed over his own saddle.

Phlai Ngam drew himself up and slashed down with his sword, clattering Phetkla's skull, raising a dark bruise as big as a turtle shell. Thai troops cheered and clapped loudly.

Lao stared apprehensively at their chief who was almost dead but still able to gallop his horse away. He enchanted saliva and applied it to make the swelling disappear, then spurred his horse back into the fray.

The two horses whirled around like windmills, whinnying loudly. The two men exchanged stabs and slashes. The two horses wheeled and separated.

Phlai Ngam waved his sword and feinted to fool the Lao into making a thrust. Phlai Ngam's body flashed where it was struck as if Phetkla's spear had stabbed onto diamond. He was unscathed, but the spear shattered.

Phlai Ngam swung hard across Phetkla's chest, almost severing his body and putting stars in his eyes.

Phlai Ngam hit down again on his skull. Phetkla spluttered, his face blackened, and tears oozing from his eyes. He galloped away.

Phlai Ngam called out, "Hey, Phetkla, your spear is broken. Go and fetch a new one." Phetkla changed his spear with his mind in turmoil. Phlai Ngam pondered back and forth.

"If I attack quickly now, I should be able to slash him, and he'll have no reputation as a warrior in the future." He called out, "Hey, look over here, Phetkla. Surely you can stab my little mouse!"

Phetkla thrust but the blade did not enter. "How come this Thai's skin is so tough. However hard I stab, it doesn't pierce. I've never fought anyone like this Thai."

Phlai Ngam's men roused one another to cheer. Maddened by rage, Phet-

---

23. อีสัง เย่อ เง่อ มา ขบ ม้า สวน, *i sang yoe ngoe ma khop ma suan*, whole speech in Lao.

kla went to stab again. "Tcha! Stabbing doesn't touch this villain." Phlai Ngam turned back into the attack and hit hard,

slashing open Phetkla's side. Phlai Ngam galloped away, turned his horse on its tail, gnashed his teeth, and charged. The Lao fled away in a cloud of dust.

Phlai Ngam summoned up his powers,[24] and hurled his sword, slicing into Phetkla, who fell, rolled on his back, and died. The crowd of Thai roared. Kamkong rode up.

Lao troops charged the Thai, making the forest resound with gunfire. Thai cheered in return and rode their horses forward. The two sides slashed and stabbed at each other bloodily at close quarters.

Thao Mueang Maen did a war dance and charged at Phra Thainam, who wielded his sword fiercely. The Lao thrust his spear into Phra Thainam,

but it did not pierce, "This old fellow is tough." Phra Thainam lashed back with his sword, hitting Mueang Maen hard, then lashed again and lopped his head off.

Ko Kalamphak galloped up. Ta-Lo hurled a Lawa pike into his chest. The Lao dropped from his horse and died in a pool of blood.

Kamkong cried out, "Ha, Phlai Ngam. I don't fear you Thai!" and galloped forward. Phlai closed with him, stood up in the stirrups, summoned up his powers, and hurled a pike.

Kamkong was hit in the chest, cried out loud, fell headlong to the ground, and writhed to death. The Lao army broke. Thai chased after them, slashing and slicing. Severed arms and lopped heads were scattered everywhere.

The thrusts and gunshots of the Lao did not pierce the Thai. With powder and shot exhausted, the Lao vanguard retreated. The Thai followed slashing until they reached the main Lao army.

Saen Rahu, commander of the main Lao army, well-versed in lore, battle-hardened, invulnerable, and fearless, divided his troops into crow's wings.

He mounted an elephant as leader of the conscript troops, and called those hidden to come out to the front. He waved his hand to hold back the Thai with lore while he set up a base for the battle.

He caught sight of the fine figure of Phlai Ngam, the army commander. "This young fellow, just come of age, deserves to be a soldier of Ayutthaya."

---

24. เรียก อยู่คง มา, *riak u-khong ma*, literally, summoning up his invulnerability, probably by intoning a mantra.

He shouted out, "Hey, little Thai! Aren't you afraid of me? Don't you realize you're about to die? If you're afraid, get down and pay me respect. [25]

I'm Saen Rahu, the army chief. Any city I attack is reduced to dust. How come you were bold enough to kill our prison warders and armorers?

If you bow and submit to Chiang Mai, you'll be pardoned and raised to high status. If you refuse, you'll be captured and tormented until you die."

Phlai Ngam called out, "Lao lord, don't brag about your intentions. A real man does not malign another man. In the past, you had easy victories—but against box turtles!

This is a battle of man against man, a real fight. Even a crab knows how to nip a hand. You're like a big battle-hardened tiger that did not expect to meet a tigress.

You're wrinkled down to your neck, your teeth are broken, and your hair is so grey even spirits find you haunting. You tempt me to your city but I'd only cause devastation among you Lao."

The Lao lord became even more perplexed. "This child is so contemptuous of me. I've defeated more than five countries but never been defied by anyone like these Thai.

They're so feeble, like a riverbank that's eroded to the point of collapse—can't support a single crocodile.[26] Bring twenty-five elephants quickly. Fill them with liquor to make them fierce."

The elephants were strong, daring, battle-hardened, and able to understand language like humans. Drunk on liquor, they raised their trunks, rolled their red eyes, swayed from side to side, trumpeted, and rushed at the Thai.

Phlai Ngam yelled a mantra that the twenty-five elephants could not stand. In shock, they scattered away, shitting themselves, and trampling Lao to death in piles.

Saen Rahu saw Phlai Ngam's unusual powers and grew worried. "If I continue to attack, it's not beyond my skill to win,

but people will say I only won over a little boy! My reputation will be greatly diminished." With these thoughts, he arrayed his troops, pushing the daring ones forward to engage the enemy.

---

25. บ่อ ยั่น ค่อย สัก เตื้อ เหลือ เจียว หวา ดุตุ บ่อฮู่ จะ มรณา แม็น วาสูยั่น จง กราน ลง, *bo yan khoi sak tuea luea jiao wa du tu bo hu ja morana maen wa su yan jong kran long*, "Aren't . . . . respects" in a mixture of Lao and Thai.

26. These two sentences in Lao.

He called out for them to fire guns at will, and they let fly with volleys. He advanced his elephant to halt at the flag. "Aim the guns at the little Thai."

Phlai Ngam rode with his seat raised out of the saddle. "Tcha! You're an army of beasts, of dogs!" The Lao soldiers shouted and took aim. "Shoot at his thing!" [27]

They sprayed him with shot but missed. "Not a single bullet hit the mark!" [28] The Thai hollered loudly. Ta-Lo stabbed and shouted, "Hey! You dare to shoot at our chief."

Phlai Ngam spurred his horse into the fray and slashed hard at Phlia Phet. The pair swirled around, feinting, attacking, and dodging in the middle of the battlefield. The Lao stabbed but missed. The Thai slashed the Lao.

At the sound of the chop, blood oozed like the white sap of a caladium when a leaf is peeled away. [29] Phlia Phet shuddered. The horse tripped over his long spear and stumbled.

Taking the advantage, Phlai Ngam slashed again. Horse and rider collapsed on top of each other. Phlia Phet writhed to death on the spot. "Off with his head! That Lao shit is done for."

Comrades rushed to help but were too late. Phra Thainam again slashed at the corpse. A Lao appeared riding an elephant with massively long tusks. Ta-Lo hurled a Lawa pike.

The elephant fled with its tail in the air, trumpeting, dropping turds, and splashing piss. Phra Thainam's men stabbed it repeatedly. "Quick, Ta-Lo, take him!"

Ta-Lo attacked standing in the stirrups and hurling a pike into the beast's side. Muen At Narai came to join in, riding a horse and whirling his blade around.

Lao fell flat down dead on the spot, spurting red blood and rolling like forest monkeys. Saen Jop Phaenchang came riding on a horse, with the lore to be invulnerable.

Ai-Mo Pho-khao-phok raised a spear, and the two exchanged pulverizing blows but none of them pierced. Ai-Thong and Ai-Phon Mue Kluang approached from behind and thrust hard.

Ai-Suea stabbed as hard as he could, leaping into the attack, hollering, "You shit-wiping Lao!" They separated and circled one another in the middle of the battlefield with dead bodies covered in red blood scattered around them.

While the Thai did not spare a single Lao, they themselves lost not even a

---

27. อี ฉัง จ้า ยิง หั้น ของ มัน, *i chang ja ying han khong man*, in Lao.

28. บ่อ ถูก มัน สัก ยาด พลาด ถีบ เห, *bo thuk man sak yat phlat thip he*, in Lao.

29. บอน, *bon*, has a thick, white, sticky sap.

single hair. The Lao were decimated, their troops thrashed. The main army came to give support and turn them back into the battle.

Khun Phaen, great valiant, saw the fight had been long, tough, and hectic. He advanced his mantra dummies[30] to allow his son a rest.

He chanted a Phraya mantra, bringing the Lao troops to a standstill as if planted. They gazed at the Thai troops come in all their splendor. They had fought previously at the time of the Chiang Thong affair.

The spirits of the army commander ran ahead and captured the spirits of those whom the Thai had already killed. *Phi pop* and *phi jakla*[31] ran up, but the Thai spirits murderously chased them away into the forest.

Saen Rahu, the commander, seated on an elephant amidst his troops, watched the Thai army coming with reinforcements, and felt hard-pressed. "This Thai chief is good.

I haven't yet seen this Thai's style, so if I attack it will be like a blind man fumbling an elephant in confusion.[32] I may lose to Thai trickery, which would be terrible.

Now! I'll go and observe if he has any devices. If he doesn't, I'll crush him to death." He advanced his elephant and called out, "Here, Thai chief. I thank you.

Let us proceed according to ancient tradition. There's no need for the troops to engage. What great wrong have they done to make them enemies? To trade their lives I think is wrong.

Excuse me, what's your name? What interest do you have here? That little fellow with good speech and manners rather like yours—what's his name?"

The expert and war-hardened Khun Phaen thought carefully before replying amiably, "My name is Phraya Phaen the steadfast. I'm an army chief in Ayutthaya.

That's my son called Phlai Ngam. We are to chase down the King of Chiang Mai and kill him. If he submits and hands over Soithong, his life will be spared

on grounds he has renounced his error. But if he doesn't bow in submis-

---

30. หุ่น มนต์ ผ้า พยนต์, *hun mon pha phayon, hun mon* is a dummy or puppet created by a mantra, and *pha phayon* is a general term for movable objects created by lore.

31. ผี ปอบ, *phi pop*, a malevolent spirit which resides inside people and eats away their innards until they die; ผี จะกละ, *phi jakla*, a forest spirit in the form of a cat.

32. In a famous proverbial story, several blind men feel separate parts of an elephant and come to very different conclusions about the nature of the animal.

sion, he'll die and be reduced to dust. As for you, soldier, who came boldly out here, what's your name?"

"I'm called Saen Rahu. My answer is that I'm in royal service as an army chief. Like an elephant, I'll not cede to anyone. You, my cocky Thai, have no hope.

Saying you'll capture the Lao is a false claim. Do not think that this realm lacks troops. We came out here on orders and will oppose the Thai forces without fear.

Why should we deliver up Soithong? Her hand was requested for marriage by our king. The Thai came up here to seize her and so were captured. This case is known everywhere.

We're all-conquering soldiers. Don't threaten us, as we'll not run away like cowards. You'll see our powers before the day is out." He summoned his crowd of spirits, but they had disappeared.

"What's this? You miserable curs of spirits! Where have you wandered off to instead of fighting?" He promptly pronounced a mantra summoning a great, violent storm

to blow all the Thai away. The sky was shrouded in darkness. Trees bent and broke in a gale. Grass was torn into shreds.

Khun Phaen intoned a mantra to prevent the wind from blowing. In a flash, the storm disappeared and the light returned. The Lao was inflamed with fury.

Using a mantra he had employed before and trusted, he enchanted a disk of leather like a bullet, artfully rolled the disk in the palm of his hand like a prayer bead,

and blew the disk away from his hand while bellowing a mantra as loud as Ai-Tue the elder.[33] But the device hit a *rang* tree and left the Thai in the vicinity untouched.

The Thai jeered. "We just fended it off and it flew up into that *rang* tree." They beckoned with their hands and noisily taunted the Lao to advance.

Saen Rahu drew on his knowledge and expertise as a soldier to chant another mantra. Ten large elephants appeared,

all powerful males, trumpeting, swaying from side to side, and thrusting their tusks around like windmills. They surged forward

to stab and gore the Thai, using their exceptional powers as elephants. The

---

33. อ้าย ตื้อ เถร, *ai tue then*; obscure.

Thai were trampled and scattered away. Some daring fellows came out with pikes to offer resistance.

Others brought out wheeled guns and fired at close range, but the shot bounced back uselessly, while pikes crumpled or shattered, and the Thai collapsed unconscious.

Some called out to the Mother Goddess[34] for help. Some raised their hands in wai and implored the spirits. "I'll offer whatever ducks and chickens I have! Let me survive and return alive to my wife!"

The adept Khun Phaen saw his men scatter in trembling confusion. "These ten elephants conjured up by the Lao are causing havoc."

He took some pan and lime and enchanted them using his great knowledge. A giant person came stomping up, breaking the earth's crust into long fissures.

His big black body was the size of a rice barn. His face was sunken with eye sockets as white as an ancestral storage pot. His mouth hung open some two to three fathoms long.

His teeth were huge, white, and pointed. His nose was huge, and his eyes hollow as caves with pupils red as the sun. He bounded after the elephants, slapping with his hands,

making cracking sounds as loud as thunder, sending them hurtling to the ground. He caught one by the tail and hurled it away with a crash. He bit into the beast, breaking its neck,

and chewed briefly before swallowing until all slipped down his throat, leaving nothing behind. He popped an elephant in his cheek like a wad of *miang*.[35] Cocking his head, he peered around for more to stuff into his mouth.

The other elephants made by the Lao mantra all ran off into the forest. The giant captured Lao running around on the ground and popped them into his mouth to eat in hundreds.

One Lao fled out through the giant's ear, scrambled down his body hair, and tumbled to the ground. "What is this? I'm so scared." He dripped tears. "I've never met anything as awful!

What is this? I fear so much I can't open my eyes. It eats an elephant just like eating a frog! It's beyond us to fight back." Crowds of Lao fled away to hide.

---

34. แม่ ซื้อ, *mae sue*, a deity believed to protect children, propitiated at the time of birth and other occasions. Phya Anuman translated the term literally as the Purchasing Mother. He speculated that the name arose because people believed spirits would claim a good-looking newborn baby after three days but could be deceived into believing the baby had already been purchased by this deity (Anuman, *Essays*, 279–81).

35. Fermented tea leaves, chewed like tobacco.

Saen Rahu the army commander watched countless numbers of elephants being destroyed. "Fighting with mantra is hopeless. This Thai's knowledge is better.

In former battles, mastery like this lad's just now was never used. The Thai who have come this time are exceptionally strong, bold, able, and daring.

But I still have knowledge that can neutralize their power." He chanted a mantra and ten huge tigers appeared,

their growls echoing around the forest. They thrust their paws into the ground and soared up, making noise like thunder.

They opened their mouths and roared loudly and strangely to intimidate people. Eyes bulging, the Thai fled away to hide in a swamp.

One mistook his comrade for a watching tiger, stood up, and hit him on the head. His friend called out, "A tiger is dragging me off." Then he grabbed the other's head and said, "You elbowed me?"

Khun Phaen watched the Lao create the tigers. "He's able, superhuman, with mantra devices." After thinking of the possibilities, he reached for his buffalo charm, enchanted it with a mantra seven times,

and hurled it away. Around fifteen huge buffaloes appeared, all tall, strong, sturdy, and as big as the sacred mountain.

They charged around, showing off their youth and agility, raising their heads and tossing their horns which were sharp, shiny, and beautifully curved.

They attacked to gore the tigers with their horns. The two sides clashed, smashing into one another in confusion at close quarters. Some tigers were gored and fell dead.

Others scattered and fled into the forest to hide or to die. Lao also ran away, almost at death's door, crawling along with bulging eyes, calling out, "I'm scared!"[36]

Saen Rahu pondered. "These Thai soldiers have powerful devices. Killing them is very tricky as they're good with knowledge."

In a rage, he stood with his head raised and neck thrust forward, urging his troops to advance. Gnashing his teeth, he banged a gong as a signal to drive his forces forward to engage the Thai army.

Lao troops poured into the attack on horse and elephant, hollering loudly, ignoring the swish of blades, shooting their bows and crossbows in volleys, firing guns, creating uproar and smoke.

---

36. ยันเด, *yan de*, in Lao.

They spread shields, and wielded javelin, spear, lance, pike, and sword into the attack. They stabbed at the Thai, making enough thunderous noise to shake the earth.

Khun Phaen advanced his mantra troops on horseback with spirits to give them protection. Human troops in support shouted enough to make the earth collapse.

Mantra dummies bounded into battle with the Lao troops, leaping up onto the stirrups and pulling the riders down. Some broke the necks of horses or drove in their chests with kicks.

A Lao drove an elephant to stab but a spirit pulled out its tusk. The elephant lowered his head to the ground and was chased away. Spirits took possession of soldiers, making them attack one another,

unable to tell who was on which side because Lao and Thai were all muddled together. Lao were slaughtered without hope of escape. Those still surviving expired on their backs all over the ground.

Others gave up in frustration that their blows were useless. In panic, they broke and scattered away to the rear en masse.

Looking on, Saen Rahu saw the Lao either being slaughtered or scattering away into the forest.

"However much they are shot, slashed, or stabbed, the Thai don't die. Perhaps the power of their spirits is sacred power, created with knowledge and very effective. It was a mistake to think these were people.

Right! I'll use a special mantra. Under its power, if these people are dummies, their weapons will all fall from their hands,

and they'll disappear in a shudder. Even though they're spirits, they'll be annihilated." He cut a handful of grass, enchanted it with the mantra of a powerful teacher,

and scattered it around. The grass turned into weapons that battled on their own without dummies. But the humans and spirits were invulnerable to these weapons, and reduced each one to a pile of dust.

As Khun Phaen had provided them with protection, nothing whatever could harm them. The army of mantra dummies still ran hollering to attack the Lao.

Saen Rahu witnessed this unusual power and pondered fretfully to himself. "I know special lore too. I won't run off into the forest and let him beat me easily.

I think countering him with troops is useless. I must use a tactic to trick him. As I'm invulnerable, I'll challenge him to fight one on one.

If he dies, his troops will all scatter. Let it appear for all to see. I'll ride out, capture him, and drag him by the hair to our jail."

He turned his elephant in musth to the front, and divided his army into crow's wings in the old way. Holding his lance, he raised his head and said, "Hey, troops! I'll go after their chief."

He shouted out to the Thai commander, "Hey! I've been thinking that it's laughable. We've been using our troops as barriers. We've not yet seen which of us has the better powers.

If we two do battle, the weaker one will lose his life. Stop depending on your troops. Let your own sacred power be seen."

Khun Phaen heard Saen Rahu and laughed. "He wants to fight with me!" He instructed his army to divide into crow's wings, and rode Color of Mist out in front of the troops.

When he drew Skystorm out of its sheath, the sword shook with power in a hair-raising fashion. Even someone with invulnerability could not do battle against this weapon,

but would be cut in two like the stalk of a banana because the sword was instilled with the malevolent power of countless spirits. Khun Phaen beckoned with his hand. "Hey, my good fellow, come on!" He urged the horse forward, brandishing his sword.

As Saen Rahu looked on, the sword flashed in his eyes, making him almost faint, and the weapon's instilled power took possession of him. "My karma is to die, so let it be."

Saen Rahu's elephant in musth turned its head, both eyes rolling wildly, tail arched, ears spread, looking forward intent on nothing but attack.

Because it was in musth, it raised its tusks and roared like thunder. Oil spread over both its fore and rear quarters. Saen Rahu clicked his tongue and called, "Hey, you villain!" Trumpeting madly, the elephant charged into the attack.

Looking sturdy and strong, Saen Rahu raised his lance with a flourish ready to thrust, and drove his elephant forward shouting, "Hey, ha! Let's fight."

Color of Mist held his ground. He was invulnerable to the thrusts of the elephant's tusks and could be seen only as a shadow. The elephant repeatedly tried to gore him without success.

The elephant trumpeted, closed its eyes, and placed his tusks badly. The horse closed on its flank to let the riders fight. Saen Rahu quickly thrust with his lance. Khun Phaen parried and returned a blow with his sword.

Saen Rahu raised his lance in defense. With a chopping sound, both lance and person were severed. Saen Rahu fell dangling down the side of the elephant, blood flowing from his severed neck.

Khun Phaen galloped away to attack the Lao troops, scattering them away. Mantra dummy troops stormed into the fray. Phlai Ngam advanced his men into the battle. Phra Thainam rushed in to slash at the Lao.

To the sound of swishing blades, the Lao were cut down or ran off in uproar. The Thai hollered loudly as they chopped and slashed. None of the Thai were killed, only the Lao.

Those who escaped sat wai-ing repeatedly, or fled before guns could be cocked and fired, riding horses and elephants away from the Thai army amid a din of shouting, hollering, and trumpeting.

30: KHUN PHAEN AND PHLAI NGAM CAPTURE THE KING OF CHIANG MAI

Now to tell of Khun Phaen, slender and expert warrior. He discussed matters with youthful Phlai Ngam and Phra Thainam.

"The Lao who came to fight with us today have broken and fled into the forest. We have been on royal service for many days. The king will be waiting all this time.

We must take the troops to besiege the city and capture the King of Chiang Mai in person." They all agreed.

At an auspicious time for victory, the troops marched off, firing guns and raising three cheers.

They were arrayed in order, with Phlai Ngam assigned to the vanguard, bald Nai Bua on the right flank, and brave Nai Thong Men on the left.

Phra Thainam led the way, looking magnificent. Khun Phaen, the army commander, rode the elephant Phlai Song Narai[1] at the head of the force, holding a lance-goad.

After contemplating the situation, the knowledgeable Khun Phaen and Phlai Ngam summoned the troops and sent five hundred phrai and militiamen

to cut elephant grass and plait fifty thousand dummies. The troops went off as ordered, plaited the dummies, brought them back,

and piled them up as high as a mountain. Khun Phaen blew a mantra with powerful lore, and the grass dummies changed into humans,

a great rowdy crowd with weapons in hand. Khun Phaen ordered five female spirits to hurry into the city.

"Don't attack and kill ordinary people because we can use them on royal service later. Wait for a signal from the big gun that it is an auspicious time, and then advance.

Surround the city in three layers and give them a fright, but do not attack them yet. When we have the advantage, we'll make our entrance."

---

1. ทรงนารายน์, mount of Vishnu.

The lady spirits and dummies raced off. Humans and dummies surrounded the city in three layers,

hollering loudly and firing guns as if to rend the sky. The sound of fifty-six thousand dummies' voices was earsplitting.

Created with the power of mantra lore, the dummies generated a thunderous noise as if the world were collapsing. The sound of spirits hollering and crying echoed around.

The people of Chiang Mai were greatly alarmed. Those on the fortifications all around the city could see the attacking army.

At the sight of countless troops, they shook their heads in fright. People climbed up onto the fortifications all round the city,

and fired through slits in the battlements, keeping up an endless crackle of gunfire. They heated gravel and sand, and prepared the blades of spears and swords.

Large teak logs were brought and suspended from the walls, ready to drop on attackers when they approached.

Great quantities of rocks, lead ore, and lime were collected and piled up in readiness. Cannons were placed at every aperture, all set to fire on the approaching Thai.

Officers were posted on the battlements. When they saw the Thai besiegers approaching, soldiers fired from the ramparts. "The Thai want to break down the city wall!"

The Thai spirits led the assault, followed by the dummies in huge numbers hollering war cries. Under attack, many of the defenders broke and fled. Cannon in the city fired without a break,

pouring down shot on the dummies and blowing them away in all directions. But the dummies immediately picked themselves up, did a war dance, and returned in greater force like an army of ants.

They leaned ladders against the city walls and swarmed up them. The Lao on the walls stabbed downwards, but the Thai were not intimidated and kept on climbing.

The defenders released sand and gravel, hurled bricks, and cut teak logs to tumble down on the attackers, breaking their heads and knocking them off the ladders.

Some lost their cloths and fell on their backs. Some hung on safely. Others dangled down from the ladders. The Lao kept bombarding them.

Those who had fallen down picked themselves up and climbed back upwards, scaling the ladders and throwing themselves fearlessly onto the defenders, shouting to their comrades to come in support.

The sound of hollering, and the crackle and boom of guns and cannons, continued until near evening when the army commanders discussed calling a halt.

"In the dark we may slash our own men dead by mistake. At midnight when the moon is bright, we'll advance again. Withdraw the army to rest. Keep a watch on the Lao in the city."

At night, Khun Phaen, great valiant, thought the matter over and went to talk with Phra Thainam.

"Forcing entry into their camp will be difficult and will cost many lives. Instead, I'll go in to intimidate and capture the king.

I'll put the King of Chiang Mai and all his military officers to sleep with the power of mantra lore. Then I'll capture and imprison the whole city.

In the morning all of us will be able to saunter into the town in a big crowd. If not, we'll slash them all down, and raze the palace, the walls, the whole city."

After the discussion, Khun Phaen and his son Phlai Ngam took leave of Phra Thainam and went off. Khun Phaen grasped Skystorm and mounted a horse.

Phlai Ngam rode along behind. When they came close to the city, they halted to talk and sent the servants back with the horses.

"Feed them with grass so they'll be strong." Khun Phaen and Phlai Ngam decked themselves out to look fierce, took some wood to serve as a ladder, climbed onto the wall, made themselves invisible, and sneaked in.

As none of the crowds of guards on duty could see them, Khun Phaen entered without fear of anybody. Phlai Ngam followed behind.

Khun Phaen pronounced a Great Subduer mantra, putting everybody to sleep. The father and son went to the palace[2] gate and halted.

Khun Phaen opened a packet of fragrant herbal medicine, pronounced a Mahakhlang[3] verse seven times, and went into the palace. He ordered his spirits

to put every one of the forbidden ladies[4] to sleep, including those in the royal apartments. "Don't let anyone remain awake, including King Chiang In. If anyone wakes, I'll cut your heads off."

---

2. ไพรชน (SS), ไพรชนต์ (WK), possibly ไพชยนต์, *phaichayon*, a distortion of Wetchayan, the name of a chariot and palace of Indra, used poetically to mean a palace.

3. มหาคลัง, of great supernatural power.

4. สาวห้าม, *sao ham*, or นางห้าม, *nang ham*, a conventional phrase for royal consorts, forbidden to others.

His spirits took the order, saluted, and prostrated at the feet of Khun Phaen. They went around sending everyone to sleep and snore, then rushed to keep guard on the king.

The King of Chiang Mai, valiant and splendid, was fast asleep on a grand royal bed as if dead to the world. Khun Phaen of great mastery,
along with his beloved young son, Phlai Ngam, boldly used a Loosener to open the closed doors. Father and son followed each other in and saw inner ladies fast asleep throughout the palace.
Each room was lit brightly with crystal lanterns and fine lamps. They walked through every room full of palace ladies, looking around enthralled.
There were magnificent golden ornaments, glittering tables and salvers in nak and gold, splendidly elegant curtains and mosquito nets. The inner ladies lay close together, sleeping soundly,
in a long brick building that was not partitioned into rooms but divided by screens. Lamps lit the scene as brightly as daytime. The palace ladies slept packed together.
Every face was fair and invited love. Some ladies wore dazzling earrings along with uppercloths of purple *mot* in shining silk, fetchingly edged in pink.
All were young with fair and lovely faces, and hair swept up in fitting and attractive style. Some slept soundly with their uppercloth slipped from their breasts,
firm and full enough to burst. A flower inserted between them would not slip through. They seemed sculpted onto their chests, and they shone in the light of a full moon.

Phlai Ngam hung behind and stopped to admire. "They stand out like the breasts of *kinnari* figures." With his mind in turmoil and lust aroused, he turned back, sat down,
and embraced one of the ladies, feeling her all over with his hands, kissing her cheeks in a daze. He was still a youth and totally carried away. Khun Phaen turned back to see him,
and called out, "What are you doing, Phlai Ngam? These are forbidden ladies. You shouldn't touch. It'll harm your knowledge. Just look at them to please the eye."
Phlai Ngam replied, "I'm not doing anything. I just came over here to light some tobacco, Father." Khun Phaen said, "You're full of tales. I saw you with my own eyes but you won't admit it."
Phlai Ngam stood up and came over. "I'm not doing anything naughty with

these sleeping people. I won't harm my knowledge." He walked along with his father.

They saw many servants of the forbidden ladies, sleeping close together, some dreaming and sleeptalking. A sentinelle, sitting on watch by a lamp,

had dozed off and kicked over the lamp in her sleep, spilling all its oil. Some couples had fallen asleep, laughing side by side. Some were sprawled over their friends.

One had fallen asleep while eating, with mouth open and bowl in hand. Another had dozed off holding a fish. Another was mumbling in her dreams.

Others had collapsed squashed together, with fish between their teeth, or bananas in their open mouths, and eyes closed in sleep. Some mumbled about playing together in the evening, going into the cabin of the gatekeeper.

Cloths had slipped away from their bodies. One slept on her back, dribbling spittle. Another sighed, ground her teeth in frustration, tossing and turning out of a mosquito net.

Another mumbled about asking for the return of some money, saying "It's mine." Another snored with her hand holding a sac.[5] Another blearily gripped a fan to swat mosquitoes. Father and son looked and passed on by.

They saw a single prominent building and thought it must be the residence of the King of Chiang Mai. The door was closed fast, but they opened it wide with a Loosener and walked in.

The room was scented with a carpet of flowers, and suffused with camphorwood, sandal, and eaglewood. The walls, paneled with crystal, were dazzling. Elegant folding screens were arranged as ornament,

hung with garlands of fragrant flowers. On the ceiling, crystal lamps shone brightly. Half-moon tables were laid with articles for worship. They walked up to a magnificent golden bed.

Parting the curtains to admit light, they saw two ladies lying on the bed, very much alike, both of outstanding beauty, grace, and elegance.

Their complexions were fair and radiant, strikingly beautiful in a way that caught the eye. Their ears were as pretty as lotus petals, eyebrows plucked into attractive arches,

and eyes in sleep as handsome as a portrait. They seemed different from the usual forbidden ladies. Their lips looked fresh and red as if rouged, their hair was styled charmingly

---

5. See p. 766, note 17.

in chignons, and held by hairpins encrusted with flashing rubies. Necklaces and breast chains encircled their bodies. Fine golden bangles decked their arms.

The fingers of both hands glittered with rings. Their exceptional beauty was fitting for royalty. Even fast asleep, their quality was evident. Father and son whispered together.

"From the appearance of these two, the older is the queen for sure, and yet is still attractive in every way. The other must be the princess."

Phlai Ngam's heart was thumping with desire to couple with her. He approached, torn by indecision, wanting a little touch, yet scared of his father.

He trickily pretended to see something, and nudged his father to look at a screen beside the wall. When his father turned away as hoped, he made a grab but knocked over some worship offerings with a crash.

Khun Phaen turned and said, "Phlai Ngam, don't create trouble, damn you. She's a royal princess. Don't make a racket. A sword will jump up and take your neck."

Phlai Ngam mumbled an excuse, "She's just like Simala, Father." He stepped away and stood waiting. When his father walked off, he leapt back,

and came beside the bed where the princess was sleeping. Thinking of his father's warning not to bother her, he loosed a huge sigh. "She's the child of a king.

If her father loses his capital, she'll probably become a consort at Ayutthaya. Or perhaps this is Princess Soithong.

I volunteered to be a soldier. It's not fitting to couple." But he stayed there looking with his mind in turmoil, the two towers thrusting upwards inviting his caress.

He stood sighing and groaning, itching to put out his hand. "Oh, lightning strike! If I didn't think of my king and his support, I wouldn't pass this up. Though Father scolds, I'm not taking any notice."

Khun Phaen looked over, "Ha, Phlai Ngam. You've already made a racket, you trickster. Though you stole a meal at Phichit, I can see you're not heeding my warning."

With this complaint, he walked over to look at his son. Phlai Ngam was so mesmerized, he did not notice his father was standing right beside him, watching,

as he laid his hand down on the princess. Khun Phaen rapped him on the head. "Mm! Phlai Ngam, you're not frightened. I should deal with you right now, you villain."

Phlai Ngam said, "I was about to go off for a pee. Why did you turn up here like a hungry ghost hit by a mantra? I hadn't been for the pee when you came."

"You're good at quick thinking. This is like your peeing at Phichit." Khun Phaen grabbed his son's hand and dragged him away.

In single file, Khun Phaen and Phlai Ngam arrived at the bedchamber of the King of Chiang Mai. Using a Loosener, they walked in. The light of the lamps was dazzling.

Strewn on the floor was a group of forbidden ladies, sleeping packed together. Beyond them were the attendants on fanning duty, fair of face, slight and slender, beautiful.

Outside a curtain beside the royal bed, the attractive players and singers of a *mahori* ensemble were stretched out asleep on suitably fine mattresses and pillows. Inside on the bed was King Chiang In.

Father and son drew back the golden curtains, walked up to the splendid royal bed, and saw the king fast asleep.

His body was stout, his face fair with a blonde tinge, and his apparel magnificent. Several royal swords were placed beside the bed, and another sharp, white, short sword to his right.

Father and son looked at the King of Chiang Mai. "Though his royal wealth should be enough to satisfy him, the fruit of his karma will cause him to lose so many consorts and palace ladies."

Phlai Ngam hid away the royal swords. Khun Phaen boldly concealed the short sword, and ordered his spirits to relax their power and allow the king to wake up.

The spirits complied. Khun Phaen stood on the magnificent golden royal bed. Phlai Ngam, the valiant warrior, stood beside the lord of the city.

Khun Phaen drew Skystorm and stood poised to pounce and chop the king dead. He bellowed like a lion, "Heigh! Ha! Impetuous king,

we are soldiers of Ayutthaya, come to bring your life to a close because you have not adhered to justice but committed grave and major offenses.

His Majesty the King of Ayutthaya has vast power that subdues the world, so that everyone in the ten directions fears him greatly and renders up beautiful golden flowers.[6]

The King of Si Sattana, faithful to the ten principles and loyal without parallel, resolved to bow low and present Princess Soithong in recognition of His Majesty's merit.

---

6. See p. 169, note 10.

But the King of Chiang Mai impetuously failed to pay respect to His Majesty. In addition, he seized the princess, imprisoned Thai in his city, and sent a missive with a challenge to an elephant duel.

There are cities tributary to the Thai that are greater than yours, yet you arrogantly commit these wrongs. Hence the king has sent some skilled enforcers to put an end to your life today.

If you have anything to say, then speak. To whom does the city of Chiang Mai belong? Don't lie there on your back with closed eyes, thinking all is well, you villain. Come out to explain, or to fight!"

The King of Chiang Mai felt as if thunder and lightning had split the palace asunder. He leapt up and grasped for his swords but found nothing and almost died.

Then he roared like a lion, and stamped his foot hard enough to crush the earth to pieces. Feeling as if the Lord of Darkness were scorching him to death, he jerked around in a fit of shame.

Unable to lay his hands on a sword, he felt devastated enough for his chest to crack open. He let out a great sigh of terror, and his face turned ashen.

But in the manner of a king, he did not abase himself. Feeling sad enough to die, he fell fearfully silent as if possessed by a spirit.

Khun Phaen, great romancer, magnificent in mastery, brandished Skystorm to flash like the sun, and bellowed,

"I am the Lord of Darkness come to destroy your life. What are you thinking? Speak quickly. Are you contemplating another fight? Tell me if you're going to resist.

I'll summon the palace guards and slash them to dust, finish off all of Chiang Mai, no survivors. Your life will end at any moment."

He leapt up and shouted loud enough to shake the palace. "Why won't you speak? Don't delay. Any moment now you'll writhe to your death."

The King of Chiang Mai was in shock, as if his heart had suddenly stopped. "I beg for my life, and beg pardon for my error. Everything now depends on your mercy.

Chiang Mai is yours already. I also offer my beloved daughter and piles of silver and gold in return for my life. I'm guilty, deserving of death.

You say I'm in the wrong, and I can't deny it. The fruit of karma led me into this action. The lovely Soithong is still very much a child. There has been no lovemaking.

I present everything to your king including phrai, troops, countryside, and city, along with myself to be his servant until I die."

He swore an oath, "If I am not honest, may I fall into hell and burn, may you slash me to death. I cannot fight. I beg for my life."

Khun Phaen, great savant, heard the Lao lord's words and smiled. "If you're faithful to your promise, you have nothing to fear. Your punishment will not be severe."

He ordered the spirits to relax the mantra. All around, men and women stirred. Khun Phaen returned the royal short sword to the king. The two officers invited him

to proceed to the splendid audience hall. They released the restraint on the nobles, officials, and courtiers in attendance,

both inside the palace and at the front. In all the residences of the palace ladies, people rushed wildly around, still bleary with sleep, looking for their friends, their hearts as hot as raging fire.

Once released from the mantra, the Lao officials fled, trembling, shouting and screaming, pouring out through the gates,

crashing into one another in confusion, and falling flat on face and back. The Thai soldiers did not let them escape, but grabbed some by the hair and dragged them off, still bleary and not fully conscious.

Some saw the Thai soldiers and tried acting dead, but still were grabbed by the hair and elbowed with a lot of loud shouting. Phra Thainam's people joined in, crowding around to punch and beat.

Anyone who resisted or ran away was hit and elbowed in the back until they could not cry out. The soldiers besieging the city immediately ran to gather up goods and round up people.

One soldier caught a Lao, pulled his hair, and commanded, "Tell me where your silver and gold is kept or I'll set fire to your arse!" The Lao said, "Hold off! I can't stand heat. Take the money."

Muen At Narai got hold of an old lady and stuck her up on a frame with legs splayed. She cried, "You can dig the money out of those jars of fermented fish." He whooped and hollered for joy.

Captives were made to sit in groups, "Now, don't be mean and try to hide your money and goods." The soldiers felt around in the twists of their lowercloths, or went up into their houses and searched everywhere.

Ai-Phut dragged off a Lao girl and mounted her. "If you'd like to sleep, I'll sing you a lullaby. It's been ages since I enjoyed a roll. I won't abandon you to be alone."

The Lao girl cried out, "I won't consent. This lullaby singer is an evil spirit with a head as high as the roof." Ai-Thong called out, "Oh damn! You're giving him such a hard time the rain's dried up."

Eventually people submitted and peace reigned. Every single Thai got some money. Some also carted off cloth,

or hauled away buffaloes and oxen by their harness. "I'm taking them as a gift for the mother of my little girl." Phra Thainam gave orders for building lodgings, and then sat to discuss with his phrai.

"Just now Khun Phaen and Phlai Ngam went into the palace. We haven't yet had any news. Be on alert until we hear.

If there's trouble in the palace, we'll have to surround it, capture people, and kill them to prevent the enemy besting us. Get ready at once."

At the sight of the two officers leading the king out of the royal residence, the queen and Soi Fa felt as if they were being burned alive.

Fearing the king would be slashed dead, the queen sobbed uncontrollably, embracing her daughter. "I think we're done for, Mother's jewel.

Our enemies have got in. They've captured Father and will kill him. We're destroyed, my precious. Pity us, our lives will be snuffed out.

Oh, lord and master of mine, why did you let your heart lead you astray to carelessly provoke this war?

You seized the Princess Soithong and, for better or worse, did not heed your wife's warnings. Our city was a beautiful place to live, but you stirred up trouble by issuing a challenge for an elephant duel.

Through listening to flatterers, you became confused and lost. We can't match the Thai at all. We sent our best soldiers to bar their way, but within a day our men had broken, fled, or died.

Yesterday evening, their troops came to our city, and the Thai vanished from the jail. Guards were killed with their necks lopped off. Many horses, elephants, and weapons were taken.

The only thing remaining for them was to capture you, yet you still did not give up your arrogant attitude. Now that they've found you, I've no idea who can provide protection.

Oh my lord and master of the world, your wife is sad enough to die. This is the fruit of karma catching up with you—bad deeds from the past drove you on.

However much I warned, you didn't listen—you didn't listen at all. Lust alone took over your mind, and you forgot your love for the consorts and palace ladies.

Even Soifa here, on whom you dote, could not stop you. You were groaning after Soithong so much that you abducted her and imprisoned the Thai.

The powerful guardian spirits of the city didn't protect you but stood idly by in every direction, and allowed the golden umbrella to be broken without mercy, not helping the city survive.

Oh, when will Chiang Mai rise again! Every night, it will die away like the stars. There is no happiness any more. Everybody will be scattered afar.

In the past you governed the city without a trace of trouble. Now you'll die, and nobody will remain alive in this palace.

You'll be parted from my breast and will face only heartbreaking hardship. When will I see my beloved daughter again?" She lowered her face, racked with sobs.

The consorts and governesses were bent over with weeping, feeling as if fire were burning the earth, altogether creating a great commotion.

They ran around in circles, falling over and scrambling up again. They went outside and saw the queen coming to the royal residence.

Three of them bowed and addressed the queen. "Ma-am, don't be sad about His Majesty.

I think gold and silver flowers will be all they want.[7] They'll probably govern Chiang Mai rather than destroying it. The whole royal dynasty should survive." The queen and princess heard these words and felt somewhat relieved.

The Lao nobles and officials, also as shocked as if on fire, made obeisance to the King of Chiang Mai, and prostrated to Khun Phaen.

Looking at Phlai Ngam and Phra Thainam, their faces darkened, their hair stood on end, and their heads seemed to swell like great baskets, all in turmoil, all weeping loudly out of self-pity.

In fear of the three officers, the Lao nobles cried, "Nobody can offer resistance." "Haul away carts piled up with silver and gold, but please spare the lives of our wives and mothers."

"Our daughters and granddaughters, we offer to you." "We'll hand over elephants, horses, and servants so you have enough for yourselves and for presenting to your wives, but please spare us nobles, good sirs."

---

7. Meaning, Chiang Mai will become a tributary, and make regular presentation of gold and silver flowers as symbolic recognition of this status (see p. 169, note 10).

Seeing his officers weeping, the King of Chiang Mai was in despair. He spoke. "Don't be troubled. We'll survive due to the mercy of these three officers.

We must arrange a residence suitable for them with roof, curtains, blinds, lanterns, lamps, and everything.

Set up screens, curtains, and blinds as partitions. Find big clear mirrors to make it bright. Spread the floor with smart carpets. Furnish the interior with beds and bedding.

Provide betel, *miang*, liquor, sweet and savory foods, tables, salvers, water bowls, mattresses, and pillows. Scent with camphorwood, sandal, and eaglewood to overcome the heat. Garland around with flowers.

Carry in water for drinking and for bathing. Hang ornaments in the main apartment. Decorate the ceiling with bright stars. String up garlands of flowers.

Have ladies on duty to dance and sing, and make sure they are very beautiful young ladies, according to Lao custom, and skilled at playing the pipe and drum."

After everything was arranged, the officers returned and informed the king, "All is provided in profusion." Khun Phaen and Phlai Ngam took their leave of the king and walked out together.

Servants and phrai surrounding them closely, holding guns. As if being attacked by tigers, Lao scattered to let them through, running off, falling over and bumping into one another, crying desperately, "I'm scared."[8]

A woman pulled her cloth over her head and ran away, bashing her head into a fence. The Thai volunteers shouted and cheered. All of them went happily up into the residence.

Lao nobles ordered, "Hey, bring in lots of food." Four Lao ladies of good appearance brought in water bowls and golden salvers.

The King of Chiang Mai had food brought for Khun Phaen and his son to eat at a head table. Phra Thainam was seated further down.

Phlai Ngam sat beside his father, and the Lao brought trays of food for them. The volunteers got merrily drunk and chatted away, wreathed in smiles.

Phra Thainam ate at a big table, sitting cross-legged and speaking loudly with his head thrown back. Khun Phaen chatted and drank liquor. Phlai Ngam smiled sweetly all the time.

All the soldiers drank liquor, and those that got drunk laughed and chattered away. Some enchanted liquor to give invulnerability and then bit bowls to display their lore. Others challenged their friends to slash and stab them.

---

8. ข้อย ยั้น เด, *khoi yan de*, in Lao.

Some gnashed their teeth and roared. Some showed off their mantra lore, leaping up and striking poses with red eyes, "I'll try out my strength riding a Lao girl!"

A Lao woman cried out, "I'm done for!"[9] and ran off white-eyed. Ta-Rak drew his sword and flashed it around. The Lao cried pitifully with staring eyes.

Some soldiers stabbed themselves for the Lao to see they were invulnerable to piercing. Chisel, drill, axe, and hoe were brought, but their bodies were no more hurt than by being pinched with fingernails.

The Lao were shocked. Khun Phaen reprimanded his men. "Don't make so much noise. You're showing off so people will talk. Is that a good thing to do?"

Hearing Khun Phaen's words, the soldiers became embarrassed and trembled in fear. Those who had been drinking lost their drunkenness. Silence fell and nobody spoke.

The three officers sat comfortably on a low bench, and Lao served them attentively from left and right. Ladies were summoned to sing, dance, and let the guests gaze on their fair and lovely faces.

Ta-Rak nodded to his friends to watch. He pointed to a girl with an indigo uppercloth, breasts like sidebags, chubby cheeks, earrings, and a good singing voice. "If the boss didn't forbid it, I'd put it in her for several rounds."

Forgetting his body was old, Ta-Lo ran across and tripped over a water bowl, drenching his clothes like an infant. Ta-Plok got up and danced with a Lao girl,

tripping back and forth, then hugging her round the neck. His friends roared with laughter. They struck poses from the mask play and sang boat songs. With no room left for them to dance, the Lao girls sat down.

---

9. ข้อย ตาย เด, *khoi tai de*, in Lao.

The three officers, Khun Phaen, Phlai Ngam, and Phra Thainam, held a discussion. "We'll send a message cylinder to Ayutthaya,

stating that the King of Chiang Mai acted wrongly but has begged to be spared, and has given piles of silver and gold in exchange for his life. He is also looking after our troops attentively.

In this way we'll help ensure his punishment is not as heavy as it might have been." Khun Phaen turned his face and said, "Hey, men! Although he did wrong, don't seek revenge.

From now onwards, let bygones be bygones." All the troops agreed. A missive was prepared explaining events in a roundabout fashion, with truth inextricably mixed up with falsehood.

When it was done, the missive was stamped with a seal, folded and placed in a cylinder, and sent to Nai Jan Samphantueng with the orders,

"Hasten down to Ayutthaya within fifteen days and deliver this missive without fail. Once it is delivered, wait to hear the reply."

Nai Jan Samphantueng made his farewell and plunged off. He dressed himself quickly, mounted a horse, slung a sidebag over his shoulder, and departed.

Digging in his heels, he galloped furiously, speeding along at a powerful rate. Lao bowed and saluted him along the way.

He hastened into the deep forest, eating up the track with long strides. He passed through Thoen,

and in seven days arrived at Kamphaeng. He informed the local officials who quickly made arrangements to receive him, and conscripted phrai to find a boat

while Nai Jan hit on liquor to the full, shouting "We fixed those northerners!" They seized a boat belonging to a Mon salt seller, I-Moei-Duea, who fell into the water with a splash.

Her cloth slipped off completely as she thrust her head above the surface. "Oh, my cunt! Lord fuck me! Oh mother![1] Damn you!" She doubled over with

---

1. แหงน บิชิ ตอก ขมิ อุ้ย ย่าย, *ngaen bi chi tok khami ui yai,* in Mon.

her bottom in the air, stark naked, shrieking "I'm drowning!"[2]

She was given two baht for the liquor. Officials took the boat, saying, "Let's go." It was a good *khon* boat with a canopy. They loaded rice, and ordered the oarsmen to paddle off,

singing boat songs loudly in chorus as they went. The officers sat in state under the canopy, pouring liquor in turns. Rowing strongly, they reached the city in seven days

and moored at the regular landing. Nai Jan washed and dressed, picked up the missive cylinder, put a cloth round his belly, and went off, trailed by servants carrying a sidebag.

He arrived at the inner official sala, went in, looked around, and made inquiries. As soon as he found a senior official, he produced the missive and related what had happened.

The duty officer went to wait on the chaophraya. With people in attendance all around, the cylinder was broken open, and the message read out for all to hear.

The almighty king, eminence of the magnificent city, monarch of the capital of Ayutthaya, ruler of immense authority,

slept on an exquisite bed, with masses of palace ladies arrayed around. When the moon and stars had slid behind the clouds, he awoke from sleep immediately,

and proceeded to his ablutions. He was bathed in water sprinkled from a crystal shower, anointed with splendid scents,

and arrayed in raiment to look dazzling. He walked out to the balcony of the palace to the sound of music playing.

All the courtiers were present in groups according to position, as was the regular practice at audience. They raised their arms in salute.

Chaophraya Jakri had the floor and promptly addressed the king on the contents of the missive. "My liege, my life is beneath the royal foot.

Khun Phaen and Phlai Ngam report on the war for which they volunteered. Nai Jan was deputed to bring a letter. Phra Thainam affixed a seal with their names.

On the first waxing day of the fourth month,[3] we fought and killed the Lao

---

2. ทะแล(ด) อา, *thalae(t) a*, from Mon, *a* means "to go" but the previous word is unidentified and the translation guessed from context.

3. If this is lunar months, the date would fall in February. But these may be months counted

of the border post, and swarmed ahead to the great lake.[4] After we established a base camp, the sun set.

At seven in the evening, Chiang Mai received information about our arrival, and placed its troops on alert. Phra Thainam and his men were all in jail, surrounded by guards and bonfires.

At dawn, they intended to execute Phra Thainam and his men. Hence at the second watch, Khun Phaen and Phlai Ngam entered the city,

put all the warders to sleep, unlocked the manacles, and removed all the cangues. Five hundred persons were released and went to slash the jailers.

Then they left the jail, put the staff of the stables to sleep, took away horses, broke into the armory,

and equipped everyone with weapons. Phra Thainam led his troops skillfully. Next morning, the lord[5] of Chiang Mai sent out an army of almost thirty thousand men.

They cut a road and made camp at the edge of the forest. In command of a vanguard of almost ten thousand troops, Phetkla made an assault on our camp to eliminate our forces.

Saen Rahu, commander of the main army, attacked in support like a deluge. Phlai Ngam rode a horse at the head of his troops to engage the enemy at close quarters.

Khun Phaen advanced an army of dummies to provide rear support for the defense. Phlia Phetkla on horseback engaged with Phlai Ngam,

who fought back with his sword and slashed off the enemy's head in the middle of the battlefield. Saenyi Kamkong followed into the fray, and both sides joined battle in force.

Not a single Thai was felled, while the Lao were slashed and cut to pieces. Saen Rahu attacked the talented Khun Phaen,

who slashed Saen Rahu to death. Countless Lao died, cut down by the Thai, and five hundred were captured.

Survivors fled to the city and took up positions at every location. Khun Phaen rode his horse at the head of the troops to invest the walls.

The Lao unleashed gunfire with red flashes like lightning and loud reports like thunder. The Thai responded with hollering and gunfire.

The hail of spears and gunfire did not hit any of the Thai troops, causing the

---

from Songkran (see p. 1319, note 35), in which case it is July.

4. Old European maps of Siam showed a fictitious large lake in the vicinity of Chiang Mai from which the Chaophraya River was thought to originate. Perhaps this "great lake" is part of the same tradition.

5. In this missive, and during his time at Ayutthaya, the ruler of Chiang Mai is referred to as เจ้า, *jao*, rather than พระเจ้า, *phrajao*. This is translated as "lord."

lord of Chiang Mai to be greatly shocked. He decided to raise a white flag.

As a result we withdrew and watched. Quickly the gates of the city were opened and an ambassador was sent out to beg for their lives as servants of the Thai.

Then the Princess Soifa and Princess Soithong were presented. Nothing had happened. The two were too young to know anything. Khun Phaen thus pardoned Chiang Mai.

The Princess Soithong had not been summoned for lovemaking. The Thai forces entered the city. The troops of Phra Thainam were offered compensation

of silver and gold in great quantity along with gifts of cloth. Phra Thainam did not wish to continue the karma and so did not exact any revenge.

Gifts presented to His Majesty include five thousand pieces of silver, and almost two hundred pieces of gold, along with great quantities of elephants, horses, and other goods including families and articles of tribute,

five hundred tusks of large and small sizes, guns, weapons, and military equipment. The lord of Chiang Mai was placed under the five irons. We await the royal orders."

The king, seated on a magnificent throne, looked up wreathed in smiles, spoke thunderously,

and clapped his hands loudly enough to shake the palace, making the audience hall sway back and forth. "It was no waste to employ these soldiers. Let the lord of Chiang Mai be brought down under restraint.

Let word spread to cities great and small that I will let this pass and not exact punishment if his city submits and becomes tributary to glorious Ayutthaya. To call this a revolt by our law,

given that his is a primary country and was not tributary to my city in the past, and given that he confesses his guilt without question, would be like beating fish at the mouth of a trap.[6]

Let it be known into the future that anyone subject to Ayutthaya who acts wrongly and dishonestly will be condemned to death.

In the sealed order, do not follow what I have just said. Prepare a secret missive to inform the army commander that the miscreant's punishment will not be death."

The chaophraya took the order. Courtiers prostrated and crawled out. At the sala at the end of the pond,[7]

---

6. A proverbial phrase with meaning similar to "shooting ducks in a barrel."

7. ศาลา ท้าย สระ, *sala thai sa*, probably the new inner official sala built in the 1680s to the

duty officers were summoned to prepare an order on cut sheets of paper, affixed with the Ratchasi seal. The missive was rolled up and placed in a cylinder that was closed and inscribed with a seal.

When it was done, Nai Jan was ordered to hurry away. "Have the ruler of Chiang Mai brought under restraint. Let the army return immediately along with the Lao families."

Nai Jan took the sealed missive and went down to a boat. He made the oarsmen holler, shout, and sing boat songs while he poured liquor. They crashed into the boat of an old man,

who leapt up and danced about naked, calling out, "A spirit has broken my neck!" The soldiers sat bent over watching him, forgetting all about paddling the boat.

Arriving at Bang Lang, they seized some liquor. Chinaman Kao shouted out, "Cunts!"[8] as they hauled some over into the long boat, hollering. In shock the Chinaman cried, "Oh shit,[9] help me!"

At a river junction, they passed some fish nets and Nai Jan asked, "I'm going on royal business. Let me have some fish." They slowed the boat, went close, and his men grabbed some. The villagers protested, "Oh, look here![10] We're finished!"

Reaching Chawai, they went into a sugar plantation and carried off many sticks of cane. The guards of the plot ran away in fear but they caught some and made them wrestle and dance to a *thon* drum.

Be forgiving, but this is customary for an army. They create the kind of chaos you see in a mask play. Even though they think they're good, it's as crude as a robber getting a wife by capture and rape.

Description will take too much time and the story will be long and tiresome if you listen to every syllable and every line. They won't tell the wife they had a fling along the way.

In fifteen days they came to Rahaeng. The district officials flocked around. Nai Jan took his travel document to inform the governor seated in the central sala.

The governor arranged dried rice, betel, popped rice, and sweets for his

---

north of the new Banyong Ratanat Audience Hall (KLW 205–7; KCK 207; APA, 59; see p. 540, note 22).

8. จีไบ๋, *ji bai*, in Hokkien (see p. 43, note 69).

9. ไส่บวย, *sai buai*, in Hokkien (see p. 43, note 69).

10. อา อุมิ ชิ, *a umi chi*, in Mon.

waist pouch, and provided post horses as of old so he could hurry ahead as it was royal business.

Nai Jan Samphantueng took leave and hastened onward, accompanied by four phrai, all on horseback, with waist pouches and bags swaying and slapping a rhythm as they went.

They reached the outpost at Tha Kwian and stopped to rest. The officers of the outpost shouted to Nai Jan in greeting, provided white liquor, and carried over food including fish and turtle.

As soon as they were full, they mounted and sped off with wind racing from their ears. At Thoen, where they turned in to be fed, snakeskin and liquor were sent over

along with elephant meat, fishcakes, and boiled eggs, carried by a line of people swaying to and fro. Once happily full, they mounted and went off hollering,

drunk on the liquor and dribbling spittle. They blurrily saw elephants the size of pigs, "Let's fight!" They came across Lao walking on their own and dragged them along to sing and dance wild chicken songs.

Nai Jan arrived at Chiang Mai, found Khun Phaen, saluted him with a wai, and handed over the sealed cylinder. Khun Phaen took it and read it.

He folded the secret missive and kept it. Replacing the open message in the canister, he let his son and Phra Thainam have a look, then summoned Lao ironsmiths

to make chains and manacles. Khun Phaen went to find the lord of Chiang Mai and read him the sealed royal message stating that he had to go down under the five irons.

The King of Chiang Mai was as shocked as if his neck had been chopped off. "I depend utterly on you to help me talk to the king so I may avoid death.

I have firmly committed to be loyal. If not, I would already be dead. Please help to gain my pardon for certain. Please petition the king for relief so I may survive."

On hearing the Lao lord's words, the wise Khun Phaen smiled and laughed. "Don't worry. On the way down, you won't be under restraint—only when you are seen arriving there.

We'll do just enough to avoid my master's anger. Have no fear. I'll ask for pardon on your behalf so you may soon return to Chiang Mai. Whatever I say, the king will believe."

The army was told they would leave in three days. The front and rear brigades were all made ready. Servants were sent around banging gongs loudly and calling out, "Day after tomorrow, the chief orders us to march."

Among the soldiers, some sang, while others played flutes and banged drums in joy that the army was returning home and they would see their wives again.

Ta-Lo said, "Sir, I'm not sad. Though my old woman is sick and ailing, I've got a young Lao girl as wife." Giggling and jiggling his head, he stumbled away.

Young men with young wives worked the rice pounder,[11] push and pull, up and down, back and forth. Some couples pounded together. One old and decrepit husband pounded in place of his wife,

while she prepared betelnut to give to her stooped husband. Young lads gathered around to cheer. "Good on you, old fellow, for being kind to your wife. The old husband laughed and spat beteljuice, enjoying their praise.

Some packed crates and cases for porterage. Some went to get snakehead fish, beheaded them, and either grilled them or made them into *tomyam*. Others busily harnessed up buffaloes.

The King of Chiang Mai went into the palace to get everything ready. "Today a sealed order has come for us to travel. The army commander has undertaken to get a pardon

for certain, which is comforting. It can't be helped that they have ordered us to be put under restraint. He'll help us in any way he can. He's taken this upon himself for sure.

On arrival, we'll have to be seen under restraint or else the king will be angry enough to reduce us to dust. The commander will petition the royal foot for pardon so we can return up to our city.

I saw the sealed report that was sent down. It will help us in no small way. He's like a father to us. How do you feel about this?"

Nang Soi Sumali wept at her husband's words, hugging Soifa, and said, "However much I warned, you did not listen.

If the Thai soldiers had not spared your life, you'd be dead by now with your neck lopped off. By the force of karma, we must be parted from this palace. Bad deeds from the past have caught up with us.

It's said that a dog won't defecate where there's no rubbish,[12] and a debtor

---

11. The image is of a rice pounder like a seesaw, worked by foot.
12. A proverb with the same meaning as "There's no smoke without fire."

is always pursued, my lord. People flattered you so much that you got carried away and had the princess seized by force.

When they're lifting a pig, don't push your pole in too.[13] Your eyes are so red and almost blind, yet you boasted about fighting the king in an elephant duel. Is Ayutthaya bereft of good people?[14]

Their king employed only subjects of military lineage. We could not match them so we were knocked down rolling in the dirt. If he pardons your life and does not slash you to death, that's true kindness.

Now you're to be sent down to the lower city, rattling with chains." She embraced her daughter, crying pitifully. "Oh my beloved, your mother's in grief.

This Soithong was like a decoy bird, luring your father to get caught in a net. He was so excited and hopeful he got trapped and had his feathers plucked.

He paid no thought to his age, but was drooling at the thought of having a young girl, and so led his own daughter into distress." She embraced her daughter and grieved on and on.

Soifa listened to the queen's lamentation. "You brought up this child. Now fate has intervened, and I don't blame anybody.

Dear Mother, don't blame Father out of anger. This has come about because of karma from the past. Just avoiding death makes me happy. I feel sorry for the phrai of our city.

They used to be happy but now face hardship as hot as if roasted in fire. They must leave their homes because of us. They'll be quiet, lonely, doubled over with the pain of sorrow.

Like plants in a drought, they'll wilt and wither under the light of the sun. Where the flowers used to spread their fragrant pollen, fallen leaves will scatter all over the earth.

And this sorrow alone will not be the whole of it. They'll be roasted by forest fires. Just as we are separated from the city, the ordinary people will be sorrowful in the same way."

The lord of Chiang Mai continued to lament in desolation. "Why did it turn out like this?[15] Oh karma, truly karma has caught up with me. I shall suffer and sorrow so much from parting.

No one born a man can escape peril. This suffering is no joke. This time everybody will die. Karma is the cause. Nobody is to blame."

---

13. A proverb meaning "Don't poke your nose into other people's affairs."
14. See p. 1019, note 5.
15. ก่น แต่ เว้า เป็น หยัง บีสัง หั้น, *kon tae wao pen yong bi sang han*, in Lao.

He comforted his daughter. "Listen to your father's words, and don't cry. When karma leads, we are helpless. You should realize that you'll be a servant of the Thai king.

You must look after him well. When attending on him, do nothing wrong. When far from his eyes, be thoughtful and set your mind to respect his royal wishes.

If he's enraged, do not be angered in return. Whether he's right or wrong, observe his mood and refrain from opposing him. If there's anything that can be done to calm him, then do it, but don't try to put out a fire in a strong wind.

Be loyal, and love the king until death. Do not have bad thoughts—sweet on the outside but bitter inside. Though your mother and father will be far away and out of sight, we'll think of our beloved child with love.

You're like a priceless jewel. Help your father as if allowing him to be born again. Have a care for me and the city. Please avert the danger I'm facing,

and save the phrai, officials, and your kinsfolk. Our city has already fallen, Father's jewel. Bow your face and go to be a servant of the Thai king."

Soifa listened to her father, sobbing pitifully, her eyes flooded with tears. "What ill fate has caused that I should leave?

You brought me up in the palace. Now ill fate from the past has brought catastrophe, like a junk hit by a storm, that is smashed by waves and sinks down in the water.

Oh, going down to the southern city will be just like falling into the depths of a stormy ocean. Will this little ship stay upright when the waves hit?

I fear it will sink amid the buffeting. Who can help save my life? At my wits' end I'll probably die." She grieved heavily as if her life would slip away.

"Oh, god of the golden umbrella, please beat and batter me to death so I can escape the hardship that heaps on top of me. I don't cling to life for another day or night.

From now on I'll have no happiness, like a jewel that's fallen low." She grieved and lamented, sobbing on and on, still and unmoving.

Her mother and father were desolate with pity. They put both arms around her body, with both eyes flooded with tears.

Father said, "Oh poor daughter." The queen said, "You'll be established as a wife." Father said, "Your leaving this city is like someone gouging out my own eye."

Soifa said, "Oh my lord and master, parting from you to go south feels like someone plucking out my own heart. Forced to be far away, I'll be forced to stifle my tears."

Mother said, "The city will deteriorate, with no one to revive it." Father said, "May you have a long life, and may I regain realm and city because of beloved you."

Soifa said, "I must leave, feeling miserable enough for my heart to break." The three were overcome with sorrow and tears for a long time.

Beyond sorrow, beyond weeping, beyond strength, beyond thought, beyond voice, beyond life, the three grieved in the sandalwood residence.

All the ladies of the jeweled palace were plunged in sorrow. Sounds of sad lamentation filled the air. Wherever they looked they saw others grieving.

At that time in the city of Chiang Mai, it seemed as if a great heavenly storm was pouring down wild torrents of water, submerging everything, and filling the waterways throughout the territory.

Nobles, officials, and people of village and city were flooded with tears. All did nothing but lament to the end of their strength. No one had the ability to hold back their grief.

At this point, listeners may be wondering why Soithong has not made some appearance. When the political matters had been resolved, she was immediately brought into the Thai camp,

and a pavilion was built for her amid the army, surrounded by rings of protection. Her retinue from Lanchang was also brought over with her.

Phra Thainam and the phrai who had been her escort were deputed to guard and look after her. Phlai Ngam supervised.

At this point, listeners may be wondering why the masterful Elder Khwat[16] did not volunteer to attack and destroy the army using unusual methods of warfare.

If the Thai army had not attacked immediately and won victory on the battlefield, he could have disrobed and volunteered to fight. But the attack was unexpected.

The lord of Chiang Mai pledged his word, bringing the affair to a close. All that remained was to prepare to face the rigors of travel along with the families.

---

16. Khwat plays a prominent part in the sequel after Wanthong's death (chs. 37 to 43). This section seems to have been inserted as a link to that story.

At cockcrow in the streaky golden light before sunrise, the King of Chiang Mai sent for his daughter and sadly ordered her to get dressed.

Princess Soifa sobbed so pitifully that no one could provide relief. She did not want to bathe. Only when her kinsfolk gathered around did she manage to overcome her sorrow a little.

"Calm yourself, mistress. Don't be miserable. Please bathe to cheer yourself up." Forbidden ladies crowded around, comforting her. They brought water,

infused with the fragrance of foreign flowers, dressed her splendidly with glittering golden bracelets,

powdered her face white and radiantly pure, and styled her hair beautifully. She wore a shimmering golden breast chain beautifully studded with gems,

a lowercloth with a cross-branch pattern in gold on a light green background and a red border of flowers and cones. Her hair was wound into a chignon held by a good hairpin. She walked to audience.

The King of Chiang Mai and his beloved wife, sadly swallowing their tears, led their daughter to walk away from the sandalwood palace, followed by palace ladies,

to the sounds of weeping and wailing loud enough to fill the whole palace. The king said, "Don't be sad. I will go for a year or so and then return to our city.

Those remaining here, listen to my instructions. Look after the palace as you did when I was here. Don't neglect any corner, room, or door." Palace governesses took the order, bathed in tears.

"We servants of the foot who remain here will do nothing but sorrowfully weep and wail while waiting. Only when Your Majesty returns will the sorrow wane."

I-Mai[17] said, "I don't want to stay. I wish to go with you to face death, come what may, wherever in the world. Don't protest. I'm determined to go along."

Phra Thainam and Khun Phaen drew up the mass of troops in fine order, readied horses and elephants, and provided officers with post horses to oversee the army.

Khun Phaen came back to give orders to the Chiang Mai nobles to look after the city. Elephants, horses, troops, and people were crowded tightly together. Khun Phaen guarded the king.

---

17. Mai becomes the personal servant of Soifa in Ayutthaya.

At an auspicious time, they hollered, beat gongs loudly, and fired large guns as a signal. The reports echoed around.

With lines of flags and pennants fluttering overhead, units and brigades moved off. Families, oxen, and buffaloes were herded along under the control of the Thai.

Elder Khwat and Novice Jiw[18] walked up to join the column with begging bowls slung across their shoulders. "Please let us go along to help with remedies." They mounted on a tusker with a howdah.

The elder sat in the middle and Novice Jiw at the back. The elephant surged forward, chomping its mouth. For Soifa and her mother, an elephant was harnessed with a howdah equipped with golden curtains to screen them from view.

The king rode a saddled elephant, enclosed by a brilliant golden curtain and canopy. Khun Phaen kept guard on him. Masses of families followed along, some riding horses, elephants, buffaloes, and oxen in noisy turmoil. Phra Thainam led the army. Soithong grieved under a golden canopy.

Phlai Ngam rode a horse as guard. The troops hollered and loosed shots. Flags flew over the units and brigades. Gongs and drums echoed around.

King Chiang In, eminence of the world, wept sadly with a heavy heart. Leaving through a city gate,
he turned his face to look at the peak of the palace spire, glittering with fine gold. The more he looked the more he felt chilled with fear, and his tears flowed down as if to submerge the spire.

"Oh, I feel pity for the palace. Before it was full of light and happiness, but now who will look after it? When it deteriorates, who will make repairs?

Oh, I pity the crystal-paneled walls which will lose their color within days. I pity the nine-jeweled spire which must crack, crumble, and fall.

Oh, I feel pity for leaving the royal apartments, once always lively, but now sad and gloomy, day and night. I feel pity for the forbidden ladies who sat on their regular watch, and the singers and dancers who performed every day.

The bedchamber will sadly lose its golden color. The crystal mounting place will become a pile of brick and stone. Where we sat in the cool of the evening will be lonely and cold. Where we sat in the heat will crumble away.

The audience hall will deteriorate into forest and grass. The courtyard will sprout weeds. The crystal lake, once filled with lotus, will be choked with water spinach.

---

18. Jiw is Khwat's acolyte and partner in mischief in chapters 37 to 43.

I feel pity for the fruit trees in the garden of the right, the brilliant jasmine and double jasmine, fivegold, smiling lady, camphorwood, sandal flowers,

night jasmine, rosewood, heartache, teak, pine, ivorybell, gem jasmine, milkwood, pupil, *phayom, masang, jampa,* and *jampi,* whose fragrance we used to enjoy, wafting on the wind.

Insects, wasps, and bees used to swarm around the pollen of the flowers. Crickets trilled rhythmically every day. What a pity I now have to depart!

Oh Buddha! Only recently we used to enjoy all this but now have to be parted without saying farewell." His mind swirled with sorrow, and tears streamed from his eyes as he stared at the city.

The army drove the Lao families along. If they stopped walking, they were beaten and berated to keep moving. One Lao cried, "I'm truly afraid," [19] dashed ahead in alarm, and ran into an elephant.

Some were frightened by the din of guns, gongs, drums, and wild shouting. A young girl and her old widowed mother slipped off the back of a buffalo and hung down the sides, losing their lowercloths and dangling along.

A phrai of the army whooped wildly, "Oh my! Fair and lovely is just right!" Elephant mahouts drove their mounts along, plodding and nodding and chomping in rhythm.

Cartwheels creaked, squeaked, sighed, and groaned, as they bumped and bounced along. Little kids trailed after their mothers, weeping, whining, and wailing.

The King of Chiang Mai and his beloved daughter looked at the phrai and troops with their eyes streaming in sadness, loneliness, and regret. He turned back to look again at the city.

The more he looked the farther it receded from his eyes. He felt his life would not last until his return. The paddy fields, city, palace, and trees would all be destroyed.

"They're carting away our troops, elephants, horses, people, and everything else like trapped frogs. Whatever they found, they took without a thought— young girls, old ladies, or widows.

In fear of death, father, mother, child, and husband must leave. Some will fall dead, thinking of their abandoned homes far away."

He watched monkey and langur running and leaping; gibbon swinging through trees, this way and that, returning home as the sun sank; and orioles flying to find a roost.

---

19. ยั้น จริง, *yan jing,* in Lao.

"Oh poor us! We never went without, but now have to part from the city where our hopes reside. That golden peacock on the wing cries like a horn or conch playing in the forest.

The female partridge perched on a *khontha* calls out in greeting and swoops away. An elephant wrenches a tree that breaks with a crack, sending birds swooshing into the air, just like us.

When the army broke, the city was lost, and people scattered to hide up in the hills. Oh, who is like us, not even caring to eat rice and fish?"

Reaching Chomthong, the main army banged gongs to call a halt. The sound of gunfire echoed around. The whole army dismounted from horses and elephants.

Saen Kham Maen[20] cocked his head and sat shifting from side to side with mouth agape, then rushed off with his wife to meet the army and welcome their son-in-law.

The young women of Chomthong carried many presents along. Every single house brought something in a great crowd,

happy to see the son-in-law of the village head. The headman and his wife, dressed in their best, heaved themselves into litters, telling their servants to carry the gifts in an orderly fashion.

The village head reclined on a litter, looking intently ahead. Behind came phrai packed together in a big crowd as far as the eye could see. Khun Phaen lifted his head to look,

and saw his parents-in-law coming. He called out a welcome and walked to meet them. The two old folk clopped along in shoes and sat looking grand.

Khun Phaen and his son quickly prostrated. The couple greeted them and handed over gifts, asking questions one after another. Khun Phaen gave them many kinds of cloth,

two bowls of gold and silver, cartwheels, elephants, horses, cattle, buffaloes for his mother-in-law, and five salvers of cloth along with a betel tray, a golden border cloth embroidered with circles,

a footed and covered betel tray, betel boxes in good-quality lacquerware, pikes, swords, guns, spears, lances, rolled mats, and pillows embroidered with gold thread. His parents-in-law roared with laughter, showing their red mouths.

"We heard you won victory and took the city. Son-in-law has given us so many things." The old man shook with laughter, slapping his thigh, "If I could fly, I'd go to a palace in the heavens!" Both sat jiggling with joy.

---

20. Laothong's father (see ch. 10).

Towards evening, the old couple made their farewells. Khun Phaen and his son reciprocated. "We leave at the crack of dawn."

Some troops were assigned to make a camp. All slept guarded safely within a circle. The masterful Khun Phaen,
along with his troupe of famous spirits, stood guard on the lord of Chiang Mai. Thainam and the Lanchang Lao were put in charge of the two princesses and their people.

Phlai Ngam and the five hundred phrai stood guard all around, while the thirty-five volunteers went to lie down, keeping watch on the principal elephants.

Muen At Narai and two hundred phrai lay on watch as scouts in the forest. If anyone tried to enter or leave at the wrong time, they were captured and held by the troops.

In the evening at torch-lighting time after the sun set and darkness fell, the troops in charge of bonfires kept watch, beat gongs, and made inspections.

Phlai Ngam patrolled to check if any bonfire went out. As night fell, Thai soldiers who had got themselves wives went in to sleep,
and called their wives into the mosquito net, "Come and take care of me." Some laid out mattresses and pillows, and massaged one another. One tried teaching his sulky young wife to pray saying "I-ii."[21]

The Lao girl said, "You're no young bull." "I used to teach I-Duek and she didn't complain." The Lao girl lowered her face and said "I-ii." The husband chuckled and cuddled her.

Ta-Lo said, "Oh, you two start early in the evening! This will make old folk like me unable to restrain ourselves. Young I-Toe, why are you lying quietly there? Come in and massage me for a bit."

Young Toe, who was deaf, replied sharply, "Tomorrow I can't walk, my legs are so stiff. If you can get me an elephant to ride, I'll love you. All of us have busted legs."

Ta-Lo was angry. "See here, I dislike you, you deaf bat, enough to throw up, to vomit, to heave." "Leaves?" I-Toe cried, "I'd like leaves in a curry."

Friends laughed, "Oh Ta-Lo, don't bother her. This isn't your home ground. Whatever you say, she can't hear. Not everybody has gone to sleep yet, old fellow."

Ta-Lo laughed and cried out, "In a minute, I'm coming over and dragging her off." He got out of the mosquito net, walked over, grabbed I-Toe's hand, and pulled her along.

---

21. Meaning humming, usually with eyes closed, as an exercise to still and concentrate the mind. Perhaps he is urging her to relax and be less sulky.

I-Toe screwed up her face and said, "I'm very hungry. Stop dragging me along. I'm not willing." Ta-Lo said, "Get up in there." He went into the mosquito net and mounted her.

I-Toe shrieked and wriggled. Her lowercloth was ripped to pieces. Just when Ta-Lo was getting into position, I-Toe stood up. Ta-Lo said, "You're really uncontrollable. It's worse than herding buffaloes."

He gripped her neck with both hands. She kicked at Ta-Lo's throat, knocking him down. With bleary eyes, Ta-Lo readied to grab her. She shouted, "I'm scared to death!"[22] and sprawled down flat.

I-Toe could not match his strength. Ta-Lo said, "Wonderful, like jelly." Friends laughed, and Ta-Lo stabbed away until he reached the end of his strength and dozed off.

In the pitch dark of midnight, the Thai were fast asleep. Some lay embracing their wives and breathing softly. The Chiang Mai Lao were dead to the world.

Six women who had old husbands picked up their gold and valuables and sneaked away in a group with bodies trembling. They went outside the fence, found the entrance to a path,

and walked until they came across some people sitting on the road. Ai-Pu with the cauliflower ears leapt up and gave chase. His mates cried out, "Lao or Thai? Male or female? Where are you running to?"

The soldiers caught them and recognized their faces. "So the Lao from the main army are off to the fair! This is Ta-Lo's wife!" He laughed out loud. "Tie her up and put her in my mosquito net.

It's our bonus payment. Why should we catch people for nothing? Let's give them a pounding through to dawn. Is this a moneybag or what, tied round her belly?" He tugged an end, and the string came of its own accord.

The gang of friends laughed as the cloth slipped down. "Damnit, hair up to her ears." "Make her dance the forest dance." "That would be a sight." They cheered in chorus.

In the morning they delivered the prisoners to the army officers. "Let their husbands come and collect them." Phlai Ngam and Khun Phaen ordered the vanguard to raise flags

and fire off volleys. They marched through the lofty forest, bristling with guns and spears, then left the forest and came to deciduous woods.[23]

---

22. ยั่น ตาย พ่อ แล้ว, *yan tai pho laeo*, in Lao.

23. ป่าแดง, *pa daeng*, the red forest.

People, horses, elephants, cattle, and buffaloes felt comfortable in the shade with dry ground underfoot and water in the streams. As the red sun was hidden by the trees, they set up camp to sleep.

Next morning they ate and then marched, herding the crowd of Lao families along, across the deep forest on the uplands, past the city of Lampang, and beyond.

The great phalanx of people went through Thoen, back into the forest, and through the defile. The families were patrolled all the time.

In that region the path went up steeply among gorges and overhangs where people could hide. Close guard was kept. Any Lao caught escaping was beaten to death.

Guards with gongs stood watching at each one hundred paces. If anyone went into the defile, hid, and did not reappear, a gong was beaten as a signal. Lao who strayed off were warned to keep to the path.

Past the defile, some almost lost their footing. Flocks of birds perched on trees in the broad forest. Along the way, the King of Chiang Mai looked at the birds and trees.

Heron perched on a tall *krasang*. A lordly peacock spread its wings on a *yang* tree. Parrots sat in pairs on an upright *kalang*. Crake pecked at bunches of *anchan*.

Imperial pigeons crouched on a crystal mango. A pygmy owl perched peering from a cinnamon tree. Mynas massed on branches of *inthanin*. Orioles called through the forest.

The sun stooped towards evening. Flocks of birds flew through the forest, swooping down to find somewhere to roost, or bringing prey for the young in their nests.

Some flew to eat in the wild, while their nest fellows waited, then flew back to where their young waited sleepily on the end of a branch.

Weaverbirds and warblers whirled around chattering. One looted material from a nest, like drawing silk thread. The owner of the nest saw, swooped across, and attacked, pecking and noisily complaining.

"What a pity! Even birds have anger. If one does something wrong, another attacks. I've lost Chiang Mai, city and palace. There's nobody left to help me fight."

He watched the tree leaves fluttering in the wind, *yang* leaves falling, and a branch swaying and breaking, spreading a cloud of pollen.

His spirits sank as the sun dropped and the light faded. A gibbon hid on a branch, whooping for its mate. The more he thought of Chiang Mai the more he shivered and mumbled plaintively like a spectral.

"In the city where I once happily lived and played, I never listened to a gibbon whooping. I used to hear the strains of horns, but now I listen to crickets in the deep forest."

The sun slipped down and set. Bird calls rang crisp and clear in the silence. A breeze blew his heart almost as cold as death. His eyes were glutted with sad tears.

Soifa and the queen followed the path through the forest, sobbing and grieving for their city. "Pity us, we've wandered many days.

I used to see palace spires, but now all I see are forest trees. I used to be surrounded by fort, camp, and pillar. Now all around are hills.

We used to enjoy the fragrance of perfume, now only the scent of flowers. We had ladies to fan and comb us, now we are buffeted by the wind.

At times for bathing, we had fragrant water. Now we suffer the dew along the way. For light, we were lit by brilliant lamps, but here we make do with the moon.

Once we listened to the ensemble of pipe, conch, and horn but here the only sounds are the birds. Once we saw dances regularly, now our eyes are full of the dancing of peacocks.

Once we heard fiddle, *khaen*, and plaintive flute playing in harmony. Oh, we left the city because of karma and now must listen to the call of the gibbon,

an unfamiliar and hair-raising sound. Here, strange spirits and spectrals soar around. Cicadas trill in the undergrowth so faintly it sounds fearful in the forest.

Oh gods of the woods and the great hills, of every thicket and stream, of every hollow with herbs and horsetail creepers, please help to protect us against peril.

Oh lord spirits and guardian spirits, great powers of the hills, of the great ironwood, *thakian, yanang, yang,* and *phayom* of every forest, please drive away the fearful wild animals.

When we return to Chiang Mai, we'll make two *baisi*, and feed you with liquor, duck, chicken, liver of buffalo and ox, and turtle, both head and tail. I fear the sounds of the gibbons and the spirits in the forest.

Please make their calls disappear, and silence reign." The two ladies raised their hands to embrace each other, and wept along the way.

Phlai Ngam rode his horse at the head of the troops, seeing the beautiful and lofty *sak,*[24] *son, ngao, ngio, ding, takhian, yung, yang, pring, prang, pru, prong, prayong, sai,*

phikun, kaeo, ket, kum, chumsaeng, yang daeng, oi chang, hang lai, takhop, khoi, khae, khang, krangkrai, lamyai, yisun, pip, jampa,

mafo, faep, mafueang, mafai, khai-nao, dipli, plao, taorang, philang-kasa, sak, sik, sa-uek, masang, kradang-nga, pheka, prakham-kai, khrai, khroe,[25]

chalut, liap, rabiap,[26] *khla, hua phluang, takhrai, khruang,*[27] *tumka, ta-suea, khanun, khanan,*[28] *phanjam, maklam, makla, makluea, maduea, rakam, kral-ampho, salaengphan,*

tum,[29] *tat, hat, hiang, krathum-thong,*[30] *taeo, tong,*[31] *takhop, makham, nam-han, pip, peng, talingpring, chingchan, nomsawan, jan, in, krathin-phiman.*

Admiring the trees, Phlai Ngam rode his horse along, cutting across forest, stream, and river. The troops, elephants, and horses were given a long rest. They passed the outpost of Tha Kwian,

and entered Sawankhalok. Local officials gathered. The troops stayed for half a day before continuing straight through the deep forest.

Families, oxen, buffaloes, elephants, horses, and porters were weighed down with goods. At Phitsanulok, the governor came out happily to welcome the army to stay. The oxen, buffaloes, elephants, and horses were exhausted.

In three days they had recovered and set off again, with masses of elephants and horses jogging along, carrying supplies.

Among the Lao, young, old, and widows were wasted almost to death and could walk no further. Suffering from bellyache and diarrhea they cried out, "When will we reach Ayutthaya?"

Some were so weak from hunger they dropped asleep in the forest. "Father and mother far away cannot look after me!" "At home we had baskets of rice, but in the forest there are only tamarind fruit." "I brought nothing so I'm starving."

Babes in arms fell sick. Without banana or sugar, they had to suffer eating sap or wild yams. Hungry, desperate, starving, staggering, people shouted out, "We're down to skin and bones!"

---

24. As in the example in chapter 21, this is a poetic exercise to string tree names together to fit the rules of rhyming.

25. A generic name for a vine or creeper.

26. Not found as a flora name. Means "order, neatness." Perhaps just rhyming with *liap*.

27. ครวง, unidentified.

28. ขนัน, unidentified, but given in Bradley as a tree, and often linked with *khanun*.

29. ตุม, perhaps ตุมกา, *tumka*.

30. Assumed to be a variant of *krathum*, but not identified.

31. ต้อง, not identified.

"In our city of Chiang Mai, anyone sick is looked after by their parents. They feed them fish and rice, morning and evening, and hold ceremonies to propitiate the spirits by day and night."

"Our grandfathers and grandmothers, when they died, were placed in a coffin, with the rat-tat-tat of many *thon* drums. Here people are left curled up with an empty stomach for the vultures to pick at their eyeballs."

"We eat rice alone. " "We lie down but don't sleep because we're famished." "For ages, we've been without betel, without pan, without tobacco, without rice, without fish, without chili dip."

"I haven't put a big helping of sticky rice in my mouth for ages." "Since leaving Chiang Mai, I've had no water to wash in." "I'm covered in stripes and streaks both back and front where I've been beaten badly by the Thai lads."

"Can't walk along without being shoved forward and shoved back." "Can't walk, can't listen, can't even squat down for a shit." "Walk off the path and, bang, bang! Every time." "Stop for a bit and they beat you to death. Oh poor Lao!"

The Thai hollered and shouted. "We're getting close to Phichit, Pa!" Phlai Ngam dug in his heels and galloped ahead, excited at the thought of his sweetheart in her home.

"Oh, right now is Simala grieving to see her lover's face? Who can look after my beloved? When I reach the house, I can comfort you.

You're like a lotus flower blooming atop a stem. I left you to blossom in the room. Nobody else should possess and fondle the flower while its owner is away in the hills.

Swarms of bees will fly up and cluster round to take the pollen. I feel sorry for the beautiful lotus.

At times for sleeping, do you walk around for ages reciting *nirat*? Oh eye's delight, right now are you sleeping in the house, or sitting with face poised ready for something,

or plaiting a garland of jasmine, or combing your hair, or grieving? Or is my precious in a waiting mood,

constantly glancing at the gate of the residence? Are you still suffering from missing me right now? Or are you nothing but joy and laughter? The more I think, the more I sigh, shake, and grieve." Riding along, he was almost crazed with longing.

He saw Lao soldiers looking hungry and tired, some injured badly and unable to walk. The more he looked, the more he felt distressed. "This lot is slowing us down.

Ai-Mi, why aren't you moving, you lowlife? If you don't walk I'll slash you a hundred times. How about that?" He turned his horse back to drive them along. Khun Phaen rode over.

"Hey, Phlai Ngam, what did they do to you? Why do you want to attack them? Are you missing your wife, damn you?" Phlai Ngam called out, "It's infuriating.

There's only a little way to go, but nobody's moving." Some had stopped and could walk no farther but only gaze at the tree line ahead. Some sat crying, while others panted and wheezed.

Khun Phaen punched him in the head. "If you can fly, then why don't you, damn you? You're like a spider or lizard that sees a hole and wants to leap in as fast as it can."

Reaching Phichit in the cool of the evening sun, they dropped their loads, tethered the horses and elephants, released the oxen and buffaloes, and relaxed.

The mass of people swarmed down to bathe. Just before nightfall they were rounded up to pitch camp. Huts and shelters were set up in rows, and people busily steamed rice, grilled fish, and made curry.

Some went to collect vegetables and banana flower shoots, or snatch ducks and chicken from anywhere. "I'll go to spear a pig to give us some strength." A Jek protested noisily.

A large pavilion was erected for the King of Chiang Mai and his beloved wife. Soithong and her Thai retinue were lodged alongside.

Officers and men of the army were placed on guard. Phra Phichit hurried over with local officials and had the army make camp at the edge of the forest outside the town.

The villagers of the district kept careful watch. After curfew, they would not let people come and go. Horses, elephants, buffaloes, and oxen were placed around the outside. Guards sat with pikes and guns.

Soifa and Soithong were screened from view, and nobody was allowed to enter or leave without being questioned by the guards every time.

Khun Phaen and Phlai Ngam walked to the residence. Phra Phichit, Busaba, and Simala came to welcome them.

Servants carried water up to fill a tub. One fell and broke a bucket.[32] Inside the kitchen, people made curry and chopped pork and beef for the meal.

---

32. ครุ, *khru*, a bucket made with bamboo and lined with dammar (Wibun, *Phojananukrom hatthakam*, 85–86).

Father and son bathed and powdered their faces. Servants carried in the meal, and the two were invited to eat.

When they had finished, betel and pan were served. Father and son gave Phra Phichit a large share of the goods. Silver, gold, and cloth were brought over, along with many elephants, horses, oxen, buffaloes,

carts, howdahs, and people. Several men and women were selected. Then they related the story of the battle with the Lao. "On their side, the men were all able and skillful.

If someone other than me had gone as army commander, he wouldn't have made it back here. Only because my son had knowledge and bravery were we able to attack and win victory."

Phra Phichit laughed. "I knew that already. If it'd been anyone other than you, the attack wouldn't have come off. If hundreds and thousands of others had gone up there, they wouldn't have matched the enemy's skill."

The three chatted away until the last light of the sun. Birds flocked around, flying in pairs to roost.

Phra Phichit ordered his servants to find mattresses and pillows. "Khun Phaen can sleep in the sitting hall with a screen of mosquito net and curtains." Khun Phaen went in and slept.

Phra Phichit went off to his room. Phlai Ngam's thoughts turned to gentle Simala. Becoming aroused, he rushed off to find her.

He opened the door, entered the room, and sat down close beside her. He embraced her, hugged and kissed, and then spoke. "While I've been far away, I put love out of my mind.

I had no happiness, only suffering—unable to eat, unable to sleep, as if a mountain had split asunder and fallen on my chest. When Chiang Mai surrendered the city to us,

and the war was over, only then was I happy. We hastened back through the forest with the great army, not stopping but always rushing onward, in order to see the face of my beloved bedfellow.

We reached Phichit today, and I thought of coming to find you at once but I was afraid of my father. He was getting at me along the way."

With these words, he hugged her close, cradled her breasts which looked full, budding, and tight, and caressed them to arouse her.

Simala pushed his hands away and complained, "Don't come here with your fancy talk. I'm not listening so don't go on.

Saying that you were thinking deeply of me—you shouldn't talk such tricky, deceptive words. At the start, you thought of me for about half a day. After that you were carried away by the Lao.

At Chiang Mai you ate sticky rice. Why should you think back to ordinary rice? You attacked Chiang Mai and took it in one attempt. Did you get excited over the Lao girls among the war prisoners?

All good-lookers, not bad! Am I to think that you hate and fear girls so much you ignored them? Or could you restrain yourself like a barren monk? I don't believe you. Stop trying to fool me."

Phlai Ngam embraced her, caressed and comforted her with his hands, and replied with a smile, "I'm not like you say.

The Lao country is full of young women, but I don't fancy them. Were I given one, I would not want her. In my eyes, I find them hateful.

You say I was eating sticky rice, but I didn't chew. I thought about myself and feared I'd have backache. I was there a year and didn't eat it even once. All through, I've just been grieving to hurry back here.

When a missive reached the army, I was happy that I was returning to see your face. This is the truth. I'm not just saying it, Simala. Don't be suspicious."

While speaking, he pulled her close and embraced her lovingly, caressing to arouse her confusion. A great storm blew in with a crash of rain.

The sky exploded and rain sluiced down, though out of season and late at night. Thunder rumbled across the world, breaking with a great crack and gradually fading away.

Meeting after a long time, both joined in joy. Whirled around by the full force of love, they clung close together until both fell asleep.

In the bright sunlight of dawn, as each had the other on his mind, Khun Phaen and Phra Phichit awoke at the same time.

After washing their faces, they came to the central hall, and sent for all the nobles to discuss dispatching the princesses down. "By land I think it's impossible because of the difficulties.

We must prepare and send down a missive requesting officers to bring up a victory[33] barge with curtains, tall regalia, horn, conch, and gong."

They all agreed and promptly prepared a missive, affixed a seal, and ordered Khun Phaeng to take it down.

Khun Phaeng received the order, took leave, went to a six-fathom boat, backed away from the landing, and left. Servants paddled along strongly,

---

33. เอกไชย, *ekkachai*, primary victory.

hurrying past many cities, towns, and districts, reaching Ayutthaya in seven days. They halted at the landing by the Rattanachai Tower Gate.[34]

Khun Phaeng disembarked and called his servants to take the missive up immediately. They went into the inner official sala where all the chaophraya were gathered.

Khun Phaeng informed one of the chaophraya, who promptly broke open the cylinder, read the missive, and realized its importance. He spoke with the others to enter and inform the king.

The king, eminence of the city, resided in the excellent crystal palace, enjoying perfect contentment at all times.

When the sun had reached nine o'clock, he came out to the audience hall at the front with all his senior officials in attendance without exception, making a great assembly.

A chaophraya made obeisance and addressed the king on the current matter. He produced and unfurled the missive, and read its contents from the beginning.

"At present Khun Phaen, the army commander, has marched back with swarms of families, and halted at Phichit, a city with a fine landing. He sends down a missive with this information.

It is now the season of the sixth month.[35] Rain is falling and water from the north is flooding the forests. To march the army overland to the city will weaken elephants and horses and cause them pain.

Enough boats can be requisitioned from people here to dispatch the families down. But to send the radiant Soithong and Soifa down by canopy boat,

there is a lack of golden curtains to screen them from view, and we fear this may displease Your Majesty." At the end of the missive, the chaophraya prostrated three times and waited for the king's order.

The king had heard in full the contents of the missive. He ordered officials to quickly oversee the dispatch of boats,

including procession boats, guard boats, and outlier boats along with everything required such as tall regalia and golden curtains to screen from view. The king then returned inside.

---

34. หอรัตนไชย, *ho rattanachai*, a watergate at the northeast corner of the island. The *ho rattanachai* or Tower of the Jewels of Victory first appears in the Ayutthaya chronicles around 1564 (RCA, 41; gate no. 10 in KCK, 198; see map 8).

35. If this were lunar months, it would be around April, at the height of the hot dry season. These must be months counted from Songkran, making it around September.

The senior officials took the order, went out to sit at the main inner sala, and dispatched orders to officeholders everywhere to arrange

throne barges for sitting, barges of honor, and everything needed for each position in a flotilla. Oarsmen of strong build were conscripted to man the craft wearing red shirts.

The river echoed with the sounds of preparation. Oarsmen rowed strongly up to the northern cities, beating the timing loudly, and churning the water into foam with their paddles.

In ten days and ten nights of racing along, they reached Phichit, moored at a landing with a covered passageway coming down to the river, and waited to prepare the flotilla.

Khun Phaeng disembarked from the main boat, hurried to find Khun Phaen and Phra Phichit in the governor's residence, and informed them of all the details.

Once the two had been informed, Khun Phaen said that he would go to the lodging of King Chiang In.

He entered and imparted all the news. "At present, His Majesty the King is concerned over the journey.

As this is the rainy season, the families will not be able to go overland. Hence His Majesty has sent royal boats to take the princesses down to the city.

Tomorrow there is an auspicious time at eleven. Please go to Soithong and inform her of all this by the end of the day. Also inform the troops and families—everybody."

The King of Chiang Mai trembled and wept in fear of the punishment awaiting him. "This time I'm done for, Khun Phaen. Please help.

If you don't give me some assistance on this occasion, I think I won't survive with my life. When I go down south, I don't know what will happen.

Please look after everything until we reach the city." Khun Phaen said, "Don't be troubled. I should be able to talk a way out of this for you, make the king's anger disappear, and have him support you.

I don't think there's a problem achieving that much." He went down to the landing to have all the boats prepared. Soithong was invited to embark on a royal barge.

Soifa and the King of Chiang Mai boarded another. The troops hollered, beat gongs, and shouted loudly. At an auspicious time, they departed.

Khun Phaen and his son said farewell to Phra Phichit who came to see them off at the landing. Phlai Ngam turned to tell Simala, "Soon I'll come back to fetch you."

With tears falling in deepening misery, Simala raised her hands to wai her husband. The boats moved away to the sound of drum, conch, and horn echoing across the water.

Khaek drum, flute, *ranat*, and gong played in clear and sweet harmony. The oarsmen sang boat songs, all with strong voices. Entering the stream, the boats passed through Phichit,

where villagers and townsfolk massed to watch, standing packed together on the landings, chattering away to one another. "Never seen a water procession like this. My oh my!"

At Boraphet while waiting for other boats, some Lao saw groups of villagers selling fish. Feeling hungry, they tried to snatch some. One grabbed at a catfish,

and fumbled around, trying to grip its tail, but the fish jumped up and flopped about. Granny Suk shouted out, "None of your tricks!" A hungry man with a head like a coconut shell took some fish anyway.

At Nakhon Sawan, *thon* drums, barrel drums, horn, and conch played magnificently. At Trok Phra they went downstream to Nam Song. Villagers ran up noisily to make merit.

Through Hua Daen, Hua Dan, Khung Thaphao, and Chi Dak Khanon, onlookers were packed together, pushing and shoving, rushing round in circles, and shouting at one another.

They halted to spend a night at Chainat where a *klongyon* was played by loud barrel drums, horn, conch, Khaek drum, and Java flute.

Rather late in the afternoon, they moored at a royal jetty. The governor and local officials came in a crowd to offer gifts to the princesses.

Villagers swarmed on both banks to catch a glimpse of the procession in all its beauty and variety. Young women sat at three rows of shops beside the governor's house, showing off their pretty figures.

Lao and Thai disembarked to go shopping. Vegetables and fish were available in profusion on both banks. The young Lao men went off to flirt, swaggering into the market,

swishing their lowercloths to reveal their black legs. One showed off his fine limbs to a southern lady but she turned her face away, saying, "You villains with black legs and northern beads,

babbling away and eyeing us up, with your dirty hair like clowns in a mask play." She looked over, saw his balls dangling, and ran slap into the shop of an old Mon lady.

"Oh mother, oh lord![36] You spilled a bowl of shrimp paste. You tousle-headed shit-eater, why don't you look, bashing in like that all the time?[37] Opening your lowercloth is shameful."

⦈

Now to tell of the king at Ayutthaya. He summoned all the chaophraya. "Arrange for our city to be beautifully decked out to look splendid,

so that the Chiang Mai people fear our power as if this were the abode of the fatal Lord of Darkness. Have all the traders, great and small, moor their junks along the banks of the river

together with all the rafts so that the place looks busy. On both sides of the roads, have rows of shops crammed together. Make sure all the troops are on duty.

Let them see the might of the Thai city so that they are as shocked as if they were being killed by Lord Matjurat, and will all want to flee in panic."

The chaophraya took the order and made obeisance to take leave. Courtiers followed behind, chattering. Officials bustled around, intent on responding to the royal order promptly.

Call-up papers were issued. Elephants and horses were busily organized. Crowds of people rushed hither and thither to get everything arranged.

⦈

Now to tell of Khun Phaen, in command of the Lao army. At dawn he set off to the sound of hollering, cheering, gongs, drums, and flutes.

The rows of oarsmen paddled in time with the beating of a staff. They came downstream through Ban Ngio and Hua Wang, hollering loudly and making a great racket. To describe the journey in detail would take too long,

so we will hurry ahead with an economical account of places along the route. Everywhere, people rushed in great numbers to sit and watch.

The crowds were big at Mueang In, Mueang Phrom, Phla Mu, Ban Oi, and Phra Ngam. All the way to the river mouth at Bang Phutsa, masses of people sat to watch them pass.

They went through Ban Kaeo and Ban Ri without stopping. Villagers from the district of Tha To came out to look. Mon people from around there powdered their faces, put on lowercloths, and rushed to watch.

---

36. อุย ย่าย อุย ขมิ, *ui ya ui khami*, in Mon.

37. อะ ด่า ราว ยอง เนาะคะเมะ เคลิง, *a kha rao yong no khamo khloeng*; from "bashing" in Mon, translation speculative.

The inhabitants of Ban Kup and Ban Tanim collected in a fine crowd along the waterway. At the entrance to the Maha Sang River, they went past hollering, and approached the river junction.

Crowds of Mon called out "Oh lord!"[38] and ran down frantically. "Oh mother! Oh father!"[39] They knocked into one another and fell over, giving themselves black faces and bleary eyes.

The flotilla reached Three Bo Trees, where the crowds were raucous. The oarsmen sang boat songs and beat their paddles loudly on the water. At Ban Lao they found themselves among woman traders who left their breasts bare, tying cloths only around their waists.

The traders crowded around to get a look, pushing and shoving, dropping betel and pan all around, climbing down the riverbanks with babes in arms strapped on their waists and wailing.

At Wat Rak Khae, young men and women watched in crowds, pushing and shoving, shouting loudly, scolding at their parents, waving hands up and down with chopping movements.

They reached the elephant enclosure,[40] a Mon locality. The throng shouted, "Over there! Oh mother! Look at the boats."[41] Mon fell over, picked themselves up, ran off, and cursed one another. "Your mother![42] Your cane hit my arse."

The leading boats moored at the landing of the Red Gate, and others moored below the walls right up to the end. People packed every gate and landing, watching open-mouthed.

A jetty broke and crashed down into the water. Granny Mak was bewildered and looked as if she would throw up. Granny Sa, a nun, opened her mouth wide and screamed. Elder Duang cried, "My shoulder robe has been ripped off!"

Granny Ma Rattana, a nun, fell down. Novice Khong and Elder Ngok managed to escape, but Nang Baen and Nang San were done for. Abbot Koeng looked on, jiggling his whole body around.

Jek Lok fell flat on his back, hitting Granny Phon. She grabbed him by mistake, thinking it was her husband, Old Leadhead. "Well, he'll do!" Others bashed their heads on stumps or got covered in mud. That's enough of that.

---

38. อุย แหล่ง, *ui laeng*, in Mon.
39. อุย ย่าย อี ต, *ui yai ita*, in Mon.
40. See p. 729, note 39.
41. อิเนาะ กะม่อน อุมิ ฉิ กำปั้น, *ino kamon u-mi chi kampan*, in Mon.
42. อ้าย ตอก ขะย่าย, *ai dok khayai*, in Mon.

Officials, high and low, including astrologers, together with servants, phrai, and nobles' retainers, were frantically making arrangements as the sound of boat songs approached the landing.

A chaophraya went to fetch palace governesses and a big crowd of sentinelles. Seats were placed beside the royal landing for receiving the princesses on arrival at the Floating Pavilion.

Once Soithong and Soifa were received, palace governesses guarded them closely, and arranged for them to be bathed and dressed, ready for presentation once the king had risen.

Chaophraya Yommarat arranged fierce executioners, all carrying swords ready to slash. The best royal punishers[1] from the palace guard carried Enforcer canes bound as thick as an arm.

To escort the lord of Chiang Mai, they wore tight sompak and belts strapped crosswise on their chests, hefted large pikes, trussed the bound canes together with the pikes,

and carried whipping equipment including leather lashes. Ngam Mueang, several prison warders, Ratchasak, a deputy of the palace, Pradaengjan, and a group of jail guards were all present.[2]

Elephants and horses stood by. The lord of Chiang Mai went up first. His wife and I-Mai walked in chains.

Military officers guarding the Lanchang princess looked around to left and right. The more they saw, the more they were amused. One got so carried away that he collided with a shop.

A young girl cried out, "Ugh! Truly shameful. You fall and roll around like a lump of charcoal." The Lao dusted off his head and said, "Never mind.[3] Just bruised my head." He hitched up his cloth Khmer-style and left.

---

1. See p. 709, note 3.

2. Pradaengjan is a *samian tra* under Yommarat, *sakdina* 600 (KTS, 1:230). For the other officials, see p. 709, note 5.

3. ข้อย ยั่น, *khoi yan*, in Lao.

The King of Chiang Mai, his wife, and I-Mai were in a pitiful state. Their faces were pale with fear and set in a crazed look. They babbled about apologizing and fearing the royal power.

At the sight of the executioners and punishers, they thought their lives would not be spared. Sweat bathed their bodies. People crowding around like an army of ants struck them with alarm.

They walked along in procession, disheartened and desolate, bowing their faces in prayer with tears plopping down. I-Mai slobbered in panic. Her shit shrank and fart fled, replaced by fever and wind.

Pradaengjan gnashed his teeth, seized her hand, and growled, "Your breasts are pretty big. If you get sent to jail, I'll have fun. Put you in a cangue, and I won't sleep a wink."

Khun Phaen turned and said to the King of Chiang Mai, "Don't lose heart. I'll not abandon you so don't be concerned." The king relaxed somewhat.

When they arrived at the inner sala, a warder made obeisance and informed Phraya Yommarat, "I'm delivering the prisoner."

The senior Lanchang military officers who had been in charge of escorting the princess were sent for. "Whatever your lordship orders."

Chaophraya Jakri,[4] Chaophraya Yommarat, and the military chiefs greeted one another with smiles and conferred together on how to present the matter to the king.

Khun Phaen, Phlai Ngam, and Phra Thainam, followed by their servants, came to pay their respects. Khun Phaen bowed and crawled in. Reaching the senior officials, he spoke to them in a whisper.

"Please help the lord of Chiang Mai to avoid heavy punishment. Please arrange matters with the king so that he escapes the lash and is reprieved.

I'll provide thirty beautiful Lao girls as reward for your lordships' assistance." The ministers were pleased and laughed so hard

that they bent over double, bashed their heads together, and bumped their bottoms into one another. They stopped whispering and spoke out loud, "So you say that royal horse is dead?"

Khun Phaen replied, "Indeed, sir." A minister said, "I'll tell His Majesty." As it was close to the time of the king's appearance, they put on their sompak and bustled off.

---

4. Here called Ratchasi, the symbol on the seal of Mahatthai.

The king, adherent of the Buddha, summit of the world, was bathed comfortably, anointed with floral scents,

and arrayed with regalia including a crystal sword with filigree and diamonds. Accompanied by a bevy of inner ladies,

he went up to the Phihan Somdet[5] Audience Hall looking like the beautiful three-eyed lord of the *truengsa* heaven[6] with crown and ornaments highlighting his face. Music played loudly three times.

Palace guards chased people away as the king emerged. Outside was a great commotion. The chaophraya awaiting the audience went in to prostrate and wai together.

Chaophraya Jakri paid respect and addressed the king. "My liege, Chiang Mai has come in chains and cangue, the five irons.

Along with his wife and a female servant, he has been detained in chains in the city. He is crying for love of self and in fear of death. He looks like a simple-minded provincial,

a leader of the forest Lao, brutish of manner, prepared to leap into a fire and die for nothing, unmindful of the sin and karma he makes. He's like a short stick stuck in excrement.

What purpose does it serve to support him? As your humble servant, I see no gain, only loss. Following him, even towards heaven, would end up in mud. He fully deserves to be executed.

This brave fellow would like Your Majesty to simply pardon him. He'll make a petition, leaving matters out, adding on the end, and changing things around to secure a reduction in his punishment.

The beauteous Princess Soithong has been installed in the palace along with the princess of Chiang Mai. May Your Majesty proceed inside.

Khun Phaen, Phlai Ngam, and Phra Thainam are guarding Chiang Mai. They harbor anger and resentment and wish Chiang Mai be put to death."

The almighty king smiled, threw back his head, and laughed. "Chaophraya, don't sow confusion. This scoundrel is like a mackerel.

I won't condemn him to be chopped to pieces, but I'll threaten him first to make him weary. Have Thainam, who caused this matter, brought here for

---

5. The Wihan Somdet or Somdet Mahaprasat Audience Hall was built by King Prasat Thong to replace a hall burned down in 1643. It had a roof tiled with tin, five gilt spires, and a porch with stone statues of Chinese warriors and Chinese pillars at the eight directions. It was used for coronations and other royal ceremonies (KLW, 202; *Boranasathan*, 1:231; see map 9).

6. ตรึงษา, meaning Traitrueng (see p. 711, note 7).

questioning, along with the father and son."

The chaophraya took the order and sent a guard to run out, wielding a bundle of canes and shouting, "Where's Thainam? Bring him here, along with Khun Phaen and his son. Quickly."

Phra Thainam trembled in despair. Because of his failure, he feared a major punishment. He put on a sompak clumsily, and fumbled around with the tail flap, leaving it dangling.

People around tried to stifle their laughter. Ta-Lo said, "Oh sir, it's too much." Phra Thainam said, "Keep your words to yourself, you lowlife. It's the tail of my cloth." He tugged his cloth to hide it.

Khun Phaen and his son went ahead with Thainam stumbling along behind, tying a white prostration cloth untidily round his belly. He clumsily prostrated three times.

The king, eminence of the city, sublime in authority, called, "Heigh! Khun Phaen and Phlai Ngam,

you did not soil the reputation of the lineage of Khun Krai, the most valiant soldier on the battlefield. This time I sent you to war with thirty-five phrai.

Chiang Mai had over two hundred thousand phrai but still you could crush the Lao and put them to flight. This Chiang Mai didn't have the courage to resist. I've got my troops back and gained a dependency because of you.

From the time you marched from Ayutthaya, how many days did it take to reach there? I know you had a great battle at the end of the lake. Tell us the whole story without mumbling."

Khun Phaen, great savant, made obeisance. "My liege, Your Victorious Majesty, my life is beneath the royal foot.

I volunteered to go on this occasion with thirty-five able soldiers. Making a good pace, we reached the city of Chiang Mai in a month and a half.

At the great lake we halted, dug a moat, set out spikes, and made a base camp. After consultation and agreement, I and my son, just the two of us,

disguised ourselves as Lao, went in to the city at the third watch, and sent everyone to sleep and snore. Phra Thainam's men had nothing to fear. Seven hundred were released.

They slashed the warders and palace guards to death in large numbers, entered the armory to seize weapons, and stole horses from the palace stables for everybody.

We departed by the gate and returned to camp. That afternoon, the Lao brought a great army, and I arrayed our troops to confront them. The Lao army was crushed and completely destroyed.

This can be seen in detail. It is not hearsay. In the evening, the city was put to sleep and the lord of Chiang Mai captured." Ending his account, Khun Phaen prostrated.

The king was delighted to hear this account. "Khun Phaen, you did well on this occasion. You deserve to be made a phraya."

He ordered the Inner Treasury to arrange a betel tray, golden bowl, shirts, cloth, a saber with a gold handguard, many other articles, and cash of twenty chang as reward.

"I hereby appoint you to the illustrious rank of Phraya Surin Luechai, governor of Kanburi, as is fitting for gaining such a victory."

The king turned his face to address Phlai Ngam. "On this occasion, you have won great favor. In warfare, you resemble your father. You both boldly volunteered to go on campaign.

You are still just a youth with a slender build, but you are skilled in mantra lore that makes people quail. I will bestow on you an illustrious rank, and reward you as befitting your achievement.

You become Muen Wai Woranat, lieutenant of the pages on the right. I bestow on you a valuable saber, and various silkwool cloth,

also cash of fifteen chang, flask, insignia, fine sword[7] with handguard, and nielloware tray with golden accoutrements,[8] all fine things as reward for Muen Wai."

Next the king instructed Chaophraya Yommarat to issue orders to the district officer to commandeer some land. "Find somewhere big and spacious in the city center. Make sure it's close to the palace."

He gave orders to a department head of the palace guard, "Build a house for Wai with about five apartments, along with a kitchen, and surrounding fence. Don't delay. Finish it quickly."

The king turned his face to Phra Thainam, and became angry enough to kill. He roared like a lion, "Mm! You did beautifully, Thainam!

It was a waste to favor you as a phraya. I did not realize you were such a cowardly lowlife. I trusted you to go to war but you let the Lao catch you like a monkey on a string.

You didn't even put up a fight but gave up in fear. Tcha! Your heart is like a woman's. You let them overpower and capture you so shamefully.

If I did not fear the karma, I'd have you thrashed with two canes. You brought

---

7. บั้ง จะหรี่ (SS), จะรี่ (WK), perhaps จรี, *jari*, a Khmer word for a knife, sword, or spear.
8. Probably a betel set.

shame to your master, you slave. Issue an order to reduce him to the status of phrai, and put him to work as a gatekeeper."

The king gave orders to a department head of the main guard, "Bring the lord of Chiang Mai for me to threaten." The guard took the order, crawled quickly away, and rushed down to the boat.

He informed the warders, "The king orders the lord of Chiang Mai be brought." He was hoisted left and right, and carried into the audience.

The king roared like a lion. "Heigh! You evil-minded lord of Chiang Mai! Your behavior has displeased me.

Seizing the princess. Capturing the Thai. And on top, sending a missive with a challenge to war that was so crude and arrogant. Should not your punishment be your life?"

The lord of Chiang Mai shivered fearfully in every hair. His chest felt burned with fire. Sweat dripped from him. He wanted to disappear into the earth.

Composing himself, he made obeisance and addressed the dust beneath the royal foot. "Your Majesty, great Vishnu, over my head, as I boldly violated your royal authority, the punishment is to forfeit my life.

But I plead with Your Gracious Majesty to pardon your servant who has done wrong. Your Majesty's power is beyond estimation. Let me offer my life beneath the royal foot.

Henceforth let me truly be a servant under the dust of the royal foot along with my whole solar lineage. Let me depend on the royal foot henceforth."

The king was pleased to hear this. He said, "Ha! Heigh! Lord of Chiang Mai, today I'll pardon you but in the future do not overreach yourself."

He gave orders to his senior officials. "Mahatthai, Kalahom, and the military, take the lord of Chiang Mai off to swear fealty by drinking the water of allegiance.

Then requisition money and cloth for the thirty-five phrai who went on campaign. Make them exempt from construction and other royal works. When there's another war, they'll be sent.

Have an official order prepared to exempt them from collection of farmed taxes and market dues. Make a roster of their names with a unit head, and place them all under Muen Wai.

As for the phrai who escorted Soithong, including Kueng Kamkong, requisition money and cloth for them, and send them all back to Vientiane.

As for the Lao families and Chiang Mai officials, let them all stay in royal houses. Do not let anyone mistreat them." With the matter complete, the king returned to the inner palace.

Luang Phaen and his brave son, Phlai Ngam, left carrying their great quantity of royal gifts, and went to stay in the house with Phaen's mother.

Kalahom, Mahathai, and all the nobles took the lord of Chiang Mai off to administer the water oath of fealty.

Petty officials rushed off to erect posts to mark a house plot. Palace troops built a house with wooden walls. All the royal orders were executed.

The king, crown of Ayutthaya, resided in a glittering crystal palace among consorts and palace ladies offering their respects.

At sundown as the chariot of the moon gently glided aloft, and stars glittered across the sky, illuminating the surface of the earth

and the precious trees in the garden of the right,[9] a wind wafted fragrant and refreshing scents, uplifting the royal mind as on no other day.

"Soithong, the daughter of Lanchang, is said to be radiantly beautiful, of an appearance unseen elsewhere in all the three worlds.

And this little Soifa, daughter of the Chiang Mai lord, how dazzling is her appearance?" With these thoughts, he ordered the head palace governess,

"Fetch Soithong and Soifa up here." The governess made obeisance and left. She told the two princesses to get dressed and powder their faces to be as brilliant as a full moon.

They wound their hair into chignons that suited their faces, fixed them with golden hairpins, inserted heavenly flowers, hung sparkling earrings from both ears,

encircled both wrists with golden bracelets, slid nine-jeweled rings on both left and right hands, and clad them in uppercloths with an attractive golden stripe and lowercloths with a *kanok* pattern.

Looking as strikingly beautiful as *kinnari*, they followed one another out with the governess leading the way into the golden palace where they prostrated to the dust of the royal foot.

The governess made obeisance and raised her hands in wai above her head. "Princess Soithong is prostrating on the right, while the body prostrating to the royal foot on the left is Princess Soifa."

---

9. See p. 684, note 24.

The king looked at both ladies, their manners, and attitude in every detail. The manner of each was different.

He examined Soithong. She had a soft face, superb figure, and gentle manners—perfect in every way. "So this is the one with such fame in the Lao country."

She seemed quiet and reserved, with a youthful beauty and friendly manners befitting a young lady. "So this was why she became so famous in the Lao country that Chiang Mai came to know and tried to seize her."

Then he turned to examine Soifa and saw she had an affected manner. "Her poise and bearing are truly good. Her only fault is that she looks sulky.

Her eyes are very sharp and they dart around. After a quick glance, I feel bored. She looks really very young and pretty in every way, but seems like a drama actress.

Soithong, the daughter of Lanchang, has both rank and good manners. But this Princess Soifa looks frightening." The king said to the head governess,

"At present Wai has won favor and been given the position of Muen Wai along with a house, servants, and everything, but he still has no wife to carry water.

I'll give little Soifa to him. Muen Wai is a handsome fellow. Soifa is like a dancer. If she behaves badly, she can be reprimanded.

Head governess, how do you feel about this? As Wai has just proved himself by winning a victory, I should give him a reward to encourage him in royal service."

The head governess prostrated to the dust of the royal foot to receive the royal inquiry, and gave her reply. "It is most fitting for the king to present her to Phra Wai.

Just now he won a victory and took the Lao country. His fame has spread to every town. If Your Majesty grants him Soifa as wife, it will strengthen his loyalty."

Hearing this, the king smiled brightly. "Yes, governess, I like what you say. Wai is a suitable match for Soifa."

He turned to speak to Soithong. "I'll support you befitting your rank. You'll be presented with betel boxes in gold and nielloware, fifty chang of silver, diamond rings,

silk and cloth, and a residence in the large group of brick buildings." Everything was presented to Soithong, including a snake ring and glittering diamond earrings with each stone fine and valuable.

Next he spoke to Soifa. "You need not fear. I'll not let you be shamed but will support you well by giving you as the wife of Muen Wai.

For when you go out to be seen in public, I'll provide you with silver, gold, silk, and cloth befitting for both husband and wife. Do not feel sorry. If in the future, you face poverty, come and speak to me."

The king went out to the front. The mass of senior officials all around prostrated and crawled forward. The king was seated on a throne
under a white umbrella to speak on affairs of state. Nobles crowded around to address the king according to his wish. Seeing him looking glum, the king mused that the lord of Chiang Mai had been there for some time.

So he said, "Ha! Heigh! Lord of Chiang Mai, I'm sending you back home. Also I'm returning the families, men and women, and palace ladies to travel home with you.

Go to look after your palace and territory. Protect them against military threats from north and south. If an enemy who is beyond your powers appears in any direction, send a missive down here."

The lord of Chiang Mai felt he was flying in the sky with happiness. He bowed and prostrated to the king. "May I serve the royal foot until death.

If in the future I break my word and incur your anger, have me executed. As guarantee that I'll not lapse, may I offer my daughter beneath the royal foot."

The king smiled and laughed. "Go to your city, lord of Chiang Mai. You can come and go to see her with no problem.

About your daughter, do not worry. I appreciate greatly that you give her to me, lord of Chiang Mai. Do not feel belittled by what I'm about to tell you. Allow me to give Soifa to Phlai Ngam.

The pair are very suitable for each other. Soifa's appearance is enchanting. Phlai Ngam's knowledge is excellent. The two are very alike in their beauty.

Don't be disappointed that she is given to someone of lower rank. I love Phlai Ngam very much, and have appointed him as a lieutenant of the royal pages. I ask you not to harbor resentment against me."

The lord of Chiang Mai heard the king's request. His heart lurched and he felt desolate at the loss of honor for his solar lineage. Trembling, he could not speak.

"Oh precious daughter of mine, why is there so much bad fortune? If I object, I fear it will irritate the royal foot." Out of necessity, he prostrated in gratitude.

"I've presented you with my daughter to be a servant of the royal foot until death. If the king grants her to Phra Wai, that is according to the royal wish.

This Phra Wai has gained honor. He's a shrewd, talented fellow of military lineage. He has become a lieutenant of the pages in royal service. I'll depend on him from now on."

The king went up inside. Nobles returned home. The lord of Chiang Mai went to his lodging and informed his wife about the royal order.

Nang Soi Sumali was happy to hear from her husband that they would return home, but sad about her daughter, her life's jewel.

She sent I-Mai to find her. "Go and call Soifa immediately." I-Mai rushed off and told Soifa to come.

Arriving at her father's residence, Soifa raised her clasped hands and prostrated at his feet. The lord of Chiang Mai hugged his daughter and wept, saying, "Your father and mother will leave you and return home.

Because we had you to present to the king, his anger abated and our city was returned. But you'll stay in his capital. He wishes to present you to Phra Wai. I'm beyond sorrow, my jewel."

Soifa was grief-stricken. She wai-ed, bowed her head, gripped her father's foot with her left hand and her mother's with her right.

"Lord and master of your child, you will say farewell to your daughter and flee. The king has given me to Phra Wai. Nobody loves me. It's unbearable.

That you presented me to the king to save lives, I do not mind, Father. Even if you had me fetch water or carry a palanquin, I would not refuse but would repay my debt of gratitude."

She sobbed in great sorrow. "I do not object, and I can face it, but I'm shocked that I will end up in the Thai city. Whether I sicken, live, or die, you will not see.

From the time I was tiny until I was grown—oh Buddha!—I never left the palace to go anywhere.[10] The distance is so great that we will not see each other. Whichever way I look, there'll be only the Thai.

I'll see neither Father nor Mother. I'll meet only strangers and find no warmth. I used to play happily but now face hardship. Father will abandon me and return to the palace.

In times of hardship, I'll pick grassflowers to decorate my hair. Even though the smell is bitter and not sweet, it won't matter.[11] I'll worry and pine for you throughout life. I'm at my wits' end and will probably die."

---

10. บ่อ ได้ เคย จาก วัง ปี หยัง หั้น, *bo dai khoei jak wang pi yang han*, "I . . . anywhere" in Lao.
11. บ่อ เปน สัง, *bo pen sang*, "it won't matter" in Lao.

Nang Soi Sumali embraced Soifa, streaming with tears. "Don't be sorrowful on one point, my precious. Though you do not love Phra Wai, this arrangement is necessary

because we've fallen to be servants of the king. Please think carefully, Daughter, and you'll see. Please entrust yourself to your husband morning and evening. Minister to him every day and night.

At times for eating, serve savory and sweet. Even if there's nothing, you must somehow provide. At times for sleeping, minister to him as a matter of course. Think of yourself as a servant, darling child.

Though Phra Wai may acquire minor wives, don't be too critical. It's inappropriate to make a scene. Your husband will probably be kind."

Soifa sadly took her mother's instructions on her head.[12] "When you go away, Mother, may you be well. When a year has passed, send someone

to let me know whether things go well or badly. I'll wait to hear. You both return to govern the city. May your lives last ten thousand years."

The lord of Chiang Mai and his beloved wife saw that their daughter's face was deeply miserable, and he pitied her greatly. "It's almost time to go into the palace."

He took off a nine-peaked ring and gave it to her, saying "This is worth fifteen chang. If I had more to give, I would, but now I'm poor and helpless."

He chose Lao servant girls for her, including I-Mai to be their head, and four or five others of good appearance. "Keep them as your friends, my darling."

Then the queen gave strict orders to Mai. "Don't consider yourself as a servant but think of her as your younger sister from the same womb. Try to look after each other and teach each other.

It's almost time they close the gate, my jewel. Hurry back into the palace. May you be eternally happy. May danger and evil not cross your path."

Soifa felt her chest would crack apart. She prostrated at the feet of her mother and father with tears flowing down in heartbreak.

"It's very late. I can stay no longer. I'm sorry I have to rush into the palace but the sun has almost set and there'll be concern if I don't go."

The palace matrons warned it was getting dark. Soifa shuddered and sighed at having to leave her parents, and kept on grieving until she entered the palace.

---

12. She made a wai and moved her hands above her head, as if placing the instructions there, signaling acceptance.

The lord of Chiang Mai and his queen, seeing their daughter walk away, almost lost their minds. Gradually they controlled their sorrow, entered the lodging, and gave orders to prepare for departure.

All kinds of weapons were bundled up. Articles of nak, gold, silver, and clothing were placed in chests and securely fastened.

Four duty officers of the Ministry of the Palace wrote out records, and the goods were carefully checked against the manifests. People were sent to carry goods to the boats.

The King and Queen of Chiang Mai along with all their palace ladies boarded a *maepa* boat[13] at sunset.

✦

With Venus rising in the golden light of approaching dawn, the moon descended into the forest. Cocks beat their wings and their crowing echoed around the city.

Coels uttered their sweet and plaintive calls. Yellow rays of the sun filtered through the clouds. The lord of Chiang Mai was feeling unsettled, lonely, sad, and regretful.

"Oh, the sun is up already. From tomorrow I'll not see my beloved child. Because of karma we're parted, and I must be far from my darling daughter.

Oh, from when she was small until now, I and her mother took care of her and were never ever separated. It's a pity that karma has forced us apart.

The more I think, the more it's unthinkable." Once the sun had dawned brightly, the lord of Chiang Mai, with his wife following,

went up into Khun Phaen's house. Khun Phaen, Phra Wai, Grandmother, Laothong, and Kaeo Kiriya were all there.

The lord of Chiang Mai sobbed. "I take leave to go back to Chiang Mai. We'll not meet again in one hundred years, one hundred thousand days, one hundred thousand months.

May I entrust my precious Soifa to you. Until her dying day, she'll not return to me because the king has ordered her to be with Phra Wai."

Khun Phaen and Phra Wai comforted the lord of Chiang Mai to dispel his

---

13. เรือ แม่ ปะ, also known as เรือแมงป่อง, *ruea maengpong*, scorpion-tail boat, a flat-bottomed dugout boat with a cabin amidships and a distinctive high stern, rowed by four oarsmen, used on the Ping River. In 1906, Prince Damrong reported that he had earlier traveled on the Ping in a *maepa* boat belonging to the ruler of Chiang Mai but that such craft had "now almost disappeared" (Damrong, *Nithan borankhadi*, 406–9).

sorrow. "When Soifa comes to be with Phlai Ngam, I'll look after her like my own child.

Even in sickness, I'll not abandon her. Everything that can be given her will be given, without fail. I'll support her until death. There's no need for any concern."

Hearing Khun Phaen, the lord of Chiang Mai gradually overcame his sorrow. He bade farewell, got up, and went down to the boat, feeling miserable.

Khun Phaen and Phlai Ngam followed down to the jetty to send him off. The lord of Chiang Mai said with tearful eyes, "Allow me to take my leave."

His Lao phrai and servants made ready the paddles and rudder. The *maepa* boat set off. The boats of the retinue left at the same time.

They glided away and disappeared from sight. His tears fell in streams, and he lay down to grieve. "From now on I'll be far from my dear daughter."

They paddled hard against the current. "Now you'll be looking out for your father, and expecting him to return home and stay there. You'll be even more disheartened and possibly die."

Rowing against the current, they reached the elephant enclosure. He felt desolate at the sight of the posts and pens in rows. "That bull elephant followed the herd and fell into a trap.

Now he rests his trunk on his tusks and stands lonely by the *talung* posts. His eyes gaze gloomily at nothing. Tears bathe his face and fall in pools. He has no wish to eat grass, no wish to stab with his tusks.

Oh Buddha! He used to have friends in the wild, friends with strong hearts who feared nobody, who would charge anything with their own strength. But he was lured by the herd into a trap,

not knowing he was being tricked, and for the love of a female, lost everything. His wife and child face ruin without him. He just stands here alone, gazing through eyes bleary with tears.

Oh Buddha! We used to live in Chiang Mai and had the best of everything. Our wealth was dazzling. Nobody caused us difficulty or distress.

Because I became lost in love for Soithong, I wronged and angered the king in an extreme way. My wife and child had to be parted from their home. I'm angry that Soifa will not return.

The more I think, the more I'm lonely and sad in the soul." His tears flowed down with sobbing. They came to Ban Maen, where a group of Mon were standing, wearing lowercloths and watching.

They wore uppercloths embroidered in patterns, and had earrings in their ears and long hair wound up on their heads. One young and fair lady stood watching. "She's like my own little Soifa—

slender waist, slight build, rounded arms, hair done to suit her face." When he looked more closely, he saw it was not his dear child. She spoke in Mon and stood with breasts jutting out.

They came to Three Bo Trees and he looked at the bo. "Oh darling, you'll never come to me. The bo trees have grown rounded like sculptures. The tree in the middle has shed its leaves,

and its branches and twigs look sad, while the other two are lush and pretty—like we two who must travel up to Chiang Mai while our child suffers like the central bo."

He came to the river mouth at Bang Prasop.[14] "In years I'll not meet Soifa at all." He thought of his beloved child along the way. They came to Bottleneck Village[15] and he felt still more disheartened.

"Why have they dug out this channel so that we can pass? What a pity. Thinking of my daughter my heart is ever heavier. May the boat hit on the bottleneck so I die!"

They passed Mueang In and Mueang Phrom. "Where have In and Phrom[16] gone? Both have disappeared. Help retrieve my daughter to relieve my sadness. On arrival home. I'll make offerings."

They passed Chainat and Koeichai. "Who built this beautiful mounting platform, just like the old one in our capital? For years, Soifa will never mount it again."

At Phichit he gazed at the residence where they had stayed earlier. "Your father's heart is empty, my darling. Even though the boat stops, my tears will not stop flowing. At this rest house, we rested for many days.

Morning and evening we saw each other, bringing happiness to relieve any sadness. Oh, today from morning until evening we'll not see each other. In that room my little daughter once slept.

The bedclothes were tied with fragrant garlands. Now they've all gone—pillows, mats, mattresses, everything." He grieved along the way, not sleeping through to sunrise.

After fifteen days, they reached Rahaeng[17] and moored beside a jetty. He called his wife to disembark, bringing their possessions along. They continued by elephant and horse.

Reaching a defile in the hills, the lord of Chiang Mai shed tears, thinking

---

14. They have been traveling up the Bang Lang Canal. Probably this is where that canal meets the Lopburi River close to Wat Sop Sawan, 3 kms south of Bang Pahan (see map 3).

15. บ้าน ขวาง ท่า คอ, Ban Khwang Tha Kho, Village of obstruction-landing-neck, now Ban Khwang, on the east bank of the Bang Kaeo Canal, 5 kms east of Ang Thong (see map 3).

16. Thai versions of the gods Indra and Brahma.

17. Though traveling up the Nan River through Phichit, they have managed to arrive at Rahaeng on the Ping River, far to the west.

ever more sadly of his daughter, feeling lonely as they entered the forest.

He heard the eerie sound of birds screeching loudly through the woods. A coel called out clearly from a sandal tree, sounding like the voice of his daughter,

making him start in false expectation. He parted the curtains and looked out but found it was not Soifa. He closed the curtain, turned his face, and wept floods.

At night they did not halt but hurried on across river, marsh, and forest. In a month they reached Chiang Mai as intended, and entered the city along with their servants and phrai.

Word spread to all the Lao of Chiang Mai that the king of the Thai capital had graciously sent the Lao lord back to enjoy his city.

PART 4

PRINCE DAMRONG'S PREFACES

The edition of *KCKP* that has become the standard was first printed in 1917–18 in three volumes. Prince Damrong Rajanubhab, who oversaw the editing, wrote a preface spread across the three volumes. For the second edition in 1925, he revised the preface and changed some of his opinions. However, all reprints contain only the first edition's preface. Below is a full translation of both versions. There is some repetition between the two, but this has not been touched. Where text is quoted from an external source more than once, it is not repeated. Some explanatory footnotes have been inserted, labeled (T). Where the same material appears in both versions, the footnotes have not been repeated in the second version.

PREFACE TO THE FIRST VOLUME

The tradition of reciting *sepha* existed from the Ayutthaya era, but when it began and why the *Khun Chang Khun Phaen* story was rendered in *sepha* verse is still not clearly explained. It is not even known what language the word *sepha* came from and what it means. Besides being used for *Khun Chang Khun Phaen*, the word *sepha* appears elsewhere in the names of three *piphat*[1] songs known as the *sepha nok* (outer *sepha*), *sepha nai* (inner *sepha*), and *sepha klang* (mid *sepha*), respectively. This has led to speculation that *sepha* was the name for a song whose rhythm was used for recitation of *Khun Chang Khun Phaen*. But music experts assert that the rhythm for reciting *sepha* does not resemble the *sepha* song. For these reasons, the meaning of the word *sepha* remains unclear. However, I have tried to collect information appearing in certain books, matters related to me by important and senior people, observations on the poetry and wording in certain books on *sepha*, along with my own conjectures and opinions, to compile a history of the *sepha* of *Khun Chang Khun Phaen* that presents my opinions along with explanations to clarify matters for all of you.

THE ORIGINS OF *SEPHA*

Although the origins are not known for certain, we can conjecture that *sepha* was used for relating folktales (*nithan*) to audiences in a tradition that goes back a long way. The text *Sarattha samutchai*,[2] written over seven hundred years ago, explains the origin of the Mongkhon Sutta by stating that during the Buddhist era in the cities of Machimprathet[3] there were professional reciters of folktales who performed for audiences at places such as rest-houses for travelers. As a result, the people heard only these folktales and a problem arose of whether this was a blessing (*mongkhon*). This problem became known to the gods who

---

1. ปี่พาทย์, a music ensemble; the instruments are described below in the section "History of sepha in the Third Reign" in the second preface. (T)

2. A text believed to originate from Sri Lanka in the reign of Parakramabahu I (1123–1186). (T)

3. A term in the traditional geography of the *Traiphum Phra Ruang* (Three Worlds of King Ruang) and similar works, referring to central India. (T)

went to consult Buddha, who thus created the Mongkhon Sutta.[4] This tradition of reciting stories for an audience has existed in Siam since antiquity as a form of entertainment at ceremonies. For example, at tonsure ceremonies, such recitations took place in the evening after the monks had finished chanting prayers. Arranging such recitals for guests was an old custom that survived down to the Bangkok era. *Sepha* was a form of such recitation and appeared in the same ceremonies alongside the recitation of folktales. Thus I think *sepha* is related to the telling of folktales. But *sepha* recitation differs from other storytelling in the use of verse, special intonation, and telling only the *Khun Chang Khun Phaen* story. These are the sole differences. If we speculate why people invented the *sepha* as something different from normal recitation, it was probably simply because recitation of folktales had existed for ages and had become stale, so some people invented something different by composing verse that was more listenable and melodious. Only the *Khun Chang Khun Phaen* story was used, probably because in Ayutthaya times the story was more popular than any other story owing to the fact that it was amusing, captivating, and supposedly a true tale.

THE STORY OF *KHUN CHANG KHUN PHAEN*

Khun Chang Khun Phaen is a true story that took place in the Ayutthaya era. It appears in the book, *Testimony of the Inhabitants of the Old Capital*,[5] which is considered a form of royal chronicle, as follows.

Subsequently, the royal sons, grandsons, and dynasty of King U Thong Ramathibodi[6] ruled in the city of Thepthawarawadi[7] for many succeeding reigns until a king appeared named Phanwasa, known in Burmese as King Wattathong, meaning a thousand years. This king had an elaborate history but it is unanimously agreed he had a queen named Suriyawongsathewi with whom he had a son called Phra Borom Kuman.

Later the King of Lanchang wanted close relations with Ayutthaya and thus sent a daughter of exceptional beauty and just sixteen years of age along with

---

4. Mangala Sutta, a short teaching on the Buddhist approach to living a good life. (T)

5. คำให้การชาวกรุงเก่า, *Khamhaikan chao krung kao*, believed to be testimony recorded from Siamese prisoners taken to Ava in 1767, first printed by the Wachirayan Library in 1910 and 1925 (KCK, 58–63). (T)

6. The founder of Ayutthaya according to the royal chronicles. (T)

7. "Divine city of gates," meaning Ayutthaya, referring to Dvaravati, possibly a prior state in the Chaophraya Plain about which very little is known.

a retinue of female attendants, a great many articles of tribute, ambassadors carrying royal missives, and military officers to present the princess to King Phanwasa at Ayutthaya. While they were on the way, the news spread to Chiang Mai, whose ruler of the time, King Pothisan Ratchakuman, wanted Lanchang to ally not with Ayutthaya but with Chiang Mai instead. Thus he dispatched an army to seize the princess. The Lanchang forces were defeated and fled back to inform their king.

News of these events reached King Phanwasa of Ayutthaya, who was enraged. He instructed his officials that the Chiang Mai ruler had insulted his power, was a person without justice, and had seized a lady pledged to him in contravention of ethical human behavior. The ruler of Chiang Mai had to be crushed and made to respect the ability of Thai soldiery so he would not act in such an insulting and immoral way in the future. Orders were thus sent to prepare an army, and for Pramuen Si, an old royal page and close noble retainer, to select valiant, skilled, and battle-proven soldiers to serve.

Pramuen Si informed the king that among Thai troops at that time there was no more excellent soldier than Khun Phaen who was an expert in lore, supremely valiant, and incomparably loyal to the king. At that time Khun Phaen was in jail for a criminal offense. If the king wished Khun Phaen to lead the attack on Chiang Mai, victory would be gained easily without need for both a main army and reserve army.

King Phanwasa remembered that Khun Phaen was a soldier of proven prowess. He issued a royal pardon and ordered Pramuen Si to bring Khun Phaen to audience immediately. Pramuen Si informed the minister of the capital to release Khun Phaen from prison, and brought him to be presented before the throne in the hall of royal audience. King Phanwasa asked: "Khun Phaen, will you or will you not volunteer to take the army to attack Chiang Mai in order to crush the criminal ruler of Yonok,[8] let him know the capacity of the Thai army, and bring back the princess?" Khun Phaen replied, "As a humble soldier, my life is under the dust of the foot of the king's great power and patronage, as with my father and grandfather before me. Your servant begs to volunteer to attack Chiang Mai, crush the Yonok ruler so he quails before Your Majesty's power, and bring back the Lanchang princess. If I fail to take Chiang Mai, may I offer my life in forfeit." King Phanwasa listened to Khun Phaen and was well pleased. He thus appointed Khun Phaen as army commander to lead the assault on Chiang Mai. Khun Phaen led the army to Phichit and called on the ruler of Phichit to hand over the extraordinary sword and horse that Khun Phaen had

---

8. A semi-legendary kingdom prior to the emergence of Lanna, and the name of a chronicle of its early history. (T)

left there so they might be used in the campaign. Khun Phaen's extraordinary sword later came to be known as *Fa fuen*, "Skystorm," with great powers, and his extraordinary horse was called *Si mok*, "Color of Mist," as it could gallop into battle evading enemy warriors with great agility and strength. Having acquired the extraordinary sword and steed, Khun Phaen took his leave of the Phichit ruler and quick-marched the army to the outskirts of Chiang Mai city. Hearing an Ayutthaya army had arrived, the Chiang Mai ruler sent his troops out to face them. Khun Phaen skillfully commanded the Thai troops to attack the Lao Yuan of Chiang Mai. The Chiang Mai troops broke and fled in defeat back into the city, but failed to close the gates on the causeway in time. Khun Phaen followed them into the city, killing many of the Lao troops. The Chiang Mai ruler was shocked at this invasion and fled from the city. Khun Phaen surrounded the palace, and captured Akkasathuthewi, the Queen of Chiang Mai, her daughter named Chao Waen Fa Thong, and many of the Chiang Mai king's consorts. He invited Nang Soithong, the Lanchang princess who had been seized by the Chiang Mai ruler, to leave the golden palace, and brought them all back with the army to present to the King of Ayutthaya. When he reported the victory of the army, King Phanwasa was well pleased. Thinking of the Ten Royal Virtues, he said that, as the ruler of Chiang Mai could not match the capability of the Thai troops but had fled his city leaving it without government, causing great hardship to the monks, Brahmans, and people, he was appointing a senior official as governor who would go and appease the Chiang Mai population so they did not scatter in confusion. He would also have the Chiang Mai officials invite their ruler to return to govern the city as before.

At that time, the king conferred silver, gold, and useful articles on Khun Phaen as army commander and on a great number of other courageous officers and troops who had gone on the campaign. The king made Princess Soithong of Lanchang into his great queen of the left, and Nang Waen Fa Thong, daughter of the ruler of Chiang Mai, into a consort of the first rank. But this lady's mother, the Queen of Chiang Mai, requested to return to Chiang Mai with her retainers and troops. By royal grace, the male and female slaves from Lanchang and Chiang Mai were settled to make a living in various locations in Ayutthaya.

Khun Phaen was celebrated as a great soldier in Ayutthaya at that time. Later when he felt he had become aged, he brought his extraordinary sword to present to King Phanwasa to be a royal weapon from then on. The king accepted it, gave it the name of Enemy Crusher, and also renamed another regalia sword from the time of Phraya Kraek as the Sword of Glorious Victory. He ordered pages to carry these two swords on his left and right when he traveled. He also ordered the image of Phraya Kraek and his crown to be placed in the Royal Hall of Worship in the palace, where they remain until this day.

King Phanwasa ruled for twenty-five years from age fifteen until his death at age forty.

In the *Testimony of the Inhabitants of the Old Capital*, the story of *Khun Chang Khun Phaen* appears as this and no more. Apart from the *Testimony*, there are some other books authored in the Ayutthaya era that refer to *sepha*, but none has yet been found that tells the story of *Khun Chang Khun Phaen*. In the *Northern Chronicles*, it states only that King Phanwasa ruled at a certain time. "Phra Phanwasa" was probably an honorific of the king at one time, like "Somdet Phrajaoyuhua" today, not the name of a specific king. In some later reigns similar names were used as honorifics for the king's mother as "Somdet Phraphanpi Luang" and the queen as "Somdet Phraphanwasa." For instance, the queen of King Borommakot of Ayutthaya, and Somdet Phrasisuriyentra Borommarachachonani[9] in the Bangkok Second Reign were both called "Somdet Phraphanwasa." It clearly was not the name of any specific king in the past.

The above story of *Khun Chang Khun Phaen* from the *Testimony* has evidence about the dating of the story. At one point it states that King Phanwasa was the father of Phra Borom Kuman, and that when Phra Borom Kuman ascended the throne he had a queen by the name of Si Sudajan who, when her husband died, attempted to put her lover on the throne. In the *Royal Chronicles*, Phra Borom Kuman is called King Chairachathirat, and thus King Phanwasa is King Ramathibodi II. These sources suggest that Khun Phaen lived during the reign of King Ramathibodi II (r. CS 853–91, CE 1491–1529). The Chiang Mai chronicle states that in that era, King Mueang Kaeo, the ruler of Chiang Mai, went to war against Ayutthaya several times. Further, at the start of the poem itself, the date of Khun Phaen's birth is given as "147." If we assume this was formerly written as "847" (CE 1485) but subsequently miscopied, then Khun Phaen was born in the reign of King Trailokanat (r. 1448–?1488), was six years old when King Ramathibodi II succeeded, and entered government service in that reign.[10] This seems to fit. But elsewhere in the *Testimony* it states that Thao Phothisan was the ruler of Chiang Mai at the time. In fact Thao Phothisan was ruler of Lanchang, and the son-in-law of the Chiang Mai ruler. He was the father of King Chai Chettha who asked for the hand of Princess Thepkasatri at the time of the

---

9. Chaofa Bunrot, 1767–1835, cousin of King Rama I, queen of King Rama II, mother of the future King Rama IV (Mongkut) and of Front Palace King Phrapinklao. (T)

10. Phiset Jiajanphong thinks that 147 is the year the Buddha is supposed to have achieved nirvana, and also is the last date given in the Singhanavati chronicle of Lanna, and that it is used here to mean "a long time ago" (Phiset, "Sakkarat"; Sujit, *KCKP*, 53). (T)

war against King Bayinnaung of Pegu in the reign of King Maha Chakkaphat (r. 1548–1569). The use of the name Thao Pothisan should not discredit the evidence that the story of *Khun Chang Khun Phaen* can be placed during the reign of Ramathibodi II between 1491 and 1529. However, the *sepha* probably appeared much later, after the story had been retold orally and had become a folktale. If we estimate that the *sepha* appeared later, probably not before the reign of King Narai (r. 1656–1688), I think that would not be wrong.

The story of *Khun Chang Khun Phaen* as it appears in the *Testimony*, though brief, clearly differs from the version in the poem. This is not at all surprising, seeing that the poem was passed on orally as a folktale for several hundred years. Only later was it written into *klon* verse, adapted to become more entertaining, and steadily lengthened. The *sepha* version probably differs greatly from the original, though retaining some core of the old story. If we try to reconstruct the original, as far as it can be done logically, the early part of the story was probably the same as in the *sepha* version, namely that Khun Chang, Khun Phaen, and Nang Wanthong were from Suphan, that Wanthong was the lover of Khun Phaen at the time he was still called Phlai Kaeo, and that they seemed to be settling down together but had not yet married when Phlai Kaeo was conscripted into the army (not necessarily as its commander) and was absent for a long time. During this time, Khun Chang tried successfully to get Wanthong as his wife. Phlai Kaeo returned from the army with the name of Khun Phaen Saensathan and the position as *palat* of the left in the department of the city guard (*tamruat phuban*). He abducted Wanthong, and Khun Chang gave chase. Khun Phaen wounded Khun Chang in some fashion, and Khun Chang filed a complaint. King Phanwasa sent nobles after Khun Phaen, who killed them and fled to the northern cities, but eventually presented himself to the ruler of Phichit, who informed the capital. Possibly it was at this point that Wanthong was condemned to death by the king for being of two minds, and Khun Phaen was imprisoned for killing an official but given remission on account of his confession. At this point war broke out with Chiang Mai, and during recruitment, Pramuen Si recommended Khun Phaen to the king, resulting in Khun Phaen being pardoned and sent off to fight. He gained a victory and became famous. This was probably the original story of *Khun Chang Khun Phaen*. The remainder was added later when it was a folktale and *sepha*.

KHUN CHANG KHUN PHAEN IN WRITTEN FORM

Khun Chang Khun Phaen is not the only old text produced by adapting a folktale into *klon* verse for recitation. Various legends (*tamnan*) and Jataka stories that had been passed on by word of mouth were also written down in *klon* for recital in the wat. This is why they are called "*o-e-wihanrai*," tales read for an audience. Such texts existed long before *sepha*, and spread as far as Lao cities in the north. While both legends and Jataka stories were adapted into texts for recitation in this way, *Khun Chang Khun Phaen* probably did not follow this model, but originated from the practice of reciting folktales in the villages.

Folktales passed down from ancient times to the present differ from the Jataka stories adapted into texts for chanting in one key respect: folktales are coarse and uncouth. This is not because reciters and their listeners had a general disposition to like coarseness, but in truth probably arose from old beliefs about protective lore (*athan*). If a spirit takes a liking to someone and wants to possess that person, it will cause that person to die, and take the person away to look after and put to work in the spirit world. To combat this, the spirit has to be convinced that the person is coarse and uncouth and thus not appropriate to be abducted and adopted. This belief gave rise to several kinds of behavior that survived into later times. For example, in Chiang Mai children of royalty and nobles were often given two names—one the usual name, the other something like Toad or Frog to put off the spirits. In the performance of chicken-flapping *phleng* or *thepthong*,[11] crude interplay, even to the point of publicly slandering the ancestors, is similarly believed to have originated from the intention to make somebody or something objectionable to the spirits. For this reason, *thepthong* is an indispensable part of the festival to celebrate the arrival of a white elephant in the capital down to the present day. Tying a lingam on a child, or using a lingam as an offering to a spirit, are not done because spirits appreciate the lingam, but must have come from a similar idea to make the spirits dislike the child or the person making the offering so they are not taken off to the land of the spirits. In rites to call back the soul, such as during the tonsure ceremony, crude tales are recited in order to make the spirits dislike the child undergoing tonsure. By the same thinking, folktales recited for entertainment tended to be coarse. This was tolerated because of the above traditions, and eventually became customary and almost humorous. At the time that *Khun Chang Khun Phaen* was still recited as a folktale, it was probably coarse, and the *sepha* versions still recited in the localities are rather coarse, but not as bad as other tales. Besides, the story of *Khun Chang Khun Phaen* is entertaining, and appeals to people more than any other tale, thus accounting for its unique popularity.

---

11. เพลง, *phleng* was the generic name for popular performances of verse play which came in many varieties, usually improvised, and often involving exchanges between a couple or small group of players. *Prop kai*, "chicken flapping," was one of the most popular variants. *Thepthong* was another. (T)

In the first stage of the development of *Khun Chang Khun Phaen* as *sepha*,[12] I assume that only certain important passages were written in verse. When the tale was recited, certain passages about lovemaking, lament, admiring female beauty, and admiring the forests were composed in verse, rather in the manner of an "elaborate" folktale (*nithan song krueang*). Let me explain why I believe this was so. In its past as a folktale, *Khun Chang Khun Phaen* was usually recited from beginning to end, either by one person or several in sequence. As the tale is very long, it would take a long time to adapt into verse form, and be impossible to recite the resulting whole story in one night. So I assume that at the first stage of its development as *sepha*, only certain passages in the key chapters were adapted into verse and the remainder was told as a tale. The verses were probably improvised on the spot during the telling. Once this appealed to audiences, at the next stage poets adapted the whole story into meter to be recited as *sepha*, and written versions appeared. But as the story is so long, as already noted, the version in meter for stylized recitation could not be completed in a single night. Hence it was divided into chapters that were each the right length for a single night. Once this idea took hold, many different people adapted their favorite passages into verse for recitation. For this reason, the old *sepha* from Ayutthaya (or even that from early Bangkok which followed the Ayutthaya model) was in bits and pieces, not continuous like a drama script. There are records to show that these fragments were not amalgamated into a book until later, around the Bangkok Third Reign, as will be explained below.

Sepha texts composed in the Ayutthaya era have almost all disappeared. The fate of *sepha* texts has been different from that of drama scripts or prayer chants that depended on the text. Drama players needed a script or else they could not play, and prayer books were required in the same way. But *sepha* was different. The texts were used to help the reciters to memorize, and thereafter were not needed. Those who composed the texts in order to make a living probably concealed the texts, allowing only their own students to read them, for fear that others would become their rivals. Hence there were few *sepha* texts, and they were hidden. Consequently they deteriorated easily and rarely survived, unlike drama scripts and prayer chants from the Ayutthaya era.

Some Ayutthaya *sepha* survived into the Bangkok era because some *sepha* reciters from the Ayutthaya era survived, but they retained only a few passages either as texts or memory to serve as the seeds of the *sepha* recited in the Bang-

---

12. As Damrong states, *KCKP* was the original *sepha*. Hence in the Thai original of this preface, he uses "*sepha*" sometimes to refer to the form and genre, and sometimes to mean the *KCKP* story. In this translation, we have often added the words "*Khun Chang Khun Phaen*" to make this less ambiguous. (T)

kok era. Even these old versions, under close examination, are all believed to have been recomposed in the Bangkok era.

For the history of *sepha* in the Bangkok era, there are adequate sources to provide more detail than for the Ayutthaya era in several ways. I know two documents that can be counted as records of the *sepha*. The first is a passage by Sunthon Phu in the chapter of *Khun Chang Khun Phaen* about Phlai Ngam's tonsure ceremony. The second is the final verse of an invocation paying respects to teachers by an unknown author. Nai Yu, a *sepha* master of Ang Thong, recited it for me to record in writing. These two documents allow us to determine many things about the history of the *sepha*, as will be explained below.

SUNTHON PHU'S VERSE

The abbot acknowledged, and went back to the wat.
A music ensemble played. Thong Prasi's family and friends
had sought the very best masters of *sepha*.
Ta-Mi, a firecracker maker, excelled at fight scenes,
his throat swelling with sound as he recited.
Old people liked to hear him and declared he knew everything.
Ta-Rongsi was good at being funny, and knew every trick.
He clacked the claves while clowning around and rolling his eyes.
Nai Tang with a loud booming voice
made the quarreling scenes very amusing.
Nai Phet had lots of tricks, and dragged the choruses out
to three fathoms and two cubits, as long as a long gun.
As for Nai Ma from the retinue of Phraya Non,[13] he was a comedian
good at bawdy improvisation who made people laugh heartily.
Ta-Thongyu knew how to recite in Lao
and sing background music[14] in a drone.

PAYING RESPECT TO TEACHERS

Now let us pay respect to old teacher Son,
a gatekeeper, and a teacher of people from all over.
Next comes teacher Mi, a maker of firecrackers,
and teacher Pheng, good at the parts about Suphan.
Pay respects to old teacher Le who likes to have fun;

---

13. In the second version of the preface, Damrong clarified that this means Ma, a retainer of Phraya Non. (T)

14. กราวเชิด, *krao choet*, rousing background music played on various occasions such as fights, marches, travel. (T)

Phan Raksa Ratri, good and hardworking;
old Thongyu, drama teacher, composer of major verses;
old Luang Suwan Rongsi who has died.
At the time of the previous reign,
sepha was not yet recited along with music.
Now in the time of the present king,
good people have been born in Ayutthaya.
For *prop gai, khrueng thon,*[15] and verse,
I'm not skilled, having only just begun to learn.
The one who is quick-witted is
the teacher by name Ma, of Phraya Non.
He can play comedy, mask play, shadow play, everything,
gong, *ranat*, nothing missing.
For studying, he is the teacher of everyone,
renowned until death.

Now let us pay respect to teachers of *piphat*,
skilled on gong, *ranat*, horn, and *shenai*;
both teacher Kaeo and teacher Phak, pillars of victory;
teacher Thong-in who has no equal,
and whose hand moves so flexibly;
old Phun, a Mon, good and diligent;
teacher Mi, a Khaek fellow, is also good,
he tootles the *thayoi* fluently
in tune with old Ket, quick and supreme at *sepha*,
and teacher Noi whose words people revere;
also teacher Jaeng whose compositions are so famous;
and teacher On who spreads Phim's fame widely.
To talk more will make us late.
Now I'll perform the *sepha* following how the teachers have taught.
If I make mistakes in the verse,
please excuse me and don't complain.[16]

The *sepha* masters who appear in Sunthon Phu's verse were famous in the
Second Reign. Sunthon Phu had heard them recite and knew their styles. Those

---

15. ครึ่งทอน, a form of local folk song. (T)

16. Analysis suggests this was composed in two parts. The first part about *sepha* masters seems
to have been composed long before the verse for paying respect to the *piphat* masters. The names
of later *sepha* masters such as Khru Jaeng are muddled into the section on *piphat* masters.

in the invocation verse seem to be a collection of the names of famous *sepha* players, old and new, alive and dead. Several names appear in both lists, and the second extract is obviously later than the first as it mentions that some on Sunthon Phu's list, such as Nai Ma of Phraya Non, had now died.

In total these two extracts name fourteen *sepha* masters and five *piphat* masters. Only some of their biographies are known.[17]

1. Khru Thongyu appears in both extracts, and he is known to have been important. During the First Reign, he was a leading actor for Prince Thep-harirak.[18] Then during the Second Reign, he was a member of the royal drama troupe, and head teacher for major royal drama productions such as the *Inao* of Chao Jom Manda Yaem.[19] He is also said to have been a consultant of Prince Phithakmontri[20] on the design of dance dramas that are still played to this day. At that time, when the king composed a drama script, he sent it to Prince Phithakmontri who set up a big mirror and, along with Khru Thongyu, arranged choreography to fit the script. When the choreography was settled, Khru Thongyu had the task of training the dancers. Later in the Third Reign, Khru Thongyu became the teacher for almost all the dramas staged in various palaces. He could be called the drama teacher of the whole city, and his name is still honored in drama circles today. There was another lady teacher called Khru Rung who was his partner. She could not recite *sepha*, but Thongyu was good at it, and was one of two famed teachers of *sepha*.

2. Khru Jaeng was of a later generation, and lived into the Fifth Reign. His home was behind Wat Rakhang. At first, he was famous for *phleng* and his name appears in the passage of *Khun Chang Khun Phaen* on the funeral of Wan-thong where Nai Jaeng (meaning this Khru Jaeng) was sought out to perform *phleng* with Granny Ma. Khru Jaeng and Granny Ma were celebrated *phleng* performers in the Third Reign. During one performance, Granny Ma made fun of the mother of Khru Jaeng in some way, and Khru Jaeng was unable to come up with a satisfactory riposte. This made him so angry that he stopped performing *phleng* and turned to *sepha* and prayer chanting. He composed many passages that appear in this book. His verse was good but tended towards

---

17. Prince Naritsranuwattiwong helped research the biographies of these *sepha* and *piphat* teachers.

18. 1759–1805, son of King Rama I's sister Sisudarak with Chao Khrua Ngoen; prominent patron of drama; origin of the Thephasadin family. (T)

19. 1814–1857, eighteenth of the thirty-six consorts of King Rama III; famed as a performer and teacher of drama. (T)

20. 1870–1922, Jui, younger brother of Prince Thep-harirak (see note 18 above); minister of the palace and Mahatthai in the Second Reign; poet and craftsman, producer and choreographer for drama; origin of the Montrikun family. (T)

crudity, probably because he was used to playing chicken-flapping *phleng*. He also composed some *lamsuat*[21] that were chanted later. Khru Jaeng counts as another of the major masters of *sepha*.

3. The *piphat* master Khru Mi Khaek—meaning a Khaek called Mi—is said to have played almost every musical instrument, and been good at music composition as well. Examples of his famous compositions include *thayoi nai* and *thayoi nok sam chan*, still played today by all orchestras. Anyone who cannot play these two songs is considered not yet accomplished. Khru Mi was especially skilled on the flute, as appears in the invocation verse above: "teacher Mi, a Khaek fellow, is also good, he tootles the *thayoi* fluently." The *thayoi* here is not the *thayoi nok* or *thayoi nai* mentioned above, but a Khru Mi composition for a single flute known among *piphat* players as the solo *thayoi*. He was prominent from the Third Reign. During the Fourth Reign, many royalty including Front Palace King Phrapinklao,[22] Prince Thewet,[23] and Prince Wongsa[24] brought several *piphat* masters together for contests. Khru Mi was the *piphat* master for Phrapinklao, who gave him the title of Phra Pradit Phairo and the posts of deputy head of the royal pages and head of the *piphat* department of the Front Palace. He lived into the Fifth Reign when he was a *mahori* master for Princess Sudarat Naratprayun.[25]

Now let me tell the story of the *sepha* that can be ascertained from the two verse extracts. Starting furthest back, there was a *sepha* master called Nai Son, who was a gatekeeper. He may have been a *sepha* player from the Ayutthaya era who became a *sepha* master in the First Reign, and died before Sunthon Phu wrote the above verse, hence his name is not mentioned there. The fact that he was known as a *sepha* master in the First Reign suggests there were *sepha* players from the Ayutthaya era who were the seeds of later development in the Bangkok era. The six named by Sunthon Phu were *sepha* masters in the Second Reign. Their ages suggest they were probably not born early enough to be *sepha* players in Ayutthaya, but were the first generation to perform in Bangkok. In the Third Reign, there was a better generation of *sepha* masters, many of whose names appear in the invocation excerpt.

21. A sermon delivered in verse spontaneously improvised. (T)

22. 1808–1866, Prince Chudamani, son of King Rama II and younger brother of King Rama IV (Mongkut). (T)

23. 1798–1863, Kunchon, son of King Rama II; head of the Department of Horses in the Third Reign, and also of elephants in the Fourth Reign; origin of the Kunchon family. (T)

24. 1808–1871, Nuam, forty-ninth son of King Rama II; studied Western medicine from American missionaries; minister of Mahatthai in the Fourth Reign when he acquired the full title as Prince Wongsathiratsanit. (T)

25. 1818–1861, Lamom, daughter of King Rama III. (T)

Members of this group did not only recite *sepha* but also composed and hence were elevated as *sepha* masters. They were probably authors of the first texts of *sepha* that appeared in Bangkok. One example that survives in several printed *sepha* is the first chapter of this book (which here has partly been revised). It is noticeably like Ayutthaya verse in which rhyme is not so important, and the content is rather clumsy. As in the Ayutthaya era, the *sepha* composed as verse in early Bangkok was limited to certain passages. The line from Sunthon Phu's verse above that "Ta-Mi . . . was good at fight scenes" means that he liked to recite the passages where Phlai Kaeo goes to attack Chiang Thong, or where Khun Phaen attacks Chiang Mai; "Master Thongyu knew how to recite in Lao" means that he liked to recite the passages about Laothong, Soifa, and Simala; "Teacher On spreads the fame of Phim" means that he liked to recite the passage where Phlai Kaeo makes love to Phim.

Sepha texts only became more prized in the Second Reign. This is known because of evidence in the invocation excerpt:

At the time of the previous reign,
sepha was not yet recited along with *piphat*.
Now in the time of the present king,
good people have been born in Ayutthaya.

This means that, before the Second Reign, *sepha* was recited like folktales without musical backing. It is understood that recitation was shared between two people who alternated passages to give each other time to rest. Alternatively, in the case of very skilled *sepha* players, the host would choose just a single passage to recite, improvising both sides of an interchange, like in chicken-flapping *phleng*. This was known as *sepha don*, improvised *sepha*. I have heard that this was the old style. When the musical backing was introduced, there was only a single reciter who rested while the music played.

In the Second Reign, the structure of the *sepha* did not change, only the musical backing was added, and much of the *sepha* was revised. Almost all of the *sepha* that today is considered special was recomposed in the Second Reign, some by King Rama II himself. I once asked Prince Bamrap Borabak,[26] "I have heard it said that this *sepha* was composed by King Rama II. Is that true?" He replied, "Yes, he composed, but not openly, and several other people helped." I took note of this answer. It was a pity that I did not ask more. If I had asked

---

26. 1819–1886, son of King Rama II with a daughter of Chao Inthawong of Vientiane; earlier known as Chaofa Chai Klang; served in the palace, rising to superintend all the palace treasuries and chair the dynastic council; origin of the large and powerful Malakul clan, and the related Aphonkun family. (T)

the names of all the authors and who wrote what section, it would have been very good. Now we can only guess from the style. King Rama III also composed before he ascended the throne. But the style that can be recognized for sure is that of Sunthon Phu, who composed the passage on the birth of Phlai Ngam, from the birth until he becomes a page. It is undoubtedly Sunthon Phu's style. King Rama II is said to have composed the passage when Phlai Kaeo becomes the lover of Nang Phim in chapter 4, and the passage when Khun Phaen goes into Khun Chang's house and enters the room of Kaeo Kiriya in chapter 17. The passage in chapter 13 when Wanthong is jealous of Laothong after Khun Phaen returns home also seems to be King Rama II's composition. The two passages of Khun Chang asking for the hand of Phim, and Khun Phaen flee-ing with Nang Wanthong are believed to be by King Rama III.[27] The *sepha* composers in the Second Reign, even though not all are known, are believed to be among the famous authors of the time, those whom the king consulted when composing poetry, or in other words, the same group of authors who composed the Second Reign dramas such as *Inao* and *Ramakian*. The good verse in *sepha* is clearly similar to those in the dramas of the Second Reign. The only major difference is that the *sepha* verse has fewer restrictions than the verse for drama that had to be composed to fit with the movements of the dancers. Whether a passage of *sepha* is short or long is up to the composer. If he wants to say something, he can say it completely. Another important point is that *sepha* is composed like the telling of a folktale. It must appear realistic. For example, the style of dialogue and the words used must approximate the way such a person would speak. Even the geography mentioned is realistic. I once tracked down the various places referred to in the *sepha* and found that most are correct. It seems that to compose a *sepha* one had to know a certain amount of geography. The composition had more room to maneuver than in drama. The story of *Khun Chang Khun Phaen* is entertaining and offers room to play around in many ways. The fact that the authorship was not disclosed gave the authors full freedom. For this reason, authors showed off their skills without restraint in their work on *sepha*, and this work displays the style of various authors at their best. Hence the *sepha* is a distinctive type of poetic work, different from earlier genres, and different from other genres of the same era. No other work is comparable. That is the charm of *sepha*. Both in the past and present day, any reader is captivated.

The *sepha* texts recomposed in the Second Reign were confined to certain

---

27. In the part of the preface that first appeared in the first edition of the second volume, Prince Damrong changed his mind on this, attributing the flight (chapter 18) to King Rama II and the subsequent chapter on Khun Chang to King Rama III. (T)

passages which authors selected because they liked them. Examining the texts shows that each seems to have been the right length for one night's recitation, or two volumes of *samut thai*. These compositions are known to have been presented at court on major occasions, beginning a tradition of *sepha* recitation on such occasions. Later, when King Mongkut ascended the throne, he followed the model of the Second Reign, and commissioned poets to render the royal chronicles into *sepha* for presentation on major occasions. The identity of the authors is unknown, but Sunthon Phu was still alive and was among them. Unfortunately the *sepha* version of the chronicles composed at that time has completely disappeared, except for some passages that were remembered and that Phraya Boranratchathanin (Phon Dechakup)[28] assembled into a publication. But they could not rival the *sepha* of *Khun Chang Khun Phaen* as the contents of the chronicles are not as suitable to the form. Apart from the chronicles, the story of *Chiang Miang* or *Si Thanonchai*[29] was rendered as *sepha*, probably also in the Fourth Reign, but when and by whom is not known. There is only an original text in the Royal Library in which the style of the verse and the orthography suggest the Fourth Reign. In the Fifth Reign, King Chulalongkorn commissioned a *sepha* on *Nithra chakhrit*[30] in the same manner as in the Second and Fourth Reigns. Eleven people contributed:

Chapter 1   Luang Phisanuseni (Tongyu, the *sepha* master), later
             Phra Ratchamanu
Chapter 2   Phraya Maha-amnat (Run)
Chapter 3   Khun Wisutseni (Chang)
Chapter 4   Khun Phinitchai (Yu) later Luang Phiromkosa
Chapter 5   Luang Banhan Atakhadi (Sut) later Phra Phiromracha
Chapter 6   Khun Wisutthakon (MR Nu) later Phraya
             Itsaraphansophon
Chapter 7   Phraya Sisunthonwohan (Noi)
Chapter 8   Khun Thongsue (Chuang) later Luang Mongkhonrattana

---

28. 1871–1936, son of a royal page; as a youth spent time in service of Prince Vajirunhis and Prince Damrong; teacher and then official in the new Ministry of Education; governor of Ayutthaya from 1898 to 1929, responsible for pioneering discovery and restoration of Ayutthaya's historical remains; author of several works on Ayutthaya. (T)

29. A collection of tales about a trickster who constantly outwits a king. (T)

30. "The Sleeper Awakens," a story from the *Arabian Nights* or *One Thousand and One Nights*. In 1879, King Chulalongkorn composed this work from an English translation of the *Arabian Nights* (not Burton's, which appeared six years later), and distributed it to members of the royal family for the new year celebration (Mattani, *Dance, Drama, and Theatre*, 109–10). Abu Hasan awakens one day to find himself in the palace in the clothing of the caliph. He starts to believe he is the caliph. Next day, he wakes to find himself in his own house, but persists in believing he is the caliph, despite his mother's denials. He returns to sleep, refusing to face the world. (T)

Chapter 9   Luang Seniphitak (Uam) later Phraya Ratchawaranukun
Chapter 10   Luang Samosonphonkan (Tat), now Phraya
             Samosonsanphakan
Chapter 11   Luang Jakkaraphani (Ruek Prian) who composed *Nirat
             phra pathom chedi*

The four works mentioned above[31] are known as the royal *sepha*. However, the *sepha* of *Nithra chakhrit* in the Royal Library has only the first five chapters. If anyone has other chapters and would agree to have them copied for keeping in the Royal Library, I would be very grateful.

The text of *Khun Chang Khun Phaen* as read today was not totally composed in the Second Reign. From internal evidence, we know that several passages were composed in the Third Reign. I will give several examples of such internal identification. In the passage in chapter 7 on the marriage of Phlai Kaeo and Nang Phim, when Khun Chang is dressing to go as one of the groom's party, it says: "With these thoughts, he bathed and dressed in a golden yok that Phraya Lakhon had given him." This indicates composition in the Second Reign as there was someone with the title Phraya Lakhon only in this reign, while in the First and Third Reigns, the equivalent person was a chaophraya.[32] Later when Khun Phaen enters Khun Chang's house, it says "piled with glittering crystal, double screens, curtains, and blinds," suggesting this passage dates to the Second Reign when crystal was fashionable. Other passages have internal evidence of being written in the Third Reign. For example, the passage on the funeral of Nang Wanthong says: "Nai Jaeng came to play chicken-flapping songs / jigging his shoulders up and down and singing "cha cha." / He performed with Granny Ma, each trying to outdo the other, / and making people laugh uproariously." Nai Jaeng was a *sepha* master who lived until the Fifth Reign, but was famous for his *phleng* during the Third Reign, hence we know this passage was composed then. There is other such internal evidence but I have not examined the whole poem in detail to ascertain

---

31. *KCKP*; *Chiang Miang* or *Si Thanonchai*, the royal chronicles; *Nithra chakhrit*. (T)

32. Damrong seems to have got this wrong. Phat, the ruler of Nakhon from 1784 to 1811, held chaophraya rank. So did his son Noi, who ruled the city until 1839, and who by legend was actually the son of King Taksin of Thonburi by a wife presented to Phat when already pregnant with Taksin's child. Throughout this era, Bangkok was concerned that Nakhon might attempt to gain its former near-independence, or even collude with the British in Malaya. When Noi was succeeded by his son Noi Klang in 1839, the rank was reduced to phraya. So this reference suggests the chapter may have been written in the latter part of the Third Reign. The Nakhon governorship was elevated back to chaophraya rank at the next succession in 1867 (Munro-Hay, *Nakhon Si Thammarat*, 167–219). (T)

which portion was composed in the Second Reign and which in the Third, as the internal evidence is fragmentary. The style of verse did not differ between the Second and Third Reigns as most of the poets of the Second Reign survived into the Third. There were also several poets who emerged in the Third Reign and who could rival the compositions of their forebears. The legendary assumption that King Rama III ended dancing and recitation at court is true, but he did not put a ban on others, so other royalty and senior officials arranged performances in many places. These included dramas, *mahori*, and *piphat* in which *sepha* was chanted, so *sepha* was still widely played. The royal *sepha* from the Second Reign was still performed for audiences at this time, and many new pieces appeared. The authors are not known except for Khun Dan, a son of the King of Thonburi, who was in government service and held the title of Luang Mongkhonrattana. He was famous for shadow puppetry, *phak* recitation, and good conversation as he was a poet who crafted his own words. Apart from Khun Dan who composed good poems, there were many others skilled at verse such as the composer of *Phlengyao Wat Phra Chetuphon*. The set of royal *sepha* was probably completed in the Third Reign, and almost all of the old *Khun Chang Khun Phaen* had been recomposed by this time. At this point in the Third Reign, some royalty or senior noble who played *sepha* and music had the idea of assembling all the chapters together in sequence as the book we know today.[33]

The reason it is known that this assembling was done at this later period is because passages identifiable with different periods such as before the Second Reign, Second Reign, Third Reign—on grounds of style and certain evidence presented above—are interleaved together, with passages composed later sometimes appearing ahead of those known to have been composed earlier. For example, Sunthon Phu's composition on the birth of Phlai Ngam comes before the passage on the ruler of Chiang Mai asking for the hand of Soithong, which is in an earlier style. If the compilation had been made earlier, the sequence of style would probably match the sequence of periods. Examining the compilation shows that older pieces are scattered throughout. Authors chose passages at will without any coordination, and often with inconsistencies including the naming of characters. For example, the elders who ask for Wanthong's hand on behalf of Khun Chang are initially called Granny Kloi and Granny *Sai*, but later appear as Granny Kloi and Granny *Sa*. There is credible evidence that the *sepha* was composed in disparate sections, and only later compiled together. I estimate this compilation was in the Third Reign on grounds that some of the

---

33. In his revised preface of 1925, Damrong altered this opinion and placed the compilation in the Fourth Reign. (T)

passages are known to have been composed in that reign, and that the *sepha* compilation in the Capital Library,[34] of which there are eight copies (not counting partial copies) totaling some two hundred *samut thai* volumes, has not one volume written in orthography as old as the Second Reign. The oldest, which came from the royal palace, is in the orthography of the Third Reign in the form of *samut thai* but written with white *dinso* powder. If it was not the king's copy, then it belonged to some other royalty such as Princess Apson Sudathep[35] who is known to have liked books. Hence I conclude that the compilation of the *sepha* was made in the Third Reign, or at the latest in the Fourth, and that the initial compilation was only thirty-eight volumes of *samut thai* running from the beginning of the story up to Soifa's flight to Chiang Mai, as the text ends at that point.

In the Fourth Reign, after the *sepha* compilation had been made but not yet printed, there were few copies, mainly in the possession of people of high rank. As a result, the *sepha* performed in the localities was recited in two versions. Most performers still used the old version, and only a few adopted the royal one. Many poets continued the Third Reign practice of adapting passages into verse, including the passage on Crocodile Khwat, and that on Phlai Phet and Phlai Bua. Several of Khru Jaeng's compositions can be dated to this time on grounds of their style. These later verse compositions play a lot with internal rhyming on the model of Sunthon Phu, but their attention to geography is not as accurate as in the earlier generation. During the Fourth Reign, there was another compilation of the *sepha* all together like a printed book, up to the episode of Phlai Phet and Phlai Bua, adding an extra four volumes of *samut thai* for a total of forty-two.

Celebrated *sepha* masters in the Fourth Reign were as follows.

1. Khru Jaeng, mentioned earlier, who was famous more as a *phleng* master in the Third Reign, became celebrated as a *sepha* master in the Fourth.

2. Khru Sing was father of Nai Sungchin Piphat, who died in London where he went with a *piphat* ensemble during the Fifth Reign, and father of Nai Thongdi who later became Luang Sanoduriyang. During the Fourth Reign, Khru Sing is said to have had no rival in reciting the passage on Crocodile Khwat.

3. Luang Phisanuseni (Thongyu, known as Luang Phetchalu) is said to have been accomplished in many ways—recitation, composition of *sepha*, and vocal with music—and was especially known for recit-

---

34. See p. 905, note 63. (T)
35. A favorite daughter of King Rama III who died at age thirty-five in 1845. (T)

ing the passage where Khun Phaen goes to fight in Chiang Mai. He
became a leading master in the Fifth Reign.

4. Khru Inyu reputedly had a very beautiful voice and liked to recite
   the lovemaking scenes. He was a partner with Luang Phisanuseni
   (Thongyu).

5. Khru Muang, the *sepha* master of Somdet Chaophraya Borommaha
   Phichaiyat,[36] was reputedly unrivaled for playing the claves to accom-
   pany the recitation.[37]

In the Fourth Reign, *sepha* was adapted for performance along with a music
ensemble. This form was performed widely because people liked both the reci-
tation and the music equally, and did not listen to *sepha* alone as before.

Dr. Smith printed the *sepha* for the first time in 1872 during the Fifth Reign.
Now that the royal version was easy to purchase, more performers adopted this
version, and those using the old versions steadily diminished. No new chapters
were composed. The music made the *sepha* diverge even further from the old
version. For example, *sepha* was now performed with dancing like a drama,
but with *sepha* recitation rather than a drama script, and a pair of performers
interleaving recitation, dialogue, and comedy. The recitation of the *sepha* story
was shortened. Although the old style of *sepha* performance did not disappear,
the celebrated *sepha* players in the Fifth Reign were mostly famous for other
things, not composition of *sepha*. Research shows that these famed *sepha* play-
ers of the Fifth Reign were as follows.

1. Luang Phisanuseni (Thongyu), known since the previous reign, was
   promoted as Luang Ratchamanu and became the most respected *sepha*
   master. There is a story about a certain tonsure ceremony. The host
   had a friend with a *piphat* ensemble that had recently formed and
   was not yet accomplished, but since it would only have to accompany
   prayer chanting the friend agreed to the assignment as the ensemble
   was at least up to that. After the prayers, the head of the ensemble
   spotted Luang Phisanuseni, realized the host intended to have *sepha*,
   and was shocked because the reciter was an important master. He did
   not know what to do, so went over, paid respect to Luang Phisanuseni,
   and said: "Sir, my *piphat* ensemble has only just started to rehearse."

36. That Bunnag, 1791–1857, son of a close associate of King Rama I; leading member of one
the most powerful noble families from the Second to Fourth Reigns; oversaw foreign trade in
the Fourth Reign. (T)

37. Material on the history of *sepha* masters in this era and later came from Phra Pradit
Phairo (Tat).

Luang Phisanuseni turned to ask, "What songs can you play?" The head of the ensemble said, "Only one song, 'Crocodile with a long tail,' sir." Luang Phisanuseni lowered his face and stood stock still. At the *sepha* that evening, Luang Phisanuseni played "Crocodile with a long tail" all through the night, saving the ensemble's skin.

2. Ja Phen Phayongying (Khom, known as Ja Khom), younger brother of Luang Phisanuseni (Thongyu), played *sepha*, was good at composition of verse, and knew many *lam*, but was mainly a narrator for *mahori* and composer of *sakkawa*.[38]

3. Luang Phisanuseni (Klom Karawek) was formerly a prayer chanter with a fine voice, hence his name.[39] After leaving the monkhood, he became a versifier[40] of *sakkawa* for Prince Bodinthon Phaisansophon.[41] His method of singing was very precise and his voice beautiful. He could recite *sepha*, but was not famous in the development of *sepha*.

4. Nai Joem Mahaphon became famous for chanting *Mahaphon*[42] while in the monkhood. Once he composed and played the part of a *kinnon* who followed the army that went to fight against the Ho.[43] Chaophraya Mahin,[44] who had led this army, was angry, and Joem had to stop. After leaving the monkhood, he went to stay at Ban Bang Tanaosri.[45] He had considerable skill at *sepha* recitation, and knew many *lam* songs. *Piphat* players were in fear of him. If their playing was only average, they did not dare play *sepha* with Nai Joem.

5. Khun Phonsongkhram (Pho), the *kamnan* of Ban Sai, Ang Thong, lived until the end of the Fifth Reign, played *sepha* in the old style, and reportedly very well, though I never heard him.

6. Phra Saenthongfa (Pong) from Ratchaburi was a *sepha* player for Som-

---

38. A kind of song playing in which poems are improvised as lyrics for the performance of a music ensemble; often enjoyed in boats on moonlit nights during the rainy season. (T)

39. *Klom* means lullaby, and *karawek* is a mythical bird with a beautiful call. (T)

40. ต้นบท, *ton bot*, someone who reads the script to guide the dancers. (T)

41. 1826–1906, son of King Rama III; oversaw the Royal Scribes Department during the Fourth Reign; origin of the Singhora family. (T)

42. The *Great Forest*, one of the episodes of the *Mahachat*, or Great Birth, the Jataka story of Prince Wetsandon. (T)

43. In 1884–85 and 1885–87, Bangkok sent troops to oppose armed bands, remnants of the Taiping rebellion, which were raiding south from Yunnan. (T)

44. Pheng Phenkun, Chaophraya Mahintharasak-thamrong. Pheng's father was assigned to look after the future King Mongkut when both were in the monkhood. Mongkut subsequently adopted Pheng, who rose to be head of the pages, deputy of the 1857 diplomatic mission to Queen Victoria, minister of the rolls, and head of one of the four armies sent to Nong Khai against the Ho in 1875. Chaophraya Mahin also developed the first commercial theatre. (T)

45. In Nonthaburi province. (T)

det Chaophraya Borommaha Sisuriyawong.[46] He had a good voice, and melodious recitation. While I was preparing this book, he was still alive, aged over eighty, and still playing *sepha*. But *piphat* players smiled among themselves that his rhythm tended to be faulty.

THE REVISION FOR THE 1917 PRINTED EDITION

In the Library there are four major sets of the *sepha* of *Khun Chang Khun Phaen* that were consulted: 1. a set that came from the palace, written in the orthography of the Third Reign; 2. a set from Somdet Chaophraya Borommaha Phichaiyat, written in the Fourth Reign; 3. a royal collection from the Fifth Reign, written in 1869; 4. a set belonging to Somdet Chaophraya Borommaha Sisuriyawong written in the Fifth Reign in 1869, thought to be the version that Dr. Smith printed. Unfortunately not one of these versions is complete from beginning to end, but they are very useful for studying the old wording, style, and usage of verse. This revision mainly used these four sets. But it is noteworthy that even across these four major versions, there are differences in the verse and wording. Hence it must be assumed that when all the *sepha* was initially assembled in text form, the compilers could not find one manuscript with all the chapters. In particular, there were few manuscripts in the Ayutthaya style. For some passages, *sepha* players had to be brought in to recite for transcription. So the mistakes and poor memorization of the reciters were reproduced in the first compilations of texts. Later versions made by copying and concatenating were probably not edited, except perhaps some checking and correction by *sepha* reciters. Probably the errors were exacerbated in this process, resulting in the discrepancies among the various printed versions sold today. The *sepha* texts can be called a mess because they were corrected by people who did not value the old style, who changed old wording because they liked internal rhyming, who altered words that they did not understand, and who generally increased the errors. When these texts were printed, the editing was not meticulous, creating another layer of textual disasters. For all these reasons, the editing of this volume of *sepha* was much more difficult than other books.

This Wachirayan Library[47] edition of the *sepha* appears to be the first that has undergone scrutiny and correction. But may I beg you all to understand

---

46. Chuang Bunnag, 1808–1883, head of a trader-official lineage of Persian origin; a uniquely powerful noble during the Fourth Reign. (T)

47. See p. 905, note 63. (T)

that the committee of the Library has the aim of preserving poetic works that are good examples of Thai language, rather than trying to preserve the story of *Khun Chang Khun Phaen*. For this reason, the committee analyzed the existing old texts of *sepha*, and found that those in which both the poetry and the story were good amounted to just thirty-eight volumes, understood to be the first ever compilation of the *sepha*, running from the beginning of the story until Soifa's flight to Chiang Mai. Hence it was decided to revise and print only this material. Subsequent passages, whether about Phlai Yong going to China, or about Phlai Phet and Phlai Bua, are considered to have no value as literature and so are not included in the printed edition.

But when the Library collected the *sepha* together, it acquired manuscripts of many other passages composed by poets in the past. Some passages had new stories, for example about Crocodile Khwat; and some passages expanded on what was in the old *sepha*, for example the passage about the birth of Goldchild (*kuman thong*), son of Buakhli. Many of these passages were well written and worth hearing. They were understood to have been based on old folktales rather than being new inventions. It would have been a pity to throw them away, so it was seen appropriate to select the good passages for inclusion in the Wachirayan Library edition. But this would mean deleting some old passages that were duplicative, hence decisions had to be made on whether the original or new version should be dropped. However, after close examination, it was found possible to combine the older and newer versions together by cutting only a small number of clumsy passages in the old version, and not a single passage deemed to be good. Thus it was decided to insert several of these fragments, and to indicate clearly at printing which passages these were.

This Wachirayan Library edition of the *sepha* amounts to forty-three volumes of *samut thai*, about the same length as the earlier printed versions, but different because of the insertions and deletions. It can be guaranteed that this edition is superior in both the storyline and the poetry. It has preserved the good things in the *sepha*, without a single omission or mistake. In addition, this version is divided in a new way because the old division into *samut thai* volumes is not suitable for a printed book. The division into chapters better reflects the plot, and also the differing styles of the authors. The whole story is presented as forty-one chapters printed in three volumes.[48]

As for language, this Wachirayan Library edition was made with the intention of retaining the old wording composed by the earlier poets, but it was necessary to make some amendments for the following reasons.

1. In some places, the old version has crude passages intended to make the

---

48. As explained below, this actually became forty-three chapters. (T)

audience laugh. As Sunthon Phu wrote in the poem, "As for Nai Ma from the retinue of Phraya Non, he was a comedian good at bawdy improvisation who made people laugh heartily." These crude passages probably predate the royal version. They made readers dislike the *sepha*, and in the past women were even forbidden to read it. In this revision, these crude passages have been deleted with the aim of overcoming this prejudice against the *sepha*. But such passages have not been completely smoothed away, because by its very nature *sepha* poetry is based on everyday dialogue that often includes obscenity and abuse. Deleting everything considered crude would ruin the style of the *sepha*, hence discretion has been used.

2. The plot of the *sepha* has a lot of humor, but on top of that the composers inserted many comic passages. For example, in the account of the cremation of Khun Siwichai and Phan Sonyotha, there was a comic passage about prayer chanting in twelve languages. These comic passages were probably improvised during recitation, but are not funny on the printed page, and detract from the work. Such comic passages have also been cut out.

3. There are connecting passages that seem to have been added when the *sepha* was assembled as a single work. Sometimes these are disconnected, poorly integrated, repetitive, or contain mistakes. Some have been amended for better continuity.

4. In the case of unusual words or verses, where possible they have been corrected by reference to an old version. Otherwise they have been amended on the basis of personal opinion, with care taken to correct only those that are certainly wrong.

This Wachirayan Library edition of the *sepha* has failed on one point. The opening line—"Now respects to teachers have been paid, a start be made on this old saga"—indicates that there originally was a preface honoring teachers. This should be included in the printed edition. However, all efforts to locate a volume with this preface failed to bear fruit. Inquiries were made with *sepha* reciters both in the capital and provincial towns to find someone who had a written or memorized version of the preface that would be suitable. It can be assumed that there was a preface honoring teachers in the first chapter, probably composed in the Ayutthaya era, and probably making offerings to the deities in the manner of *saiyasat*. But it is not known whether it was short or long, or how it began and ended, as it has almost completely disappeared. Only two lines survive in a later preface:

Ganga and Yamuna, the foundations;
Mount Meru, the lofty pillar of the world;
earth, water, wind and fire, the certainties,
that survive and endure.

These two lines are probably found in prefaces honoring teachers that everybody can remember. But apart from this, not a single other line that makes sense can be found anywhere. A preface from Phak Hai, Ayutthaya, which is more complete than others, is given below so that you can see an example.

Ten fingers raised above the head,
Pay respects to the Buddha and the *thamma* overarching the world;
the Sangha which preserves the precepts carefully;
Ganga and Yamuna, the foundations;
Mount Meru, the lofty pillar of the world;
earth, water, wind and fire, the certainties,
that survive and endure.
Pay respects to the merit of fathers and mothers,
all the teachers of language;
also to Lord Narai, who presides over the great ocean
using the naga king as his crystal throne,
who will not awaken without cause.
Holding the conch and the mighty wheel,
the avatar[49] became Lord Rama.
Also pay respects to him of great lineage
who rides on a swan and flies in the sky.[50]
Pay respects to Lord Isuan, the lord of the universe,
Phra Narai Ramathibodi.
Pay respects to powerful rishis and heavenly musicians,
the magnificent Lord Wisanukam[51]
who blesses the instruments in the world
that exist from the past.

Nai Yu's preface honoring teachers of *sepha* and *piphat* seems to follow this. I have researched prefaces honoring teachers from the Ayutthaya era only to this extent, and cannot include one at the start of this *sepha*.

The checking and revision work on this Wachirayan Library edition of the *sepha*, from the beginning of the project to the time of printing, has been a collaboration between Prince Krommuen Kawipot Supricha[52] and myself for

---

49. Waikunt, the vehicle of Vishnu (Narai), but used in Thai to mean avatar. (T)

50. Brahma. (T)

51. Visvakarma, the great artificer. (T)

52. 1881–1927, son of Prince Wichaichan, Front Palace King at the center of the Front Palace crisis of 1874–75; earlier titled Prince Kalyanprawat; wrote several books of poetry; edited the journals *Wachirayan* and *Thesaphiban*, King Chulalongkorn's travel memoir, *Klai ban*, Far From Home, and Damrong's memoir, *Khwam songjam*, Memories; his descendants use the surname

over two years. We hope it will meet with favor from all of you.

Signed: Damrong Rajanubhab
Director
Wachirayan Library
7 August 1917

PREFACE TO THE SECOND VOLUME

In the first printed volume of *Khun Chang Khun Phaen*, I related the history of the *sepha*, and explained the nature of the revision of the Wachirayan Library edition at length. There is no need to repeat that material here. I will relate only certain differences that the reader should be aware of in a few chapters of this second volume.

Chapter 16, the birth of Goldchild, son of Buakhli. The version printed here was composed by Khru Jaeng. It was popular among reciters of *sepha* but is understood never to have been printed. In the old version, Khun Phaen went to find a spirit (*hong phrai*) in a graveyard, and met two spirits called I-Ma and I-Phet-kong who had died while pregnant. Khun Phaen asked for one of the children from their wombs to raise as a *kuman thong*. The old version was short, only four pages. Khru Jaeng expanded it. He added the story of Khun Phaen marrying Buakhli and living together until she was pregnant, and then the incident when Buakhli died along with the baby in her womb, making it possible for Khun Phaen to acquire a *kuman thong* who was his own true child. After this story came the stories about Khun Phaen forging the Skystorm sword and purchasing his horse, Color of Mist. Khru Jaeng also recomposed these, following older versions but trying to outdo them. The story of the sword is well written both in the Khru Jaeng and earlier versions. In the older version it appears before the *kuman thong* story, but Khru Jaeng placed it later. I consider this is not an important enough passage to merit disrupting the sequence, so I use Khru Jaeng's version throughout including the passage on the Skystorm sword. But the old version of purchasing Color of Mist is good, and Khru Jaeng's version cannot compete with it, so I include the old version beginning

Kalyanawong. Prince Bidya called him "one of the finest poets of his day" (Bidyalankarana, "*Sebha* Recitation," 10). (T)

from "Luang Songphon and Phan Phan" to the end of the chapter.

Khru Jaeng's version uses words that are believed to come from the Fourth Reign such as *patsatan* on page 316, line 4. This means gunpowder and bullet wrapped in paper ready for loading into a percussion-cap gun such as the Enfield. These are understood to have come to Siam in the Fourth Reign.

In general, Khru Jaeng is an esteemed poet as the preface honoring teachers mentions "teacher Jaeng whose compositions are so famous." His verses were well composed in the sense that they met with the approval of ordinary people. But given a chance, he tended towards crudity. There are two places in this chapter 16 where such crudity had to be excised—where Sijan instructs Buakhli, and in the "wondrous scene"[53] of Khun Phaen in Buakhli's room.

Chapter 17, in which Khun Phaen goes up into Khun Chang's house and enters the room of Kaeo Kiriya, is said to have been composed by King Rama II. The style of the poetry appears inconsistent across the chapter. The king's composition probably begins where Khun Phaen reaches Khun Chang's house with the words "Arriving at Khun Chang's house, he entered the huge compound and saw a strong embankment and surrounding moat," and continues to late in the chapter. Another style seems to begin at "Hit by the mantra, Wanthong forgot her anger. She sat next to him with one hand on the floor and her head bowed." The royal composition seems to end at the stanza, "Are you losing your biting eloquence?" The rhythm of the verse seems to be designed for playing with a *phinphat* ensemble.

Chapter 18, in which Khun Phaen flees with Wanthong, seems to be in the same style as chapter 17. If that chapter is a royal composition then this seems to be also. But the passage from where Wanthong laments over her condition up to the end of the chapter seems to be in another style. This passage of lament, as printed in this book, appears only in the *sepha* of Somdet Chaophraya Borommaha Sisuriyawong. In other versions it is shorter.

Chapters 17 and 18 are considered the high point of *Khun Chang Khun Phaen*. People like to listen to these chapters and to memorize them more than others, and they are widely recited. Phra Saenthongfa (Pong) told me that Somdet Chaophraya Borommaha Sisuriyawong would listen only to this passage. Phra Saenthongfa was later asked what happened if he recited to the very end where Khun Phaen descends from Khun Chang's house. He replied, "Well, I have to go back to where Khun Phaen enters the house again." The reason why these two chapters are greatly liked is because they have many moods—admiration, lovemaking, complaint, grief, humor, anger—combined

---

53. บทอัศจรรย์, *bot atsajan*, the term for love scenes employing extravagant metaphors, a literary convention of this era. (T)

in one passage. Authors had the opportunity to display many moods and to put their feelings into the composition. If anyone has to choose a single passage for listening, no other passage can compete with these two chapters. But revising these two chapters for the printed edition was more difficult than any others in the work because they are better remembered than others. Moreover, the versions that could be found, both in text form and in the memory of people such as Phra Saenthongfa, all had different wording. Hence it was necessary to make choices. This was done with a great deal of effort, but criticism is inescapable because the wording in the printed edition cannot follow what is memorized by every reciter. Some will say this is wrong, and some will say that is wrong, since each believes his own memory is correct. There is no duty like that of a book editor.

Chapter 19, in which Khun Chang follows after Wanthong, seems to be in the same style as the passage in which Khun Chang asks for the hand of Phim, printed as chapter 5 of the first volume. If the chapters in which Phlai Kaeo becomes the lover of Phim and in which Khun Phaen goes into Khun Chang's house are by King Rama II, I believe that the two chapters about Khun Chang are by King Rama III. Both chapters follow a chapter by King Rama II, and the rhythm and style of the verse seem similar to the drama script of *Sangsinchai*.[54] This is my conjecture for you readers to evaluate.

Chapter 23, in which Khun Phaen is jailed, has one passage known to have been composed in the Second Reign. When Khun Chang plays chess with Sonphraya, the latter says "Even the teacher couldn't match you. It's stupendous to take something on the king's rank."

This is similar to a *Ramakian* drama script composed by King Rama II on the coronation of Ram, when Sangkakari goes to invite Phra Wasit Rishi who is playing chess and says "when young at that time and still diligent / the teacher could match even Indra."

Chapter 24 on the birth of Phlai Ngam is easily identified as the work of Sunthon Phu by anyone who knows his poetry. Nobody else could achieve this style. Study shows that Sunthon Phu composed the whole chapter very carefully so that it could not be outdone by other versions. In no other work, even *Phra Aphaimani*[55] or *Laksanawong*, did Sunthon Phu compose as meticulously as in this chapter of the *sepha*.

Chapter 25, in which the King of Lanchang presents Nang Soithong to King Phanwasa, is an old version that I believe dates from before the Second Reign

---

54. An old story composed as an outer drama during the Second Reign, possibly by the future King Rama III. (T)

55. Sunthon Phu's most famous work, a picaresque fantasy about a wandering prince. (T)

and could be another example to recognize the old style as mentioned in the history of the *sepha* above.

The *sepha* printed in the second volume needs only these points of special explanation. Apart from this, in the process of revision, some parts had to be deleted and replaced for the same reasons to do with connecting passages, crudity, and errors that were explained in the preface of the first volume.

The old versions of *sepha* texts were divided according to *samut thai* volumes, that is, chapters ended where the *samut thai* volume ended, not according to the plot. This division is not suitable for a printed book, and so was replaced with division into chapters according to the story. Previously it was estimated there would be forty-one chapters but on investigation it proved more suitable to divide into forty-three. This printed edition is in three volumes divided according to the storyline, hence the number of chapters and pages in each volume is different. The first volume has fourteen chapters, the second twelve, and the third will have seventeen. This will complete the Wachirayan Library edition of the *sepha*.

Signed: Damrong Rajanubhab
Director
Wachirayan Library
16 December 1917

PREFACE TO THE THIRD VOLUME

Study of the verse style in the well-known version of the *sepha* printed by Dr. Smith suggests that the revision of the *sepha* by various poets during the Second Reign went only up to the birth of Phlai Ngam which is chapter 24 in the second volume of this Wachirayan Library edition. Another revision by various poets in the Third Reign began from the marriage of Phra Wai, which is chapter 33 in this third volume, up to the story of the ordeal by fire of Soifa and Simala in chapter 42. In these two periods, there was no revision of the middle part about the Chiang Mai campaign—from the point where the King of Chiang Mai asks for Soithong up to where King Phanwasa releases the King of Chiang Mai to return home. This middle part remained in an old version that was rather rough and discontinuous, unlike the earlier and later sections. This point was obvious to the authors when they assembled the whole poem into one story. As a result, during the Fourth Reign, authors such as Khru Jaeng worked to create a revised version of this middle section about the attack on Chiang Mai that would be better than the old version. When making this Wachirayan Library edition, several manuscript versions were found, some too good to be overlooked. As the committee of the library overseeing this edition has the aim of preserving good books of literature, it examined these rival versions, compared them to the older version, and adopted any that were found to be of higher literary value. One example is the chapter on the birth of Goldchild, son of Buakhli, printed as chapter 16 of the second volume.

In this third volume, the following chapters are these replacement versions.

Chapter 27, Phlai Ngam volunteers. The author is unknown. The opening uses the old version. The new version, that starts where King Phanwasa becomes angry because nobody volunteers to go to attack Chiang Mai, makes the story of Phlai Ngam volunteering more subtle.

Chapter 28, Phlai Ngam gets Simala. The style is the same as chapter 27, and the content differs from the old version on one point. In the old version, when Khun Phaen and Phlai Ngam reach Phichit, the ruler of Phichit invites a priest to perform their marriage ceremony, suggesting that Phlai Ngam asked for her hand and won acceptance. In the replacement version, Phlai Ngam catches sight of Simala, falls in love, and thus steals in on her. This amendment seems to fit better, as later when the army returns home, King Phanwasa appoints Phlai Ngam as Muen Wai and orders him to marry Simala. Khun Chang comes to attend the ceremony and gets into a dispute. If they had married at Phichit, why would they have married again? In the old version, Khun Phaen even addresses the king: "When Phra Wai went with the army, he had Simala, the child of Phraya Phichit. Though they were in love, they had not yet married. The ceremony was postponed until the fourth month." The revised version seems more appropriate. But the original manuscript of this version is missing a passage where Phlai Ngam goes to the bed of Simala. This passage had to be composed jointly at the Library, up to the point where Phlai Ngam admires the forest. From there to the end of the chapter is Khru Jaeng's version.

Chapter 29, in which Khun Phaen and Phlai Ngam release Phra Thainam, was composed by Khru Jaeng. This is probably the best of Khru Jaeng's work on the *sepha*. He made certain changes from the older version, for example about the course of the fighting and the name of the Chiang Mai army commander, but these were only details.

Chapter 30, in which Khun Phaen and Phlai Ngam subdue the King of Chiang Mai, was composed by Khru Jaeng like the previous chapter.

Chapter 31, in which Khun Phaen and Phlai Ngam take the army home, was also composed by Khru Jaeng, but had to be slightly amended in the Library at the point where Khun Phaen and Phlai Ngam arrive back at Phichit to make the story of Simala accord with chapter 28.

Chapter 32, on the presentation of Soithong and Soifa, is the old version with small additions by Khru Jaeng. However in the final part where the ruler of Chiang Mai goes lamenting back to his city, Khru Jaeng wrongly used the geography of Bangkok so this was rejected in favor of the old version.

This third volume of the Wachirayan Library edition has six chapters that have never previously been printed—five on the attack on Chiang Mai and one on Crocodile Khwat. Otherwise, the chapters are all from the old version with some editing for smoothness.

Chapter 43 on Crocodile Khwat is really an insertion, probably composed in the Third Reign. The extant manuscripts have three versions. One seems to be in old style with poor poetry. The second is a revised version that reads smoothly but is short. Khru Jaeng expanded this and made it more fantastic, creating a third version which is better than the two earlier ones and which was thus chosen for this volume.

The Wachirayan Library edition of the *sepha* of *Khun Chang Khun Phaen* ends with this third volume. The committee believes that subsequent chapters continuing beyond this ending are of no literary value in either story or poetic style and thus will not be revised and printed.

Damrong Rajanubhab
Director
Wachirayan Library
1 October 1918

HISTORY OF *SEPHA* (1925)

ABOUT THE OLD *SEPHA*

In the first edition of the "History of *sepha*," I discussed what language the word "*sepha*" came from and what it meant. Many people had pursued this matter without result. Since my discussion was published, a new generation of students has made it their business to assist the research. They advised me that the Sanskrit dictionary by Sir Monier Williams (1899 edition, p. 1247) gives several definitions of *seva* including a type of worship.[56] There is a related word, *sevakaku*, defined as "change of voice in service (i.e. sometimes speaking loudly, sometimes softly, sometimes angrily, sometimes sorrowfully)." These students thus think that *sepha* may come from the Sanskrit *seva*. I think this is ingenious. *Sepha* could indeed come from the Sanskrit *seva*. This is evidence that the origins of *sepha* recitation in our country may have come from India, just like the *khon* mask play, *lakhon* drama, and many other kinds of performance. Examination of the nature of *sepha* at present reveals traces of what is mentioned in the dictionary. Worship of Brahmanical gods is found in the invocation of teachers. The rhythm of reciting *sepha* can vary from loud to soft depending on the characters in the story. But Kuppuswami Ariya, a Brahmin, Sanskrit expert, and native of the state of Kalinga (Orissa) who used to be on the staff of the Library, explained that *seva* means any kind of worship of gods using articles of any kind. It is not the word for a particular form of ceremony. All this information is still not consistent and so no conclusion can be made on the translation of the word *sepha*. When Kuppuswami Ariya died, his position at the Library was occupied by Subramania Sastri, who came from Madras. On being asked about the word *seva*, he explained that in southern India the Tamils have a ceremony practiced until today called *serawai* or *hariserawai*. To worship a god or deity, they recite a hymn of praise accompanied by music and sometimes also dancing. Perhaps the word *serawai* is a Tamil distortion of the word *seva* mentioned in the Sanskrit dictionary. This information seems sufficient to resolve that the Thai custom of reciting *sepha* came from India.

As for the history of *sepha*, there is evidence that it existed in Siam around

---

56. Monier-Williams gives an umbrella definition as "going or resorting to, visiting, frequenting," and then five sub-definitions including "worship, homage, reverence, devotion to"; other sub-definitions are "service, attendance on," "to be in the service of," "sexual intercourse with," and "addiction to, indulgence in, practice or employment of, frequent enjoyment of" (online version at www.indica-et-buddhica.org). (T)

five hundred years ago. In the Palatine Law instituted in the year of the rat, B.S. 2011 (1468) during the reign of King Boromtrailokanat, the timetable of royal activities includes the statement: "at midnight, *sepha* and music; at 1 a.m., folktales."[57] This suggests that at the time the Palatine Law was established, *sepha* was appreciated, and that *sepha* was distinguished from "folktales" (reciting stories). As for the nature of *sepha* at that time, we can only surmise on the basis of the clues available. The fact that *sepha* was different from "folktales" suggests that *sepha* was recited, and that the form was verse. But the Palatine Law also mentions music. This may have one of two meanings: first, music could have been an element of the *sepha*; or second, music could have been something separate, and the king had the option to listen to *sepha* or music. Of these two possibilities, I suspect music was an element of *sepha* as, according to ancient practice, music accompanied recitation or singing, as in *Kaki* where the *khonthan*[58] "takes up the *phin* to accompany his lament." This also accords with Subramania Sastri's information that *serawai* in India included music. On this basis, I think the reciter of the *sepha* mentioned in the Palatine Law played the *phin* or fiddle, or else there was a separate musical ensemble, in the manner of *khap mai*, a trio that still figures in royal ceremonies down to the present day with one reciter, a fiddle player, and a third with a *banto* hand-drum[59] for rhythm. Perhaps also, the old *sepha* was improvised on the spot in the old tradition of singing without a script (in the same way that *phleng* and the Nora drama are still improvised to this day). The important qualities of the old *sepha* may have been the creativity of the verse and the harmony of the recitation, while music was simply a supporting element, or an entertainment that allowed the reciter to have some time to rest. In the past, the story was not taken from *Khun Chang Khun Phaen* which appeared much later, but perhaps from tales in praise of the gods such as the *Mahabharata* or the *Ramakian*, occasionally substituted by local tales in praise of the king. Later at the end of the Ayutthaya period, *Khun Chang Khun Phaen* became so popular that it was used exclusively for *sepha*.

---

57. See in full in Ratchaburi Laws, vol. 2, p. 93 (KTS, 1:131 (T)).

58. Heavenly musicians, *gandharva*. (T)

59. บัณเฑาะว์, *bando*, a small double-ended drum with strikers attached by cord, played by flipping in the hand. (T)

THE STORY OF *KHUN CHANG KHUN PHAEN*

Khun Chang Khun Phaen is a true story that took place in the Ayutthaya era. It appears in the book, *Testimony of the Inhabitants of the Old Capital,*[60] which is considered a form of royal chronicle, as follows.

[see above, pp. 1342–45, for the extract]

The above story of *Khun Chang Khun Phaen* from the *Testimony* has evidence about the dating of the story. At one point it states that King Phanwasa was the father of Phra Borom Kuman, and that when Phra Borom Kuman ascended the throne he had a queen by name Si Sudajan who, when her husband died, attempted to put her lover on the throne. In the Royal Chronicles, Phra Borom Kuman is called King Chairachathirat, and thus King Phanwasa is King Ramathibodi II. These sources suggest that Khun Phaen lived during the reign of King Ramathibodi II (r. cs 853–91, ce 1491–1529). The Chiang Mai chronicle states that in that era, King Mueang Kaeo, the ruler of Chiang Mai, went to war against Ayutthaya several times.[61] And there is another intriguing point in the opening stanzas of the *sepha*:

This is the story of Khun Phaen, Khun Chang,
and the fair Nang Wanthong.
In the year 147,
the parents of these three people of that era . . .

The date 147 does not correspond to any calendar, apparently because a leading word has been lost. If we assume this was formerly written as "847" (1485) but subsequently miscopied, then Khun Phaen was born in the reign of King Trailokanat, was six years old when King Ramathibodi II succeeded, and entered government service in that reign. This seems to fit. On this basis, there is evidence that the story of *Khun Chang Khun Phaen* took place during the reign of King Ramathibodi II. However, it must be noted that the story was not performed as *sepha* until at least a century later after the story had been passed down orally and transformed into a folktale. If we estimate that *Khun Chang Khun Phaen* was first popular as *sepha* performance around the reign

---

60. This book has the testimony of Thai captured at the fall of Ayutthaya in 1767, recorded in Burmese. The library acquired a copy and had it translated into Thai. It was printed for the first time in 1910, and again in 1925.

61. But where the *Testimony* mentions Thao Phothisan as the King of Chiang Mai is wrong, as Thao Phothisan was King of Lanchang and son-in-law of a later Chiang Mai king.

of King Narai, I think that would not be far off.

The tale of *Khun Chang Khun Phaen* as summarized in the *Testimony* above is clearly not identical with the *sepha*. This is not at all surprising, given that the story was probably passed down orally as a folktale before it was performed as *sepha*. And even later when it was written down as a poetic text for *sepha* performance, it was probably made more entertaining and gradually lengthened as well. It's likely that the story in the *sepha* has greatly deviated from the true story, yet still retains some trace of the original. If we try to reconstruct the original, as far as it can be done logically, the early part of the story was probably the same as in the *sepha* version, namely that Khun Chang, Khun Phaen, and Wanthong were from Suphan, that Wanthong was the lover of Khun Phaen at the time he was still called Phlai Kaeo, and that they seemed to be settling down together but had not yet married when Phlai Kaeo was conscripted into the army (not necessarily as its commander) and was absent for a long time. During this time, Khun Chang tried successfully to get Wanthong as his wife. Phlai Kaeo returned from the army with the name of Khun Phaen Saensathan and the position as *palat* of the left in the department of royal guards (*tamruat phuban*). He abducted Wanthong and Khun Chang gave chase. Khun Phaen wounded Khun Chang in some fashion, and Khun Chang filed a complaint. King Phanwasa sent nobles after Khun Phaen who killed the nobles and fled to the northern cities, but eventually presented himself to the ruler of Phichit who informed the capital. Possibly it was at this point that Wanthong was condemned to death by the king for being of two minds, and Khun Phaen was imprisoned for killing the nobles, but given remission on account of his confession. At this point war broke out with Chiang Mai and during recruitment, Pramuen Si recommended Khun Phaen to the king, resulting in Khun Phaen being pardoned and sent off to fight. He gained a victory and became famous. This was probably the original story of *Khun Chang Khun Phaen*. The remainder was added later when it was a folktale and *sepha*.

Personal names that appear in the *sepha*, such as the word "Phlai" in Phlai Kaeo, have been the subject of debate and some misunderstanding. As *phlai* is the term for a bull elephant, some people have questioned why this name was used, and some have asserted that it should really be "Phrai" because he is an expert with spirits (*phut, phi, hong, phrai*). I have found an explanation in a clause of the Criminal Law[62] that mentions "Phlai Changai, close retainers of the king," who used their royal association to seize goods and cause suffering to people. The law prescribes: "have that person clapped in chains and take the case to the king, who will deal with the matter." This suggests that Phlai Changai

---

62. See further in the Ratchaburi edition of the laws, volume 2, p. 223 (KTS, 4:91 (T)).

was the name for a group of bold youths that the king kept as close retainers, like pages. Probably when Khun Phaen first entered service, King Phanwasa placed him in this group. As his old name was Kaeo, he was now called Phlai Kaeo. He was promoted to Khun Phaen when he was given a position as *palat* of the provincial guard (*tamruat phuthon*). In the old government roster, the *palat* of the department of the right was titled Khun Phitsanusaen, and that of the left was Khun Phaen Sathan. In the *sepha* it appears as Khun Phaen Saen-sathan but surprisingly, in the later edition of the roster, the name was changed to Khun Phlaeng Sathan.[63] This seems to have been a recent change as it lost the rhyming connection with Khun Phitsanusaen. When and why it was changed is unknown, but possibly in order to differentiate the official name from the name in the *sepha*. The name Khun Chang is really not a personal name but an official title, meaning a head of the Department of Elephants. The title "Khun Chang" appears in the Palatine Law, and ancient poems have lines such as "Khun Chang rode an elephant with fine tusks." In the *sepha*, Khun Chang's father, Khun Siwichai, was head of the provincial division of the Department of Elephants and would have held the title "Khun Chang." When he died, his son would have taken the name in his stead. Whatever name the son had earlier, he became Khun Chang when he took over the office in place of his father, and was probably called as such in Suphanburi at the time. The name that Khun Chang was given by his mother is not found in the *sepha*.

SEPHA IN LATE AYUTTHAYA

In the late Ayutthaya period, *sepha* was a widespread form of entertainment both in the capital and the nearby provincial centers. Anyone who had a merit-making ceremony at home, such as a topknot shaving, liked to have *sepha*. Monks would be invited to chant prayers in the evening, and guests would begin to gather from that time. After the chanting, the guests would be fed and then in the early night would listen to *sepha* until the gathering ended. Probably *sepha* was favored because it was easier and less expensive than other entertainments such as *phleng* singing or *lakhon* drama, which required many people and a stage, whereas *sepha* required only a single person and could be performed in a house without erecting anything. Even someone with few resources could have *sepha* and hence it was popular. Given this popularity,

---

63. In the Three Seals code, Khun Phitsanusaen is the *palat* of the right in the provincial guard, but Khun Phlaeng Sathan is the *palat* of the left in a sister department, the city guard (*tamruat phuban*; KTS, 1:226). (T)

there were many people who could make a good living from performing *sepha* in the localities. The form of *sepha* performance in late Ayutthaya, and how it changed, can be studied from surviving old records, as I will now explain.

1. *Sepha* was performed only on auspicious occasions, not in ceremonies to make offerings to the spirits. Probably this was laid down in old manuals that limited *sepha* to auspicious ceremonies.

2. *Sepha* was performed only in the evening, not during daytime. Probably this was an old rule. The Palatine Law shows that the king listened to *sepha* late at night along with folktales. I have heard that the practice of reciting folktales was confined to night time because the gods would become angry if the tales were recited in daytime when the gods went to pay court to Phra Isuan (Siva) and hence missed them. Old tradition probably laid down that both *sepha* and folktales were night-time entertainments.

3. *Sepha* later had only one reciter with claves for rhythm, and no musical accompaniment. This was the practice from the Narai reign.[64] It probably arose because when the *sepha* became a local entertainment, it was difficult to find musical accompaniment and instruments, and so two people alternated between recitation and rest periods. The tradition of *sepha* with a *piphat* ensemble arose only in the Bangkok Second Reign, as will be related below.

4. The only story performed as *sepha* was *Khun Chang Khun Phaen*. How did this come about? It can be surmised from the evidence presented above that *sepha* and folktales used to be popular for domestic merit making ceremonies. Probably these two forms had always gone together, as seen in the Palatine Law. When these became local entertainments, they could both be staged easily. But the two had different principles. In *sepha*, the main point was the versifying and the recitation, whereas in folktales the main point was the story and the realism and humor of the storytelling. The content of *sepha* and folktales was thus different. The *sepha* could use a tale that was already known, or could present one episode from a longer story, since the versifying and delivery were more important then the plot. But a folktale needed to be a story that was different and unknown to the audience or else it would be unexciting. Also a folktale had to be related from beginning to end since the important thing was the story. Probably *Khun Chang Khun Phaen* used to be recited as a folktale, but once the plot was widely known it became unexciting. However, it was suitable to be performed as *sepha* for several reasons including the fact that the story was entertaining, and the setting was local. Performing

---

64. As described in the book on Siam by the French envoy, M. La Loubère, chapter 12, page 68, which calls the sepha reciter "Tchang cap." (ช่างขับ. The page reference is to the 1693 English-language version of *A New Historical Relation of the Kingdom of Siam*. (T))

this story in verse with all its romance, quarreling, and lamentation appealed more deeply to the audience than stories from abroad such as *Ramakian*. In addition, according to the old *sepha* manual, *Khun Chang Khun Phaen* was a story in praise of the king, namely King Phanwasa's victory over Chiang Mai, and hence suitable for performance as *sepha*. For all these various reasons, the audience for *sepha* appreciated *Khun Chang Khun Phaen,* and hence reciters elaborated and lengthened it to the point that no other story could compete, and so *Khun Chang Khun Phaen* alone was performed as *sepha*.

SEPHA IN THE BANGKOK ERA

In early Bangkok, there is evidence to suggest that *sepha* was performed in the same way as in late Ayutthaya. The evidence appears in two passages of verse, the first by Sunthon Phu about Phlai Ngam's topknot ceremony in chapter 24 of the *sepha*, and the second in an old invocation of teachers, as follows:

[see above, pp. 1349–50, for the extracts]

These two passages list the names of good *sepha* teachers. Four appear in both passages, namely Khru Mi, the firework maker; Khru Thongyu; Khru Rongsi (who later became Luang Suwan); and Khru Ma, a retainer of Phraya Non. Another two mentioned only by Sunthon Phu are Nai Thung[65] and Nai Phet. Another four mentioned in the invocation verse are Khru Son, Khru Pheng, Khru Re, and Phan Raksa-ratri. Altogether there are ten names. It seems that Sunthon Phu knew six players well enough to relate what each was good at. But the author of the invocation verse knew only three, namely Khru Re, described as someone "who likes to have fun," Khru Thongyu who liked to play "major verses," and Khru Ma of Phraya Non who had been the author's own teacher but had since died. For the other five, he gives only names that he had been told. This suggests that this invocation was written later.

There are some other known historical details about the good *sepha* performers celebrated in these two passages. The timing of one of them is known for sure. Khru Thongyu was a player of the *Inao* drama in the troupe of Prince Thep-harirak at the start of the First Reign. In the Second Reign he became a

---

65. This may be the same Nai Thung as the father of Nai Choi (blind in both eyes), who was a famous *ranat* player. In the Fifth Reign there was a story that Nai Thung played both *piphat* and *sepha*, and ordered his son Nai Choi to play only *sepha*, not *piphat*, but Nai Choi practiced *piphat* in secret and became an accomplished *piphat* player, as his father discovered.

royal drama teacher, and performed dramas in almost every house and home. That is why he is described as "old Thongyu, drama teacher" in the invocation verse. He died in the Third Reign. The inclusion of his name indicates that the people mentioned in these two passages were the good *sepha* performers of the First and Second Reigns. Sunthon Phu composed verse from the First Reign onwards and thus had heard all six names mentioned. But one name found in the invocation verse, Khru Son the gatekeeper, celebrated as "a teacher of people from all over," was not mentioned by Sunthon Phu, maybe because he had already died before Sunthon Phu had a chance to hear him. This suggests that Khru Son may have been a *sepha* player from the Ayutthaya era, who became a master in early Bangkok. Probably there were other *sepha* players of the Ayutthaya era but none as outstanding as Khru Son and hence they were not mentioned in the invocation. Yet the sole reference to Khru Son is enough to indicate that the *sepha* performed at the end of the Bangkok First Reign probably followed the late Ayutthaya form, that is, it was an entertainment for night time, especially for household ceremonies such as topknot cutting, played after the prayer chanting and dinner until late in the night, and using sections from *Khun Chang Khun Phaen* chosen by the host or at the preference of the audience or the performers' capabilities. This can be seen from Sunthon Phu's verse that Khru Mi was "good at the fight scenes," and Nai Thongyu "knew how to recite in Lao," meaning that Khru Mi was expert at the passages where Phlai Kaeo went to attack Chiang Thong or Khun Phaen went to attack Chiang Mai, while Khru Thongyu excelled in the passages about Laothong or Soifa. It seems that in late Ayutthaya and the Bangkok First Reign, if the host wanted to hear a specific passage of *Khun Chang Khun Phaen*, he could find a performer who excelled in that type of passage since there were many to choose from, including some from the lower classes such as gatekeepers like Nai Son who had become "a teacher of people from all over" in early Bangkok. This suggests that *sepha* was a widespread entertainment in late Ayutthaya.

THE HISTORY OF *SEPHA* IN THE FIRST REIGN

Scripts for *sepha* performance are thought to have become important in the Bangkok First Reign. Prior to that, according to tradition, *sepha* had to be improvised on the spot without a script. But when sepha performance became widespread in the localities, some *sepha* scripts probably appeared because, among the many performers, some had a good voice and delivery but were not skilled at versification, and thus requested others to write scripts for them to memorize. Some performers who could improvise verses were also probably happy to prepare scripts and commit them to memory because it was convenient and the verses were finer than those improvised. Hence *sepha* scripts probably appeared in the Ayutthaya era, but were kept secret as the performers wanted to give the impression they were extemporizing, and were reluctant to let anyone else read or copy their scripts. For these reasons, the Ayutthaya *sepha* scripts were probably few in number. This can be seen from the fact that, unlike drama scripts and other types of texts in verse, the *sepha* that survived down to the Bangkok era was only what people could remember and a few retained texts. Almost everything had to be recreated in Bangkok.

King Rama II (Loetla Naphalai) is said to have enjoyed listening to *sepha*, and to have encouraged the writing and revising of some old passages. The chapters that he is believed to have composed include: when Phlai Kaeo becomes the lover of Phim (chapter 4); and when Khun Phaen enters Khun Chang's house (chapter 17). But judging from the style in the existing *sepha* text, he also composed other passages, such as the quarrel between Laothong and Wanthong, and Khun Phaen abducting Wanthong from Khun Chang's house.

On the episode of Khun Phaen entering Khun Chang's house, the Library has both old manuscripts[66] as well as the royal composition. For comparison, here are excerpts of the passage where Khun Phaen admires the tapestries, and of the passage where Khun Phaen laments.

ADMIRING THE CURTAIN, OLD VERSION

[See this volume, pp. 1128–29, from "Khun Phaen stood up and looked at the cross hall" to ". . . cutting the string of her curtain to fall in a heap."]

THE ROYAL COMPOSITION

[See the main volume, p. 342, from "Holding Skystorm, he walked up to the central hall" to ". . . but hurried on to find Wanthong."]

KHUN PHAEN LAMENTS, OLD VERSION

[See this volume, p. 1148, from "Khun Phaen, great romancer, said angrily to Wanthong" to "that almost fell off because I let you sleep on it."]

THE ROYAL COMPOSITION

[See the main volume, pp. 348–49, from "Angered by her words, Khun Phaen said," to "to knock me down dead—really."]

---

66. This old version is usually known as *samnuan kao 1*. It was first published as *Khun Chang Khun Phaen chabap khwam kao* (Bangkok: Sophon Phiphannathanakon, 1925), and reprinted in 1990 and 1998. (T)

I once asked Prince Bamrap-borabak about King Rama II's composition of *sepha*. He replied, "Yes, he composed it, but not openly, and several other people helped." I regret that I did not ask for further details on what passages the king composed, and who composed what. As I only wanted to know whether it truly was a royal composition, I was satisfied with this answer. Now that I would like to know further, I can only surmise. The fact that the king concealed his authorship was probably because he composed for performers to use as their own style. The style of *sepha* must convey realism, and in some passages of quarreling, the words used are coarse, and hence the royal authorship was not disclosed. I also surmise that it was composed while he held various posts during the First Reign, as once he had ascended the throne he did not have the opportunity to go and listen to *sepha* in royal palaces and noble houses as before. If he composed only for performance for the king at court, he would not have had to conceal his authorship. During the First Reign, he would just have had to command *sepha* performers not to tell anyone it was a royal composition, but among the poets themselves it was probably not concealed since it would be difficult to prevent other poets recognizing a person's style. The statement that "several other people helped" in the composition probably means that King Rama II encouraged others to compose *sepha*, and poets of high status who were close to the king probably used the king's compositions as a model for composing other passages. They also did not disclose the authorship because they wanted to use strong words in the same way. Competition to compose the very best poetry for the *sepha* was one source of amusement among poets at that time. Any performer probably considered it an honor to perform *sepha* composed by King Rama II or by other royalty and senior nobles. And those who got to hear good compositions would have come to appreciate the *sepha* more. Hence the composition of *sepha* gradually became more popular. The future king's stimulus to the composition of *sepha* during the First Reign can be called the origin of the use of written texts from then on.

THE HISTORY OF *SEPHA* IN THE SECOND REIGN

Though King Rama II composed dramas, he did not give up listening to *sepha*. For example, the custom of having *sepha* performed during the king's hair cutting began in the Second Reign. The king later ordered changes in the *sepha*, especially the creation of a royal version, and accompaniment by a *piphat* ensemble.

Probably the passages composed by the king and other poets during the First Reign were rather few, and often were just improvements of old versions and not very meticulous. In the Second Reign, the king seems to have ordered the court poets to divide up the work, each taking one or two passages of a length suitable for performance over a single night, or around one *samut thai* manuscript book. These were then performed for the king. These compositions were linked together as a continuous sequence for the first time, and were meticulous throughout. For example, the references to places and routes in Ayutthaya and Suphanburi, such as when Khun Phaen and Wanthong flee, are all correct (I once had them checked). Even the court customs in the passages on King Phanwasa's expedition to hunt buffalo in Suphanburi and on the reception of the envoy from Lanchang are correct according to the manual, something beyond the capability of someone outside the court. In addition the wording is not coarse like the versions performed in the localities. Even at points where the style should be coarse, double meanings are used, as if the intention was that women should no longer be prohibited from listening to the *sepha* as in the past. Regrettably, it is not known who composed which passages, and it can only be deduced from the style. It is generally known that the chapter on "The birth of Phlai Ngam" (chapter 24) is in the style of Sunthon Phu without any doubt. Apart from this, some passages are known to be in the style of poets who helped to compose royal drama scripts in the Second Reign. Some excerpts can be compared as evidence. For example, in the chapter on the marriage of Phlai Kaeo, Thong Prasi goes to ask for Phim's hand and Siprajan responds as follows:

> "Let me ask the elders one thing:
> in what way is this son of yours any good?
> Does he gamble, drink liquor, or get giddy on ganja?
> Does he smoke opium at all?
> Is he tall or short, dark or fair?
> So far I haven't seen him with my own eyes. Please tell me the truth."

In the royal version of the *Ramakian* drama, when Hanuman goes to present the ring to the king, the rishi Narot speaks as follows:

> This crooked ten-faced fellow,
> this monitor lizard, has abducted the wife,
> by name Sida.
> The appearance of that lady is excellent.
> He deviously wooed her with words,
> but she cursed him that she was not willing.
> Now she was sent to live in the soul garden
> and cannot be found in the city.
> Is she tall or short, dark or fair?
> So far I haven't seen her with my own eyes. Please tell me the truth.

The two passages seem to have been composed by the same author.

Apart from the fact that the style seems the same, there are other indications that passages were composed during the Second Reign. For example when Khun Chang joins the bridegroom's party at Phlai Kaeo's marriage:

> With these thoughts, he bathed and dressed
> in a golden yok that Phraya Nakhon had given him,
> and an upper cloth of wool embroidered with gold.
> The servants followed in a gaggle.

The governor of Nakhon Sithammarat during the First and Third Reigns had the title of Chaophraya, and only in the Second Reign was a Phraya. Thus the mention of Phraya Nakhon here indicates composition during the Second Reign.

These compositions made or commissioned by the king should be called the "royal *sepha*" because they were created in the court. Examination of the words and style helps to date them. It seems the royal *sepha* composed during the Second Reign ended at the death of Wanthong. The subsequent part was done during the Third Reign.

The creation of the royal *sepha* divided the performance into two types: one still using improvisation in the old style, known as *sepha don*, and the other following a poet's composition, known as *sepha rueang*. As everyone liked to hear the royal *sepha*, the *sepha don* gradually lost popularity and by now has virtually disappeared.

The *piphat* accompaniment of *sepha*, which is said to have begun in the Second Reign, is attested in the verse invoking teachers:

> at the time of the previous reign
> *sepha* was not yet recited along with *piphat*
> now in the time of the present king
> it has come to pass in Ayutthaya[67]

It seems that the written text of the royal *sepha* was performed by a single reciter who tended to get tired, and hence the king introduced interludes of *piphat* playing to allow the reciter some time to rest. The *piphat* ensemble was similar to that used for the drama, not the type that accompanied the *sepha* later. The evidence for this is found in an old manuscript of royal *sepha* that has instructions for music and vocalization, using similar instructions as in

---

67. The last line in the quotation differs from the wording in Damrong's first preface, and this one makes more sense. The line is a pun on a famous phrase, and in the earlier preface the famous phrase rather than the punning version somehow got printed. (T)

the drama. At certain points in the recitation there are instructions to sing—
sometimes four words, sometimes more. The songs are chosen to match with
the story, as in the drama. At points there are indications to sing slowly, or play
"a slow flute," or "Phraya Sok,"[68] or a *phatcha*.[69] At some points at the ends of
chapters, the ensemble is told to play *choet*, play loudly, or play a lullaby. The
music is matched to the story as in drama. What I am describing here seems
to be the same as Sunthon Phu's verse above about singing "background music
(*krao choet*) in a drone." When the royal *sepha* began to have *piphat* accom-
paniment, it became common for others to copy the practice, and so *piphat*
became a customary element of *sepha* from then on.

HISTORY OF *SEPHA* IN THE THIRD REIGN

There is evidence on the history of *sepha* in the Third Reign in the latter part
of the verse invoking teachers quoted above:

> [see above, p. 1350, from "Now let us pay respect to teachers of *piphat*" to
> "please excuse me and don't complain."][70]

Not one of the names of the *sepha* masters referred to in this verse appear
in Sunthon Phu's passage or the earlier invocation, as they belonged to a later
generation that only became famous in the Third Reign. More is known about
one of them from other sources. That is Khru Jaeng. Earlier he was famous
as a *phleng* performer, as mentioned in the passage on Wanthong's cremation
in chapter 36:

> Nai Jaeng came to play chicken-flapping songs,
> jigging his shoulders up and down and singing "cha, cha."
> He performed with Granny Ma, each trying to outdo the other,
> and making people laugh uproariously.

Khru Jaeng and Granny Ma were said to play *phleng* well together. During
one performance, Granny Ma made fun of the mother of Khru Jaeng in some
way, and Khru Jaeng was unable to come up with a satisfactory riposte. This

---

68. A composition for the *ranat* by Luang Pradit Phairo (mentioned below). (T)

69. A genre of song. (T)

70. Analysis suggests this was composed in two parts. The first part about *sepha* masters
seems to have been composed long before the verse for paying respect to the *piphat* masters.
The names of later *sepha* masters such as Khru Jaeng are muddled into the section on *piphat*
masters.

made him so angry that he stopped performing *phleng* and turned to *sepha* and prayer chanting. He came to be famous for both because he composed *sepha* very well. He lived until the Fifth Reign.

There is further historical information about another of the *piphat* masters mentioned in the invocation verse. Khru Mi Khaek—a Khaek called Mi—is said to have played almost every musical instrument, and been good at music composition as well. Examples of his famous compositions include *thayoi nai* and *thayoi nok sam chan,* still played today by all orchestras. Anyone who cannot play these two songs is considered not yet accomplished. The Chinese *choet* played by *piphat* to this day is another of Khru Mi's compositions. But the passage in the invocation verse that he "tootles the *thayoi* fluently" is a different song to the *thayoi nai* and *thayoi nok* mentioned above. It is also a Khru Mi composition, played on a single flute and called the solo *thayoi.* In the Fourth Reign, several royal personages such as the Front Palace King Phrapinklao,[71] Prince Thewet, and Prince Wongsathirat, put together their own *piphat* ensembles. Khru Mi was the music master for Phrapinklao, and was given the title Phra Pradit Phairo[72] and a post as a deputy supervisor in the royal pages. He remained the music master of the Front Palace until the Fifth Reign when he became the *mahori* master of Princess Sudarat Naratprayun, and subsequently died.[73]

The second part of the invocation suggests that the nature of the *sepha* changed again in the Third Reign. *Sepha* and *piphat* became paired together, or had to be performed together. Unlike the Second Reign, when *sepha* was the main event and *piphat* a supporting element, now *sepha* had to have *piphat,* and *piphat* had to have *sepha.* On examination, the story of the *sepha* in the Third Reign resembles that of the drama in the same reign. In the Second Reign, King Rama II had brought the drama to its peak both in terms of script and performance. King Rama III (Nangklao) did away with the royal drama troupe, but other royalty and senior officials still appreciated the royal drama in the Second Reign style, and hence it was still widely performed. The pattern for *sepha* was similar. King Rama III stopped royal performance of *sepha* as well as drama, but *sepha* remained popular in the localities as it was easier to stage than drama. During the Third Reign, royalty and senior officials kept up *sepha* in the royal style of the Second Reign. At first, *sepha* was the main element and

---

71. Prince Chudamani, 1808–66, son of Rama II and younger brother of King Rama IV. (T)

72. Mi Thuriyangkun was born during the First Reign and died in the Fifth. He composed many classic pieces. (T)

73. The history of Khru Mi was told to me by Somdet Chaofa Kromphra Naritsaranuwat-tiwong.

piphat only a support as in the Second Reign, but once it was performed in many places, there arose competition and efforts to improve the *piphat* until it became as important as the *sepha*. The Second Reign style of royal *sepha* was thus at its best in the Third Reign.

Judging from the style, many passages of the *sepha* were composed in the Third Reign. But since this composition was not done at royal command as in the Second Reign, any poet with the ability could compose at will. Some people thought up extensions to the story of *Khun Chang Khun Phaen*, and composed chapters adding to the royal *sepha* of the Second Reign. Some like Khru Jaeng recomposed old chapters as if to compete with the royal version, perhaps because the royal version was not available. Hence in the Third Reign, several versions of the *sepha* were in existence, both in the vulgar (*chaloeisak*) style and in the style of the court poets of the Second Reign. Yet it seems that all the *sepha* chapters composed later than the Second Reign, however good the style, make mistakes over the geography of places and routes, lacking the accuracy of the Second Reign compositions, because nobody checked thoroughly. People took less care than when the *sepha* was being performed for the king. The *sepha* chapters composed in the royal style in the Third Reign are probably those following Wanthong's cremation, up to the point where Soifa returns to Chiang Mai, and where Phlai Chumphon is affected by the love charm. In addition, two other chapters were composed. One is on Elder Khwat transforming his body into a crocodile and coming to take revenge on Phlai Chumphon. This is said to have been composed by Khru Jaeng during the Fourth Reign. The other is on Simala's sons, Phlai Phet and Phlai Bua, fighting with Phlai Yong, the son of Soifa. On examination, this chapter is of poorer style and for this reason was not popular for performance, but appears in the royal version of the Fourth Reign. It was thus probably a Third Reign composition. At that time there was no Thai language printing. All the *sepha* chapters, both new and old, were handwritten and thus varied according to whoever composed or performed the passages. Throughout the Third Reign, nobody seems to have assembled the chapters of the *sepha* of *Khun Chang Khun Phaen* and edited them as a continuous work from beginning to end. This is evident from the fact that all the old *sepha* texts in the Library which from the style ofwriting date back to the Third Reign, consist of isolated passages.[74]

---

74. In the "History of *sepha*" written in 1917, I said there was a royal version of the *sepha* written by the royal scribes in the Third Reign. That was incorrect. On more detailed examination, it is the work of scribes from the Fourth Reign. Hence I must give a new opinion that there was no collected version in the Third Reign.

From ancient time until the Second Reign, a *piphat* ensemble consisted of five instruments: flute (*pi*), *ranat ek,* a gong circle (large), *taphon* drum, and drum. For accompanying the *sepha* in a house, the *taphon* and drum were too loud, so a *songna* two-faced drum[75] was used instead. Then in the Third Reign when *sepha* and *piphat* were played together, someone had the idea of doubling up the instruments, namely adding a second flute, a *ranat thum* to pair with the *ranat ek*, and a small gong circle to pair with the large one, giving rise to a new form of *piphat* called the "paired instruments," while the old type was called the "*piphat* five."

HISTORY OF *SEPHA* IN THE FOURTH REIGN

In the Fourth Reign, King Mongkut (Chomklao) liked to listen to *sepha* in the same way as King Rama II had. He brought back the tradition of playing *sepha* during the royal hair cutting. He had Sunthon Phu compose another *sepha* based on the royal chronicles, and had someone else unknown compose a *sepha* of Si *Thanonchai*. Two new royal *sepha* thus appeared during the Fourth Reign.

There is evidence to suggest that the compilation of the *sepha* of *Khun Chang Khun Phaen* as a continuous sequence from beginning to end, as appeared in the printed book version, was done at the royal command of King Mongkut as the earliest version was written by royal scribes during the Fourth Reign. In addition there are several other manuscripts in the Library, such as that of Chaophraya Borommaha Phichaiyat, and that of Somdet Chaophraya Borommaha Sisuriyawong, in handwriting of the Fourth Reign or later. There are none in handwriting earlier than of the Fourth Reign. These sets of manuscripts consist of forty or more *samut thai* volumes. If there had been such a set prior to the Fourth Reign, some trace should remain. In addition, the style in these sets is not consistent throughout. Some passages are coarse; for example, the passage where Khun Phaen goes to do battle with Chiang Mai (in the version printed prior to that of the Library) is clearly a vulgar version in a style unsuitable for performance in the court. Possibly a passage of this style was inserted because the royal version of this segment from the Second Reign had gone missing, and thus someone used another version. This is another factor indicating that the assembly of the *sepha* into the story read to this day only began in the Fourth Reign.

The performance of *sepha* changed in the Fourth Reign in several ways that resulted in a decline of the model from the Second Reign. After *sepha*

---

75. A double-ended drum placed horizontal on a stand. (T)

was paired with *piphat* in the Third Reign, royalty and senior officials in the Fourth Reign came to like *piphat* even more, giving rise to a "large scale" ensemble with a metal *ranat thum* and a metal *ranat ek* (or *ranat thong*) added to the paired ensemble. Competition among *piphat* ensembles continued to increase. Although *sepha* was still performed in conjunction with *piphat* as before, hosts preferred to reduce the performance of *sepha* and give more time for the *piphat* to show off its skill. *Sepha* was forced to have songs that the host wanted the *piphat* to play, not songs that matched the storyline as before. The music at the end of a chapter was eliminated. Thus the *piphat* was now the main event, and the *sepha* became only a supporting element. The *sepha* was played to give the musicians in the single *piphat* ensemble time to rest, and not vice versa.

There were other reasons for *sepha*'s decline. Female drama troupes became widespread in the Fourth Reign. Previously, in a tradition that originated in the Ayutthaya era, the only female drama troupe belonged to the king. The troupes of other royalty and nobles were all male. I have heard that when the king's female drama troupe was disbanded in the Third Reign, some nobles put on female dramas, claiming that there was no reason to prohibit other troupes now that the royal troupe no longer existed. But as there was no royal permission given, the female drama was not performed openly but in secret all through the Third Reign and into the Fourth. King Mongkut reinstated the king's female drama troupe but also gave permission for others to stage female dramas, removing the earlier restriction. As a result, female drama became widespread, both among those of high rank and among common people who acted for a living. Some troupes with all women, and others with both male and female actors, sought out new plots to please the audience. Some theatres, such as that of Nai Tai and Nai Net, staged dramas of *Khun Chang Khun Phaen*. When female drama became widespread, and especially when *Khun Chang-Khun Phaen* was played as drama in competition with *sepha*, people came to prefer the drama, contributing further to *sepha*'s decline. But there were still some devotees of *sepha*, such as King Mongkut who not only liked *sepha*, as already noted, but who had the royal female *mahori* troupe perform Sunthon Phu's *sepha* of the royal chronicles. In addition senior figures who did not participate in drama still probably performed *sepha* among themselves with a *piphat*. In the localities also, *sepha* probably persisted. Hence *sepha* declined but did not disappear. There were still several good performers whose names are known from the Fourth Reign, as follows.

Luang Phisanuseni (Thongyu) was a royal *sepha* performer, expert in both the *don* and *rueang* types. He was considered a great master of *sepha* down to the Fifth Reign.

Nai In-u, who performed in partnership with Luang Phisanuseni (Thongyu), was said to have had a very fine delivery.

Nai Sing (father of Nai Sangjin, a *piphat* master who died in London, and father of Luang Sanoduriyang, Thongdi, a royal *piphat* master in the Fifth Reign) was said to perform Crocodile Khwat very well.

Nai Mueang, a performer for Chaophraya Borommaha Phichaiyat, was said to be unequalled in playing the claves to accompany the *sepha*.[76]

THE HISTORY OF *SEPHA* IN THE FIFTH REIGN

In the Fifth Reign, King Chulalongkorn (Chulachomklao) liked to listen to *sepha* as King Mongkut had. He encouraged some government servants who were poets, such as Phraya Sisunthonwohan (Noi),[77] to compose a *sepha* on the story of Abu Hasan as a royal composition called *Lilit nithra chakhrit.* This gave rise to another royal *sepha.* Performance of *sepha* in the localities continued as in the Fourth Reign with the *piphat* more important than the *sepha.* The performance of *Khun Chang Khun Phaen* as a drama became even more widespread than before, though only certain episodes were played, especially the marriage of Phra Wai, Wanthong warning about the army,[78] and Phlai Phet and Phlai Bua fighting with Phlai Yong. The performance of *Khun Chang Khun Phaen* as dance was another form that appeared in the Fifth Reign, with a reciter and *piphat* musicians in the same manner as *sepha* performance (sometimes with *mahori* instead of *piphat*) but with some costuming for the actors and dialogue in drama style rather like a comedy. It was performed widely as it was easy to stage without the high investment needed for a drama. Yet this practice still added to the decline of the *sepha*, as did other factors. At some point during the Fifth Reign, several other entertainments appeared such as *li-ke*,[79] *lakhon rong*,[80] and cinema, diminishing the popularity of old-style *sepha*. Yet there were still

---

76. The history of *sepha* masters of the Fourth Reign comes from Phra Pradit Phairo (Tak).

77. Noi Ajaryangkun, 1822–1891, native of Chachoengsao, poet and artist, author of an early primer of the Thai language. (T)

78. Wanthong's apparition as a netherworlder in chapter 40. (T)

79. A form of dance-drama that developed from earlier folk styles (the exact derivation is disputed) and became very popular. (T)

80. "Dance-drama operetta (originated in the Fifth Reign) in contemporary settings. The actor-dancers sing and speak their parts and perform some dance movements to demonstrate the lyrics. The stories are usually translations from, or adaptations of, foreign tales or contemporary incidents and situations. The costumes are contemporary as well" (Mattani, *Dance, Drama and Theatre,* 276). (T)

some good and well-known *sepha* performers. Luang Phisanuseni (Thongyu) continued as a *sepha* master for a long time in the Fifth Reign and was accorded a higher title as Phra Rachamanu. Phra Saenthongfa (Pong) from Ratchaburi, who had formerly been a *sepha* performer for Somdet Chaophraya Borommaha Sisuriyawong, and who had a good voice and delivery, performed for the king in both the Fifth and current Sixth Reigns, living to the age of eighty-five. Luang Phon Songkhram from Ban Sai, a local official in Ang Thong, was another famed for his voice though I never heard him. Also Nai Joem from Talat Khwan performed the *Mahaphon* episode of the *Mahachat* while in the monkhood and was famed for his fine recitation. He was invited to perform for the king at Bang Pa-in, playing the part of a *kinnon* who followed the army that went to fight the Ho. As this angered Chaophraya Mahintharasakdi-thamrong, who had been the army commander at the time, Nai Joem disrobed and went into hiding for a time, but then returned as a *sepha* performer. He had a good voice, but in the *piphat* circle, people were afraid of Nai Joem because he was so knowledgeable about recitation. An ensemble that was not truly proficient would not dare to accompany Nai Joem.

One important point in the history of *sepha* that occurred in the Fifth Reign was the first printed version which appeared in the year of the monkey, 1872. Dr. Smith, owner of the Bang Kho Laem press, used Chaophraya Borommaha Sisuriyawong's manuscript of the *sepha* (which had been copied from the royal version) to print and sell at one salueng per volume (equivalent to one volume of *samut thai*).[81] Previously, everybody had known the *sepha* from hearing the recitation of certain episodes. Performers knew only certain chapters which they performed, and the only complete versions of the manuscript were in the possession of the court and a few royalty or senior officials. Once the *sepha* was printed and sold, it was read widely. Performers converted to using the royal version. Students of literature came to like reading the script of *Khun Chang Khun Phaen* as it was a poetic work known to almost everyone in Bangkok as an exemplary collection of refined verse that was not at all boring, and unique in being consistently good. Hence *Khun Chang Khun Phaen* became an important book in Thai literature from the Fifth Reign onwards.

---

81. In fact, Smith sold the publication in installments containing four *samut thai* volumes priced at one baht. The Wat Ko edition of 1890 was printed as single *samut thai* volumes sold for one salueng. (T)

THE HISTORY OF *SEPHA* IN THE SIXTH REIGN

In the present reign, King Vajiravudh (Mongkutklao) appreciates *sepha* as his predecessor did, and has it performed during the royal hair cutting and when he visits provincial centers as in the previous reign. In addition he has added a new royal composition of *sepha* on the story of Phya Ratchawangsan,[82] and given a royal command for a new form of *sepha* performance called *sepha samakki sawek* that has dance performances of various subjects on a stage, accompanied by *piphat* with no singing or dialogue. The *sepha* is recited to tell the story before opening the curtain for each dance episode in order to explain the dance to the audience, and also as entertainment during scene changes so that the musicians and dancers have time to rest. The first *sepha samakki sawek* appeared in 1914.

The printing of the Library edition of *Khun Chang Khun Phaen* should also be counted as a new event in the history of the *sepha* during the Sixth Reign as this edition differs from prior printed editions of the *sepha* both in the content and the editing, as I shall now explain.

EXPLAINING THE LIBRARY EDITION OF THE *SEPHA*

The reason why the committee of the Wachirayan Library wished to print *Khun Chang Khun Phaen* as a new library publication was because they had heard it constantly said that it was a pity that a good edition for reading could not be found since at present there were only editions that various presses have printed by copying Dr. Smith's edition three or four times, accumulating more errors each time. Were this to continue, it was feared that an excellent book in Thai verse might be lost. Some people asked whether the Library, which has published a few books, had given some thought to revising the *sepha* of *Khun Chang Khun Phaen* for a new publication. On examination, the committee agreed, and felt it would be appropriate to revise and publish a new edition of *Khun Chang Khun Phaen*. Moreover, no place was more suitable for this task than the Library as it has a much more complete collection of the original manuscripts of the *sepha*, including both royal and popular versions, than anywhere else. For these reasons, the committee of the Library began the work of revision from the year 1914 onwards.

---

82. Adaptation of an excerpt from *Othello* which Rama VI first performed as a drama and later as *sepha*. (T)

Several facts about the history of the *sepha* were learned through this process of revision, as explained above. But there were also several problems that had to be resolved. The first was the old view that women should not read *Khun Chang Khun Phaen* because it is an obscene book. On examination of the original manuscripts, chapters which are from the royal *sepha*, or which were composed later on the same model, were found to have no obscenity at all. The obscene wording is found only in passages from the vulgar versions which probably came to be inserted at the time when the whole work was assembled because certain chapters from the royal version had disappeared. Hence if those vulgar chapters were to be excised and replaced by other versions that are not obscene, it would result in *Khun Chang Khun Phaen* becoming readable by both men and women without the former prejudice. On grounds of style, the portions that had to be excised were no loss, as better replacements could be found. Thus several passages, where the style is common and obscene were selected for excision and were replaced by other versions considered to be good. There are four segments by Khru Jaeng: chapter 16 on the birth of Goldchild, chapter 29 when Khun Phaen frees Phra Thainam, chapter 30 when Khun Phaen captures the King of Chiang Mai, and chapter 43 on Crocodile Khwat. It was agreed that Khru Jaeng's verse is good and though he liked to include some obscenity, it could be corrected. Another chapter that was changed was chapter 28 where Phlai Ngam gets Simala. The author of the replacement version is unknown, and, as it was incomplete, some additional parts had to be composed in the Library. In addition, the beginnings of some chapters were newly created in the Library but only small linking passages. The substitution of some passages and the additions mentioned above make this edition of the *sepha* differ from previous printed editions, and hence this is called the Library Edition of *Sepha Khun Chang Khun Phaen*.

Though the passages on Phlai Phet and Phlai Yong have been omitted on grounds of poor quality, this edition still includes over forty *samut thai* volumes. To print and sell as separate chapters on the model of Dr. Smith's publication would contradict the purpose of the Library. When the revision of the first volume was complete, it coincided with the time that Prince Asdang[83] was moving to a new palace at Suan Kulap,[84] and wanted to publish a book for

---

83. Chaofa Asdang-dechawut kromluang nakhon ratchasima, 1889–1925, Prince of Nakhon Ratchasima, son of King Chulalongkorn by Queen Saowabha; became the heir apparent on the death of his brother, Chakrabongse, in 1920, but died a few months before King Rama VI. (T)

84. At the junction of Ratchasima Road and Si Ayutthaya Road, in the southwest corner of the Dusit grounds. Built in European style, the palace was originally intended as a temporary residence, but was later extended and occupied by Prince Asdang until his death in 1924. Later it served as Government House.

distribution as a gift at the ceremony. When he learned that the committee of the Library was revising *Khun Chang Khun Phaen,* he was happy to sponsor printing of the first volume for distribution as a gift on 6 October 1917. In December of the same year, Prince Prajadhiphok[85] celebrated his twenty-fifth birthday. A message came to the Library from the Parusakawan Residence[86] that they wished to print a book as a gift, and if the committee of the Library could have the second volume of *Khun Chang Khun Phaen* ready in time, the prince would be happy to distribute it. Thus the second volume was printed in time for the distribution on 16 December 1917. A year later, when Prince Devawongse[87] celebrated his sixtieth birthday and moved to the Thewet Palace,[88] the Library received a message that he wished to sponsor printing of the third volume for distribution as a gift on that day. The committee thus arranged the printing for the prince to distribute on 1 October 1918, completing the publication of the Library edition of *Khun Chang Khun Phaen.*

Since the Library edition of *Khun Chang Khun Phaen* has appeared, many people have found it better than any previous printed version and believe it will be the canonical version. In a short time, the first printing was exhausted and the resale price rose. Hence the committee of the Library feel it is time for a new printing that we hope will meet with everybody's approval.

---

85. Chaofa Prajadhiphok-sakdidet kromluang sukhothai-thammaratcha, the future King Rama VII. (T)

86. Not the Parusakawan Palace (on Phitsanulok Road), occupied by Prince Chakrabongse, but a building then in the same grounds, sometimes called the Suan Chitlada Residence. (T)

87. Somdet-prachao borommawongthoe kromphraya thewawong-worapakon, 1858–1923, half-brother of King Chulalongkorn, minister of foreign affairs almost continuously from 1885 to 1915; origin of the Devakul family. (T)

88. Built in Italianate style by King Chulalongkorn for Prince Devawongse on the riverside, completed in 1914, later occupied by the Health Ministry, and now housing a museum for the Bank of Thailand whose headquarters are in the adjacent Bangkhunphrom Palace.

PART 5

FLORA, FAUNA, COSTUME, WEAPONS, FOOD

FLORA

This is a complete listing of plants mentioned in *KCKP* in the Prince Damrong edition, the Smith/Wat Ko edition, and the additional episodes included in this edition. Asterisks denote translations that we have invented, explained in the Notes column. The Index column refers to Gardner, *Field Guide to Forest Trees*.

In the text	Thai	Transliteration	Botanical name	Index	Notes
amora*	รัก	rak	*Gluta usitata, etc.*	301	Burmese lacquer tree, black-varnish tree; sap a source of lacquer; *same word as "love"
anchan	อัญชัน	anchan	*Clitoria ternatea*		butterfly pea; a vine with deep blue flowers used to make food dye
angelbreast*	นมสวรรค์	nomsawan	*Clerodendron paniculatum*	629	pepangil, pagoda flower, borneo sunset, Kashmir bouquet; *close translation
aporosa	กลม, เหมือดโลด	klom, mueat lot	*Aporosa villosa*	697	
armorbark*	กันเกรา	kankrao	*Fagraea fragrans*	606	tembesu, Burma yellowheart; *echoes word for armor
arum	บุก	buk	*Amorphophallus rex, etc.*		low forest plants that in the rainy season sprout fleshy leaves and flowers, some of which can be eaten
baelfruit	มะตูม	matum	*Aegle marmelos*	187	fruit with sweet flesh used in cooking and medicine
bamboo	ไผ่	phai	*Bambusa vulgaris, etc.*		general term for bamboos
bamboo	ผาก	phak	*Gigantochloa hasskarliana*		a clump bamboo, native to Java
banana	กล้วย	kluai	*Musa (various)*		general term for bananas
banyan	ไทร	sai	*Ficus annulata, etc.*	767	
bean	ถั่ว	thua			general term for beans
betel	หมาก	mak	*Areca catechu*	860	areca
blackwood	ชิงชัน	chingchan	*Dalbergia oliveri*	366	rosewood
bo	โพธิ์	pho	*Ficus religiosa*	785	pipal, bodhi
bombax	ง้าว	ngao	*Bombax anceps*	114	white flower variant
bombax	งิ้ว	ngio	*Bombax ceiba, etc.*	115	red flower variant; kapok tree, cotton tree
bottle gourd	น้ำเต้า	nam tao	*Lagenaria siceraria*		wild bottle gourd

braidflower*	ผกากรอง	phakakrong	Lantana camara		large-leaved lantana, red sage; *close translation
caladium	บอน	bon	Araceae (various)		flowering waterside plants, some green, some with multicolor leaves
camphor-weed	หนาด	nat	Blumea balsamifera		ngai camphor; shrub with medicinal leaves
camphor-wood	จวง	juang	Cinnamomum porrectum	668	different from camphor tree; fragrant oil, extracted from the leaves, bark, and roots, is combined with sandal as a skin cosmetic
casumunar*	ไพล	phlai	Zingiber casumunar, purpureum		a tuberous root used for treating wounds, nausea, and headaches; *based on botanical name
chalut vine	ชะลูด	chalut	Alyxia reinwardtii		vine used for medicine and fragrance
chamma-liang	พุมเรียง, ช่ามะเลียง	phummar-iang, cham-maliang	Lepisanthes fruticosa		mid-size tree with sweet purple fruit
chanan	ฉนาน, perhaps ขนาน, กะหนาน	chanan, perhaps khanan, kanan	Pterospermum acerifolium	138	
changnao	ช้างน้าว	changnao	Gomphia serrata; Ochna integerrima	209	
chanuan	ฉนวน	chanuan	Dalbergia nigrescens	362	
chili	พริก	phrik	Capsicum (various)		general term for chili pepper
Chinese ivorybell*	กระดังงา จีน	k(r)adang-nga jin	Artabotrys hexapetalus, uncinatus		vine with very fragrant bell-like yellow flower with tusk-like petals; *close translation of name based on appearance
chingchi	ชิงชี่	chingchi	Capparis micracantha		a bush with thorns and white flowers
chongkho	ชงโค	chongkho	Bauhinia purpurea, etc.	336	a bush with large leaves and white or reddish purple flowers
chumsaeng	ชุมแสง	chumsaeng	Xanthophyllum glaucum		
cinnamom tree*	โมง, อบเชย	mong, opchoei	Cinnamomum iners, tammala, bejolghota, etc.	670	*bark has strong cinnamon smell
citron	ส้มซ่า	som sa	Citrus medica		
climbing jasmine	มะลิวัน มะลิวัลย์	maliwan	Jasminum adenophyllum, bifarium, gracilimum		petals smaller than regular jasmine, fragrant overnight
coconut	มะพร้าว	maphrao	Cocos nucifera		
coral tree	ทองหลาง	thonglang	Erythrina fusca, stricta, etc.	357, 358	large dipterocarp with buttresses
cottonrose hibiscus	พุดตาน	phuttan	Hibiscus mutabilis		cotton rose, changable rose; flower changes from white to pink to red over a day
couch grass	หญ้าแพรก	ya phraek	Cynodon dactylon		Bermuda grass
cowitch	หมามุ่ย	mamui	Mucuna gigantea		cowage, horse-eye bean, a vine whose hanging seedpods have highly irritable hairs
crowvine*	กาฝาก	kafak	Helixanthera cylindrica		birdvine; a parasite that grows on trees, seeds spread by birds; *close translation
crystal mango*	มะม่วง แก้ว	mamuang kaeo			a type of mango; *direct translation

cucumber	แตงกวา	taeng kwa	Cucumis sativus		common cucumber
cucumber tree	ตะลิงปลิง	talingpling	Averrhoa bilimbi		very sour cucumber-like fruit
custard apple	น้อยหน่า	noina	Annona squamosa		
cutch	สีเสียด	si siat	Acacia catechu		black cutch; sap, rich in tannin, chewed with betelnut and used in medicine
dam	ดำ	dam	Diospyros brandisiana		
damascene	ยี่สุ่น	yisun	Tagetes putala; Phlox drummondii; Rosa damascena		African marigold, damascene rose
deer's ear*	หูกวาง	hu kwang	Terminalia catappa	391	Indian almond, tropical almond; big leaves like deer's ear; *direct translation
diamond-on-anvil*	ว่านกาเพ็ชนาทั้ง	wan ka phet na thang			unidentified; *direct translation
dipli	ดีปลี	dipli	Piper chaba		sort of pepper
double jasmine	มะลิซ้อน	mali son	Jasminum sambac		
duckweed	จอกแหน	jok nae	Lemna trisulca		ivy leaf, star duckweed
duk	(มะ)ดูก	(ma)duk	Beilschmiedia roxburghi-ana		
eaglewood	กฤษณา	kritsana	Aquilaria agalocha, crassna	685	aloes, aloewood, agar wood
ebony	ตะโก, ตะโกนา	tako, takona	Diosporos rhodocalyx, etc.	556	an ebony used for topiary
eggplant	มะเขือ	makhuea	Solanum (various)		aubergine
elephant cane*	อ้อยช้าง	oi chang	Lannea coromandelica	309	liked by elephants; *close translation
evening-bloom*	บานเย็น	banyen	Mirabilis jalapa		marvel of Peru; *direct translation
faep nam	แฟบน้ำ	faep nam	Hymenocardia wallichii		
fenugreek	ซัด	sat	Trigonella foenum-graecom		seeds used to make dye and fragrance
fig	เลียบ, มะเดื่อ	liap, maduea	Ficus lacor, hispida, etc.	779, 780	
finger banana	กล้วยไข่	kluai khai	Musa suerier		
fishtail palm	เต่าร้าง เต่ารั้ง	taorang	Caryota mitis, obtusa	855	
fivegold*	เบญจมาศ	benjamat	Wedelia urticifolia		Chrysanthemum family; *direct translation
frog herb*	ว่านกบ	wan kop			unidentified; *direct translation
gardenia	พุด	phut	Gardenia collinsae; Tabernaemontana cumingiana		name for several species of gardenia, mostly with fragrant white flowers
gem jasmine*	แก้ว	kaeo	Murraya paniculata	185	orange jasmine, China box tree, mock orange; small evergreen with flowers like a citrus; *gem is direct translation
giant reed	อ้อ	o	Arundo donax		a tall perennial reed
goodwood*	มะริด	marit	Diospyros discolor, philippensis		Macassar ebony, Andaman marblewood; *name sounds like Thai for "success"

gooseberry tree	มะยม	mayom	Phyllanthus acidus	740	Otaheite gooseberry, Malay gooseberry, Tahitian gooseberry, etc.
gourd	แฟง	faeng	Cucurbita pepo		broad term for squash and gourd
han	หัน(ช้าง)	han (chang)	Knema laurina	650	wild nutmeg
hang lai	หางไหล	hang lai	Dalbergia abbreviata		
happy-shade*	สุกรม	sukrom	Shorea roxburghii	103	central region name for phayom; *close translation
hat	หาด	hat	Artocarpus chaplasha	761	chaplash, a fig
heartache*	โศกระย้า	sok raya	Saraca indica		beautiful flowering tree; name from "Asoka"; *elided form is homophone for sorrow
hiang	เหียง	hiang	Dipterocarpus obtusifolius	99	
hibiscus	ชบา	chaba	Hibiscus rosa-sinensis, etc.		rose-mallow
hidden-lover*	ซ่อนชู้	sonchu	Polianthes tuberosa		tuberose; bush with white flowers, often used at funerals, hence associated with sorrow; *direct translation
horsetail creeper	ลดาวัลย์	ladawan	Porana volubilis		
hundred-tongue*	ร้อยลิ้น, perhaps กัดลิ้น	roi-lin, perhaps gat-lin	perhaps Walsura robusta	217	*direct translation
in-jan	อิน, จัน	in, jan	Diospyros decandra, etc.	565	name for several Diospyros variants with small fragrant yellow fruits; in has round fertile seeds, while jan has flat infertile seeds. The two appear separately in the poem but are amalgamated in the translation, partly because "in" is easily misunderstood.
inthanin	อินทนิล	inthanin	Lagerstroemia macrocarpa, etc.	449	pride of India
ironwood	ตะเคียน	takhian	Hopea odorata, etc.	102	Malabar ironwood, thingwa; hard wood used in construction, but associated with ghosts because the wood oozes sap for a long time
ivorybell*	กระดังงา	kradang-nga	Cananga odorata	31	ylang-ylang; bell-shaped flower with tusk-like petals; *direct translation
ivy gourd vine	ตำลึง	tamlueng	Coccinia grandis		shoots eaten as a vegetable, seeds spread by birds
jackfruit	ขนุน	khanun	Artocarpus heterophyllus		
jaeng	แจง	jaeng	Maerua/Niebuhria siamensis		small plant with smooth dark grey bark and elliptical yellow fruit
jakajan	จักจั่น	jakajan	Millettia pubinervis	375	"cicada"
jambolan	หว้า	wa	Syzygium cumini, etc.	426	Java plum, jamun, black plum, faux pistachier, Indian blackberry
jampa	จำปา	jampa	Michelia champaca	7	champak, orange champak; Magnolia family
jampi	จำปี	jampi	Michelia alba	8	white champaka; Magnolia family; name translates as "remembered for years"

jan	จัน	jan		565	see in-jan
jan hom	จันทน์หอม	jan hom	Mansonia gagei; Tarenna hoaensis		coffee family
jan khana	จันทน์คณา, จันทน์คันนา	jan khana, jan khanna	Psychotria adenophylla	479	coffee family
janthana, jan khao	จันทนา จันทน์ขาว	janthana, jan khao	Tarenna hoaensis; Xantonnea quocensis		(white) sandal tree, dracena
jewel vine	เปรียง	priang	Derris/Dalbergia scandens		
jik	จิก	jik	Barringtonia acutangula, coccinea, etc.	436	Indian oak
jujube	พุทรา	phutsa	Zizyphus mauritiana	261	monkey apple, Indian jujube, Chinese date; legendarily spread from seeds of fruits dropped by invading Burmese soldiers
k(r)athok-rok	ก(ร)ะทกรก	k(r)athok-rok	Passiflora foetida		red-fruited passion flower
kaelae	แกแล	kaelae	Maclura cochinchinensis		
kaffir lime	มะกรูด	makrut	Citrus hystrix		fruit used as astringent in cooking, and as air deodorant
kalampho	กะลำพอ ตะลุมพอ	kalampho, talumpho	Randia uliginosa		
kalong	กาหลง	kalong	Bauhinia acuminata		snowy orchid tree
kamyan	กำยาน	kamyan	Styrax benzoides	575	styrax benzoin, benzoin
kaphrao	กะเพรา	kaphrao	Ocimum sanctum		a basil
karaket	การะเกด	karaket	Pandanus tectorius, furcatus	846	hala, screwpine
khae	แค	khae	Dolichandrone serrulata; Pterospermum (various)	618	
khae foi	แคฝอย	khae foi	Stereospermum cylindricum/fimbriatum	622	snake tree
khai nao	ไข่เน่า	khai nao	Vitex glabrata	641	
khanang	ขานาง	khanang	Homalium tomentosum	65	Moulmein lancewood
khang	คาง	khang	Albizzia lebbekoides	322	woman's tongue tree, black siris
khansong	คันทรง	khansong	Colubrina asiatica		bush with yellow flowers
khla	คล้า	khla	Schumannianthus dichotomus		general name for Calathea herbs
khlak	คลัก	khlak	perhaps a Pterospermum		unidentified
khondinso	โคนดินสอ, คนที(สอ)	khondinso, khonti(so)	Vitex trifolia	637	
khontha	คนทา	khontha	Harrisonia perforate	207	
khrai	ไคร้	khrai	Glochidion daltonii, kerrii, etc.	720	evergreen shrub
khwat	ขวาด	khwat	Garcinia speciosa; Syzygium longiflora	53	
khwit	(มะ)ขวิด	(ma)khwit	Feronia limonia	188	elephant apple
kra	กระ, พระ	kra, phra	Elateriospermum tapos		
krai	ไกร	krai	Ficus concinna, superba		type of fig
krajae	กระแจะ	krajae	Naringi crenulata; Ochna integerrima	209	wood and bark steeped to make scented skin preparation
krajao	กระเจา, กระเชา	krajao, krachao	Holoptelea integrifolia	751	Indian elm

krak-khi	กรักขี	krak-khi	Cudrania javanensis		
krang	กร่าง	krang	Ficus altissima, etc.	765	type of banyan
krapho	ก(ร)ะพ้อ	k(r)apho	Licuala spinosa, paludosa, etc		
kraphrao-ton	กระเพราต้น	kraphrao-ton	Cinnamomum glaucescens		a laurel
krasang	กระสัง	krasang	Peperonia pellucida		
krathin	กระถิน	krathin	Leucaena leucocephala, glauca, etc.		lead tree, white popinac
krathin-phiman	กระถิน พิมาน	krathin-phiman	Acacia tomentosa		
krathom	กระท่อม	krathom	Mitragyna speciosa		leaves chewed as a narcotic
krathum	กระทุ่ม	krathum	Anthocephalus chinensis	481	
kruai	กรวย	kruai	Horsfieldia irya		a tree with yellow flowers
kum	กุ่ม	kum	Crateva religiosa (kum bok) or Crateva magna (kum nam)	40, 41	garlic pear, temple plant
lady's fingernail	เล็บมือนาง	lep mue nang	Quisqualis indica, conferta		Rangoon creeper
lalang grass	(หญ้า)คา	(ya)kha	Imperata cylindrica		lalang, cogon, imperata grass
lamduan	ลำดวน	lamduan	Melodorum fruticosum	15	devil tree, white cheesewood; small, very fragrant flowers
lamphaen	ลำแพน	lamphaen	Sonneratia alba, ovata		
lan	ลาน	lan	Corypha umbraculifera	851	talipot palm, source of bailan
langling	ลางลิง, กระไดลิง	langling, kradailing	Bauhinia scandens		pinanga vine
langsat	ลางสาด	langsat	Aglaia domestica		a berry-like fruit with a fawn skin and translucent white flesh
laurel	รก, รกฟ้า	rok, rokfa	Terminalia tomentosa/alata	396	
lemongrass	ตะคร้าย, ตะไคร้	takhrai	Cymbopogon citratus		a culinary herb
lian	เลี่ยน	lian	Melia azedlarach	221	bastard cedar, Persian lilac, chinaberry
lightleaf*	มะสัง	masang	Feroniella lucida	188	tree with glossy, fleshy, composite leaves, spiny branches, and a small sour fruit, similar to makhwit; very popular as bonsai; *from botanical name
lion's tail*	สร้อยหาง(สิง)โต	soi hang to, perhaps soi hang singto	perhaps a Lycopodium		*direct translation
longan	ลำไย	lamyai	Dimocarpus longan	270	
lotus	บัว	bua			general term for lotus
lotus	บุษบัน	busaban			poetic word for lotus or lily
lychee	ลิ้นจี่	linji	Lichi chinensis		
maduea	มะเดื่อ	maduea	Ficus hirta, hispida, racemosa, etc.	779	name for several fig species
maduk	มะดูก	maduk	Siphonodon celastrineus	257	
mafai	มะไฟ	mafai	Baccaurea ramiflora	700	baccaurea

mafo	มะฝอ	(ma)fo	Trewia nudiflora	747	
mafueang	มะเฟือง	mafueang	Averrhoa carombola		star apple, fruit, carambola
makhaen	หมากมาศ, มะแข่น	makmat, makhaen	Zanthoxylum budrunga	197	green-brown berry-like fruits used in cooking
makham pom	มะขามป้อม	makham pom	Phyllanthus emblica	737	ambal, emblic myrabolan, fruits chewed to quench thirst
maklam	มะกล่ำ	maklam	Adenanthera pavonina, etc.	315	
makluea	มะเกลือ	makluea	Diospyros mollis	559	
mango	มะม่วง	mamuang	Mangifera indica, etc.		
maprang	มะปราง	maprang	Bouea macrophylla, burmanica	289	Marian plum
marigold	ดาวเรือง	daorueang	Tagetes erecta		African, American, Mexican, Aztec marigold
masang	มะทราง, มะซาง	masang	Madhuca pierrei	543	mahua
matong	มะต้อง, กระท้อน	matong, krathon	Sandoricum indicum, koetjape	227	
miang	เมี่ยง	miang	Camellia sinensis		tea (northern Thai word), leaves fermented for brewing and chewing
milkwood*	เกด	ket	Manilkara hexandra	366–69	evergreen with hard, heavy wood; Ceylon ironwood, milkey tree, khirni; *milky sap
misery-plum*	ระกำ	rakam	Salacca wallichiana, rumpii		thorny bush with thorny fruits; *word also means suffering, hardship
mok	โมก	mok	Wrightia religiosa, pubescens, etc.	601, 603	wild water plum, water jasmine
montha	มณฑา	montha	Talauma candolei; Manglietia garrettii	14	magnolita; Magnolia family, yellow flower, fragrant in morning
mukman	มูกมัน โมกมัน	mukman, mokman	Wrightia tomentosa	600	
mulberry	ยอ	yo	Morinda citrifolia	490	Indian mulberry, noni; fruit and leaves used in cooking
nam-han	หนาม หัน	nam-han	Acacia comosa		
nettle vine	ตำแย	tamyae	Laportea interrupta		
night jasmine	กรรณิกา	kannika	Nyctanthes arbor-tristis		hursinghar
nutmeg	จันทน์เทศ	jan thet	Myristica fragrans		
nymph lotus	บัวเผื่อน	bua phuean	Nymphaea nouchali		white lotus, white water lily
orangegold*	แทงทวย, คำแสด	thaengthuai, khamsaet	Mallotus philippensis	735	kamala, monkeyface tree; *more commonly called khamsaet, which translates as golden orange
orchid	กล้วยไม้	kluai mai			general term for orchids
ottelia vine	สันตะวา	santawa	Ottelia alismoides		
pacifier*	ระงับ	rangap	Breynia glauca		*close translation
pan	พลู	phlu	Piper betel		vine leaf used for wrapping betelnut
pandan	เตย	toei	Pandanus helicopus, kaida		screwpine

paperbark	เสม็ด	samet	Melaleuca cajuputa, leucadendra		cajuput, paper bark, swamp tea, milkwood
paper-wood*	ข่อย	khoi	Streblus asper	755	toothbrush tree, Siamese rough bush; rough leaves used to clean teeth; *bark used to make paper
parting palm*	จาก	jak	Nypa fruticans		atap, nipa; *homophone for "leaving"
pecking plum*	ตะขบ	takhop	Flacourtia indica	66-8	rukam, governor's plum; *khop means peck
peng	เป้ง	peng	Phoenix humilis, loureiri, etc.	863	
persimmon	(มะ)พลับ	(ma)phlap	Diospyros malabarica, areolata	555	a relative of the Chinese persimmon; oval fruits, 3–5 cm across, ripen to orange
phak hom	ผักโหม, ผักขม	phak hom, phak khom	Amaranthus lividus		general term for Amaranthus family
phak wan	ผักหวาน	phak wan	Phyllanthus geoffrayi, etc.		a wild vegetable
phanjam	พันจำ	phanjam	Vatica odorata	94	a dipterocarp
phayom	พยอม	phayom	Shorea roxburghii	103	white meranti
pheka	เพกา	pheka	Oroxylum inducum	626	
philang-kasa	พิลังกาสา	philang-kasa	Ardisia pendulifera, polycephala	531	
phluang	พลวง	phluang	Dipterocarpus tuberculatus	100	eng gurjin oil tree
phobai	โพบาย	phobai	Sapium baccatum; Balakata baccata	742	
phokphai	โพกพาย	phokphai	Pachygone dasycarpa		
phrom	พรม	phrom, namphrom	Carissa carandas, cochinchinensis	589	
phutthachat	พุทธชาด	phutthachat	Jasminum auriculatum		
pine	สน	son	Pinus merkusi, etc.	871	general term for pines
pip	ปีบ	pip	Millingtonia hortensis	627	tree jasmine, Indian cork tree
plantain	กล้าย	klai	Musa paradisiaca		
plao	เปล้า	plao	Croton argyratus, etc.		general name for croton
pomelo	ส้มโอ	som-o	Citrus maxima		large grapefruit-like fruit
pondweed	สาหร่าย	sarai	Najas graminea		bushy pondweed, water nymph
pradu	ประดู่	pradu	Pterocarpus macrocarpus	360	Burmese rosewood/ebony
pradulai	ประดู่ลาย	pradulai	Dalbergia errans	363	
prakham-kai	ประคำไก่	prakham-kai	Drypetes roxburghii		
pralong	ประโลง, โปรงขาว	pralong, prongkhao	Ceriops decandra		
prayong	ประยงค์, พยงค์	prayong, phayong	Aglaia odorata, lawii	228	Chinese rice flower, Chinese perfume plant
pring	(มะ)ปริง	(ma)pring	Bouea oppositifolia	105	
pru	ปรู	pru	Alangium salviifolium	463	
pumpkin	ฟักทอง	fak thong	Cucurbita moschata		

pupil*	พิกุล	phikun	Mimusops elengi		named after Bakula, a disciple of Buddha; fragrant cream flowers; bulletwood, kabiki, baula medlar, Spanish cherry;*Bakula and echo of name
pussbosom*	นมแมว	nom maeo	Rauwenhoffia siamensis	15	a medium-size tree with small flowers, fragrant at night; *direct translation
rachaphruek	ราชพฤกษ์	rachaphruek	Cassia agnes	351	pink cassia
rain tree	ซึก, จามจุรี	suek, jamjuri	Albizzia lebbek; Samanea saman	317	
rak-khi	รักขี	rak-khi	Cudrania javanensis		
rambutan	เงาะ	ngo	Nephelium lappaceum		fruit with spiny red casing
rang	รัง	rang	Shorea siamensis	105	lauan, meranti; a dipterocarp
rattan	หวาย	wai	Calamus (various)		cane
red lotus	โกมุด	komut			poetic name for red lotus
red lotus	สัตตบงกช	sattabongkot			poetic word for a lotus with a squat bud
red yang	ยางแดง	yang daeng	Dipterocarpus turbinatus	97	gurjun
rhino's hoof*	ว่านกีบแรด	wan kip raet	Angiopteris evecta		dark-leafed crossandra, Philippine violet; *direct translation
ronthong	ร่อนทอง	ronthong			unidentified type of wan medicinal herb
rose	กุหลาบ	kulap	Rosa (various)		general name for roses
rose apple	ชมพู่	chomphu	Syzygium (various)		rose apple
rosewood	พยุง	phayung	Dalbergia cochinchinensis		Siamese rosewood
saba	สะบ้า	saba	Entada pursaetha, rheedii		a vine with large seeds
sacred lotus	บัวหลวง *	bua luang	Nelumbo nucifera		
sadao	สะเดา	sadao	Azadirachta indica	222	margosa, nim, neem
sadao daeng	สะเดาแดง	sadao daeng	Ganophyllum falcatum		
sago palm	ปรง	prong	Cycas circinalis, pectinata, etc.	872	or similar cycads known as sago palm or fern palm
sak	ซาก	sak	Erythrophloeum teysmannii		
sakae	สะแก	sakae	Combretum quadrangulare, etc.	400	
salaengphan	แสลงพัน	salaengphan	Bauhinia binata		
samae	แสม	samae	Aegiceras corniculatum, etc.		
samo thale	สมอทะเล	samo thale	Sapium indicum		
samun-waeng	สมุลแว้ง	samun-waeng	Temmodaphne thailandica		
sandal	จันทน์	jan	Myristica (various)		name for several tree with fragrant flowers, fruits, or bark used for making perfume
sangkorani	ว่านสังกรณี	wan sangkorani	Barleria strigosa		barleria; shrub with pale mauve flowers
santol	กระท้อน(ป่า)	krathon (pa)	Sandoricum koetjape	227	red and yellow edible fruits

sappan-wood	ฝาง	fang	Caesalpinia sappan	312	brazil wood; red wood used to make dye
saraphi	สาระพี	saraphi	Mammea siamensis	60	
sattaban	สัตตบัน	sattaban	Alstonia scholaris	594	lotus devil tree, blackboard tree, devil's bark; also known as tin pet, duck's feet tree because of the shape of its leaves
satue	สตือ สะตือ	satue	Crudia chrysantha		
sa-uek	สะอึก	sa-uek	Ipomoea maxima		
secretscent*	ซ่อนกลิ่น	sonklin	Polianthes tuberosa		see hiddenlover (same species); *direct translation
secretspirit*	หิงหาย, ติ่งหาย	hinghai	Crotalaria laburnifolia, bracteata		a flowering shrub, bird flower; *sounds close to "a spirit disappears"
sesame	งา	nga	Sesamum indicum		
shieldvine*	กันภัย	kanphai	Afgekia mahidolae		*sounds like "shield from danger"
sik	ซิก, จามจุรี	sik, jamjuri	Albizzia lebbek; Samanea saman	317	rain tree
smilinglady*	นางแย้ม	nang yaem	Clerodendrum fragrans; Volkameria fragrans	629	fragrant clerodendrum; *direct translation
sparrow's brinjal	มะแว้งเครือ	mawaeng khruea	Solanum trilobatum, sanitwongseii		nightshade
star lotus	บัวสาย	bua sai	Nymphaea, various		
sugar palm	ตาล	tan	Borassus flabellifer		toddy/sugar palm, palmyra
sugar reed*	แขม	khaem	Saccharum arundinaceum		a reed in the sugar family; *invented
sugarcane	อ้อย	oi	Saccharum officinarum		
sweet potato	มัน	man	Ipomoea batatas		
sweet-passion*	เสาวรส	saowarot	Passiflora laurifolia		a variant of passion fruit sometimes called a water lemon; *the Thai word also means tasty, luscious.
ta tum	ตาตุ่ม	ta tum	Excoecaria agallocha, bantamensis		eye-blinding tree
tabaek	ตะแบก	tabaek	Lagerstroemia calyculata, cuspidate, etc.	443–46	
taeng	แตง (แดง)	taeng (daeng)	Xylia xylocarpa	328	
taengtaeo	แตงแตว	taengtaeo			unidentified; perhaps a Tricosanthes, vines with edible leaves
taeo	แต้ว	taeo	Cratoxylum maingayi	627	tree jasmine, cork tree
tamarind	มะขาม	makham	Tamarindus indica, etc.		astringent used in cooking
tangerine	มะจุก	majuk	Citrus reticulata		a dialect word
taro	เผือก	phueak	Colocasia esculenta		
tasselfern	ยมโดย	yomdoi	Lycopodium squarrosum		rock tassel fern, a fern-like type of club moss
tat	(มะ)ตาด	(ma)tat	Dillennia indica	6	
teak	สัก	sak	Tectona grandis	631	
teng	เต็ง	teng	Shorea obtusa	106	sal chammaliang, Siamese sal

thornweed*	ผักหนาม	phak nam	Lasia spinosa		waterweed with spiny stem; *close translation
tiger-eye*	ตาเสือ	ta suea	Dysolxylum cochinchi-nese, etc.	223–26	*direct translation
trabao	ตระเบา, กระเบา	trabao, krabao	Hydnocarpus kurzii, etc.	64	fruit believed to counter leprosy
trabian	ตระเบียน, กระเบียน	trabian, krabian	Hydnocarpus ilicifolia; Gardenia turgida	64	
trumpet-flower*	ดอกลำโพง	dok lam-phong	Centranthera brunoniana		a bush with large trumpet-shaped flowers that have inspired the Thai word for a loudspeaker; *close translation
tumka	ตุมกา	tumka	Strychnos nux-blanda, minor	607	fruits are source of strychnine
turmeric	ขมิ้น	khamin	Xantonnea quocensis, etc.		
turtleweed*	ตับเต่า	taptao	Mimulus orbicularis		Asian frog's bit; an edible water plant with round leaves and pale purple flowers; *direct translation
ulok	อุโลก	ulok	Hymenodictyon orixense, excelsum	478	
victoriflora*	ชัยพฤกษ์	chaiyaphruek	Cassia fistula, renigera	341	yellow cassia, golden showers; *chaiya means victory and phruek is a Sanskrit-derived word for plants
waitinglady*	สาวหยุด	saoyut	Desmos chinensis		*close translation
walking-lady*	นางไกร	nangkrai			unidentified, appears also in other literary works; *direct translation
water chestnut	กระจับ(บก)	krajap(-bok)	Trapa bicornis		
water hyacinth	ผักตบ	phak top	Monochoria hastata		
water peony*	จอก	jok	Pistia stratiotes		*flower is like a peony
water primrose	แพงพวย	phaeng phuai	Jussiaea repens		
water spinach	ผักบุ้ง	phak bung	Ipomoea aquatica		a common vegetable
waterweed	ไคล	khlai			bryophyte; general term for waterweed
white mulberry	หม่อน	mon	Morus alba	753	
wild olive	สมอ	samo	Terminalia chebula, etc.	390	myrobalan; term used for several varieties with olive-like fruits
wild olive	สมอไข่, perhaps สมอไทย	samo khai, perhaps samo thai	Terminalia chebula	390	unidentified, maybe a mistake for samo thai
wild water-fern*	ผักกูด	phak kut	Diplazium esculentum; Dryopteris amboinensis; Asystasiella neesiana		*invented
wild yam	กล้อย กลอย	kloi	Dioscorea hispida		
yanang	ย่านาง	yanang	Tiliacora triandra		a vine
yang	ยาง	yang	Dipterocarpus alatus	98	gurjun
yung	ยูง	yung	Dipterocarpus grandi-florus	100	

Index: Gardner, Field Guide to Forest Trees.

FAUNA

This is a complete listing of animals mentioned in *KCKP* in the Prince Dam-rong edition, the Smith/Wat Ko edition, and the additional episodes included in this edition. Asterisks denote a translation that we have invented, explained in the Notes column. A key to the Indexes is found at the foot of the tables.

BIRDS

In the text	Thai	Translitera-tion	Scientific name	Indexes		Notes
adjutant stork	ตะกรุม	*takrum*	*Leptopilos javanicus, dubius*	K52	B471	lesser adjutant
barbet	โพระดก	*phoradok*	*Megalaima* (various)	K486–90	B92–100	
barn owl	แสก	*saek*	*Tyto alba*	K385	B202	
barred owlet	เค้าโมง	*khaomong*	*Glaucidium cuculoides*	K402	B220	Asian barred owlet
bulbul	กรอด ปรอด	*krot, prot*	*Hypsipetes* (various)	K609–43	B729–48	
buttonquail	คุ่ม	*khum*	*Turnix* (various)	K197–99	B52–54	general term for small pheasants and quail
cockatoo	กระตั้ว	*kratua*	*Cacatuidae* (various)			not native to Thailand
coel	ดุเหว่า, โกกิลา	*duwao, kokila*	*Eudynamis scolopacea,*	K374	B174	common coel, Asian koel
coppersmith barbet	ค้อนทอง	*khonthong*	*Megalaima haemacephala*	K497	B105	
cottonteal goose	คับแค	*khapkhae*	*Nettapus coromandelianus*	K87	B33	cotton or white-quilled pygmy-goose
crake	อัญชัน	*anchan*	*Porzana* (various)	K206–12	B264–74	
crow	กา, อีกา	*ka, i-ka*	*Corvus macrorhynchos*	K681	B529	
crow, house	แก	*kae*	*Corvus splendens*	K677	B530	smaller and greyer
darter	งัว	*ngua*	*Anhinga melanogaster*	K19	B438	oriental darter
dove	เขา	*khao*	*Streptopelia* (various)	K341–44	B237–42	
drongo	แซงแซว	*saeng saeo*	*Dicrurus macrocercus*	K646	B561–64	

egret	ยาง	yang	Egretta (various)	K31–36	B442–47	
egret	สร้อยอิร้า	soi ira				now called ra or nangra
fish-owl	ทืด, ทิ้งทูด	thoet, thingthut	Ketupa zeylonensis, ketupu	K397–99	B215–16	brown and buffy fish-owl
greenpigeon	เปล้า	plao	Treron (various)	K321–25	B249–54	
hawk	เหยี่ยว	yiao	Loiculus vernalis, etc.	K115–45	B390–408	general term for buzzards, hawks, harriers, etc.
hill myna	ขุนทอง	khunthong	Gracula religiosa	K1099	B691	
ibis	ค้อนหอย, ช้อนหอย	khonhoi, chonhoi	Threskiornis melanocephalus, etc.	K53–56	B462–65	
imperial pigeon	กระลุมพู	kralumphu	Ducula aenea, etc.	K330	B257–59	
khla	คล้า	khla				unidentified
kingfisher	กระเต็น	kraten	Alcedo, halcyon (various)	K445–60	B128–43	general name for kingfishers
kot	กด	kot				appears often in literature, variously identified
laughingthrush	ก(ร)ะลาง	k(r)a lang	Garrulax (various)		B824–34	
little grebe	เป็ดผี	petphi	Podiceps ruficolis, cristatus, etc.	K2–4	B436–37	
lory	โนรี	nori	Loriculus vernalis	K354	B180	general name for parrots of Lorius/Loriidae genus, not native to Thailand
magpie	สาลิกา	salika	Cissa chinensis, hypoleuca	K664	B520–21	common green magpie
magpie robin	กางเขน	kangkhen	Copsychus saularis	K879	B650	oriental magpie robin
myna	เอี้ยง	iang	Acridotheres tristis, etc.	K1093	B686	
night heron	แขวก	khwaek	Nycticorax nycticorax	K37	B456	
openbill	ปากห่าง	pak hang	Anastomus oscitans	K46	B473	Asian openbill
oriole	ขมิ้น	khamin	Oriolus (various)	K654	B532–37	
painted stork	ผักบัว	fak bua	Mycteria leucocephala	K45	B470	
parakeet	กระลิง กะลิง	k(r)aling	Psittacula finschii	K353	B184	grey-headed parakeet
parrot	แก้ว	kaeo	Psittinus (various)			general term
parrot	หก	hok	Psittinus (various)	K353–5	B179–81	short-tailed parrots
partridge	กระทา	kratha	Francolinus pintadeanus	K159	B1	general term for small partridges, especially the Chinese francolin
peacock	ยูง	yung	Pavo muticus	K196	B24	green peafowl

peacock-pheasant	พญาลอ	phya lo	Polypectron bicalcaratum	K191	B21	grey peacock pheasant
pelican	กระทุง	krathung	Pelecanus philippensis	K11	B468	
pheasant	ไก่ฟ้า	kai fa	Lophura (various)	K187–88	B16–19	
pygmy owl	เค้าแมว	khao maeo	Glaucidium brodiei	K400	B219	collared owlet or collared pygmy owl
quail	ปักก้อ	pakko	Coturnix (various)	K3–5	B162–64	term for quail, based on the call
rainbow lorikeet	เบญจ-วรรณ	benjawan				similar to lory, often now called lorikeet
red turtle dove,	เขาไฟ	khao fai	Streptopelia tranquebarica	K342	B239	red-collared dove
rosefinch	คิริบูน, คีรีบูน	khiribun	Carpodacus (various)	K1163–68	B971–73	general term for rosefinches and similar birds
stork	กระสา	krasa	Ciconia (various)	K44–50	B474–78	
swift	อีแอ่น	i-aen				general name for swallows and swifts
tailorbird	กระจิบ	krajip	Orthotomus (various)	K975–79	B788–92	
vulture	แร้ง	raeng	Gyps bengalensis, etc.	K109	B85	
weaver bird	กระจาบ	krajap	Ploceus (various)	K1144–46	B957–9	
wild cock	ไก่เถื่อน, ไก่ป่า	kai thuean, kai pa	Gallus gallus	K186	B15	red junglefowl
wind-eater	วายุภักษ์	wayuphak				a legendary bird with a spectacular tail, sometimes identified as a bird of paradise
woodpecker	กระไน	kranai				general term for woodpeckers

LAND ANIMALS

In the text	Thai	Transliteration	Scientific name	Index	Notes
bandicoot	หนูพุก	nu phuk	Bandicota savilei, indica		
bear	หมี	mi	Ursus (various)	M85–86	
boar	หมูป่า	mu pa	Sus scrofa	M124	Eurasian wild pig
buffalo (domestic)	ควาย	khwai	Bubalus bubalis		
buffalo, wild	กระบือ	krabue	Bubalus arnee	M133	distinct species, larger and more aggressive than the domestic buffalo
chaman deer	ฉมัน, สมัน	chaman, saman	Cervus schomburgki	M132	Schomburgk deer, a deer with spectacular antlers, named after a British consul in Bangkok in 1857–64; declared extinct in 2006
chameleon	กิ้งก่า	kingka	Calotes mystaceus, etc.		
chicken	ไก่	kai			
civet	อีเห็น	i-hen	Paradoxurus hermaphroditus, etc.	M102–104	
cobra	งูเห่า	ngu hao	Naja (various)		
deer	กวาง, เนื้อ	kwang, nuea			general terms
deer	มฤคี	maruekhi	.		poetic word
elephant	ช้าง	chang	Elephas maximus	M119	
elephant	กุญชร	kunchon			poetic word
field turtle	เต่านา	tao na	Damonia subtrijuka	T90	Malayan snail-eating terrapin
fishing cat	เสือปลา	suea pla	Prionailurus viverinnus	M111	stocky, mainly nocturnal cat with olive-grey fur and dark spots; inhabits wetlands and lives off fish
gaur	กระทิง	krathing	Bos gaurus	M135	a massive wild buffalo of dark grey or black color, weighing around a ton when fully grown
gibbon	ชะนี	chani	Hylobates (various)	M20–23	
green snake	งูเขียว	ngu khiao			
jackal	(หมา) จิ้งจอก	(ma) jingjok	Canis aureus	M83	
jingjok	จิ้งจก	jingjok	Hemidactylus (various)		small house lizard
lamang deer	ละมั่ง	lamang	Cervus eldii	M131	thamin, brow-antlered deer, Elds deer; named after a British Indian army officer in 1844; facing extinction in Thailand
langur	ค่าง	khang	Semnopithecus (various)	M16–19	
lemur	บ่าง	bang	Cynocephalus variegatus	M9	sunda colungo, Malaya flying lemur
linsang	ชะมด	chamot	Viverricula indica, etc.	M97–106	a type of civet

lizard, butterfly lizard	แย้	*yae*	*Lioleps belliana*		ground lizard, tree monitor, with yellow spots on back
macaque	ลิงแสม	*ling samae*	*Macaca mulatta*	M12	long-tailed or stump-tailed macaque
mole	ตุ่น	*tun*	*Talpa micrura*	M8	
monkey	ลิง	*ling*	*Macaca mulatta, etc.*	M11–15	general term for macaques
paddy frog	อึ่งนา	*ueng na*			
porcupine	เม่น	*men*	*Hystrix brachyuran, atherurus macrourus*	M59–60	
rabbit	กระต่าย	*kratai*	*Lepus peguensis*	M26	Siamese hare
rhinoceros	แรด	*raet*	*Rhinoceros sondaicus*	M122	Javan rhinoceros; extinct in Thailand
rhinoceros	ก(ร)ะซู่	*k(r)asu*	*Dicerorhinus sumatrensis,*	M123	Sumatran rhinoceros; a smaller species, now virtually extinct in Thailand
sambar	กวางป่า	*kwang pa*	*Cervus unicolor*	M130	
sand deer	กวางทราย	*kwang sai*	*Cervus porcinus*	M127	hog deer
serow	เยียงผา, เลียงผา	*yiang pha, liang pha*	*Naemorhedus sumatraensis*	M138	goat antelope, southern serow; a small goat antelope found mainly in steep limestone terrain
squirrel	กระรอก	*krarok*	*Callosciurus (various)*	M29–31	
tiger	เสือ	*suea*	*Panthera tigris*	M118	
tiger	พยัคฆ์	*phayak*			poetic word
treeshrew	กระแต	*kratae*	*Tupaia glis, etc.*	M1–5	similar to a squirrel with a pointed snout and long tail
tukkae	ตุ๊กแก	*tukkae*	*Gecko gekko*		large house lizard with distinctive call, captured in the name
wild dog	หมาใน	*ma nai*	*Cuon alpinus, rutilans*	M84	dhole, Malay wild dog; a fox-like animal that hunts in packs

INSECTS

In the text	Thai	Transliteration	Scientific name	Notes
ant	มด	mot	Oecophylla (various)	
bee	ภมร	phamon		poetic term
bug, bedbug	เรือด (เลือด)	rueat, lueat	Cimex lectularius, hemipterus, etc.	
carpenter bee	แมลงภู่	malaeng phu	Xylocopa latipes, caeruleus, etc.	
caterpillar	บุ้ง	bung		
cicada	จักจั่น	jakkajan	Dundubia intermerata, etc.	
cicada	จิ้งหรีด	jingrit	Acheta bimaculatus, gryllus testaceus	
cricket	เรไร	rerai	Pomponia intermedia	
cricket	ลองไน	long nai	Tosena melanoptera	
dragonfly	แมลงปอ	malaeng po	Ordonata (various)	
emerald beetle*	แมลงทับ	malaeng thap	Coleopteran polyphaga	*distinctive green casing
firefly	หิ่งห้อย	hinghoi	Lampyridae	
fly	แมลง	malaeng	general term for flying insects	
hairy caterpillar	ร่าน	ran	Arctiidae, lymantriidae, lasiocampidae	general name for large hairy caterpillars
midge	ริ้น	rin	Culicoides orientalis, Leptoconops spinosifrons, etc.	general name for small insects
mite	ไร	rai	Dermanyssus, Tetranychus (various)	general name for small blood-sucking insects
mosquito	ยุง	yung	Culicidae (various)	
red ant	มดแดง	mot daeng	Oecophylla smaragdina	
spider	บึ้ง	bueng	Melopeus albostriatus, Nephila maculate	a big edible spider over 3 cms long, edible
spider	แมงมุม	maeng mum	Pholcus (various)	
termite	ปลวก	pluak	Isopteran (various)	
winged termite	แมลงเม่า	malaeng mao	Ephermerida (various) ·	

WATER ANIMALS

In the text	Thai	Transliteration	Scientific name	Index	Notes
anabas	หมอ	mo	Anabas testudineus	P199	
apple snail	หอยโข่ง	hoi khong	Pila ampullacea		
blackear catfish	เทโพ	thepho	Pangasius larnaudii	P178	
box turtle	เต่าฝา	tao fa	Cuora amboiensis	T84	Siamese box terrapin
catfish	ดุก	duk	Clarias batrachus, macrocephalus, etc.	P184	
crab	ปูแสม	pu samae	Neoepisesarma (various)		samae crab; small crab that lives in mangroves; used in somtam
crocodile	จระเข้	jorakhe	Crocodylus siamensis		
crocodile	กุมภา	kumpha			poetic term
crocodile	ตะโขง	takhong	Tomistoma schlegelii		a large, russet-brown crocodile, now found only in the south
eel	ไหล	lai	Futa alba, Ophichthys microcephalus, etc.	P189	
featherback	กราย	krai	Hototerus chitala, Chitala omata	P115	spotted featherback
frog	กบ	kop			general term
giant catfish	เทพา	thepha	Pangasius sanitwongsei	P179	
giant catfish	บึก	buek	Pangasianodon gigas	P176	Mekong giant catfish; world's largest fresh-water fish, up to 2.5 meters long, now an endangered species
giant snakehead	ชะโด	chado	Channa micropeltes	P205	
grey featherback	สลาด	salat	Notopterus notopterus	P116	
horse fish*	ม้า	ma	Boesemania microlepis	P193	Boeseman Croaker, Smallscale Croaker; *direct translation
java carp	ตะเพียน	ta-phian	Puntius javanicus, etc.	P137–38, 143	
leaf fish	สลิด	salit	Trichogaster pectoralis	P201	snakeskin gourami
mackerel	ทู	thu	Rastrelliger kanagurta		Indian mackerel
mud carp	นวลจันทร์	nuanjan	Chanos chanos, Cirrhinus microlepis	P148	
mud snail	จุ๊บแจง	jupjaeng	Cerithidea obtusa		horn snail, obtuse horn shell, blunt creeper
mussel	หอยแครง	hoi khraeng	Anadara granosa		
porpoise	โลมา	loma	Peponocephala electra	M74	
puffer fish	ปักเป้า	pakpao	Monotrete cochinchinensis, fangi	P111–12	general term for the Monotrete family of puffer fish, probably Monotrete fangi, which has the ability to swell up, and is poisonous

red catfish*	ต้อง, นง	dong, nong	Pterocryptis cochinchinensis	P175	*descriptive
river snail	หอยขม	hoi khom	Vivipara doliaris		
scissortail	ซิว	sio	Rasbora trilineata, etc.	P128	
small frog	เขียด	khiat	Rana nigrovittata, limnoch, etc.		general term for small frogs
snakehead	ช่อน	chon	Channa striata	P206	
soft-shell turtle	ตะพาบน้ำ	ta-phap nam	Trionyx cartilageneus	T136	common Siamese soft-shelled turtle
spotted featherback	กราย	krai	Chitala ornate	P115	
striped catfish	สวาย	sawai	Pangasianodon hypophthalmus	P177	
sweetlip	สร้อย	soi	Dangila leptocheila		
toad	คางคก	khangkhok	Bufo melanostictus, etc.		
turtle	เต่า	tao			general term
turtle	กริว	krio			poetic term
whale	วาฬ	wan		M75–80	
whisker sheatfish	เนื้ออ่อน	nuea on	Ompok krattensis	P174	

Index guide:

K   King, *Field Guide to the Birds of South-East Asia.*
B   Boonsong, *Nok mueang thai*
M   Parr, *Guide to the Large Mammals*
P   Chawalit, *Pla nam juet*
T   Wirot, *Turtles of Thailand*

This table lists garments, types of cloth, patterns and motifs, personal orna-
ments, and protective devices worn on the body.

anklet กำไลใส่เท้า *kamlai sai tao*—Any ankle ornament, especially heavy silver
anklets for children.

appliqué หักทองขวาง *hak thong khwang*—"Break-gold-athwart," an embroidery
technique used on royal regalia such as fans and umbrellas. A pattern
is made by laying cut lengths of golden silk thread perpendicular to the
weave, and attaching them by overstitching.

appliqué flowers ฉลุดอกลอย *chalu dok loi*—"Floating flowers," embroidery cut
so the flowers "float" above the surface of the fabric.

attalat อัตลัด—A satin fabric, originally from Persia. In Persia, the term *atlas*
covered plain, striped, and sumptuously gold-and-silver brocaded vari-
ants worn in the court. In Siam, *attalat* usually meant a satin fabric from
Persia or Bengal with gold and sometimes also silver brocade motifs
placed in the weave at intervals. A popular design used an oval motif
representing a mango tree.

bandeau ประเจียด *prajiat*—A piece of cloth inscribed with a yantra design, worn
to convey invulnerability. It should be made with cloth given to a monk
as a funeral donation that has been washed, impregnated with herbs,
polished with a *saba* seed, inscribed by an adept using ink mixed with
enchanted powder, and activated with further formulas. It may be tied
around the neck, upper arm, chest, or head.

banphap บานพับ—An ornament, often a lozenge-shaped piece of brocade, that
accompanies the *sangwan* breast chain, hanging at the waist, especially
as part of drama costume.

beaded wristlet/necklace ประคำ, ปะวะหล่ำ, บ้าหว่า *prakham, pawalam, bawa*—A
string of beads worn on neck or wrist, and sometimes used for count-
ing prayers like a rosary.

belt ปั้นเหน่ง *pan-neng*—Javanese word for a belt, now principally used for
items worn as part of costumes for traditional dance; usually strips of
brocade or other heavy fabric, around 10 to 15 cms wide.

bodice ก่อง *kong*—An ornamental bodice, now usually associated with costume for traditional dance.

bracelet กำไลมือ *kamlai mue*—General term for wrist jewelry.

breast chain สังวาล *sangwan*—A long chain or sash worn either around the neck, looped over the shoulders, or crosswise on the breast, as a mark of status for gods, kings, or nobles. It probably originated from India where it was called a *sankal* and appeared as the regalia of several gods, especially Ganesh.

britches สนับเพลา *sanap phlao*—Close-fitting trousers ending below the knee, often with a flared cuff, now seen mostly as part of the costume for traditional dance.

cat's eye แก้วตาแมว *kaeo ta maeo*—A semi-precious stone believed to be the eye of a dead cat, miraculously transformed. Usually green, translucent, and sparkling, it conveys invulnerability and other benefits.

chain, necklace สาย, สร้อย *sai, soi*—General term for a chain worn round the neck or waist.

chalang **pattern** ลายฉลาง *lai chalang*—A type of patterned cloth, possibly from Thalang, Phuket.

charm, amulet เครื่องราง *khrueang rang*—General collective term for amulets and other protective devices.

chemise ฉลององค์ *chalong-ong*—Term for an outer shirt worn by a king.

chicken-skin silk แพรหนังไก่ *phrae nang kai*—A fine silk that creases like chicken skin.

chili-shaped charms พริกเทศ *phrik thet* —Decorative pieces, usually on a bracelet or anklet.

choker สร้อยนวม *soi nuam*—A neck ornament formerly worn by royalty and nobility, or in stage costume.

clashing-circles pattern แย่งชิงดวง, ดวงแย่ง *yaeng ching duang, duang yaeng*—A pattern based on adjacent or overlapping circles, usually combined with floral motifs.

cone pattern กรวย, กรวยเชิง *kruai, kruaichoeng*—A pattern of elongated cones, used as a border on cloth or other decorations such as wat pillars.

conical hat ลอมพอก *lomphok*—A tall, tapering conical hat with an upturned brim decorated with golden flowers. It originated from Persia where it was known as *taj* and was formerly a royal headdress that later became a standard part of court attire. It became part of Siamese noble regalia during the era of King Narai as recorded by the illustrators of the French diplomatic missions in the 1680s.

coral-pea pattern ตามะกล่ำ *ta maklam*—A dark-colored cotton cloth with a small woven pattern resembling the seed of a *maklam ta nu, Abrus pre-*

catorius, crab's eye, rosary pea, or coral bean—a vine with long pods containing seeds of brilliant red with a black spot.

cross-branch pattern ก้านแย่ง *kanyaeng*—A pattern with lines of intertwined flowers and stems dividing the area into a grid of squares or diamonds. In the eighteenth century, cotton dyed in this pattern was made on the Coromandel Coast of India for shipment to Siam.

duck-egg stone ไข่เป็ดเป็นหิน *khai pet pen hin*—A stone, usually light green, found in the egg of a duck (or chicken). When placed on a shrine and worshipped, it will fulfill any wishes.

earrings กุณฑล *kunthon*—General term for earrings (sometimes *kunthon* means a hairpin).

epaulet อินทรธนู *inthara thanu*—Now a shoulder epaulet on military uniform but uncertain what it meant in the past. Literally, Indra's bow.

gardenia pattern พุด *phut*—A pattern based on a flower of the Gardenia family, especially *Gardenia collinsae*.

Garuda stepping on Wasukri motif สุบรรณบินเหยียบวาสุกรี *suban bin yiap wasukri*—Motif of Garuda, the mythical bird mount of Vishnu, gripping in its claws Wasukri, a king of the nagas. Garuda is a symbol of kingship.

girdle ราตคด, ราตะคด, รัดประคด *rattakhot, ratprakhot*—A girdle or monk's belt.

hair ornament จุฑามณี *juthamani* sometime pronounce *julamani*—General term for hair ornaments.

hairpin ปิ่น, กุณฑล *pin, kunthon*—General terms for pins to hold the hair in a topknot or chignon.

handkerchief ผ้าเช็ดเหงื่อ *pha chet nguea*—Literally, cloth to wipe sweat.

hat, helmet หมวก *muak*—General term for hat or helmet.

headcloth โพก *phok*—Any cloth tied around the head.

helmet ตุมปี่ *tumpi*—Probably from the Sanskrit *topi*, meaning hat, the root of (solar) topee; a general word for military headgear, not any particular shape.

helmet พระมาลา *phra mala*—A helmet with a straight, stiff brim and an ornate crown.

herbal amber เทียนคล้า *thian khla*—A hard, apparently metallic core naturally occurring in *khla*, shrubs of the Calathea genus, worn as a protective device.

hibiscus motif ดวงพุดตาล *duang phuttan*—A popular design motif based on a hibiscus flower with stalk and foliage.

inscribed shirt เสื้อเครื่อง *suea khrueang*—A shirt inscribed with yantra diagrams.

intertwined vines pattern เครือลดา, เครือเถาวัลย์ *khruea lada, khruea thaowan—* A pattern with many variants, based on vines with foliage.

jackfruit-spine pattern หนามขนุน *nam khanun—*A checkered pattern produced by tie-dye or batik technique, used on cloths imported from India or Japan and worn by nobles. Alternatively, a method of weaving silk to produce a stretchy, bobbly fabric used for sashes, supposedly reserved for the families of the senior ministers.

jap-ping จับปิ้ง *jap-ping—*A protective ornament tied round an infant girl's hips. The form may originate from India where it is known as *mudi-thagadu*, and the name may come from Malay where it is *caping*.

jiwon จีวร *jiwon—*One of a monk's three robes: the outer robe.

kanok **pattern** กระหนก *kanok—*A motif, based on a flame, with many variants.

kanok-**and-vine pattern** กนกเป็นเครือวัลย์ *kanok pen krueawan—*A pattern combining *kanok* motifs with foliage, often in slanting lines dividing the space into a mesh of diamond shapes.

Khmer-style ขัดเขมร *khat khamen—*A way of hitching up a lowercloth by tucking the lower edge in the waist and rolling up the sides. The result is a bit like a pair of shorts.

kimkhab เข้มขาบ *khemkhap—*Silk with gold thread in the warp, and longtitudinal brocade patterns made with a fine strand of flattened metal wound over a core of silk, using yellow silk under gold, and white silk under silver. The cloth originated from Persia (where the term means gold cloth), but was later made extensively in northern India.

kinnari **motif** กินรี *kinnari—*A motif of a mythical creature, half woman, half bird.

krajang **motif** กระจัง *krajang—*A motif like a lotus petal used in horizontal frieze designs.

leggings กางเกง *kangkeng—*Leggings often worn inside a lowercloth.

lowercloth ผ้านุ่ง, ภูษา *pha nung, phusa—*Any cloth worn on the lower body by men or women, usually a simple oblong wrapped around and tucked in the waist.

medallion ตระพอง *traphong—*An ornament on a waist sash.

medallion ตาบ *tap—*A flat, round or square ornament worn at the neck or on the breast.

mercury amulet ปรอท *parot—*Usually a small enclosed metal cylinder filled with mercury. Because mercury is a metal that acts unnaturally (like a fluid), it is one of the most common substances considered *khlang*, of intrinsic power, believed to convey invulnerability by flowing to that part of the body that is threatened with piercing.

meshwork กรองทอง, กรองตาชุน *krong thong, krong ta chun*—Fine, loosely woven cotton, often woven or embroidered with gold thread, usually in a mesh (*ta khai*) pattern. Reserved for auspicious occasions, it was worn by men draped over the left shoulder or tailored into a long tunic, and worn by women over a sabai.

mondop **ring** แหวนมณฑป *waen monthop*—A ring with gems arranged in a pyramid shape similar to a *mondop* roof over a shrine with stacked layers diminishing to a peak.

mori โมรี *mori*—A type of green cloth from India.

mot โหมด *mot*—A check fabric of Indian origin, principally from Rajasthan, made by rolling diagonally and tie-dyeing to create a checked pattern. The term comes from *moth*, a lentil, in reference to the usually small checks. In Siam, this term was applied to Indian fabric woven with silk, silver and gold thread, and silver and gold paper, probably first imported in the early Bangkok era.

naga kings entwined motif แย่งนาคราช *yaeng nakharat*—A motif of entwined snakes.

nine jewels เนาวรัตน์, นพรัตน์, นพเก้า *naowarat, noppharat, nopphakao*—A combination of diamond, ruby, emerald, topaz, garnet, sapphire, moonstone, zircon, and lapis lazuli.

nok yang นอกอย่าง *nok yang*—Cloth imported from India that did not conform to patterns prescribed by the Siamese court. The latter were called *pha lai yang*. *Nok yang* cloth was considered of lower quality. Often the pattern was based on a Thai original but less well executed and sometimes clearly influenced by Indian style.

offertory-rice pattern (พุ่ม)เข้าบิณฑ์ *(phum) khao bin*—A motif based on popped rice in a folded leaf or almsbowl in a shape resembling a lotus bud.

open style ห่มดอง *hom dong*—A way of wearing all three monk's robes, usually only inside the wat at ceremonies and formal occasions. The *jiwon* is worn over the left shoulder with the right shoulder left bare; the *sangkati* is draped over the left shoulder and fastened with a belt round the waist.

Pakthao ปักเถา *pakthao*—Possibly a weaving center in China.

parrot's-eye pattern ตานกแก้ว *ta nok kaeo*—Unidentified.

peeled lotus pattern ตาบัวปอก *ta bua pok*—A printed cloth with a square pattern, popular in the court.

phakhaoma ผ้าข้าวม้า *phakhaoma*—Originally a waist sash from Persia, now a general-purpose cloth for bathing, but in *KCKP* an uppercloth of high value.

Phakhawam ภควำ—An image of Gavampati, an early disciple of the Buddha, usually depicted covering his eyes and perhaps other bodily orifices with extra hands; a powerful, protective amulet, often very small.

pha-muang ผ้าม่วง *pha-muang*—Silk woven with stiff yarn in dark colors (blue, purple, or green), generally worn in tuck-tail (*jongkraben*) style. It was made locally, but the most popular and probably original type came from China.

phirot **ring** (พระ)พิรอด *(phra) phirot*—Cloth or paper inscribed with yantra, then rolled and twisted into something that could be worn, and perhaps hardened with lacquer. Larger ones were worn as a belt, or on the upper arm, and smaller ones on the finger as a ring.

prayer beads ปะวะหล่ำ, ข้าหว่า—See beaded wristlet/necklace.

prostration cloth ผ้ากราบ *pha krap*—Originally a cloth for placing on the ground for prostration by nobles and monks, it evolved into a narrow sash tied around the waist or chest as a mark of status.

pum **silk** ปูม *pum*—A silk with a floral pattern made with *ikat* weaving, originating from Gujarat where it is known as Patola, adopted into Siam from Cambodia, presented to nobles by the king as a mark of rank.

quatrefoil pattern ประจำยาม *prajam yam*—Literally "usual for the time," a pattern based on a flower with four leaves, often used in borders, found in decorative design reaching back to the Dvaravati era, nominally reserved for royalty.

ring ธำมรงค์ *thammarong*—General term for a finger ring.

robe ครุย *krui*—A light robe worn as a sign of office, often made of muslin or similar light fabric, knee-length with long arms, open at the front, perhaps with decoration denoting rank on the collar, cuffs, and lower hem. The term probably derived from the Persian *khel'at,* meaning the bestowal of a robe of office or other regalia, suggesting the garment was introduced in the era of Persian influence at court in the seventeenth century.

sabai สไบ, ผวย *sabai, phuai*—Uppercloth worn by both men and women. Also in *KCKP* used for the upper robe of a monk (today usually called *sangkhati*).

sabong สบง *sabong*—One of a monk's three robes: an inner lower cloth extending from waist to shin.

sacred thread มงคล *mongkhon*—A cord of plaited cotton tied around the head.

Salapatun, Sappadun สละปะตุ่น, สับปะดุน *salapatun, sappadun*—A contraction of Machilipatnam (Masulipatam), a port on India's east coast that traded cloth through Mergui to Siam. Since at least the late sixteenth century, some of the cloth was made specifically for the Siamese market with Siamese designs.

sangkhati สังฆาฏิ *sangkhati*—One of a monk's three robes: the breastcloth.

saphak สะพัก *saphak*—An elevated word for the sabai or uppercloth, used especially when worn by ladies of the court at ceremonial events. The basic form is wound once round the body with one end thrown over the shoulder, leaving the other shoulder and midriff bare. The more elaborate form is a longer cloth wound crosswise over the breasts with the two ends thrown over the two shoulders.

sash เจียระบาด *jiyarabat*—A waist sash tied with the ends hanging in front.

sash with tail โจงหาง *jong hang*—A way of tying the lowercloth to leave a decorative "tail."

seamed uppercloth เพลาะ *phlo*—An uppercloth made by joining two cloths.

serge ประสะตุ, ปัสะตุ *p(r)asatu, patsatu*—A type of twilled fabric.

sesame seed pattern เมล็ดงา *malet nga*—An intricate flower pattern on dark cloth, imported from India, or brought by cart traders from Khorat.

shirt เสื้อ *suea*—General term for a tailored upper garment.

shoulder cloth อังสะ *angsa*—A cloth worn by a monk over the shoulder.

silkwool ปูมส่าน *pumsan*—A high-quality fabric used for sompak presented to nobles by the king (see *pum* and *san*).

sin ซิ่นยก, ผ้าซิ่น *sin yok, pha sin*—A tubular style of lowercloth worn by women in Lanna and the Lao country.

snake ring แหวนงู *waen ngu*—A ring in the form of a snake coiled around the finger.

sompak สมปัก *sompak*—A lowercloth worn by nobles while attending at court, especially while attending audience, sometimes called *pha kiao*. The term derives from the Khmer *sombuat*, meaning any kind of cloth. Usually this cloth was presented by the king at the time of appointment, and the design and quality of the cloth were marks of the nobles' specific status. The sompak was generally made by sewing two pieces of cloth together, resulting in a cloth much larger than normal that must be worn in a more elaborate style, with the pattern showing at both ends.

spiral ring เนื่อง *nueang*—A gold ring of many spirals.

spirit-skull belt ปะขมองพราย, ขมองโขมด *pa khamong phrai, khamong khamot*—A belt made from the skull of a corpse of someone who died a violent death, sawn into strips, woven in a checkered pattern, and inscribed with formula.

subduing charm ลูกสะกด *luk sakot*—A seed-shaped amulet made with metal left over from casting a Buddha image, threaded on a string tied round the waist.

Surat สุหรัด—A port and weaving center in Gujarat, western India, which became a major supplier of printed cotton textiles designed specifically for the Siamese market in the eighteenth and nineteenth centuries. The goods were mostly white cloth of English origin, hand-printed with wooden blocks.

takrut ตะกรุด *takrut*—A protective device made from thin metal, inscribed with yantra, rolled around a cord, and worn around the neck, arm, or waist. The size varies from about 3 to 15 cms long. Its power comes from the yantra inscribed on the metal by a teacher while simultaneously intoning formulas. Sometimes the yantra are so complex they are spread across several *takrut* worn as a set.

Tani ตานี *tani*—Probably a style of cloth originating from Pattani, perhaps made by a settlement of Pattani weavers and dyers in Ayutthaya. Alternatively, this might mean *yantani*, a word probably derived from the Persian *jamdani* or *jamdari*, a fine-quality cloth brocaded with gold.

tat ตาด *tat*—A silk brocade of Middle-Eastern origin, reserved for higher nobility, made with flat metal strips of gold-plaited silver, or gold-plaited copper, or silver and silver-plaited copper.

toggle buttonhole รังดุมหูไหม *rang dum hu mai*—Fastening on a monk's inner robe.

topknot ornament เกี้ยว *kiao*—General term for ornaments on a child's topknot.

tuck-tail style โจงกระเบน, โจงหาง *jongkraben, jonghang*—A lowercloth worn with a long "tail" passed between the legs and tucked in the waist at the back giving a pantaloon-like appearance. This was a popular style among the nobility in the nineteenth century.

uppercloth ห่ม *hom*—Any cloth worn on the upper body by men or women, usually a simple oblong, worn in various styles.

Vietnamese stripe ริ้วญวน *rio yuan*—Unidentified.

votive-deity motif เทพพนม *thepphanom*—A motif with a deity sitting with crossed legs and hands in wai, often used in cross-branch designs.

waist pouch ไถ้ *thai*—A tubular pouch tied around the waist, often to carry food on a journey.

waist sash เกี้ยว *kiao*—General term for a waist sash.

waist chain สะอิ้ง *sa-ing*—Usually a fine chain of silver.

waistcoat เสื้อกัก *suea kak*—A hunter's garment.

wasp-nest ring แหวนรังแตน *waen rang taen*—A ring with stones arranged in a hexagonal shape like a wasps' nest.

waving flowers ดอกไม้ไหว *dok mai wai*—Artificial flowers, usually made of cloth, on flexible wire stems, inserted in hats or hair.

white linen โขมพัตร *khommaphat*—A Sanskrit-derived word for white linen.

wool, woolen ส่าน *san*—From the Persian word *shal* (and possibly further back from Syriac, *sa'r*), the origin of the English word shawl. *Shal* meant a patterned twill-woven fabric made from spun wool using a technique similar to European tapestry weaving. Earlier the word applied to rough, thick fabrics but later was mainly used for cloth made from fine goat hair, such as those known as cashmere or pashmina. In Siam, the term seems to have acquired a broader meaning as a fine, expensive fabric, generally made from wool or similar material. In modern Thai, the word means "wool."

wrist chains with sema เสมาปะวะหล่ำ *sema pawalam*—A bracelet with links in the shape of *sema*, the stones that define the sacred area of an ordination hall; an inverted-shield shape.

yok (ผ้า)ยก *(pha) yok*—A high-quality lower cloth, usually brocade, worn by both men and women. *Yok* means to raise or lift, and the pattern is raised in the weaving process.

WEAPONS AND MILITARY TERMS

ambush brigade กองซุ่ม *kong sum*—A unit for surprise attack, sometimes also used for scouting.

armor เกราะ *kro*—General term for armor, usually of leather.

armorer จ่าดาบ *ja dap*—A junior officer in charge of weaponry.

artillery พลปืน *phon puen*—Soldiers equipped with guns.

athamat อาทมาต *athamat*—Probably a word used to describe spies, especially those working across the border into Burma.

bayonet ปลายหอก *plai hok*—A blade affixed to a gun.

bomb หม้อดิน *mo din*—Literally "earthen pot"; a pot filled with gunpowder with a fuse.

bow ธนู, เกาทัณฑ์ *thanu, kaothan*—General term for a bow.

buckler เขน *khen*—A round shield.

cannon ปืนใหญ่ *puen yai*—General term for large guns.

cleaver ดาว *tao*—Probably the same as *dao*, a straight, heavy, square-ended, chisel-edged blade, narrowest at the hilt, used by tribals in northeast India.

club ตะแบง, กระบอง *tabaeng, krabong*—General term for a crude wooden weapon.

commissariat เกียกกาย *kiakkai*—Unit or officer responsible for provisions.

crossbelts ตะแบงมาน *tabaengman*—Belts worn crosswise on the body (adopted from European military uniform).

crossbow หน้าไม้ *na mai*—". . . about five feet long; it is passed through a stock about three or four feet long, tipped with hard wood, or iron. The leaf of a palm supplies the place of a feather to the arrow. The bow-string is drawn to the notch by the united exertion of the feet and arms, and the arrow is shot off by a trigger." (Low)

crow's wings ปีกกา *bik ka*—A military formation with both wings spread like a crow. The term is used today for a curly bracket (}) which gives an idea of the shape.

crupper ซองหาง *song hang*—A strap from the saddle under a horse's tail.

dagger กั้นหยัน *kanyan*—A twin-edged knife or short sword of Chinese origin.

discus จักร *jak*—Circular disk carried by deities.

flanchard แผงค้าง *phaeng khang*—Panels of cow or buffalo leather to protect a horse's flanks, often decorated by painting or tooling.

flank elephant ช้างกันแซง *chang kansaeng*—Elephants placed along both sides of a procession as protection.

flintlock guns ปืนคาบหิน, ปืนคาบศิลา *puen khap hin, puen khap sila*—Gun fired by a flint throwing a spark into the powder.

fore cloth ปกตระพอง *pok traphong*—A decorative cloth placed over the humps on an elephant's head.

fore elephant ช้างดั้ง *chang dang*—Elephants positioned at the front center of a column or procession.

fore harness ผ่านหน้า *phan na*—A strap passing under the neck and over the back of an elephant.

frizzen หน้าเพลิง *na phloeng*—"Fire face," a metal flap over the priming pan of a flintlock that is struck by the flint to spark the powder.

fuse ชนวน *chanuan*—A fuse for firing a matchlock gun.

fuse box เต้าชนวน *tao chanuan*—A container for fuses, slung on a belt.

guard ตำรวจ *tamruat*—General term for those who guard and police the palace, city, etc.

gun ปืนไฟ *puen fai*—General name for hand-held guns.

harpoon ชนัก *chanak*—A short spear with an arrow head and a retaining rope, used for hunting.

heron-leg gun ปืนขานกยาง, *puen kha nok yang*—A gun with a barrel over a meter long and a tripod to support it. Low described it as "a short piece which one or two men can carry. When it is to be fired, it is supported on a sort of tripod of wood. It is either a wall or a field-piece."

javelin แหลน *laen*—A light spear for throwing or stabbing, usually wooden.

kris กริช *krit*—Malay word for a dagger with a distinctive wavy blade; a weapon and status object in the Malay world.

lance ง้าว *ngao*—A curved blade around eighteen inches long mounted on a long handle, wielded with a slashing movement; primarily a foot soldier's weapon, but also used on horse or elephant.

lookouts แมวเซา, แมวมอง *maeo sao, maeo mong*—"Peering cats," a unit for keeping watch.

mace คทาธร *khothathon*—A club carried by gods and demons in legend.

machete พร้า *phra*—A large knife.

militia, militiaman อาสา *asa*—A term derived from Khmer meaning "forward troops," generally applied to the "six militia units," the only standing army.

mobile fort ปิลั่น *pilan*—Perhaps a ring of men carrying palisades or long shields.

palace watch ล้อมวัง *lom wang*—"Surround the palace," an elephant unit, originally to guard the king's elephant, later deployed in battle.

pennant ธงฉาน *thong chan*—A triangular flag with insignia.

pike หอก *hok*—A stabbing weapon with a straight metal blade like a twin-edged knife on a long, usually wooden handle; a foot soldier's weapon.

pipe flag เที่ยว *thiao*—A flag in the form of a cylinder.

post horse ม้าเร็ว, ม้าใช้ *ma reo, ma chai*—Horse for delivering messages.

powder horn แขนง *khanaeng*—A container for powder, often made from animal horn.

priming pan หูลับ *hu lap*—"Secret ear," the ignition chamber of a flintlock gun.

procession horse ม้าแซง *ma saeng*—A horse for use in processions.

quartermaster ยกกระบัตร *yokkrabat*—An officer responsible for supplies.

quiver แล่ง *laeng*—A container for arrows.

rear elephant ช้างกัน *chang kan*—Elephants positioned at the rear center of a column or procession.

recruiter ประแดง *pradaeng*—A recruitment officer; word based on the Khmer term *kamarateng*, used in Siam for various official posts.

regal sword พระแสง(น้อย) *phrasaeng (noi)*—A short sword, especially one that is a part of royal regalia.

saber กระบี่ *krabi*—A one-handed sword with single-edged curving blade and a short handle.

saddle pad เบาะอาน *bo an*—A cloth, sometimes quilted, placed on an elephant's back.

scouts เสือ ป่า *suea pa*—"Forest tiger," a unit that often went ahead of the main army to gather intelligence.

sentinel กะลาบาต *kalabat*—A division of the guard defined as those who stand watch by the lamps, with a duty to stand posted along the routes of royal processions.

sheath ปลอก, ฝัก *plok, fak*—General terms for containers for swords.

shield โล่, ดั้ง *lo, dang*—An oblong shield with handle, usually of wood. A *dang* is longer than a *lo*.

short sword ขรรค์ *khan*—A sword with twin-edged blade and a short handle to be gripped one-handed, for regalia.

signals brigade กองแล่น *kong laen*—A unit of messengers, literally "runners," but may be mounted on horses.

six militia units อาษาหกเหล่า *asa hok lao*—A collective term for six permanent military units whose main role was to guard the city.

spear ทวน *thuan*—A simpler, lighter form of pike, often a bamboo shaft tipped with a cone of metal.

spear หลาว *lao*—A stabbing weapon consisting of a wooden staff with sharpened point.

spikes กวาก *kwak*—"... crow's feet, made of bamboo sharpened, and then hardened by fire, or of iron, and so constructed that on being cast on the ground one spike remains nearly upright" (Low).

stave ไม้พลอง *mai phlong*—A heavy stick.

stiletto กระเบา *krabao*—A dagger with a very narrow blade.

sword ดาบ *dap*—Usually a sword with a longish (e.g., 60 cm) handle designed to be gripped with both hands, and a curved blade, usually slightly longer than the handle.

throwing knife เสน่า *sanao*—Any knife for throwing.

trident ตรี, ตรีศูล *tri, trisun*—A three-pronged weapon carried by deities.

victory brigade กงชัย *kong chai*—Possibly an elite fighting unit.

victory flag ธงชัย *thong chai*—A pennant or ensign.

This table includes all prepared foods, excluding simple descriptions like "fried pork" or "grilled catfish."

cake sugar น้ำตาลงบ—Sugar formed into round cakes.

caramel ขนมกะละแม *khanom kalamae*—Rice flour, coconut milk, and sugar boiled and stirred until viscous and black.

chamot **sweet** ขนมชะมด *khanom chamot*—Coconut rolled in sugar, coated with flour, and fried.

chili dip แจ่ว *jaeo*—A characteristically Lao dip, usually made with a base of red onion, fermented fish (*pla ra*), chili, and lime juice.

chili paste น้ำพริกปรุง *nam phrik prung*—Chili pounded with other spices and dried fish or prawn, usually eaten with rice and fresh vegetables.

chup-chu ชุบชู—Miniature imitation fruit made from bean paste, dipped in coloring, served floating in syrup.

clam sweets ครองแครง *khrong khraeng*—Flour paste shaped as cockleshells, then either cooked in coconut milk, or dusted with sugar and fried.

crisped rice ข้าวตาก *khao tak*—Leftover cooked rice, sun-dried or toasted to prevent mold.

cured fish ปลาจ่อมเจ่า *pla jom jao*—*Pla jom* is small fish and prawns mixed with salt and dry fried rice, and left to cure until sour. *Pla jao* is river fish cured in the same way and then cooked in coconut milk with garlic, red onion, and chili.

curry แกง (หมู ไก่ ขม บวน แตงเต้า แย้ ฟักทอง ตะพาบน้ำ) *kaeng*—A general term for soup or curry (pork, chicken, river snail, pork offal, bottle gourd, lizard, pumpkin, softshell turtle).

dancing prawns กุ้งเต้น *kung ten*—Lime juice, chopped chili, and other ingredients are poured over freshly caught live prawns, causing them to twitch or "dance."

dry curry ฉู่ฉี่ (กุ้ง) *chuchi (kung)*—A dry curry made with kaffir lime leaves (prawn).

earth flower sweet ดอกดิน *dok din*—A sweet made with the herb, *Aeginetia indica*, sometimes called forest-ghost flower. A paste of flour, sugar, banana, and the herb is steamed in leaf-cups and served with coconut.

The herb gives an unusual, deep purple color.

egg custard สังขยา *sangkhaya*—A custard made with eggs, coconut milk, and sugar.

fermented fish ปลาร้า *pla ra*—Fish mixed with salt and dry fried rice, and left to cure.

golden drops ทองหยอด (หยอด) *thong yot*—Adapted from the Portuguese sweet, *ovos moles* (soft eggs), made with flour, sugar, egg yolk, and jasmine water mixed into a paste, formed into balls, and cooked in syrup.

golden pinch ทองหยิบ *thong yip*—A mixture of beaten egg yolk, sugar, and flour, dropped into boiling syrup in disk shapes, creased by the fingers into a mold in the shape of a small flower. Probably based on the Portuguese sweet Fatias de Tomar, though the original recipe precooks the egg yolk in a larger mold and then drops it, in slices, into the syrup.

golden puffs in syrup ทองพลุ *thong phlu*—A stiff batter of wheat flour, butter, eggs, jasmine water, and salt, formed into small balls and deep fried to be crisp and hollow. Of French origin.

golden spray ฝอยทอง *foi thong*—Beaten egg yolk squeezed from a banana-leaf cone into boiling syrup as a mat of yellow strands. *Foi thong* is based on the Portuguese sweet, Fios de Ovos, though the Thai version has slightly finer strands made as a mat rather than a pile.

homok ห่อหมก—"Wrap and bury," originally a mixture of fish and herbs, wrapped in banana leaves, covered with mud, and baked with charcoal in a hole in the ground.

jelly วุ้น (ลายสายเลื่อม) *wun*—A translucent, soft sweet, originally made from water weed, often in many colors.

kaeng-om แกงอ่อม—A characteristically northern curry of deer, buffalo, beef, chicken, or offal made with bitter gourd, chili onion, garlic, galangal, lemongrass, coriander root and seed, fish paste, and kaffir lime leaf.

kaolao เกาเหลา—A soup-base of Chinese origin.

khanom bueang **pancakes** ขนมเบื้อง—Small pancakes spread with a sweet or savory filling, then folded.

khanom jin ขนมจีน—Thin, round noodles, like angel-hair spaghetti, made from slightly fermented rice, usually eaten with a curry of fish pounded to a smooth paste (*namya*).

khanom ko ขนมโก๋—A Chinese sweet made with rice flour.

lap ลาบ (เนื้อสมัน)—A preparation with raw or nearly raw meat, finely chopped and heavily spiced (deer).

masaman มัสหมั่น (มัสมั่น)—A sweet, rich, and slightly sour curry, probably with remote Arabic origins (the name derives from Mussulman).

miang เมี่ยง—Fermented tea, or a snack made with various chopped foods wrapped in a leaf.

namya jin น้ำยาจีน—A curried fish sauce, often eaten with *khanom jin*, a form of rice noodles. The sauce is made with coconut milk, dried chili, galangal, lemongrass, kaffir lime peel, ginger, shallots, garlic, coriander, several herbs and edible leaves, dried fish, and snakehead fish.

paengji **waffles** แป้งจี่ *paengji*—A deep-fried pancake made of glutinous rice, coconut, salt, and sugar.

palm nuts in syrup ลูกตาลเชื่อม *luk tan chueam*—A sweet.

patties ทอดมัน (กุ้ง ปลา) *thotman*—Fish or prawn meat pounded with chili and herbs into a paste, kneaded into small, flat patties, and deep-fried (prawn, fish).

phanaeng พะแนง (ไก่)—A thick red curry, probably named after Penang (chicken).

phla พล่า (เต่า เนื้อ)—A sour and spicy mixed dish, rather like *yam*, but with raw meat, raw shrimp, or similar base (turtle, meat).

pla krim **sweet** ขนมปลากริม *khanom pla krim*—Rice flour rolled into a fish-like shape around 5 cms long, cooked in thick coconut milk and palm sugar, and garnished with fried sesame.

popped rice ข้าวพอง *khao phong*—Rice popped by roasting or dry-frying.

rice cake ข้าวตู *khao tu*—A sweet made with leftover rice that is dried and pounded, along with sugar, grated coconut, coconut milk, and a jasmine flower, then cooked and pressed into shapes using a mold.

rice crackers ข้าวตัง *khao tang*—Rice that stuck to the pan, further sun-dried, cut into disks, and fried to a crisp.

rice fritters (นาง)เล็ด *(nang) let*—Sticky rice steamed, formed into disk shapes, sun-dried, fried, and coated with palm-sugar syrup.

salty eggs ไข่พอก *khai phok*—Eggs steeped in rice husk, ash, and brine.

sausage ไส้กรอก *sai krok*—General term for sausage.

soup ต้ม (ปลาร้า) *tom*—A boiled soup (fermented fish).

sour salad ส้มยำ (เต่า) *som yam*—A spicy salad similar to *yam* (turtle).

spicy salad ยำ (ปลา แย้) *yam*—A base of meat or fish with sliced vegetables, flavored with lime or other sour taste, chili, and fish sauce (fish, lizard).

sweet eggs ไข่หวาน *khai wan*—Eggs poached in a syrup made with palm sugar and floral water.

sweet-in-attap ขนมห่อใบจาก *khanom ho bai jak*—Sticky rice, sugar, and grated coconut, wrapped in an attap leaf and grilled.

thian **sweets** ขนมเทียน *khanom thian*—A dough of rice flour and sugar, rolled into a cylinder in a banana leaf, and steamed. Nowadays these sweets are stuffed with yellow beans and formed into a pyramid shape.

thick curry แกงคั่ว *kaeng khua*—A curry thickened with pounded dry-fried rice.

tomyam ต้มยำ *tomyam*—A spicy and sour soup made with lemongrass, chili, fish sauce, and lime.

touchstone sweet หินฝนทอง *hin fon thong*—A round sweet with a dimpled top filled with some grated coconut, named for similarity to a goldsmith's touchstone.

ua อั่ว—A spicy pork sausage from the north.

Vietnamese sausage แนมญวน *naem yuan*—Chopped raw pork mixed with cooked, rice, and garlic, and left to ferment slightly.

water peony sweet ดอกจอก *dok jok*—A paste of rice flour pressed in a mold in the shape of a water peony flower, and deep-fried.

wheel sweet ขนมกง *khanom kong*—A paste made from green or yellow beans, flour, palm or coconut sugar, coconut milk, and duck's eggs, shaped into a Buddhist wheel of the law (*chakra*) and deep-fried.